EMOTIONS IN PSYCHOPATHOLOGY

SERIES IN AFFECTIVE SCIENCE

Series Editors

Richard J. Davidson
Paul Ekman
Klaus Scherer

EMOTIONS IN PSYCHOPATHOLOGY

Theory and Research

Edited by
William F. Flack, Jr., &
James D. Laird

New York   Oxford
Oxford University Press
1998

Oxford University Press

Oxford   New York
Athens   Auckland   Bangkok   Bogota   Bombay   Buenos Aires
Calcutta   Cape Town   Dar es Salaam   Delhi   Florence   Hong Kong
Istanbul   Karachi   Kuala Lumpur   Madras   Madrid   Melbourne
Mexico City   Nairobi   Paris   Singapore   Taipei   Tokyo   Toronto   Warsaw

and associated companies in
Berlin   Ibadan

Copyright © 1998 by Oxford University Press, Inc.

Published by Oxford University Press, Inc.
198 Madison Avenue, New York, New York 10016

Oxford is a registered trademark of Oxford University Press

Library of Congress Cataloging-in-Publication Data
Emotions in psychopathology : theory and research / edited by William
F. Flack, Jr. and James D. Laird.
p.   cm. — (Series in affective science)
Includes bibliographical references and index.
ISBN 0-19-509321-6
1. Emotions.   2. Psychology, Pathological.   3. Affect (Psychology)
I. Flack, William F.   II. Laird, James D.   III. Series.
[DNLM: 1. Mental Disorders—psychology.   2. Emotions.
3. Psychological Theory.   WM 140 E54 1997]
RC455.4.E46E466   1997
616.89—dc20
DNLM/DLC
for Library of Congress   96-32150

1 3 5 7 9 8 6 4 2
Printed in the United States of America
on acid-free paper

Acknowledgments and Dedications

WFF: I acknowledge the support of the Department of Psychiatry at Baystate Medical Center in Springfield, Massachusetts, the Frances L. Hiatt School of Psychology at Clark University and its chairman, Jim Laird, and the Behavioral Sciences Division of the National Center for PTSD at the Boston V.A. Medical Center.

To my family.

JDL: To Nan, who once again contributed more than she knows.

Both editors acknowledge the work and patience of all contributors to this volume, the series editors, Paul Ekman, Richard Davidson, and Klaus Scherer, and our editor at Oxford, Joan Bossert.

Contents

PART IV. DISORDERED PERSONALITY

Contributors

John Altrocchi, Ph.D., Department of Psychiatry and Behavioral Sciences, University of Nevada School of Medicine, Reno, Nevada, USA

Jack J. Blanchard, Ph.D., Department of Psychology, The University of New Mexico, Albuquerque, New Mexico, USA

George W. Brown, Ph.D., Medical Research Council, Department of Social Policy and Social Science, Royal Holloway and Bedford New College (University of London), London, England

Ross Buck, Ph.D., Department of Communication Sciences, University of Connecticut, Storrs, Connecticut, USA

Lorraine A. Cavallaro, Ph.D., Mental Hygiene Clinic, Worcester Outpatient Clinic, Psychology Service, Brockton/West Roxbury Department of Veterans Affairs Medical Center, and Department of Psychiatry, Harvard Medical School, Worcester, Massachusetts, USA

Luc Ciompi, M.D., Social-Psychiatric University Clinic, Berne, Switzerland

Monique de Bonis, Ph.D., National Center for Scientific Research, Paris, France

Joseph de Rivera, Ph.D., Frances L. Hiatt School of Psychology, Clark University, Worcester, Massachusetts, USA

Caroline J. Easton Ph.D., Department of Psychiatry, University of Connecticut Health Center, Hartford, Connecticut, USA

Heiner Ellgring, Ph.D., Institut für Psychologie, Universitat Würzburg, Würzurg, Germany

Seymour Epstein, Ph.D., Department of Psychology, University of Massachusetts at Amherst, Amherst, Massachusetts, USA

William F. Flack, Jr., Ph.D., Behavioral Sciences Division, National Center for PTSD, Boston V.A. Medical Center, and Department of Psychiatry, Tufts University School of Medicine, Boston, Massachusetts, USA.

David D. Franks, Ph.D., Department of Sociology and Anthropology, Virginia Commonwealth University, Richmond, Virginia, USA

Eva Gilboa, M.A., Department of Psychology, Northwestern University, Evanston, Illinois, USA

Cheryl K. Goldman, Ph.D., Department of Psychology, Gettysburg College, Gettysburg, Pennsylvania, USA

Leslie S. Greenberg, Ph.D., Department of Psychology, York University, North York, Ontario, Canada

Susan M. Heffernan, B.A., Department of Sociology and Anthropology, Virginia Commonwealth University, Richmond, Virginia, USA

Jill Hunziker, M.A., Department of Psychology, Long Island University, Bronx, New York, USA

Rick E. Ingram, Ph.D., Doctoral Training Facility, Department of Psychology, San Diego State University, San Diego, California, USA

Jennifer M. Jenkins, Ph.D., Institute of Child Study, and Department of Psychology, University of Toronto, Toronto, Ontario, Canada

Susanne Kaiser, Ph.D., Faculty of Psychology and Educational Sciences, Department of Psychology, University of Geneva, Geneva, Switzerland

Ernest Keen, Ph.D., Department of Psychology, Bucknell University, Lewisburg, Pennsylvania, USA

Sandra Kerr, Ph.D., Department of Psychology, Northern Illinois University, De Kalb, Illinois

Rainer Krause, Ph D., Faculty of Psychology, University of Saarlandes, Saarlandes, Germany

Ann M. Kring, Ph.D., Department of Psychology, Vanderbilt University, Nashville, Tennessee, USA

James D. Laird, Ph.D., Frances L. Hiatt School of Psychology, Department of Psychology, Clark University, Worcester, Massachusetts, USA

William Lyons, Ph.D., F.T.C.D., Department of Philosophy, Trinity College, University of Dublin, Dublin, Ireland

Carol Magai, Ph.D., Department of Psychology, Long Island University, Bronx, New York, USA

Paul McReynolds, Ph.D., Department of Psychology, University of Nevada, Reno, Nevada, USA

Joerg Merten, Ph.D., Faculty of Psychology, University of Saarlandes, Saarlandes, Germany

Daniel R. Miller, Ph.D., Department of Psychology, Wesleyan University, Middletown, Connecticut, USA

Gregory A. Miller, Ph.D., Departments of Psychology and Psychiatry and Beckman Institute, University of Illinois at Urbana-Champaign, Champaign, Illinois, USA

Susan Mineka, Ph.D., Department of Psychology, Northwestern University, Evanston, Illinois, USA

Patricia Moran, M.A., Medical Research Council, Department of Social Policy and Social Science, Royal Holloway and Bedford New College (University of London), London, England

John M. Neale, Ph.D., Department of Psychology, State University of New York at Stony Brook, Stony Brook, New York, USA

Keith Oatley, Ph.D., Center for Applied Cognitive Science, Ontario Institute for Studies in Education, and Department of Psychology, University of Toronto, Toronto, Ontario, Canada

Sandra C. Paivio, Ph.D., Department of Psychology, University of Saskatchewan, Saskatoon, Canada

Pierre Philippot, Ph.D., Research Unit for Clinical and Social Psychology, University of Louvain, Louvain-la-Neuve, Belgium

Robert Plutchik, Ph.D., Department of Psychiatry, Albert Einstein College of Medicine, Bronx, New York, USA

Jill H. Rathus, Ph.D., Department of Psychology, Long Island University–C. W. Post Campus, Brookville, New York, USA.

Bernard Rimé, Ph.D., Research Unit for Clinical and Social Psychology, University of Louvain, Louvain-la-Neuve, Belgium

Peter Salovey, Ph.D., Department of Psychology, Yale University, New Haven, Connecticut, USA

William Sanderson, Ph.D., Cognitive Behavior Therapy Program, Department of Psychiatry, Albert Einstein College of Medicine, Montefiore Medical Center, Bronx, New York, USA

Theodore R. Sarbin, Ph.D., Department of Psychology, University of California at Santa Cruz, Santa Cruz, California, USA

Thomas J. Scheff, Ph.D., Department of Sociology, University of California, Santa Barbara, California, USA

Klaus R. Scherer, Ph.D., Faculty of Psychology and Educational Sciences, Department of Psychology, University of Geneva, Geneva, Switzerland

Walter D. Scott, Ph.D., Department of Psychology, University of Miami, Coral Gables, Florida, USA.

David A. Smith, Ph.D., Department of Psychology, Ohio State University, Columbus, Ohio, USA

Marcia C. Smith, Ph.D., Department of Psychology, University of Portsmouth, Portsmouth, United Kingdom

Nanciann Norelli Smith, M.S., Department of Psychology, University of Connecticut, Storrs, Connecticut, USA

Evelyne Steimer-Krause, Ph.D., Faculty of Psychology, University of Saarlandes, Saarlandes, Germany

Martha S. Stretton, Ph.D., Private Practice, Chester, Vermont, USA

E. Keolani Taitano, M.A., University of Illinois at Urbana-Champaign, Champaign, Illinois, USA

Burkhard Ullrich, Ph.D., Faculty of Psychology, University of Saarlandes, Saarlandes, Germany

Drew Westen, Ph.D., Department of Psychiatry, The Cambridge Hospital, Harvard Medical School, Cambridge, Massachusetts, USA

William F. Flack, Jr., & James D. Laird

Introduction

The idea for this book began to take shape during two symposia, one at the International Congress of Psychology in Brussels (Flack & Krause, 1992), and the other during the centennial meeting of the American Psychological Association in Washington, DC (Flack & Laird, 1992). In the course of discussions both during and following those meetings, it became apparent that there was a groundswell of important and exciting work going on at the interface of research on emotions and psychopathology. All participants at the two meetings agreed that the time was ripe to gather together a broad sampling of this work, both to assess the state of the art, and to stimulate new thinking and empirical efforts. This book is the result.

Although the two symposia involved only empirically minded psychologists, we decided that a broader net should be cast to include as wide a range of theoretical perspectives as possible. Thus, the reader will find chapters written by workers from a number of professional disciplines, including clinical, developmental, social, and personality psychology, psychiatry, sociology, and philosophy. The sampling of theoretical perspectives and empirical methods is even more diverse, ranging from the philosophical, speculative, and wholistic, to the statistical, hypothesis-testing, and reductionistic. We were not able to include all possible perspectives in a finite volume, of course, and thus we have chosen not to call it a "handbook," or to refer to it as "comprehensive." Still, we believe that this collection is a fair sampling of the diversity of informed opinion and methods of investigation in research on emotions and psychopathology at the present time.

The book is divided into four parts. The first is devoted to some general issues in the field. These include consideration of the meaning of emotion as a concept (Lyons), biological mechanisms and theories (Kaitano & Miller), early development (Jenkins & Oatley), the self (Epstein), regulation of social interaction (Krause, Steimer-Krause,

Merten, & Ullrich), psychotherapeutic interaction (Scheff), social sharing of emotion (Phillippot & Rimé), and social constructivism (Sarbin & Keen).

The three subsequent parts contain reports of research focused on emotions in specific psychological disorders. Part II includes chapters on "normal" emotions and their relationships to psychopathology (Franks & Heffernan; Neu), and on psychological disorders that are, primarily, "emotional"—namely, depression (Brown & Moran; de Bonis; Scott & Ingram; Mineka & Gilboa; Paivio and Greenberg) and anxiety (Kaiser & Scherer; McReynolds; Mineka & Gilboa; Paivio; Rathus & Sanderson; Stretton & Salovey). Part III consists of chapters on emotions in schizophrenia and in other psychotic disorders (Ciompi; Buck, Goldman, Eastman, & Norelli Smith; Flack, Laird, Cavallaro, & Miller; Ellgring & Smith; Blanchard; Neale, Blanchard, Kerr, Kring, & Smith). Part IV contains chapters on emotions in disorders of personality, including ego functioning (Plutchik), borderline disorder (Magai & Hunziker; Westen), multiple personality (Altrocchi), and false memory syndrome (de Rivera).

Our hope for this volume is that it reflects a balanced account of the current state of research on emotion and psychopathology. If it stimulates further thinking and investigation, so much the better.

References

Flack, W. F., Jr., Laird, J. D. (1992, August). *Emotions in psychopathology*. Symposium presented at the 100th annual convention of the American Psychological Association, Washington, DC.

Flack, W. F., Jr., & Krause, R. (1992). Nonverbal communication and severe psychopathology [Abstract]. *International Journal of Psychology, 7*, 443–444.

Part I

GENERAL ISSUES

William Lyons

Philosophy, the Emotions, and Psychopathology

Introduction: Your Theory of Emotion Matters

It matters a great deal what theory of emotion is presumed by anyone involved in psychopathology. Putting this another way, I should make it clear that there can be no such things as free-standing or theory-neutral definitions, including those in psychopathology. Definitions always involve theory. Coming to an agreed definition, at least at its best, involves argument, evidence, and decision. Even to define such an ordinary, uncontroversial thing as a rabbit involves theorizing of a quite involved sort. To define *rabbit* (as does the Oxford English Dictionary [OED]) as "burrowing rodent of hare family, brownish grey in natural state" already presupposes a host of theoretical decisions, decisions such as what is to count as a rodent: "animal of the order *Rodentia* with strong incisors and no canine teeth" (says the OED). So, agreeing on what a rodent is depends on a decision about how we are to pick out *orders*, a decision about why having incisors and no canine teeth is to be considered a sufficiently salient difference so as to be the basis of an *order*, and so on.

With emotions the matter is no different. Wittingly or unwittingly, the definition (or presumed definition) of *emotion* or *affect* in a textbook of psychiatry has been the result of a host of theoretical decisions. Not the least of these will be the decision about how we are to separate emotions from nonemotions, and how we are to differentiate one emotion from another. Discussion and decision about the answers to be given to such questions are the very core of theorizing about the emotions. As I will endeavor to make clear in the next section, no subject area contains more theorizing on this topic than does philosophy.

It seems to me that, in the area of theory, philosophy is very useful as a prophylactic against possible distorting influences. It is a purely theoretical subject with no immediate applied or practical demands to bend the direction of its speculations. On the other hand, by the very nature of the demands on their time, psychotherapists of any discipline are confronted by patients—those who are suffering some form of mental illness. Thus, in the area of emotions, the clinician sees emotions only from a very circumscribed area, emotions such as anxiety, anger, mania, depression, and fear. Moreover, he or she sees only disturbed or pathological versions of these emotions. So, it would be extraordinary if the psychiatric view of emotion was not colored by these clinical encounters with emotions.

I begin this chapter proper with a truncated outline of the history of philosophical theorizing about the nature of emotion. It is truncated because I begin at the beginning of the twentieth century and ignore the period intervening between Plato and this century. It is nothing more than the merest outline because to do otherwise would require much more than one section of an essay.[1] The main aim of this outline is to make clear how and why most philosophers have come to believe that a cognitive theory of the emotions, as distinct from a Cartesian (or feeling) theory, a behaviorist theory, a psychoanalytic theory, or any other theory, is, the best theory going. There is some special pleading involved at this point, as what I end up with is one particular version of a cognitive theory of emotion. This version is the one I myself have argued for since the 1970s. Like all theories, a cognitive theory of emotion is revisable when confronted with contrary evidence or cogent critique. Over the last 20 years, however, the criticisms of cognitive theories and the consequent revisions have been comparatively minor. So, what I end up presenting is an account of one particular current and reasonably well known version of a cognitive theory of emotion.

The Emergence in Philosophy (and Psychology) of CognitiveTheories of Emotion

In the history of philosophy—and the twentieth century has been no exception—for the most part theories of emotion have been considered to be a subtext of more general theories about the nature of mind. If you were an unreformed Cartesian dualist about minds and bodies, then this would have been reflected in your account of emotion. If you were a behaviorist, then you would have felt that you must generate a behaviorist account of the emotions. However, let me go back as far as the turn of this century to try to make sense of the comparatively recent development in philosophy (and psychology) of cognitive theories of emotion.[2]

At the beginning of this century, in both philosophy and psychology, William James's account of emotions was the orthodoxy. James's account, in effect, was "export quality" Cartesianism machined to high standards by means of nineteenth-century positivism. James, at least when he published his masterpiece, *The Principles of Psychology*, in 1890, was more or less a regular nineteenth-century adherent of Cartesian substance dualism, or the view that humans were composed of an intimate alliance and interplay between a mental substance or soul, whose essence was consciousness, and a material substance or body, whose essence was extension. In *The Principles* James wrote, famously, that "*bodily changes follow directly the perception of the exciting fact, and that our feeling of the same changes as they occur is the emo-*

tion. Common sense says, we lose our fortune, are sorry and weep. . . . The hypothesis here to be defended says . . . that we feel sorry because we cry" (emphasis in original, James, 1890/1950, pp. 449–450; see also James, 1884). That is, our feeling of sadness, which is the emotion, is our conscious experience of our weeping. More generally speaking, we act and react automatically after the perception of something, at least sometimes. If these actions and reactions involve physiological arousal, say, increased heart beat, increased respiration rate, sweating, pallor, and so on, then most often we will be conscious of this bodily upset. The gestalt (conscious) feeling of this complex upset or pattern of arousal is the emotion.

James, and his colleague in this area of research, the Danish physiologist Carl Lange, believed that they had improved on Descartes's account of emotion—as the "feeling in the soul" of our bodily actions and visceral reactions—by showing how the study of emotion could become scientific. Since each emotion was nothing but the mirror-feeling of some complex pattern of bodily arousal (some pattern of physiological changes), then all you needed to do to distinguish and describe the various emotions was to study the physiological details of each pattern of arousal. The psychology of emotion was, in effect, now a part of physiology, and so as "hard-nosed," "tough-minded," and scientific an enterprise as you like.

Of course, matters were not really as simple as this; they never are. When investigated with the ever-increasing skills of the new science of psychology, brought about by the ever-increasing subtlety of instrumentation and experiment, it was discovered that the physiological patterns associated with emotion were not sufficiently diverse and distinct to give us any clear and distinct listing of emotions (see, e.g., Cannon, 1927; Mandler, 1975; Munn, 1961; Schachter, 1971).[3] Furthermore, there were some gaps in the theory as well. How could we be sure that the emotion—the feeling in the soul or at least in the privacy of one's own stream of consciousness—that you have when you are running away from a Rottweiler is the same as the one I have when I am in the same situation? How can a comparison be made, if only you have access to your feeling and only I have access to mine? If in the final analysis love, for example, becomes just a "lovey-dovey feeling," and every other emotion is similarly characterized by the quality of some inner private feeling, then no one could ever be quite sure whether it was love, anxiety, or indigestion that was keeping him or her awake at night, for there could be no "feeling police" to ensure that your labeling of your particular present feeling had been correctly done. Indeed, the whole notion of a correct labeling of such inner, essentially private feelings has no purchase.

In that disturbed decade from 1910 to 1920, there was a permanent sea change in the subject of psychology, to be followed not long afterward by a similar one in philosophy. In psychology the old Cartesian experimental method—of subjects introspecting their stream of consciousness with their "mental eye" and reporting on their discoveries about the mind and mental events, albeit under strict laboratory conditions—was being castigated for having produced little or nothing of value. No "discoveries" were being made. Besides, the whole enterprise seemed altogether too subjective and uncheckable, that is, altogether too dubious, to be the mainspring of a scientific psychology. While agreement might sometimes be reached concerning some claim about human psychology within the confines of one school or one particular laboratory, it was notoriously impossible to reach any agreement across schools and in a number of laboratories. If one school of introspectionists said that you could have thoughts that were not mediated by one of the senses, that is, that you could have thoughts that were not in the form of visual images or heard speech or some such, another school would claim that the evidence from their introspectionist laboratory told a different story. With their morale sapped by such controversies and by a lack of any real, observable, incontrovertible gains in the accumulation of facts about human psychology, the introspectionists fell easy victims to the invading behaviorist army.

In effect, J. B. Watson produced the behaviorist manifesto when he wrote his exciting and combative paper "Psychology as the Behaviorist Views It," in *The Psychological Review* of 1913. There he declared that

> psychology as the behaviorist views it is a purely objective experimental branch of natural science. Its theoretical goal is the prediction and control of behavior. Introspection forms no essential part of its methods, nor is the scientific value of its data dependent upon the readiness with which they lend themselves to interpretation in terms of consciousness. The behaviorist, in his efforts to get a unitary scheme of animal responses, recognizes no dividing line between man and brute. The behaviour of man, with all its refinement and complexity, forms only a part of the behaviorist's total scheme of investigation. (p. 158)

At a stroke, from being the science of mind, psychology had been redefined as the science of behavior. The way to study humans, including human psychology, was to employ just the same methods as you would use to study nonhuman animals, that is, by means of scientifically controlled, objective observation and experiment, and by taking no account of any alleged introspective access to a mind or soul.

Regarding the investigation of human emotions, somewhat surprisingly, Watson did not produce an account in terms of human behavior as did later behaviorists, such as B. F. Skinner, but in terms of patterns of physiological changes. Indeed, his account of emotion is really William James's account shorn of any reference to feelings or any other sort of conscious state. Whereas James had said that an emotion is the feeling that is the record or imprint in consciousness of the distinctive pattern of physiological reactions or changes in the body, Watson held that the emotion is nothing but the pattern of physiological reactions or changes. Furthermore, as human infants are the obvious bridge between humans and other primates since they can be described as animal-like humans, the best research strategy is to study the emotions of the newborn. Thus, in his book *Psychology from the Standpoint of a Behaviorist* (1919), Watson declared:

> A formulation which will fit a part of the emotional group of reactions may be stated as follows: An emotion is an hereditary "pattern reaction" involving profound changes of the bodily mechanism as a whole, but particularly of the visceral and glandular systems. By pattern reaction we mean that the separate details of response appear with some constancy, with some regularity and in approximately the same sequential order each time the exciting stimulus is presented. (p. 195)

Thus, in his book *Behaviorism* (1930), Watson describes shame in an infant as involving "heightened blood pressure, superficial dilation of the capillaries of the skin known as flushing, among many other [physiological changes]" (p. 187).

Psychological behaviorism was one of the major sources of philosophical behaviorism, but there were other sources. The most important of these latter sources was logical positivism, which amounted to nineteenth-century positivism machined with the modern logic of Frege, Russell, and Wittgenstein, and fashioned into a philosophical methodology. Nineteenth-century positivism was a hymn to natural science, extolling it as the sole repository of real, factual, or positive knowledge. Thus, the only genuine knowledge was scientific knowledge, and the only genuine method of gaining knowledge was the scientific method of producing and testing causal hypotheses by reference to observation and experiment. The most important aspects of the logical positivists' version of positivism were the beliefs that logic was the chief tool of philosophy as mathematics was of science, that the only worthwhile task for a scientific philosophy was to work alongside natural science by providing an account of the logical and conceptual foundations of science, and that the language of less basic sciences could be reduced, at least ultimately, to the language of the basic science, physics. Thus, in the course of their scrutiny of the language of psychology in the pursuit of their aim of ultimately reducing the language of psychology to the language of physics, the logical positivists found that at present the hoped-for reduction could proceed no farther downward than a reduction of the vocabulary of psychology to the vocabulary of behavior. Thus, only temporarily it was hoped, positivists often found common cause with mainstream behaviorism.

One of the central figures in the logical positivist movement was the German philosopher Rudolph Carnap. One of his most famous essays, "Psychology in Physical Language"(1931), was first published in *Erkenntnis*, the house journal of the Vienna Circle, the best-known group of logical positivists, who met regularly for discussion in Vienna before the Second World War. In this essay Carnap wrote that "all sentences of psychology describe physical occurrences, namely the physical behaviour of humans and other animals" (Carnap, 1931/1959, p. 165). The "sentences" referred to are not the sentences psychologists themselves may employ, for they may be unredeemed introspectionists, but the sentences into which, Carnap believed, any meaningful sentences employed by psychologists could and should be translated. In due course these sentences describing the physical behavior of humans would be translated into statements in the language of physics, the fundamental science. Thus, said Carnap, "Now it is proposed that psychology, which has hitherto been robed in majesty as the theory of spiritual events, be downgraded to the status of a part of physics"(Carnap, 1931/1959, p. 168).

When he came to the task of delineating the details, Carnap admitted that at present one could not go much farther than a translation of, say, "He is excited" into something like "His body is characterized by a high pulse rate, and respiration rate, by the occurrence of agitated movements, by vehement and factually unsatisfactory answers to questions, etc." (adapted from Carnap, 1931/1959, pp. 170–173). In short, Carnap was under no illusion about what sort of "translation" work was possible. Regarding psychology, including the psychology of the emotions, he realized that his "translations" had advanced no farther than those of the psychological behaviorists. What he believed was important was seeing the task as one of translating one language—strictly speaking, one vocabulary—into another.

There was yet another source of behaviorist analyses in philosophy of emotion. This source was linguistic analysis, which in turn was markedly anti-Cartesian in spirit. One of the central figures in mid-century British philosophy was Gilbert Ryle, and he is often considered to be the most notable member of the philosophical movement called linguistic analysis. One of the sources of this movement was logical positivism. Others were the Cambridge philosophers Moore and Wittgenstein. Wittgenstein, in particular, saw philosophy as the task of untying knots in our thinking, where the knots resulted chiefly from philosophers' own misuse of ordinary language when they employed it in the more exacting tasks of philosophy. In 1932 Ryle wrote an essay entitled "Systematically Misleading Expressions," which has sometimes been called the manifesto of linguistic analysis. At the end of that paper, Ryle wrote:

> Philosophy must then involve the exercise of systematic restatement. . . . I conclude, then, that there is, after all, a sense in which we can properly enquire and even say "what it really means to say so and so". For we can ask what is the real form of the fact recorded when this is concealed or disguised and not duly exhibited by the expression in question. And we can often succeed in stating this fact in a new form of words which does exhibit what the other failed to exhibit. I am for the present inclined to believe that this is what philosophical analysis is and that this is the sole and whole function of philosophy. (p. 61)

For Ryle, then, philosophical achievement lay in correcting the category mistakes, or mistakes in our understanding of concepts, that philosophers perpetrated when they mishandled ordinary language in the course of propounding and defending philosophical theories or theses, and in substituting a correct understanding of the concepts under scrutiny.

Ryle described his masterpiece, *The Concept of Mind* (1949), as a sustained piece of hatchet work on the Cartesian doctrine of mind, that is, on Cartesian dualism. Cartesian dualism, he said, was one big category mistake because the Cartesian dogma explained the meaning of mental terms and expounded mental concepts in terms of inner mental faculties, such as the intellect and will, each of which produced its own proprietary activities. Ryle argued that, generally speaking, the real explanation of our mental terms and concepts was in terms of dispositions. To be intelligent, for example, is not to possess a special faculty in the mind or soul that is able to do clever calculations in a private mental arena and occasionally publishes its findings in speech and behavior. To be intelligent is to be disposed to do certain specifiable actions in certain circumscribed environmental conditions. It is to be disposed to accomplish successfully tasks that we consider to be intellectual ones. To take another example, to be a hypocrite is not to say one thing and believe another thing in the privacy of one's own mind, but to do one thing overtly and then soon afterward to do something that gives the very opposite impression, furtively and covertly. A hypocrite is the village atheist who secretly goes to church in another village. So, whether it be to animals or humans, we attribute mental terms on the basis of the *ordinary observation of ordinary behavior,* not on the basis of some alleged inner introspective observation of some alleged private inner mental events.

Ryle had also read his Watson and Carnap, and his account of emotion is a product of the triad of influences: psychological behaviorism, logical positivism, and anti-

Cartesianism. Thus, in chapter 4 of *The Concept of Mind*, Ryle puts forward an account of emotions as being behavioral dispositions. To be afraid is not to undergo a private Cartesian experience such as a feeling, but is to be disposed to act and react in a certain way in certain circumstances and to have that disposition activated. To be in love is not to harbor a private feeling of a special sort in one's mental parlor but to be prone to doing quite ordinary and observable things such as to talk about someone to the exclusion of other topics, to overpraise that person, to defend him or her against any criticism, to seek out that person's company in an overweaning way, and so on. In short, Ryle produced an account of emotion that was not very different from the answers that the psychological behaviorists gave, though for very different reasons. Where behaviorists in psychology were behaviorists for reasons of methodology, those in philosophy were so for logicolinguistic reasons.

Ryle also added to his account of emotion something that was peculiar to linguistic analysis. He set about exposing the ambiguity in our ordinary use of the term *emotion*, explaining that, depending on the context, it meant inclinations or motives, moods, agitations or commotions, or feelings. The first three usages should be analyzed as referring to dispositions; the latter (feelings) in terms of ordinary bodily sensations such as itches, twinges, and tickles.

Generally speaking, then, behaviorism and behaviorist accounts of emotion appeared in philosophy much later than they appeared in psychology. On the other hand, behaviorism and behaviorist accounts of emotion were jettisoned in philosophy much earlier than they were in psychology. Ryle himself admitted that there was a permanent gap in behaviorist analyses in general, namely, in their inability to give any account, as he memorably put it, of what "Le Penseur" ("The Thinker," as depicted in Rodin's statue) is doing, for here we have a person to whom we readily apply the paradigm mental predicate "thinking," yet no behavior is taking place, no noticeable physiological agitation is occurring, and no notice is being taken of what is going on in the immediate environment. All the usual ingredients for a behavioristic analysis are simply not available.

Another very basic problem for behavioristic analyses, which shows up all too clearly in the context of the emotions, is what might be called "the problem of diffuseness." Any account of an emotion stating that "emotion X" is to be analyzed as "a disposition to behave in manner a, b, and c in context p" will encounter an intractable problem. The behavior that, in fact, we associate with any particular emotion cannot be circumscribed in a neat, definitive, and packaged way. For example, one person might display anger by banging the table, shouting, and slamming the door. Another might display it by being unusually quiet and undemonstrative, and by closing the door with studied carefulness as he leaves the room with exaggerated courtesy. What an angry person will do will depend on what sort of temperament he has, what culture he is part of, what context he finds himself in, and so on. What an angry person might do, then, is "open-ended" rather than "neatly parceled."

The very profuseness and unpredictability of emotional behavior, unless we know a great deal about the subject of the emotion in question, is an indication that we consider behavior to be a quite variable manifestation of an emotion rather than all that an emotion is. Indeed, unless we considered it thus, how could we decide that slamming the door and shouting, or tightening the muscles of the face, narrowing the eyes, and speaking in an unnaturally even tone of voice, or going red in the face and weeping, or some other pattern of behavior, is angry behavior but picking your nose or scratching your neck is not? Behavior does not come hallmarked with the name of some emotion. We need to link behavior to some emotion or to learn that this behavior is a symptom of that emotion. We have to learn that giggling is a sign of nervousness in Japanese people and not a sign of frivolity. We have to learn that sobbing can be a sign of relief as well as grief.

If behavioristic accounts can be described as "peripheralist" ones, in that they emphasize and make essential reference to the peripheral or behavioral aspects of humans, then the reaction to behaviorism in both philosophy and psychology might be called "centralist." The main theories of mind and emotion, which superseded behaviorist ones, gave accounts that emphasized what they believed was going on inside human heads and so was central to the human organism. This reaction was not a return to Cartesian dualism. I doubt if there ever will be a reaction of that sort, for contemporary philosophers and psychologists tend to be uncompromising materialists. All there is to humans, just as all there is to animals, is physiology organized so as to act and react in a certain way. For a time, from roughly 1960 to 1980, the guiding metaphor in philosophy of mind was the digital computer. The mind is to the body, so the slogan went, as a computer's program or software is to its electronics or hardware. The study of human psychology amounts to the investigation of the human program. Evolution is both the programmer of the software and the designer of the hardware. It is up to humans to unravel what evolution has knitted.

The pendulum has swung back. Psychology and philosophy of mind were seen once again as mental science but with the "mentalism" removed. Human psychology was first and foremost what went on inside human heads. The core of theoretical psychology, as a discipline, was the scientific account of human cognition and appetition, or "cognitive science" for short. In philosophy of mind and philosophical psychology—the latter term was increasingly being substituted for the former as once again philosophers and psychologists found common cause—this "centralism" took the form of making it legitimate once again to talk about beliefs, desires, hopes, and wants. On the other hand, there arose soon enough an uncompromising and unrelenting debate about the correct account of such terms as *belief, desire, want, hope,* and so on. Do these terms, it was asked, refer literally to neuronal states of the brain? Or do they refer to functional tasks that are performed by the brain? Or are such terms really just a useful "folk" way of talking about what goes on inside human heads that must not be taken literally?

These mainstream core debates in philosophy of mind are not our concern here. What is our concern is that the centralist reaction against the behavioristic accounts of emotions produced what came to be known as cognitive accounts. The core of emotions, as Aristotle had claimed long ago, is beliefs, including evaluative beliefs, and desires, which, in the rather inexact modern jargon, came to be lumped together under the label "cognitions."[4] Now emotions were viewed once again as complexly psychosomatic; that is, emotions were analyzed in terms of physiological changes, feelings, behavioral actions, and reactions, as well as beliefs, desires, wants, and wishes. Indeed, the latter were held to be the core of emotional states. What differentiated one emotion from another, and an emotional state from a nonemotional state, was a cognitive "something." Which sort of "cognitive" state—belief, evaluation, or desire—was the essential one was itself a matter of considerable debate, and still is to some extent. Some saw the essential cognitive state or item to be beliefs, others argued that it was judgments, others desires, and still others appraisals or evaluations that seem to hover between pure beliefs and pure desires.

In my attempt to get to the essentials when describing the demise of behaviorism and the rise of cognitivism in philosophy and psychology, no doubt I have tidied up the story a little too much. Certainly the move away from behavioristic accounts of emotion to so-called cognitive accounts was a slow and unspectacular affair. The beginnings are probably to be found in a series of careful but undramatic essays that drew attention to the shortcomings of noncognitive accounts of emotion and to the attractions of bringing "cognitions" into the analysis of emotional states. Though it is not easy to chart the exact beginning of this progress, some of the early and influential discussions were the following: Errol Bedford's article "Emotions" (1956–1957), Terence Penelhum's article "The Logic of Pleasure" (1956–1957), R. S. Peters's book *The Concept of Motivation* (1960) and his subsequent article "Emotions and the Category of Passivity" (1961–1962), Anthony Kenny's book *Action, Emotion and Will* (1963), George Pitcher's article "Emotion" (1965), and William Alston's encyclopedia entry "Emotion and Feeling" (1967). Much later, in the 1970s, I myself set out to work up these and later piecemeal gains into a full, clear, and elaborated cognitive account of emotion that was published as *Emotion* (Lyons, 1980/1993).

In *Emotion* I pointed out that emotion terms are sometimes used *dispositionally* and sometimes *occurrently*. *Rage*, for example, is always used occurrently; that is, it is always used to refer to an actual here-and-now bout or state of extreme anger in some person. The term *irascible*, on the other hand, is a purely dispositional term, for it means that the person to whom it is applied is disposed or liable to fits or bouts of anger "at the drop of a hat." *Love* is another term that is used almost always in a dispositional sense, while the term *excited* is used almost always in an occurrent sense. I suggested that, since an emotional disposition amounts to being disposed to be in an occurrent or here-and-now emotional state of some sort in certain circumstances, then the focus of investigation and theoretical discussion should be occurrent emotional states, for they are "the full case." Whatever it is that is latent in an irascible person, which makes that person irascible, will still be there, though now activated, in a person who is now angry. In addition, the other "parts" of emotional states—the feelings, behavior, physiological changes, expressions—will now be present.

I argued for *a causal-evaluative* (and in that sense "cognitive") account of emotional states, namely, that a subject is in an emotional state if and only if he is in an abnormal physiological state caused by his evaluation of the context in relation *to* himself." *Abnormal*, in relation to physiological changes, is defined as "*departing significantly from a human's normal physiological states in either direction*" that is, in the direction of arousal or perturbation, or in the direction of unusual dampening down or calm. *Evaluation* is defined as "*a grading of the situation according to a wide spectrum of possible gradings or values.*" For example, the subject of an emotional state will be in an emotional state because he or she has evaluated the situation as dangerous to himself, or insulting, or exciting, and so on. Thus, the subject is *afraid* if he *evaluates the situation as dangerous and this evaluation effects him physi-*

ologically, that is, if it makes his heart beat faster, his respiration rate increase dramatically, his hands sweat, and his jaw tighten. This realization of danger, if the danger in question is the appearance of a Rottweiler from around the corner, will also quite likely make him want to avoid or escape the danger, which in turn will make him want to run away or call for help. But it might not. He might be knowledgable about dogs and know that if he stands stock-still and speaks to the dog in a soft and even voice, with lots of phrases like "Nice doggy" and "Aren't you a handsome fellow," the dog will eventually lope off.

The evaluation, which is at the heart of each emotion, is also what differentiates one emotion from another. Your agitation is to be labeled *anger* rather than *fear* if you believe that he has insulted you rather than that he is about to attack you. In fact, your evaluation of the situation may be wrong. He is about to attack you and he was not the person who insulted you. Nevertheless, your emotional state is still one of anger rather than fear, for your emotion is caused by what you "cognize" about the situation and its relevance to you, not what some objective observer guesses or even knows about the situation.[5]

A cognitive-evaluative approach to the explanation of emotions also makes emotions out to be part of the deliberative, thoughtful, and rational side of humans rather than, as Plato had claimed, the animal-like foe of reason. Our evaluations of particular situations express our personal values, which in turn will very often be influenced by our culture. Our values are, usually, things we hold dear for good reasons, and the things by which we order our life at its deepest levels. Emotions, indeed, are probably a better guide to what we really approve and disapprove of than are our words and actions, for we can readily simulate the latter but not the former. When we speak of our fearlessness, our physiology, gestures, and behavior may contradict us. When we say "no matter," our flushing or blushing may say it matters very much.

A cognitive-evaluative account of emotion solves "the problem of diffuseness." We call this behavior emotional and that behavior not, and this behavior angry behavior rather than anxious behavior, because we know or guess that the subject of the behavior considers that he himself or someone dear to him has been insulted or the victim of some outrage. It is the emotional person's "cognitions" in the broad sense[6] that we employ as a sieve to sift out the behavior that stems rationally and appropriately and so typically from those "cognitions." It is this link that enables us to label a piece of behavior as typically angry behavior or as a symptom of anxiety or a sign of embarrassment. It is the failure to discover any such discernible link that forces us to decide that this other action or reaction more likely to be a symptom of fatigue or stomach upset, that is, the effect of a noncognitive cause. To put this in another context, no noncognitivist account can explain why both running away and dieting can be a sign of fear. Only a cognitivist account, which makes it clear that we can view dogs as liable to attack people and look upon obesity as a danger to health, can explain how we can have both a fear of dogs and a fear of getting fat.

A cognitive account of emotions also explains how emotions are motives and how emotional behavior is rational, appropriate behavior. If the core of the emotion of anger is an evaluative belief that one has been insulted or is in some sense a victim of outrage, then it makes sense that an angry person will lash out vengefully, verbally or otherwise, at the author of the insult or outrage. Contrariwise, if the core of the emotion in question is an evaluation of someone as possessing special personal characteristics such as beauty, charm, or goodness, or all three, then it makes sense to say that the appropriate and so likely response of someone who is in the grip of that emotion will be the opposite of a vengeful lashing out.

Put more generally, only a cognitive account of emotion seems to make sense of emotions as not merely motives behind our actions but as subtle, rational, finely tuned motives. A cognitive account can make the "cognitive core" of any particular emotional state as complex and as "thick" as you like. "She cried because she was sad" can be thickened to "She cried because she was sad that Mary had died" to "She cried because she was sad that Mary had died because Mary was her friend" to "She cried because she was sad that Mary had died because Mary was her friend and because Mary was so young" and so on. The reaction is seen, at least very often, as the result of more than one emotion, as, for example, the result of sadness, affection, and loneliness, all mixed in. Sometimes these emotions can clash. Sometimes we are ambivalent in our emotional responses. Sometimes we are emotional about our emotions. Only a cognitive account seems able to make sense of such subtleties.

Of course, feelings and physiological changes are an integral part of emotions. Rather, the point is that they must not be seen in isolation. They are "smeared with cognition." However, there are theoretically interesting cases when feelings can be absent from emotional states. As William James pointed out, feelings are consciously experienced happenings in our bodies and so part of our conscious attention. When a person's attention is wholly taken up by something important, then there can be no "attention room" left over for feelings. On the other hand, the "something important" will often generate an emotional state but one with no room for feelings. For example, during a philosophical discussion about politics, I might become very angry at someone's claiming that I am a crypto-something-or-other but, because my attention is wholly taken up by the discussion, my being physiologically aroused will escape my attention. My arousal will not enter my consciousness as feelings (though it may be very noticeable to others). I am emotional but, owing to the circumstances, do not in fact feel anything. Of course, feelings are most often a part of emotional states. Indeed, it would be very odd if someone claimed that they were overcome by love, anger, anxiety, or hate but felt nothing at all. We would doubt the sincerity of their claim.

More generally speaking, the lack of emphasis on feelings in the cognitive account of emotion is another sign of the long retreat from a Cartesian subjectivist view of emotions. Feelings are subjective experiences while evaluations and physiological changes are not. While a cognitivist account of emotion is a centralist account, and thereby in conflict with any behaviorist or peripheralist account, it is not a return to subjectivism. Evaluations are objective items. It may be possible in the future, given advances in neurophysiology, to identify them with neurophysiological events (see, e.g., the attempt by Gray, 1981). Such a correlation makes some sense, at least initially, precisely because evaluations are much more objective than, say, feelings. Correlations involve co-relating *two* things. To do this successfully, we need to be able, first of all, to identify, separately, each of the items to be eventually correlated. We can identify evaluations in an objective way because we attribute evaluations "from the outside." We, observers, say that he believes (or, if we are doing philosophy, "he has the evaluative belief") that he is in danger of being robbed *because* we see him carefully put his money into a money belt, check it every few minutes, continually look around to see if anyone is following him, and become nervous if someone accidentally brushes against him. We attribute beliefs, including evaluative ones, in other words, on the basis of observable behavioral and contextual evidence (which, of course, may include what the subject claims, verbally, is his belief). We cannot identify feelings in an objective way, because we cannot attribute them to someone "from the outside." Only the subject of feelings can say that he or she has some feeling and what it is like. Because feelings, unlike beliefs, are items in a subject's stream of consciousness, feelings are known "from the inside" or subjectively. There is no way that an observer can check your claim about whether you have a feeling and what it is like.

Having said all that, it may now be clear why I believe that it is a mistake to attempt to reify evaluations in such a crude, reductive, one-to-one way. *Evaluating* seems to be a term that is properly employed only at a higher, macro, functional level of description, which takes into account a whole panorama of items, such as the perceived environment, a person's cognitive reaction to his perception of the environment, and his subsequent behavioral responses to his cognitive reaction. What the term *evaluating* describes is a highly complex relation of ordinary items at the ordinary everyday level of events observable by ordinary humans as a result of the application of their ordinary senses.

Perhaps this can be made clearer by approaching it from a slightly different angle. Regarding what it refers to, *evaluation* should be categorized as a complex term rather than a simple one. What I mean by this might be made clear by means of an analogy. *Slippery* as applied to roads is not a simple perceptual term on a par with *wet*, though it may appear to be so, for *slippery* means "the level of wetness that in the past has been found to make the tires of vehicles, which travel on such a surface, lack adhesion and so slide across the surface." Similarly, *evaluating* seems not to be a comparatively straightforward term like *perceiving* but a highly complex one. Thus, it may not make sense to look for a single area in the brain, or easily circumscribed pattern of brain activity, that could be labeled *evaluative center* or *evaluative cortex*, in the way that there is a visual cortex. However, this does not mean that evaluations are any the less objective. It just means that their explanation will not be as simple and straightforward.

It is probably fair to say that cognitivism is still the orthodoxy in philosophy of the emotions today. However, the cognitive theory of emotion may be modified in the future, perhaps quite radically, when philosophers and psychologists settle the current debates about the status of beliefs and desires or, in general, of *cognitions*.

Cognitive Theories of Emotion and Psychopathology

Good theoretical work has its effect, if at all, at a very basic level. It may eventually guide someone's search for crucial experiments or indicate new areas of investigation, but it is unlikely to do so immediately or directly. I have no reason to believe that in psychopathology matters are any different.

In this section I will confine myself to bringing forward some speculative considerations that result from my long-standing advocacy of cognitive theories of emotion.

While Affective Disorders Are Cognitive Disorders, They Are Not Necessarily Generated at a Cognitive Level

If the core of emotions is a cognition of some sort, such as, as I have suggested, an evaluative belief, then disordered emotions will almost always involve disordered evaluative beliefs. For example, a patient may have an unbudgeable phobia about earthworms. Or else the patient suffers from severe incongruity regarding his or her emotions; he laughs at his mother's funeral and cries all day on his own birthday, or she is unbudgeably manic one day and depressed the next.

However, unfortunately, it does not follow that the way to cure such disorders is to reason the patient out of his inappropriate evaluation of the situation. Indeed, the contrary is the case. The inappropriate fear, elation, sadness, or depression is pathological precisely because it is impervious to the ordinary level of "talking out" cure. The patient usually knows this himself. He knows also all the usual reasons why earthworms are not dangerous, why the deaths of loved ones are sad, and why birthday celebrations should be occasions of joy.

So what is the answer? The answer I believe, lies in the direction of realizing that rational deliberation is only *one* of the ways in which humans form their beliefs including their evaluative ones. Very often the "reasoning" that does produce our beliefs is not logical. It is not how the logic textbooks recommend that you reason to conclusions. But then, logic is an artificial "pure" system, like algebra. It is pure *in*human reasoning.

Unfortunately, perhaps, we humans are also psychosomatic creatures. We are not just reasoning minds, so just as anxiety or thinking about the examination tomorrow can bring us out in a rash, so can a rash cause anxiety. Beliefs, evaluations, and desires can be caused by drugs, poor diet, trauma, or disease. They can also be caused by disorder at the genetic level. The switches from mania to depression, and back again, in severe cases of manic-depression are often so swift, cyclical, context-independent, and far-reaching and fundamental in their effects, altering both behavior and perception itself to a severe degree, that almost certainly it is caused at a very fundamental biological level.

Another rich source of our beliefs is the subterranean world of embedded and repressed memories, often ingeniously "rewired" by our imagination. Her fear of earthworms is really her fear of the man next door who, in her childhood, did something terrible to her while she was playing with earthworms. Or his sudden uncontrollable outbursts of rage are an expression of an otherwise inexpressible desire to be helped regarding some difficulty.

Part of any serious and thoroughgoing account of belief will include an account of the myriad and amazing ways in which beliefs can be engendered. Part of any serious and thoroughgoing account of emotion will include an account of the myriad and amazing ways in which the evaluative beliefs, which are at the heart of emotion, can be engendered.

While Affective Disorders Are Cognitive Disorders, They Are Not Necessarily Curable at One Particular Level That Takes Precedence Over Others

There is an increasingly favored view in philosophy that reductionism about beliefs, including the evaluative beliefs, or evaluations, at the core of affective states, is misguided. Beliefs are not to be identified with some neurophysiological item such as a brain state, process, neural network, or activated cell assembly. It would be extraordinary if it turned out that our terms *belief, desire, evaluative belief,* and their like were the labels of isolatable states or processes in the brain, for it would mean that, while our earliest ancestors probably employed our ordinary "folk psychological" vocabulary of belief and desire and their relatives, they had by some extraordinary serendipity also been doing very sophisticated neuroscience without realizing it. Without knowing it, they had employed a psychological vocabulary that had correctly carved nature at its neurophysiological joints.

To put it bluntly, and paradoxically, I do not believe that story about beliefs. I do not think they can be reduced to items or processes at the level of the brain without absurdity.[7] For I think that the true account of beliefs is closer to the way behaviorists described them. To say "She believes it is going to rain" or "Lassie believes there is a bone buried in the corner of the garden" is to attribute something to someone *from the outside,* and on the basis of observation of "input" to that person, their presumed perceptual information about the environment, and "output," their observed actions and reactions. We say she believes it is going to rain because we might have seen her look up at the sky, then go back into the house, and then reemerge with an umbrella. We did not at any time gain a privileged look into her brain.

We attribute emotions, via an attribution of their core evaluative beliefs, in the same way. We say that "She is afraid of dogs" if we see her cross the street whenever she sees a dog, says "Keep that animal away from me" in an emotional tone of voice whenever she is invited to pat a dog, and so on.

Talk about beliefs, including evaluative beliefs, and about other such attitudes, such as hope, desire, intention, or decision, is an indispensable, *macro* account of the cognitive life of humans. And it no more makes sense to reduce our talk about beliefs to talk about the physiology of the brain, or talk about anything else at a "lower" level for that matter, than it makes sense to reduce an economist's talk about an increase in the money supply causing inflation to talk about causes and effects at the level of physics and chemistry.

Crude reductionism about beliefs, including evaluative beliefs, is out, and, for the same reason, so are crude reductionist cures of affective disorders. You will not be on the road to any clean, neat, and quick cure of affective disorders by first reducing the emotions or affects to brain states or processes, and then altering these brain states or processes. Beliefs, and so emotions, at the heart of which are evaluative beliefs, are realities that are only picked out at the macro level of description-from-the-outside.

It follows, also, from what I have said about the many ways in which beliefs can arise, that there are many ways in which disordered evaluative or affective beliefs can arise. The causes will be many and varied, and will arise along different routes at different times. In turn, these different routes will have different sources, and these different sources may be found at different levels. Thus, the only way to cure the affective disorders will be the painstaking and messy one of working out, *in each particular individual case*, how, from what direction, and at what level the disordered belief arose, and then trying to undo the damage.

Annoyingly, perhaps, psychopathology is always going to be much more difficult because it is more individualistic than other areas of medicine, because the disorders of evaluative belief can and do arise in a large number of ways. You have to look carefully at individual cases. There is not going to be a single cure, say, a drug or an alteration of a gene, as there might be for arthritis or leukemia. And to ignore this difficulty may only do untold damage, not merely to the patients but also to psychopathology and psychiatry.

Acknowledgments I am greatly indebted to Professor Marcus Webb, Professor of Psychiatry at St. James's and St. Patrick's Hospitals in Dublin, for his most perceptive comments on the first draft of this essay, and to my colleague, Dr. David Berman, for his advice and encouragement.

Notes

1. I begin my book *Emotion* (Lyons,1980/1993) with two chapters on the history of theorizing in philosophy about the nature of emotion.

2. Arguably, however, modern cognitive theories of emotion could be considered to be a reworking of Aristotle's account of emotion in the *Rhetoric* (trans. 1941, Bk. II).

3. There are those who would say that these failures to discover distinct physiological patterns for each distinct emotion were due to weaknesses in measurement technique (e.g., see Ax, 1971; Izard, 1972; Plutchik & Ax, 1967; Stanley-Jones, 1970).

4. Strictly speaking, the term cognitions is crude and inexact. Cognition, from the latin *cognoscere*, meaning "to know," implies knowledge or knowledge-type states. But the core states regarding emotion are evaluative beliefs that are in the nature of assessments or appraisals of what we know, or think we know, rather than further knowledge. Factual beliefs and appetitive states (such as desires, wants, and wishes) also play a part, but the crucial part is that played by evaluations (i.e., evaluative beliefs). I stick with the term *cognitions*, then, solely because it has become set in cement in the psychological literature.

5. This view, besides having the philosophical sources already acknowledged in the text, owes some inspiration to the work of the psychologists Arnold, Schacter and Singer (see Arnold, 1945, 1960; Schachter 1971; and Schachter & Schachter 1962).

6. See note 4 above.

7. My own view is that these terms, such as *belief, desire, wish, want,* and *evaluative belief,* do pick out realities but not simple biological or neurological ones. They form part of a long-standing common-sense psychology that picks out complex relations between humans and their environment. The parts of the relations, encompassing both what is inside human heads and what is outside human heads, as well as the imprint of the latter on the former and the dispositions of the former regarding the latter, are very complex indeed and so very messy when one sets out to analyze them in detail. In our talk of beliefs, desires, and other attitudes, we are more sophisticated than we know. But this is true of most bits of us that have evolved over time. Our commonsense psychology is no exception.

References

Alston, W. (1967). Emotion and feeling. In P. Edwards (Ed.), *The encyclopedia of philosophy* (Vol. 2) (pp. 479–486). New York: Collier Macmillan.

Aristotle. (trans. 1941). *Rhetoric*. In R. McKeon (Ed.), *The basic works of Aristotle* (trans. W. D. Ross) New York: Random House.

Armon-Jones, C. (1991). *Varieties of affect*. New York: Simon & Schuster.

Arnold, M. B. (1960). *Emotion and personality* (2 vols.). New York: Columbia University Press.

Ax, A. F. (1971). Review of neurophysiology discovers the mind. *Contemporary Psychology, 16*, 365–367.

Bedford, E. (1956–1957). Emotions. *Proceedings of the Aristotelian Society, 57*, 281–304.

Carnap, R. (1959). Psychology in physical language. In A. J. Ayer (Ed.), *Logical positivism* (pp. 165–198). New York: Collier Macmillan. (Original work published 1931).

Gray, J. (1981). *The neuropsychology of anxiety: An enquiry into the functions of the septo-hippocampal system*. Oxford: Oxford University Press.

Izard, C. E. (1972) *Patterns of emotions: A new analysis of anxiety and depression*. New York: Academic Press.

James, W. (1884). What is emotion? *Mind, 9*, 188–205.

James, W. (1950). *The principles of psychology* (Vol. 2). New York: Dover. (Original work published 1890).

Kenny, A. (1963). *Action, emotion and will*. London: Routledge & Kegan Paul.

Lyons, W. (1993). *Emotion* (facsimile reprint). Adlershot, UK: Gregg Revivals. (Original work published 1980).

Oakley, J. (1992). *Morality and the emotions*. London: Routledge.

Penelhum, T. (1956–1957). The logic of pleasure. *Philosophy and Phenomenological Research, 17*, 488–503.

Peters, R. S. (1960). *The concept of motivation*. London: Routledge & Kegan Paul.

Peters, R. S. (1961–1962). Emotions and the category of passivity. *Proceedings of the Aristotelian Society, 62*, 117–134.

Pitcher, G. (1965). Emotion. *Mind, 74*, 326–364.

Plutchik, R. & Ax, A. F. (1967). A critique of "Determinants of Emotional State" by Schacter and Singer (1962). *Psychophysiology, 4*, 79–82.

Rorty, A. (Ed.). (1980). *Explaining emotions*. Berkeley, CA: University of California Press.

Rose, S. (1976). *The conscious brain* (rev. ed.). Middlesex, UK: Penguin.

Ryle, G. (1949). *The concept of mind*. London: Hutchinson.

Ryle, G. (1971). Systematically misleading expressions. In G. Ryle, *Collected Papers: Vol. 2. Collected Essays 1929–1968*. London:Hutchinson (Original work published 1932).

Schachter, S. (1971). *Emotion, obesity and crime*. New York: Academic Press.

Schachter, S., & Singer, J. (1962). Cognitive, social and physiological determinants of emotional state. *Psychological Review, 69*, 379–399.

Schoeman, F. (Ed.). (1987). *Responsibility, character, and the emotions: New essays in moral psychology*. Cambridge: Cambridge University Press.

Skinner, B. F. (1953). *Science and human behaviour*. New York: Macmillan.

Solomon, R. (1978). *The passions:The myth and nature of human emotion*. New York: Anchor Books.

Stanley-Jones, D. (1970). The biological origin of love and hate. In M. B. Arnold (Ed.), *Feelings and emotions: The Loyola Symposium* (pp. 25–37). New York: Academic Press.

Strongman, K. T. (1987). *The psychology of emotion* (3rd. ed.). New York: Wiley.

Taylor, J. (1971/1974). *The shape of minds to come*. St. Albans, UK: Panther.

Watson, J. B. (1913). Psychology as the behaviourist views it. *The Psychological Review, 20,* 158–178.

Watson, J. B. (1919). *Psychology from the standpoint of a behaviorist*. Philadelphia: Lippincott.

Watson, J. B. (1930). *Behaviorism* (rev. ed.). Chicago: University of Chicago Press.

Some Further Reading

Arnold, M. B. (1945). Physiological differentiation of emotional states.*Psychological Review, 52,* 35–48.

Cannon, W. B. (1927). The James-Lange theory of emotions: A critical examination and an alternative theory. *American Journal of Psychology, 39,* 106–124.

Cotman, C. W., McGaugh, J. L. (1980) *Behavioral neuroscience: An introduction*. New York: Academic Press.

Descartes, R. (1911–1912). *The passions of the soul*. In E. L. Haldane & G. R. Ross, (Eds. & Trans.), *The philosophical works of Descartes*. Cambridge: Cambridge University Press.

de Sousa, R. (1987). *The rationality of emotion*. Cambridge, MA: MIT Press.

Gelder, M. Gath, D., & Mayou, R. (1991). *Oxford textbook of psychiatry* (2nd. ed. with later revisions). Oxford: Oxford University Press.

Gordon, R. M. (1986). The passivity of emotions. *Philosophical Review, 95,* 371–392.

Greenspan, P. (1988). *Emotions and reasons: An inquiry into emotional justification*. London: Routledge.

Gregory, R. (Ed.). (1987). *The Oxford companion to the mind*. Oxford: Oxford University Press.

Hart, B. (1930). *The psychology of insanity*. Cambridge: Cambridge University Press. (Original work published 1912)

Irani, K. D. & Myers, G. E. (Eds.). (1984). *Emotion: Philosophical studies*. New York: Haven.

Lange, C. (1922). Om sindsbevaegelser (Engl. trans.). In K. Dunlap (Ed.), *The emotions*. Baltimore: Williams and Wilkins. (Original work published in 1885)

Lyons, W. (1992). An introduction to the philosophy of the emotions. In K. T. Strongman (Ed.), *International review of studies of emotion* (pp. 295–313). New York: Wiley.

Mandler, G. (1975). *Mind and emotion*. New York: Wiley.

Munn, N. L. (1961). *Psychology: The fundamentals of human adjustment*. London: Harrap.

Plato. (trans. 1955) *The republic* (H. D. P. Lee, Trans. & Ed.). Middlesex, UK: Penguin.

2

Keolani Taitano & Gregory A. Miller

Neuroscience Perspectives on Emotion in Psychopathology

Many opportunities exist to bring neuroscience to bear in studies of the role of emotion in psychopathology. Unfortunately, psychological approaches to psychopathology often seem to ignore compelling biological issues and findings, and biological approaches to psychopathology are often equally parochial with respect to psychology (Churchland, 1986). The divide that often separates biological and psychological approaches to both emotion and psychopathology fosters a variety of philosophical errors, barriers to collaboration, and even competitive pressures among subdisciplines. A consideration of the range of available measures of biological phenomena, however, provides encouragement. Such measures may of course take the form of direct recording of biological events, such as heart rate changes, brainwave patterns, cortisol levels, or regional metabolic rate, but they may also take the form of direct recording of behavioral events used as a basis for inference about biological events, such as overt performance on a neuropsychological test. Thus, the distinction between "biological" and "psychological" measures is less clear than it may appear.

In this chapter we provide a survey of some promising "biological" methodologies and initiatives, and we consider some challenging issues they raise. We emphasize a number of conceptual and methodological issues that must be faced in bringing neuroscience to bear on the study of emotion in psychopathology. Finally, we highlight some promising findings and conceptualizations.

Some Conceptual and Definitional Issues

Domain of Measurement versus Domain of Inference

A frequent confusion that arises when bringing biological methods to bear on the study of psychological phenomena concerns the purpose and status of the biological measures. What kind of story is being constructed: Are we interested in a psychological account, or a biological account, of psychopathology? It is often assumed, though it is not at all necessary to assume, that biological measurements best serve biological questions. On the contrary, biological measures can be equally appropriate for addressing psychological questions. For example, electrophysiological measures are playing a major and growing role in the service of mental chronometry in cognitive psychology (e.g., Coles, 1989). There, the questions are purely psychological; the goal is not to localize functions in the brain but to model the structure and timing of cognition. Conversely, the behavioral data that a neurologist collects in a standard exam may be invaluable in addressing very biological questions. Although brain localization can be helpful to cognitive psychology and vice versa, these are different domains, and their distinct goals must be understood. Neither biological nor psychological models are necessarily diminished by ignoring phenomena in the other domain (Strauss & Summerfelt, 1994). For example, it is not necessary to know the generator of a brain-wave component to employ it fruitfully to study psychological phenomena. Such a measure can have the same status as any other measure, such as reaction time—an index of some process or event that is meaningfully related to the concepts of interest. On the other hand, no model can be considered comprehensive as long as it leaves out interesting, relevant phenomena, and ultimately psychological and biological models will have to converge in order to be comprehensive (Churchland, 1986).

A related confusion is based on the assumption that it is possible, with a sufficiently thorough biological account of some kind of psychopathology, to provide an adequate account of that psychopathology. A classic example is the so-called dopamine theory of schizophrenia (Davis, Kahn, Ko, & Davidson, 1991). This is an important and impressive theory, but it can never be a satisfactory theory of (all of) schizophrenia. It is a theory about dopamine *in* schizophrenia, an account of biochemistry in schizophrenia, not a comprehensive account of schizophrenia. *Schizophrenia*, as a term, refers to a host of things not reducible to a set of synaptic events. By definition, thought disorder is a phenomenon in the domain of psychology. It may indeed be that an excess of dopamine receptors is common in schizophrenia, or even invariably present. But thought disorder is not accomplished by *neural* systems, it is accomplished by *cognitive* systems. This is a matter of semantics, not in the sense of word games but in the sense of paying attention to the proper meanings of words. The converse point can also be made: Given the compelling data for a genetic role in schizophrenia, for enlarged ventricles, for diminished P300 (a component of the event-related brain potential), and for a variety of other biological findings, a purely psychological account that deals with thought disorder will necessarily be inadequate as a comprehensive model of schizophrenia.

This argument warrants elaboration because it is so often unappreciated. As another example, depressives' memory bias (Mineka & Sutton, 1992) may involve certain consistencies in the neural events involved across individuals and occasions, but the bias clearly persists in the face of neural implementations that vary enormously across people and situations. Even if we are able to outline what goes on at a neural level, we will still refer to the entire phenomenon as a *memory bias* (a purely psychological term). It would be inefficient and unclear to refer only to an indefinite set of neural operations that happen to implement such a bias, just as it would be inefficient and unclear to replace concepts in chemistry with concepts from physics or to replace the concept of a mousetrap with an enumeration of examples (Fodor, 1968; Kozak & Miller, 1982; Miller & Kozak, 1993). Even a prominent champion of reductionism (the potential for reduction of psychology to neuroscience) allows mental phenomena to remain after reduction has been achieved (Churchland, 1986). In fact, Churchland concedes that some mental phenomena as currently conceived may not be reducible to brain states.

Brain Localization

With that general caveat about psychology-biology relationships in mind, we turn to several issues in the effort to identify brain tissue involved in implementing specific psychological functions that are important in considering the role of emotion in psychopathology. Emotion functions appear to be lateralized, and appreciation of this is rapidly growing. Lateralized processing in the brain can be approached methodologically in at least three ways. First, stimulus presentation can be lateralized. Tones may be presented monaurally, or visual stimuli can be presented to one hemifield. This forces lateralized processing at least at initial stages. Second, one can directly measure biological events that are themselves lateralized, such as regional brain metabolism or components of the visual event-related brain potential (ERP) arising from primary visual cortex. Third, one can measure phenomena believed to be dependent on lateralized processing, even though the phenomena measured directly are not themselves lateralized. For example, the P300 component of the ERP is generally maximal at midline electrode sites but may be driven by processing that occurs predominantly in one hemisphere. A measure such as heart rate is clearly not lateralized, but there is evidence of lateralized innervation of heart rate (Wittling, 1995).

Important methodological constraints should be recognized regarding research on hemispheric differences in the processing of emotion. For example, task demands and differences in methodology can contribute substantially to visual-field differences in recognizing or judging facial emotion (for a review, see Hellige & Sergent, 1986). Task difficulty is one highly influential factor. Adequate task difficulty is required to avoid the potential problem of a ceiling effect in performance on single-hemisphere trials, which would make it difficult to demonstrate a differential rather than a global performance deficit (Banich, 1995; Chapman & Chapman, 1978). However, if the task is very difficult, a number of processes may come into play that are not involved in easier tasks, and these could result in reduced group differences in task performance or a shift in strategies from those that are more typically pursued by one hemisphere to those of the opposite hemisphere. There is some evidence that the left hemisphere may become more dominant with increased task difficulty (Goldberg & Costa, 1981; Kinsbourne, 1974; Tucker & Williamson, 1984). Greater task difficulty can also result in an advantage on across-hemisphere trials (Belger & Banich, 1992). Mode of response may also influence literality findings. Hellige and Sergent (1986) suggested that requiring a subject to produce a verbal response may selectively arouse the left hemisphere and thus bias attention toward the right visual field. Other intentional behavioral responses may also affect relative hemispheric activity, such as deliberate lateral shifts in gaze (Autret, Auvert, Laffont, & Larmande, 1985; Kinsbourne & Hicks, 1978).

A number of caveats must be recognized in research that specifically addresses cerebral asymmetries in emotion. Davidson (1993a) provided a detailed discussion arguing that asymmetries associated with different aspects of emotional processing do not directly implicate the neural substrate responsible for the production of emotion. Additionally, research indicates that each hemisphere does not function as a unitary whole. Instead, there are important differences in regional specificity within each hemisphere (Davidson, 1993a, Wood, Flowers, & Naylor, 1991).

An important distinction relevant to hemispheric localization of function is the fact that a hemisphere may be associated with a particular mood without being specialized to process information corresponding to that state (Heller, 1990). High levels of regional activity, in other words, do not necessarily indicate a specialization for the task at hand, as shown in split-brain patients when the hemisphere least suited for a task may dominate in the performance of that task (Levy, 1972), and when normal individuals tend to engage one hemisphere preferentially, regardless of the task (Levy, Heller, Banich, & Burton, 1983a; McKeever & Dixon, 1981).

The caveat here is to be wary of unnecessarily narrow notions of how to study or verify regional differences in brain function. For example, it is not only those direct measures that are themselves lateralized that may be informative about hemispheric differences in emotional processing. In a study currently underway we are recording ERPs from inpatient depressives and controls presented with a series of emotional stimuli (Deldin, Keller, Miller, & Gergen, 1996). The stimuli are presented foveally, and the primary ERP component of interest is P300. Neither of these features of the study alone can provide much information about possible group differences in lateralized processing. However, given that the stimuli consist of emotional words and emotional facial expressions, and given the evidence of differentially lateralized processing for such types of stimuli (Ahern et al., 1991; Borod, Andelman, Obler, Tweedy, & Welkowitz, 1992), we will be able to infer lateralized processing differences from certain patterns of group differences in P300.

A more general point about assessing the localization of function is that a common misstep is to conclude prematurely that the brain site directly producing an event that responds to experimental manipulation is the location responsible for the interesting processing. For example, it was thought for a time that P300 might be generated in the hippocampus. There was good circumstantial evidence for this view. But it was then found that P300 is observable after surgical removal of the hippocampus, and it was noted that the latency of P300–like activity recorded directly from the hippocampus tends to be later than the latency of scalp-recorded P300 (Johnson, 1989). In fact, biophysical modeling suggests that scalprecorded P300 cannot possibly be generated as deeply as the hippocampus and more likely comes from a broad layer of superficial cortex (Lutzenberger & Elbert, 1987). In retrospect, it is easy to fault the simplistic reasoning that, because both P300 and hippocampus seem to be related to memory, and because scalp P300 and hippocampal voltage covary experimentally, the hippocampus probably directly produces scalp P300. If anything, it is more logical to suggest that it is P300 that is driving the hippocampus. Furthermore, it is quite possible that other locations in the brain are driving both phenomena. Thus, P300 may be a manifestation of memory updating processes (e.g., Donchin & Coles, 1988), but those processes may not be reducible to, or even identifiable with, isolated brain regions or isolated brain events.

As modern brain-imaging techniques begin to be used in studies of emotion in psychopathology, it will be tempting to make similar mistakes. If two PET scans of the same slice differ at one location as a function of the subject's mood, it will be tempting to assign a causal role to that location in the generation of mood or in the service of emotional processing. Fredrikson et al. (1993) provided data amenable to such overinterpretation. They obtained PET scans of snake-phobia patients during exposure to videotapes of snakes, nonphobic aversive scenes, and neutral scenes. Blood flow in visual association cortex was elevated during phobic scenes. It might be concluded, but should not yet be concluded (and the authors did not conclude), that this region has a specific, causal role in anxiety. Interestingly, the available literature appears to be far less inclined (though it is no less plausible) to draw the causal arrow the other way: instead of reducing mood differences to activity levels in some brain region, one could attribute differences in that brain region to mood effects. Is that any less appealing?

In our search to find brain sites involved in emotional processing, there is also a need to be cautious in evaluating findings from neuropsychological research on brain-damaged individuals. As with inferences made about the meaning of EEG activity found over a region of the scalp, changes in mood or appraisal following lesion of a particular brain site could mean various things: that the excised or damaged tissue when intact produces the behavior or emotion in question, that it played a role in inhibiting that function or another function that in turn inhibited the variable of interest, or that it was a necessary component within an array of processes invoked in manifesting the measured outcome. The possibility has also been raised that hemispheric or regional specialization for type of emotion is more subtle in normal than in brain-damaged subjects and that methodologies that have been used may be obscuring such differences (Silberman & Weingartner, 1986).

The Relevance of Specific Biological Measures

A very common and unnecessarily narrow conceptualization of neuroscience in psychopathology involves the segregation of direct measures of brain physiology, such as the electroencephalogram (EEG), as being appropriate for studying cognition versus direct measures of visceral or peripheral physiology, such as pulse transit time or electrodermal activity, as being appropriate for studying emotion. Cognitive studies using peripheral physiological measures are numerous, though they are rarely noted in current cognitive neuroscience literature. Conversely, though fewer in number, studies of emotion using EEG frequency band activity and ERP components are becoming more common. Indeed, Davidson and Sutton (1995) have offered the term *affective neuroscience* as an antidote to the unnecessarily narrow view implicitly adopted in much of current cognitive neuroscience.

The unnecessary conceptual segregation of central and peripheral measures may reflect a widely held though substantially discredited view of the physiology of emotion as undifferentiated. Given the highly influential work of Schachter and Singer (1962), many lay people and even many scientists assume that there is no differential physiology for different emotions and that emotional differentiation is a purely cognitive process. Thus, one would measure peripheral physiology to assess the degree of arousal, but one must rely on self-report ratings or direct measures of brain function (as if there are no central efferents to the periphery) to study emotional specificity. However, this view overlooks the vast literature on the psychophysiological differentiation of emotion (for a brief but compelling review, see Levenson, 1992). There are many dozens of studies showing clearly that different emotional states are associated with different physiological states (e.g., Levenson, Ekman, & Friesen, 1990; Miller et al., 1987), although there are relatively few studies primarily aimed at that question. As a result of this oversight, the full range of physiological measures available to study emotion is often not considered.

What Underlies What?

All too frequently one encounters phrases like "the underlying neural pathology" in discussions of psychopathology or "underlying brain mechanisms" in discussions of emotion. From where comes the assumption that it is neural events that underlie psychological events? Positing such a relationship between neural and psychological events is certainly possible theoretically but is not necessary logically. The converse—that psychological events underlie neural events—is equally available, and there are other ways in which neural and psychological events may relate to each other. For example, we need not assume that an excess of dopamine receptors proposed for schizophrenia (Davis et al., 1991) "underlies" thought disorder. It could very well be that a history of thought disorder disrupts the dopamine system in a way that fosters excess receptor development. Thus, it could be thought disorder that "underlies" dopamine abnormality.

Along these lines, it is also common for the assumption to be made that biological findings reflect innate properties of the individual, sometimes even genetic factors. It is just as feasible, however, that environmental factors contribute as much or more to the variance observed in biological measures of emotion. Furthermore, the premise that it is possible or necessary to distinguish between genetic and environmental causes is highly questionable, as a variety of work has shown the very complex and dynamic nature of the interplay between genetic and environmental effects (Wahlsten, 1994). Thus, returning to the example of schizophrenia, early interactions with a caretaker may influence the development of the neural pathology or protective factors observed at later stages.

Where to Intervene

To expand on that point briefly, a pitfall in bringing neuroscience perspectives to bear on psychopathology is the temptation to assume that dysfunctions viewed biologically warrant interventions viewed biologically and conversely for dysfunctions and interventions viewed psychologically. For example, from suspecting an excess of dopamine receptors in schizophrenia it does not necessarily follow that one should treat schizophrenia with dopamine receptor agonists. Psychosocial interventions may be better not only in treating schizophrenia generally but in manipulating the behavior of dopamine receptors specifically.

What Is Emotion?

A very general issue to consider is the range of views on what emotion *is*. First, emotion theorists differ in adopting a dimensional (e.g., Lang, Bradley, & Cuthbert, 1990) or categorical/discrete (e.g., Levenson et al., 1990) model of the emotions. This choice has major implications not only for the measures one might select to study emotion but for the experimental designs deemed appropriate. (See Cacioppo, Klein, Berntson, & Hatfield [1993] for a model of emotion that attempts to integrate peripheral and central along with discrete and dimensional aspects of the processing of emotional experience.)

Second, the specificity of the concept of emotion varies greatly in different studies and theories. For example, the time frame of "an emotion" is in dispute. Some writers distinguish a brief emotion from a sustained mood. Other writers employ yet other time frames for these same terms. Similarly, writers differ in their definition of emotion relative to related words; some, but not all, distinguish emotion from affect or feeling. The boundary between emotion and motivation is also variable. Again, the problem is not that the potential distinctions are meaningless but that they are inconsistent across writers, although individual writers will speak as if a particular lexicon is widely shared. This sets up false or misleading conflicts between theorists and between data sets.

Third, against the traditional assumption of a nonspecific physiological arousal, there is overwhelming evidence that such a unitary concept of arousal is not generally useful (Lacey, 1967; Lang, 1968; Nitschke, Miller, & Heller, 1996) and that, instead, a conceptualization allowing for more specific kinds of arousal, or more localized areas of activation, is appropriate (e.g., Davidson, 1978, 1992a, 1993b; Heller, 1990, 1993; Tucker & Williamson, 1984; Venables, 1984). In fact, terms such as *arousal* or *activation*, deprived of their connotation of generalized mobilization, are now effectively reduced to meaning nothing more than activity in a particular measure or a particular brain region. As a result, the baggage associated with the traditional terms unnecessarily clouds modern writing. It would be far preferable to talk about regional activity than regional activation, when it is unclear what additional meaning, if any, is intended by the latter term.

Fourth, it should be noted that the locus of emotion is talked about very inconsistently. Sometimes emotion is that which one perceives, sometimes it is that which one expresses, and sometimes it is that which one experiences. Writers differ considerably in their emphasis, creating major barriers to a synthesis of the empirical literature. For example, what is the impact of a stimulus slide showing an angry face? Conceivably, at a biological level, the regions of the brain that work to classify the face as "angry" may be different from the regions that directly produce the viewer's own emotional response to the face (Heller, 1990). Similarly, at a psychological level, the processing undertaken to evaluate the poser's mood may differ from the processing that produces the subject's emotional response to the poser. A further complexity is that the coupling of perception and response may vary greatly as a function of individual learning history and predisposition. Does the sight of an angry face prompt anger, or fear? Is it possible to undertake perceptual processing of emotional stimuli without inducing some degree of emotional experience? Such questions may be central to a study of emotion in psychopathology. For example, there is growing interest in facial expression in schizophrenia, both its perception and its production (Berenbaum & Oltmanns, 1992, Blanchard, Kring, & Neale, 1994; Stolar, Berenbaum, Banich, & Barch, 1994; see also Blanchard, chap. 24, and Neale, Blanchard, Kerr, Kring, & Smith, chap. 25 in this volume). What, then, is the actual experiment being performed? Is the angry face, in effect, a means of mood induction? And, if so, is it equally effective across subjects? Whether the independent variable is patient diagnosis or a more traditionally biological phenomenon, do observed group differences reflect differences in the encoding of the facial stimuli or differences in the production of facial emotion given identical encoding? More studies are needed to look at the relationship between these aspects of emotional processing.

Is Emotion a State?

Previously we noted the issue of the duration of an emotional state as a major source of variance in terminology and conceptualization about emotion. We should take a further step and question the common assumption that emotions and moods are states that one enters and exits. Beyond interesting issues about entrance and exit phenomena, or the duration of the period in between, it is apparent that this assumption views emotion as something one "has." But it is instead possible to view emotion as something one "does." In line with an issue raised earlier in this chapter, is emotion a fundamentally biological or psychological phenomenon? Something the brain produces, causes, or (merely) implements? Either way, is there an important or causal role for emotional *experience* as a state? If, for example, one adopts the view that the physiological efference that accompanies an emotion is actually *part of*, not a *response to*, the emotion (Lang, 1979, as explicated in Miller & Kozak, 1993), then an *emotion* need not be viewed as a state but as an activity. This choice of perspective has immediate implications for the applicability of a variety of features of cognitive neuroscience. Typically, cognition is seen as something one "does," rather than as a state. Although in the cognitive literature it is often said that one can adopt an attentional bias or set, which sounds much like a state, even that sort of bias is seen as a disposition to act (to process) rather than as something the subject "has," as something the subject does, not as something that happens to or comes over the subject.

How one views the interaction of cognition and emotion is greatly affected by whether one adopts the common assumptions that the former is an activity and the latter is a state in which that activity occurs. For example, how one would test proposals regarding memory bias in depression or attentional bias in anxiety would depend on what one thinks emotion is and how one believes it can be engaged. Terms such as *emotional processing* (Foa & Kozak, 1986; Rachman, 1980) begin to recast emotion more in accord with modern cognitive neuroscience. In fact, it may be worthwhile to adopt a processing approach in conceptualizing emotion and, furthermore, not to distinguish between cognition and emotion at all — to attempt to model emotion phenomena with what are formally the same kinds of models that are used to model cognition (see Laird, 1989, for a somewhat similar view).

What Gold Standard?

If one prefers the emotion-as-state assumption, one must confront a particularly difficult problem: verification of emotional state. Imagine all of the measures and correlates of emotion one might have available. In a given study, a subset of them will be designated independent variables, and a separate subset will be designated dependent variables. What guides the choice of which is which? One's theory might, but one's theory might be prejudging what should go where. In any case, there is little consensus on this question among current emotion theorists. Going a step further, in a study of emotion it would be highly desirable to designate a third subset of variables to serve as a manipulation check: how the scientist knows that the emotion of interest is actually present, that the state has been entered and sufficiently and uniformly sustained. Again, how shall we sort our measures into independent variables, dependent variables, and manipulation checks? Davidson, Ekman, Saron, Senulis, and Friesen (1990) proposed an extremely stringent set of criteria that a study of emotion (in a mood/state sense) must meet. Their argument is compelling, but virtually no available study meets their criteria.

Is Biology Better?

Finally, it is problematic that there is often an unjustified privileging of certain kinds of measures over others. Claims are frequently made about psychophysiological measures being more "objective" or less subject to demand characteristics, but such claims are probably groundless (Miller & Ebert, 1988). On the other hand, some writers seem to assume, at least implicitly, that self-report is the gold standard for measures of emotional state. It is sometimes said to have more direct access to subjective experience or to permit finer grained analysis than physiological or behavioral measures. Such claims are not supportable given considerable evidence from psychophysiological measurement of internal mental processes (Coles, 1989).

Biological measures are often employed for the wrong reasons, leading to inappropriate claims about what they demonstrate. Biological measures should not be pursued because of a mistaken faith in their superiority over psychological measures. It is precisely because they are *not* special that they are useful in studies of emotion in psychopathology. They are of the same logical status as more conventional self-report and observational measures; that is why they can join with those measures in converging operations.

A Selective Survey of Neuroscience Methods and Findings

Having surveyed some difficult conceptual and methodological problems in the application of biological measures to the study of emotion in psychopathology, we now provide a survey of some promising directions in that field. The survey is necessarily highly selective, as the body of literature is quite large. These are directions we find particularly exciting. In some cases they are not the hottest technologies available. In several cases they are, instead, some of the more mature.

Production of Facial Expression

One of the most influential methodological developments contributing to affective neuroscience is the Facial Affect Coding System (FACS) of Ekman and Friesen (1975). Facial coding is not normally considered as part of neuroscience, but it warrants such consideration for two reasons. First, as noted earlier, we do not assume that measures of biological phenomena must involve directly biological measurement. One can measure facial behavior via electromyography (EMG) of the facial muscles or by ratings based on visual inspection. The former is probably better at detecting subthreshold actions and the latter at classifying socially meaningful patterns of action. Either way, the raw phenomenon measured is biological: muscle activity. The second reason to consider FACS within neuroscience is that it provides an appealing gold standard as a manipulation check on emotion induction methods. It has a validity that is directly relevant to some emotion theories. For example, it is favored by Davidson et al. (1990) as a manipulation check in studies of emotion and regional brain activity. There is nothing inherent in FACS that makes it a more valid standard than, say, self-report or brain-wave or cardiac measures of emotion (with facial behavior thus cast in the role of dependent measure). But FACS and similar systems deserve some air time in affective neuroscience applications in psychopathology. This is true not only on methodological grounds—it is a well-designed, well-researched method—but on substantive grounds. For example, as noted above, there is considerable interest in the perception and production of emotional facial expression in schizophrenia. Schizophrenics with flat affect have been compared with right-brain-damaged patients using facial as well as vocal measures of expression and were found to perform less accurately than normal controls and nonlateralized brain-damaged patients but similarly to right-brain-damaged patients (Borod et al., 1989). Unipolar depressed patients have been found to be significantly impaired relative to normals in the accuracy and intensity of the emotional facial expressions they posed—especially regarding positive expressions, as rated by naive judges (Jaeger, Borod, & Peselow, 1986).

Gross Regional Brain Activity

The investigation of the relationship between psychopathology and regional differences in brain activity occurs in the context of a long tradition of neuropsychological studies attempting to locate areas of the brain contributing to differences in mood. These studies have tended to find changes in emotional expression in patients following left or right cerebral lesions (Deglin & Nikolaenko, 1975; Flor-Henry, 1979; Gainotti, 1972; Hécaen, 1962; Robinson, Kubos, Starr, Rao, & Price, 1984), with an indifferent or inappropriately euphoric mood associated with unilateral right-hemispheric damage and a depressive or catastrophic reaction following left-hemisphere damage (Sackeim et al., 1982). Findings fairly consistent with these have been provided by anesthetizing one hemisphere in individuals being prepared for surgery to treat epilepsy and observing behavior that occurs while the anesthesia is in effect (intracarotid sodium amobarbital; Alema & Donni, 1960; Alema & Rosadini, 1964; Lee, Loring, Meader, & Brooks, 1990; Perria, Rosaclini, & Rossi, 1961; Terzian, 1964; Terzian & Cecotto, 1959; but see also Fedio & Weinberg, 1971; Tengesdal, 1963; Werman, Christoff, & Anderson, 1959). Unilateral electroconvulsive therapy has replicated this pattern of change in affect (Deglin & Nikolaenko, 1975).

A well-developed area of research furthering the affective neuroscience of psychopathology is the assessment of brain-region-specific activity as a trait and state variable. Much of this work has been done by Davidson and colleagues (for reviews, see Davidson, 1992a, 1993b; Sponheim, Allen, & Iacono, 1995), employing scalp-recorded EEG and measures of regional activity levels indexed by the alpha band of the EEG. Generally, high amounts of alpha are interpreted as reflecting low amounts of activity in nearby cortex. A substantial literature has established that depressives show a lateral asymmetry of activity in the frontal lobes. Of particular interest to psychopathologists is that this asymmetry appears to persist after remission of a major depressive episode (Henriques & Davidson, 1990). Thus, frontal asymmetry is a candidate vulnerability marker for depression.

In addition to these between-subject findings, within-subject differences for different emotions have been documented. In EEG studies during different emotional states higher activity in the left frontal region has been associated with cheerful emotions and higher activity in the right frontal region with sad or depressed emotions (e.g., Davidson & Tomarken, 1989; Henriques & Davidson, 1990; Tomarken, Davidson, Wheeler, & Doss, 1992). Four other independent laboratories have also reported a relationship between types of negative affect (e.g., disgust and fear) and greater relative activity over the right frontal region than was found for comparably intense positive affects (Ahern & Schwartz, 1985; Dawson, Klinger, Panagiotides, Spieker, & Frey, 1992; Fox, 1991; Tucker, Stenslie, Roth, & Shearer, 1981). Davidson and colleagues proposed that fundamental motivational differences underlie the differential roles of the left and right frontal lobes in emotion, such that the left frontal region is associated with approach behavior, and the right frontal region is associated with avoidance behavior (Davidson, 1992a; Davidson & Tomarken, 1989).

Related but distinct theoretical formulations have been offered in this area by Heller (1990, 1993) and Tucker (1981). Heller's model is based in part on evidence that the right hemisphere plays a determining role in the control of emotion according to its level of arousal (Levy et al., 1983a) and on more recent work supporting the possibility that the right hemisphere controls levels of arousal for both hemispheres (Levy, Wagner, & Luh, 1990). Heller's model involves a dynamic, reciprocal pattern of regional brain activity associated with differences in mood state. In this model, frontal regions are associated with the valence dimensions of mood, as proposed by Davidson and colleagues. However, in contrast to the latter group, Heller proposed that activity of the right parietotemporal region is directly associated with more self-report arousal. Her model is consistent with findings derived from multidimensional scaling and factor-analytic studies suggesting that arousal and valence are fundamental dimensions representing emotional experience (e.g., Lang, 1985; Russell, 1980;

Russell & Bullock, 1986). Depression is therefore associated with a reciprocal pattern of low activity in the right parietotemporal region and high activity in the right frontal lobe. Heller proposed that anxiety would be associated with increased activity in both the right parietal and right frontal regions.

Tucker (1981) proposed a model wherein cortical lesions release inhibition of ipsilateral subcortical regions, which results in an exaggerated display of the emotional tone of that hemisphere. He interpreted the finding that damage to the left cerebral cortex results in more negative affect as reflecting the negative tone of left subcortical regions. Insult to the right cerebral cortex is associated with a more "positive, symptom-denying emotional state" due to the disinhibition of the more positive-emotionally toned right subcortical regions (Tucker, 1981, p. 35). This model thus views the effect of a lesion as activating ipsilateral subcortical regions. Such models offer considerable promise for integrating emotion, neuropsychology, and brain science in the service of psychopathology.

Perceptual Asymmetries

The assessment of differences in hemispheric activity has also been accomplished by investigating biases in attention that can be reflected in a number of ways, such as by a characteristic horizontal shift in gaze to either the left or the right (Day, 1964; Teitelbaum, 1954; but see Ehrlichman & Weinberger, 1978, for a critique of the lateral eye movement literature). For example, individuals with predominantly rightward eye movements (greater inferred left-hemisphere activity) scored significantly higher on a measure of difficulty in identifying, communicating, and attending to one's own emotions (collectively termed *alexithymia*) than individuals with predominantly leftward eye movements (Parker, Taylor, & Bagby, 1992). These data suggest that greater relative left-hemisphere activity is associated with difficulty in processing emotional information.

Assessment of relative differences in activity of the hemispheres has also been accomplished through a free-vision test of perceptual bias (the Chimeric Faces Test [CFT]; Levy, Heller, Banich, & Burton, 1983b). The CFT has proven to be a useful self-report assessment of attentional bias that provides a reliable measure from which to infer characteristic individual differences in relative hemispheric activity. This task requires the subject to decide which member of a pair of face chimeras presented in free vision looks happier, the one with the smile to the left or its mirror image with the smile to the right. It is inferred that subjects exhibiting greater, left-hemispatial biases on the CFT (perceiving faces with the smile on the left as happier) have relatively greater right-hemisphere activity. Individual differences in characteristic perceptual asymmetry have been found to account for nearly half of the variation on lateralized tachistoscopic tasks (Kim, Levine, & Kertesz, 1990). Thus, the effects of characteristic differences in relative hemispheric activity are believed to be superimposed upon those accounted for by the functional specialization of each hemisphere. Since variations in perceptual asymmetries on the CFT are highly correlated with data obtained from tachistoscopic tasks requiring the functions of the parietotemporal regions of the brain (e.g., Kim & Levine, 1991, 1992) and reliably predict performance on cognitive tasks that depend on one hemisphere more than the other (Banich, Elledge, & Stolar, 1992), the CFT appears to be a potentially useful measure for investigating emotion and psychopathology.

This potential has been revealed in recent research. For example, unipolar depressives were found to show significantly smaller left-hemispace biases on the CFT than did normal controls (Jaeger, Borod, & Peselow, 1987), a finding consistent with Heller's (1990) proposed relationship between depression and decreased activity of the right parietotemporal area of the brain. Heller, Etienne, and Miller (1995) found depression and anxiety to be associated with opposing biases in perceptual asymmetry scores obtained on the CFT. Depressed subjects had smaller left-hemispatial biases than control subjects. However, when anxiety was present depression was not associated with a difference in hemispatial bias relative to controls, supporting a relationship between anxiety and increased right parietotemporal activity. This work contributes to our understanding of the comorbidity of anxiety and depression and may explain conflicting data when samples differ in their levels of these often comorbid pathologies. In addition, the fact that a measure found to reflect characteristic differences in hemispheric involvement is sensitive to levels of depression and anxiety raises questions about the degree to which these disorders of mood are trait related.

Characteristic differences in relative hemispheric activity have also been linked to other individual differences in emotional processing. An association between greater left-hemisphere activity and high levels of alexithymia was recently reported by Berenbaum and Prince (1994), who found that extremely alexithymic individuals exhibited a right-hemispatial (left-hemisphere) bias on the CFT. Recent work (Taitano & Heller, 1996) found the CFT to be significantly correlated with scores on a general distress factor derived from a principal component analysis of a widely used symptom checklist (SCL-R-90: Derogatis, 1977), indicating that left-hemisphere bias was positively associated with reported psychological and physical distress. The hypothesis that reduced characteristic right-hemisphere involvement would be associated with psychological as well as physical complaints was therefore supported.

Other measures of perceptual asymmetry appear promising as well. Using a tachistoscopic dot enumeration task as such a measure, Bruder et al. (1989) were able to distinguish bipolar from unipolar depression. Bipolar patients did not show the left-visual-field advantage found for unipolar patients and normal controls on this task. Another measure of perceptual asymmetry, the dichotic listening task, has produced significant effects for certain psychological disorders. When different stimuli are presented simultaneously to both ears the difference in accuracy of performance for the material sounded in the right and left ears is referred to as the ear advantage or perceptual asymmetry. College students scoring high on the Perceptual Aberration or Magical Ideation scale, or both, devised by the Chapmans to identity psychosis-prone individuals (Chapman, Chapman, & Raulin, 1976, 1978; Eckblad & Chapman, 1983; Edell, 1995; Fernandes & Miller, 1995; Miller & Yee, 1994) showed a right-ear advantage on a consonant-vowel task and a reduced left-ear advantage on a tone task compared to normal controls (Overby, 1992). Bruder (1988) reported abnormal perceptual asymmetry in patients with depressive disorders, and Bruder et al. (1989) further found that patients with Diagnostic and Statistical Manual of Mental Disorders (3rd ed.; hereinafter DSM-III) diagnoses of melancholia had abnormal perceptual asymmetry for dichotic tasks involving nonsense syllables and complex tones. In contrast, patients in the latter study with nonmelancholic, atypical depression did not differ from normal controls. The use of emotional stimuli with this pardigm could provide another means to explore ways in which different modes of emotional processing are involved in psychopathology.

Recognition of Emotion: Asymmetries in the Processing of Facial Expression

Research in the 1970s and early 1980s explored hemispheric differences in the perception of emotion with the use of the tachistoscopic, divided-visual-field paradigm. Some studies found a left-visual-field (right-hemisphere) superiority for emotional versus nonemotional judgments (Buchtel, Campari, de Risio, & Rota, 1978; Ley & Bryden, 1979; McKeever & Dixon, 1981; Suberi & McKeever, 1977), and a left-visual-field (right-hemisphere) advantage in the recognition of facial expressions of emotion (Buchtel et al, 1978; Hansch & Pirozzolo, 1980; Ley & Bryden, 1979; Strauss & Moscovitch, 1981; Suberi & McKeever, 1977). Other studies, however, reported a right-visual-field (left-hemisphere) advantage in accuracy when subjects were required to detect which of a pair of faces was emotionally expressive and when stimuli were exposed for longer durations (Reuter-Lorenz & Davidson, 1981; Reuter-Lorenz, Givis, & Moscovitch, 1983). As mentioned previously, data obtained with the divided-visual-field paradigm can be strongly affected by subtle methodological differences.

The few studies that have investigated the judgement of the degree and valence of emotionality of facial stimuli reported conflicting results (Campbell, 1978; Heller & Levy, 1981; Levy et al., 1983b; Natale, Gur, & Gur, 1983), probably due to methodological differences. The first three studies above, finding a left-visual-field effect, requested subjects to contrast chimeric faces. The fourth study, reporting a right-visual-field effect, required subjects to judge the predominant mood of similar stimuli. These different task demands are likely to have elicited different kinds of processing.

In addition to task factors, subject factors can influence the degree and direction of results from divided-visual-field studies of emotional appraisal. Some contradictory findings of sex differences (Ladavas, Umilta, & Ricci-Bitti, 1980; Safer, 1981) may be explained by other factors, such as cognitive style (Pizzamiglio, Zoccolotti, Mammucari, & Cesaroni, 1983). Handedness has also had an effect on findings (Heller & Levy, 1981; Levy et al., 1983b). The sensitivity of this paradigm to these influences can create obstacles to clear interpretation but can also provide an interesting means for assessing the subtle ways in which many within- and between-subject factors interact with processes of emotional appraisal.

Lateralized tachistoscopic methods and free vision tasks requiring lateralized processing have been applied more recently to the investigation of psychopathology. Suppressed right-hemisphere activity has been observed in sad or depressed individuals as reflected in performance on tachistoscopic tasks (Bruder et al., 1989). Depressed patients have also exhibited specific impairments on right-hemisphere tasks associated with parietotemporal functions (e.g., Banich, Stolar, Heller, & Goldman, 1992). Schizophrenics with flat affect performed significantly less accurately than normal controls but similarly to right-brain-damaged patients on tasks assessing the perception of facial emotion (Borod et al., 1993). As with investigations involving nonclinical samples, a careful consideration of methodological and subject factors is needed when interpreting these results.

The Startle-Probe Paradigm

An increasingly popular psychophysiological paradigm in both basic and clinical research is the two-stimulus startle-probe procedure. In general, two stimuli are presented in close temporal proximity, with the first stimulus altering the processing of the second—increasing or decreasing the amplitude or latency of a variety of psychophysiological measures. The second stimulus is typically very intense, eliciting the startle reflex. The stimulus parameters of the paradigm have been thoroughly researched (Graham, 1979), showing, for example, interesting cross-modal attentional effects (Anthony & Graham, 1985; Hackley & Graham, 1983, Haerich, 1994). An animal model of fear in the startle-probe paradigm has been well established (Davis, 1989). The paradigm has also been used fruitfully with subjects believed to be at risk for psychopathology (Dawson, Schell, Hazlett, Filion, & Nuechterlein, 1995; Fernandes & Miller, 1995; Simons & Giardina, 1992). Related paradigms construed as backward-masking (Braff et al., 1978) or conditioning-testing (Adler et al., 1982) procedures have revealed fairly specific information processing deficits in schizophrenia. Of particular interest to emotion researchers in psychopathology is a variation on the paradigm in which the first stimulus is replaced by, in effect, a mood-induction stimulus such as an emotional slide. Startle stimuli are then presented during the slide, and inferences are made about emotional processing as a function of the startle reflex elicited at various points during slide presentation (for review, see Lang et al., 1990). For example, whereas control subjects show a monotonic increase in the amplitude of the startle response as the emotional valence of the slide becomes more negative, psychopaths' startle-probe responses to very negative slide material are no larger than their responses to neutral stimuli (Patrick, 1994). In effect, psychopaths do not appear to find aversive stimuli to be as aversive as control subjects do. The startle-probe paradigm is unusually promising because it is relatively easy to set up, some of the relevant neurophysiology is relatively well known, and impressive, clinically relevant findings are already available.

Resource Allocation

To support our suggestion above that cognition and emotion not be too readily distinguished, we propose that the traditionally cognitive research in resource allocation can also provide a productive paradigm for investigating emotional processes. Speculations about cognitive resource abnormalities have arisen with increasing frequency in the psychopathology literature, including schizophrenia (Nuechterlein, 1990), depression (Yee, 1995), anxiety (Mineka & Sutton, 1992), and at-risk populations (Miller & Yee, 1994). Sometimes it is overall amount of resources that are believed to be deficient. More interestingly, an anomaly in the deployment or allocation of resources is sometimes suggested.

Several studies in our laboratory have looked at ERP measures during cognitive tasks, including those involving emotional stimuli. Yee (1995; Yee & Miller, 1994) studied dysthymic and anhedonic nonpatients in a dual-task paradigm requiring distinct patterns of resource allocation to nearly simultaneous visual, auditory, or both memory tasks. Within each condition, subjects' reaction-time performance equalled that of controls, but their P300 responses suggested a considerably different resource-allocation strategy. Controls' P300 declined as fewer processing resources were devoted to the visual task, when asked to devote more to the auditory task. In contrast, the other two groups' P300 was small and invariant across conditions. This pattern suggests that those groups' cognitive resources are taxed even under conditions that are not demanding for controls. A recent study by Keller, Deldin, Miller, and Gergen (1996) evaluated the N400 and P300 components of the ERP measured in inpatient depressives in response to sentences that ended with either typical, anomalous, or emotionally valenced words. Preliminary analyses showed that depressives produced significantly attenuated N400s under some conditions, suggesting a reduced appreciation for the meaningfulness of ordinary discourse. Planned P300 analyses will evaluate the extent to which these effects are attributable to resource allocation differences.

Other Cognitive ERP Paradigms

A number of studies have found significant ERP amplitude differences in response to words and pictures differing in emotional value (Begleiter, Gross, & Kissin, 1967; Begleiter & Platz, 1969; Begleiter, Porjesz, & Garrozo, 1979; Johnston & Wang, 1991; Klorman & Ryan, 1980; Williamson, Harpur, & Hare, 1991). Specifically, the latency of P300, which is sensitive to a subject's expectation for an event (Duncan-Johnson & Donchin, 1977), varies systematically with requirements for stimulus evaluation, and is a more reliable measure of complete stimulus evaluation time than is reaction time (Kutas, McCarthy, & Donchin 1977), has also been found to be sensitive to the emotional value of stimuli. Naumann, Bartussek, Diedrich, and Laufer (1992) reported a larger P300 for positive and negative words than for neutral words. Johnston, Miller, and Burleson (1986) found two late positive components (P3 and P4) that varied with the emotional value of slides.

Another endogenous component, N400, formerly considered mainly as an index of linguistic processing (Garnsey, Tanenhaus, & Chapman, 1989; Kutas & Van Petten, 1988), has recently been found to be responsive to the conceptual mismatching of nonverbal stimuli (Barrett & Rugg, 1990), including those involving faces (Barrett & Rugg, 1989). Whereas only slight N400 mismatch effects were observed in one study that matched faces on the basis of their expressions (Potter & Parker, 1989), Pecchinenda, Ferlazzo, and Kappas (1994) recently found an enhanced negativity of an ERP component at around 400 ms that was larger when prototypical facial expressions failed to match. An unexpected finding was that an even larger negativity followed prototype-blend pairs (with expression blends created via computer morphing), with increased negativity to the mismatch condition of these pairs. Thus, blends may concurrently activate more than one emotional category in memory.

These methods have been useful for exploring emotional processes in emotionally disordered individuals. Anhedonics have been shown to have reduced P300 amplitude in comparison to controls in response to stimuli predicting subsequent slides of emotional interest (nude women and/or men; Miller, Simons, & Lang, 1984; Simons, MacMillan, & Ireland, 1982). P300 (along with P200, N200, and O-wave components) has also been found to distinguish between dysthymics experiencing high and low levels of fear in response to cued pleasant and unpleasant slides (Yee & Miller, 1988). Later components have been found to distinguish between depressives and normals. Williamson et al. (1991) reported a diminished distinction among psychopaths between emotional and neutral words in a P300-like component. Ivanitsky, Kurnitskaya, and Sobotka (1986) measured ERPs in depressives and normals in response to winning or losing a tennis video game and found that N600 increased in the left posterior associative cortex to winning and P800 decreased at right frontal cortex to losing. Depressives showed a larger negativity of the right posterior and left frontal area for both winning and losing the game. Thus, in contrast to common assumptions that brain-wave measures are more appropriate for addressing cognitive than emotional questions, it is clear that ERPs can be sensitive to the emotional content of stimuli for both affectively normal and disordered individuals and can differentiate such individuals.

Although confident inferences about localization of function require a convergence of different measures rather than reliance on ERPs alone, there is evidence that ERPs are sensitive to the asymmetric involvement of the hemispheres in emotion. As mentioned previously, laterality can be an important factor even when direct measures are not lateralized. For example, abnormally long P300 latencies have been recently found for typical depressives (melancholia and simple mood reactive depression as diagnosed by DSM-III criteria) in response to a spatial task but not a temporal task, with abnormal lateral asymmetry found in longer P300 latency for stimuli presented in the right but not the left hemifield (Bruder et al., 1991). Atypical depressives in this study, however, did not differ from normals on either index of P300 latency.

In summary, a small but growing body of literature demonstrates the responsiveness of ERP components to emotional stimuli. Although even fewer studies to date have used clinical samples, the variety of paradigms showing ERP effects for emotion already is substantial, and this appears to be a very promising area to pursue. The challenge will be to design paradigms that go well beyond merely demonstrating ERP differences as a function of diagnostic groupings or emotional manipulations and instead explicate the psychological and biological significance of those differences.

Conclusion

This chapter emphasizes common, difficult, and underrecognized methodological and conceptual problems facing the application of biological measures to the study of emotion in psychopathology. Nevertheless, it also highlights a few of the many promising biological methods available in that field. This is a growing area that among other virtues, stands a reasonable chance of bridging the often substantial gap between biological and psychological analysis in psychopathology, a bridging that we believe will be essential for the field.

Acknowledgments   Preparation of this chapter was supported in part by NIMH Grant F31 MH10970 to Keolani Taitano and by NIMH Grant R01 MH39628 to Gregory A. Miller. We thank Howard Berenbaum, Wendy Heller, and the editors for comments on an earlier draft.

References

Adler, L. E., Pachtman, E., Franks, R. D., Pecevich, M., Waldo, M. C., & Freedman, R. (1982). Neurophysiological evidence for a defect in neuronal mechanisms involved in sensory gating in schizophrenia. *Biological Psychiatry, 17*, 639–654.

Ahern, G., Schumer, D., Kleefield, J., Blume, H., Cosgrove, G., Weintraub, S., & Mesulam, M.-M. (1991). Right hemisphere advantage for evaluating emotional facial expressions. *Cortex, 27*, 193–202.

Ahern, G. L., & Schwartz, G. E. (1985). Differential lateralization for positive and negative emotion in the human brain: EEG spectral analysis. *Neuropsychologia, 23*, 745–756.

Alema, G., & Donni, G. (1960). Sulle modificazioni cliniche ed elettroencefalografiche da introduzione intracarotidaea di iso-amil-etil-barbiturato di sodio nell'uomo. *Bollettino Societa Italiana Biologia Sperimentale, 36*, 900–904.

Alema, G., & Rosadini, G. (1964). Donnees cliniques et E.E.G. de l'introduction d'Amytal sodium dans la circulation encephalique concernant l'etat de conscience. *Acta Neurochirurgica, 12*, 240–257.

Anthony, B. J., & Graham, F. K. (1985). Reflex modification by selective attention: Evidence for modification of automatic pressing. *Biological Psychology, 21*, 43–59.

Autret, A., Auvert, L., Laffont, F., & Larmande, P. (1985). Electroencephalographic spectral power and lateralized motor activities. *Electroencephalography and Clinical Neurophysiology, 60*, 228–236.

Banich, M. T. (1995). Interhemispheric processing: Theoretical considerations and empirical approaches. In R. J. Davidson & K. Hugdahl (Eds.), *Brain asymmetry* (pp. 427–450). Cambridge, MA: MIT Press.

Banich, M. T., Elledge, V. C., & Stolar, N. (1992). Variations in lateralized processing among right-handers: Effects on patterns of cognitive performance. *Cortex, 28*, 273–288.

Banich, M. T., Stolar, N., Heller, W., & Goldman, R. (1992). A deficit in right hemisphere performance after induction of a depressed mood. *Neuropsychiatry, Neuropsychology, and Behavioral Neurology, 5*, 20–27.

Barrett, S. E., & Rugg, M. D. (1989). Event-related potentials and the semantic matching of faces. *Neuropsychologia, 27*, 913–922.

Barrett, S. E., & Rugg, M. D. (1990). Event-related potentials and the semantic matching of pictures. *Brain and Cognition, 14*, 201–212.

Begleiter, H., Gross, M. M., & Kissin, F. (1967). Evoked cortical response to affective visual stimuli. *Psychophysiology, 6*, 91–100.

Begleiter, H., & Platz, H. (1969). Cortical evoked potentials to semantic stimuli. *Psychophysiology, 6*, 91–100.

Begleiter, H., Porjesz, B., & Garozzo, R. (1979). Visual evoked potentials and affective rating of semantic stimuli. In H. Begleiter (Ed.), *Evoked brain potentials and behavior* (pp. 127–141). New York: Plenum Press.

Belger, A., & Banich, M. T. (1992). Interhemispheric interaction affected by computational complexity. *Neuropsychologia, 30*, 923–929.

Berenbaum, H., & Oltmanns, T. F. (1992). Emotional experience and expression in schizophrenia and depression. *Journal of Abnormal Psychology, 101*, 37–44.

Berenbaum, H., & Prince, J. D. (1994). Alexithymia and the interpretation of emotion-relevant information. *Cognition and Emotion, 8,* 231–244.

Blanchard, J. J., Kring, A. M., & Neale, J. M. (1994). Flat affect in schizophrenia: A test of neuropsychological models. *Schizophrenia Bulletin, 20,* 311–325.

Borod, J. C., Andelman, F., Obler, L. K., Tweedy, J. R., & Welkowitz, J. (1992). Right hemisphere specialization for the identification of emotional words and sentences: Evidence from stroke patients. *Neuropsychologia, 30,* 827–844.

Braff, D., Stone, C., Callaway, E., Geyer, M., Glick, I., & Bali, L. (1978). Prestimulus effects on human startle reflex in normals and schizophrenics. *Psychophysiology, 15,* 339–343.

Bruder, G. E. (1988). Dichotic listening in psychiatric patients. In K. Hugdahl (Ed.), *Handbook of dichotic listening: Theory, methods and research* (pp. 527–653). Chichester, UK: Wiley.

Bruder, G. E., Quitkin, F. M., Stewart, J. W., Martin, C., Voglmaier, M. M., & Harrison, W. M. (1989). Cerebral laterality and depression: Differences in perceptual asymmetry among diagnostic subtypes. *Journal of Abnormal Psychology, 98,* 177–186.

Bruder, G. E., Towey, J. P., Stewart, J. W., Friedman, D., Tenke, C., & Quitkin, F. M. (1991). Event-related potentials in depression: Influence of task, stimulus hemifield and clinical features on P3 latency. *Biological Psychiatry, 30,* 233–246.

Buchtel, H., Campari, F., de Risio, C., & Rota, R. (1978). Hemispheric differences in discriminative reaction time to facial expressions. *Italian Journal of Psychology, 5,* 159–169.

Cacioppo, J. T., Klein, D. J., Berntson, G. G., & Hatfield, E. (1993). The psychophysiology of emotion. In M. Lewis & J. M. Haviland (Eds.), *Handbook of emotions* (pp. 119–142). New York: Guilford Press.

Campbell, R. (1978). Asymmetries in interpreting and expressing a posed facial expression. *Cortex, 19,* 327–342.

Chapman, L. J., & Chapman, J. P. (1978). The measurement of differential deficit. *Journal of Psychiatric Research, 14,* 303–311.

Chapman, L. J., Chapman, J. P., & Raulin, M. L. (1976). Scales for physical and social anhedonia. *Journal of Abnormal Psychology, 85,* 374–382.

Chapman, L. J., Chapman, J. P., & Raulin, M. L. (1978). Body-image aberration in schizophrenia. *Journal of Abnormal Psychology, 87,* 399–407.

Churchland, P. S. (1986). *Neurophilosophy: Toward a unified science of the mind/brain.* Cambridge, MA: MIT Press.

Coles, M. G. H. (1989). Modern mind-brain reading: Psychophysiology, physiology, and cognition. *Psychophysiology, 26,* 251–269.

Davidson, R. J. (1978). Specificity and patterning in biobehavioral systems: Implications for behavior change. *American Psychologist, 33,* 430–436.

Davidson, R. J. (1992a). Anterior cerebral asymmetry and the nature of emotion. *Brain and Cognition, 20,* 125–151.

Davidson, R. J. (1993a). Cerebral asymmetry and emotion: Conceptual and methodological conundrums. *Cognition and Emotion, 7,* 115–138.

Davidson, R. J. (1993b). Parsing affective space: Perspectives from neuropsychology and psychophysiology. *Neuropsychology, 7,* 464–475.

Davidson, R. J., Ekman, P., Saron, C. Senulis, J., & Friesen, W. V. (1990). Approach/withdrawal and cerebral asymmetry: Emotional expression and brain physiology, I. *Journal of Personality and Social Psychology, 58,* 330–341.

Davidson, R. J., & Sutton, S. K. (1995). Affective neuroscience: The emergence of a discipline. *Current Opinion in Neurobiology, 5,* 217–224.

Davidson, R. J ., & Tomarken, A . J . (1989). Laterality and emotion: An electrophysiological approach. In F. Boller & J. Grafman (Eds.), *Handbook of neuropsychology* (Vol. 3, pp. 419–441). Amsterdam: Elsevier.

Davis, K. L., Kahn, R. S., Ko, G., & Davidson, M. (1991). Dopamine in schizophrenia: A review and reconceptualization. *American Journal of Psychiatry, 148,* 1474–1486.

Davis, M. (1989). Neural systems involved in fear-potentiated startle. *Annals of the New York Academy of Sciences, 563,* 165–183.

Dawson, G., Klinger, L. G., Panagiotides, H., Spieker, S., & Frey, K. (1992). Infants of mothers with depressive symptoms: Electroencephalographic and behavioral findings related to attachment status. *Developmental and Psychopathology, 4,* 67–80.

Dawson, M. E., Schell, A. M., Hazlett, E. A., Filion, D. L., & Nuechterlein, K. H. (1995). Attention, startle eye-blink modification, and psychosis proneness. In A. Raine, T. Lencz, & S. A. Mednick (Eds.), *Schizotypal personality disorder.* Cambridge: Cambridge University Press.

Day, M. E. (1964). An eye-movement phenomenon relating to attention, thought and anxiety. *Perceptual and Motor Skills, 19,* 443–446.

Deglin, V. G., & Nikolaenko, N. N. (1975). Role of the dominant hemisphere in the regulation of emotional states. *Human Physiology, 1,* 394–402.

Deldin, P. J., Keller, J., Miller, G. A., & Gergen, J. A. (1996). *Mood congruence and emotional memory in depression.* Manuscript in preparation.

Derogatis, L. R. (1977). *SCL-90 R (revised) version manual: I.* Baltimore, MD: Johns Hopkins University School of Medicine.

Donchin, E., & Coles, M. G. H. (1988). Is the P300 component a manifestation of context updating? *Brain and Behavioral Sciences, 11,* 357–374.

Duncan-Johnson, C. C., & Donchin, E. (1977). On quatifying surprise: The variation of event-related potentials with subjective probability. *Psychophysiology, 14,* 456–467.

Eckblad, M., & Chapman, L. J. (1983). Magical ideation as an indicator of schizotypy. *Journal of Consulting and Clinical Psychology, 51,* 215–225.

Edell, W. S. (1995). The psychometric measurement of schizotypy using the Wisconsin Scales of Psychosis Proneness. In G. A. Miller (Ed.), *The behavioral high-risk paradigm in psychopathology* (pp. 3–46). New York: Springer-Verlag.

Ehrlichman, H., & Weinberger, A. (1978). Lateral eye movements and hemispheric asymmetry: A critical review. *Psychological Bulletin, 85,* 1080–1101.

Ekman, P., & Friesen, W. V. (1975). Measuring facial movement. *Journal of Environmental Psvchology and Nonverbal Behavior, 1,* 56–75.

Fedio, P., & Weinberg, L. K. (1971). Dysnomia and impairment of verbal memory following intracarotid injection of sodium amytal. *Brain Research, 31,* 159–168.

Fernandes, L. O. L., & Miller, G. A. (1995). Compromised performance and abnormal psychophysiology associated with the Wisconsin Psychosis-Proneness scales. In G. A. Miller (Ed.), *The behavioral high-risk paradigm in psychopathology* (pp. 47–87). New York: Springer-Verlag.

Flor-Henry, P. (1979). On certain aspects of the localization of the cerebral systems regulating and determining emotion. *Biological Psychiatry, 14,* 677–698.

Foa, E. B., & Kozak, M. J. (1986). Emotional processing of fear: Exposure to corrective information. *Psychological Bulletin, 99,* 20–35.

Fodor, J. A. (1968). *Psychological explanation.* New York: Random House.

Fox, N. A. (1991). If it's not left, it's right: Electroencephalograph asymmetry and the development of emotion. *American Psychologist, 46,* 863–872.

Fredrikson, M., Wik, G., Greitz, T., Eriksson, L., Stone-Elander, S., Ericson, K., & Sedvall, G. (1993). Regional cerebral blood flow during experimental phobic fear. *Psychophysiology*, *30*, 126–130.

Gainotti, G. (1972). Emotional behavior and hemisphere side of lesion. *Cortex*, *8*, 41–55.

Garnsey, S. M., Tanenhaus, M. D., & Chapman, R. M. (1989). Evoked potentials and the study of sentence comprehension. *Journal of Psycholinguistic Research*, *18*, 51–60.

Goldberg, E., & Costa, L. D . (1981). Hemisphere differences in the acquisition and use of descriptive systems. *Brain and Language*, *14*, 144–173.

Graham, F. K. (1979). Distinguishing among orienting, defense, and startle reflexes. In H. D. Kimmel, E. G. van Olst, & J. F. Orlebeke (Eds.), *The orienting reflex in humans* (pp. 137–167). Hillsdale, NJ: Erlbaum.

Hackley, S. A., & Graham, F. K. (1983). Early selective attention effects on cutaneous and acoustic blink reflexes. *Physiological Psychology*, *11*, 235–242.

Haerich, P. (1994). Startle reflex modification: Effects of attention vary with emotion valence. *Psychological Science*, *5*, 407–410.

Hansch, E. C., & Pirozzolo, F. J . (1980). Task relevant effects on the assessment of cerebral specialization for facial emotion. *Brain and Language*, *10*, 51–59.

Hécaen, H. (1962). Clinical symptomatology in right and left hemispheric lesions. In V. B. Mountcastle (Ed.), *Interhemispheric relations and cerebral dominance* (pp. 215–243). Baltimore: Johns Hopkins Press.

Heller, W. (1990). The neuropsychology of emotion: Developmental patterns and implications for psychopathology. In N. L. Stein, B. L. Leventhal, & T. Trabasso (Eds.), *Psychological and biological approaches to emotion* (pp. 167–211). Hillsdale, NJ: Erlbaum.

Heller, W. (1993). Neuropsychological mechanisms of individual differences in emotion, personality, and arousal . *Neuropsychology*, *7*, 1–14.

Heller, W., Etienne, M. A., & Miller, G. A. (1995). Patterns of perceptual asymmetry in depression and anxiety: Implications for neuropsychological models of emotion. *Journal of Abnormal Psychology*, *104*, 327–333.

Heller, W., & Levy, J. (1981). Perception and expression of emotion in right-handers and left-handers. *Neuropsychologia*, *19*, 263–272.

Hellige, J. B., & Sergent, J. (1986). Role of task factors in visual field asymmetries. *Brain and Cognition*, *5*, 200–222.

Henriques, J. B., & Davidson, R. J. (1990). Regional brain electrical asymmetries discriminate between previously depressed subjects and healthy controls. *Journal of Abnormal Psychology*, *99*, 22–31.

Ivanitsky, A. M., Kurnitskaya, I. V., & Sobotka, S. (1986). Cortical topograpy of event-related potentials to winning and losing in a video tennis game. *International Journal of Psychophysiology*, *4*, 149–155.

Jaeger, J., Borod, J., & Peselow, E. (1986). Facial expression of positive and negative emotions in patients with unipolar depression. *Journal of Affective Disorders*, *11*, 50.

Jaeger, J., Borod, J. C., & Peselow, E. D. (1987). Depressed patients have atypical hemispace biases in the perception of emotional chimeric faces. *Journal of Abnormal Psychology*, *96*, 321–324.

Johnson, R., Jr. (1989). Auditory and visual P300s in temporal lobectomy patients: Evidence for modality-dependent generators. *Psychophysiology*, *26*, 633–650.

Johnston, V. S., Miller, D. R., & Burleson, M. H. (1986). Multiple P3s to emotional stimuli and their theoretical significance. *Psychophysiology*, *23*, 684–694.

Johnston, V. S. & Wang, X. T. (1991). The relationship between menstrual phase and the P3 component of ERPs. *Psychophysiology*, *28*, 400–409.

Keller, J., Deldin, P. J., Miller, G. A., & Gergen, J. A. (1996). *Mood congruence and semantic processing in depression.* Manuscript in preparation.

Kim, H., &: Levine, S. C. (1991). Inferring patterns of hemispheric specialization for individual subjects from laterality data: A two-task criterion. *Neuropsychologia, 29*, 93–105.

Kim, H., & Levine, S. C. (1992). Variations in characteristic perceptual asymmetry: Modality specific and modality general components. *Brain and Cognition, 19*, 21–47.

Kim, H., Levine, S. C., & Kertesz, S. (1990). Are variations among subjects in lateral asymmetry real individual differences or random error in measurement? *Brain and Cognition, 14*, 220–242.

Kinsbourne, M. (1974). Mechanisms of hemispheric interaction in man. In M. Kinsbourne & W. L. Smith (Eds.), *Hemispheric disconnection and cerebral function* (pp. 260–285). Springfield, IL: Thomas.

Kinsbourne, M., & Hicks, R. E. (1978). Functional cerebral space: A model for overflow, transfer and interference effects in human performance: A tutorial review. In J. Requin (Ed.), *Attention and performance* (vol.7, pp. 345–362). Hillsdale, NJ: Erlbaum.

Klorman, R., & Ryan, R. M. (1980). Heart rate, contingent negative variation, and evoked potentials during anticipation of affective stimulation. *Psychophysiology, 17*, 513–523.

Kozak, M. J., & Miller, G. A. (1982). Hypothetical constructs versus intervening variables: A re-appraisal of the three-systems model of anxiety assessment. *Behavioral Assessment, 14*, 347–358.

Kutas, M., McCarthy, G., & Donchin, E. (1977). Augmenting mental chronometry: The P300 as a measure of stimulus evaluation time. *Science, 197*, 792–795.

Kutas, M. & Van Petten, C. (1988). Event-related brain potential studies of language. In P. Ackles, J. R. Jennings, & M. G. H. Coles (Eds.), *Advances in psychophysiology* (Vol. 3, pp. 139–187). Greenwich, CT: JAI Press.

Lacey, J. I. (1967). Somatic response patterning and stress: Some revisions of activation theory. In M. H. Appley & R. Trumbull (Eds.), *Psychological stress: Issues in research* (pp. 14–37). New York: Appleton-Century Crofts.

Ladavas, E., Umilta, C., & Ricci-Bitti, P. E. (1980). Evidence for sex differences in right hemisphere dominance for emotions. *Neuropsychologia, 18*, 361–367.

Laird, J. D. (1989). Mood affects memory because feelings are cognitions. *Journal of Social Behavior and Personality, 4*, 33–38.

Lang, P. J. (1968). Fear reduction and fear behavior; Problems in treating a construct. In J. M. Shlien (Ed), *Research in psychotherapy* (Vol. 3, pp. 90–102). Washington, DC: American Psychological Association.

Lang, P. J. (1979). A bio-informational theory of emotional imagery. *Psychophysiology, 16*, 495–512.

Lang, P. J. (1985). The cognitive psychophysiology of emotion: Fear and anxiety. In A. H. Tuma & J. D. Maser (Eds.), *Anxiety and the anxiety disorders* (pp. 131–170). Hillsdale, NJ: Erlbaum.

Lang, P. J., Bradley, M. M., & Cuthbert, B. N. (1990). Emotion, attention, and the startle reflex. *Psychological Review, 97*, 377–395.

Lee, G. P., Loring, D. W., Meader, K. J., & Brooks, B. B. (1990). Hemispheric specialization for emotional expression: A reexamination of results from intracarotid administration of sodium amobarbital. *Brain and Cognition, 12*, 267–280.

Levenson, R. W. (1992). Autonomic nervous system differences among emotions. *Psychological Science, 3*, 23–27.

Levenson, R. W., Ekman, P., & Friesen, W. V. (1990). Voluntary facial action generates emotion-specific autonomic nervous system activity. *Psychophysiology, 27*, 363–383.

Levy, J. (1972). Lateral specialization of the human brain: Behavioral manifestations and possible evolutionary basis. In J. A. Kiger, Jr. (Ed.), *The biology of behavior: Proceedings of the thirty-second annual biology colloquium* (pp. 159–181). Corvalis, OR: Oregon State University Press.

Levy, J., Heller, W., Banich, M. T., & Burton, L. A. (1983a). Are variations among right-handed individuals in perceptual asymmetries caused by characteristic arousal differences between hemispheres? *Journal of Experimental Psychology: Human Perception and Performance, 9,* 299–312.

Levy, J., Heller, W., Banich, M. T., & Burton, L. A. (1983b). Asymmetry of perception in free viewing of chimeric faces. *Brain and Cognition, 2,* 404–419.

Levy, J., Wagner, N., & Luh, K. (1990). The previous visual field: Effects of lateralization and response accuracy on current performance. *Neuropsychologia, 28,* 1239–1249.

Ley, R. G., & Bryden, M. P. (1979). Hemispheric differences in processing emotions and faces. *Brain and Language, 7,* 127–138.

Lutzenberger, W., & Elbert, T. (1987). Assessment of the effects of weak DC currents on brain and behavior. In K. H. Schmidt (Ed.), *Safety assessment of NMR clinical equipment* (pp. 36–45). Stuttgart: Thieme.

McKeever, W. F., & Dixon, M. S. (1981). Right-hemisphere superiority for discriminating memorized from nonmemorized faces: Affective imagery, sex, and perceived emotionality effects. *Brain and Language, 12,* 246–260.

Miller, G. A., & Ebert, L. (1988). Conceptual boundaries in psychophysiology. *Journal of Psychophysiology, 2,* 13–16.

Miller, G. A., & Kozak, M. J. (1993). A philosophy for the study of emotion: Three-systems theory. In A. Öhman & N. Birbaumer (Eds.), *The structure of emotion: Physiological, cognitive and clinical aspects* (pp. 31–47). Seattle: Hogrefe & Huber.

Miller, G. A., Levin, D. N., Kozak, M. J., Cook, E. W., McLean, A., & Lang, P. J. (1987). Individual differences in imagery and the psychophysiology of emotion. *Cognition and Emotion, 1,* 367–390.

Miller, G. A., Simons, R. F., & Lang, P. J. (1984). Electrocortical measures of information processing deficits in anhedonia. *Annals of the New York Academy of Sciences, 425,* 598–602.

Miller, G. A., & Yee, C. M. (1994). Risk for severe psychopathology: Psychometric screening and psychophysiological assessment. In J. R. Jennings, P. K. Ackles, & M. G. H. Coles (Eds.), *Advances in psychophysiology,* (Vol. 5, pp. 1–54). London: Jessica Kingsley.

Mineka, S., & Sutton, S. K. (1992). Cognitive biases and the emotional disorders. *Psychological Science, 3,* 65–69.

Natale, M., Gur, R. E., & Gur, R. C. (1983). Hemispheric asymmetries in processing emotional expressions. *Neuropsychologia, 21,* 555–565.

Naumann, E., Bartussek, D., Diedrich, O., & Laufer, M. E. (1992). Assessing cognitive and affective information processing functions of the brain by means of the late positive complex of the event-related potential. *Journal of Psychophysiology, 6*(4), 285–298.

Nitschke, J. B., Miller, G. A., & Heller, W. (1996). *The physiology and psychology of extraversion: An attentional-neuropsychological replacement for arousal theory.* Manuscript submitted for publication.

Nuechterlein, K. H. (1990). Methodological considerations in the search for indicators of vulnerability to severe psychopathology. In J. W. Rohrbaugh, R. Parasuraman, & R. Johnson, Jr. (Eds.), *Event-related potentials: Basic issues and applications* (pp. 364–373). New York: Oxford University Press.

Overby, L. A. III. (1992). Perceptual asymmetry in psychosis-prone college students: Evidence for a left-hemisphere overactivation. *Journal of Abnormal Psychology, 101,* 96–103.

Parker, J. D. A., Taylor, G. J., & Baghy, R. M. (1992). Relationship between conjugate lateral eye movements and alexithymia. *Psychotherapy and Psychosomatics, 57,* 94–101.

Patrick, C. W. (1994). Emotion and psychopathy: Startling new insights. *Psychophysiology, 31,* 319–330.

Pecchinenda, A., Ferlazzo, F., & Kappas, A. (1994, October). *Modulation of ERPs during categorization of prototypical and mixed emotional facial expressions.* Paper presented at the annual meeting of the Society for Psychophysiological Research, Atlanta, GA.

Perria, P., Rosadini, G., & Rossi, G. F. (1961). Determination of side of cerebral dominance with Amobarbital. *Archives of Neurology, 4,* 173–181.

Pizzamiglio, L., Zoccolotti, P., Mammucari, A., & Cesaroni, R. (1983). The independence of face identity and facial expression recognition mechanisms: Relation to sex and cognitive style. *Brain and Cognition, 2,* 176–188.

Potter, D. D., & Parker, D. M. (1989). Electrophysiological correlates of facial identity and expression processing. In J. Crawford & D. M. Parker (Eds.), *Developments in clinical and experimental neuropsychology* (pp. 137–150). New York: Plenum Press.

Rachman, S. (1980). Emotional processing. *Behavior Research and Therapy, 18,* 51–60.

Reuter-Lorenz, P. A., & Davidson, R. J. (1981). Differential contributions of the two cerebral hemispheres to the perception of happy and sad faces. *Neuropsychologia, 19,* 609–613.

Reuter-Lorenz, P. A., Givis, R. P., & Moscovitch, M. (1983). Hemispheric specialization and the perception of emotion: Evidence from right-handers and from inverted and noninverted left-handers. *Neuropsychologia, 6,* 687–692.

Rohinson, R. G., Kuhos, K. L., Starr, L. B., Rao, K., & Price, T. R. (1984). Mood disorders in stroke patients: Importance of location of lesion. *Brain, 107,* 81–93.

Rossi, G. F., & Rosadini, G. (1967). Experimental analysis of cerebral dominance in man. In C. H. Millikan & F. L. Darley (Eds.), *Brain mechanisms underlying speech and language* (pp. 167–184). New York: Grune & Stratton.

Russell, J. A. (1980). A circumplex model of affect. *Journal of Personality and Social Psychology, 39,* 1161–1178.

Russell, J. A., & Bullock, M. (1986). On the dimensions preschoolers use to interpret facial expressions of emotion. *Developmental Psychology, 22,* 97–102.

Sackeim, H. A., Greenberg, M. S., Weiman, A. L., Gur, R. C., Hungerbuhler, J. P., & Geschwind, N. (1982). Hemispheric asymmetry in the expression of positive and negative emotions: Neurological evidence. *Archives of Neurology, 39,* 210–218.

Safer, M. A. (1981). Sex and hemisphere differences in access codes for processing emotional expressions and faces. *Journal of Experimental Psychology: General, 110,* 86–100.

Schachter, S., & Singer, J. E. (1962). Cognitive, social, and physiological determinants of emotional state. *Psychological Review, 69,* 379–399.

Silberman, E. K., & Weingartner., H. (1986). Hemispheric lateralization of functions related to emotion. *Brain and Cognition, 5,* 322–353.

Simons, R. F., & Giardina, B. D. (1992). Reflex modification in psychosis-prone young adults. *Psychophysiology, 29,* 8–16.

Simons, R. F., MacMillan, F. W., & Ireland, F. B. (1982). Anticipatory pleasure deficit in subjects reporting physical anhedonia: Slow cortical evidence. *Biological Psychology, 14,* 297–310.

Sponheim, S. R., Allen, J. J., & Iacono, W. G. (1995). Psychophysiological measures in depression: The significance of electrodermal activity, electroencephalographic asymmetries, and contingent negative variation to behavioral and neurobiological aspects of depression. In G. A. Miller (Ed.), *The behavioral high-risk paradigm in psychopathology* (pp. 222–249). New York: Springer-Verlag.

Stolar, N., Berenbaum, H., Banich, M. T., & Barch, D. (1994). Neuropsychological correlates of alogia and affective flattening. *Biological Psychiatry, 35,* 164–172.

Strauss, E., & Moscovitch, M. (1981). Perception of facial expressions. *Brain and Language,*
13, 308–332.

Strauss, M. E., & Summerfelt, A. (1994). Response to Serper and Harvey. *Schizophrenia*
Bulletin, 20, 13–21.

Suberi, M., & McKeever, W. F. (1977). Differential right hemispheric memory of emotional
and non-emotional faces. *Neuropsychologia, 15,* 757–768.

Taitano, K., & Heller, W. (1996). Individual differences in psychological and somatic distress and characteristic patterns of perceptual asymmetry. Manuscript in revision.

Teitelbaum, H. A. (1954). Spontaneous rhythmic ocular movements, their possible relationship to mental activity. *Neuology: 4,* 350–354.

Tengesdal, M. (1963). Experiences with intracarotid injections of sodium amytal: A preliminary report. *Acta Neurologica Scandinavia, 39,* 329–343.

Terzian, H. (1964). Behavioural and EEG effects of intracarotid sodium amytal injections.
Acta Neurochirurgica, 12, 230–239.

Terzian, H., & Cecotto, C. (1959). Determinazione e studio della dominanzaemisferica
mediante iniezione intracarotide di amytal sodico nell'uomo: I. Modicficazioni cliniche.
Bollettino Societa Italiana di Biologia Sperimentale, 35, 1623–1626.

Tomarken, A. J., Davidson, R. J., Wheeler, R. E., & Doss, R. C. (1992). Individual differences in anterior asymmetry and fundamental dimensions of emotion. *Journal of Per-*
sonality and Social Psychology, 62, 676–687.

Tucker, D. M. (1981). Lateral brain function, emotion, and conceptualization. *Psychologi-*
cal Bulletin, 89, 19–46.

Tucker, D. M., Stenslie, C. E., Roth, R. S., & Shearer, S. L. (1981). Right frontal lobe activation and right hemisphere performance: Decrement during a depressed mood. *Ar-*
chives of General Psychiatry, 38, 169–174.

Tucker, D. M., & Williamson, P. A. (1984). Asymmetric neural control systems in human
self-regulation. *Psychological Review, 91,* 185–215.

Venables, P. H. (1984). Cerebral mechanisms, autonomic responsiveness, and attention in schizophrenia. In R. A. Dieusthier, W. D. Spaulding, & J. K. Cole (Eds.), *Current theory and*
research in schizophrenia (Vol. 31, pp. 47–91). Lincoln, NE: University of Nebraska Press.

Wahlsten, D. (1994). The intelligence of heritability. *Canadian Psychology, 35,* 244–260.

Werman, R., Christoff, N., & Anderson, P. J. (1959). Neurological changes with intracarotid
Amytal and Megimide in man. *Journal of Neurology, Neurosurgery, and Psychiatry, 22,*
333–337.

Williamson, S., Harpur, T. J., & Hare, R. D. (1991). Abnormal processing of affective words
by psychopaths. *Psychophysiology, 28,* 260–273.

Wittling, W. (Ed.). (1995). Brain asymmetry in the control of autonomic physiological activity.
In R. J. Davidson & K. Hugdahl (Eds.), *Brain asymmetry.* Cambridge, MA: MIT Press.

Wood, F. B., Flowers, D. L., & Naylor, C. E. (1991). Cerebral laterality in functional
neuroimaging. In F. L. Kitterle (Ed.), *Cerebral laterality: Theory and research* (pp. 103–
115). Hillsdale, NJ: Erlbaum.

Yee, C. M. (1995). Implications of the resource allocation model for mood disorders. In
G. A. Miller (Ed.), *The behavioral high-risk paradigm in psychopathology* (pp. 271–288).
New York. Springer-Verlag.

Yee, C. M., & Miller, G. A. (1988). Emotional information processing: Modulation of fear
in normal and dysthymic subjects. *Journal of Abnormal Psychology, 97,* 54–63.

Yee, C. M., & Miller, G. A. (1994). A dual-task analysis of resource allocation in dysthymia
and anhedonia. *Journal of Abnormal Psychology, 103,* 625–636.

3

Jennifer M. Jenkins & Keith Oatley

The Development of Emotion Schemas in Children

Processes That Underlie Psychopathology

Functions of Emotions and Their Role in Psychopathology

Observations of children with psychopathology make it clear that emotions are important in the difficulties they suffer. Childhood psychopathology is generally divided into two classes, externalizing and internalizing disorders. A child with an externalizing disorder, such as conduct disorder, is aggressive and destructive apparently without adequate provocation. He (boys show much higher rates of conduct disorder than girls) will react to other children's playful or friendly overtures with hostility. He steals from his parents without regard to their feelings. He taunts and teases until his sibling starts to cry. Such behaviors have an emotional quality. He seems to be angry with the world and he maintains a mode of retaliation. A child with an internalizing disorder behaves differently. She (girls have a somewhat higher prevalence of internalizing disorders than boys) may withdraw from many situations because they make her feel frightened. She often feels lonely, and feels that others do not like her. Her mood is often low and she is unlikely to initiate activities with peers.

Exactly how everyday emotions, which are short-lived, relate to long-term patterns that we call psychopathology is unclear, and there are as yet few empirical data that bear on this issue. Some investigators have emphasized the child's inability to regulate emotional arousal, whereas others have emphasized mismatches between the child's affective response and the environmental demand (Cole, Michel, & O'Donnell Teti, 1994). Others have hypothesized that one particular emotion becomes prominent in the life of the individual: A depressed person experiences high levels of sadness; an anxious person experiences high levels of fear (Malatesta & Wilson, 1988; Tomkins, 1963). It is this last theoretical perspective that we adopt in this chapter.

The idea that one emotion is more readily experienced than others is useful for explaining the patterns of stability that are seen in child psychiatric disorders as well as for understanding the link between risk factors in children's lives and psychopathology. We argue that children develop biases of emotional responding. These develop because particular emotions are repeatedly elicited in their environment, and because certain emotional expressions serve a function in that environment. We call this patterning of appraisal and response an emotion schema. Schemas are structures of knowledge and readiness, prompting people to experience and express one kind of emotion rather than others.

Until recently theories of emotions that were popular among psychologists had not focused on function. For instance, the most popular theory has been that of William James (1890), who argued that emotions occur as a coloring of experience after a response to an event had occurred. Others have argued that emotions had no necessary functional importance in our lives. Darwin (1872/1965), for instance, saw emotions as vestiges derived from our evolutionary history, which occur whether or not they are of any use.

More recent understandings have taken a quite different form. In developmental psychology, informed by the work of Bowlby (e.g., 1969), and in cognitive psychology prompted by the work of Tomkins (1962) and Simon (1967), emotions are seen as functional. They function to establish, maintain, change, or terminate particular modes of relationship to the environment because of issues that are important to us (Campos, Mumme, Kermoian, & Campos, 1994). So, central to our conception of emotion is the idea of goals. Emotions signal the status of our goals, to ourselves and often also to others. Another important aspect of emotions is the way in which they serve instrumental functions in interpersonal achievement of goals (Tronick, 1989). Angry shouts from a child whose toy has been taken function to get the other child to return it. A child's crying summons the mother and elicits actions from her that alleviate distress.

Like Frijda (1986), we take the position that emotions function to organize readiness. Some theorists argue that emotional life is based on a few, genetically based, patterns of action and interaction (Oatley, 1992). These patterns have been evolutionarily selected, and can be thought of as instinctive outline patterns of interpretation linked to appropriate repertoires of response to certain recurring kinds of events that are important in the life of the individual. The function of an emotion is to set the brain into a specific mode of readiness for a particular kind of action. The emotions most often referred to as basic are happiness, sadness, fear, and anger. Happiness is an emotion of making progress toward some objective, or of maintaining proximity to an attachment figure or peer. It functions interpersonally to elicit affiliative behaviors from others. Sadness is an emotion of loss or defeat, that elicits caregiving from others. Fear is an emotion of response to threat or danger, that also elicits protection from others (Bowlby, 1980). Anger occurs when a goal is frustrated and when another individual is seen as responsible (Stein & Levine, 1987). It has the interpersonal function of establishing dominance (Goodall, 1986).

The main advance in understanding children's psychopathology in the last 30 years has been from epidemiological studies that define what kinds of environments put children at risk. Onsets of psychopathology in childhood are most strongly associated with adverse environments. Externalizing and internalizing psychopathology in children can be seen as providing functional outline structures of readiness to act in these adverse environments. We propose that externalizing psychopathology is based on an affective organization in which anger predominates; internalizing psychopathology is based on an affective organization in which fear and/or sadness predominate.

A Functional View of Emotions

In conceptualizing the relationship between emotion and psychopathology we refer to functionalist conceptions of emotion. The functionalist argument is that in order to understand why emotions are elicited we need to refer to how a person is trying to affect their environment. Instead of defining emotion as a feeling state, or in terms of facial expression or physiological response, we see it in terms of goal orientation toward an environment. Anger, then, is not primarily a facial expression, but an orientation toward the world in which frustration is experienced, and dominance over the other person is sought. A conduct disordered child may decide to laugh when his toy is taken away by an older boy, but later steals money from the older boy's locker. Although he briefly expresses "happiness" by laughing, his orientation is one of anger and retaliation.

By taking this perspective we can integrate notions of short-lived emotions with longer term emotional patterns that occur in psychopathology. Children with externalizing psychopathology act to deny the rights of others; they act against other people, sometimes with aggression, but sometimes with more subtle defiance. The goal orientation of such children is to move against the world. The symptoms of children with internalizing disorders involve loneliness, fears, and sadness. Their goal orientation is to withdraw, to move away from the world. We have taken these phrases from Caspi, Elder, and Bem (1987, 1988).

In relation to internalizing psychopathology there has been a long-standing debate about whether disorders of anxiety and depression are different from one another in childhood, since they frequently occur together (Finch, Lipovsky, & Casat, 1989). Here we view the basic affective organization of internalizing disorder as an orientation to withdraw. Comfort and protection are the principal interpersonal goals. Some children, however, focus more on the aspects of the situation that suggest loss and defeat, leading predominantly to sadness. Others focus more on threat and danger, leading predominantly to fear. Within the internalizing orientation, the adverse environments of depressed children will predominantly have involved loss, while those of anxious children will often have involved threat.

This kind of functionalist perspective is informed by a study by Jenkins (1995). Observations were made of children's facial expressions of emotion at school. Psychopathology ratings were provided by mothers, teachers, and peers. Externalizing symptoms were found to be strongly associated with more frequent facial expressions of anger in response to immediate goals being blocked. Externalizing psychopathology was also associated with facial expressions of happiness while saying cruel and provocative things to other children, that is, taunting. We reasoned that the goal of the emotion expression when the child was taunting was to achieve submission of the other child in much the same way as the interpersonal goal of anger is to get a goal reinstated. Had we just treated the facial expression of emotion as the marker variable for emotion, it would not be easy to relate patterns of psychopathology to particular emotional states. If emotion is defined in relation to the goals of the individual, then the patterns of affectivity that children show can more easily be interpreted.

Stability of Emotion Schemas Over Time

We suggest that individuals show stability over time in their affective orientations toward others. Some develop characteristic feelings of being frustrated, or of loss, or of threat. They also develop characteristic ways of expressing emotions that serve them instrumentally—for instance, "If I cry, I will be protected." We interpret expressions of emotion as functioning in the service of goals. In this section we review evidence for behavioral continuities, and suggest that underlying these are continuities in goals.

In normal development, continuities in affective expression have been found over relatively brief periods: Hyson and Izard (1985) observed children in Ainsworth, Blehar, Waters, and Wall (1978). Strange Situation test when they were 13 months and then again at 18 months of age. There were high correlations between these two occasions for interest expressions ($r = 0.90$), anger expressions ($r = 0.61$), and total negative expressions ($r = 0.90$). Worobey and Blajda (1989) assessed children at 2 months and again at 1 year of age. They reported correlations between the two occasions of $r = 0.46$ for positive reactivity and $r = 0.50$ for negative reactivity. So, there are continuities in normal emotionality, but the empirical evidence has shown this over short periods.

Patterns of affectivity in psychopathology are also stable and here there have been studies over much longer periods, both within the childhood years and from childhood to adulthood. In a follow-up study of children in the general population who suffered from psychiatric disorders, Graham and Rutter (1973) found that none of the children who had shown an externalizing disorder at age 10 years showed an internalizing disorder at age 14. Also consistent with our argument about stability is the finding that 75% of the children who had an externalizing disorder at age 10 still showed the disorder 4 years later. The stability of aggressiveness is almost as high as the stability of IQ (Olweus, 1979). Even lower level angry behavior, such as ill temperedness in early childhood, has been found to predict angry orientations in adulthood, 30 years later, with long-term consequences on lifestyle (Caspi, et al. 1987). In a long-term follow-up of children with conduct disorder, Robins (1978) found that approximately half of the children with conduct disorder in childhood went on to show antisocial personality disorder as adults.

Internalizing orientations of fear or sadness are also stable, although less so than externalizing orientations. Caspi et al. (1988) found that children who were shy in childhood were also shy in adult life. Rubin (1993) reported a correlation between shyness at age 7 and at age 14 of $r = 0.5$ and found that shy children developed into adolescents who showed more internalizing psychopathology. In a follow-up study of children with depressive symptomatology, Harrington, Fudge, Rutter, Pickles and

Hill (1990) found that if individuals showed any psychopathology in adult life it was most likely to be depression.

If children had been found to switch from internalizing disorder to externalizing disorder or vice versa over the course of months or years, it would make little sense to talk about an underlying affective organization. But this is not the case. Moreover, the stability found in types of psychopathology extends beyond the childhood home to other environments, so continuing patterns of behavior do not merely reflect continuation of environmental elicitation. Such behavioral consistency implies mediation by emotional schemas, or by some other enduring organization. The stability in types of psychopathology reflects a stability of goal states toward other people.

Next we review briefly relevant factors associated with psychopathology in childhood, and try to explain them in terms of how events in children's lives result in an orientation toward anger, fear, or sadness.

Emotion Mechanisms in the Development of Psychopathology

Epidemiological studies carried out over the last 30 years have given us a good understanding of circumstances associated with the onset of psychopathology in children. Factors that have repeatedly emerged as important in externalizing and internalizing disorders in children are poverty, marital conflict, parental psychiatric disorder, physical and sexual child abuse, hostile parenting, poor temperament in the child, and developmental delays (Costello, 1989; Rutter, Tizard, & Whitmore, 1970).

Innate differences of temperament contribute to the patterning of affect in psychopathology (Rende, 1993). Thus, some children have a lower threshold for anger, and others are temperamentally shy. Such individual differences are obvious starting points for interactions with others, and are essential for understanding some of the goal orientations that develop. Without denying these effects, we concentrate in this chapter on environmental risks.

The known environmental risks for childhood disorder are usually described in global terms, for instance, parental depression or marital discord, but these give little information about the mechanisms by which an emotional orientation is formed. In this section we go beyond global descriptors to describe specific mechanisms of emotion elicitation. Studies have yet to be done that directly relate risk factors found in epidemiological studies with fine-grained analyses of emotion elicitation. So, some of what we say is speculative, but hypotheses of the kind we propose will be essential in understanding the relationship between emotions and psychopathology.

Elicitation of Emotion

By the time children are 5 years old, most emotions that can be observed in them are responses to obvious happenings in the world (Fabes, Eisenberg, Nyman, & Michealieu, 1991; Jenkins & Oatley, 1996). When someone approaches a child with an offer to play or a warm greeting, this usually elicits an expression of happiness in the child. When another child takes something away or blocks them from doing something, a negative emotion is expressed. We hypothesize that children in normal families are exposed to a wider range of elicitors, and to a higher proportion of positive to negative elicitors, than children in troubled homes.

Consider how global factors such as abuse, exposure to violence, and loss of a parent may elicit emotions. We propose that such stressors are associated with disorder because of the repeated elicitation of the same negative emotion. Events associated with psychopathology are not single events, but events that have long-term repercussions, or are often repeated. For instance, death of a parent was previously thought to be associated with increased risk of psychopathology, but closer investigation suggests that it is not so much the event of losing a parent, but the increased neglect and abuse occasioned by the loss that constitutes the risk for the child (Brown & Hams, 1993). Tomkins (1979) suggested that single events build on one another as similarities across situations are perceived. He hypothesized that single events, or scenes, became magnified by subsequent experiences in which similar emotions are elicited. A negative script is formed that includes more and more events, which were previously ambiguous, but are subsumed later under one kind of interpretation.

How might an anger schema develop? Anger is experienced when goals are blocked and when there seem to be possibilities of reinstating them. Factors that are strongly associated with onsets of externalizing disorders such as poverty (Costello, 1989) and hostility of a parent toward the child (Stubbe, Zahner, Goldstein, & Leckman, 1993) can be conceptualized in this way. As poor children compare their opportunities with those of wealthier others, they experience frequent frustration of their own goals. Poverty is also associated with increased parental hostility toward children (Radke-Yarrow, Richters, & Wilson, 1988). Parental hostility is associated with parents being less facilitating of children's goals (Crockenberg, 1985). When anger has been repeatedly elicited the child will build a schema of the other as intentionally stopping them from doing what they want.

Sexual and physical abuse can lead to internalizing patterns. For example, a child who is repeatedly abused by a parent frequently feels frightened. A sense of loss and feelings of sadness can also occur because the child lacks a trusted caregiver. Women who have been sexually abused in childhood have greater anxiety and depression in adult life (Brown & Harris, 1993). So, we suggest that repeated experiences of threat and loss can lead to the development of internalizing schemas.

Consequences of Emotional Expression

Emotions function as a means of communication: One person's expression of emotion affects the emotions of others. We suggest that children learn to display emotions that work well for them in relationships and attenuate emotions that work badly. Goldberg, MacKay, and Rochester (1994), using Ainsworth et al.'s (1978) Strange Situation procedure, found that mothers of securely attached infants responded to a wider range of affects than mothers of insecurely attached infants. Mothers of avoidant infants were most likely to ignore negative expressions of emotion. Mothers of ambivalent infants were most responsive to negative affect and least responsive to positive affect. If, as attachment theorists argue, mothers' caregiving practices are the principal causes of the attachment styles of their babies, some babies had learned that expressions of negative emotions did not further the satisfaction of their goals, and attenuated these expressions. Others learned that negative expressions were the best way of eliciting care.

In families with children who have externalizing disorders, anger may function to reduce subsequent aversive interaction. Patterson (1982) has suggested that the most important mechanism in the development of externalizing disorders is that long chains of escalating aversive interactions occur: in such families parents withdraw and stop their coercion in response to the child's aggression. Angry aggression is thus reinforced because it serves to reduce aversiveness, and aids in the reinstatement of the child's goals.

In families in which a child has internalizing psychopathology, we propose that fear and sadness can function positively to reduce aversiveness. Hops et al. (1987) observed the affect of family members when mothers were depressed. They found that when mothers expressed high levels of sadness, their spouses expressed less hostility and aggression toward them. A child in such a family may learn that this is a good way of stopping hostility. Indeed, Dadds, Sanders, Morrison, and Rebgetz (1992) found that parents of depressed children responded to increases in their child's depression by attenuating their own aggression. By contrast, parents of conduct-disordered children were found to increase their aggression when their child's depression increased. Thus, one reason that internalizing emotion schemas may become instantiated in some, but not all, aversive families is that in these families sadness or fear reduces aversiveness.

A given pattern of emotionality may satisfy one goal, but make another impossible. A child with an externalizing disorder can frequently get others to withdraw or defer, but though this may be effective it often occurs at the expense of affiliation and affection.

Modelling of Emotion

Another mechanism that is important in the establishment of a child's goal orientation is emotional contagion. Malatesta and Haviland (1982) have described how mothers model emotions to their children, and how the children adopt the same patterns. Nondisordered mothers usually show their children a large amount of happy affect and rarely display negative emotions. Parents with psychiatric disorders such as depression, however, show more sadness and anger to their children (Cohn, Campbell, Matias, & Hopkins, 1990).

In general, the evidence is that children tend to show patterns of affective expression similar to those of their parents. Thus, antisocial parents are most likely to have children with externalizing disorders (Frick et al., 1992). Children who are exposed to high rates of anger, either from having hostility directed at them (Dodge, Bates, & Pettit, 1990) or from observing conflict between their parents (Jenkins & Smith, 1991), are, in turn, likely to be aggressive in their interactions with peers. Parents who are depressed are more likely to have depressed children than children with other psychiatric disorders (Hammen, Burge, Burney, & Adrian, 1990). Those with anxiety disorders are most likely to have children with anxiety symptoms (Rosenbaum, Biederman, & Gersten, 1988). Genetic transmission may play a part in such parent-child correspondences (Rutter et al., 1990). We know from experimental studies, however, that children randomly assigned to a condition in which they are exposed to displays of anger between adults show increased aggression toward peers directly afterward, as compared with those who did not witness the display (Cummings, 1987). Similarly, children exposed to sad displays show more lethargy and withdrawal (Field et al., 1988).

In human evolutionary history, contagion enabled one person to communicate an evaluation of events to others, and hence establish action readiness in a social group. For instance one person's fear signals to others to take flight. Children living with a depressed parent, for instance, are at risk because they are exposed to deviant levels and a narrowed range of emotional expression. Through emotional contagion, their own goal orientation toward the environment may become similar to those in their family.

Learning of Appraisals

Modeling of appraisals by parents is another way in which parents influence their children's goal orientation. An emotion is experienced when an event is appraised as being relevant to a goal, and different appraisals lead to different emotions (Lazarus, 1991). One means by which children learn appraisals is by watching them being made by others. By 10 months of age infants show evidence of paying attention to the appraisals of their parents and by 12–13 months they alter their behavior according to their parents' expression of affect (Walden & Ogan, 1988). This phenomenon is known as social referencing.

Appraisal biases are common in children with psychopathology (Quiggle, Garber, Panak, & Dodge, 1992). Events in the world are interpreted to make negative emotions more likely. Although there are, as far as we know, no data on the appraisals made by parents of aggressive children, we know that aggressive children are likely to have aggressive parents, and that such parents have more positive attitudes toward aggression (Dodge, Pettit, & Bates, 1994). It is therefore likely that parents of aggressive children more often attribute hostile intentions to the neutral behavior of other people, and that such biased appraisals have been learned by example. For depression there is more direct evidence: Radke-Yarrow Belmont, Nottlemann, and Bottomly, (1990) examined the speech of depressed and nondepressed mothers to their toddlers. Mothers who made more negative appraisals about their children had children who made more negative appraisals about themselves.

Emotion Schemas as Relational Constructs

With some exceptions, such as some fears of nonpersonal things (of novelty, of the dark, of illness), by far the greater part of our emotional life is interpersonal. We are happy with friends or with a loved one. We are angry at being thwarted by others. We are sad at losing love or respect. Emotion schemas grow out of transactions with people: They represent goal orientations toward others.

We build cognitive models of our relationships with others (Baldwin, 1993). People internalize their experience from previous relationships and carry it with them into new ones. Knowledge acquired through previous experience is used to anticipate and act planfully. Children can represent how their expressions of emotions will affect other people, as well as the kinds of affective events they are likely to meet in their environment. Attachment theorists have elaborated the idea of internal models of relationships: Children form their models of what to expect in close relationships, based on how parents have responded to their distress. We propose that many other kinds of affective experience in the home influence what we expect from ourselves and others in the affective domain. When children watch two parents scream at one another in frustration, or hear the hostile attributions that each makes toward the other, they learn about affect in interaction.

Here we build on the formulation suggested by Tomkins (1979): Events of central significance to the person, eliciting a particular affective reaction, can become an organizing structure for subsequent experiences. We base our view on epidemiological research about the kinds of environments that raise the risk of psychiatric disorder in children, and have discussed (above) the emotional reactions that occur repeatedly in such environments. In our proposal, the goal structure of the individual is partly constructed as an emotional response—angry, depressed, fearful—to an early environment. Later this habitual response can become a fulcrum around which subsequent experiences turn. The goal structures of a child with an externalizing disorder involve the child in thinking that others block their goals, and that dominance is the most important aspect of a relationship. For a child with an internalizing disorder, the goal structure involves protecting the self from danger and loss, and achieving this through withdrawal, vigilance, and attempts to recruit aid.

Goal structures based on schemas of anger or fear-sadness develop and become established through experiences that occur over and over again. In one sense such structures are useful. Like other habits, they give children readily available responses to deal with the environment. Once established, however, they become entrenched and elaborated. People who are anxious attend to threats in the world that maintain their anxiety (Mathews, 1993). People who are depressed have memories of past failures or losses coming to mind, which provide further cause for feeling depressed (Teasdale, 1988).

Then comes the most difficult and problematic aspect of children's psychopathology. Schemas constructed for functional reasons in one environment are exported to other environments in which a new set of people, reacting to the deviance of a child's emotional responsiveness, can exacerbate the very same patterns. Children who are hostile and aggressive are treated more negatively by teachers (Sroufe & Fleeson, 1988) and are more likely to be rejected by peers (Coie & Kupersmidt, 1983). Children who are anxious are faced with unfamiliar and taxing experiences that make them yet more fearful and avoidant. So, emotion schemas learned in the family are taken first to school where they are reenacted. There they are made ready to be carried into adulthood.

Acknowledgments   We thank the Social Sciences and Humanities Research Council of Canada for grants that assisted in the preparation of this chapter.

References

Ainsworth, M. D. S., Blehar, M. C., Waters; E., & Wall, S. (1978). *Patterns of attachment: A psychological study of the strange situation.* Hillsdale, NJ: Erlbaum.

Baldwin, M. (1993). Relational schema's and the processing of social information. *Psychological Bulletin, 112,*461–484.

Bowlby, J. (1969). *Attachment and loss: Vol. 1. Attachment.* London: Hogarth Press.

Bowlby, J. (1980).*Attachment and loss: Vol. 3. Loss: sadness and depression.* London: Hogarth Press.

Brown, G. W., & Harris, T. O. (1993). Aetiology of anxiety and depressive disorders in an inner-city population, 1. Early adversity. *Psychological Medicine, 23,* 143–154.

Campos, J. J., Mumme, D. L., Kermoian, R., & Campos, R. C. (1994). A functionalist perspective on the nature of emotion. *Monographs of the Society for Research in Child Development, 59*(Serial No. 240), 284–303.

Caspi, A., Elder, G. H., & Bem, D. J. (1987). Moving against the world: Life course patterns of explosive children. *Developmental Psychology, 23,*308–313.

Caspi, A., Elder, G. H., Bem, D. J. (1988). Moving away from the world: Life-course patterns of shy children. *Developmental Psychology, 24,*824–831.

Cohn, J. F., Campbell, S. B., Matias, R., & Hopkins, J. (1990). Face-to-face interactions of postpartum depressed and nondepressed mother-infant pairs at 2 months. *Developmental Psychology, 26,* 15–23.

Coie, J. D., & Kupersmidt, J. D. (1983). A behavioral analysis of emerging social status in boys' groups. *Child Development, 54,*1400–1416.

Cole, P., Michel, M. K., & O'Donnell Teti, L. (1994). The development of emotion regulation and dysregulation: A clinical perspective. *Monographs of the Society for Research in Child Development 59*(Serial No. 240), 73–103.

Costello, E. J. (1989). Developments in child psychiatric epidemiology. *Journal of the American Academy of Child and Adolescent Psychiatry, 28,* 836–841.

Crockenberg, S. (1985). Toddlers reactions to maternal anger. *Merrill Palmer Quarterly, 31,* 361–373.

Cummings, E. M. (1987). Coping with background anger in early childhood. *Child Development, 58,* 976–984.

Dadds, M. R., Sanders, M. R., Morrison, M., & Rebgetz, M. (1992). Childhood depression and conduct disorder: II. An analysis of family interaction patterns in the home. *Journal of Abnormal Psychology, 101,* 505–513.

Darwin, C. (1965). *The expression of emotions in man and animals.* Chicago: University of Chicago Press. (Original work published 1872).

Dodge, K. A., Bates, J. E., & Pettit, G. S. (1990). Mechanisms in the cycle of violence. *Science, 250,* 1678–1683.

Dodge, K. A., Pettit, G. S., & Bates, J. E (1994). Socialization mediators of the relation between socioeconomic status and child conduct problems. *Child Development, 65,* 649–665.

Fabes, R. A., Eisenberg, N., Nyman, M., & Michealieu, Q. (1991). Young children's appraisals of others' spontaneous emotional reactions. *Developmental Psychology, 27,* 858–866.

Field, T., Healy, B., Goldstein, S., Perry, S., Bendell, D., Schanberg, S., Zimmerman, E. A., & Kuhn, C. (1988). Infants of depressed mothers show "depressed" behavior even with nondepressed adults. *Child Development, 59,*1569–1579.

Finch, A. J., Lipovsky, A. J., & Casat, C. D. (1989). Anxiety and depression in children and adolescents: Negative affectivity or separate constructs? In P. C. Kendall & D. Watson

(Eds.), *Anxiety and depression: Distinctive and overlapping features* (pp. 171–196). New York: Academic Press.

Frick, P. J., Lahey, B. B., Loeber, R., Stouthamer-Loeber, M., Christ, M. G., & Hanson, K. (1992). Familial risk factors to oppositional defiant disorder and conduct disorder: Parental psychopathology and maternal parenting. *Journal of Consulting and Clinical Psychology, 60*, 49–55.

Frijda, N. H. (1986). *The emotions*. Cambridge: Cambridge University Press.

Goldberg, S., MacKay, S., & Rochester, M. (1994). Affect, attachment and maternal responsiveness. *Infant Behavior and Development, 17*, 335–339.

Goodall, J. (1986). *The chimpanzees of Gombe: Patterns of behavior*. Cambridge, MA: Harvard University Press.

Graham, P. J., & Rutter, M. (1973). Psychiatric disorder in the young adolescent: A follow-up study. *Proceedings of the Royal Society of Medicine, 66*,1226–1229.

Hammen, C., Burge, D., Burney, E, & Adrian, C. (1990). Longitudinal study of diagnoses in children of women with unipolar and bipolar affective disorder. *Archives of General Psychiatry, 47*, 1112–1117.

Harrington, R., Fudge, H., Rutter, M., Pickles, A., & Hill, J. (1990). Adult outcomes of childhood and adolescent depression. *Archives of General Psychiatry, 47*, 465–473.

Hops, H., Biglan, A., Sherman, L., Arthur, J., Friedman, L, & Osteen, V. (1987). Home observations of family interactions of depressed women. *Journal of Consulting and Clinical Psychology, 55*,341–346.

Hyson, M. C., & Izard, C. E. (1985). Continuities and changes in emotion expressions during brief separation at 13 and 18 months. *Developmental Psychology, 21*, 1165–1170.

James, W. (1890). *The principles of psychology*. New York: Holt.

Jenkins, J.M. (1995). Parental conflict, peer relationships, and development of anger schema in children. Paper presented at the Society for Research in Child Development, April 1995. Indianapolis, Indiana.

Jenkins, J.M., & Oatley, K. (1996). Everyday emotions in the playground. Manuscript in preparation.

Jenkins, J. M., & Smith, M. A. (1991). Marital disharmony and children's behaviour problems: Aspects of a poor marriage that affect children adversely. *Journal of Child Psychology and Psychiatry, 32*, 793–810.

Lazarus, R. S. (1991). *Emotion and adaptation*. New York: Oxford University Press.

Malatesta, C. Z., & Haviland, J. M. (1982). Learning display rules: The socialization of emotion expression in infancy. *Child Development, 53*, 991–1003.

Malatesta, C. Z., & Wilson, A. (1988). Emotion/cognition interaction in personality development: A discrete emotions, functionalist analysis. *British Journal of Social Psychology, 27*, 91–112.

Mathews, A. (1993). Biases in emotional processing. *The Psychologist: Bulletin of the British Psychological Society, 6*, 493–499.

Oatley, K. (1992). *Best laid schemes: The psychology of emotions*. New York: Cambridge University Press.

Olweus, D. (1979). Stability of aggressive reaction patterns in males: A review. *Psychological Bulletin, 86*, 852–875.

Patterson, G. R. (1982). *Coercive family process*. Eugene, OR: Castalia.

Quiggle, N. L., Garber, J., Panak, W. F., & Dodge, K. A. (1992). Social information processing in aggressive and depressed children. *Child Development, 63*, 1305–1320.

Radke-Yarrow, M., Belmont, B., Nottlemann, E., & Bottomly, L. (1990). Young children's self-conceptions: Origins in the natural discourse of depressed and normal mothers and their children. In D. Cicchetti & M. Beeghly (Eds.), *The self in transition* (pp. 345–361). Chicago: University of Chicago Press.

Radke-Yarrow, M., Richters, J. & Wilson, W. E (1988). Child development in a network of relationships. In R. A. Hinde and J. Stevenson-Hinde (Eds.), *Relationships within relationships* (pp. 48–67). Oxford: Clarendon Press.

Rende, R. D. (1993). Longitudinal relations between temperament traits and behavioral syndromes in middle childhood. *Journal of the American Academy of Child and Adolescent Psychiatry, 32*, 287–290.

Robins, L. N. (1978). Sturdy childhood predictors of adult antisocial behavior: Replications from longitudinal studies. *Psychological Medicine, 8*, 611–622.

Rosenbaum, J. F., Biederman, J., & Gersten, M. (1988). Behavioral inhibition in children with parents with panic disorder and agoraphonia. *Archives of General Psychiatry, 45*,463–470.

Rubin, K. H (1993). The Waterloo longitudinal project: Correlates and consequences of social withdrawal from childhood to adolescence. In K. H. Rubin & J. Asendorpf (Eds.), *Social withdrawal, inhibition and shyness in childhood* (pp. 291–314). Hillsdale, NJ: Erlbaum.

Rutter, M., Macdonald, H., Le Couteur, A., Harrington, R., Bolton, P., & Bailey, A. (1990). Genetic factors in child psychiatric disorders. II. Empirical findings. *Journal of Child Psychology and Psychiatry, 31*, 39–84.

Rutter, M., Tizard, J., & Whitmore, K. (1970). *Education, health and behavior.* London: Longman.

Simon, H. A. (1967). Motivational and emotional controls of cognition. *Psychological Review, 74*, 29–39.

Sroufe, A. L. & Fleeson, J. (1988). The coherence of family relationships. In R. A. Hinde & J. Stevenson-Hinde (Eds.), *Relationships within families: Mutual influences* (pp. 27–47). Oxford: Clarendon Press.

Stein, N. L., & Levine, L. (1987). Thinking about feelings: The development and organization of emotional knowledge. In R. E. Snow & M. Farr (Eds.), *Aptitude, learning, and instruction* (pp. 165–197). Hillsdale, NJ: Erlbaum.

Stubbe, D. E., Zahner, G. E. P., Goldstein, M. J., & Leckman, J. F. (1993). Diagnostic specificity of a brief measure of expressed emotion: A community study of children. *Journal of Child Psychology and Psychiatry, 34*, 139–154.

Teasdale, J. D. (1988). Cognitive vulnerability to persistent depression. *Cognition and Emotion, 2*, 247–274.

Tomkins, S. S. (1962). *Affect, imagery, consciousness: Vol. 1. The positive affects.* New York: Springer.

Tomkins, S. S. (1963). *Affect, imagery, consciousness: Vol. 2. The negative affects.* New York: Springer.

Tomkins, S. S. (1979). Script theory: Differential magnification of affects. In H. E. Howe & R. A. Dienstbier (Eds.), *Nebraska Symposium on Motivation, 1978* (pp. 201–236). Lincoln, NA: University of Nebraska Press.

Tronick, E. Z. (1989). Emotions and emotional communications in infants. *American Psychologist, 44*, 112–119.

Walden, T. A., & Ogan, T. A. (1988). The development of social referencing. *Child Development, 59*, 1230–1240.

Worobey, J., & Blajda, V. M. (1989). Temperament ratings at 2 weeks, 2 months, and 1 year: Differential stability of activity and emotionality. *Developmental Psychology, 25*, 257–263.

4

Seymour Epstein

Emotions and Psychopathology from the Perspective of Cognitive-Experiential Self-Theory

It is no accident that mental illnesses are also referred to as emotional disorders. Laypeople and professionals alike recognize that emotions lie at the heart of many disorders in living. It is noteworthy, in this respect, that the three primary negative emotions (in the sense that they are observable in nonhuman animals), fear, sadness, and anger, have their counterparts in major classes of psychological disorders, namely, anxiety disorders, depression, and anger-hostility-related disorders, including paranoia and antisocial personality.

The purpose of this chapter is to examine from the perspective of cognitive-experiential self-theory (CEST) the relation of emotions to psychopathology. CEST substitutes for the conventional contrast between emotions and cognition a contrast between two cognitive systems, experiential-intuitive and rational-analytical. The former is assumed to be intimately associated with emotions, whereas the latter is assumed to be affect-free. This seemingly small change of substituting two cognitive systems for the usual contrast between emotions and cognition will be demonstrated to have important implications for the relations between unconscious processes, emotions, and psychopathology.

There is a logical flaw in the usual contrast between emotions and cognition that assumes that they are constructs at comparable levels of complexity. As it is widely recognized that emotions include a cognitive as well as other components, such as physiological and expressive reactions, it makes no more sense to contrast emotions with cognitions than to contrast emotions with physiological reactions or with expressive movements. One way of circumventing this difficulty is to substitute the word *affect* (the subjective feeling component of emotion) for the word *emotion*. It would then be appropriate to contrast affective with cognitive responses as they are both basic components of emotion. However, something of importance would be lost in this process, because the reason that emotions are normally contrasted with cognitions is that they are presumed to identify two fundamental ways of knowing, an emotional way and an intellectual way. This distinction is widely assumed to have important implications for understanding information processing in general, and normal and abnormal adjustment and psychotherapy in particular (Epstein, 1994).

Unfortunately, there is considerable cognitive slippage in the assumption that emotions as well as cognitions are ways of knowing, as, by definition, only cognitions are capable of knowing. To assume that there is a cognitive way of knowing is obviously redundant, and to assume there is a noncognitive way of knowing is a contradiction in terms. What is implicit in the distinction between emotional knowing and cognitive knowing that is worth retaining is that there are two different cognitive modes of knowing, one that is associated with emotions and one that is not. CEST makes this implicit distinction explicit by postulating two conceptual systems, experiential and rational. One important consequence of making such a distinction is that it draws attention to the importance of identifying the distinguishing attributes of the two cognitive modes of information processing, shortly to be described.[1]

Cognitive-Experiential Self-theory

Before proceeding further, it will be helpful to provide some background information on CEST. More detailed information can be found elsewhere (Epstein, 1990, 1991a, 1994). Consistent with modern cognitive theory, CEST assumes that most human information processing occurs automatically, outside, or at the fringes of, human awareness.

CEST differs from other cognitive theories in two major ways. First, it is a psychodynamic theory in that it assumes that the cognitions in the experiential system are primarily emotionally driven. Second, it assumes that automatic, heuristic thinking is organized into an overall integrated adaptive system, the experiential system, and is not simply a set of independent heuristic rules that are incorporated in a broader system that includes more organized conscious, deliberative processing.

The label *experiential system* was selected because the system is considered to be a learning system that derives its schemata from emotionally significant past experiences. This is in contrast to a rational system that operates by a person's understanding of conventional rules of logic and evidence. Unlike the essentially maladaptive Freudian unconscious, which is assumed to operate according to the principles of the *primary process* (associationistic thinking, wish fulfillment, symbolic representation, displacement, and condensation) and is better suited for understanding dreams and psychotic delusions than adaptive behavior, the experiential system *is* an adaptive system. To be sure, it has its limitations, but this should be weighed against the consideration that its adaptive properties have been fashioned over many millions of years of evolution. As evolution does not give up its hard-earned gains easily, it is assumed that the same mode of information processing that is used by higher order subhuman animals is also employed by humans, albeit more complexly. Because of its ease and efficiency, information processing in the mode of the experiential system is considered to be the default option.

The Role of Emotions in CEST

According to CEST, people automatically construct an implicit theory of reality in their experiential system that contains two major divisions, a self-theory and a world-theory, and connecting propositions (e.g., "If I do this, the world will do that," "If the world does this, I will feel that and I should do something if I wish to prevent such feelings and something else if I wish to have the feelings"). People do not construct a theory of reality for its own sake, but in order to make life liveable, meaning as emotionally satisfactory as possible under the circumstances. Thus, the experiential system is an emotionally driven psychodynamic system.

Emotions can be viewed as ready-made, cognitive-affective modules that predispose people to respond to certain critical life events in ways established to be adaptive in the course of evolution. Included are feeling frightened and fleeing when threatened by a larger animal, feeling angry and attacking when threatened by a smaller one, avoiding risks and disengaging from the immediate environment when sad, and welcoming challenges and increasing one's engagement with the environment when happy.

Infants do not begin with a tabula rasa; they begin with cognitive-affective modules that become increasingly differentiated, integrated, and extensive through interactions with the environment. Emotions can thus be viewed as providing nuclei around which an integrative model of the world is constructed. If all goes well, a child will construct an implicit theory of reality in the experiential system in which all of the basic emotions play important roles, in which they are all appropriately acculturated, and in which they interact harmoniously with processing in both the experiential and rational modes.

Emotions are important not only because they provide initial organizational structures, but also because they are an important source of intrinsic motivation. There is a vast difference between affect-driven motives in the experiential system and intellectually driven motives in the rational system. The former provides a source of passion in living and occurs naturally and spontaneously, whereas the latter reflects a person's conceptualization of duty and is a product of self-discipline.

Emotions both influence cognitions and are influenced by them. When people are in a particular emotional state, they think thoughts consistent with that state. A deeply saddened person recruits memories, interprets present events, and anticipates future ones in a manner that is consistent with an overarching view of the world as hostile or rejecting, and of the self as unworthy, inadequate, and helpless. The same person when angry or frightened thinks thoughts that are consonant with those feelings. Moreover, when a person is deeply immersed in one emotional state, it is difficult for that person to imagine another. In these respects, emotions are similar to multiple personalities. People, in fact, do behave as different people when they are experiencing different emotional states. It follows that if people were to change their predominant emotions, they would change who they are. They would experience the world differently and they would behave differently.

Turning to the influence of cognitions on emotions, with rare exception emotions in everyday life are instigated by automatic cognitions. People react not to objective events, but to their subjective construals of events (e.g., Averill, 1980; Beck, 1976; Ellis, 1973; Epstein, 1973). Robert is angry because he interpreted a remark as a threat that warrants, even demands, a counterattack. If he interpreted it as a threat for which flight was more appropriate, he would feel fear, not anger. Note that, unlike other views concerning the influence of cognition on emotions, the critical consideration in CEST is on people's automatic construals of desired responses (e.g., flee, attack, disengage), not on their construals of stimulus-situations per se (threatened, attacked, loss of relationship). This follows from the assumption in CEST that the essence of an emotion is an action tendency (Epstein, 1984). Under most circumstances, of course, interpretations of stimulus-situations and of desired actions are highly related.

Emotions in CEST are viewed as the royal road to the implicit cognitions in a person's implicit theory of reality. By treating their emotions (of which people are usually aware) as cues for attending to the preconscious cognitions that preceded the emotions, people can become aware of the important schemas in their experiential systems that automatically direct their lives. As cognitive therapists (e.g., Beck, 1976; Ellis, 1973) have long recognized, this has important implications for psychotherapy.

The Operating Principles of the Experiential System

The distinguishing characteristics of the experiential system are listed in Table 4.1. A considerable body of research has provided support for most of these (Catlin & Epstein, 1992; Denes-Raj & Epstein, 1994; Denes-Raj, Epstein, & Cole, 1995; Epstein, 1990, 1993a, 1994; Epstein, Denes-Raj, & Pacini, 1995; Epstein, Lipson, Holstein, & Huh, 1992; Epstein & Morling, 1995; Kirkpatrick & Epstein, 1992). It is evident from Table 4.1 that the experiential system is ideally suited for the rapid and efficient appraisal and direction of behavior.

The experiential system is assumed to operate in the following manner. When a person experiences an event of some personal significance, the experience is automatically associated with past similar experiences, and on that basis elicits either subtle, vague feelings, referred to in CEST as "vibes," or full-blown emotions. If the vibes or emotions are pleasant, they motivate thoughts and behavior anticipated to reproduce the previous outcomes, including feelings, and if they are unpleasant they motivate thoughts and behavior anticipated to avoid a repetition of the outcome and feelings. Thus, the acquisition and further development of schemata in the experiential system are assumed to always be driven by affect. However, as thoughts and behavior become proceduralized through practice, they tend to lose their affective loading (Anderson, 1982).

Although the experiential system is an associationistic system that encodes events in the form of concrete exemplars and is ideally suited for simple learning, it is also capable of more complex learning, generalizing, encoding, and organizing of information in the form of directives for goal attainment through the use of prototypes, metaphors, scripts, and narratives. There is reason to suspect, however, that these processes, at least at the more complex levels, involve a contribution from the rational system (Bucci, 1985; Epstein, 1994; Labouvie-Vief, 1990).

Table 4.1 Comparison of the experiential and rational systems

Experiential System	Rational System
1. Holistic	1. Analytic
2. Automatic, effortless	2. Intentional, effortful
3. Affective: pleasure-pain oriented (what feels good)	3. Logical: reason oriented (what is sensible)
4. Associationistic connections	4. Logical connections
5. Behavior mediated by "vibes" from past events	5. Behavior mediated by conscious appraisal of events
6. Encodes reality in concrete images, metaphors, and narratives	6. Encodes reality in abstract symbols, words, and numbers
7. More rapid processing: oriented toward immediate action	7. Slower processing: oriented toward delayed action
8. Slower and more resistant to change: changes with repetitive or intense experience	8. Changes more rapidly and easily: changes with strength of argument and new evidence
9. More crudely differentiated: broad generalization gradient, stereotypical thinking	9. More highly differentiated
10. More crudely integrated: dissociative emotional complexes; context-specific processing	10. More highly integrated: context-general principles
11. Experienced passively and preconsciously: we are seized by our emotions	11. Experienced actively and consciously: we are in control of our thoughts
12. Self-evidently valid: "experiencing is believing"	12. Requires justification via logic and evidence

Note. Adapted with permission from Epstein, 1991.

The Basic Functions of the Experiential System

Almost every major theory of personality proposes a single need that is more basic than any other. The needs that have been most widely proposed are to maximize pleasure and minimize pain, to maintain a stable, coherent conceptual system, to maintain or establish relatedness, and to enhance self-esteem (Epstein, 1993b). According to CEST, the above needs are equally important, and their joint influence must therefore be taken into account in any comprehensive attempt to understand human behavior. This has interesting implications for adaptive and maladaptive behavior, for it means that, depending on how needs are fulfilled, the satisfaction of some may result in the frustration of others. It follows that good adjustment requires a synergistic fulfillment of needs, and that a competitive strategy in need fulfillment is self-defeating. For example, a poorly adjusted person may fulfill the need for self-enhancement in a manner that alienates others, whereas a better adjusted person is more likely to do so in a manner that increases others' attraction to him or her.

By taking into account the interaction of multiple needs, behavior that otherwise appears to be anomalous can be accounted for. For example, based on evidence that normal individuals in a wide variety of circumstances make unrealistically enhancing judgments about themselves and unrealistically optimistic judgments about events, some have concluded that the importance of reality awareness as a criterion of mental health has been overrated, and that good adjustment is better served by positive illusions (see review in Taylor & Brown, 1988). A consideration of the interaction of multiple needs suggests a different interpretation. Namely, the moderately unrealistic favorable judgments that people often make represents a compromise between the needs for self-enhancement and for maintaining a realistic, coherent model of the world. If the latter did not moderate the former, everyone would suffer from delusions of grandeur. Thus, the appropriate conclusion is not that reality awareness is unimportant, but that it is only one among other important needs.

The above example leads to another important generalization that follows from the interaction of multiple needs: that the needs serve as checks and balances against each other. When an attempt to fulfill a need, such as for self-enhancement, becomes excessive, it is normally moderated by the other needs. For example, if a person becomes grandiose, not only will it violate fulfillment of the need to maintain a realistic, coherent conceptual model of the world, but it will tend to alienate other people, and it will also be a direct source of displeasure, as unrealistic expectations are likely to lead to frustration. If one need is fulfilled at the expense of others, the pressure to fulfill the others mounts until, under most circumstances, they moderate the fulfillment of the first need. Should this mechanism fail because of a desperate involvement with fulfilling a particular need, pathology follows, the nature of which is influenced by the particular needs that are involved.

According to CEST, needs are dealt with in two fundamentally different ways that involve either a fulfillment or a defensive orientation. In a fulfillment orientation, a person accepts the risk of negative outcomes in order to achieve positive outcomes. A defensive orientation is characterized by a risk-avoidance strategy, with the person forgoing the opportunity of positive outcomes in order to minimize the possibility of negative ones.

For the motive of maximizing pleasure and minimizing pain, a fulfillment strategy would be oriented toward maximizing pleasure and a defensive strategy toward minimizing pain. For the motive of maintaining a realistic, coherent conceptual system, a fulfillment orientation would involve behaving and thinking in ways that contribute to an increasingly differentiated, integrated, and expansive implicit model of the world. It would entail seeking new experiences and knowledge, engaging in new thoughts, and being willing to take risks. A defensive orientation would consist of "battening down the hatches" in an attempt to preserve the existing system. It would entail avoiding new experiences, knowledge, and thoughts, and defending and rigidifying old ones. For relatedness, a fulfillment orientation would involve developing new relationships, particularly with people different from one's own identification group, and risking increased commitment in current relationships. A defensive orientation would involve attempts to reduce the possibility of rejection by avoiding new relationships and deep attachments, and by clinging desperately to old ones. For self-enhancement, a fulfillment orientation would involve seeking success, whereas a defensive orientation would be more concerned with avoiding failure, which could be accomplished not only by setting low standards, but also by setting standards that are so unrealistically high that failing to reach them could not be taken seriously.

Good adjustment is normally associated with a fulfillment orientation and poor adjustment with a defensive orientation. This is not meant to suggest that a defensive orientation is maladaptive. It is adaptive when used in a paced manner that allows individuals to gradually cope with threatening events within the capacity of their current resources.[2] It is maladaptive when rigidified into a chronic way of adapting to the world.

Relation of Emotions to Psychopathology from the Perspective of Cognitive-Experiential Self-Theory

According to CEST, there are at least six major ways in which emotions are related to psychopathology. These include sensitivities and compulsions, fixation on specific emotions, alienation from emotions, an imbalance in mode of processing, incoherence within and between the experiential and rational systems, and failures in need fulfillment.

Sensitivities and Compulsions

In contrast to psychoanalysis, which emphasizes repression, CEST considers the most basic source of maladjustment to be the development of sensitivities and compulsions. Sensitivities refer to reactions to certain kind of situations with undue distress. Such reactions are learned from past experience, and are encoded into schematic networks that exert an important influence on the construal of events. They have a low threshold for activation by situations that are no more than tangentially relevant, and they therefore bias the interpretation of events in the manner of fear-fulfilling hypotheses. Compulsions refer to driven, fixated, learned responses for coping with sensitivities. They were initially learned because they reduced the distress produced by sensitivities, and they have been maintained because they continue to function in this capacity, are well-practiced, high-priority responses, and have often acquired secondary gains. Sensitivities and compulsions are maladaptive because they predispose individuals to automatically interpret and respond to events in ways that were appropriate in the past, but are not in the present. Moreover, as gross overgeneralizations (the experiential system overgeneralizes in proportion to the emotional intensity of experiences), sensitivities and compulsions lack the fine-tuning and flexibility that is required for effective adjustment (Epstein, 1990, 1991a; Epstein & Brodsky, 1993).

Fixation on Particular Emotions

Emotional responses are no different from other responses with respect to the importance of flexibility. A psychologically healthy person is capable of responding to situations with the full range of appropriate emotions. An important source of maladjustment is responding predominantly with a particular emotion. A person who is predominantly sad, fearful, or angry not only experiences more distress in living than others, but is bound to behave inappropriately. Such fixated emotional states correspond to major diagnostic categories.

There are at least three ways in which propensities to react with particular emotions can develop. First, there is direct reinforcement. Some parents admire aggression as a way of solving life's problems, and reinforce their children whenever they express anger or behave aggressively. Others, who value caution, teach their children to be fearful by reminding them of the many ways in which they can be hurt and by praising them when they behave cautiously. Another way in which parents influence children is through modeling. Children tend to imitate the behavior of the significant others in their lives. For this reason, holding all other factors constant, happy parents are likely to have happy children, sad parents sad children, and so on.

I suspect, however, that the most important reason why people become fixated on the use of particular emotions is that they have been repeatedly exposed to the conditions that elicit those emotions. Because of their assimilating power as cognitive-affective-behavioral modules, when emotions are repeatedly practiced, their range of applicability expands. Repeatedly exposing a child to frightening experiences, including uncertain, unpredictable situations, is likely to make the child anxiety prone. With practice, the anxiety response becomes an increasingly well-learned response, with a low threshold for its arousal, and it becomes increasingly well established in an increasingly elaborated cognitive network within the experiential system. What is true of anxiety is no less true of other emotions. For anger, the provoking situations include the frustration of basic needs, jealousy-arousing situations, and behavior, particularly punishment, construed as unfair. The conditions that predispose children to sadness and depression include loss of relationships, negative evaluation, and conditions of helplessness.

A serious source of pathology consists of creating the conditions for experiencing an emotion, while preventing its acknowledgment and/or expression. This results in alienating people from their emotions, a topic to which we turn next.

Imbalance Between the Two Processing Modes

Good adjustment requires a balanced and harmonious relation between the experiential and rational systems. Each has its advantages and disadvantages, and we could not function without either. It is just as meaningless to attempt to determine which is more important, the experiential or the rational system, as it would be to judge which is more important, eating or breathing.

Overreliance on either system and suppression or avoidance of the other is associated with its own form of pathology. Prototypical examples of extreme reliance on one mode of processing at the expense of the other are conversion hysteria (excessive reliance on the experiential mode) and obsessive compulsive reactions (excessive reliance on the rational mode).

An important area for future research is the determination of the correlates of processing in each of the modes, and the consequences of different degrees of imbalance between them. Such research should be expedited by our recent development of a self-report measure of processing in each of the modes (Epstein, 1994;

Epstein, Pacini, Denes-Raj, & Heier, 1996). In support of the assumption in CEST that these are two independent modes of information processing, responses to the scales that measure the two modes, despite reasonably high reliability, are not significantly related to each other and are associated differentially with measures of personality and adjustment (Epstein et al., 1996).

Alienation from Emotions

The basic needs, or motives, in the experiential system can be moderated and shaped according to culturally acceptable forms of expression, but they cannot be completely suppressed, and attempts to do so are likely to have pathological consequences. It is important, in this respect, to distinguish between construing situations in a manner that does not evoke particular emotions, and denying the emotions once they have been aroused, as can be verified by physiological and expressive reactions. The former is highly adaptive, and a mark of maturity, whereas the latter is a source of alienation from emotions and a source of pathology.

According to Horney (1950), the major source of neurosis is the development of a false self. Although Horney does not define false and true selves, it appears that the false self corresponds, in the language of CEST, to a rational self that is incongruent with the experiential self. The true self, she notes, is driven by a life force that will not be denied. Attempts to suppress it by substituting intellectual, duty-driven motives from the false self for the more spontaneous motives of the true self, acquired directly from emotionally significant experiences, simply drives the true self underground. This results in a loss of spontaneity and enthusiasm for living, and in the development of compensatory defenses and symptoms. The individual with a false self is driven by will and duty to pursue goals that produce neither enthusiasm nor joy in the undertaking, nor a sense of accomplishment and fulfillment if accomplished.

Failure to Fulfill Basic Needs

The view that good adjustment is characterized by a synergistic fulfillment of basic needs, and poor adjustment by a fulfillment of some needs at the expense of fulfillment of others has interesting implications for different forms of psychopathology. Depending on which needs are fulfilled and which are sacrificed, particular syndromes of symptoms occur.

In depression, there is an attempt to maintain a tight hold on a conceptual system that realistically interprets reality at the expense of maintaining self-esteem, of fulfillment of the pleasure-pain principle, and of maintenance of satisfactory relationships; that is, depressives frequently alienate others. In contrast, in schizophrenic disorganization the situation is reversed: The sacrifice of a coherent, realistic conceptual system functions to reduce psychological pain in general, and threats to self-esteem and relatedness in particular. Given the disorganization of a personal theory of reality, there is no longer a conceptualization of a self that can be loathed, a world that can be cruel, and loved ones who can be rejecting. In extreme states of disorganization, the person experiences a psychological void, which can be viewed as a net gain over experiencing intense dysphoric emotions (Epstein, 1979).

In paranoia with delusions of grandeur, the needs for self-esteem enhancement and maintenance of a coherent conceptual system are fulfilled at the cost of maintaining a realistic conceptual system and positive relationships with others; that is, people tend to avoid those who regard them as inferior. In paranoia with delusions of persecution, the coherence of a conceptual system threatened by disorganization is buttressed by a preoccupation with external threats. The focus on external threats increases the stability of the conceptual system, but at the cost of a narrow and unrealistic view of the self and the world. Delusions of persecution also contribute to the enhancement of self-esteem, as to be persecuted, almost always by important others, implies that one must be of considerable importance oneself. Sacrificed is the fulfillment of the need to maintain a realistic model of the world, a component of the need to maintain a realistic, coherent conceptual system. Parenthetically, paranoia informs us that the need to maintain a coherent, realistic model of the world is not entirely a unitary need, for coherence can be achieved by sacrificing reality.

Posttraumatic stress disorder (PTSD) can be understood from the perspective of CEST as a reaction to invalidation of basic beliefs in a personal theory of reality. When a person has experiences that threaten the most fundamental beliefs in his or her implicit theory of reality, such as that the world is predictable, controllable, and benign, and that the self is morally good and capable of coping with whatever situations arise in daily life, the conceptual system is placed under pressure to disorganize. Unlike the situation in schizophrenia, where disorganization of the conceptual system actually occurs, in PTSD disorganization rarely takes place. There are three major types of symptoms of PTSD: direct manifestations of overwhelming stress and of inhibitory attempts to contain it, abortive attempts to assimilate the unassimilable experience, and manifestations of failures in satisfying the four basic needs. Included in the latter are problems with self-esteem and maintaining satisfactory relationships, confusion and a lack of direction in one's life, and the widespread experience of dysphoric emotions, including anger, fear, and depression. In other words, in PTSD, the ability to fulfill all four basic needs is deeply compromised, with the greatest threat being to the maintenance of a coherent conceptual system. (For similar views that were influenced by CEST, see McCann & Pearlman, 1990; Janoff-Bulman, 1992; also see Horowitz, 1976.)

The question may be raised, given the above analysis, as to why everyone subjected to experiences that seriously threaten the stability of their conceptual systems does not become schizophrenic. A possible answer is that schizophrenia may require a disposition to disorganization based either on genetic vulnerability, or on the construction of a fragile foundation of the conceptual system in early childhood, or both. That is, holding the amount of external threat to the organization of the conceptual system constant, some individuals, for genetic or early environmental reasons, have a lower threshold for disorganization than others. In a similar vein, the kind of stimulation that precipitates schizophrenic disorganization may be more related to vulnerabilities in early-childhood relationships, such as those produced by perceptions of rejection by significant others and threats to self-esteem, rather than by threats to life and limb.

Incoherence Within and Between the Two Systems

According to CEST, a major cause of psychopathology consists of incongruence within and between the two systems. With respect to the latter, since both systems occupy the same body, they must function in some degree of harmony, or people would continuously be torn in different directions. In other words, they would frequently experience conflicts between the heart and the mind, between what they feel like doing and what they believe is the reasonable or moral thing to do.

Even more important from the perspective of CEST are inconsistencies within the experiential system itself, for such reactions threaten the very stability of the experiential system, or in the terms of Horney, of the *true self*. According to CEST, all emotionally significant experiences are automatically encoded in the experiential system. If they are assimilable within the extant conceptual system, they are included in the theory. This may require a greater or lesser amount of accommodation in order to make the assimilation possible. This is the normal way in which personal theories grow, becoming increasingly differentiated, integrated, and extensive in the process. If events are extremely arousing and unassimilable, there are two possible reactions that can occur, disorganization of the conceptual system, and dissociation. By dissociating the unassimilable experiences, the integrity of the remainder of the conceptual system is preserved. However, dissociations are like time bombs waiting to explode under appropriate conditions, such as confrontation with cues reminiscent of the initial experience. If dissociations break down, the entire personality structure is jeopardized. Thus, dissociations are a permanent source of vulnerability.

Because of the inherent need to construct and maintain a coherent theory of reality, there is a continuous pressure on dissociated material to be assimilated into a single, organized conceptual system. As a result, the dissociated material often appears in displaced form in dreams and in behavior, and is a continuous source of stress, as it tends to be repeatedly activated until assimilation may ultimately occur (Epstein, 1991b; Horowitz, 1976).

Summary and Conclusions

CEST integrates the cognitive unconscious of modern psychology with the psychodynamic unconscious of psychoanalysis by assuming that the former is emotionally driven. The result is that an adaptive unconscious that operates automatically by principles of learning and is consistent with evolutionary principles is substituted for the Freudian maladaptive unconscious that operates by the primary process and is indefensible from an evolutionary perspective. CEST replaces the usual way of thinking about two ways of knowing in terms of emotions versus cognition with two cognitive systems, an experiential system that is intimately associated with emotions and a rational system that is affect free, and indicates the principles by which each system operates. The implications of the theory for an understanding of emotions, psychopathology, and their interaction is discussed. At the very least, the theory provides a new perspective for examining the nature of emotions and their role in adaptive and maladaptive behavior.

Notes

1. It is important to be aware that the experiential system is not isomorphic with an emotional system. For one, the experiential system, although it interacts with emotions, is strictly cognitive. Second, not all the schemas in the experiential system, such as those that have become habituated or "proceduralized," contain an affective component.

2. See Epstein (1983) for a discussion of graded stress inoculation as a natural healing process for coping with stress.

References

Anderson, J. R. (1982). Acquisition of cognitive skill. *Psychological Review, 89,* 369–406.

Averill, J. R. (1980). A constructionist view of emotion. In R. Plutchik & H. Kellerman (Eds.), *Emotion, theory, research, and experience: Vol. 1. Theories of emotion* (pp 305–339). San Diego: Academic Press.

Beck, A. T. (1976). *Cognitive therapy and the emotional disorders.* New York: International Universities Press.

Bucci, W. (1985). Dual coding: A cognitive model for psychoanalytic research. *Journal of the American Psychoanalytic Association, 33,* 571–607.

Catlin, G., & Epstein, S. (1992). Unforgettable experiences: The relation of life-events to basic beliefs about self and world. *Social Cognition, 10,* 189–209.

Denes-Raj, V., & Epstein, S. (1994). Conflict between experiential and rational processing: When people behave against their better judgment. *Journal of Personality and Social Psychology, 66,* 819–829.

Denes-Raj, V., Epstein, S., & Cole, J. (1995). The generality of the ratio-bias phenomenon. *Personality and Social Psychology Bulletin, 10,* 1083–1092.

Ellis, A. (1973). *Humanistic psychotherapy.* New York: Macmillan.

Epstein, S. (1973). The self-concept revisited, or a theory of a theory. *American Psychologist, 28,* 404–416.

Epstein, S. (1979). Natural healing processes of the mind: I. Acute schizophrenic disorganization. *Schizophrenia Bulletin, 5,* 313–321.

Epstein, S. (1984). Controversial issues in emotion theory. In P. Shaver (Ed.), *Annual review of research in personality and social psychology* (pp. 64–87). Beverly Hills, CA: Sage.

Epstein, S. (1990). Cognitive-experiential self-theory. In L. Pervin (Ed.), *Handbook of personality theory and research: Theory and research* (pp. 165–192). New York: Guilford Press.

Epstein, S. (1991a). Cognitive-experiential Self-theory: An integrative theory of personality. In R. Curtis (Ed.), *The relational self: Convergences in psychoanalysis and social psychology* (pp. 111–137). New York: Guilford Press.

Epstein, S. (1991b). The self-concept, the traumatic neurosis, and the structure of personality. In D. Ozer, J. M. Healy, Jr., & A. J. Stewart (Eds.), *Perspectives in personality* (Vol. 3A, pp. 63–98). London: Jessica Kingsley.

Epstein, S. (1992). Cognitive-experiential self-theory: An integrative theory of personality. In R. C. Curtis (Ed.), *The relational self: Theoretical convergences in psychoanalysis and social psychology.* (pp. 111–137). New York: Guilford Press.

Epstein, S. (1993a). Emotion and self-theory. In M. Lewis & J. Haviland (Eds.), *Handbook of emotions* (pp. 313–326). New York: Guilford Press.

Epstein, S. (1993b). Implications of cognitive-experiential self-theory for personality and developmental psychology. In D. Funder, R. Parke, C. Tomlinson-Keasey, & K. Widaman

(Eds.), *Studying lives through time: Personality and development* (pp. 399–438). Washington, DC: American Psychological Association.

Epstein, S. (1994). An integration of the cognitive and the psychodynamic unconscious. *American Psychologist, 49,* 709–724.

Epstein, S., & Brodsky, A. (1993). *You're smarter than you think: How to develop your practical intelligence for success in living.* New York: Simon & Schuster.

Epstein, S., Denes-Raj, V., & Pacini, R. (1995). The Linda problem revisited from the perspective of cognitive-experiential self-theory. *Personality and Social Psychology Bulletin, 11,* 1124–1138.

Epstein, S., Lipson, A., Holstein, C., & Huh, E. (1992). Irrational reactions to negative outcomes: Evidence for two conceptual systems. *Journal of Personality and Social Psychology, 62,* 328–339.

Epstein, S., & Morling, B. (1995). Is the self motivated to do more than enhance and verify itself? In M. H. Kernis (Ed.), *Efficacy, agency, and self-esteem* (pp. 9–29). New York: Plenum Press.

Epstein, S., Pacini, R., Denes-Raj, V., & Heier, H. (1996). Individual differences in intuitive-experiential and analytical-rational thinking styles. *Journal of Personality and Social Psychology, 71,* 390–405.

Horney, K. (1950). *Neurosis and human growth.* New York: Norton.

Horowitz, M. J. (1976). *Stress response syndromes.* New York: Jason Aronson.

Janoff-Bulman, R. (1992). *Shattered assumptions.* New York: Free Press.

Kirkpatrick, L. A., & Epstein, S. (1992). Cognitive-experience self-theory and subjective probability: Further evidence for two conceptual systems. *Journal of Personality and Social Psychology, 63,* 534–544.

Labouvie-Vief, G. (1990). Wisdom as integrated thought: Historical and developmental perspectives. In R. J. Sternberg (Ed.), *Wisdom: Its nature, origins and development* (pp. 52–83). New York: Cambridge University Press.

McCann, I. L., & Pearlman, L. A. (1990). *Psychological trauma and the adult survivor: Theory, therapy, and transformation.* New York: Bruner/Mazel.

Taylor, S. E., & Brown, J. D. (1988). Illusion and well-being: A social psychological perspective on mental health. *Psychological Bulletin, 103,* 193–210.

5

Rainer Krause, Evelyne Steimer-Krause,
Jörg Merten, & Burkhard Ullrich

Dyadic Interaction Regulation, Emotion, and Psychopathology

In our research we have been dealing with questions and problems usually centered around the psychoanalytic concepts of *transference* and *countertransference*. Laplanche and Pontalis (1972) define transference "as the process through which unconscious wishes are actualized with specific objects within the frame of specific types of relations, having been relevant for these objects" (p. 550). According to this definition transference must encompass strategies to create specific relationship patterns. In addition, according to this psychoanalytic assumption, these patterns should be repetitions of past experiences with significant others. Most, if not all, schools of psychotherapy would agree that mentally ill people can be characterized by high degrees of negentropy within their cognitive-affective organization. The related phenomena are called "Klischee" (Freud, 1912), schemas (Horowitz, 1994), or role relationship models (Horowitz, 1991).

Moreover, there is overwhelming evidence that a specific form of emotional interactive climate within families fitting these relationship models is the best predictor for a relapse to acute psychosis of formerly hospitalized schizophrenic patients (Olbricht, 1994). In depressives we find more and more evidence for similar predictors. Given this state of affairs, we could expect a great deal of research and knowledge about the nature of the social processes being governed by these maladaptive, highly negentropic schemas and keeping them alive, by forcing the interaction partners to confirm them. This, however, is not the case. The research on expressed emotion within families is purely inductive and based mainly on rating procedures (Hahlweg, Feinstein, Müller, & Dose, 1988).

Within psychoanalytic theory neither the interpersonal side of transference nor the social strategies, which create specific relationship patterns, were systematically studied. Instead, transference was considered conceptually, at least at the beginning, within an intrapsychic monadic model (Thomä & Kächele, 1988), in which the focus was on the patient and his or her wishes and defense mechanisms. Only reluctantly was the interpersonal side of this process theoretically valued by including the role of the therapist (Gill, 1982), as well as the realization that the transference wish of the patient includes the object's reply and the patient's fantasies and desires (Sandler, 1976). In addition, not enough of the empirical research on social exchange processes and strategies was recognized within the psychoanalytic field.

Our research group has worked since 1973 within that field. We were searching for the links between patients' unconscious wishes and their "implantation" in the social field by influencing their interaction partners. At the beginning of this research we did not know whether such enactments would exist, nor did we have detailed ideas about what kind of messages the patients might use (Krause, 1982, 1983). Our clinical experience and first promising results concerning the interactive and especially the affective behavior of stutters and their partners, showing a tremendous influence of stutterers on their partners, even if they could hide the speech disfluency (Krause, 1981), encouraged us to study in a more systematic way the interactive affect-exchange processes in different nosological groups. Following the psychoanalytic tradition, we used the separation of *neurotic disturbances*, centered around intrapsychic conflicts, like hysteria, compulsion, and so on, from *structural disturbances*, centered around enduring alterations of the ego functions, like in schizophrenia or severe psychosomatic disturbances. This separation is quite common in the German psychoanalytic community (Heigl-Evers, Heigl, & Otto, 1993). Each of these two nosological groups should have typical deviations in the social regulation of intimacy, power, and erotic seduction. In what have been termed structural disturbances, which include psychoses and in particular schizophrenia as well as severe psychosomatics, deviations presumably concern the regulation of intimacy and distance (Krause, Steimer, Sänger-Alt, & Wagner, 1989, p. 1).

Questions of Research and Hypothesis

Formulated in a more precise way, our questions were as follows.

1. Do patients with neurotic versus structural mental disturbances show different relationship patterns? The structural disturbances should be characterized by a general reduction of cathexis and intimacy, whereas the neurotic patients should enact specific conflicts without a general reduction of cathexis and intimacy. Alternatively, specific affect-exchange processes, if they exist, could be a function of the severity of the sickness as experienced by the patient disregarding our dichotomous classification. We were quite convinced that there is no built-in connection between symptomatology and the experienced severity of the sickness. So, it is often mentioned that psychosomatic patients describe themselves as feeling remarkably well, despite the severity of their illness, whereas anxiety patients, which can be treated easily with whatever technique, experience themselves as very disturbed and sick. Finally, it could be the symptomatology per se, as diagnosed on Axis I of the *Diagnostic and Statistical Manual of Mental Disorders* (3rd ed.; hereinafter DSM-III; Wittchen, Saß, Zaudig, & Köhler, 1989) or the International Classification of Diseases, 10th edition (ICD-10; Dilling, Monbour & Schmidt, 1992).

2. Do healthy subjects react specifically in their behavior and fantasies, if they interact with patients showing different patterns of enactment, even if they are not informed about the patient's sickness?

3. If so, how is it that the patients manage to influence the healthy subjects?

Methodology

For the investigation of these questions we ended up with the following setting: Two people of the same age, sex, and education unknown to one another met in our laboratory and discussed politics for 20 minutes. In particular, they had to agree on the four most important problems to be solved in the next year in the Federal Republic of Germany.

One of the partners was always healthy, and the other partner was suffering from one of the following problems: schizophrenia (in- and outpatients: 20 males), ulcerative colitis (10 males and 10 females), and 10 male subjects suffering from functional spine disturbance with a neurotic etiology. The control group consisted of healthy individuals (20 males and 20 females). The diagnosis was made according to the revised DSM-III (Wittchen et al., 1989) and in recent times the ICD-10 (Dilling et al., 1992). The patients with functional spine disturbance were included because they can be subsumed conceptually under the heading of a neurotic disturbance. According to the ICD-10 the number is F45 .4 (*anhaltende somatoforme Schmerzstörung*, continuous psychosomatic pains). Since the schizophrenics were not acutely psychotic, their partners did not consciously realize that they were talking to sick people. We analyzed facial, kinetic, paraverbal, and verbal behavior on an individual as well as a dyadic level and their temporal organization. Facial expression was analyzed with the help of Ekman and Friesen's methodology on facial measurement (Ekman & Friesen, 1978; Friesen & Ekman, 1986). The internal representation of the affect was rated by the subjects themselves using the *Differentielle Affekt Skala* (Merten & Krause, 1993). We related facial behavior to the ratings on the experienced feelings within each subject of the dyad, and to the assumptions of how their partner would feel.

Results

The first question about *specificity* can be answered in the following way: Males suffering from schizophrenia (paranoid hallucinatoric without open exacerbation) or ulcerative colitis showed severe reduction of facial movements compared to the control group (healthy subjects talking to one another) neurotic patients (Frisch, Schwab, & Krause, 1995; Krause et al., 1989; Steimer-Krause, Krause & Wagner, 1990).

The reduction is mainly a consequence of the scarcity of felt happiness expression as well as speech-related frontalis movements usually being a sign of involvement. With the schizophrenics this is only partly due to the neuroleptic medication, the amount of which correlates negatively with the amount of facial movements ($r = -.30$), but not with facial affect per se. The neuroleptic medication affects mainly the speech-related involvement indicators such as the frontalis innervations, not the affect expression per se.

Since the general reduction is only indicative for the schizophrenic and psychosomatic disturbances, not for the patients with underlying neurotic conflicts, we conclude that it is the underlying *structure* that governs the alterations. Neurotic conflicts are somehow visible in the affect system of the face. The structural disturbances can be characterized by an absence of affective expression. Some of these observations have been confirmed independently by Ellgring (1995). Nevertheless, in the case of schizophrenia, as a structural disturbance, one affect, namely, contempt, is heightened against all others. We have speculated elsewhere (Krause, Steiner-Krause, & Huffnagel, 1992) how this lead affect might be tied to the process of projection as a specific form of externalization. Among the patients with neurotic conflicts, facial activity and affect are heightened. There is an excess of different negative and positive affects of conflicting nature, for example, contempt/happiness. *We conclude that there are specific forms of affective schemas for structural and neurotic disturbances.*

The second question was whether the partners of the patients unknowingly *react* to the patients' offers. The most convincing and surprising result was that the *amount* of facial affectivity of the patients and their healthy partners was nearly identical. These results do not imply causal influence. It is, however, highly unprobable that the schizophrenics adapted downward to healthy subjects since the healthy subjects talking to one another show significantly more facial affect than the ones being engaged with the patients with structural disturbances.

Concerning the third question about the *underlying process* of this "adaptation," we thought of several possibilities. The healthy subjects could mimic unconsciously the affect of the patients. This explanation can be ruled out as a major source of influence. In the case of the structural disturbances, the healthy subjects would mimic a nonreaction, a process for which the term *mimicry* is not very suitable. In addition, the healthy subjects do not mimic the lead affect of the schizophrenics. Despite this severe reduction, the healthy partners, like the control group, show most frequently felt happiness and not contempt, as did their disturbed partners. The most frequent negative facial affect of the inpatient schizophrenics' partners was anger, not contempt. Contrary to the schizophrenic patients, the nomothetic variability of the affects used by the partners remained high despite the reduction in quantity.

Another explanation would be that the healthy subjects had realized consciously that they were talking to mentally ill people. Then the alteration of their pattern could follow the layman s theory of "schizophrenia" or "neurosis." This can be ruled out since the healthy subjects never told us they had realized they were talking with a mentally disturbed person, in an intensive interview after the discussion. Some of the partners of the schizophrenic inpatient group admitted feeling slightly bewildered.

Finally, the affective internal representation of the situation could have changed during the interaction without any conscious knowledge. This seems to be the case. The schizophrenic patients experience themselves as significantly more anhedonic than the control group. They attribute to their partners a maximum of negative affect, which is correct since the partners rate themselves as more sad and fearful than the control group and the patients themselves. So, somehow the patients managed to change the internal affective life of their partners dramatically. Maybe this is because they were confronted with severely reduced happiness, a very reduced facial affective signaling, and so much contempt.

The partners of the schizophrenics are the only ones who show what they feel. They feel angry and they show anger. This is usually not the case among healthy people talking to one another—there are no substantial correlations between expression and experiencing on the level of group statistics. This is a consequence of the fact that in situations like the one we had choosen the affect is usually neither "attached" to the partner nor to the self, but to the objects they are talking about. That means that the anger face is related, say, to the person they are "angrily" talking about. This is usually not the partner but mental objects like politicans. That means the more negative affect they show, the happier they feel ($r = +.60$, between anger expression and self-rating happiness). The happiness expression, however, is tied to the partner and the self. This can be clearly demonstrated through a context analysis of different streams of behavior like mutual gaze, affect expression, and speaking (Merten, 1995). The high amount of shown happiness excludes the attribution of negative affect to the partner.

Also, for the schizophrenic inpatients there is no congruence between expression and experiencing. Again, we find a strong negative correlation between their preferred affect signal—contempt—and the attribution of negative affect to the self structure, which means they are feeling better the more contempt they show. For their interaction partners it is the other way round—the more contempt they show, the worse they feel. Keeping in mind that the partners of these patients are the only group that shows congruence between expression and experiencing, which again induces the fear and sadness feelings on the side of the schizophrenics (Hufnagel, Steimer-Krause, Wagner, & Krause, 1993), we might postulate a positive feedback loop resulting in situations in which the interaction has to be interrupted because the negative affect becomes unbearable for both interaction partners. This happened sometimes: both subjects sitting mute in their chairs for longer periods of time. Another possibility would be that they switch to physical violence, or that the patient would decompensate into a psychotic spell.

The complete regulation system might work in the following way: The schizophrenic patients *feel* very bad, especially fearful. They mostly *show* contempt, however. The more contempt they show, the better they feel. In psychoanalytic terms we could consider that part of the process the visible enactment of *projection* as a defense mechanism. From the experiential side it is *relieving* to ridicule the partner instead of the self. In the long run the process is not successful, because the partners are unwilling to accept the projected role. They react to the contempt expression with fear and experienced anger; they show the anger. Within the verbal parts of the interaction the healthy partners very often take over an active part, keeping the discussion going, through metaregulation statements like "Why don't you make a proposal, I have talked a lot up to now" (Villenave-Cremer, Kettner, & Krause, 1989). The shown anger of the partner creates more feelings of inferiority, fear, and other negative affects in the patient, and the necessity to project grows stronger; as a consequence, they have to express more contempt. So, the patient is under the influence of his own projected impulses coming back to him from the partner's face.

This can be shown empirically: For the schizophrenic inpatients 60% of the variance of the affective experience can be explained through their partner's facial expression, especially their unhedonic affects. In addition, the amount of shown happiness signals of the patient's partner correlates with the patient's self-attribution of contempt, disgust, and anger. So, the meaning of the partner's felt happiness face is turned into its contrary. The patient attributes "gloating." In healthy subjects the facial happiness signaling has, contrary to that, a suppressor effect on the amount of experienced negative affect, as well as on the attribution of negative affect to the partner. The amount of variance of the affective experiencing that can be interpreted through the partner's facial expression is 20% within healthy dyads and is centered around the happiness expression. The patients feel how their partners look, but they themselves induce this appearance. This process was sometimes called projective identification, assuming that they identify with their own projections. It is more adequate to call it cycles of projection and reintrojection.

A detailed analysis of dyadic gaze behavior, facial affect, and speaking versus listening in the course of time comparing the healthy dyads and those with a schizophrenic patient, as it was done by Merten (1995), led to the following algorithm governing the enactment process:

The schizophrenic's behavior in the first part of the projective process

Negative affect in the partner is induced by the following behaviors of the schizophrenic patient:

- Display of negative facial affects while both interaction partners are looking at each other. This mutual gaze pattern raises the probability that the negative affect is attached to the partner, not to the mental object they are talking about.
- Continuous gaze at the partner, even when talking (within healthy dyads the speaker usually does not look, besides switching-pauses).
- Augmentation of contempt in the listener position.
- Rupture of mutual gazing with proceedings or successive negative facial affect.
- Manipulation of the partner to look away by showing negative affect during mutual gazing.
- Complete reduction of mutual gazing during speaker turns with no partner being prepared to take over the floor.

The partner's behavior in the second part

The healthy partner as a "container" of the projected states: Experiencing intense negative affect, the partner starts to display negative facial affect, especially anger, while looking at the schizophrenic. Furthermore, the partner smiles when the schizophrenic looks away, which rather serves as a sign of contempt than one of affiliation. In these cases, the partner acts in accordance with the projected feelings.

The first and second parts of the projective process describe a positive feedback loop, which has to be terminated; otherwise, the interaction would escalate in the way we described it above.

There are three other variations in how the dyadic interaction regulation can continue. One of them is that the healthy partner augments the positive involvement through forced happiness expression to stabilize the relationship and the partner. This strategy, of course, is not successful because the patient attributes that kind of behavior as contempt. Another variant is that the partner does not intensify the involvement in the relationship but tries to take over the discussion. This, however, is detrimental to the self-esteem of the patient. The third variant is that the healthy partner clarifies the reference of the shown negative affects to the objects, to avoid the misinterpretation that they are indicative for the affective state of the relationship or the self. This is done by showing a specific gazing pattern while displaying the negative affect, which is described in detail elsewhere (Merten, 1995). Using this technique, the interaction can go on with a bearable amount of negative feelings.

Another source influencing the enactment of affective schemata is synchronization. Synchronization was operationalized in our studies as all those events during which one subject shows a facial response within a maximum temporal delay of 1 second to a facial movement of his partner. The schizophrenic patients and their normal partners showed less synchronization reactions as compared to the healthy control group interacting with each other. This result remains even if we take into account the reduced total expressiveness in dyads with patients as compared to that of the healthy subjects.

If we are relating the synchronization reactions of one partner to those of the other within each dyad, we can find very high correlations, no matter whether the dyads consist of healthy people only ($r = .88$) or of a schizophrenic outpatient and a healthy partner ($r = .89$). But this high interdependence within each dyad is determined very differently in the two groups.

For the dyads with healthy people the number of synchronization reactions both partners are showing is determined equally by both partners' expressivity. The total expressivity of both partners influences the amount of their own synchronization reactions as well as those of their partners. So, this is real reciprocity. Based on the correlations in the dyads with the schizophrenic patients, there must be another form of interconnectiveness. Here, so it seems, the amount of synchronization reactions both partners are showing is steered by the expressivity of the schizophrenic patient. How expressive the healthy partner is has no effect on his own synchronization behavior or on that of the patient. Again, we have reasons to assume that the feelings this behavior creates in the partner are negative (Steimer-Krause, 1994).

Obviously the organization of the microsynchronization is something essential for the relationship regulation. Since most of these processes are on time schedules below reaction time, they require anticipatory knowledge of the partner's action, which is a form of basic empathy in the realm of the body. These kinds of processes are reminiscent of mother-child interactions, and maybe their absense has something to do with specific experiences of that time.

Despite the general reduction of facial affectivity in the colitis ulcerosa patients, the relationship regulation is different. First, there is no strong induction of negative affective *experience* like in the dyads with a schizophrenic patient. Instead of getting angry, their partners get bored. We do not yet know how to explain this. For the time being, we have data that the psychosomatic patients overemphasize the resemblance of themselves and their partners. They have very high intercorrelations between the affect ratings about themselves and those attributed to the partners. Their partners have no significant correlations between their self-rating of affect and the attribution of affect to their partners. We have interpreted this as a form of cognitive denial. We do not yet know how this denial might be related to the other nonverbal behavior patterns.

The patients with neurotic conflicts use very different forms of enactment. Again, the partners of the neurotic patients feel very bad, nearly as bad as those of the schizophrenic patients, but the induction of these feelings is very different. There is no general reduction in involvement and cathexis; instead, the patients somehow manage to superimpose very peculiar themes, for example, the most important problem is to protect truck traffic against railway transportation. The healthy subjects usually cannot agree with them if they want to fulfill the task of the discussion. As a consequence, there is a lot of anger centered around the selection and ranking of themes. Facially the neurotic patients show a lot of blends and a lot of facial idiosyncratic activity that cannot be interpreted using our dictionary. The enactment seems to be much more specific to conflicts, not the relationship regulation per se, as in the structural disturbances.

Discussion

We are still far from understanding the processes governing the relation of psychopathology, its social origin, and its maintenance. At least some things we can say. Naive laymen react very strongly to the specific behavior mentally ill people offer. These processes are preconscious or unconscious on both sides. The main source of influence is the expressive affect system, be it in the face or, in the voice, imbedded in the dia- and synchronous context of gaze, speech, and bodyshifts. For the structural disturbances the main common influence is a reduction in engagement and joy on the behavioral level. The introspective experiential part is not reduced in the anhedonic spectrum of feelings. The partners of the schizophrenics usually feel very angry; those of the colitis ulcerosa patients' bored. The regulation of the dyadic enactment with the severe psychosomatic colitis patients has yet to be clarified. We assume that it is centered around denial but we do not understand the underlying processes. Within dyads with neurotic patients we find again high influence on the healthy partners' feelings. They feel nearly as bad as the schizophrenic patients, but again, the way these feelings are enacted seems to be very different. It is much more cognitively bound and the expressive patterns are more closely related to the underlying unconscious cognitive structure. The patients manage to superimpose specific themes onto the discussion that, from the point of view of the healthy subjects, make it nearly impossible to fulfill the task adequately. These themes are related to the unsolved neurotic conflicts. Again, we do not yet know the details of the enactment. However, there is no reduction in facial affect. The conflict seems to be visible.

Based on our research, we have developed a taxonomy using the following six variables:

1. facial signal person x,
2. facial signal person y,
3. affect rating x (self),
4. affect rating x (other),
5. affect rating y (self),
6. affect rating y (other).

Using these variables and their interrelations we define the following terms, which we have used quite successfully for operationalizations of interactive, psychodynamic processes (Schwab & Krause, 1994).

1. *Affect-induction, ideomotoric reactions:* high correlation between facial signals of person x and person y.
2. *Congruence:* high correlation between the expression of person x and self-rating of person x.
3. *Projection:* high correlation of facial signals of person x with the affect rating of the same person x about the person y. Person x shows what he thinks that his partner feels.
4. *Denial in perception:* high negative correlation between the facial affect of person x and the attribution of emotion to person x by partner y (person x attributes in a systematic but wrong way internal mental states to person y; e.g., the schizophrenic attributes contempt whenever he sees felt happiness in this partner).
5. *Missing of empathy* can be characterized as no systematic relation between expression of person x and the attribution of emotion to person x by person y.
6. High correlations between self-rating of person x and object rating of the same person x can be characterized as subjectively attributed *resemblance*. Based on this measure we defined *denial in cognition* as high differences of resemblance ratings of the two persons, for example, those we found in psychosomatic patients: If person x rates himself as very resembling person y and person y has no resemblance ratings with x at all, we assume that person y denies the existing differences cognitively.
7. A high correlation between the object rating of person x and self-rating person y we characterized as *validity* of the affective rating.
8. Finally, *enactment power* is defined as the amount of variance in the affective self-ratings of person x that can be explained by the facial affect of person y. As we have seen, the healthy partners have a very high enactment power on to the schizoprenic patients.

Using these measures we could predict and investigate the relation of mental and body emotion processes within different groups of psychosomatic patients (Schwab & Krause, 1994), as well as between healthy men and women. For the time being, healthy women show significantly more facial affect than healthy men. This difference (Frisch, 1995), however, disappears if the men talk to the women. Then, the men augment their facial affectivity to the level of the women. Within the psychosomatic patients, gender overrides the sickness; nevertheless, the colitis women had significantly less facial affect than the healthy women talking among themselves. Within the schizophrenics, gender has no impact on the reduction of facial affectivity (Ellgring, 1995).

We have proposed a diagnostic decision tree, taking into account the results we describe here (Krause, Steimer-Krause & Ullrich, 1992). In the meantime, we started a research project on the process of psychotherapy and its nature. Using the same methodology, we could predict 50% of the variance of therapeutic outcome using the dyadic facial affective behavior of patient and therapists within the first session (Anstadt, Ullrich, Merten, Buchheim, & Krause, in press; Merten, Krause, Ullrich, & Buchheim, in press).

References

Anstadt, T., Ullrich, B., Merten, J., Buchheim, P., & Krause, R. (in press). Remembering, acting in, acting out. Studies about the core conflictual relationship theme. *Psychotherapy Research*.

Dilling, H., Monbour, W., & Schmidt, M. H. (1992). *Internationale Klassifikation psychischer Störungen. ICD 10.* Göttingen: Huber.

Ekman, P. & Friesen, W. V. (1978). *Facial action coding system (FACS)*. Palo Alto, CA: Consulting Psychologists Press.

Ellgring, H. (1995). Psychopathology and facial expression. Paper presented at the sixth European conference on facial expression, measurement and meaning, Universidad Autonoma, Madrid, Spain June, 1995.

Freud, S. (1912). *Zur Dynamik der Übertragung. Studienausgabe, Ergänzungsband: Behandlungstechnik* (pp. 157–168). Frankfurt: Fischer.

Friesen, W. V. & Ekman, P. (1986). *Emotional facial action coding system (EMFACS)*. Unpublished manuscript.

Frisch, I. (1995). Mimisches Verhalten von Frauen und Männern in gleichgeschlechtlichen dyadischen Interaktionen. *Zeitschrift fur Differentielle und Diagnostische Psychologie, 16*, 33–42.

Frisch, I., Schwab, F., & Krause, R. (1995). Affektives Ausdrucksverhalten gesunder und an colitis erkrankter männlicher und weiblicher Erwachsener. *Studien zur Psychosomatik. Zeitschrift für Klinische Psychologie, 24*, 1–9.

Gill, M. M. (1982). *Analysis of transference*. New York: International University Press.

Hahlweg, H., Feinstein, E., Müller, U., & Dose, M. (1988). Folgerungen aus der Expressed-Emotion-Forschung für die Rückfallprophylaxe Schizophrener. In W. P. Kaschka et al. (Eds.), *Die Schizophrenien, biologische und familiendynamische Konzepte zur Pathogenese* (pp. 201–210). Berlin: Springer-Verlag.

Heigl-Evers, A., Heigl, F. S., & Otto, J. (1993). Abriß der Psychoanalyse und der analytischen Psychotherapie. In A. Heigl-Evers, F. S. Heigl, & J. Otto (Eds.), *Lehrbuch der Psychotherapie* (pp. 1–284). Stuttgart: Fischer-Verlag.

Horowitz, L. M. (1991). *Person schemas and maladaptive interpersonal patterns*. Chicago: University of Chicago Press.

Horowitz, L. M. (1994). Person schemas, psychopathology and psychotherapy research. *Psychotherapy Research, 4*, 1–19.

Hufnagel, H., Steimer-Krause, E., Wagner, G., & Krause, R. (1993). Facial expression and introspection within different groups of mental disturbances. In J. W. Pennebaker & H. C. Traue (Eds.), *Emotional expression and inhibition in health and illness* (pp. 164–179). Göttingen: Hogrefe

Krause, R. (1981). A social psychological approach to the study of stuttering. In C. Fraser & K. R. Scherer (Eds.), *Advances in the social psychology of language* (pp. 77–122). Cambridge: Cambridge University Press.

Krause, R. (1982). Kernbereiche psychoanalytischen Handelns. *Der Nervenarzt, 53*, 504–512.

Krause, R. (1983). Zur Onto- und Phylogenese des Affektsystems und ihrer Beziehungen zu psychischen Störungen. *Psyche, 37*, 1015–1043.

Krause, R., Steimer, E., Sänger-Alt, C., & Wagner, G. (1989). Facial expression of schizophrenic patients and their interaction partners. *Psychiatry: Interpersonal and Biological Processes, 52*, 1–12.

Krause, R., Steimer-Krause, E., & Hufnagel, H. (1992). Expression and experience of affects in paranoid schizophrenia. *European Review of Applied Psychology, 42*, 131–138.

Krause, R., Steimer-Krause, E., & Ullrich, B. (1992). Use of affect research in dynamic psychotherapy. In M. Leuzinger-Bohleber, H. Schneider, & R. Pfeifer (Eds.), *Two butterflies on my head. Pschoanalysis in the interdisciplinary scientific dialogue* (pp. 277–291). Heidelberg: Springer-Verlag.

Laplanche, J., & Pontalis, J. P. (1972). *Das Vokabular der Psychoanalyse*. Frankfurt: Suhrkamp.

Merten, J. (1995). *Affekte und die Regulation nonverbalen interaktiven Verhaltens*. Bern: Peter Lang.

Merten, J., & Krause, R. (1993). *Differentielle Affekt Skala. DAS*. [Arbeiten aus der Fachrichtung Psychologie No. 173]. Saarbrücken: Universität, Institut für Psychologie.

Merten, J., Krause, R., Ullrich, B., & Buchheim, P. (in press). Affect expression and experiencing within the therapeutic process. *Psychotherapy Reseach*.

Olbricht, R. (1994). Risikofaktoren für Rezidive schizophrener Erkrankungen. *Zeitschrift für Klinische Psychologie, 23*, 153–162.

Sandler, J. (1976). Countertransfrence and role-responsiveness. *International Review of Psychoanalysis, 3*, 33–42.

Schwab, F. & Krause, R. (1994). Über das Verhältnis von körperlichen und mentalen emotionalen Abläufen bei verschiedenen psychosomatischen Krankheitsbildern. *Zeitschrift für Psychotherapie, Psychosomatik, Medizinische Psychologie, 44*, 308–315.

Steimer-Krause, F. (1994). Nonverbale Beziehungsregulation in Dyaden mit schizophrenen Patienten. Ein Beitrag zur Übertragungs-Gegenübertragungs-Forschung. In U. Streeck & K. Bell (Eds.), *Die Psychoanalyse schwerer psychischer Erkrankungen. Konzepte, Behandlungen, Erfahrungen* (pp. 209–228). München: Pfeiffer-Verlag.

Steimer-Krause, E., Krause, R., & Wagner, G. (1990). Interaction regulations used by schizophrenic and psychosomatic patients. Studies on facial behavior in dyadic interactions. *Psychiatry: Interpersonal and Biological Processes, 52*, 1–12.

Thomä, H., & Kächele, H. (1988). *Handbook of psychoanalytic therapy* (Vols. 1 & 2). New York: Springer.

Villenave-Cremer, S., Kettner, M., & Krause, R. (1989). Verbale Interaktion von Schizophrenen und ihren Gesprächspartnern. *Zeitschrift für Klinische Psychologie und Psychotherapie, 37*, 401–421.

Wittchen, H. U., Saß, H., Zaudig, M., & Köhler, K. (1989). *Diagnostisches und Statistisches Manual Psychischer Störungen. DSM-III-R*. Weinheim: Beltz.

6

Susanne Kaiser & Klaus R. Scherer

Models of "Normal" Emotions Applied to Facial and Vocal Expression in Clinical Disorders

Most clinicians, reflecting on their experience, readily admit to the fact that nonverbal cues, and especially vocal and facial patterns, have a strong effect on their overall evaluation of a client. They regularly use the facial and vocal behavior of their patients as diagnostic indicators of type of disorder, of transient shifts in mood state, and of improvement during therapy. However, the use of these nonverbal diagnostic indicators is almost always of a very intuitive nature, which is quite different from a trained skill in differentially utilizing specific vocal and facial cues.

One reason for this discrepancy between a widely, and often successfully, used intuitive approach and a trainable skill based on an established body of knowledge can be found in the dearth of well-controlled empirical studies on nonverbal diagnostic indicators that use sufficiently large and homogeneous groups of patients, appropriate control groups, and established measurement procedures. In part, the scarcity of research is due to the absence of explicit models of affect disturbance that include differential predictions of the facial and vocal expression patterns likely to accompany various disorders. In this chapter, it will be argued that approaches to the psychological study of "normal emotional functioning," specifying the relation between specific affect states and the related facial and vocal patterns, may provide a useful theoretical framework for concrete hypotheses on plausible nonverbal indicators of specific clinical disorders.

Emotion theories adopting a functional approach to conceptualizing emotion seem to be the most promising for this purpose (e.g., Frijda, 1986; Izard, 1991; Plutchik, 1980; Scherer, 1994a; Tomkins, 1984). Within a functional approach, emotion is considered as a phylogenetically continuous mechanism for flexible adaptation, serving the dual purpose of rapid preparation of appropriate responses to events and of providing opportunities for reevaluation and communication of intent in the interest of response optimization (see Scherer, 1984, 1985). This approach draws a description of both "normal" and "pathological" emotional functioning by systematically assessing the functionality or appropriateness of different emotional states and the behaviors generated by these. Following Darwin's (1876) view of expressions as rudiments of adaptive behavior that have acquired important signaling characteristics, a functional approach to the study of emotion and its disorders presumes that motor expressions are both reliable external manifestations of internal affective arousal and social signals in the service of interpersonal affect regulation (Ekman, 1992; Fridlund, 1994; Krause & Lütolf, 1988; Scherer, 1984).

In line with this approach, we review the functions of emotions and potential disturbances with respect to the two interrelated regulatory processes in which emotions are involved: the *intraindividual regulation* of thoughts and behavior and the *interindividual regulation* in social interactions. In the first part of the chapter the intraindividual regulative function of emotions is discussed in the theoretical framework of Scherer's *component process model of emotion*. The second part of the chapter is devoted to the interindividual regulative function of emotion and the need for interactive approaches. Facial and vocal expressions can be seen as an interface between these two regulatory processes or systems. They are expressions of the internal regulation process and, simultaneously, vehicles for the regulation of the interaction. On the basis of the theoretical framework and empirical data, we have formulated specific hypotheses concerning the expressivity and the symptomatology of different groups of affectively disturbed patients. We outline potential disorders in the two regulatory systems that can be predicted in the context of the theoretical framework proposed here. Though this framework is admittedly speculative, the detailed predictions can be tested empirically and could stimulate systematic, hypothesis-guided clinical research.

The Component Process Model of Emotion

Scherer (1993a) has suggested that emotion can be defined as an episode of temporary synchronization of all major systems of organismic functioning represented by five components (cognition, physiological regulation, motivation, motor expression, and monitoring/feeling) in response to the evaluation of an external or internal stimulus event as relevant to central concerns of the organism. It is claimed that while the different subsystems or components operate relatively independently of each other during nonemotional states, dealing with their respective function in overall behavioral regulation, they are recruited to work in unison during emergency situations, the emotion episodes. These require the mobilization of substantial organismic resources in order to allow adaptation or active responses to an important event or change of internal state. The emotion episode begins with the onset of synchronization following a particular stimulus evaluation pattern and ends with the return to independent functioning of the subsystems (although systems may differ in responsivity and processing speed). Since stimulus evaluation is expected to affect each subsystem directly and since all systems are seen to be highly interrelated during the emotion episode, regulation is complex and involves multiple feedback and feedforward processes. For this reason, it is assumed that there is a large number of highly differentiated emotional states, of which the current emotion labels capture only clusters or central tendencies of regularly recurring *modal* states (Scherer, 1994b).

A central feature of the component process model is the notion that the elicitation of an emotion process and its differentiation into different types of emotional qualities such as fear, anger, or joy is determined by a process of evaluation or appraisal of stimuli, events, or situations. This theoretical approach is increasingly widespread in emotion psychology. Following pioneering work by Arnold (1960) and Lazarus (1968), a number of theorists have independently developed models of emotion-antecedent appraisal, all attempting to predict emotion elicitation and differentiation on the basis of a limited number of cognitive dimensions or criteria (Frijda, 1986; Scherer, 1984, 1993b; Smith & Ellsworth, 1985). There is a surprising convergence of many appraisal theories with respect to some of the central dimensions postulated in almost all of the models.

Component process theory (see Scherer, 1984, 1986a, for details) posits relatively few basic criteria and assumes sequential processing of these criteria in the appraisal process. Table 6.1 shows the major "stimulus evaluation checks" (SECs), as well as the related dimensions proposed by other theorists that are considered to be sufficient to account for the differentiation of all major emotions.

The nature of the emotional reaction or response is expected to be shaped directly by the outcomes of this appraisal process. Rather than assuming that appraisal processes will evoke one of several discrete emotions with their specific response patterning (Ekman, 1992; Izard, 1991; Tomkins, 1984), component process theory suggests that the result of each stimulus evaluation check will have a direct effect on each of the other emotion components, such as autonomic nervous system functioning and motor expression (Scherer, 1984, 1986a). Well-known examples of this assumption are the orienting reflex for novelty appraisal and the defense reflex for unpleasantness appraisal. Given the assumed sequentiality of appraisal, this process will lead to cumulative changes in the different response domains, with the effect of each subsequent check being added to the effects of prior checks. Scherer (1993a) has suggested that subjective experience or feeling can be conceptualized as the reflection of the changes in all other emotion components, including the different neurophysiological and motor subsystems as well as changes in motivation and particularly the cognitive appraisal system. Leventhal and Scherer (1987) have made a first attempt to illustrate the way in which Scherer's stimulus evaluation checks could be performed on the sensory-motor, the schematic, and the conceptual level. Obviously, the nature of the resulting emotion is likely to be quite different depending on the level of its antecedent appraisal, particularly with respect to the conscious experience of the episode.

Conceptualizing Affect Disturbances within the Component Process Model

Assuming that the component process model outlined above provides a useful description of normal emotion processes, how can it help to explain, describe, and facilitate the study of emotional disorder? Scherer (1986b, 1987b, 1989) has argued that many of the established affective disturbances, including stress, can be explained

Table 6.1 Theoretically Predicted Criteria for Emotion-Antecedent Appraisal Processes

Stimulus Evaluation Checks	Appraisal Dimensions[a]
Novelty	Change, attentional activity (?)
Suddenness	
Familiarity	Familiarity
Predictability	Unexpectedness
Intrinsic pleasantness	Valence, appealingness, pleasantness
Goal significance	
Concern relevance	Focality, appetitive/aversive motivation, scope/focus, importance
Outcome probability	Certainty, probability, likelihood, predictability
Expectation	Presence, prospect realization
Conduciveness	Open/closed, desirability, motive consistency, goal/path obstacle, evaluation
Urgency	Urgency, proximity
Coping potential	
Cause: agent	Intent/self-other, agency, responsibility, locus of causality
Cause: motive	Agency, stability
Control	Modifiability, controllability
Power	Controllability, power
Adjustment	
Compatibility standards	
External	Value relevance, legitimacy, fairness
Internal	Blameworthiness

[a]Frijda, 1986; Ortony & Clore, 1988; Roseman, 1984; Smith & Ellsworth, 1985; Solomon, 1976; Weiner, 1986.

as a malfunctioning of specific aspects of the mechanisms involved in the emotion process. In the following, we will discuss three possible types of long-term malfunction and the chronic emotional disturbances that can be their result: (a) inappropriate or inadequate appraisal of situation and events, (b) inappropriate or inadequate motor expression or signaling, and (c) inappropriate or inadequate relationships between different aspects of feeling.

Inappropriate or Inadequate Evaluation of Situations and Events

It can be easily demonstrated that an inappropriate object or event evaluation will produce what is generally considered an inappropriate affect; for example, we talk of neurotic anxiety in a case where most normal people would consider the object of fear to be neutral or benevolent rather than frightening. Generally, the abnormal affect is produced by an inappropriate evaluation strategy where either the relevance of an object for satisfying one's needs or reaching one's goals has been grossly misjudged, or where the coping potential of the individual has been underestimated. For example, an unrealistically low level of self-esteem and coping ability is likely to produce feelings of anxiety or depression that are regarded as inappropriate or abnormal by other people. Inappropriate situation appraisal, in particular with respect to causal attribution, for example, overestimation of self-agency, has been at the core of cognitive theories of depression etiology (Abramson, Seligman, & Teasdale, 1978; Teasdale, 1988).

One of the most serious problems for the approach advocated here is the issue of defining what is inappropriate or inadequate. The problem is well known from the difficulties encountered in attempting to classify "abnormal behavior" or "affect disturbance" in terms of its symptomatology (Reiser & Levenson, 1984). It is interesting to note, in this context, that abnormality diagnoses are often based on considering the situation appraisal of a patient as inappropriate. Thus, it would obviously be circular to diagnose an affective disorder on the basis of situation evaluation and thereby infer inappropriate appraisal.

A first attempt to define the appropriateness of event appraisal in a more objective fashion has been made by Perrez and Reicherts (1992), who have proposed a *situation-behavior approach* to stress and coping. Their theoretical framework is based on Lazarus's (1981) *transactional* conceptualization of stress and coping behaviors as *processes* related to the *appraisal* of the situation. They try to distinguish the objective parameters of situations, which are important for adaptation, from subjective perceptions and appraisal. They argue that for successful adaptation there must be a good fit between the objective situation and the subjective perceptions and appraisals. This presupposes a more or less adequate perception of the important features of the environment, for example, its controllability, as well as the choice of appropriate coping strategies to master the situation. Perrez and Reicherts suggest that there are only a limited number of situation-independent criteria of adequate coping behavior. They therefore propose *situation-specific behavior rules* for adaptive coping behavior. Actively influencing the situation and other active coping strategies might be adequate when the person is confronted with a controllable stressor. In an uncontrollable situation; however, it might be more adaptive to evade the situation or to change goals and attitudes. Perrez and Reicherts tested their situation-specific behavior rules on self-reports describing everyday life stress episodes. On the basis of these theoretically deduced and empirically tested behavior rules the authors analyzed maladaptive situation evaluations and coping strategies in clinical populations. They could show, for example, that depressed persons tend to underestimate the controllability of situations.

Scherer (1987b) suggested a preliminary typology of affect disorders based on appraisal malfunctioning. Table 6.2 shows a somewhat more elaborated version of this suggestion. Clearly, the attempt to describe the etiology of a number of affect disorders on the basis of appraisal malfunctioning remains theoretical and rather speculative. Empirical studies of appraisal processes in different clinical groups are urgently needed to evaluate the promise of this approach.

Inappropriate or Inadequate Expression of the Emotional State

Emotional disorder and abnormal affect do not necessarily imply a deficiency in expressing the related emotional state. Even if the expressive behavior is judged as

Table 6.2 Theoretical Definition of Malfunctions of Emotion-Antecedent Appraisal and Associated Affect Disorders

Stimulus Evaluation Checks	Type of Malfunction	Type of Emotional Disorder
Novelty		
Suddenness	Exaggerated sensitivity	Nervousness, jumpiness,
Familiarity		easily frightened
Predictability		
Intrinsic pleasantness	Insensitivity to intrinsic or learned valence of stimuli	Anhedonia
Goal significance		
Concern relevance	Inability to judge importance of events with respect to goals, low intensity of motivational striving	Apathy
Outcome probability	Overestimation of certainty of negative effects	Exaggerated pessimism
Expectation		
Conduciveness	(a) Bias in the direction of detecting discrepancy between events and goal/plans, (b) conduciveness bias	(a) Chronic dissatisfaction/frustration, (b) euphoria
Urgency	(a) Underestimation of need for action, (b) overestimation of urgency	(a) Lethargy, (b) overreaction, panic
Coping potential		
Cause: agent	(a) External attribution bias, (b) internal attribution bias	(a) Paranoia, (b) unrealistic feelings of shame and guilt
Cause: motive	Overestimation of intent	Paranoia
Control	Underestimation bias	Hopelessness, depression
Power	(a) Underestimation bias, (b) overestimation	(a) Helplessness, depression, (b) mania, panic
Adjustment	Underestimation	Panic
Compatibility standards		
External	Tendency to (a) overestimate, (b) underestimate discrepancy of own behavior with social norms	(a) guilt neurosis, (b) antisocial behavior
Internal	Tendency to (a) overestimate, (b) underestimate discrepancy of own behavior with ego ideals	(a) shame neurosis, (b) shamelessness

inappropriate by an external observer it might nevertheless express the internal state adequately. In this case, expression and state correspond. For example, Ellgring (1989) has argued that "a low amount of active nonverbal behavior obviously expresses a depressed state in an adequate way" (p. 181). The reduced nonverbal activity corresponds to the reduced emotional variety experienced during depression. Accordingly, one would expect an increase of nonverbal activity with recovery. Ellgring (1989) has studied how the nonverbal activity of endogenous depressed and neurotic depressed patients changes over time and with improvement of the disorder. He recorded and analyzed the facial behavior of the patients during interviews at the moment of admission, release, and some weeks later. Ellgring found the expected reduction followed by substantial increase for endogenous depressed patients, but for a considerable proportion of the neurotic depressed patients general facial activity remained at a low level or even declined with improvement of subjective well-being. According to Ellgring one would assume an *"encoding" disturbance* for these patients since their state cannot be inferred from their behavior. In the case of an encoding disturbance, expression and state do not correspond. A lack of correspondence can be due to neurophysiological malfunctions or it can be a result of control and defense mechanisms.

Desynchronization between expression and state is often found in stutterers. In the scope of a clinical research project, designed to develop and test a new therapeutic approach (see Krause, 1981), Bänninger-Huber (1991) analyzed the nonverbal behavior of stutterers in interactions with nonstutterers. She found that the facial expressions that occur during the stuttering phases of speech are often very intense and involve all parts of the face. These so-called *full-face expressions* (e.g., Ekman & Friesen, 1975) are found very rarely in interactions of nonstutterers. Contrary to what one would expect on the basis of the extraordinary intensity of these facial expressions, stutterers did not report any emotion during these phases but claimed to have been absorbed by their attempts to produce an utterance. The expressive patterns differed notably between stutters but almost always there were facial indicators of negative emotions involved. For example, the typical facial pattern of a female stutterer included trembling and protruding of the lower lip, lowering of the lip corners, and squeezing the eyes, a pattern found in weeping. Another stutterer showed a pattern including raising of the eyebrows, bulging eyes, and a stretched open mouth, a pattern found when someone is afraid or gasps for breath. During therapy it was possible to detect a focal conflict and an associated affective pattern for each stutterer that could be related to the specific facial patterns occurring during the stuttering periods. Krause (1981) has proposed a theoretical model that conceptualizes stuttering as an emotion regulation disturbance rather than a speech disturbance. Many stutterers speak fluently when they can avoid emotional involvement. According to Krause this disturbance has its roots in a rigid educational style of emotion control, which is especially intrusive in the phase of speech acquisition. Whereas most parents are not overly worried by the speech problems that typically occur in this phase particularly when children are emotionally aroused, parents of stutterers may tend to assign excessive importance to fluent speech in their children. This may include instructions such as "First calm down and then say it again!" that might bring about correct speech but that at the same time may suppress all affective and interactive signals. Abiding by such rules makes it difficult for the child to express his or her emotions appropriately and requires the building up of strong control and defense mechanisms to avoid affective involvement. The expression of emotions is thus not only separated from speech but also from the conscious component of the emotional experience.

Inappropriate or Inadequate Relationships Between Aspects of Feeling

The subjective experience or feeling component of emotion often has been considered to be the central feature of emotion, largely because it is the obvious basis for the verbalization of a feeling state, allowing the social sharing of emotional events in conversation (Rimé, Mesquita, Philippot, & Boca, 1991). Unfortunately, the topic is complex and hardly accessible to objective empirical research given that one needs to rely exclusively on subjects' verbal reports. Yet, it is likely that this component of emotion represents an important aspect of inappropriate emotional processing due to a disintegration of different aspects of the feeling component.

As mentioned above, Scherer (1993a) conceptualizes the feeling component of emotion as a "monitoring subsystem," reflecting the changes in *all* other components. The states of the different organismic subsystems that are monitored are seen to acquire meaning mostly through the reflection and interpretation of the cognitive appraisal processes. However, assuming multilevel processing, it is highly likely that not all of the appraisal processes are accessible to consciousness. Furthermore, it is to be assumed that some of the reflections of the neurophysiological and motor systems, as well as changes in motivation, are not completely accessible to consciousness. Thus, it is necessary to distinguish grossly between an unconscious and a conscious part of "feeling" in the sense of a total monitoring representation of emotional processing. One can further assume that the conscious part of feeling goes beyond the overall unconscious reflection. In the sense of active, constructive cognitive processing, it could be partly *constructed* by schemata, scripts, or social representations that can add meaning in the process of rendering unconscious material conscious. Thus, as shown in figure 6.1, we can depict these parts of the feeling component as two partially overlapping Venn circles. The *verbalization* of the conscious part of feeling can be represented by a third circle partially overlapping the other two. Again, the use of linguistic labels or expressions to describe the conscious part of feeling will not cover all of what is conscious, partially because of the absence of appropriate verbal concepts. It will also add surplus meaning, in the sense of adding content, due to the denotational and connotational meaning of the concepts used in the verbalization. These aspects of meaning which are part of the pragmatics of language may not always be totally appropriate to the conscious feeling state.

The Venn circle approach suggests seven areas or aspects of feeling: (a) total overlap of unconscious and conscious appraisal appropriately verbalized; (b) unconscious appraisal is consciously represented but cannot be verbalized; (c) unconscious appraisal is intuitively verbalized without being consciously represented; (d) a constructed conscious representation, not based on any unconscious appraisal, is verbalized—the classic case of stereotype; (e) unconscious appraisal that rests inaccessible; (f) constructed conscious appraisal that is not verbalized; (g) surplus meaning provided by the use of verbal labels not based on conscious representation.

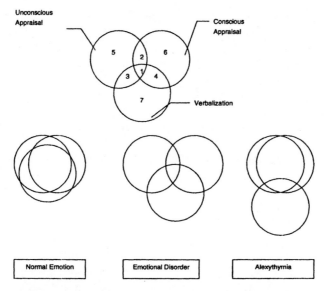

Figure 6.1 Theoretically predicted relationships between unconscious, conscious, and verbalizable aspects of feeling under normal and disturbed affect states. Note: For the explanation of the areas see text.

Under normal circumstances, the three aspects of feeling, as illustrated by the Venn circles for normal emotions in figure 6.1, tend to overlap rather strongly. In other words, much of the emotional processing is accessible to consciousness, in particular the cognitive appraisal of pertinent events, giving appropriate significance to the affective experience, and much of this can be adequately verbalized for the purposes of social communication. Affective disorder, on the other hand, could be characterized by increasing dissociation of these feeling aspects. Thus, much of the appraisal processes that have actually generated a particular emotional state may remain inaccessible to consciousness, due to repression or other defense mechanisms, to attentional deficits, to neurological malfunctioning, or to other factors. The surplus meaning in the conscious representation of feeling may thus be determined to a very large extent by extraneous factors unrelated to the actual appraisal processes, such as compulsive ideas, in the form of schemata or scripts that the person might hold with respect to the self or the social or physical environment. Similarly, verbalization may represent only a very small part of the conscious feeling component, and thus be considered to be bizarre and inappropriate by the social environment, as for example in the case of alexythymia shown as an example of emotional disorder in figure 6.1.

Need for Research in Interactive Settings

The approach advocated here, focusing on the dynamic nature of emotion as a process of continuously changing states in several components, requires the microanalytic study of the ongoing changes in the pertinent emotional response modalities. It is further suggested that researchers investigate the process of normal emotions as well as of disturbed affect in naturalistic social contexts, particularly *interactive* settings such as conversations, interviews, or therapy sessions. There are two major arguments that can be advanced to justify the need for research in interactive settings: (1) the essentially social nature of emotion elicitation, and (2) the social regulation of emotional expression with potential feedback on other emotion components (e.g., facial feedback hypothesis).

1. The majority of emotional episodes occur in social interactions and are elicited by other persons (Scherer, Wallbott & Summerfield, 1986). This seems to be equally true for emotional disorders. Clients often complain about difficulties in getting along with other people. Plutchik (1993) points to the fact that "when such complaints are examined closely, it becomes evident that emotions are at the heart of them as well. Parents make them feel guilty, bosses resentful, children disappointed, lovers anxious." (p. 54).

If affective disturbances, as argued above, are due in part to the malfunctioning of emotion-antecedent appraisal one might expect that this will be particularly manifest in interpersonal contexts. Thus, to diagnose habitual appraisal biases or errors it would seem necessary to study patients in interpersonal, particularly socially interactive, settings that are likely to make biases in situation and person evaluation appear.

2. Ever since the pioneering writings of Darwin (1876) and Wundt (1874) it has been recognized that while emotional expression externalizes internal states it is a fundamentally social phenomenon, serving important signaling functions. Given this close linkage between externalization and signaling, a phylogenetically continuous phenomenon found in all socially living species, expressions occurring in solitary individuals are difficult to evaluate. Even more than other behavioral phenomena, expressive behavior seems to require study in interactional contexts to attain ecological validity (Fridlund, 1994). The study of expressive behavior is rendered particularly difficult by the powerful role of regulation and control of expression through explicit and implicit social norms and expectations (Ekman & Friesen, 1975; Wundt, 1874). It is important to take such regulation efforts into account when operationalizing expressive behavior as externalization of internal affect states.

For example, in clinical disorders that are characterized by a particular core affect, like depression or anxiety disorders, patients also experience other emotions that may be externalized in expression. In Ellgring's (1989) study on endogenous depressed and neurotic depressed patients, an unexpected variety of facial patterns was found for the depressed patients compared to rather homogeneous patterns shown by the controls. Concerning the emotional quality of these expressions, Ellgring states "that the content of these affect displays can be interpreted as pointing to the emotions of fear and anger. There were no clear indications for sadness or grief." (p. 80). A possible explanation could be that the patients try to control the emotional experience that threatens them. Presumably, the central negative affect would be most controlled whereas minor affects would be less controlled and then become apparent in expression. Ekman and Friesen (1975) describe such phenomena as *nonverbal leakage*.

Many affect disorders are not only characterized by an inappropriate emotional state but also by inappropriate expression of this state and/or communicative handicaps. We already mentioned possible encoding disturbances and desynchronization between feeling and expression in the section on inadequate expression of the emotional state. Clearly, disassociation between feeling and expression occurs very often and is quite normal. Below, we will provide examples of normal disassociation and possible reasons for it, contrasted with what we consider examples of disturbed disassociation. Finally, we will examine possible malfunctions resulting from the interdependence between the intraindividual and the interindividual emotion regulation systems.

Many of the facial or vocal patterns that occur during an interaction are not "true," spontaneous expressions of emotional experience or a disturbed affective state but serve other functions such as conversational marking (Ekman, 1979; Scherer, 1980). In addition, we often find *expression-management* serving self-presentation (Goffman, 1959) or, as mentioned above, *expression-control* demanded by sociocultural norms, such as "display rules" (Ekman & Friesen, 1975; Wundt, 1874).

Facial and vocal cues can also constitute communicative acts, comparable to "speech acts" directed at one or more interaction partners (Bänninger-Huber, 1992). They can be meant as a signal to the interaction partner to keep on joking, for example, in the case of a happy expression, or to stop it, in the case of an angry expression. Thus, individuals often use expressive behaviors more or less consciously in order to achieve a social goal, for example to obtain attention or support. Here, the subjective feeling of the person and his or her facial expression may not necessarily correspond. For example, if a woman is angry with her husband but wants him to help with the housework, it might be a better strategy to smile rather than to shout. However, if her anger is too strong the conflict between her feeling and her communication strategy might become visible in the face, constituting nonverbal leakage in the sense of Ekman and Friesen (1975).

More severe discrepancies between feeling and communicated expression can be found in clinical disorders. Krause and Lütolf (1988) present an example of a patient who shows a "paradoxical" communication strategy. The patient tends to display nonverbal signals that provoke exactly the emotional reaction in his interaction partners that he consciously wants to avoid, namely, that the partner becomes angry and "picks on him." As Krause and Lütolf point out, while the feeling of this patient might be described as worry or fear, the facial signals that seem to provoke the emotional reaction of the partner can be described as a mixture of a constant submissive smile with sporadic "micromomentary expressions" (Ekman & Friesen, 1975) of contempt and anger. Psychoanalysts describe this phenomenon as *Wiederholungszwang* (repetition compulsion). With such an obviously unconscious strategy the patient "proves" that his fears and worries are "true."

Cases where the interdependency between intraindividual and interindividual emotion regulation can build up into a vicious circle are very severe, "early" disturbances (e.g., psychoses or borderline disturbances). In these disturbances, the synchronization between the components of emotion (the intraindividual regulation system) seems to be fundamentally disturbed. According to Krause (1990), a possible consequence of early affect disorders can be a reduced capability to encode affects (expression component), which makes it difficult for others to understand the behavior of these patients. Therefore, the interaction partners do not adapt their behavior appropriately and possible conflicts cannot be solved. As a further consequence, physiological reactions of the patient may become chronic, which reduces the specificity of the physiological reaction. According to Krause (1990), this lack of specificity can affect the subjective feeling component of the emotion and produce feelings of diffuse or even artificial emotional arousal instead of clearly differentiated emotional experience patterns.

Given the high cost of research using microanalytic techniques in interactive settings, particularly with respect to the time needed to objectively measure and analyze facial and vocal behavior, only a few such studies have been conducted up to now (for a review see Bänninger-Huber and von Salisch, 1994). Examples of such interactive studies in the domain of clinical disorders are discussed in greater detail in the chapters by Ellgring and Smith (chapter 23) and Krause, Steimer-Krause, Merten, and Ullrich (chapter 5) in this volume.

Predictions for Vocal and Facial Indicators of Affective Disorders

In the final section of this chapter we attempt to demonstrate how a "normal emotions" approach to affective disorder can be used to develop hypotheses concerning the nature of facial and vocal expression patterns characteristic of specific syndromes. The key for the predictions to be ventured below is the conceptualization of emotion as a component process that serves to recruit all of the organismic systems in the preparation of appropriate responses to relevant situational demands. Following Darwin's (1876) original suggestion, expressive behaviors are considered both as rudiments of adaptive actions and as social signals informing the social surround of the organism's reaction and action tendencies.

If this reasoning is correct, the theoretical predictions resulting from this approach can be made to serve at least two diagnostic aims in the area of affective disturbance: (a) using expression in addition to verbal report as indices of malfunctioning appraisal processes, and (b) using expression as the basis for differential diagnoses of specific affect disturbance syndromes. In what follows, these two approaches will be briefly illustrated for both vocal and facial expression.

Vocal Indicators

Using the component process principles discussed above, Scherer (1986a) arrived at detailed theoretical predictions of the changes in voice production (and their ensuing acoustical results) that should be expected as a consequence of each of the appraisal checks. Assuming typical appraisal profiles for a number of "modal emotions" (Scherer, 1994b), predictions were made for states such as rage and irritation, anxiety and fear, sadness and despair, contentment and joy. The results of a number of empirical studies have confirmed many of these predictions for normal emotions (Banse & Scherer, 1996).

Applying the same reasoning to habitually malfunctioning appraisal processes and the resulting affect disturbances, Scherer (1987b, p. 78) proposed a set of theoretical predictions concerning the patterns of acoustic parameters expected to characterize the full-blown state of a number of affect disorders. Even though some predictions are equivocal since the voice production mechanisms involved exert opposing effects, and thus requiring empirical assessment of the relative strength of the opposing forces, the majority of the predictions yield clear-cut profiles that, in many cases, correspond to clinical intuition. For example, manic patients are expected to show exaggerated range and level of fundamental frequency (F0; heard as pitch; indicative of extreme muscular tension), very strong intensity, an extended spectral frequency range, and fast speech tempo. Patients in states of panic or agitated fear may show similar F0 characteristics. However, in this case the frequency range shows a strongly elevated energy component in the higher frequencies, making the voice sound strident or sharp. Intensity is also expected to be high, and speech tempo to be fast. In contrast, states of helplessness and hopelessness, as in many cases of depression, are predicted to be characterized by reduced range and variability of F0. It should be noted that this does not necessarily entail a lower level of F0 or reduced spectral range. This is due to the fact that hopelessness and helplessness often go hand in hand with an appraisal of failure, producing tense voice, and of powerlessness, producing thin voice. These voice types are characterized by relatively high F0 and proportionally higher energy in the high-frequency range. Intensity is expected to be very low and tempo to be slow (for further details see Scherer, 1987b).

If at least some of these predictions can be confirmed by empirical results, as has been the case for normal emotions (Banse & Scherer, 1996), one could reasonably consider using vocal analysis more systematically, to unobtrusively diagnose appraisal habits of patients that might be difficult to verbalize, to differentially diagnose specific affect disturbance syndromes, and to monitor therapeutic effectiveness (see Scherer, 1987b, 1989). Unfortunately, this type of clinical research not only requires intensive interdisciplinary collaboration and access to clinical settings but also sizable groups of patients with comparable diagnoses. Since none of these conditions is easily met, it is not surprising that the testing of the hypotheses described above does not advance more rapidly.

Facial Indicators

Most studies on facial expression of emotions have been conducted by researchers within the tradition of discrete emotion theories (e.g., Ekman, 1984; Izard, 1991). These theories claim that there is only a limited number of so-called fundamental or "basic emotions" and that for each of them there exists a prototypical, innate, and universal expression pattern. In this tradition, the variability of the observable emotion expression patterns is explained by a process of mixing or blending of the basic expression patterns. Compared to this rather molar approach, the work of the pioneers in this area, particularly Duchenne (1872/1990) and Darwin (1876), seem to be more molecular, focusing on individual muscles and their functions. Their molecular approach is highly compatible with the component process approach, which assumes that the facial muscle configuration that is activated as the result of a particular emotional state is the result of a combination of effects linked to emotion-antecedent cognitive appraisal and associated action tendencies (Scherer, 1992). Theoretical considerations as well as empirical results found in the literature provided the basis for predictions on facial expressions resulting from specific stimulus evaluation checks (Scherer, 1987a). Some initial empirical evidence for the presumed link between the evaluation of a stimulus as being obstructive to a goal and corrugator innervation, resulting in a frown, has been provided by Smith (1989). Applying these predictions to the model illustrated in table 6.2, we can formulate hypotheses concerning possible facial indicators of affect disturbances (see table 6.3). These predictions have been formulated in the terminology of the Facial Action Coding System (FACS) as developed by Ekman and Friesen (1975) because it is ideally suited to the approach advocated here. FACS allows the reliable coding of any facial action in terms of the smallest visible unit of muscular activity, so-called action units (AU), each referred to by a numerical code. As a consequence, coding is independent of prior assumptions about prototypical emotion expressions. The predictions in table 6.3 are presented as short-hand descriptions of the postulated facial actions as well as the respective AU numbers.

FACS has been widely used in studies of facial indicators of clinical disorders (e.g., Ellgring, 1989; Krause & Lütolf, 1988). Since the basic emotion patterns these researchers have described are presented as combinations of AUs, their results can be used to look for some clinical evidence for the predictions based on appraisal patterns.

One of the problems with the concept of basic emotions is that the prototypical full-face expression patterns as used in research on the universality of facial expression (Ekman & Friesen, 1975; Izard, 1991) may occur only occasionally in "real" life. Even if actors are asked to portray one of the dozen or so basic emotions, the resulting patterns look very different, generally involving only a subset of AUs (Gosselin, Kirouac, & Doré, 1995). In consequence, researchers trying to find indicators of basic emotions tend to use the presence of subsets or even single AUs that are part of the full pattern as evidence for the presence of a full-blown basic emotion. This may be misleading, however, since a single AU or even a combination of several units can be found in several emotions as well as in nonemotional expressions, such as conversational markers (Ekman, 1979). The most obvious example is AU4 (corrugator), which is typically interpreted as an indicator for anger in this tradition. In contrast, the component process model predicts that corrugator innervations indicate the evaluation of an event as discrepant with respect to important goals, needs or expectations (Scherer, 1987a, 1992).

By associating single AUs not to basic emotions but to appraisal dimensions, as suggested by the component process model, we can address an important empirical finding that, at first sight, seems counterintuitive. Above, we cited Ellgring's (1989) report concerning the facial expressions of the depressive patients he studied: "the content of these affect displays can be interpreted as pointing to the emotions of fear [AU20] and anger [AU24]. There were no clear indications for sadness or grief" (p. 80; AUs in square brackets inserted by the present authors). Using a componential approach, we would propose another explanation. Rather than arguing that AU20 is an indicator of fear, it could be interpreted as a sign of appraising one's coping ability as rather limited, specifically as "low power." Similarly, AU24 can be seen as a sign of appraising an event or a situation as unpleasant. Obviously, both of these appraisal patterns can be easily related to depression. Thus, the use of a componen-

Table 6.3 Facial Action Units Predicted as Indicators of Selected Types of Affect Disorder

Affect Disorders	Inadequate Appraisals	Related Action Units (Shorthand Descriptions)
Euphoria	Excessively positive pleasantness and conduciveness evaluation	5 (lids up), 26 (open mouth), 38 (open nostrils); or 6 (crow's feet wrinkles), 12 (lip corners up), 25 (lips part)
Anhedonia	Excessively negative pleasantness evaluation	4 (brow lowering), 7 (lid tightening), 9 (nose wrinkling), 10 (upper lip raising), 15 + 17 (lip corner down + chin raised), 24 (lip press), 39 (nostrils closed)
Chronic dissatisfaction, frustration	Strong bias toward habitual negative conduciveness evaluation	4 (brow lowering), 7 (lid tightening), 17 (chin raised), 23 or 24 (lips tight or pressed together)
Indifference, apathy	Malfunctioning of conduciveness check	Hypotonus of facial musculature
Mania	Overestimation of power and control	4, 5 (eyebrows contracted, eyes widened), or 7 (lids tight, eyes narrowed); 23, 25 (lips tight and parted, bared teeth)
Hopelessness	Underestimation of control	15 (lip corner depression), 25 or 26 (lips part or jaw drop), 41 or 43 (lids droop or eyes closed), if tears 1 + 4 (inner brow raised and contracted)
Helplessness	Underestimation of power	1, 2, 5 (brows and upper lid raising), 20 (mouth stretch), 26 (jaw drop), or 32 (lip bite)
Anxiety disorders	Excessive concern about adequacy of power	4 (eyebrows contracted), 1, 2, 5 (brows and upper lid raising), 20 (mouth stretch), 23, 24 (lips tight or pressed), 32, 37 (lip bite or wipe)

tial approach may provide diagnostically useful information on both appraisal and interpersonal action tendencies.

Conclusions

Given space constraints, this chapter could not do justice to the complexity of the theoretical and clinical issues raised, and thus some of the suggestions might seem inordinately speculative. However, we believe that the case for approaching affect disorders through an analysis of deviations from normal emotions, particularly in interactive settings, and using facial and vocal expression as a royal road to studying the underlying processes, is basically sound.

Clearly, this approach allows one to generate a large number of theoretical predictions that can be solidly based on earlier work on normal emotion. These predictions are concrete and testable. Unfortunately, so far empirical testing of theoretical predictions made on the basis of a component process model approach has been rare in the domain of affect disturbance.

The reasons for this are many. One of the major problems that we have encountered in our own work on clinical populations (Scherer, 1989; Scherer & Zei, 1988; Tolkmitt, Helfrich, Standke, & Scherer, 1982), is the difficulty of obtaining groups of clinical subjects that can be considered to be minimally homogeneous with respect to the underlying affect disturbance syndrome. Thus, the general label *depression* often covers a wide variety of different clinical profiles. Much of the problem, however, is due to the hesitation of many clinical practitioners and researchers to engage in the expensive and time consuming activities of behavioral research requiring extensive videotaping of patient behavior in interactive settings and systematic coding of complex expressive behavior patterns. It is true that having standard scales or symptom checklists filled out routinely by clinical staff is more a economical procedure, in terms of both time and money. Unfortunately, the amount of information that can thus be gathered on the malfunctioning of emotion-antecedent appraisal or inappropriate emotional expression, which may account for severe interactional handicaps, is quite limited. One might expect more rapid progress in this area if intensive collaboration between behaviorally oriented emotion researchers and clinicians convinced of the value of using a "deviation from normal emotions" approach were to become more widespread.

References

Abramson, L. Y., Seligman, M. E. P., & Teasdale, J. (1978). Learned helplessness in humans: Critique and reformulation. *Journal of Abnormal Psychology, 87*, 49–74.

Arnold, M. B. (1960). *Emotion and personality* (vols. 1 & 2). New York: Columbia University Press.

Bänninger-Huber, E. (1991). Stottern—eine Emotionsstörung: Die Wirkung nonverbaler Ausdrucksmuster auf den Interaktionspartner. In G. Lotzmann (Ed.), *Aggressionen und Angste im stimm- und sprachtherapeutischen Prozess* (pp. 125–137). München: Profil.

Bänninger-Huber, E. (1992). Prototypical affective microsequences in psychotherapeutic interactions. *Psychotherapy Research, 2*, 291–306.

Bänninger-Huber, E., & von Salisch, M. (1994). Die Untersuchung des mimischen Affektausdrucks in face-to-face Interaktionen. *Psychologische Rundschau, 45*, 79–98.

Banse, R. & Scherer, K. R. (1996). Acoustic profiles in vocal emotion expression. *Journal of Personality and Social Psychology, 70*, 614–636.

Darwin, C. (1876). *The expression of the emotions in man and animals*. London: Murray.

Duchenne, G. B. A. (1990). *Mechanisme de la Physionomie Humaine: Ou, analyse electrophysiologique de l'expresion des passions* [The mechanism of human facial expression]. (R. A. Cuthbertson, Ed. and Trans.). Cambridge: Cambridge University Press. (Original work published 1872)

Ekman, P. (1979). About brows: Emotional and conversational signals. In M. von Cranach, K. Foppa, W. Lepenies, & D. Ploog (Eds.), *Human ethology* (pp. 169–202). Cambridge: Cambridge University Press.

Ekman, P. (1984). Expression and the nature of emotion. In K. R. Scherer & P. Ekman (Eds.), *Approaches to emotion* (pp. 319–344). Hillsdale, NJ: Lawrence Erlbaum.

Ekman, P. (1992). An argument for basic emotions. *Cognition and Emotion, 6,* 169–200.

Ekman, P., & Friesen, W. V. (1975). *Unmasking the face.* Englewood Cliffs, NJ: Prentice Hall.

Ekman, P. & Friesen, W. V. (1978). *Manual for the facial action coding system.* Palo Alto, Calif.: Consulting Psychologist Press.

Ellgring, H. (1989). *Nonverbal communication in depression.* Cambridge: Cambridge University Press.

Fridlund, A. J. (1994). *Human facial expression: An evolutionary view.* San Diego: Academic Press.

Frijda, N. (1986). *The emotions.* New York: Cambridge University Press.

Goffman, E. (1959). *The presentation of self in everyday life.* Garden City, NY: Doubleday Anchor.

Gosselin, P., Kirouac, G., & Doré, F. Y. (1995). Components and recognition of facial expression in the communication of emotion by actors. *Journal of Personality and Social Psychology, 68,* 1–14.

Izard, C. E. (1991). *The psychology of emotions.* New York: Plenum Press.

Krause, R. (1981). *Sprache und Affekt. Das Stottern und seine Behandlung.* Stuttgart: Kohlhammer.

Krause, R. (1990). Psychodynamik der Emotionsstörungen. In K. R. Scherer (Ed.), *Enzyklopädie der Psychologie: Band 3. Psychologie der Emotion* (pp. 630–690). Göttingen: Hogrefe.

Krause, R., & Lütolf, P. (1988). Facial indicators of transference processes within psychoanalytic treatment. In H. Dahl, H. Kächele, & H. Thomä (Eds.), *Psychoanalytic process research strategies* (pp. 257–272). Berlin: Springer.

Lazarus, R. S. (1968). Emotions and adaptation: Conceptual and empirical relations. In W. J. Arnold (Ed.), *Nebraska Symposium on Motivation* (Vol. 16, pp. 175–270). Lincoln: University of Nebraska Press.

Lazarus, R. S. (1981). The stress and coping paradigm. In C. Eisdorfer, D. Cohen, A. Kleinman, & P. Maxim (Eds.), *Models for clinical psychopathology* (pp. 174–214). New York: Spectrum.

Leventhal, H., & Scherer, K. R. (1987). The relationship of emotion to cognition: A functional approach to a semantic controversy. *Cognition and Emotion, 1,* 3–28.

Ortony, A., Clore, G. L., and Collins, A. (1988). *The cognitive structure of emotions.* New York: Cambridge University Press.

Perrez, M., & Reicherts, M. (1992). *Stress, coping, and health.* Toronto: Hogrefe & Huber.

Plutchik, R. (1980). *Emotion: A psychobioevolutionary synthesis.* New York: Harper & Row.

Plutchik, R. (1993). Emotions and their vicissitudes: Emotions and psychopathology. In M. Lewis & J. M. Haviland (Eds.), *Handbook of emotions* (pp. 53–66). New York: Guilford Press.

Reiser, D. E., & Levenson, H. (1984). Abuses of the borderline diagnosis: A clinical problem with teaching opportunities. *American Journal of Psychiatry, 141,* 1528–1532.

Rimé, B., Mesquita, B., Philippot, P., & Boca, S. (1991). Beyond the emotional event: Six studies on the social sharing of emotion. *Cognition and Emotion, 5,* 435–465.

Roseman, I. J. (1984). Cognitive determinants of emotion: A structural theory. In P. Shaver (Ed.), *Review of personality and social psychology: Vol. 5. Emotions, relationships, and health* (pp. 11–36). Beverly Hills: Sage Publications.

Scherer, K. R. (1980). The functions of nonverbal signs in conversation. In R. St. Clair & H. Giles (Eds.), *The social and psychological contexts of language* (pp. 225–244). Hilllsdale, NJ: Erlbaum.

Scherer, K. R. (1984). On the nature and function of emotion: A component process approach. In K. R. Scherer & P. Ekman (Eds.), *Approaches to emotion* (pp. 293–318). Hillsdale, NJ: Erlbaum.

Scherer, K. R. (1985). Vocal affect signalling: A comparative approach. In J. Rosenblatt, C. Beer, M. Busnel, & P. J. B. Slater (Eds.), *Advances in the study of behavior* (pp. 189–244). New York: Academic Press.

Scherer, K. R. (1986a). Vocal affect expression: A review and a model for future research. *Psychological Bulletin, 99,* 143–165.

Scherer, K. R. (1986b). Voice, stress, and emotion. In M. H. Appley & R. Trumball (Eds.), *Dynamics of stress* (pp. 159–181). New York: Plenum Press.

Scherer, K. R. (1987a). Toward a dynamic theory of emotion: The component process model of affective states. *Geneva Studies in Emotion and Communication, 1,* 1–98.

Scherer, K. R. (1987b). Vocal assessment of affective disorders. In J. D. Maser (Ed.), *Depression and expressive behavior* (pp. 57–82). Hillsdale, NJ: Erlbaum.

Scherer, K. R. (1989). Emotion psychology can contribute to psychiatric work on affect disorders: A review. *Journal of the Royal Society of Medicine, 82,* 545–547.

Scherer, K. R. (1992). What does facial expression express? In K. Strongman (Ed.), *International review of studies on emotion* (Vol. 2, pp. 139–165). Chichester: Wiley.

Scherer, K. R. (1993a). Neuroscience projections to current debates in emotion psychology. *Cognition and Emotion, 7,* 1–41.

Scherer, K. R. (1993b). Studying the emotion-antecedent appraisal process: An expert system approach. *Cognition and Emotion, 7,* 325–355.

Scherer, K. R. (1994a). Emotion serves to decouple stimulus and response. In P. Ekman & R. J. Davidson (Eds.), *Questions on emotion* (pp. 127–130). New York: Oxford University Press.

Scherer, K. R. (1994b). Toward a concept of "modal emotions." In P. Ekman & R. J. Davidson (Eds.), *Questions on emotion* (pp. 25–31). New York: Oxford University Press.

Scherer, K. R., Wallbott, H., & Summerfield, A. (1986). *Experiencing emotion: A cross-cultural study.* Cambridge: Cambridge University Press.

Scherer, K. R., & Zei, B. (1988). Vocal indicators of affective disorders. *Psychotherapy and Psychosomatics, 49,* 179–186.

Smith, C. A. (1989). Dimensions of appraisal and physiological response in emotion. *Journal of Personality and Social Psychology, 56,* 339–353.

Smith, C. A., & Ellsworth, P. C. (1985). Patterns of cognitive appraisal in emotion. *Journal of Personality and Social Psychology, 48,* 813–838.

Solomon, R. C. (1976). *The passions. The myth and nature of human emotion.* Garden City, NY: Doubleday.

Teasdale, J. D. (1988). Cognitive vulnerability to persistent depression. *Cognition and Emotion, 2,* 247–274.

Tolkmitt, F. J., Helfrich, H., Standke, R., & Scherer, K. R. (1982). Vocal indicators of psychiatric treatment effects in depressives and schizophrenics. *Journal of Communication Disorders, 15,* 209–222.

Tomkins, S. S. (1984). Affect theory. In K. R. Scherer & P. Ekman (Eds.), *Approaches to emotion* (pp. 163–196). Hillsdale, NJ: Erlbaum.

Weiner, B. (1986). *An attributional theory of motivation and emotion.* New York: Springer.

Wundt, W. (1874). *Grundzüge der physiologischen Psychologie.* Leipzig: Engelmann.

7

Thomas J. Scheff

Therapeutic Alliance

Microanalysis of Shame & the Social Bond

The concept of the therapeutic alliance is crucially important in the theory and practice of psychotherapy, but it has never been clearly defined. This issue is part of a much broader problem, the nature of social relationships in general. The idea of relationships between persons is so primitive and fundamental that it goes without saying, both in ordinary and in technical discourse. In this chapter I propose a model of the social bond, and a way of determining the momentary state of the bond, through microanalysis of verbatim discourse.

Sociologists have made a preliminary step toward defining relationships, but only in terms of types of conventional roles. The father-daughter and employer-employee relationships are examples. Role-relationships are considered to be made up in terms of reciprocal rights, duties, and rules that govern the interaction between persons in their respective roles. The idea of role relationships is helpful because it establishes the contours of the kinds of behavior that are expected to occur in different types of relationships. In a given society, we would usually find a wide consensus on these contours.

The concept of role-relationships is of quite limited use in understanding an actual relationship between particular persons, since it refers to idealized, abstract expectations rather than specific behavior. Between any father and daughter or therapist and client there is an enormous variation in what actually occurs between them. Especially if we want the nuances of a relationship, types of role-relationships are of virtually no help; because they are partial, they concern only one aspect of a whole. Much is missing from such classifications, since they are so simple. In particular, we would expect that they would miss the difference between the kind of relationship that generated a therapeutic alliance, and one that didn't.

It might help us visualize the problem of further defining the concept of a relationship if we tried to imagine a different mode of conceptualizing a relationship, the opposite limiting condition of abstractness. One opposite would be a second-by-second description of transactions between actual persons in a relationship, what was said and done by each person, and their manner. We would put the discourse that constitutes a relationship under a microscope. From such a highly particularized description, we might be able to also infer the subjective side of the relationship, what each person thought and felt at each moment. We would also need to include the biography of the relationship, and the social context. Perhaps such a holistic approach could help us understand therapeutic alliances, and how to reach them in practice.

An approximation is offered in great novels. Goethe, Doestoyevsky, and George Eliot, for example, often described in detail not only the history of a given relationship, but also the words and manner in dialogue between characters, and the accompanying thoughts and feelings. The novel itself provides careful delineation of the biographical background of each character and social context for each relationship. These descriptions go far beyond role-relationships, allowing us at least the illusion of understanding whole relationships, the motives, perceptions, and personalities of fictional persons.

In the social sciences, a comparable approach can be found in several microlinguistic studies, beginning with the work of Pittenger, Hockett, and Danehy (1960), Helen Lewis (1971), and Labov and Fanshel (1977). Although these studies deal only with parts of psychotherapy sessions, they come close to an ideal description of the complete outer behavior of persons in a transaction, the details of articulation and manner. Because they focused so intensively on brief moments in relationships, these studies were able to describe *every* sound, all verbal and nonverbal speech, that could be heard on the tapes.

The time spans in the Pittenger and in the Labov studies are so brief (Pittenger et al. is 5 min, Labov and Fanshel, 15 min) that together they make up even less than Blake's eternity in an hour. (Readers of Pittenger et al. sometimes complain about eternity when reading a five-page discussion of a single sentence.) Joking aside, the precise attention given to fine detail in these earlier studies is so great that they reward further study. In this chapter, I revisit these two studies, using them for a purpose different than those intended by their authors.

Microanalysis of therapy interaction is possible because of the invention of recording technology, and the courage and generosity of the therapists and patients who allowed their sessions to be recorded. Microanalysis approximates the goal of nineteenth-century historians like Ranke who wanted to describe history *wie es wirklich gewesen war* (as it actually happened). The emphasis of microanalysts like Pittenger et al., Labov and Fanshel, and Lewis on the nonverbal elements in communication allow us to recover crucial sequences of emotions that would otherwise have been lost.

Emboldened by their deep knowledge of the brief excerpts they studied, in many instances these authors interpreted the *meaning* of events to the subjects of their study. Especially for the patient, the authors infer thoughts and feelings. These inferences are informal, however. Neither study openly acknowledges an intention to explore inner as well as outer events. Both claim as a goal only careful description of outer behavior.

In this chapter, I outline a theory and method for studying the smallest parts and some of the *larger wholes* of relationships, using discourse from the Pittenger et al.

and Labov and Fanshel studies. Microscopic study of verbatim texts suggests that each exchange is a microcosm, implying a whole relationship. (For a discussion of part/whole analysis, see Scheff, 1990; 1997.) Building on the work of Lewis (1971), I propose that certain emotions, especially pride and shame, are directly connected to the state of a relationship. I show how cues to emotions can be used to determine the state of the social bond, and the dynamics of treatment failure and success.

To bring the features of this analysis into high relief, I first contrast them with those used in orthodox psychoanalytic thinking. Two features stand out in this comparison. First, my emphasis on shame dynamics as the key to failed and to successful therapeutic alliances. Freud did not treat shame as an elemental emotion like anxiety, guilt, or anger. For him it represented infantile regression. Consequently, it seldom appeared in his discussions. (However, the psychoanalyst Melvin Lansky (1992) has shown that shame dynamics figured in Freud's initial successes in his treatment of hysteria.) After *The Interpretation of Dreams* (1905), emotions in general and shame in particular became subsidiary to verbal analysis and interpretation.

A second difference is methodological. Although many of Freud's interpretations are brilliant, he did not take the step of demonstrating the verbal and nonverbal cues on which they were based. His methods, like most present-day qualitative analysis, were profoundly sensitive to the particular context in which the patient's expressions were embedded, but they were unsystematic. Like most practitioners of any trade, his analysis depended almost entirely on intuitive leaps. This method is swift and often effective, but difficult to teach. As Freud himself once said, "The best things you know you can't tell to the boys."

Since methods are spelled out clearly and explicitly in modern quantitative analysis, it is much more easily taught than qualitative methods like Freud's. However, quantitative methods suffer under the severe disadvantage of being acontexual: They attend only to the dialogue itself, without any reference to context whatever.

The method of discourse that I propose here seeks a compromise position. It is systematic, in that it points to clearly defined features of the verbal and nonverbal parts of discourse. But it is also sensitive to context: All interpretations are made within the context of the session as a whole. Although this method slows one down from the lightning-like leaps of intuition, it has the advantage of being teachable and verifiable. Perhaps if Freud had grounded what he told his boys in the cues that are observable in discourse, they would have made more progress than they have.

Case Study I: Failure of an Alliance

The session to be discussed here is a widely known psychiatric interview (Gill et al., 1954), which was the basis for a subsequent microlinguistic study (Pittenger et al., 1960). Because the original work was accompanied by a long-playing record, Pittenger and his colleagues were able to conduct a detailed study of the verbal and nonverbal events in the first 5 min of the interview. My analysis (for an earlier version, see Scheff, 1990) is based on and further develops that of Pittenger et al. In particular, I use techniques implied in their work, and that of Labov and Fanshel (1977), and Lewis (1971) to interpret the *message stack*. That is, I utilize the words in the transcript and the nonverbal sounds in the recording to infer the unstated implications (the *implicature*) and *feelings* that underlay the dialogue.

Message Stack: 1. Words
2. Gestures   Observables

3. Implicature   Inferences
4. Feelings

The patient is a young woman with an obvious working-class Boston accent. The therapist is a middle-aged psychiatrist-psychoanalyst with no obvious accent. The opening exchange is of great interest because it foretells much of what will happen in the session.

> (*Therapist and patient enter interviewing room.*)

T.1: (*Softly*) will you sit there.

P.1: (*Sits down.*)

T.2: (*Closes door*) What brings you here? (*sits down*)

P.2: (*Sighs*) Everything's wrong I guess. Irritable, tense, depressed. (*sighs*)

Jus' . . . just everything and everybody gets on my nerves.

T.3: Nyeah.

P.3: I don't feel like talking right now.

T.4: You don't? (short pause) Do you sometimes?

P.4: That's the trouble. I get too wound up. If I get started I'm all right.

T.5: Nyeah? Well perhaps you will.

P.5: May I smoke?

A close reading of this passage suggests several puzzles. For example, a pause of 8 s occurs after T4a. As has been noted by linguists, a pause of more than 2 s is likely to make interactants uncomfortable. In seeking to understand why the patient didn't respond to the first part of T4, we notice her preceding comment (P3): "I don't feel like talking right now." Why would the patient not feel like talking when *less than a minute* has elapsed in the interview? I suggest an answer to this question to illustrate my concept of the social bond.

Pittenger et al.'s analysis of the language and paralanguage in this passage suggests that a misunderstanding occurred during the first three exchanges, resulting in a crisis after T4a. This crisis seems rectified after T4b. Their analysis of the rest of the first 5 min, however, and mine of the rest of the interview, suggests that the crisis was averted only temporarily; the interactants failed to connect for most of the interview.

The exchange P8–T9 is typical of a large section of the interview. The patient complains at length about her husband ("He says my place is home with the children; he makes it so miserable for me that I'm in a constant stew. . . .") The therapist ignores the feelings expressed. Instead, he asks a brief factual question: "How many kids are there?" The patient answers ("Two.") The therapist asks their age. After telling him ("Three and five months"), the patient quickly returns to expressing her feelings. Again, however, the therapist's only response is to ask further factual questions.

There are 16 exchanges in the session in which the patient expresses a strong emotion, but the therapist's only response is to ask a factual question, with almost emotionless intonation. The therapist and the patient seem to have different agendas, with each responding minimally to the other's agenda. For this reason, there is little meeting of minds. The session ends somewhat abruptly, with the therapist showing little response to the final comments of the patient, who has been crying. The session does not seem successful. What happened?

A detailed analysis of virtually any part of the interview can help to explain the outcome; each segment is a microcosm, in which the same patterns of interaction recur. Individuals with highly differentiated personalities are somewhat unpredictable, since they are exactly responsive to each new situation that confronts them. But the participants in this dialogue continually repeat themselves. Their responses are like nested boxes (I am indebted to a comment by Carlos Sluzky for this idea). Each exchange is like their whole dialogue, which is like their entire relationship, which also may be much like all of their relationships. For example, the patient's response to the therapist in this case is probably very similar to her response to her husband. The therapist's response to the patient is probably much like his response to his other emotional women patients, or perhaps to all the emotional women in his life. What Freud called the repetition compulsion can be seen here in fine detail.

I will use the initial exchange as an example. Pittenger et al. suggest that a misunderstanding occurred at T4a because of T's choice of words and intonations in his first three utterances. Almost all of the words chosen are "pronominals," blank checks, and the intonations are "opaque," that is, flat. P must have heard these utterances, they say, as indicative of detachment, boredom, and disinterest: *"Here we go again! How many times have I heard this kind of thing!" (Following the convention in linguistics, an asterisk [*] signifies a hypothetical, a statement not actually made). Although unstated, these sentences are implied by the choice of words and intonations, part of the structure of communication that I refer to as *implicature.*

The authors go on to argue that P has misunderstood at least T's intent, if not his actual behavior. They say that he didn't intend to signal detachment, but neutrality: *"You can tell me anything without fear of rejection." The authors argue that during the silence after T4a, T must have realized that P had heard him as cold and detached, because in T4b, for the first time, he uses "normal" intonations; that is, he signals warmth and interest. (Perhaps he also leans forward slightly in his chair and, for the first time, smiles.)

T's understanding of P's mental state is apparently confirmed by P4: She resumes talking. To appreciate the significance of P4, it will be necessary to refer to the rhythm of turn-taking. P responds to T4 ("You don't?") with an 8–s silence. She does not say *"No, I don't," or its equivalent, signaling that she is still involved. Her silence suggests, rather, that she has withdrawn. Conversation is like a Ping-Pong game. P has put her paddle down on the table, seated herself, and folded her arms. *"If you want me to play this game, Buster, you better show me something different than what I have seen so far."

In T4b, T gets the message, and is rewarded with P4. In T5a, however, "Nyeah?," he seems to forget what he just learned, since it is delivered without intonation. This time, however, a silence from P of only 1.8 s is necessary to remind him: T5b is delivered with normal intonation.

Another confirmation of the authors' interpretation is suggested by their analysis of the paralanguage of P3 and P4. They say that P seems upset in P3, but not upset in P4. Since the issue of emotional upset will be crucial for my argument, I review and elaborate upon their comments.

Embarrassment and Anger: The Feeling Trap of Shame-Rage

Pittenger et al. (1960) interpret the paralanguage of P3 as indicative of *embarrassment* on the patient's part:

> This is a momentary withdrawal of P from the situation into embarrassment with overtones of childishness . . . (as signaled by) the slight oversoft, the breathiness, the sloppiness of articulation, and the incipient embarrassed giggle on the first syllable of talking. (p. 30)

Pittenger et al. frequently infer embarrassment in P's utterances, as well as irritation, annoyance, or exasperation. As was the case with the therapist, however, these phenomena do not figure prominently in their concerns, but are only mentioned in passing. The same thing is true of the analysis of emotion that occurs in Labov and Fanshel (1977), even though their analysis is much more sophisticated; for example, they note that signs of the compound emotion "helpless anger" appear very frequently in the patient's paralanguage. Since no explicit theory of emotions was available to them, these authors made little use of their findings concerning the emotional states of their subjects.

In my analysis, however, their references to emotional states will play a central role. I draw upon the work of Goffman (1967) on embarrassment and Lewis (1971) on shame dynamics to understand the exchanges of feeling that seem to take place in this interview.

Shame and the Social Bond: Theory and Method

Interpretive understanding (*verstehen*) involves a process between and within interactants which was referred to by G. H. Mead (1934) as "role-taking." He suggested that each party can, under ideal conditions, come very close to sharing the inner experience of the other party. By cycling between *observing* the outer behavior of the other, and *imagining* the other's inner experience, a process of successive approximation, intersubjective understanding can occur. Charles Peirce (1897) used the term "abduction" when describing a similar process in scientists. Scientific discovery, he argued, involves not induction alone (observation), or deduction alone (imagination), but a very rapid shuttling between the two.

Like Goffman's analysis, the formulations concerning *verstehen* by Dilthey, Mead, Peirce and others have been so abstract and dense that it is difficult to find out if they are useful or not. Because they offer no applications to concrete episodes, their ideas have remained somewhat mysterious.

Bruner's (1983) work on the acquisition of language is more concrete. He does not invoke the concept of *verstehen,* but refers rather to "joint attention." His examples of instances in which the mother teaches the baby the meaning of a word suggests the origins of intersubjectivity. The mother places an object (such as a doll) in the baby's line of gaze, shakes it to make sure of the baby's attention, and says "See the pretty *dolly.*" The mother intends only to teach the name of the doll, but in doing so, she also teaches the baby shared attention. I will illustrate shared attention with the incident already cited. Before doing so, it is necessary to outline a model of exchanges of feeling.

Goffman's analysis of interaction ritual suggests that embarrassment and anticipation of embarrassment are pervasive in social interaction, and particularly, that they are exchanged *between* the interactants. Lewis's analysis outlines the process of *inner* sequences, how one may be ashamed of being angry, and angry that one is ashamed, for example. Combining the two envisions the joint occurrence of emotional processes between and within, how love and hate are both psychological and social processes.

Recent studies of infant-caretaker interaction, particularly that of Stern (1984) and Tronick (1987), provide a picture of the elemental love relationship. Beginning very early in the infant's life, the infant and caretaker begin a process that might be described as falling in love. It seems to begin with taking turns at gazing into the other's eyes. This process rapidly leads to mutual eye gaze, mutual smiling, and what Stern calls mutual delight. Love can be visualized as occurring between and within the mother and child, involving meshed sequences. The perception of the mother's smile causes the baby to feel delight, which leads it to smile, which causes the mother to feel delight, which leads to a further smile, and so on, a virtuous circle.

The hate/resentment relationship can also be delineated, by using Lewis's (1971) concept of the *feeling trap.* A combination of anger and shame snowballs between and within the interactants, leading to extraordinarily intense and/or long-term relationship of hatred. These sequences are feedback loops, being ashamed, angry at being ashamed, ashamed at being angry, and so on.

In her study of four videotaped marital quarrels, Retzinger (1985; 1991) has shown in microscopic detail how shame-anger loops generate interminable or destructive quarrels. Using a coding system that she devised for verbal and nonverbal cues to shame and anger, she shows how the theory of self-perpetuating shame-anger loops accounts for all 16 of the violent escalations by her couples.

These loops may explain the extraordinary level of physical or emotional violence that can occur in families, since they have no natural limit of intensity or duration. They may also explain physical violence at a collective level (Scheff, 1994), as in feuds, vendettas, primitive and modern warfare. In the kind of hatred that occurs between avowed enemies, the shame component in the exchange of feelings is not acknowledged, but the anger is overt.

The vendetta provides a model for this kind of cycle, involving insult to honor (shaming), vengeance in order to remove the stain on honor, and mutual hatred and interminable conflict. As in the love relationship, there is a snowballing of emotional reactions between and within the antagonists: An action of one party that is perceived as insulting or rejecting by the other leads to feelings of anger and shame, which lead to a retaliation, which causes the same cycle in the other party, and so on, a vicious circle.

In relationships between intimates, elements of both love and hate often seem to be involved, as suggested by Bowlby's (1967) studies of attachment. Since the shame component in shame-anger loops is almost always disguised and denied, it requires microanalysis to reveal it. For this reason, the roots of destructive conflict are usually as much of a mystery to the participants as it they are to outside observers. To point out some of the ingredients, I return to the exchange that was discussed above.

In this interview there are several instances of attunement between the therapist and the patient. As already indicated, even though they got off to a bad start, between T4b and the end of T5b one such moment occurred. The therapist, in the silence after T4a, seems to have correctly sensed the cause of P's embarrassed withdrawal, and corrected for it. In T4b he offers the sympathy and respect missing from his initial manner. The patient responds appreciatively, relieved of her embarrassment. Such moments recur in the interview, but infrequently. For the most part, the interview is characterized by misunderstandings and feelings like those in the initial crisis at T3-T4a. Since there is little direct hostility or anger expressed, the interview is not an open quarrel, but involves many impasses.

The causes of impasse can be inferred from Pittenger et al.'s (1960) analysis. They do not attempt to characterize the mood of the interview as a whole, but they point to recurring elements in the manner of the two interactants. They repeatedly remark on the therapist's tone: "cold, remote, and detached. " They also point repeatedly to the emotionality of the patient. For example, about P6, "I'm a nurse, but my husband won't let me work," they say:

> The narrowed register, overlow, scattered squeeze, and the rasp on "work," together with the [lack of] intonation on the last phrase, mark P6 as a real complaint, invested with *real annoyance, misery, and resentment.* (pp. 50–51, emphasis added)

As already noted, the authors also identify frequent instances of embarrassment in the patient's manner (e.g., pp. 70, 101b). Finally, they note several instances of what they call "whining," "fishwifely raucousness" (pp. 82, 83b), or a "fishwifely whine" (p. 158). (These particular comments from the 1960's slander the patient's gender, social class, and emotionality: She is an emotional working class woman.) In summarizing the therapist's tactics, the authors suggest that one of the therapist's primary goals is to get the patient to reduce her level of emotionality in the session.

The paralanguage that the authors say accompanies the patient's "annoyance," "resentment," "raucousness," and "whining" is very similar to what Labov and Fanshel (1977) take to be the signs of "helpless anger," that is, shame-anger, with the shame part arising out of feelings of impotence. At the beginning of the interview, the patient is surprised, puzzled, and very soon insulted by the therapist's manner. Although there are moments of reprieve, the patient seems to remain in that state for most of the interview. Since neither the patient nor the therapist acknowledges her emotional state, the interview turns into a polite but nevertheless baffling impasse, a mixture of understanding and misunderstanding, acceptance and rejection, love and hate.

What kind of tactics might have lead to alliance rather than impasse? One possibility would have been for either participant to note that their preformed agenda was not responsive to the other person, that it was not working. (Pittenger et al. [1960] establish that the patient's initial presentation of her case seems rehearsed, and that the therapist seems to have a routine approach to patients.) The therapist might have said early on: *"I realize that you want to talk about your feelings, but in this initial interview, I need to know something about you and your background, to provide a context for the difficulties you are having. Could you bear with me for a while?" Or the patient might have said, *"I notice that you are ignoring the feelings I am telling you about to get at facts. Why is that?" Either strategy might have led to compromise and cooperation, rather than the impasse that occurred.

Communication theorists like Watzlawick et al. (1967) make a key distinction between *topic* and *relationship* talk. Topics concern objects and events in the world outside the present moment; relationship talk concerns what is going on between the participants in the present. In this session both participants stick to their agendas, which concern topics. His topics are facts, her's are feelings. Since neither participant swerves from their topics, alliance never occurs. They are stuck in topic talk.

The lack of negotiation and compromise may have emotional sources. Neither participant seems to be willing to risk making a scene by commenting on their relationship: "Wait a minute. Can we talk about what is going on here?" Such "metatalk" (talk about talk; Watzlawick et al., 1967) is unusual in ordinary conversation and, apparently, in most psychotherapy. Participants seem unready to face the possibility of the embarrassment to self or other that might occur if ongoing presentations of self are interrupted. Such a tactic would seem necessary to repair bonds damaged by unresponsive agendas.

A further emotional component in the impasse may be the lack of responsiveness of each party to the other's emotions, and lack of acknowledgment by each party of their own emotions. The patient's embarrassment when she didn't feel like talking at the beginning of the interview could have been a strong cue for the therapist, but he responds to it only in passing. Similarly, the patient, rather than discussing her feeling of embarrassment, withdraws instead. If either participant had made a point of this episode, the session might have taken an entirely different route.

It is clear that the patient feels rejected during much of the interview. But instead of discussing her feelings, she either withdraws or attacks. These tactics are probably compulsive and outside of awareness. According to the theory of shame dynamics originated by Lewis (1971), and further developed by Scheff and Retzinger (1991), if shame is evoked but not acknowledged, irrational aggression or withdrawal is generated by spirals of unacknowledged shame or shame and anger. Being ashamed that one is ashamed leads to withdrawal, and can continue indefinitely. Being angry that one is ashamed, and ashamed one is angry results in irrational aggression. Being sensitive to the other's embarrassment, and acknowledgment of one's own shame and embarrassment may be the key to developing secure bonds.

Case Study II: Therapeutic Alliance

The second case, representing the establishment of a secure bond between therapist and patient, is taken from the Labov and Fanshel (1977) study. My discussion is based in part on an earlier article (Scheff, 1989). The client, "Rhoda," is a young college student who has been diagnosed as anorexic. She had been hospitalized because of rapid weight loss, from 140 to 70 pounds. When her therapy began, she weighed 90 pounds, dangerously underweight. The session reported by Labov and Fanshel is the fifteenth in a series that went on for 2 years.

The session begins with Rhoda telling a story about a call to her mother. She points out that she tried to get help, as the therapist had suggested. Having attained the therapist's agreement that calling her mother was the right thing to do, she then re-enacts the phone call. The point that Rhoda seemed to be making was that the phone call was a complete disaster, in that her mother defeated her on all counts. She refused Rhoda's request without any ritual to protect Rhoda's "face," she won a victory in the ongoing battle over whether Rhoda is capable of taking care of herself, and she criticized Rhoda for making an inappropriate request to the wrong person. The mother's manner is forcefully rejecting.

In telling this story, Rhoda was probably trying to show the therapist how unreasonable her mother is, like all the other people she has to deal with. It is also an expression of her sense of powerless she feels in the face of the forceful, unreasonable people that are her lot. But the story also implies that, however well intentioned the therapist's advice, it didn't work.

Rhoda uses the same tactics with the therapist that she uses with her family, aggression that is disguised and denied. The therapist responds differently than the members of her family, however. Although Rhoda's disguised challenge angers the therapist, she doesn't counterattack. For this reason, the therapist was able to stay out of the quarrel.

Rhoda's first offense occurs as the session starts, omitting salutation, title and name, a hostile act. The therapist ignores this slight, but not the next one. Labov and Fanshel say that the therapist seems to have responded to Rhoda's first narrative, the dialogue with her mother, as a challenge to the therapist's *competence*: Rhoda tried out the therapist's advice, to openly ask for help, but it didn't work.

The therapist's response is to get angry. After first showing support ("Yes, I think you did, too." 2.2) agreeing that Rhoda did the "right thing," the therapist says "Well, *what's your question?*" The authors note that the intonation contours of the second sentence show repeated high stress (in linguistic analysis, stress means both pitch and loudness; in this instance the therapist's voice seems to leap at least an octave), a mark, they say, of "annoyance or exasperation" (p. 182) and "irritation" (p. 124), terms for anger.

Although the therapist apparently was angered, she didn't counterattack. The therapist's response to Rhoda's challenge was to reaffirm her original stand, the one challenged by Rhoda. The therapist might easily have blamed Rhoda for the faulty way that she approached her mother; she didn't give the therapist's advice much of a trial. However, the therapist avoids even the slightest criticism; instead she reiterates her advice. This tactic seems more rational and much less destructive than those used in Rhoda's family.

The therapist is still showing signs of anger several exchanges later. When Rhoda begins to discount the possibility that her Aunt Editha could help her, the therapist *interrupts* her with a statement which ends with an irritable assertion: "Well, what would happen if you *said* something to her—since we're in the business of talking, yes." (2.4) The authors characterize this utterance as marked by "contention" (p. 195): Both statement and manner are aggressive. Once again, the therapist gets angry, but she doesn't shame or threaten. She persists with her argument. Refusing to counter-attack, the therapist is able to gradually to build a bond with Rhoda.

Rhoda's Anger

The therapist's only extended statement occurs toward the end of the Labov/Fanshel transcript, a series of interpretations concerning anger. Until this point, she has allowed Rhoda to do most of the talking. I begin my analysis by describing the tactics used by the therapist to forge alliance, and end it by describing alternatives she might have used to have built the bond more quickly and with less risk to the alliance.

I accept one of the authors' major points about this segment: Although Rhoda gives verbal assent to the therapist's interpretation concerning anger, there are extraordinarily strong nonverbal markers, for example, silences and repeated negation, indicating that Rhoda has acknowledged anger in only the most provisional way. Her verbal agreement is undercut by her manner and nonverbal gestures.

The authors show that the therapist has qualms about making interpretations to Rhoda; she has been delaying for 15 sessions. In this session, initially supporting her, she confronts Rhoda with a loaded topic, her eating behavior. Since Rhoda constantly denies that she undereats, the therapist is running the risk of aligning herself with Rhoda's family, a dangerous step. The authors point to clues to the therapist's feelings: Her first interpretation (5.1) begins with a sharp intake of breath and a prolonged hesitation during the word "aroun-nd," before the loaded word, "dieting" "Well what they are really doing to you is so similar to what . . . apparently this goes on in the family—to what you did with them aroun-nd the dieting." Judging from clinical experience, there is good reason for the therapist's apprehensiveness. Even a single error with an anorexic patient may result in a violent reaction.

Rhoda responds to the therapist's new tactic with "a dramatic display of shock" (p. 302). In 5.13b, the therapist has finally mentioned the forbidden topic, Rhoda's weight: "Does it have anything to do with . . . your . . . weight?" Rhoda says "What?" in a whisper, as if she didn't know what the therapist was talking about. Rhoda interrupts the therapist with "a vehement denial in a falsetto squeal": "No, I don't *think* so!" (5.14d) As the therapist apparently feared, confrontation aroused violent feelings.

With what must have taken courage, the therapist persists. Although she is relentless, she tries to avoid conflict with Rhoda in a way that seems, at first glance, to be similar to the dispute tactics used in Rhoda's family: euphemisms (in 5.1, she refers to Rhoda's self-starvation as "dieting") and words so vague as to preclude understanding. In her initial statements, none of the pronouns have any referent: "*what* they are doing to you . . . apparently *this* goes on in the family . . . *this* has to be discussed in the family," and in 5.15: "All right, so why can't you stay with *that*. "

Unlike Rhoda's family, however, the therapist is using vagueness of reference not as a means of avoiding feelings, but as a Socratic method for allowing Rhoda to approach them, particularly her anger. The therapist begins her approach to the anger in Rhoda's family with a question about "feeling," a vague reference. She uses the term "feeling" in 5.17d and in 5.19b, and the term "felt" in 5.21: "In terms of how you felt?" This last question elicits from Rhoda the answer the therapist apparently wanted: "Oh, I guess I w's angry, but . . ." Success: Rhoda has acknowledged, verbally at least, a moment of anger. At this point the therapist does not press Rhoda to further accept the interpretation. The therapist shows restraint by allowing Rhoda to return to her usual storytelling.

Therapist Tactics

Let's return to the issue of the therapist's mitigating devices, her euphemisms and vagueness. The authors explain (pp. 301–302) that she was using the Socratic method as a teaching device. Rather than simply telling Rhoda her interpretation, which Rhoda might resist, she invites her participation. The therapist avoids putting answers in Rhoda's mouth. I agree, but also suggest a broader explanation.

The therapist uses *interaction ritual* (Goffman, 1967) in order to avert conflict, preparing the ground for entry into what I call "the realm of feeling. " She is showing Rhoda the same courtesy she would show anyone, trying to avoid shocking or antagonizing her by abruptly referring to feelings that are usually guarded. To explain, I review the idea of the *realm of feeling*.

In our society, there appears to be a powerful social norm concerning the discussion of feelings, which concerns the obligations of both the one who might reveal feelings (the speaker) and the one to whom they might be revealed (the listener): The speaker must not reveal feelings without permission from the listener, and the listener must not refer to them without permission from the speaker.

A commonplace example is the usual answer to the question "How are you?" No matter how the speaker feels, the expected answer is "Fine. I'm feeling just fine," or the equivalent. Any other answer might cause surprise and embarrassment. In modern societies, one's personal feelings are treated as private matters, revealed only under special circumstances.

In order to express feelings, rather than respond with the ritual answer, the speaker needs permission, which involves negotiation. The speaker may employ an assortment of devices to test the sincerity of the listener's interest. If the listener persists, refusing to be satisfied with pro forma answers, the speaker may further test the listener's determination by answering ambiguously: "Well, you know, into every life some rain must fall." If the listener passes further tests, the listener may feel permission has been granted.

Unlike Rhoda and her family, the therapist uses courtesy to *avert* conflict, rather than to *disguise* it. She does not mention anger until she obtains permission to do so. In her use of vague questions she is not only instructing Rhoda, but deferring to her. The mitigating devices the therapist uses are analogous to the testing devices that the speaker must use to obtain permission from the listener. In her role as listener, the therapist obtains permission from Rhoda to refer to her anger, by avoiding using the term until Rhoda does, and by getting her verbal assent to attributions of anger. Despite the somewhat stilted sound of her voice, the therapist's tactics are both skillful and remarkably gentle and considerate.

The therapist was able to introduce the topic of anger without precipitating conflict. Although this step probably represented an advance in the progress of Rhoda's treatment, it was a very limited advance. Rhoda's acceptance of the interpretation was superficial. In her nonverbal gestures, Rhoda gave every indication of contesting. Since we know that Rhoda did ultimately make headway over the course of

2 years, I assume that most of it would have occurred in a later session, not in this one.

Is there any way that the therapist might have made more rapid progress and, at the same time, avoided risk? At several points in her interpretation, the therapist identified herself with the family viewpoint, a step that could have alienated Rhoda. Would it be possible to proceed in a safer manner?

Shame/rage theory suggests such tactics. I describe what seems to be errors of technique in the therapist's tactics, and alternative moves. The proposals are made not to be critical of the therapist, whose performance was brilliant, but to illustrate implications of the theory.

In order to introduce the topic of anger, the therapist took unnecessary risks. For example, in 5.3, the therapist makes a statement that when voiced by Rhoda's mother or sister, she took to be a threat: "when they said you shouldn't be eating so much, *you stopped eating entirely.*" Although Rhoda ignored this statement, it was unnecessary: it was used only to introduce another topic, that is the topic of anger. The therapist avoids talking about her own relationship with Rhoda.

A safer approach would have been to made use of actual anger in the session. An entry into the topic might have been the helpless anger accompanying the dialogue with her aunt, or her sister's comments: *"What feelings are you having as you are telling me about your aunt?"

Another step would be to interpret the anger Rhoda expressed toward the therapist. The first opportunity occurred in the opening moment of the session. The therapist might have intervened after 1.4 or 1.5: *"Rhoda, I want to hear about your mother, but first, what is happening here between us? You started without greeting me, is anything going on?" Such a tactic might lead Rhoda to acknowledge some of her anger toward the therapist, with little risk of alienating her.

The next opportunity came after Rhoda had completed her narrative. As indicated above, the therapist seems to be angry at 2.2b: "Well, what's your question?" A therapeutic use of this anger would have been to call it to Rhoda's attention: *"Rhoda, can you guess how I might have felt about your story?" The other instances of Rhoda's challenging narratives, such as her stories about her aunt, would offer similar opportunities.

Interpreting anger in the session rather than in Rhoda's family has two grounds to recommend it. First, as indicated, it reduces the risk of converting the therapist into another enemy. Second, anger in the session may be more accessible to the patient than in past events: It is still occurring, it is less repressed. If the anger is the therapist's, it gives the patient the chance to see live anger that it is not lethal. If the anger is the patient's, the same possibilities occur, with the added advantage that the therapist can legitimate it. Interpretations of anger in the session help free the emotion from the topics in which it is usually embedded and disguised.

Conclusion

My discussion of these two cases has suggested a preliminary model of the therapeutic alliance as a secure social bond: A bond is secure when the parties understand each other's thoughts and feelings, and accept what they understand. The first case illustrates an insecure bond. Except for brief moments, the parties either misunderstood each other, or rejected thoughts and feelings they did understand. Not responsive to each other, the parties were unable to forge a workable alliance.

Conventional therapist-client courtesy stood in the way of coming to an understanding. Rather than developing a secure bond, the relationship between them might be called a pseudobond, based on politeness. Although polite, the parties are insensitive to each others feelings, and not revealing of their own. The shallowness of the therapist's response to the patient's embarrassment in the first case is particularly marked.

The second case illustrates the forging of a secure bond. Although the patient was aggressive and insulting toward the therapist, the therapist's tactics enabled her to avoid conflict. Moreover, although the therapist finally undercut the patient's defenses, her restraint and considerateness toward the patient enabled the patient to bring to awareness, if only briefly, some of her repressed anger. Although the therapist referred only to the patient's anger, she acted as if she also understood, at least tacitly, the patient's shame dynamics. In this case, the therapist is exquisitely respectful toward the patient's feelings, avoiding criticism and blame and all other tactics that would have been likely to generate shame.

In this chapter I have made explicit the crucial role that faulty and effective management of shame seemed to play in the two cases. Each party acknowledging their own emotions and responding to the emotions of the other seems to be crucial in forming a secure bond. In the first case, neither party acknowledged their feelings of rejection and shame. In the second case, the therapist acknowledged some of her feelings of rejection and anger, without rejecting the patient. I propose that understanding shame dynamics and awareness of shame and embarrassment cues might be a powerful tool for forging the therapeutic alliance.

This chapter suggests that the causal agent in therapeutic change is not only corrective emotional experiences (using Franz Alexander's phrase), but also corrective relational experiences. Perhaps mental illness is ultimately caused by bondlessness, the absence of secure bonds. If this is the case, even a glimpse of having a secure bond with a therapist would give patients hope for the future, as well as corrective experiences in therapy. If we consider love to be both an emotional and relational experience, this formulation would explain Freud's otherwise puzzling comment that love is the causal agent in therapeutic change.

References

Bowlby, J. (1967). *Attachment and loss*. New York: Basic Books.

Bruner, J. (1983). *Child's talk*. New York: Norton.

Gill, M., R. Newman, & F. Redlich. 1954. *The initial interview in psychiatric practice*. New York: Norton.

Goffman, E. (1967). *Interaction ritual*. Garden City, NY: Doubleday Anchor.

Labov, W., & Fanshel, D. (1977). *Therapeutic discourse*. New York: Academic Press.

Lansky, M. (1992). *Fathers who fail*. Hillsdale, N.J.: Analytic Press.

Lewis, H. B. (1971). *Shame and guilt in neurosis*. New York: International Universities Press.

Mead, G. H. (1934). *Mind, self and society*. Chicago: University of Chicago Press.

Peirce, C. S. 1896–1908. Abduction and induction. in *Philosophical Writings of Peirce* (pp. 150–156). J. Buchler (Editor), Mineola, NY: Dover.

Pittenger, H., & Danehy. (1960). *The first five minutes*. New York: Paul Martineau.

Retzinger, S. M. (1985) The resentment process: Videotape studies. *Psychoanalytic Psychology*, 2, 129–152.

Retzinger, S. (1991). *Violent emotions: Shame and rage in marital quarrels*. Newbury Park, Calif: Sage Publications.

Scheff, T. J. (1989). Cognitive and emotional conflict in anorexia: Re-analysis of a classic case. *Psychiatry*, 52, 148–161.

Scheff, T. J. (1990). *Microsociology*. Chicago: University of Chicago Press.

Scheff, T. J. (1994). *Bloody revenge: Emotions, nationalism, war*. Boulder, CO: Westview Press.

Scheff, T. J. (1997). *Emotion, the social bond, and human reality: Part/whole analysis*. Cambridge: Cambridge University Press.

Scheff, T., & Retzinger, S. (1991). *Emotions and violence*. Lexington,MA: Lexington Books.

Stern, D., Hofer, L., Haft, W., & Dore, J. (1984). Affect attunement: The sharing of feeling starts between mother and infant. In T. Field and N. Fox (Eds.), *Social Perception in Early Infancy*. New York: Elsevier.

Tronick, E. Z., Ricks, M., & Cohn, J. (1982).Maternal and infant affect exchange: patterns of adaption. In T. Field and A. Fogel (Eds.), *Emotion and early interaction*. Hillsdale, N.J.: Lawrence Erlbaum Associates.

Watzlawick, P., Beavin, J. H., & Jackson, D. (1967). *The pragmatics of human communication*. New York: Norton.

8

Pierre Philippot & Bernard Rimé

Social and Cognitive Processing in Emotion

A Heuristic for Psychopathology

Three years ago, I was deeply in love with a man, but I had never told him. Finally, I couldn't keep these feelings to myself any longer. I explained to him how much I was attracted by him. He looked very surprised and embarrassed. He told me that, although he liked me, he was not in love with me. I was petrified, and I tried to conceal my feelings but I felt very guilty and ashamed and disgusted about myself. I never told this story to anybody and I kept it secret. I felt so hurt and ashamed . After it happened, it often popped into my mind, and I felt very bad again. I tried to avoid these thoughts, but I couldn't. My whole body was aroused, but I couldn't express my emotion clearly. Now, I still think about it from time to time, and it is still painful.

Twelve years ago, I was living abroad in the same provincial little town as my in-laws. I did not like it there: There were a lot of gossips in that town and everybody knew what everybody was doing. I always felt observed. Things deteriorated quickly and I felt more and more unhappy. I always had a problem with eczema, but there, it really went very bad. My whole body, including my face, was covered with purulent scabs of eczema. I was looking so terrible that I couldn't go out anymore. I felt very depressed and lonely. My physician sent me to a specialist at the university hospital in the capital. Arriving there, I had to wait in a large room, full of other patients. I noticed that other patients had leprosy. I was terrified. I was called for examination by a young assistant physician. I had to undress. He was totally amazed by the severity of my eczema. He called his colleagues and his boss. There were a dozen of them, looking at me, naked. They had never seen such a case and there was not much they could do. They were speaking to each other, but not to me. I felt totally destroyed and humiliated. I identified myself to a rejected plague victim and, for some time, I was at the fringe of suicide. Since then, I have always considered my body as a disgusting enemy that could betray me at any time with an eczema burst or a panic attack. I never told this story to anybody but I am still haunted with the image of myself as a plague victim.

These two testimonies have a lot in common. Both are very intense emotional experiences that have been kept secret, but that are still ruminated and that still have an impact on the present life of the individual. The first testimony is from a university student who volunteered in one of our studies on emotional events kept secret. The second testimony is from an agoraphobic patient. She revealed this secret during her twelfth behavior therapy session. Incidentally, after telling this secret, her eczema problem regressed dramatically and has still not resurfaced at the 8-month follow-up. There is a difference, though, between these two testimonies. While the emotional experience depicted in the second one is obviously related to psychopathological problems, the first one is apparently not linked to any such trouble, even though it is still a painful memory.

In the recent years, we have been struck by similarities existing between emotional and traumatic responses. We have chosen to investigate what psychopathological processes could teach us about emotion, and conversely, how emotion models could help in understanding psychopathological processes. Our work is based on the postulate that there is a continuum between "normal" everyday-life emotion and traumatic dysfunctions observed in psychopathology. More specifically, we conceive of trauma as the extremity of a continuum on which emotion is located on a more intermediate position. Although differing in intensity, we propose that the processes at work in emotion and trauma are similar in nature. Up to now, we have found this approach to be a good heuristic and a source of cross-fertilization for the understanding of emotion as well as of trauma.

This chapter presents some theoretical and empirical outcomes of working with this postulate. First, we explain how considering emotion from a clinical perspective impacts on the definition and the model one holds of emotion. Second, we review our empirical findings regarding two processes that we consider central in the resolution of emotion and trauma: mental rumination and social sharing. Finally, we examine under which circumstances sharing an emotion may be functional in a recovery process.

A Working Model of Emotion

Mainstream emotion research and psychopathological research seem to have evolved independently. One is struck by a basic difference in the conception of the phenomena studied: While emotion research focuses on short-lasting processes, psychopathological research focuses on long-lasting ones. Indeed, emotion is generally conceived of as a brief and transient phenomenon. Most of emotion research focuses predominantly on processes that usually last a few seconds. For instance, Ekman (1984) states that most expressions of felt emotion last between one-half and four seconds. In contrast to this approach, psychopathological research considers recurrent processes that last over months and frequently over years. For instance, research on trauma has gathered a wealth of evidence that after very intense and negative events, people are besieged by spontaneous reminiscences of these events (for a review, see Rimé, Philippot, Boca, & Mesquita, 1992). They recurrently and automatically think about their traumatic experience, a phenomenon often called "mental rumination" (e.g., Martin & Tesser, 1989; Tait & Silver, 1989), and they also tell others about it, a phenomenon we called "social sharing" (Rimé et al., 1992). Illustrating the pervasiveness of these phenomena, Tait and Silver (1989) interviewed elderly people about the worst event they had experienced during the course of their life. Although reported events were on the average 23 years old, 71% of the participants reported still experiencing mental ruminations about them.

Postulating a continuum between emotional and traumatic processes implies that processes present in trauma should also be present in emotion, at least under attenuated forms. Thus, mental rumination and social sharing should also be observed in "normal," nontraumatic emotions. This, in turn, implies that emotion should be studied over a larger time span. Hence, in contrast with the tradition in emotion research, we propose that emotions are long-lasting phenomena that can extend over years. As illustrated in figure 8.1, the immediate emotional responses (physiological, expressive, subjective, etc.), which may indeed only last a few seconds, are modulated by regulation and coping processes. These regulation and coping processes can be intrapersonal or social. In the first case, they are based either on individuals' previous experiences (episodic memory) or on individuals' knowledge (semantic memory), which can be conceptualized as emotional schema, feeling or display rules, and so on. In the second case, individuals use the resources of their social environment: social support, advice, practical help, comfort, and so on.

Regulation and coping processes have a direct impact on the immediate emotional responses, and a feedback loop is activated until immediate responses are regulated or extinguished. This feedback loop can maintain the emotion for a much longer period of time than a few seconds. For instance, after hearing very sad news, indi-

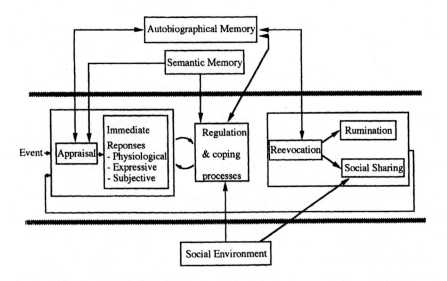

Figure 8.1 A Working Model for Long-Lasting Emotion. Intra-personal processes are represented in the top row, emotion processes in the medium row, and social process in the bottom row.

viduals can weep and sob for a long time, and try to regulate their emotional reactions for hours or even days. We stress that these regulation processes of immediate emotional responses are very different from moods, as defined by Ekman (1984). Indeed, contrary to moods, these processes are specific to an event; in a way, they are responses to responses to the emotion elicitor.

In addition, as will be documented hereafter, emotional events are almost always reevoked: Their autobiographical memories and consequences are reactivated. People ruminate about them or share them with other people. As introduced above, the first phenomenon is known as "mental rumination" and has been studied by several authors (e.g., Horowitz, 1979; Martin & Tesser, 1989; Tait & Silver, 1989; Wegner, 1989). The second phenomenon, "social sharing," has only been conceptualized and studied since very recently. Rimé (1989) has defined it as a telling about an emotional experience to some addressee in a socially shared language. In its strongest form, the social sharing of emotion occurs in the course of conversations in which individuals openly communicate about the emotional circumstances, and about their own feelings and reactions. In attenuated forms, the addressee is present only at the symbolic level, as it is the case when people write letters or diaries.

One important aspect of social sharing and mental rumination is that they reactivate the emotion linked to these reminiscences, and thus generate a new set of immediate responses at the subjective, expressive, and physiological levels. These responses need to be regulated and the circumstances of the reevocation are in turn stored into memory. Hence, by triggering immediate emotional responses, the reevocation of the original emotional event initiates a second, larger feedback loop. This feedback system can maintain emotional processes actively for months, and even years, as in the examples depicted at the beginning of this chapter.

Based on this general model, we postulate a continuity between emotion and traumatic processes. Specifically, we propose that extremely intense events will generate stronger immediate responses and, in turn, longer and more effortful regulation processes than less intense events. Because of their emotionality and their implication for the individual's concerns, the trace of these events in autobiographical memory should be stronger and more easily activated. Ultimately, these events should be reevoked more often and this reevocation should yield strong emotions. The intensity of these recurrent processes would lead to psychological dysfunctions.

The postulate of continuity between emotional and traumatic processes yields several testable empirical implications. First, the processes of social sharing and mental rumination observed in trauma should also be observed during "normal" everyday life emotional states. Second, if these processes are indeed core processes in emotion, mental rumination and social sharing should be observed during any emotion, whatever its type or valence. For instance, happiness should be ruminated and shared as much as anger or fear. Third, the continuum being differentiated by intensity, it implies that frequency, duration, and intensity of mental rumination and social sharing should be a function of the perceived intensity of the eliciting event. Fourth, as mental rumination and social sharing are triggered by the same process (i.e., the reevocation of the emotional event), they should covary, at least initially. Indeed, as it is likely that social sharing and mental rumination differentially affect the emotional memory, their time course may differ. The fourth prediction tackles the issue of the functions that might be served by mental rumination and social sharing. The present model postulates a feedback loop, but does not specify the nature of this feedback loop. On the contrary, one might wonder about the consequences of suppressing these processes: What are the consequences of keeping an event secret? Being conceived as a feedback system in which emotional reminiscences reactivate emotional responses, our general model implies that mental rumination and social sharing (or their absence) should have an effect on emotional recovery. Finally, if we consider the reevocation of an emotional memory as an emotion elicitor, it should be so for individuals telling about their emotions, but also for individuals listening to these accounts. How are such "social sharing partners" chosen? How are they affected by the description of others' emotional experiences?

In the next sections, we will attempt to address these questions. First we will describe the evidence we have gathered that emotion is indeed best conceived of as a long-lasting process characterized by intrapersonal and social reevocations. We will examine how such reminiscences are related to the intensity, type, or valence of the eliciting event. Then, we will investigate who is chosen as a sharing partner and how partners are affected by others' descriptions of emotional experiences. Finally, we will discuss the function of mental rumination and social sharing in the process of emotional recovery and the consequences of not sharing an emotion.

Emotion as a Long-Lasting Process

Recently, we have collected different types of data regarding social sharing and mental rumination in emotion. Before reporting findings, we briefly describe the different procedures we used. The first procedure was retrospective. Volunteers were instructed to briefly describe an emotional episode corresponding to a specified basic emotion that they had recently experienced. They then answered questions about their related rumination and social sharing (e.g., Rimé, Mesquita, Philippot, & Boca, 1991). We later developed a diary procedure. For several consecutive days, subjects had to report their mental rumination and social sharing in the hours immediately following an emotional event (e.g., Rimé et al., 1995). The third method proceeded by follow-up. Potential event selection biases were prevented by having the experimenters "preselecting" a target event. Subjects were contacted before an important emotional event, and were then followed up for several weeks. One such study was conducted in an emergency care clinic, with 39 subjects exposed to traffic, domestic, or work accidents (Boca, Rimé, & Arcuri, 1992) who were recontacted 6 weeks later. In another follow-up study, the target emotional event was child delivery, as experienced by 31 young mothers (Rimé et al., 1995). When leaving the maternity ward, they were given mental rumination and social sharing questionnaires to be completed during each of the 5 subsequent weeks. Finally, in a laboratory procedure, emotion was induced by exposing volunteers to movie excerpts (Philippot, 1993), and social sharing was later monitored. Luminet, Bouts, Rimé and Manstead (1996) used three movie excerpts differing in terms of intensity. Subjects, coming to the session with a same-sex friend, were randomly assigned to one of the movie conditions while their friend was assigned to an irrelevant task in another room. After the movie, subjects were left in a waiting room together with their friend. Their conversation was unobtrusively recorded and later coded for time spent talking about the movie and for number of words referring to the movie. We now turn to the description of the evidences collected with these different procedures.

Are Mental Rumination and Social Sharing Present in Mundane Everyday-Life Emotion?

In retrospective studies (Rimé, Mesquita, et al., 1991; Rimé, Philippot, & Noel, 1991), more than 95% of the subjects reported having spontaneously ruminated about the event. A considerable proportion of people (from 39% to 46%) mentioned that they have had such thoughts often or very often. Regarding social sharing, Rimé et al. (1992), in their review of eight studies totaling 1348 emotional episodes, report that 90–96% of the events were shared. Social sharing began almost immediately after the emotional event and was predominantly repetitive (Rimé, Mesquita, et al., 1991; Rimé, Noël, & Philippot, 1991). Furthermore, within the limits of investigated Western European countries, no effect of culture on global rate of social sharing was evidenced (Mesquita, 1993; Rimé et al., 1992; Vergara, 1993).

These data largely support the notion that mental rumination and social sharing are not specific to traumatic events but that they are also present, and well, in everyday-life emotions. Yet, such retrospective data are methodologically limited: Subjects were free to choose the emotional episode on which they had to report. They might have selectively remembered episodes about which they did think and talk. As mentioned above, diary procedures overcome some of these limitations. In a first diary study, 34 subjects reported the most emotional event of the day for 14 consecutive nights. Among these 461 emotional events, 58% were socially shared the day they happened. In a second study, in which 53 subjects reported every night for 3 weeks on the event that had affected them the most during that day, 67% of emotional events were socially shared. It is remarkable that these figures are slightly superior to those recorded in retrospective studies for the social sharing that took place during the day of the emotional event (i.e., 59%, Rauw & Rimé, 1990; 53%, Rimé, Mesquita et al., 1991; Rimé, Noël, & Philippot, 1991). Finally, both social sharing and mental rumination were assessed in a third diary study in which 17 subjects reported during 20 or 21 consecutive days about the most emotional event of the *previous* day. As compared to the other two studies, the delay between event and report was a bit longer. In such conditions, 74% events were socially shared, repetitively and with more than one person in most cases. Regarding mental rumination, 83 % of subjects reported having thought of the event at least once during the day. As was the case for social sharing, in spite of the shortness of the monitored period, mental rumination was clearly repetitive for 35% of the events.

The pervasiveness of mental rumination and social sharing was also evidenced with follow-up procedures. For instance, during the first and second weeks after their release from the maternity ward, the percentage of women who spoke about the delivery experience was extremely high, 97% and 90%, respectively. These figures decreased progressively during subsequent weeks, with respectively 55%, 52%, and 32%. An identical pattern was observed for mental rumination. Similar results were observed by Boca et al. (1992) following traffic or domestic accidents.

In sum, the convergence among the evidence collected with very different procedures is striking. They all indicate that more than 90% of emotional events are characterized as shared and ruminated. In more than half of the cases, these processes are activated in the hours following the eliciting event. Thus, these processes are not proper to trauma, but they are present along the entire continuum, from weak emotions to trauma. Yet, our model also postulates a positive relation between intensity of eliciting event (i.e., its location on the continuum) and intensity and frequency of mental rumination and social sharing. This issue is examined in the next section.

Relation Between the Intensity of the Triggering Event, and Mental Rumination and Social Sharing

In retrospective studies, the extent of social sharing and mental rumination was clearly related to event emotional intensity. Observing correlates of initial disruptiveness of an eliciting event, Rimé, Mesquita, et al. (1991) reported a correlation of .44, $p <$ .002, with mental rumination and a correlation of .49, $p < .001$, with social sharing. It was also observed that the more intense the shared experience, the more subjects reported (a) vivid mental images, (b) marked bodily sensations, and (c) intense subjective feelings (Rimé, Noël, & Philippot, 1991). In diary studies, positive relations were also found (Rimé et al., 1995, Study 3) and in the laboratory procedure, subjects exposed to the highly emotional movie talked about it more. Further analyses, taking into account individual differences, revealed that subjects who were more emotionally aroused by the movies later talked more about it.

Overall, our data unambiguously support the prediction that the extent of social sharing and mental rumination is a function of the intensity of the eliciting event. One might question, however, if this relation holds for positive emotions as well as for negative emotion. This issue is examined in the next section.

Relation Between Emotion Type and Valence, and Mental Rumination and Social Sharing

In our retrospective studies, subjects were instructed to report about a specific basic emotion. No differences were found among emotions regarding the amount of social sharing and mental rumination. Similarly, no differences appeared when the events reported were contrasted in terms of valence. Partly similar results were found in the diary studies. It appeared that, after partialing out the variance accounted for by the event intensity, neither emotion type nor valence could predict social sharing. Mental rumination indices, however, yielded an interesting pattern of correlations. Rumination frequency was associated with positive emotions; interest, joy, and affection. A different pattern emerged for rumination avoidance. While subjects attempted to avoid mental rumination in anger, fear, disgust, guilt, and even more importantly in sadness, they actively tried to maintain these ruminations in positive emotions (Rimé et al., 1995).

Thus, while social sharing is not related to emotion type or valence, results are mixed regarding mental rumination. While no differences were found in retrospective studies, diary studies suggest a positive relation (a) between positive emotions and rumination and (b) between negative emotions and rumination avoidance. It could be that in the hours following a negative event, people try to forget it and actively avoid thinking about it. However, such avoiding strategies might rapidly become ineffective and the active avoidance of the rumination might even trigger it (Horowitz, 1979; Wegner, 1989). Thus, in the longer term, as observed in retrospective studies, negative events would be ruminated as much as positive ones.

Conclusion: Mental Rumination and Social Sharing Are Pervasive Processes in Emotion

Using psychopathology as a heuristic for understanding emotion, we have shown that in any emotion, positive or negative, mild or intense, social sharing and mental rumination processes are present. This is true for almost any emotion, as only 5–10% of the emotional experiences are kept secret or are not ruminated. Still, it is remarkable that almost half of everyday life emotional episodes reported in diary studies were still ruminated about at the 3-week follow-up. As postulated by our general model, these reevocations also aroused an emotional state. As illustrated by Rimé, Noël, and Phillippot (1991), they elicit vivid mental images, marked bodily sensations, and intense emotion-like subjective feelings. Finally, and still congruent with our model, the intensity and frequency of mental rumination and social sharing are related to the perceived intensity of the eliciting event. The valence of the event does not affect social sharing. Immediate mental rumination, however, is affected by the valence of the event. People ruminate more about positive events and they tend to avoid ruminating about negative ones. This difference might disappear in time.

Partners in Social Sharing of Emotion

Who Is Chosen as a Social Sharing Partner?

In retrospective studies (Rimé et al., 1991a, 1992), sharing partners appeared to be confined to the circle of intimates (i.e., family, friends). Professionals (e.g., priests, physicians, psychologists) or strangers were rarely mentioned. However, within the circle of intimates, differences in partners chosen as a function of subjects' gender and age were observed. Among adolescents, family members (predominantly parents) are by far the most frequently mentioned confidants for both men and women (63%), before friends (33%). The social sharing network of young adults (18–33 years) is markedly different. First, the role played by family is dramatically diminished (22%), especially for men. Second, spouses and partners emerge as important confidants. Finally, friends are mentioned about as often as was the case for adolescents. This age group is characterized by a diversified social sharing network, with three types of partners of about equal importance. Among older adults (40–60 years), the confidant role played by family members is again markedly lower. This may be partially due to the fact that parents are no longer available. A considerable drop in the importance of friends is observed for men, but not for women. Still, at this age, spouses or partners constitute the main social sharing partners. This is especially true among men who share their emotions with their spouse or partner in more than three-quarters of the cases.

Thus, after adolescence social sharing networks evolve quite differently for each gender. While women develop a differentiated network and maintain it up to older adulthood, men's social sharing network virtually disintegrates at mature adulthood, leaving the spouse or partner as the exclusive confidant.

Social Sharing Effects on the Partner

If most emotions are shared repetitively with several partners, people must often be sought as confidants. What could be the effects of being exposed to such confidence? Several studies have shown that listening to someone confiding an emotional experience elicit marked emotional responses in the receiver, both at the physiological (Lazarus, Opton, Monikos, and Rankin, 1965; Shortt & Pennebaker, 1992) and at the subjective level (Archer & Bey,1978; Strack & Coyne, 1983). In retrospective studies (Christophe & Rimé, 1996) subjects were instructed to remember a recent instance in which they had been the recipient of social sharing. Their remembering was cued by a list of 20 events that were likely to induce emotions of either low, moderate, or high intensity. This study confirmed that hearing another's emotional account in itself constitutes an emotional experience. Indeed, people reported intense emotions while listening to the narrative of the emotional episode. As expected, low-intensity episodes had less impact on the receiver than moderate- or high-intensity episodes. Remarkably, in all three conditions, subjects rated interest at nearly maximal level. Thus, it seems that people show a great availability to act as confidants. The profile of emotions felt when listening varied according to manipulation intensity: The more intense the episode, the more it elicited negative emotions like fear, sadness, or disgust. It may be that in more intense episodes, the general openness to act as a confidant, as evidenced from ratings of interest, is counteracted by the raising of strong negative feelings. In this sense, the confidant of intense emotions may be trapped in an approach-avoidance conflict (Pennebaker, 1993). With very intense episodes, avoidance is likely to predominate, and people may attempt to elude others' confidences.

Christophe and Rimé (1996) also observed that reciprocal social sharing, in which the receiver in turn shares a personal experience resembling the one just heard was mentioned in 47% of the cases. Thus, social sharing might frequently involve social comparison. This study also investigated whether, after exposure to social sharing, receivers would themselves share the episode further with a third party, a phenomenon we called *secondary social sharing*. Indeed, it occurred in 78% of the cases. The repetitiveness of *secondary social sharing* is remarkable: It occurred "at least three or four times" in 37% of the cases, and more than six times in 13%. In the high-emotional-intensity episode, these frequencies were even higher, with 58% and 21%, respectively.

Effects of Social Sharing and Mental Rumination on Recovery from Emotion

One can speculate about the functions that mental rumination and social sharing might serve. An interesting possibility is that these processes would be spontaneous forms of emotional information processing that are instrumental in the integration of emotional experience and its recovery. The study of mental rumination and social sharing would thus have important implications for the clinical domain. In the present section, we will first briefly review the literature relevant to this topic.

Does Rehearsing an Emotion Contribute to Emotional Relief?

Conflicting theoretical views can be found in the literature regarding the question of whether rehearsing an emotion could contribute to its recovery. Some authors defend the position that rehearsal is instrumental for emotion relief. For instance, Martin and Tesser (1989) state that rumination fulfills important coping functions by helping to develop better understanding of the event, and to elaborate strategies to accommodate, or bypass the blocking of goal orientation resulting from the event. Similarly, other authors have proposed that rehearsal might help to integrate event-related information that is inconsistent with the individual's preexisting conceptual framework (Epstein, 1987; Horowitz, 1979; Tait & Silver, 1989).

Still other authors disagree with such a view. Pennebaker (1989) argued that mental rumination does not contribute to the understanding and assimilation of events. A similar view was proposed by the response style theory of depression (Nolen-Hoeksema, 1987). This theory holds that individuals who engage in ruminative responses to depressed mood will experience amplification and prolongation of the mood, whereas individuals who engage in distracting responses to their depressed mood will experience relief.

When it comes to the actual verbalization of the experience, however, some empirical evidence supports the view that rehearsal has positive consequences. For instance, Pennebaker and colleagues observed negative health consequences of not having confided traumatic experiences (Pennebaker & Hoover, 1985; Pennebaker & O'Heeron, 1984). Moreover, further studies showed that instructing people to disclose traumatic experiences had positive long-term health consequences (Pennebaker, Barger, & Tiebout, 1989; Pennebaker & Beall, 1986; Pennebaker, Hughes, & O'Heeron, 1987). These latter results suggest that sharing emotions might have positive consequences. However, contrary to this prediction, Tait and Silver (1989) have shown that communicating a major negative personal experience could reactivate the emotional disruption rather than resolve it.

In sum, opposite perspectives can be found both in the theoretical and in the empirical literature. We will now turn to our own findings relevant to this question.

Long-Lasting Rehearsal Correlates with Poor Recovery

In one diary study (Rimé et al., 1995), subjects briefly described the most emotional event of the previous day, every evening for 3 consecutive weeks, and answered a set of questions on their reactions, including emotional impact, social sharing, and mental rumination. Two to three weeks later, subjects answered additional questions about six events taken from their diary reports (three emotionally intense, three emotionally weak). When reexposed to this material, subjects rated the extent to which they had shared and ruminated the event and the emotional impact the event still had on them. A recovery index was calculated by subtracting follow-up impact from initial impact. For initially *weak* events, immediate social sharing and mental rumination were not predictive of recovery. However, the recovery index was negatively correlated with *follow-up* social sharing, $r = -.36$, $p < .01$, indicating that subjects who were still sharing the event at the followup had recovered less. For initially *intense* events, the recovery index did not relate to immediate social sharing, but well to immediate mental rumination, $r = -.30$, $p < .05$. Marked relationships were also observed between recovery and both follow-up rumination, $r = -.56$, $p < .0001$ and social sharing, $r = -.42$, $p < .005$. The latter results suggest that events still ruminated about and events still being shared at the follow-up were eliciting more emotional disruptiveness.

In sum, it seems that to rehearse an emotional experience over a period of several weeks is predictive of poorer recovery, whether this rehearsal consists of mental rumination or social sharing. This finding can be interpreted in different ways. Rehearsal might maintain emotional disruption by the feedback loop described in the model presented at the beginning of this chapter. If we consider immediate rehearsal, it was found that immediate rumination is associated with a poorer recovery. However, contrary to what was expected, initial social sharing was unrelated to the recovery index. Another explanation is that spontaneous social sharing might be rather unsystematic, varying from a few impersonal words to an in-depth self-disclosure. One could hypothesize that, to be effective, social sharing should accomplish an in-depth exploration of the meaning of the event. This hypothesis originates from findings by Pennebaker and Beall (1986), who asked subjects to write essays about unrevealed trauma in one of three conditions: They had to describe the facts of the episode, or the feelings elicited by the episode, or both facts and feelings. As compared to a fourth, control condition (writing about trivial topics), follow-up health assessments revealed positive effects for subjects who described their feelings, or their feelings and the facts, but not for those who only wrote a description of the facts. More recently, Mendolia and Kleck (1993) exposed subjects to an emotion-inducing movie, and then instructed them to talk either about the felt emotions (emotion condition) or about the sequence of movie events (fact condition). At a reexposure to the movie 48 hours later, subjects who had talked about their feelings evidenced lower levels of arousal and reported more positive affect than subjects who talked about facts only. Thus, these studies suggest that to be effective, social sharing should focus on an in-depth exploration of the feelings triggered by the event.

Psychological Effects of Social Sharing Focusing on the Feeling Dimension

We investigated how systematically exploring feelings through social sharing might have an impact on emotional recovery in the follow-up study of 31 young mothers discussed earlier in this chapter (Rimé et al., 1995). On the third or fourth day following delivery, subjects participated in a 45-min interview during which they were presented with a list of 12 emotions. Women in the experimental condition were instructed to focus on each emotion word, and to verbalize the extent to which they experienced the corresponding emotion at some moment of the delivery situation. For each emotion, the experimenter encouraged subjects to express in depth all the related feelings, thoughts, and physical sensations they had experienced during the delivery situation. Women in the control condition performed the same task, but for the emotions resulting from the impact of their pregnancy on their everyday lives. Then, for 5 consecutive weeks, subjects reported their mental rumination and social sharing related to the delivery. During the fifth week, they also rated the emotionality that the memory of the delivery still elicited in them.

Experimental subjects reported less frequent mental rumination and social sharing than control subjects. A recovery index (subtraction of follow-up emotional impact from initial impact) showed that the experimental group recovered better than the control group. In sum, this latter study demonstrates that subjects who were instructed to verbalize in great detail feelings, their causes and consequences, recovered better from the emotional event, and ruminated and socially shared it less. These results contrast clearly with those observed with spontaneous social sharing. Thus, it could be that in most instances, naturally occurring mental rumination and social sharing are ineffective for the recovery process. These processes would become beneficial only if they consist in an in-depth analysis of the feelings triggered by the event. Unfortunately, if events are complex, or elicited socially unacceptable or extremely painful emotions, such an in-depth sharing is very unlikely.

What Are the Consequences of Not Sharing an Emotional Experience?

Our previous studies consistently showed that a small proportion of emotional experiences are never shared at all (Rimé, Mesquita et al., 1991; Rimé, et al., 1992) and that 70.2 % of a sample of students could remember an emotional experience that they had never shared (Rimé et al., 1992). As far as we know the literature has not yet investigated the characteristics and consequences of emotions that are not revealed to others. Finkenauer and Rimé (1996) recently undertook a number of studies on this topic.

Psychology students were asked to report both a shared and a secret recent emotional event and to rate each event on several dimensions. Contrary to expectation, nonshared events were in no manner more intense or more arousing than shared events. Second, nonshared events evidenced higher ratings for shame and for guilt and elicited increased feelings of responsibility. Finally, contrary to expectations (e.g., Pennebaker, 1989), there was no more overall mental rumination following nonshared events than following shared ones. However, secret events elicited a more intense search for meaning and understanding. These findings were replicated, with a between-subjects design, using a large sample of subjects whose ages ranged from 16 to 70 years. In addition, this second study also indicated that, at the time of the study, subjects still did not feel the need to talk about the secret, and that talking about it would be extremely painful.

Regarding health consequences of holding secrets, Pennebaker (1989) proposes that active inhibition of thoughts and feelings represents a cumulative stressor on the body over time, which increases the probability of stress-related physical and psychological problems. Not talking about a traumatic experience is associated with more self-reported health problems (Larson & Chastain, 1990; Pennebaker &

Susman, 1988). Whether inhibition of emotional information is associated with subjective well-being is still unclear. Finkenauer and Rimé (1996) undertook a study involving the comparison of some 150 subjects having a memory of nonshared emotional experience, and 200 subjects without such memory. These subjects completed the SMU Health Questionnaire, a negative affectivity scale (Tellegen, 1982) and reported on their life satisfaction. Confirming Pennebaker's (1989) inhibition theory, subjects with a memory of nonshared emotion reported more somatic complaints than those without such a memory, while they did not differ in terms of negative affectivity. Regarding life satisfaction, subjects with memory of a nonshared emotion were overall less satisfied with their lives. The differences were especially marked for love life, physical appearance, financial situation, public self, and current life situation and were maintained when controlling for somatic symptoms, which are strongly related to life-satisfaction (Zautra & Hempel, 1984).

In sum, nonshared emotions are not more intense that shared ones. However, the former elicit more shame and guilt and generate greater efforts at understanding than the latter. In the long run, keeping secrets is associated with more health complaints and a poorer life satisfaction.

Conclusions

In this chapter, we have postulated a continuum between emotional and traumatic processes. Developing and empirically testing the implications of this postulate has changed our view of emotion and has provided a heuristic for studying the development of traumatic responses. More specifically, we have demonstrated that emotion is not limited to transient, immediate responses. It is most often a long-lasting process, characterized by cognitive and social reevocation (i.e., mental rumination and social sharing), which seem to be core features of emotion.

The postulate of a continuum between emotion and trauma is well supported by our data. Social sharing and mental rumination were consistently found to correlate with event intensity and were observed in a wide range of events, differing in terms of severity, from mundane everyday life emotions to more dramatic instances, like child deliveries or traffic accidents. To further validate this idea of a continuum, we are presently testing our model in extreme and potentially traumatic situations. The preliminary data collected so far, with severely burned patients (Frenay & Rimé, 1995), or with individuals exposed to a humanitarian catastrophe, such as the Belgian oversea volunteers who lived through the Rwandian genocide of 1994 (Sydor & Philippot, 1996), confirm our hypotheses: Mental ruminations and social sharing are present and seem to be determined by the same factors as those presented in this chapter.

An important implication of this continuum for psychopathology is that it validates the experimental use of emotion as a "low-intensity equivalent" for trauma. In other words, processes active in trauma could be studied experimentally in the laboratory using emotion induction as a paradigm. The empirically supported idea of a continuum between emotional and psychopathological processes warrants the paradigmatic use of emotion in many psychopathological domains. For instance, we have recently established the usefulness of observing laboratory-induced emotion responses for understanding the psychological effects of psychoactive drugs, such as benzodiazepines (Blin etal., 1996).

Another important aspect of our results concerns the effectiveness of social sharing and mental rumination in the process of emotional recovery. Our data clearly show that the natural occurrence of these processes does not help to reduce the emotional impact of the event. Even worse: At medium and long term, the persistence of mental rumination and social sharing is a good predictor of emotional disruption. Our hypothesis is that most often natural reevocations lack the depth necessary to work through the event. The central problem thus becomes to identify the processes that could be activated in "deeper" reevocations and that could be beneficial to emotional recovery. Pennebaker (1989) has evidenced that revealing a trauma, with a focus on elicited feelings, had positive effects on somatic well-being. Our data extend these findings to nontraumatic emotions and to psychological well-being. Still, such a procedure might activate very different processes. Investigating the processes that might be active during the systematic reevocation of an emotion, and that might be instrumental in its recovery, is clearly on the agenda of our future work.

Regarding social sharing partners, our data describe a trend during the life span that might have consequences for psychopathological problems. Indeed, in contrast to women who maintain an extended network of confidants, males over 40 years of age confide mostly to their wives. Although the question has not been investigated, it could be that this dramatic shrinking of the social network puts them at risk for psychological problems. Clearly, they would be in a particularly difficult situation in case of marital problems.

Our data also suggest that listening to someone's emotional confidence is in itself an emotional experience that might become aversive if the emotion confided is strong and negative. This might constitute a reason why natural social sharing is relatively ineffective; People might avoid revealing aspects of their experience that are too aversive. Thus, they would only reveal a part of their experience, and most likely conceal the most disrupting aspects. For instance, it is very unlikely that a young mother will tell about feelings of disgust or shame that she might have experienced during child delivery. When confronted with a disrupting experience, people might have to turn to psychotherapists with whom such confidences will be possible and even encouraged.

Finally, our "secret" data, not only confirm the established link between unrevealed trauma and somatic problems, but also extend this link to psychological well-being: Keeping secrets might have negative consequences both at the somatic and at the psychological levels. This consideration brings us back to the two testimonies that opened the present chapter. Even though many processes still need to be specified, we hope that our general framework and the research we reviewed further the understanding of the links between emotional recovery and psychological well-being on the one hand, and emotion reevocation on the other hand.

Acknowledgments   Research reported in this paper was supported by Belgian National Fund for Scientific Research FRFC Grant 8.4510.94 and by meetings sponsored by the "Maison de Sciences de l'Homme," Paris.

References

Archer, R. L., & Bey, J. H. (1978). Disclosure reciprocity and its limits: A reactance analysis. *Journal of Experimental Social Psychology, 14*, 527–540.

Blin, O., Garcia, C., Philippot, P., Auquier, P., Dutour-Meyer, A., Valli, M., Olivier, C., Rimé, B., & Bruguerolle, B. (1996, submitted for publication). *Inducing differentiated feeling states in healthy volunteers: Effects of Lorazepram.* Manuscript in preparation.

Boca, S., Rimé, B., & Arcuri, L. (1992, January). *Uno studio longitudinale di eventi emotivamente traumatici.* Paper presented at the Incontro Annuale delle Emozioni, Università di Padova.

Christophe, V. & Rimé, B. (1997). Exposure to the social sharing of emotion: Emotional impact, listener responses and the secondary social sharing. *European Journal of Social Psychology, 27*, 37–54.

Ekman, P. (1984). Expression and the nature of emotion. In K. Scherer & P. Ekman (Eds.), *Approaches to emotion* (pp. 319–343). Hillsdale, NJ: Erlbaum.

Epstein, S. (1987). Implications of cognitive self-theory for psychopathology and psychotherapy. In N. Cheshire & H. Thomae (Eds.), *Self, symptoms, and psychotherapy.* New York: Wiley.

Finkenauer, C., & Rimé, B. (1996). *Keeping emotional memories secret: Health and subjective well-being when emotions are not shared.* Manuscript submitted for publication.

Frenay, M. C. & Rimé, B. (1995). *Les grands brûlés: impact psychologique d'un événement de vie majeur.* Unpublished manuscript.

Horowitz, M. J. (1979). Psychological responses to serious life-events. In D. Hamilton & D. M. Warburton (Eds.), *Human stress and cognition* (pp. 235–263) New York: Wiley.

Larson, D. G., & Chastain, R. L. (1990). Self-concealment: Conceptualization, measurement, and health implications. *Journal of Social and Clinical Psychology, 9*, 439–455.

Lazarus, R. S., Opton, E. M., Monikos, M. S., & Rankin, N. O. (1965). The principle of short-circuiting of threat: Further evidence. *Journal of Personality, 47*, 909–917.

Luminet, O., Bouts, P., Manstead, A. S. R., & Rimé, B. (1996). *Social sharing of emotion: Experimental evidence.* Manuscript in preparation.

Martin, L. L., & Tesser, A. (1989). Toward a motivational and structural theory of ruminative thought. In J. S. Uleman & J. A. Bargh (Eds.), *Unintended thought* (pp. 306–326). New York: Guilford Press.

Mendolia, M., & Kleck, R. E. (1993). Effects of talking about a stressful event on arousal: Does what we talk about make a difference? *Journal of Personality and Social Psychology, 64*, 283–292.

Mesquita, B. (1993). *Cultural variations in emotion: A comparative study of Dutch, Surinamese and Turkish people in the Netherlands.* Unpublished doctoral dissertation, University of Amsterdam.

Nolen-Hoeksema, S. (1987). Sex differences in unipolar depression: Evidence and theory. *Psychological Bulletin, 101*, 259–282.

Pennebaker, J. W. (1989). Confession, inhibition and disease. In L. Berkowitz (Ed.), *Advances in experimental social psychology* (Vol. 22, pp. 211–244). Orlando, FL: Academic Press.

Pennebaker, J. W. (1993). Social mechanisms of constraint. In D. M. Wegner & J. W. Pennebaker (Eds.), *Handbook of mental control* (pp 200–219). Englewood Cliffs, NJ: Prentice Hall.

Pennebaker, J. W., Barger, S. D., & Tiebout, J. (1989). Disclosure of traumas and health among holocaust survivors. *Psychosomatic Medicine, 51*, 577–589.

Pennebaker, J. W., & Beall, S. K. (1986). Confronting a traumatic event: Toward an understanding of inhibition and disease. *Journal of Abnormal Psychology, 95*, 274–281.

Pennebaker, J. W., & Hoover, C. W. (1985). Inhibition and cognition: Toward an understanding of trauma and disease. In R. J. Davidson, & G. E. Swartz, & D. Shapiro (Eds.), *Consciousness and self regulation* (Vol. 4, pp. 107–136). New York: Plenum Press.

Pennebaker, J. W., Hughes, C., & Heeron, N. C. (1987). The psychophysiology of confession: Linking inhibitory and psychosomatic processes. *Journal of Personality and Social Psychology, 52,* 781–793.

Pennebaker, J. W., & O'Heeron, R. C. (1984). Confinding in others and illness rate among spouses of suicide and accidental-death victims. *Journal of Abnormal Psychology, 93,* 473–476.

Pennebaker, J. W., & Susman, J. R. (1988). Disclosure of traumas and psychosomatic processes. *Social Science and Medicine, 26,* 327–332.

Philippot, P. (1993). Inducing and assessing differentiated emotional states in the laboratory. *Cognition and Emotion, 7,* 171–193.

Rauw, M. C., & Rimé, B. (1990). [Le partage sociale des émotions chez lest adolescents]. Unpublished data.

Rimé, B. (1989) Le partage social des émotions. In B. Rimé & K. R Scherer (Eds.), *Les émotions.* (pp. 271–303). Neuchâtel: Delachaux et Niestlé.

Rimé, B., Mesquita, B., Philippot, P., & Boca, S. (1991). Beyond the emotional event: Six studies on the social sharing of emotion. *Cognition and Emotion, 5,* 435–466.

Rimé, B., Noël, M. P., & Philippot, P. (1991). Episode émotionne, réminiscences mentales et réminiscences sociales. *Cahiers Internationaux de Psychologie Sociale, 11,* 93–104.

Rimé, B., Philippot, P., Boca, S., & Mesquita, B. (1992). Long-lasting consequences of emotion: Social sharing and rumination. In W. Stroebe & M. Hewstone (Eds.), *European review of social psychology* (Vol. 1, pp. 225–258). Chichester: Wiley.

Rimé, B., Philippot, P., Finkenauer, C., Legast, S., Moorkens, P., & Tornqvist, J. (1995). *Mental rumination and social sharing in emotion: Diary investigations of the cognitive and social aftermath of emotional events.* Unpublished Manuscript.

Shortt, J. W., & Pennebaker, J. W. (1992). Talking versus hearing about Holocaust experiences. *Basic and Applied Social Psychology, 13,* 165–179.

Strack, F., & Coyne, J. C. (1983). Shared and private reactions to depression. *Journal of Personality and Social Psychology, 44,* 798–806.

Sydor, G., & Philippot, P. (1996, in press). *Prévalence du stress post-traumatique et intervention de prévention secondaire auprès de coopérants Belges exposés a une catastrophe humanitaire.* Revue Européenne de Psychologie Appliquée.

Tait, R., & Silver, R. C. (1989). Coming to terms with major negative life events. In J. S. Uleman & J. A. Bargh (Eds.), *Unintended thought* (pp. 351–382). New York: Guilford Press.

Tellegen, A. (1982). *Brief manual for the Differential Personality Questionnaire.* Unpublished manuscript, University of Minnesota, Minneapolis.

Vergara, A. (1993). *Sexo e identidad de genero. Diferencias en el conomiento social de las emociones en el modo de compatirlas.* Unpublished doctoral thesis, Universidad del Pais Vasco, San Sebastian, Spain.

Wegner, D. (1989). *White bears and other unwanted thoughts.* New York: Viking.

Zautra, A., & Hempel, A. (1984). Subjective well-being and physical health: A narrative literature review with suggestions for future research. *International Journal of Aging and Human Development, 19,* 95–110.

9

Theodore R. Sarbin & Ernest Keen

Sanity and Madness

Conventional and Unconventional
Narratives of Emotional Life

Our strategy is, first, to clarify the terms in our title, and then to offer a justification for employing the narrative as the overarching concept for conduct conventionally identified as "emotional" and also for conduct that is frequently identified with labels drawn from various psychopathological lexicons.

The juxtaposition of the terms *emotion* and *psychopathology* in the title of this volume implies that their referents are in some way connected. The received wisdom is that a causal relation exists, as exemplified in the statement: "Blank's craziness was caused by his inability to control his emotions." While statements about "emotions" causing psychopathological disorders are glibly made and uncritically accepted, the vast corpus of studies on emotion throws little light on the causality connection. The main reason for the lack of knowledge about the presumed connection is the adherence to the venerable tradition that "emotions" are proximal events; in the older language, they are "motions" taking place inside the body.

The assumed connection derives its surface validity from entrenched theories of psychopathology that had been derived from nineteenth-century medicine and its antecedents. Conduct that leads to judgments connoted by such terms as crazy, psychotic, mad, insane, abnormal, disordered, aberrant, neurotic, psychopathic, and so on, is assumed to generate inside the organism, either in the brain or in the metaphoric mental apparatus.

Except for unwanted behavior that can be attributed to the malfunctioning of brains damaged by trauma, tumors, or toxins, the diagnosis of madness is a moral judgment. That is to say, the label "madness" (or its modern equivalents, psychosis, insanity, mental illness) is assigned to persons whose conduct is offensive to the moral sensibilities of others (Leifer, 1969; Sarbin & Mancuso, 1980). Whether a sequence of actions is judged as psychopathological depends on extraorganismic factors, among them the tolerance for nonconforming behavior among the actor's social group, the social power of the judging person relative to the target person, and the readiness to assimilate the complexities of the target person's actions into one of the numerous categories of the ever-expanding *Diagnostic and Statistical Manuals* (American Psychiatric Association, 1994).

We propose to bring together the two conceptions, emotions and psychopathology, under the narrative umbrella. After introducing the narrative as the root metaphor for this chapter, we point out that the findings derived from studying "emotions" in the laboratory for the past 100 years are, for the most part, inapplicable to the study of "emotional life," a conception that refers to the narrative content and structure of actions and experience.

Our thesis is that a badly neglected but intelligible reference for conduct denoted by emotion terms is our experience as social beings. Further, such experience presents itself as plots and stories, identities and relationships, all of which are complex, to be sure, but nonetheless organized, indeed packaged, for our understanding in narrative patterns. Narrative is how we understand being a person at all, and furthermore, young children do so spontaneously and convincingly (Sutton-Smith, 1986). Socialization to an identity, and to a morality, also shapes that intensity of involvement we ordinarily call "emotional."

After making the case that emotional life is storied, we assert that some stories of emotional life fail to make sense to others, usually more powerful others, and the teller of incomprehensible stories becomes a candidate for psychopathological diagnosis. Employing narrative psychology illuminates both emotional life and judgments of madness. We also discuss briefly the implications of our analysis for psychotherapy.

Narrative Psychology

To set the stage, we offer a brief account of narrative psychology. We employ the narrative as the organizing principle for human action. Unlike such organizing principles as behaviorist stimulus/response connections or Freudian oedipal strivings, the narrative takes into account the fact that human actions are inevitably social. Human actions are not carried out in epistemological isolation but involve co-actors; thus a person's self-narrative is necessarily a collaboration.

Narrative psychology embraces contextualism, a worldview based on the historical act as root metaphor, a worldview that differs radically from the mechanistic worldview that has guided most laboratory work on "emotions. " Narrative psychology, further, is congenial with social constructionism as a theory of knowledge. Meanings are not given in events but must be constructed, negotiated, fashioned by people. Unlike older psychologies that treated human subjects as passive reactors to environmental stimuli, narrative psychology treats humans as agents who are capable of initiating action and of constructing their social worlds. In recent years, a number of books and articles have appeared that provide a warrant for the narrative as a viable organizing principle for the human sciences (see, e.g., Bruner, 1986; Gergen & Gergen, 1986; Howard, 1989; McAdams, 1985; Polkinghorne, 1988; Sarbin, 1986). Parenthetically, the expansion of interest in narrative psychology has occurred in the same time frame as many scholars' disillusionment with traditional definitions of knowledge as objective, or context-free, or perspective-free. Narratives, by definition, are socially situated.

The fundamental postulate of narrative psychology is that we live in a story-shaped world. A cursory review of everyday experiences provides initial credibility for this postulate. Our daydreams are storied; our nocturnal dream life follows narrative patterns, sometimes of mythic proportions. We fashion accounts of our everyday life in story form. The rituals of religion and the rites of passage reflect sacred stories. We anchor our memories in narrative plots. Our hopes are organized along story lines. Groups are held together by oral stories told and retold. The claim can be made that survival in a world of meanings would not be possible in the absence of skills for constructing and interpreting stories about interacting lives.

Narrative psychology illuminates both experience and action — and for that matter, knowledge and science (Polkinghorne, 1988). An example of the narrative quality of experience is given in the classic experiment by Michotte (1946/1963). Narrative plots facilitated the reporting of experience by observers who were called on to interpret films in which geometrical figures moved about in apparent random fashion. The movements of the triangles, circles, and other figures were woven into narratives about human relationships, often described with terms denoting common instances of emotional life.

We employ narrative plots to give body to everyday events. The readiness of persons to respond to the pictures of the Thematic Apperception Test (TAT) illustrates nicely the human tendency to create narratives from limited and sketchy stimulus displays. Give a person two or three household objects from everyday life and he or she will tell stories in which the objects are props or tools used by imaginary actors in furthering a plot. Such interpretations meet the criteria for stories: They have beginnings, middles, and endings, and they have a point. As we discuss later, the point is derived from implicit or explicit connections with moral rules.

Narrative plots guide the accounts that we give of our own conduct and the conduct of others. They are a necessary context in making a moral judgment. Whether the account is intended as a formal autobiography, as self-disclosure in psychotherapy, or as entertainment, we do much more than chronicle a series of discrete events. We organize, or better, we *render* the discrete events into a recognizable story. We may refer to this process as the narratory principle, the readiness to emplot or interpret apparently unconnected happenings as events in a story (Sarbin, 1986).

Besides interpretations of experience, narratives guide human actions. Actions, characterized as intentional in the sense that they are not free-floating, are directed to objects, persons, institutions. One's enculturation will influence the choice of actions in problem-solving settings, the enculturation having been mediated by narratives of many varieties: sacred stories, fairy tales, folklore, parables, fables, morality plays, adventure yarns, patriotic legends, and other story forms.

Literary scholarship has identified scores of novels in which the protagonist forms an identity through assimilating stories of historical or fictional characters and then engages in a program of action to make credible the constructed identity. The paradigm case of stories providing guides to action is Don Quixote, the protagonist in Cervantes's novel. Exclusive reading of the adventures of knights-errant of bygone centuries led Don Quixote imaginatively to construct an identity, after which he set out to seek adventures to validate that identity. This phenomenon has been aptly labeled the Quixotic Principle (Levin, 1970). Illustrations from life are not hard to find. A newly commissioned lieutenant in the Navy, a voracious reader of novels of the Old West, would call up the image of the redoubtable sheriff for guidance in dealing with unanticipated critical situations. The contents of popular spy novels provided plots for trusted government employees to engage in espionage against their country (Sarbin, Carney, & Eoyang, 1994). Many biographies recount the influence of book reading on self-narratives. Napoleon emplotted his self-narrative on stories about the legendary Charlemagne. The theologian Dietrich Bonhoeffer tried to solve personal moral problems by following the implications of the life and death of Jesus.

We identify book reading in the paradigm case, but other sources are equally potent, among them movies, television, songs, orally presented stories, and other art forms. The attempted assassination of President Reagan by John Hinckley was generated by a narrative plot constructed from overinvolvement in the film *Taxi Driver*. Other sources of imaginative involvement are orally delivered sermons, actual or vicarious acquaintance with the biographies of contemporary celebrities, and plots generated in psychotherapy discourses.

In these introductory paragraphs, we have offered propositions and illustrations to support our claim that narrative structures guide both the interpretation of experience and the choice of action in human affairs. We turn now to applying the propositions to the study of emotional life.

Emotions or Emotional Life

Traditionally, experts in the human sciences have treated "emotion" as one of the fundamental categories of behavior. Growing out of the tripartite division of the soul—intellect, passions, and will—the uncritical acceptance of emotion as a fundamental category has influenced philosophers, psychologists, and others to establish lists of emotions. Aristotle identified fifteen, Descartes offered six, Hobbes proposed seven. In more recent times, McDougal proposed seven emotions tied to seven instincts. Plutchik identified eight primary emotions; Tompkins offered nine primary emotions based on facial expressions. It is important to note that in every list, ancient or modern, the grammatical form for emotions is the noun. The use of the nominative form reflects the older psychologies' passion for reification, for taking complex human actions denoted by verbs and transforming them into literal entities denoted by nouns, with an implication of thingness. Recent positivist ideology governing psychology and psychiatry has granted ontological status to emotions as thinglike entities located within the organism.

The historical sequence of transforming descriptions of actions to thinglike entities began with observers noting the complexities of certain actions, then identifying the actions with a metaphor, and finally dropping the "as if" quality of the metaphor. Such a process results in reification. What was initially a figure of speech to aid in communication becomes the name for a literal entity (Sarbin, 1968). The linguistic history of "emotion" follows this sequence. The end result has been the social construction of emotion as a literal entity, sometimes referred to as a state of mind, sometimes as visceral reflexes, and sometimes as the responses to sensations induced by physiological processes.

This formulation reflects a widespread tendency among scholars who attempt to construct scientific theories. For example, in the eighteenth and nineteenth centuries, scientists held the belief that phlogiston was a substance emitted in the process of burning. This belief was discarded when the science of chemistry formulated and demonstrated the process of oxidation. Phlogiston was not discovered through experimentation or systematic observation but was invented by scientists who observed a similarity in burning houses, burning coal, and burning meat. They moved from the similarity rendered by the verb "burning" to constructing a noun that would convey the notion of a substance or "stuff" that was the causal agent for burning.

This understandable scientific dead end was continuous with the ideology underlying Galenic medicine, an ancient tendency to hypothesize internal substances to account for human conduct. Galen and his followers into the nineteenth century postulated that moods and personality styles reflected the distribution of humors within the body. Madness was the outcome of humors being out of temper. A human experience, intractable sadness (currently labeled *depression*), was attributed to an overabundance of black bile, hence the diagnostic label *melancholia*. The theory transmuted a profound human experience to the actions of substances inside the body.

Contemporary science continues to cope with the same mysteries that led Galen to his humoral theory. For the past hundred years or more, scientists have explored "emotion" as a causal agency for human conduct, including conduct that at various times and places has been regarded as madness. By inquiring into its properties, experts and laypersons alike have given warrant to the reified "emotion." In the nineteenth century, scholars focused their questions on how "emotion" differed from "cognition." In the twentieth century, they directed their inquiries to identifying the hormones and neurotransmitters responsible for anxiety, anger, and depression. The reification of emotions as internal bodily events has chartered the widespread practice of medicating persons who seek expert help to solve their problems in living.

If not thinglike entities in the body, what could be the referents for such terms as fear, anger, love, jealousy, pride? Phenomenological psychology tried to answer this question by breaking away from the tendency to reify and treated these emotion terms as ways of denoting subjective experience. Treating "experience" as the singular subject matter of inquiry, in the final analysis, turned out to be "experience of a social world," a world full of meanings that spring forth in many layers and from many quarters—historical, familial, cultural, political, religious, literary, and autobiographical.

The narrative approach to emotional life embraces all these meanings without becoming enchanted by the sheer impenetrable richness of subjective experience. The narrative approach goes beyond subjective experience by inquiring into the contexts in which persons engage in involved actions of the kind represented by such common words as guilt, shame, rage, anxiety, remorse, and sorrow.

We propose dropping the slavish adherence to psychophysiological symbolism (Averill, 1974) and replacing the study of "emotions" with the study of emotional life. This latter metaphor is more productive for understanding phenomena that ordinary language users characterize as guilt, shame, anger, fear, pride, grief, and sorrow.

John Doe is standing in a queue at a bank teller's window, when suddenly he hears behind him a shouting voice made unintelligible by sounds of scuffling, a slamming door, other voices expressing alarm. His body tenses, his attention is transfixed, he feels nauseous as he gasps for breath. He feels endangered. In imagination, he anticipates the staccato sounds of an assault rifle fired into the crowd, he has images of ruthless desperadoes.

What is happening here? To be sure, bodily events. But how does John Doe comprehend what he would call his "fear"? The bodily events are not the center of his fear. Such happenings would not be a part of his experience unless the sounds had meaning for him. And the meaning engages a narrative known by most participants in our culture as The Bank Robbery.

With this vignette we try to make clear that an understanding of emotional life requires a narrative construction. The events are part of a story. Being a victim in a bank robbery, falling in love, being the target of another's insult, receiving a physician's diagnosis that one has a terminal illness—these are instances of emotional life. But not any set of events constitute emotional life. We exclude from emotional life such events as increased galvanic response upon hearing a conditioned stimulus, or feeling jittery after drinking too much coffee, or being startled by an unexpected loud noise. In traditional psychology, all these instances are treated as "emotions" or aspects of emotions. The first four engage a person at the level of his or her identity, as a person in a community of persons who share common moral rules. The second set of events—the conditioned galvanic response, the reaction to coffee, and the startle reaction—do not engage a person's identity.

We therefore reserve the phrase *emotional life* for events that matter to human beings in a certain way. To speak of the galvanic reaction, caffeine overdose, or startle pattern as being "emotional" is merely to notice similarities in bodily reactions, and at the same time to make these bodily reactions criterial for "emotional." To exclude these and to restrict our study to identity-involving experiences like the first four mentioned above is to make other features criterial, namely, the common everyday life of being engaged in interacting with others. Included in "common everyday life" are the experiences of people whose problems are with life, with actions engaging other people, with moral struggles, and not with conditioned responses or chemical imbalances. These bodily processes are not irrelevant in the narrative context, but they move from the center of the discussion to the periphery; they move from the status of a central feature to that of an adjunct.

In moving away from the outworn practice of treating emotions as thinglike substances causing persons to act in certain ways, we inevitably come to grips with the distinction between "happenings" and "doings." In the older mechanistically inspired psychology, "emotions" are happenings; in the contextualist view, emotional life is guided by narrative plots in which the actors are agents.

We take for granted the proposition that human actions are embodied. In producing rhetorical acts to validate a moral position, we expect an increase in organismic involvement. A case of uxoricide can be used to illustrate. The perpetrator was a truck driver with a history of wife battering and alcohol abuse. Interviewed by a prison psychologist after having been convicted of second-degree murder, he recounted the events that led to the murder of his wife of 20 years. The marriage had been stormy almost from the beginning. The physical abuse usually occurred when he had been drinking. The beatings were justified, he said, in order "to show her who's the boss." Without proof, he would accuse her of having affairs while he was away from home on long-distance hauls. On the night of the murder, they had visited a neighborhood bar. After a few drinks, the wife struck up a flirtation with a younger man. On the way home, the truck driver accused her of infidelity.

Accusations continued after the couple returned home. During the heated quarrel, she announced that she was going to leave him and taunted him by declaring her desire to go to bed with the young man. At this point, the truck driver commenced a punching and shouting routine. Unexpectedly, his wife tried to fight back. He strangled her.

When the psychologist asked the inmate to explain his action, he reported: "I couldn't control myself. I was so mad. The anger inside me had to come out. I exploded." Later, he said that his wife's expression of desire for another man confirmed his suspicions that she had had affairs. He interpreted her desire for another man as a blot on his masculinity.

The truck driver's explanation reflects a theory of emotion that focuses on bodily states. The murderous conduct, on his theory, was caused by the "anger inside," his way of talking about bodily perturbations. From our perspective, the bodily perturbations were actually adjuncts to a narrative plot, the center of which was an insult followed by a culturally embedded response to insult, that is, retaliation. Bodily responses testify to the intense personal involvement in such an anger plot, but the plot is a whole: Insult and retaliation are parts of a narrative sequence; they do not exist separately. At the moment of the crime, the inmate did not consider that retaliation to insult has many variants. Strangling is but one option, mayhem is another. So is verbal abuse. Earlier, the duel was prescribed as the appropriate form of retaliation for real or imagined insults. Adolescent fighting on playgrounds and in streets frequently centers on insults. All options are culturally emplotted.

Analyzing the explanation offered by the truck driver leads to the conclusion that he reified a trope, or figure of speech. We are familiar with the reification of one kind of trope: metaphor. For example, the metaphor "the body is a container" has been reified by many writers who regarded the container as capable of holding psychic energy, including emotions. Another trope, metonymy, is also subject to reification. In metonymy, cause may be taken for effect, effect for cause, a sign for the thing signified, and so on. The truck driver had engaged in the figural translation of cause and effect. He, not unlike the traditional theorist, claimed that the "anger inside" was the cause of his murderous actions.

From the narrative perspective, the somatic inputs are effects, not causes, of involved action initiated by the actor in dealing with certain of life's exigencies. The truck driver's figural discourse was similar to commonly used expressions in which speakers make claims that are founded on the unwitting reification of a metonymy, "I was gripped by anger," "I was overwhelmed with grief," "The feeling of love dominated my very existence," "I was overcome with guilt."

If we examine these sentences semiotically, we find they are oblique ways of translating a set of "doings," actions performed by an agent, into "happenings," something brought about by the internal machinery. Instead of viewing the truck driver as a passive object "in the grip" of an emotion, we might say that, as an agent, he was *gripping* a narrative plot, a plot in which an exquisite insult to his masculine identity had to be answered. This dramatistic plot was part and parcel of his socialization. The insult-retaliation plot, not the internal perturbations, directed his conduct, the retaliatory actions.

In general, those cultural plots engaging one in defending one's honor, one's property, one's family—or furthering such causes—are common occasions of emotional life. As a protagonist in such cultural plots, the actor increases the vigor of his role-enactments, a by-product of which is bodily participation. Put another way, emotional life engages a person at the level of his or her identity, the sense of self as a person among a community of persons who share common moral rules about being persons.

Human behavior rarely, if ever, deviates from a format of reasoned action in which the actor examines the autobiographical past and leans into the future. Both of these must make "common sense" and be coherent in the eyes of both the actor and his or her co-actors. A crucial dimension of such common sense is that of the actor's moral status, and whether one's behavior is undermining, maintaining, or enhancing that status. We can think of practically no behavior by human beings that is not oriented to, or at the very least, sensitive to and hence constrained by these considerations.

This analysis of the truck driver's insult-retaliation narrative can be generalized to sadness, love, guilt, shame, and other narratives of emotional life. Such interpretation illustrates the postmodern critique in that it reveals the metonymy concealing the agentic nature of emotional life. What was nature (physiology acquired through evolution) becomes history (socially constructed concepts in a rhetorical context). What was seen as the center of emotion, its physiology, becomes not the whole but merely a part of a different center, human action carried out within a network of rhetorical meanings in a historical context.

The truck driver's claimed lack of volition requires examination. What is the source of the actor's narrative plot, in this case, the insult-retaliation plot? We may regard the conduct of the actor as rhetorical acts designed to enhance one's identity or to prevent the degradation of one's identity. Rhetorical acts include any action that communicates intentions: speech, gestures, violence. Rhetorical acts are of two kinds: dramaturgical and dramatistic (Sarbin, 1984). In dramaturgical acts, the actor is the author of the ongoing narrative, employing strategies of impression formation to convince others of the validity of his or her moral claims. The authorship of dramatistic acts is far removed from the actor. Dramatistic rhetoric is contained in half-forgotten cultural stories, stories that tell of trust and betrayal, honor and shame, vice and virtue, and so on. The truck driver's conduct may be cited as an instance of dramatistic rhetoric: He was following an ancient story line in which faithless wives are punished.

Conventional and Unconventional Narratives

Psychopathology is the nineteenth-century name for certain rule-breaking behavior. The name is relatively new; the behavior is not. In choosing the name, one selects from available cultural themes. "Psychopathology" thus expresses the quasi-scientific, medical themes of the nineteenth-century forerunners of contemporary psychology. The coinage of *psychopathology* reflects the passion for Greek-inspired labels, and the conceptual practices of reification dominant in our culture. Because we recognize the flaws in these themes, we prefer a name for certain rule-breaking conduct that is not associated with the older themes and practices and thus we speak of "unwanted conduct."

The history of metaphors for denoting unwanted conduct documents the shift in the sixteenth century from a demonological to a metaphoric medical convention by Teresa of Avila. She coined the metaphor *como enfermas* (as if sickness) to derail the activities of witch hunters who were about to apply the *Malleus Malificarum* to a cloister of nuns who exhibited behavior that at a later time would have been called hysterical. In time, the metaphorical marker was dropped and the literal notion of "mental sickness" took over in the eighteenth century, using a revivified version of Galen's theory of humoral pathology. Both self-reported somatic complaints and complaints by others of unwanted conduct were seen as manifestations of illness, and it fell to the doctors to explain and treat both somatic disorders and unwanted conduct. Sometimes unwanted conduct was caused by somatic conditions such as traumatic head injury; sometimes it was not ("organic" and "functional" disorders), but the practitioners, applying the early scientific theories of medicine, undertook to treat both, assimilating the "functional" to the "organic" (Sarbin, 1990). The distortions wrought in metonymy, the reifications and reductions already noted, led to the search for the causes of "mental illness," "states of mind," and the like, totally bypassing considerations of agency. This led to theories of wandering uteruses, mechanical tensions among energy-driven parts of the mental apparatus, and chemical imbalances in the brain. While these conceptualizations have sometimes been heuristic, they bypassed the agency of people who were assigned sickness labels. Further, these conceptualizations detracted from the recognition of the narrative content of their behavior and led to the uncritical acceptance of the routines of diagnosis.

Turning now to the diagnostic process, we propose that unwanted conduct is transformed into a psychiatric diagnosis (a) when an individual's conduct is incomprehensible to the diagnostician and (b) when the person's own explanation of the conduct departs from conventional plot lines. The traditional practitioner translates the incomprehensible conduct and the unconventional story into such standard psychiatric categories as thought disorder, delusional belief, hallucination, hysteria, dissociation, and so on.

Note in the following sketches of conventional and unconventional stories of emotional life, interactions ordinarily described with standard emotion names: anger, fear, guilt, shame, and so on, are common. We redefine these terms from the narrative perspective. A moment's reflection will lead the reader to the inference that no definitions of emotion terms make any sense in the absence of narrative reference. This reflection should serve as a caution to those scholars who are committed to specifying, so far without success, unique physiological components for the varieties of emotional life.

An anger plot is represented well enough by the example of the truck driver above. Did some psychophysiological entity called "anger" cause the murder? Surely not, for the bodily responses come only as an accompaniment to the interpretation of his wife's behavior as an insult to his masculinity. Had he been a member of the Ifaluk culture in the Caroline Islands (Lutz, 1986) his behavior would have been incomprehensible and referred to as "crazy." In our Western culture, however, the challenge to male sexual status is a well-known story. The truck driver's conduct and explanatory narrative are conventional; he is not given a psychiatric diagnosis but is declared to be a criminal.

The point is familiar: Standards of conduct are culturally relative—indeed, socially constructed. So are all interpretations of conduct the meanings of which always depend on the culture's stock of stories. A Plains Indian goes out on a vision quest. After fasting and praying, he returns to his community and tells stories of the visions he has seen. This is a comprehensible and conventional story to his fellows. A homeless person in New York City is brought to a psychiatric hospital when he tells a police officer on patrol of his visions. To the policeman and the hospital staff, the report of visions is an unacceptable story. "Visions" are translated into "hallucinations" and a psychiatrist's story replaces the vision-seeker's story.

We propose that unconventional stories define "psychopathology." Further, psychiatry and psychology have inserted into our library of plots narratives of psychopathology to make comprehensible in "scientific" terms what was incomprehensible in everyday language. The incomprehensibility of the mutterings and atypical beliefs of a street person becomes comprehensible when he or she is diagnosed as "schizophrenic." That comprehensibility, however, has to do with the scientist's narratives and is remarkably deaf to the narratives of the persons so understood.

Stories like vision quests are not current in modern America and hence they are incomprehensible and seen as evidence of psychopathology. Such diagnoses offer us a kind of comprehension. Conversely, some stories enacted conventionally in our culture will be seen by those from other cultures as incomprehensible as revealed in the following example.

The self-narrative of an experienced Boston policeman was one of masculine courage in the face of danger, elaborated through a thousand hours of TV watching. He had become preoccupied with fantasies of being maimed or killed in the course of duty. The recognition of his fear was grossly incongruent with the machismo coordinates of his self-narrative. He tried to meet his obligations by pretending that he was not fearful, and thus he vacillated between confidence and terror. These conflicting themes of emotional life influenced his making bad judgments on the job and also influenced his inappropriate responding to evaluations of his incompetence with heightened organismic involvement. The bad judgments, in our vocabulary, were examples of unwanted conduct. A mental health specialist examined him, found incomprehensible his stories of vague (and not so vague) fears, and he was certified as schizophrenic.

He was hospitalized and given phenothiazines for a month to reduce dopamine activity, during which dystonia and akathisia appeared, requiring benzotropine. At the end of a month, the policeman was taking these two medicines, plus a minor tranquilizer and a sleeping medication, and his subjective life was taken up with monitoring the effects of the various drugs so dosages could be adjusted and their side effects counteracted. His self-narrative now focused on that of a protagonist to whom schizophrenia "happened," interfering with his career.

What is most readily comprehensible here is a story identified in our culture as "mental illness." However, his father, an immigrant from Italy, understood his son and the pharmacological treatment the way he understood stories of his countrymen who ameliorated stress through excessive drinking. He could not understand why his son did not withdraw from his very stressful job. To the father, the son's story is that of too much pride in his fearlessness, not a story of accidental illness. Thus, not comprehending modern psychiatry, the father simply insisted that his son's job was too dangerous. However, because the son wanted to continue being a policeman, the father wondered whether his son was crazy.

The father, in our view, grasps the emotional life of his son as we do, as the product of his son's exaggerated enactment of a narrative. He suspects craziness because the narrative is more prideful than realistic. In contrast, the policeman's self-understanding is like that of his doctors, like the psychological theories of emotion as internal events, and like the theories of psychopathology that fail to see the narrative context of conduct and the agency of the person.

The doctors suspect psychosis because they neglect the narrative context of the patient's actions. The father suspects craziness because he attends to that narrative. Their conclusions may be similar, but their understandings are very different indeed. Without advanced training in reified and deterministic science, the father cannot be expected to recognize the "disease" that is obvious to the doctors. We submit, however, that his grasp of the situation of his son is more apt than that of the doctors, and further, his proposed solution is also better. Rather than changing his son's emotional life pharmacologically, the father would confront his son with the excesses of his narrative identity. His craziness is not in his failure on the job or his reactions to criticism. It is his lack of success in validating a counterfeit self-narrative.

Implications for Therapy

Life is full of difficulties, over which the natural language has thrown a variety of terms, some of which "name" emotions. Naming is the first step in a process that may result in reification. A second step is naming a disease, drawing on already reified entities. Such a sequence can be seen in the move from sadness to depression. (Because of space restrictions, we use sadness and depression as examples. The argument that follows can be generalized to other diagnoses.) The word *sadness*, being a noun, might be taken to refer to a thing, but it does not. The connotation in the natural language always points to a situation about which one is sad. On examination, the situation is revealed in a story, a drama, with multiple actors, with a beginning, a middle, and sometimes indeterminate endpoints. The same is not true when sadness is the conduct interpreted by diagnosticians as the basis for a declaration that a person suffers from "depression," a psychiatric diagnosis that connotes mysterious antecedents in one's genes or neurotransmitters or perhaps in one's early childhood, none of which is automatically implied since, like all "diseases," it is out of place, not normal, not comprehensible without special knowledge held by experts.

Ours is not the only culture to refer extremes of human experience to special experts, but ours is the most extravagant in building a profession and a technology (e.g., medications) whose interpretation of extreme emotional experiences as diseases says that such experiences are unnecessary, can be cured by experts, and refer not to situations in life but to chemical, physiological, and mysterious mental processes about which only experts have privileged knowledge. Sometimes this mystification leads to an arrogant attitude of scientific mastery of everything, including unpleasantries like having to endure stress, to bear tragedy, and to be sad. In the case of sadness, the route to the diagnosis of "depression" and its attending medical ideology from professional and pharmaceutical organizations have (a) trivialized sadness, (b) influenced therapists to turn their eyes away from the antecedent and concurrent human contexts, (c) made us deaf to understanding tragedy, and (d) worst of all, devalued traditional social rituals, like funerals, that offer communal support, defining the occasion of sadness in terms of a role of mourner. That is to say, technological (medical) solutions have replaced the "redeeming power of the social" (Jaeger, 1987) in dealing with sadness. Note that we have roles for loss of a job, loss of property, loss of one's ability to walk or to see. Insofar as we have not technologized these roles into nonexistence, they too help us understand, through a naturally occurring communal support, that tragedy is part of life.

The avoidance of dealing with a sadness narrative is a distraction from facing what it is that makes one sad, from the struggle over remembering the past and anticipating the future. This is the case when persons passively accept the role of sufferer of a psychological illness, with reassurance from all the experts that they can help fix the flawed machinery. This strategy is neither social nor redeeming. Adopting the role of patient does not engage one in a human community as much as it engages one in a dyadic contract with an expert. On the other hand, the expert who recognizes the narrative quality of experience is in a position to direct the person back to the sadness narrative, to the conditions out of which it arises, to the struggle made necessary by participating in that narrative, and to the available roles one has or can adopt within a matrix of social and communal support. This alternate view of psychotherapy bypasses the mystifications of technology in human affairs and informs the person that the exigencies of emotional life are not matters that can be "fixed" by psychopathological diagnosis and medical treatments. Whether in the psychotherapeutic context or in other social contexts, the exigencies that lead to participation in a sadness narrative must be dealt with in the same manner as one deals with exigencies that challenge or test one's other moral commitments.

References

American Psychiatric Association. (1994). *Diagnostic and statistical manual of mental disorders* (4th ed.). New York: Author.
Averill, J. (1974). An analysis of psychophysiological symbolism and its influence on theories of emotion. *Journal for the Theory of Social Behavior, 4,* 147–190.
Bruner, J. S. (1986). *Actual minds, possible worlds.* Cambridge, MA: Harvard University Press.
Gergen, K. J., & Gergen, M. (1986). Narrative form and the construction of psychological science. In T. R. Sarbin (Ed.), *Narrative psychology: The storied nature of human conduct* (pp. 22–44). New York: Praeger.
Howard, G. (1989). *A tale of two stories.* Notre Dame, IN: Academic Publications.
Jaeger, B. (1987). Language and game in psychoanalysis. In E. L. Murray (Ed.), *Second annual symposium of the Simon Silverman Phenomenology Center* (pp. 27–52). Pittsburgh, PA: Duquesne University.

Leifer, R. (1969). *In the name of mental health*. New York: Science House.

Levin, H. (1970). The quixotic principle. In M. W. Bloomfield (Ed.), *The interpretation of narrative: Theory and practice* (Harvard English Studies I). Cambridge, MA: Harvard University Press.

Lutz, C. (1986). The domain of emotion words on Ifaluk. In R. Harré (Ed.), *The social construction of emotions* (pp. 267–288). Oxford: Blackwell.

McAdams, D. P. (1985). *Power, intimacy, and the life story*. Chicago: Dorsey.

Michotte, A. E. (1963). *La Perception de la causalitieé [The perception of causality]* (T. R. Miles & E. Miles, Trans.). London: Methuen. (Original work published 1946)

Polkinghorne, D. (1988). *Narrative knowing and the human sciences*. Albany, NY: State University of New York Press.

Sarbin, T. R. (1968). Ontology recapitulates philology: The mythic nature of anxiety. *American Psychologist, 23*, 411–418.

Sarbin, T. R. (1984). Role transitions as social drama. In V. L. Allen & E. Van de Vliert (Eds.), *Role transitions: Explorations and explanations* (pp. 21–38). New York: Plenum Press.

Sarbin, T. R. (Ed.) (1986). *Narrative psychology: The storied nature of human conduct*. New York: Praeger

Sarbin, T. R. (1990). Metaphors of unwanted conduct: A historical analysis. In D. Leary (Ed.), *Metaphors in the history of psychology* (pp. 300–330). New York: Cambridge University Press.

Sarbin, T. R., Carney, R. M., & Eoyang, C. (1994). *Citizen espionage: Studies in trust and betrayal*. Westport, CT: Praeger.

Sarbin, T. R., & Mancuso, J. C. (1980). *Schizophrenia: Medical diagnosis or moral verdict?* Elmsford, NY: Pergamon.

Sutton-Smith, B. (1986). Children's fiction-making. In T. R. Sarbin (Ed.), *Narrative psychology: The storied nature of human conduct* (pp. 67–90). New York: Praeger.

Part II

NORMAL AND
DISORDERED
EMOTIONS

10

David D. Franks & Susan M. Heffernan

The Pursuit of Happiness

Contributions from a
Social Psychology
of Emotions

Every semester for ten years, the senior author of this chapter has asked students in his emotions classes to write down the purpose of life. By far the most common response—outnumbering various kinds of "success" and "serving God and others"—is to be happy. Probably most people entering therapy feel deprived of just this condition; to lack happiness is something we consider a malady. This is hardly surprising in the country whose founders forged "the pursuit of happiness" as an inalienable right in their Declaration of Independence. The purpose, of course, of the classroom exercise is to have students realize that happiness is a core cultural value, and that in this society, we give the inner life of emotion a lofty status indeed. For the majority of them, this exercise is hardly needed—the message is a truism: What other ways are there to think, and if there are other ways, why bother with them? In this chapter, we will allude to some of the other ways there are to think, and use them to shed perspective on some dangers in an unreflective preoccupation with happiness, especially as construed in currently popular ways as a subjective "feeling way down deep inside," and especially as something to acquire as we do commercial products. Without critique, beliefs such as these become the eye with which we see rather than the object seen. For example, as Gehlen (1980) points out, the priority placed on subjectivized, private states "screened away from action is a novelty of our own historical era; it is a component of the very air we breathe" (p. 76). We should mention at the outset that our intent is not in any way to devalue actual happiness; we do not toll a leper's bell! Our effort is to take it from a particular pedestal on which it is often placed and minimize unnecessary disappointment, false goals and promises, and to be happy when we can.

Several overall themes form the stage for our discussion. Much of our cultural concern with happiness is an important part of a larger ideology that insidiously serves the well-being, or at least the perpetuation, of certain economic imperatives on the social system level rather than the actual well-being of the persons so expecting and, indeed, so anxious to be in that state. Our thesis will be that happiness has become viewed popularly as an emotion, and emotions in turn have been reified in popular and some academic circles into discrete, self-sufficient physiological processes. They are then studied or "sought" as such states as if they were independent of the whole weave of a person's life. A second thread in our stage-setting is to suggest that this indigenous conceptualization of emotion, and of happiness in particular, is a part of the continued "subjectivization" of modern and postmodern mentality. One theoretical/academic consequence of this trend is that we think about emotion as being subtly, but erroneously, separated from *human action* on the world and the *relational, social context* implied herein. We will also describe, with the help of works by contemporary leaders in the study of the social psychology of emotions, how this subjectivized and fundamentally asocial inversion is part of an ideological distortion of personhood peculiar to Western culture and certainly self-serving to capitalistic economics. For many of us, this belief system ironically thwarts, rather than supports, the self-conscious pursuit of happiness that was its offspring. However this may be, it is worth repeating that giving priority to action on the world and seeing humans as primarily "doers" rather than "feelers," as crucial as the latter may be, will help to avoid the overdone cultural nominalism in our views of the person as well as emotion.

These subjectivized views reflect the inward turn of individualistic popular culture more than an advance of knowledge. They result in a passive view of the person and emotions, as well as a view that misses the social character of both. Above all, our patients and students want to feel good about themselves, others, and work. But this desire is particularly vulnerable to an anxiety over "receiving our due" out of life, and this due is increasingly seen as private feeling. Ironically, the status we grant to feeling states rather than deeds can lead to its opposite in the form of low grade depression, anhedonia, and disappointment.

As implied above, a historically tuned sociology of knowledge approach to our quest for happiness carries with it a two-horned critique. On one horn is a critique gained by a theoretical sensitivity to a millennium-old shift in mentalities, from collectively and externally oriented patterns of thought to the unfettered preoccupation with self, asocially construed, and therefore asocially *experienced*, in postmodern society. This carries forward the concerns of the work on the culture of narcissism (Lasch, 1978; Sennett, 1977) and how it enters into our professional thinking. The other horn is a critique of scientific theory of emotion that becomes simply another ideological expression on a more technical level of the same tendency toward fragmentation of personhood that we witness on the popular level.

On the Primacy of Action and Relation

The characterization of humans as primarily "doers" is a general one and must be deduced from a wide range of observations and thought. Unfortunately, it is difficult to mount a compelling argument for this characterization in a few paragraphs. Seeing human thought and emotion as subserving action goes against the bias toward fantasy and reflection in postmodernism. In the social sciences, twentieth-century metatheory has been characterized by a sustained recognition of the importance of beginning with human action in explaining the development and nature of mental phenomena such as cognition, memory, motivation, and emotion. It was fundamental that these be viewed as activities, or active processes, rather than fixed entities.

In our postmodern appreciation for the central place of human discourse and the symbolic fabrication in human experience, the line between reality-testing actions and more unconstrained constructions is blurred. In correctly stressing the importance of language in the development of human meaning, we skip over the equally important priority of action-on-the-world and the funding of further experience based on the feedback, both social and physical, that this world yields. From this point of view, symbols, which after all can mean anything, must subserve efficacious actions, that is, those particular actions that produce intended results. Here, "symbolic learning" is a misleading generalization because it obscures the true process of becoming human: the behavioral process (Becker, 1964). It is axiomatic that human meanings do not come into life "ready-made," but are created in action on the world, as problematic situations are overcome and reduced to predictable habit. Both perception and meaning are variables in this scheme, ranging from those only dimly perceived and dimly felt to perceptions and meanings that firmly "exist" in consciousness. As Becker (1964), following Dewey (1950), comments, "even physical objects merely subsist until firm behavioral patterns develop toward them" (p. 13). In sum, as problematic situations are overcome and reduced to habit, the world is converted into a meaningful behavioral environment: "[Verbal] symbols are gadflies that edge the organism on, but it is the organism that edges" (p. 15).

Too often, we forget this *primacy* of action that precedes even the child's development of the three basic cognitive distinctions between the immediate and permanent object, between self and nonself, and the related attribution of cause to self and nonself (White, 1963). Likewise, intentional actions often act as the criteria for perception. Insofar as all perception is selective, we tend to select as perceptually salient those things that answer to our materializing actions. Implicit in this view is the hypothesis that the clarity and firmness, the *sagacity* of perception, would vary with the intentional and reality-testing orientation of the person. In light of the above we can perhaps appreciate Hochschild's (1983) insistence that emotion be seen in the bodily preparation for action in the world, as the person assesses what external events mean to his or her inner, personal life.

In the final analysis, becoming and remaining human is premised on action. Marx (in Fromm, 1989), for example, emphasized action through labor and production, while Dewey's (1950) and G. H. Mead's (1938) most analogous deliberations concerned the manipulative stage of the act in the development of human meaning. For them, personal meaning was relational and dependent on action. It was built up as the physical and social world responded predictably to one's actions. Symbolic communication was simply the distinctively human means of implementing these behavioral processes. Action, then, becomes prior to thought in both time sequence and functional necessity.

After World War II, Allport (1955) and White (1959, 1963) identified an important flaw in traditional Freudian assumptions as well as in the learning theory of that time. Both assumed that the natural state of the organism was rest. Discomfort caused by unmet drives nudged the individual into "motivated" actions that reestablished the original quiescence through the satiation of drives. But empirically, it is just when all drives are satiated and theoretically infants should be at rest that they typically engage in exploratory reality testing behaviors. This challenged the assumption of equilibrium as the natural state of the organism and reaffirmed the wisdom of basing theories of learning and motivation on a more active view of early childhood. In assuming the primacy of action in the Chicago tradition of Dewey and Mead, White was joined by his Harvard colleagues M. Brewster Smith (1968) and Jerome Bruner (1966). Bandura (1977) followed with his models of efficacy based self-esteem at the same time that the sociologists Franks and Marolla (1976) and Gecas (1971) were working in the transactional tradition on efficacy based self-esteem. Despite the continuance of the primacy given to "man the doer" by scholars, postmodern society, with its emphasis on fantasy and appearance, and its focus on reality *making* rather than reality *testing*, has no doubt impeded the more hard-nosed thinking of "man the doer" following in the tradition of Marx, Mead, and Dewey. At the same time it has greatly promoted the image of the person as feeler.

Also paramount in the "action" scheme, and especially important to emotion, was the insistence on viewing these processes as relational. For example, it was crucial to avoid seeing private consciousness as existing self-sufficiently in Cartesian separation from a world of objective social and material objects. Consistent with this, in Europe, Husserl (1970) was insisting that consciousness was always consciousness *of* something. Likewise, emotion is not to be viewed as a self-sufficient state. It only arises as joined with an object of that emotion. Emotion, as distinct from sensation, is always relational. As important as sensation or feeling may be to most emotional experience, emotions are more than private, self-contained sensations. When angry, we do not literally feel "hot" around the collar as when we feel "hot" in the heat. If we are angry, we are angry "at" or "with" someone. Anger is thought dependent; unlike sensations, emotions are inseparable from their objects (Coulter, 1979). They are not just subjective feeling states, but are feelings about how the world matters to us personally. As Hochschild (1983), following Rosaldo (1984), contends, emotions are relationships that link what we care about on the inside to what is occurring on the outside. We are mad "at," "about," "toward," "with," or "over" some happening. This intrinsically relational quality of consciousness and emotion is grammatically expressed by the use of connecting prepositions. Such a relational, outward orientation is referred to as "intentionality" and differentiates emotion from individual, biologically given sensations.

Despite our lip service to the *primacy of action* in the pragmatic framework, we have failed to apply this priority systematically in our sociological thinking about emotion. The next section critiques current popular understandings of happiness from the perspective of social history. Aided by the eyes of very different ages and times, we may see through some of the ideological biases of our own age. We shall see that contemporary notions of happiness fly in the face of the knowledge base described above and reflect the influence of our economic system much more than scientific advance.

On the Modern Subjectivization of Happiness

Jan Lewis (1983) describes a shift in the meaning of happiness since Jeffersonian times. This change is from a more public, objectively measurable lifestyle assuming ownership of land and property, as well as felicity in public service. Professor Lewis traces the rapid change in the term's meaning from an objective and more collectively oriented ideal to a very vague and private emotional state. This important shift, which covers only a few generations, is only a particular part of the broader movement alluded to above. Berger, Berger, and Kellner (1973) refer to it as the "subjectivization of modern mentality." Here they borrow from Gehlen (1980) in his study of the progression since archaic times from unreflective acceptance of intrinsically justified institutional forms and the dimmest recognition of the self as a separate whole, to a more reflective consciousness of the arbitrariness of human institutions—a domain accessible only through scientific abstraction outside of direct experience (see also Baumeister, 1986; Sennett, 1977; Tuan, 1982; Westen, 1985). Subjectivization is a turning inward as the institutional world and moral codes are no longer perceived as compellingly real. This heightened emphasis on the private individual has advanced until it is threatening the public structures on which viably felt selves depend. It has been the object of a broad genre of academic studies, from Philip Rieff's (1966) *Triumph of the Therapeutic*, to Morris' (1972) *The Discovery of the Individual*, Sennett's (1977) *Fall of Public Man*, Weintraub s (1978) *The Value of the Individual*, Lasch's (1978) *Culture of Narcissism*, Gehlen's (1980) *Man in the Age of Technology*, Tuan's (1982) *Seqmented Worlds and Self*, Westen's (1985) *Self and Society*, Baumeister's (1986) *Identity*, and Wood and Zurcher's (1988) *Development of a Postmodern Self*. This list reflects an impressive variety of disciplines, ranging from cultural geography through the rest of the social sciences.

From the sociology of knowledge viewpoint, our 15-year-old rediscovery of emotions in each of the academic subfields of the humanities continues the shift in values and modes of thought that began around the late Middle Ages and spawned, as a core metaphor, "the pursuit of happiness." This shift is known variously as the rise of individualism and of personal prerogative (Berger et al., 1973; Gehlen 1980). The change in mentality and emotion occurred on the informal, interactive level of everyday European life, as well as in more formal and learned circles. From the works above, it appears that interest in the inner life of the individual, and thus in personal happiness, was negligible in archaic times and in Europe before the sixteenth century. Rather, one's sense of reality was constructed from the reified and relatively unquestioned institutions of religion, family, region, and kingship. According to Baumeister (1986), the only medieval biographies were of saints; however, even here authors were free to borrow from the miracle stories of one saint to embellish the life story of another. While we moderns find individual histories, personalities, and psychological struggles important, these themes were traditionally neglected in favor of portraying Christian ideals or stereotypes. According to Baumeister, the single human life as a unique, subjective totality was not a solidified, public idea until the end of the Middle Ages.[1]

The meaning of the term *happiness* is itself a remarkable illustration of the movement from exclusively external patterns of thought to the preoccupation with the inner, personal experience that characterizes our current age. In *Nicomachean Ethics*, Aristotle (trans. 1947) defines *eudaemonia* (translated as happiness) as an objective, if hypothetical standard: the perfections of one's potential as a rational, fully functioning human being (Averill, 1993).[2] Ryff (1989) questions the appropriateness of translating the Greek word *eudaemonia* as happiness but the issue may well be more appropriately couched in terms of differences in culturally shaped schemata than anything else. In both cases they define the broad answers to the purpose of life. The impersonal ideal suggested by *eudaemonia* may have been as close as the Greek mentality could come to our more psychologized version. This is supported by Jones's (1953) chronicle of the changing meaning of happiness in Western, and particularly American, history where there can be no issue of translation from very different languages and historical epochs. The same word is defined by various men of letters in a plethora of ways. If diversity and blatant vagary characterize the word's short history in America, one more feature is just as striking. This is the unquestioned acceptance that whatever the term *happiness* means, it is simply assumed unquestionably to be the point, the goal, of existence. With the rise of industrialization, and perhaps especially with the encroachment of the middle class against the established European monarchies, happiness becomes an irreducible, unanalyzed enabler of discourse, a primitive term that makes shared thought and discourse possible rather than the reasoned product of it. However this may be, it has certainly reflected the movement through the ages, from external and impersonally collective modes of thinking to the subjectivized and personal mentalities of today that so many writers from so many disciplines observe.

There are numerous insights to be gained from such a broad view. An important irony is that modern conceptions of emotion harbor both the dangers and the advantages of the subjectivization of mentality of which it is a part. However, critical assessment of the individualization and personalization of human beings has been forming in the works cited above. The metaphoric underpinnings of our professional theories of self are being scrutinized. Elias (1982), Baumeister (1986), Sampson (1981), and Westen (1985), for example, converge along lines of thought best expressed by the anthropologist Geertz (1974):

> The Western conception of the person as a bounded, unique, more or less integrated motivational and cognitive universe, a dynamic center of awareness, emotion, and judgement, and action organized into a distinctive whole and set contrastively both against other such wholes and against its social and natural background, is, however incorrigible it may seem to us, a rather peculiar idea within the context of the world's cultures. (p. 31)

Baumeister and Elias are suspicious of contemporary conceptions portraying self-knowledge as a search through the deep layers of self to discover preexisting desires, motives, and emotions, as if they were cookies in a jar or hidden treasure waiting for actualization. This notion is premised on what Baumeister refers to as the "spacial metaphor"—the self conceived of as an inner world, closed off from external surroundings.[3]

Guided by such nonempirical notions, moderns view emotions as innate substrata of authenticity and personal reality that reveal our true selves. Emotion is something to be discovered for what it is, then openly expressed, and through uninhibited spontaneity, channeled into self-actualizing behaviors. The historical and anthropological framework strongly suggests that we recognize our traditional view of emotion as physiological substrata of innate subjective reality, for the parochial and culturally relative conception of self and its feelings that it is (Lutz & White, 1986). According to Harré (1986) and a growing number of anthropologists, the conviction that emotions are exclusively composed of physiological states is but a peculiarly Western "account"—a culture-bound notion that many have uncritically adopted in guiding their research. Averill (1993) and Sarbin (1986) agree: The very term *emotion* arises in European history as a concept that individualized people use to make sense out of their existence, "their own and other's actions, as well as their own identity" (Crespo, 1986, p. 209).

For example, Sarbin (1986, p. 95) asked athletes to describe their feelings after winning an event. He discovered that the answers were uninformative, except insofar as a story or a self-narrative was relayed. First, the subjects formed an opinion about their poorly understood internal state. Second, after uttering the opinion ("It's a wonderful feeling"), they moved away from the task of pinning down a "feeling" and, instead, told stories about the rigors of training, the role of the coach, family support, uncertainty of outcome, and the meaning of the contest. In this context, it is not productive to posit emotions as a special kind of sensation independent of the social process.

The Fruitless Search for an Identity Composed from Within

In poignant contrast to the meaning of happiness in Thomas Jefferson's age, a sizeable number of Americans now view public events in general, and politics in particular, as beneath them. As stated above, Lewis (1983) traces the changing meaning of happiness in only a half a century to his grandson's usage. Thomas Jefferson Randolph, like many of his cohort, had come to assume that public life (which, in his case, was largely composed of salvaging what little remained of his grandfather's property) was something from which one retreated nightly. His pursuit of happiness drove him home to the privacy of his wife and children. Happiness was now more closely associated with love—love of one's intimates and love of God. "At home men and women sought salvation, and they looked for it in emotions, passions, hopes, and fears" (Lewis, 1983, p. xiv). Indeed, Lewis's book is about how such a change in feeling about feeling itself took place.

Sennett (1977) starts his volume on the fall of "public man" with a similar observation. Today, he says, "Public life has become a matter of formal obligation. Manners and ritual interchanges with strangers are looked on at best as formal and dry, at worst as phony" (p. 3). In private—at home or with our psychiatrist—we seek the nature of ourselves in what is authentic of our "feelings." The value we place on the personal aspect of our lives has led us on a quest to know ourselves and to become happier. However, as Sennett (1977), Becker (1964), Tuan (1982), and Lepenies (1992) warn, the more privatized the psyche becomes, the more it is treated as having an inner life of its own, and the more we give it a life outside of our current actions, the *less* the psyche is stimulated, and the more difficult it is for us to feel or to express feeling. Ironically, our concern with emotions, in particular anxiety about our happiness, can be a trap as likely as being a liberation. Sennett goes on to suggest that the value we place on individual experience, insofar as it leads to the measurement of all of social life in terms of personal feeling instead of deed, produces an inhibition to action and, thus, a propensity toward depression.

In a classic statement, Richard Sennett (1977, p. 9) writes, "The most common form in which narcissism makes itself known . . . is by a process of inversion," or, as Yi Fu Tuan (1982) implies, "we are prisoners of our own ineluctable subjectivity." But Sennett continues in his description of this perversion of self-consciousness:

> If only I could feel more, or if only I could really feel, then I could relate to others or have "real" relations with them. But at each moment of encounter, I never seem to feel enough [to make the encounter worthwhile]. The obvious content of this inversion is a self-accusation [low self-esteem], but buried beneath it is the feeling that the world is failing me. (p. 9, brackets added)

The important shift has taken place from belief in actions to belief in emotional states of being—a fruitless search, Sennett says, for an identity composed from within.

On Being Owed Happiness and Romantic Love

We would like to pause on Sennett's sensitivity to this idea, implied in the quote above, that life owes us things. Again, our culturally generated automatic thought patterns, as Aaron Beck (1967) would call them, encourage the unconscious assumption that this abstraction "life" has a sense of pity and justice that "it owes to us." At this point, we could benefit well from the lessons that the social historians offer. This is an age wherein, for the first time in human history, whole masses of people, not just select groups, have discovered the self and intimate emotions.[4] It is an age wherein more persons than ever before are engaged in a quest for happiness and, indeed, hold the deep-seated conviction that life owes them happiness. Many would add erotic love, the exhausting expectation of multiple orgasms and, more seriously, the ever-exciting intimacy of sharing our most secret, our most idiosyncratic thoughts with someone who can both understand and make us happy and, last but not least, turn us on sexually. When this does not happen, which for some strange reason it often does not, we need to remind ourselves that never before have such masses of people shared such lofty aims, indeed, not merely aims, but expectations (see Martin Seligman, 1988, on this point). Let us look briefly at the remarks of Denis de Rougemont (1983) on our contemporary notion of happiness as a subjective state-to-be-sought. Tricky, is it not, that our culture's very guidelines to life's meaning operate to keep such meaning at bay?

De Rougemont's description of happiness as a Eurydice, vanishing when gazed upon, should give pause for thought to a people who so frequently believe that life's meaning is in their private pursuit of happiness construed as a feeling state. If we increasingly seek a subjectivized state called "feeling good," divorced from everyday action, as our due, the inevitable conclusion that we have been sorely cheated will only escalate our already staggering rates of family and public discord, the latter because of our need for scapegoats, but even more so because of an intolerable isolation—a lack of capacity for the human bond that is a behavioral, transactional process (Scheff, 1990). In an increasingly subjectivized milieu it never occurs to us that our wider and more public social arrangements, especially those of politics and economics, may actively trade on these unrealistic expectations for their own gain and continued existence.

The generation of the 1970s listened to the lines of Peggy Lee's song "Is that all there is?" and thought, "Yeah, I have felt like that; we both need to see a shrink." More sociologically put, the problems generated by our social arrangements are typically described as individual problems—for the individuals to straighten out privately. Long ago, C. Wright Mill's (1959) suggested that social psychology had to do with a systematic linkage of private ills with their sources in social structure. More recently, Scheff (1990) has voiced what many others have also stressed, that macroconcepts such as capitalism, patriarchy, social differentiation, specialization, and stratification tend to become reified and empirically ungrounded unless we connect them point to point to the microlevel, intra- and interpersonal processes that support and maintain them.[5]

The linkage called for by Mills and Scheff is implicit in Gehlen's (1980) own critique of the crucial function of the value placed on "the pursuit of happiness" in industrial society. He sees the Enlightenment's belief in Reason as containing an inordinate readiness to plan as well as stressing the vindication of human happiness. The latter creates the individual's sense of a need to consume, which supplies the emotional underpinnings of industrialization. According to Gehlen, the industrial system has always acted to raise the living standards of the masses. Distinctively industrial products, from electricity to silk stockings, were at one point luxury items. Mass production enabled such items, once produced only for an elite, to become both perceived and objective necessities for whole societies.

Our most private restlessness, our most personal inability to be content with what we have in love, professional achievement, lifestyle, and material goods, is the emotional support, the *tax* paid in emotional currency, to our economic social arrangements.[6] We associate an enduring state of romantic, erotic love with the right to happiness and are then vulnerable to the mass media's hypnotic implication that it can be bought. People anxiously living without stable identities are led to believe that, with the paid help of professionals, they can find themselves by getting in touch with hidden emotions—emotions reified into something "there," independent of our consciousness and activities, to be discovered and, when discovered, "felt." We are told if we do not love ourselves, by purchasing the right perfumes, for example, no one else could possibly do so. Self-esteem has literally been put up as a moral obligation and then put on sale. Our inevitable dissatisfaction and high expectations make us restless and reliable purchasers.

Never before has personal happiness been so prevalent as an overriding goal of life—a goal sought in intimate relationships, albeit noncommittal ones, wherein personal prerogative is paramount (Swidler, 1980). Yet, we may expect more from intimate partnerships and the self-conscious search for emotional experiences than these pursuits can reliable give. Maybe the very pursuit of them risks "relative deprivation" and a restless inability to be satisfied. After all, from a historical viewpoint, we have only recently launched ourselves on a road that most literate people are convinced is the only one ever taken and the only one worth taking now. Yet the fact is that the quest for—and even the expectation of—happiness through romantic love and the intimate and personal has never before been available to the public on such a mass scale.[7]

As a species, we are not practiced at such individualized intimacy, regardless of how much we desire it. However, we have proceeded blithely unaware that our path is untried, that it may harbor unrealistic aspirations. It is difficult for us, caught in our cultural assumptions, to dispassionately assess the strengths and pitfalls of such novel life-expectations and forms of relationships. "The already discussed willingness to exhibit to others one's most intimate concerns . . . can be placed in relation to some distinctive features of our time: in particular to our overreflectiveness to the habitual self-consciousness of our inner existence" (Gehlen, 1980, p. 78).

Conclusions

We have waited to the end to come back to the suggestion that the "pursuit of happiness" can productively be understood as ideology. Traditionally, ideology, like personal rationalization, is seen as primarily cognitive in nature. However, the emotional quality of ideology needs recognition as well; it is absolutely essential to its functioning. How else do we make sense out of the numerous ironies in the changing meanings of "the pursuit of happiness" as a root symbol in Western history? A child of the Enlightenment and the Age of Reason, the history of its semantic promiscuity is totally antithetical to the demand for logical consistency that was so highly regarded by its early proponents. We have suggested the hypothesis that "the pursuit of happiness" as a phrase was more an enabler, motivator, or counterpoint for human discourse and action than it was an end-product of rational thought. The special capacity for shared emotion to bind people together has often been observed. Scheff (1990) discusses the notion of emotional attunement as the "mechanism" that enables people to interpret the ambiguities inherent in any human discourse and to share meanings. Certainly the strivings of the nonelite for privileges once exclusively owned by the Western monarchies would produce an emotional solidarity that moved and compelled collective action as only emotion can do. We do not mean to imply an overdrawn distinction between emotion and cognition at this point. Both are seen as drawing on each other and overlapping. This does not mean that they cannot be in tension. After presenting a physiological argument for just this interconnected view of emotion, de Sousa (1987) offers his hypothesis that emotion sets the *agenda* for thought, beliefs, and desires. Emotions, he suggests, are what we see the world in terms of; they are often described as guiding the processes of reasoning or distorting them, depending on the describer's assessment of their appropriateness. Thus, their existence grounds the very possibility of rationality. This is what we mean by suggesting that historically "the pursuit of happiness" seen as rhetoric, functioned emotionally—as a shared rallying point for political deliberation.

This chapter has identified several misconceptions implicit in "the pursuit of happiness" as the phrase is commonly used today: Happiness is often stripped of intentionality and subjectivized as a self-contained (nonintentional) sensation springing from within. For many, it not only defines their goal in life but it is their right to possess and ensure it. We have suggested that the creation and maintenance of personally meaningful pursuits is more realistic as a sine qua non of life than the securing of happiness construed as a more or less steady state. We have attempted to argue that motional states cannot be attained by bypassing the actions that produce them. In the preface to Frankl's (1992) influential book *Man's Search for Meaning*, he admonishes us:

> Don't aim at success—the more you aim at it and make it a target, the more you are going to miss it. For success, like happiness, cannot be pursued; it must ensue, and it only does so as the unintended side effect of one's personal dedication. . . . Happiness must happen . . . you have to let it happen by not caring about it. (p. 12)

Writers have, and will, disagree (Argyle, 1987). Certainly, the authors of this chapter are not uninterested in their happiness vaguely conceived. But we are misled when we subjectivize "the pursuit of happiness" as was not the case historically. It functioned emotionally to unite a middle class in its struggle for privileges deemed only appropriate to the reigning elite. It meant, in the vague but powerful medium of emotionality, an unquestionable right to what the royalty held for its exclusive possession. Stripped of this historical context and applied today as a goal of therapy, or an expectation of a relationship, or even of life itself, it is a most questionable post to hang our psychological hats.

Notes

1. The general term *emotion* (a derivative of the French *emouvoir*, to stir, move out, or to want something) did not appear in the *Oxford English Dictionary* until the end of the sixteenth century (Crespo, 1986). This does not imply that persons had fewer emotional experiences, but only that it took this long to place them in their own discrete thought category and for people to see this as intelligible and useful. Likewise, in medieval times, linguistically available concepts provided only hazy notions of self.

2. Even the psyche and the objectivization of mind in Greek thought was valued more because of its capacity for the shared, intersubjective, impersonal rules of logic rather than because of its relationship to unique differences of particular personalities.

3. See Elias (1982) concerning the current tendency to reify the boundaries of the self and the resulting unsociological view of the person as a self-sufficient, hidden entity, "encapsulated" from other people and nature.

4. As Coles observed (cited in Bellah, Madsen, Sullivan, Swidler, & Tipton, 1985), increasing numbers of people are now considering the self as "the only or main form of reality" (p. 143). Never before have so *many* people been so conscious of, and indeed, preoccupied with, the emotional quality of their inner states.

5. Macro concepts ungrounded in micro processes reify the status quo in so far as they "invoke a set of causal agents, the social norms that make up the normative structure, which have not been defined independently of the behavior they are said to explain" (Scheff, 1990, p. 64).

6. This phrase is attributed by Hochschild (1984) to Harvey Farberman in a personal conversation.

7. As implied in much of this chapter, humans can understand their relationships to each other in any number of ways. For most of our species' time we have lived in small bands with no or minimum privacy. However, this does not imply what we currently mean by

intimacy. Here one's most unique, private, and personal thoughts are shared. The value we place on the personal and private is rather recent. There is a whole section of social history devoted to the emergence of privacy (see Duby, 1988).

References

Allport, G. W. (1955). *Becoming: Basic considerations for a psychology of personality*. New Haven: Yale University Press.

Argyle, M. (1987). *The psychology of happiness*. London: Methuen.

Aristotle. (trans. 1947). *Nicomachean ethics* (W. D. Ross, Trans.). In R. McKeon (Ed.), *Introduction to Aristotle* (pp. 617–629). New York: Modern Library.

Averill, J. R. (1993). Happiness. In M. Lewis and J. M. Javiland (Eds.), *Handbook of emotions*. New York: Guilford Press.

Bandura, A. (1977). Self-efficacy: Toward a unifying theory of behavioral change. *Psychological Review, 84*, 191–215.

Baumeister, R. F. (1986). *Identity*. New York: Oxford University Press.

Beck, A. T. (1967). *Depression: Clinical, experimental, and theoretical aspects*. New York: Hoeber.

Becker, E. (1964). *The revolution in psychiatry: The new understanding of man*. New York: Free Press.

Bellah, R. N., Madsen, R., Sullivan, W. M., Swidler, A., & Tipton, S. M. (1985). *Habits of the heart: Individualism and commitment in American life*. Berkeley: University of California Press.

Berger, P., Berger, B., & Kellner, H. (1973). *The homeless mind: Modernization and consciousness*. New York: Random House.

Bruner, J. S. (1966). *Toward a theory of instruction*. New York: Norton.

Coulter, J. (1979). *The social construction of mind*. Totowa, NJ: Rowman & Littlefield.

Crespo, E. (1986). A regional variation: Emotions in Spain. In R. Harré, (Ed.), *The social construction of emotions* (pp. 209–217). New York: Blackwell.

de Rougemont, D. (1983). *Love in the western world* (M. Belgion, Trans.). Princeton, NJ: Princeton University Press.

de Sousa, R. (1987). *The rationality of emotions*. Boston: MIT Press.

Dewey, J. (1950). *Human nature and conduct*. New York: Modern Library.

Duby, G. (Ed.). (1988). *A history of private life*. Cambridge, MA: Belknap–Harvard University Press.

Elias, N. (1982). *The civilizing process: Vol. 1. Manners*. New York: Pantheon.

Frankl, V. (1992). *Man's search for meaning: An introduction to logotherapy* (4th ed.). Boston: Beacon Press.

Franks, D., & Marolla, J. (1976). Efficacious action and social approval as interacting dimensions of self-esteem: A tentative formulation through construct validation. *Sociometry, 39*, 324–341.

Fromm, E. (1989). *Marx's concept of man: With a translation and philosophical manuscripts* (with an afterword by E. Fromm). New York: Continuum.

Gecas, V. (1971). Parental behavior and dimensions of adolescent self-evaluation. *Sociometry, 34*, 466–482.

Geertz, C. (1974). From the native's point of view. *American Academy of Arts and Sciences Bulletin, 28*, 26–45.

Gehlen, A. (1980). *Man in the age of technology* (P. Lipscomb, Trans.). New York: Columbia University Press.

Harré, R. (Ed). (1986). *The social construction of emotions*. Oxford: Blackwell.

Hochschild, A. (1983). *The managed heart*. Berkeley: University of California Press.

Husserl, E. (1970). *The crisis of European sciences and transcendental phenomenology: An introduction to phenomenological philosophy*. Evanston, IL: Northwestern University Press.

Jones, H. M. (1953). *The pursuit of happiness*. Cambridge, MA: Harvard University Press.

Lasch, C. (1978). *The culture of narcissism: American life in an age of diminishing expectations*. New York: Norton.

Lepenies, W. (1992). *Melancholy and society*. (J. Gaines & D. Jones, Trans.). Cambridge, MA: Harvard University Press.

Lewis, J. (1983). *The pursuit of happiness: Family and values in Jefferson's Virginia*. Cambridge: Cambridge University Press.

Lutz, C. A., & White, G. M. (1986). The anthropology of emotions. *Annual Review of Anthropology, 15*, 403–406.

Mead, G. H. (1938). *The philosophy of the act*. Chicago: University of Chicago Press.

Mills, C. W. (1959). *The sociological imagination*. Oxford: Oxford University Press.

Morris, C. (1972). *The discovery of the individual: 1050–1200*. New York: Harper & Row.

Rieff, P. (1966). *The triumph of the therapeutic: Uses of faith after Freud*. New York: Harper & Row.

Rosaldo, M. Z. (1984). Toward an anthropology of self and feeling. In R. A. Shweder & R. A. LeVine (Eds), *Culture theory: Essays on mind, self, and emotion* (pp. 137–157). New York: Cambridge University Press.

Ryff, C. D. (1989). Happiness is everything, or is it? Explorations on the meaning of psychological well-being. *Journal of Personality and Social Psychology, 57*, 1069–1081.

Sampson, E. E. (1981). Cognitive psychology as ideology. *American Psychologist, 36*, 730–743.

Sarbin, T. R. (1986). Emotions and act: Roles and rhetoric. In R. Harré (Ed.), *The social construction of emotions* (pp. 83–97). New York: Blackwell.

Scheff, T. J. (1990). *Microsociology: Discourse, emotion and social structure*. Chicago: University of Chicago Press.

Seligman, M. (1988). Me decades generate depression. *The APA Monitor, 19*(10), 18.

Sennett, R. (1977). *The fall of public man: On the social psychology of capitalism*. New York: Vintage Books.

Smith, M. B. (1968). Competence and socialization. In J. A. Clausen (Ed.), *Socialization and society*. (pp. 271–320) Boston: Little, Brown.

Swidler, A. (1980). Love and adulthood in American culture. In N. Smelser and E. Erikson (Eds) *Themes of work and love in adulthood* (pp. 120–47). Cambridge, Massachusetts: Harvard University Press.

Tuan, Y. F. (1982). *Segmented worlds and self*. Minneapolis: University of Minnesota Press.

Weintraub, K. J. (1978). *The value of the individual: Self and circumstance in autobiography*. Chicago: University of Chicago Press.

Westen, D. (1985). *Self and society: Narcissism, collectivism, and the development of morals*. Cambridge: Cambridge University Press.

White, R. W. (1959). Motivation reconsidered: The concept of competence. *Psychological Review, 66*, 297–333.

White, R. W. (1963). Ego and reality in psychoanalytic theory. *Psychological Issues*. International Universities Press.

Wood, M. R., & Zurcher, L. A. Jr. (1988). *The development of a postmodern self: A computer assisted comparative analysis of personal documents* (Contributions in Sociology, No. 70). New York: Greenwood Press.

11

Jerome Neu

Boring from Within

Endogenous Versus Reactive Boredom

> Life, friends, is boring. We must not say so.
> After all, the sky flashes, the great sea yearns,
> we ourselves flash and yearn,
> and moreover my mother told me as a boy
> (repeatingly) 'Ever to confess you're bored
> means you have no
>
> Inner Resources.' I conclude now I have no
> inner resources, because I am heavy bored.
> Peoples bore me,
> literature bores me, especially great literature . . .
>
> (John Berryman, 1969,"Dream Song 14")

Was Berryman's mother right? Is all boredom from within? The question is in fact ambiguous. Whether or not there should always be an internal cure for boredom, there is a separate question of whether the source of boredom is itself always internal (and yet a further question of whether self-generated emotions should be regarded as pathological by virtue of their source). Mrs. Berryman may have been more concerned with cure than source. Causal treatments, treatments that get at the root of a problem, must depend on the nature of the problem, in particular its source, but symptomatic treatments come from wherever they come from and work whenever they work. The two questions are, however, surely related, for the effectiveness of inner resources in overcoming a problem may depend on just what it is that needs to be overcome. Does the world or the person, life or attitude, need to change in order to overcome boredom? Is all boredom from within?

First, what is boredom? Saul Bellow (1975), in his novel *Humboldt's Gift*, has a character begin a series of reflections on boredom pleased at having in the past stayed away from problems of definition: "I didn't want to get mixed up with theological questions about *accidie* and *tedium vitae*." But it isn't long before we find the same character saying: "Suppose then that you began with the proposition that boredom was a kind of pain caused by unused powers, the pain of wasted possibilities or talents, and was accompanied by expectations of the optimum utilization of capacities." That is not at all bad as a start. In fact, the notion of "a kind of pain caused by unused powers" is quite close to psychoanalytic definitions (Fenichel, 1934/1953; Greenson, 1953) of boredom as a state of instinctual tension in which the instinctual aims and objects are repressed. Such an approach can be illuminating.

Greenson (1953) is especially helpful on the feeling of emptiness characteristic of much boredom. One experiences

> a combination of instinctual tension and a vague feeling of emptiness. The instinctual tension is without direction due to the inhibition of thoughts and fantasies. Tension and emptiness is felt as a kind of hunger—stimulus hunger. Since the individual does not know for what he is hungry, he now turns to the external world, with the hope that it will provide the missing aim and/or object. (pp. 19–20)

With the aim and object of desire repressed, only a feeling of emptiness remains; as Greenson penetratingly puts it, "we are dealing here with the substitution of a sensation for a fantasy" (p. 16). He describes a woman patient suffering from extreme boredom, unable to find or even imagine objects worth having: "Even in masturbation the patient would get bored because she had 'nothing to think about'" (p. 11).

While an absence of fantasies is a useful way of thinking about boredom, it is no use to think one can overcome boredom simply by conjuring up fantasies and desires. The frantic pursuit of excitement is generally unsatisfying. Greenson speaks of having the "wrong" fantasies (p. 19). What this means is that satisfaction requires that desires be attached to their "true" objects. To make sense of this notion one must have, I think, a theory of human needs. (This is not a criticism. Psychoanalysis seeks to provide such a theory.) But imagination faces another obstacle, for it can play a double role in relation to boredom. On the one hand, it is one of those inner resources that may free one from or at least alleviate boredom, offering if not the "true" objects of desire at least alternatives to distract one's attention from present unappealing objects. On the other hand, imagination can also sometimes serve as a source of boredom when it brings one to see what one is doing at the moment or in one's life as a whole as but one of a number of alternatives, and an alternative less desirable or interesting than the others. One way of thinking of women's liberation (of the consciousness-raising kind) is as offering the enlightenment of boredom: getting women to see activities that they might have accepted as inevitable as really just imposed social roles that are in fact far less interesting than the alternative roles that have been made socially unavailable. The politically touchy issue is whether those who would bring enlightenment about the range of possibilities also mean to insist that women *should* feel bored or otherwise unfulfilled if they go on to choose as a matter of preference the activities and roles that had previously been simply imposed upon them. This too requires a theory of real human needs.

Returning to the main theme, the notion of repressed objects is additionally useful because it suggests a ready way to distinguish boredom from apathy or depression: If boredom can be thought of as centrally involving desire without an object, then depression can be understood as centrally involving an absence of desire. In boredom, one wants to do something, but doesn't know what. In depression, one feels will-less.

Still, the psychoanalytic understanding of boredom in terms of instinctual tension and repressed objects, despite its many advantages, is insufficiently specific, for all neuroses involve such repression, and it is so far left unclear why every neurotic is not bored. Without searching for further refinement, however, the contrast with depression mentioned a moment ago brings to mind a similarity between boredom and depression that in turn suggests another kind of limitation of the original definition. Depression is standardly distinguished into two types, depending on its believed sources. There is *endogenous depression* ("sadness without cause," Jackson, 1986, pp. 315–317), which arises somehow from within and comes to color the external world, and there is *reactive depression*, which begins as a response to particular events in the external world, such as the loss of a loved one. Similarly, there is boredom from within, which tends to color the whole of life, and there is reactive boredom, which seems to arise as a response to more particular objects.

The psychoanalytic approach tends to ignore reactive boredom. Consider Greenson's (1953) account. Defining *boredom* as "instinctual tension . . . without direction due to the inhibition of thoughts and fantasies" (p. 19), and believing this state of affairs "characteristic for all boredom" (p. 20), Greenson goes on to treat any attempt to place the source of boredom in the external world as a defensive maneuver, as denial.

> Another aspect of the denial can be seen in the readiness of bored persons to describe situations and people as boring rather than to acknowledge that the bored feeling is within. "It bores me," is more ego syntonic than "I am bored." When one is bored even the most exciting events can be felt as boring. (p. 17)

This fits well with Berryman's mother's diagnosis.

Denial doubtless occurs. And the more widespread the individual's claim that external things are boring, the more plausible the suggestion that the failure is internal. But surely sometimes things *are* boring and being bored is an appropriate reaction. The philosopher Bernard Williams (1973) puts this most strongly: "Just as being bored can be a sign of not noticing, understanding or appreciating enough, so equally not being bored can be a sign of not noticing, or not reflecting, enough" (p. 95). Williams's remark comes in the course of an argument that certain forms of repetition carried on long enough are necessarily boring. That argument may be in a variety of ways problematical, but surely a person watching Andy Warhol's movie *Sleep* who fails to be bored simply isn't paying attention. (For those unfamiliar with it, that 1963 movie consists of eight interminable hours of a fixed shot of a man sleeping. *Empire*, a 1965 Warhol film, offers a similarly endless shot of the Empire State Building.) Some things, one wants to say, are objectively boring.

"It Bores Me"

How is one to determine in a particular case whether an individual's boredom is reactive or endogenous? Obviously, whether boredom is regarded as reactive or endogenous depends on whether a feature of the object or of the person is thought to explain the state. But doesn't a reaction of boredom *always* depend on the particular person? Was John Berryman's mother perhaps right? Is all boredom from within, a sign of lack of inner resources? For it might be true that whatever the external circumstances, an appropriate shifting of attention or marshaling of internal interests should save one from boredom. But the fact that one might in certain circumstances *need* to be saved itself suggests that boredom can have an external source (even if an internal cure should always be available). What sort of features of an object are liable to cause boredom, and can they be regarded as "objective" rather than dependent on the individual's attitude (so once again blurring the line between reactive and endogenous boredom)?

Sometimes too little happens in too much time.[1] (The German word for boredom is *Langeweile*, literally "long while" — as frequently observed, time passes slowly when it is not filled with gripping events.) That is the problem with the proverbial "watching the grass grow" or the Warhol movies mentioned. The mind is given too little material to work on or to react to. Of course, diverting attention is one way to avoid boredom when the would-be object of attention is, as one might put it, "objectively boring," but the problem in the object is not thereby diminished. We are in the presence of Bellow's "pain caused by unused powers," and the problem here has an external source.

Certainly repetition can be boring. Kierkegaard wrote a rather boring book with that title (*Repetition*, 1843), and his lighthearted discussion of "The Rotation Method" in *Either/Or* (1843), which asserts that "boredom is the root of all evil" (indeed, of everything, for "the gods were bored, and so they created man," p. 282), finds the cure in change (of a special sort: limited and so inventive and intense — one must not forget that empty stimulation and novelty can be boring too; that was the problem of Greenson's patient with the tiresome affairs and the "wrong" fantasies). But repetition itself need not be bad. Nietzsche (1882/1974) reminds us of the possibility of a hopeful, even accepting and joyous response to that metaphysical extreme of repetition, eternal recurrence (§341); though Nietzsche's point, it must be admitted, has to do with the moral weight of the idea of recurrence, not the *experience* of repetition (indeed, each recurrence, being just the same as the others, bears no marks of being a recurrence).[2]

Children often find repetition desirable. They often want stories endlessly repeated in exactly the same way. (Just as dogs seem willing to go on fetching sticks long after the game has lost interest for the person playing it with them.) This is a point not overlooked by Freud in his consideration of the repetition compulsion in *Beyond the Pleasure Principle* (1920), where he notes that adults, by contrast, crave novelty (p. 35). But Freud's main concern is the repetition compulsion in relation to the death instinct, the repetition of painful experiences. It is not so puzzling that children should want to have their pleasurable experiences repeated (though that "they are inexorable in their insistence that the repetition shall be an identical one" may suggest that even such repetition can be seen as a defense against anxiety, an effort at mastery, an assertion of a kind of control); it is more difficult to understand why we keep putting our tongues into the cavities in our teeth to test whether they still hurt, when we know they will. But leaving compulsions aside, even adults can find repetition desirable in the appropriate circumstances. What circumstances? What makes for meaningful repetition rather than monotonous dullness?

We have all heard boring lectures (perhaps even given some), and even if we have not seen Warhol's *Sleep*, we have all seen boring movies or read boring books. But monotony is not by itself sufficient to explain the boredom, or monotony should always lead to boredom. But it doesn't. Repetitious prayers are meaningful for many. Chanting and meditation can produce ecstasy. (Perhaps even less patterned forms of "too little happening in too much time" can be experienced as freeing the mind from distractions and so as an aid to inner peace.) And endurance athletes seem able to engage in marathon runs or long-distance swims without getting bored. Or should we rather say that they tolerate the boredom for the sake of some further end? (When some athletes say, however, that they value a daily dose of "boredom," they may actually mean something else — perhaps what they value is "tranquility" or "absence of stimulation." It may be that "boredom" as such is necessarily painful and undesirable. But then there may be more varieties of masochism than found in the usual catalogs.) And monotony may in any case not be "objective" — it may itself lie in the eye of the beholder. Certainly variety can be experienced as monotonous, "always the same," at least by those (like the Italian poet Leopardi) so disposed.

Whether repetition, even monotonous repetition, produces boredom may be relative to one's interests. A person sufficiently interested in the content of an otherwise boring lecture may be able to focus on the content rather than its pace or the monotone in which it is delivered. Or a shift of attention may do the trick, as in Kierkegaard's (1843/1959) example of the philosophical bore with fascinating habits of perspiration while talking:

> There was a man whose chatter certain circumstances made it necessary for me to listen to. At every opportunity he was ready with a little philosophical lecture, a very tiresome harangue. Almost in despair, I suddenly discovered that he perspired copiously when talking. I saw the pearls of sweat gather on his brow, unite to form a stream, glide down his nose, and hang at the extreme point of his nose in a drop-shaped body. From the moment of making this discovery, all was changed. I even took pleasure in inciting him to begin his philosophical instruction, merely to observe the perspiration on his brow and at the end of his nose. (p. 295)

But then, can one shift interests at will? Can one choose or create "arbitrary" interests? This is not quite the same as shifting attention at will. (We are getting closer to the nature of the inner resources Mrs. Berryman wished to call upon — resources of attention, self-motivation, imagination, and perhaps tranquillity.)

Even supposing one could shift interests at will (certainly one can at least cultivate them over time), how much could one change and still be the "same" person? This is a concern of Bernard Williams in his discussion of the Makropulos case, which centers on the story of a woman in a Capek play who had lived 300 years (at the constant age of 42) and ultimately decides to end her own otherwise eternal life because immortality leaves her bored, indifferent, and cold: "In the end it is the same, singing and silence" (Williams, 1973, p. 82). Williams wishes to argue that immortal life would necessarily be boring, basically because (in terms of the immediate case) "everything that could happen and make sense to one particular human being of 42 had already happened to her" (p. 90). He assumes a relatively fixed character, and the assumption has a certain point. That one will be able to see more baseball games is not a reason for a person who hates baseball to live longer, and it is not entirely clear from what point of view an assurance that one would come to like baseball ought to be judged. Nonetheless, repetition is not necessarily always objectionable. People seem to enjoy having sex over and over again, even in the same way with the same person. And character can (and does) develop without the changes destroying an identity of concern. But without pressing issues of variation of character and stability of identity, are there objective goods that can motivate a desire to go on living (because they become the object of what Williams calls "unconditional" or "categorical" desires, that is, desires one has that are not dependent on the question of whether one will be alive)? To be objective, must they be universal? Are some things objectively good, objectively desirable in a way that makes life (interestingly, joyfully, or merely dutifully) worth living? And again, are some things objectively bad in a way that makes them intolerably boring, killing any interest in them if not in life?

Certainly it is a fact that different people react differently to the same external objects. But must a reaction to an object be universal in order to say the object causes it? After all, not everyone exposed to the tubercle bacillus falls ill. One's immune system doubtless plays a role in determining the result. Nonetheless, we can safely say the tubercle bacillus "causes" tuberculosis. And objects have colors even if some don't see them — which is not to deny that what colors one sees depends on one's individual apparatus for perception. Finally, and most relevantly, we can make sense of reactive depression though it also depends on internal (one could call them "subjective") factors, such as love for a person who has died or perhaps initial low self-esteem. We always pick out "the" cause from a multiplicity of causal factors, our explanatory or other concerns providing the grounds for picking out one from among the many necessary conditions as crucial. That something is boring may be a feature of it, a feature that explains, and is revealed by, its producing boredom in us.[3] Boredom provides one of our categories for evaluating experience — as does, perhaps more familiarly in philosophical discussions, "goodness." Insistence on a contrast between "objective" and "subjective" features may not ultimately be helpful in understanding the difference between reactive and endogenous boredom. (And we may in the end have to say something similar about the contrast between "particular" and "general" objects, the difference between being bored by something in particular and, like the grown-up John Berryman, finding life boring.)

The Good, the Bad, the Boring

The history of the philosophical understanding of the word "good" is instructive. "Good" is perhaps our most general and indeterminate term of evaluation, for things, experiences, actions, and even persons taken as a whole. Plato and many others have treated it as an almost perceptible quality of the objects evaluated. Plato understood that quality (in accordance with his general theory of meaning and value) in terms of an objective standard to be found in a supersensible Idea or Form of Goodness in which particular things in the observable world could be seen to "participate" (in different degrees). Leaving behind supersensible worlds, G. E. Moore (1903) early in this century treated "goodness" as a directly recognizable but simple and so indefinable property, like yellow. Another philosophical tradition has treated the application of the word good as an expression of individual and highly variable emotional responses. Spinoza (1677/1985) argued that to call something "good" was to record the fact that one found it pleasant, and that to call something bad was to say one found it unpleasant or painful ("insofar as we perceive that a thing affects us with Joy or Sadness, we call it good or evil," IV p. 8). Also in this line, in this century, A. J. Ayer (1936) and other so-called "emotivists" insisted that to call something good is little more than to say "I like it," a way of expressing one's (ethical) feelings and perhaps arousing similar feelings in others. In neither of these sorts of objectivist or subjectivist accounts of goodness are there definitive criteria of goodness, though there may be empirical concomitants of the characteristic, and proof or argument about value (about ends) becomes mysterious. Here as elsewhere the simply contrasting categories of objective and subjective may obscure more than illuminate. Perhaps the most plausible understanding of the meaning of "good," at least as it functions in moral argument and deliberation, can be found by going back to Aristotle. As Stuart Hampshire (1967) has summarized it, "when we praise, and reflectively criticize, things of various kinds, the more or less vague criteria of our judgment are ultimately derived from the normal, or standard, interests that things of this kind have for us" (p. 82). The relevant criteria depend on the particular kind of thing evaluated and the interests such things are designed, or meant, or taken to serve. So one may or may not be interested in clocks, but to call a clock "good" is to say it serves the function of a clock (i.e., it tells time) well. Normal human interests help provide the relevant criteria. Of course, we can also reflectively evaluate human interests and try to set some order or priority among them—and the criteria for this are neither fixable a priori nor even necessarily consistent with each other (all good things may not be compatible). This does not reduce such evaluations to reiterations of present interests, purposes, and pleasures, nor does it leave them to rest in intuitive insight into the value of things. We can and do argue intelligently about how to live and what matters.

Boredom also has a history.[4] The first citations of *boredom* and *boring* in the *Oxford English Dictionary* are surprisingly late, from the mid-nineteenth century; *bore*, in the relevant sense, does not appear till the mid-eighteenth century, and then it is first defined as "The malady of *ennui*, supposed to be specifically 'French', as 'the spleen' was supposed to be English; a fit of ennui or sulks; a dull time." In fact, one could argue boredom was invented by the French in the nineteenth century, at least in that special form of weariness known even in English as "ennui." (Perhaps Rousseau having almost single-handedly invented sincerity in the eighteenth century, it was only to be expected. Baudelaire, Stendhal, Flaubert et al. were Rousseau's children.) Certainly weariness, melancholy, spleen, dullness, apathy, listlessness, tedium, and the like have always had a place in human life, but the specific forms of detachment and sadness, the nature and understanding of that which holds or rivets attention and that which deadens passion and desire are culturally shaped and expressed (different languages even provide distinctive vocabularies, including *taedium vitae*, *Weltschmerz*, and *mal du siècle* to describe the related, but different, conditions). *Acedia, the* special form of psychic exhaustion, sloth, and spiritual dejection suffered by medieval monks, had its character and place because of a constellation of beliefs and a set of associated social structures (Wenzel, 1960). The aristocratic ennui of the French authors who have made their desolate and alienated mood a part of modern consciousness depends on a rather different set of circumstances and attitudes. Their "laments and loud yawns" (Peyre, 1974, p. 29) may have emerged partly in response to the disappointments of the revolutions of 1848 in Europe and partly in response to the ever increasing embourgeoisement of society, but whatever the explanation, their despair and gloom is now often ours. Their writing has given us a way of conceiving and so experiencing disappointing lives in a disappointing world. Some would equate the Romantic and post-Romantic concept of *ennui* with the *acedia* of the early Christian ascetics, and certainly there are similarities (Kuhn, 1976, pp. 42, 53, 55), but the modern sensibility remains in some ways distinctive. Not the least of the differences between the religious torpor of the heart and modern estrangement is to be found in the sufferer's self-understanding. While both cases may seem to an observer to be independent of external circumstances, and in that sense endogenous, the religious sufferer thinks of himself as in a state of sin: His dejection, loss of interest and joy, his sluggishness are thought of as personal faults. The sophisticated sufferer from ennui tends to think of his anguish, of the fog that descends between desire and life, as the fault of the world, especially of the established order. If the world is felt to have lost meaning, the inner emptiness is experienced as a response to a failure in the world. It does not come up to expectations. Whether the resultant state should be regarded as reactive or endogenous may thus depend on what one thinks we have a right to expect.

And so may whether the state should be regarded as pathological. Suppose one lived in a drab, gray society, say of the kind that typified Stalinist Eastern Europe not so long ago. Might not endemic boredom be the natural reaction? Societal change seems a more appropriate (and effective) remedy than individual therapy. Nonetheless, falling into desiring nothing, expecting nothing, can be a self-defeating reaction in the end indistinguishable from a self-generated despair. Of course modern boredom does not take the form only of "ennui." The mechanization of production came tied to a mechanization of life, and so made problematic the point of repetitious human activity. Why do anything more than once? But the industrial worker, Charlie Chaplin's man-as-cog in the film *Modern Times*, does not suffer from "ennui," which requires sophistication and world-weariness.[5] And one should not make the mistake of thinking that even a less pervasive reactive boredom must always be a relatively benign and passing state. It can lead to or mask impotent rage (it may look like patient waiting), and that rage can burst out in explosive aggression or implode in suicidal despair. That the boredom is in a sense imposed by external circumstances and their constraints does not make the state any less devastating and destructive.

Still, the problem remains that it may be a mistake to think the standard of health can be simply assumed. The appropriateness of an attachment to life as opposed to an overwhelming feeling of nothingness or of the vanity of ordinary pursuits may be more a matter for metaphysical disputation than clinical resolution. (The doctors, of course, must not think this.)

Pathology and the Inner

Even psychoanalysts occasionally acknowledge that boredom can be "normal" or, as Fenichel (1934/1953) also puts it, "innocent":

It arises when we must not do what we want to do, or must do what we do not want to do. . . . In pathological boredom [something expected] fails to occur because the subject represses his instinctual action out of anxiety; in normal boredom it fails to occur because the nature of the real situation does not permit of the expected detension. . . . One should not forget that we have *the right to expect* some "aid to discharge" from the external world. If this is not forthcoming, we are, so to speak, justifiably bored. (p. 301)

The familiar boredom of young children (the plaintive "I'm bored, what should I do now?") is also not pathological even though it arguably comes from within. It is more like a pervasive mood than a response to anything in particular. (More mature ennui is also typically a mood rather than a reactive and transient emotion. Neither is simply a sensation. They have and give meaning to experience.) The child is waiting for desire to crystallize, and asks help from outside. "Experiencing a frustrating pause in his usually mobile attention and absorption, the bored child quickly becomes preoccupied by his lack of preoccupation" (Phillips, 1993, p. 69). Adam Phillips usefully suggests that for a child such frustration need not mark merely an incapacity, but an opportunity, an occasion for it to take its time to discover its real interests, part of a needed "period of hesitation" in order to become more self-assured. As he puts it, "the capacity to be bored can be a developmental achievement for the child" (p. 69).

When we grow up, we are supposed of course to know (more or less) what we want, but the world can frustrate us in our desires, and we may react to that frustration in a variety of ways, including boredom. How much we are entitled to expect of the world is of course disputable. If we expect too much, we may be condemned to ennui. (And if we expect too little, joy does not necessarily follow.) If we fail to become clear about what we want, like Greenson's patient, the restless feeding of our stimulus hunger will not overcome our boredom. If everything is boring, either because of excessive expectations or uncertain desires, our state might seem clearly pathological. Certainly it is painful (and so, on Spinoza's account, bad). What kind of pain? Bellow (1975) has suggested an answer: "a kind of pain caused by unused powers." *Pleasure is a form of attention; boredom is a failure of attention.* Whether the failure is caused by a feature of the object or situation or alternatively by some internal problem or attitude is what distinguishes between reactive and endogenous boredom. But what makes an attitude wrong or pathological, when is the problem the individual's and when is it the world's? What it means for the face of the world to smile on us cannot be determined by statistical inquiry; the metaphysics of individual happiness and meaningfulness is more complex than that. So, once again the quest for an understanding of boredom makes one feel the need for a larger theory of human nature, an understanding of the cycles of desire and fulfillment, of pleasure and attention.

Freud (1915/1917) in "Mourning and Melancholia" remarks "that, although mourning involves grave departures from the normal attitude to life, it never occurs to us to regard it as a pathological condition and to refer it to medical treatment. . . . It is really only because we know so well how to explain it that this attitude does not seem to us pathological" (pp. 243–244). Where the object of someone else's boredom seems to us too without interest, whether because of monotony or other features, we accept the reaction as normal. Where the object of the boredom is everything, we must wonder about the source of the attitude. But however painful the situation, it is not clear that we can choose to have or not have such attitudes, or how one is to judge their correctness. Freud (1915/1917) states, "In mourning it is the world that has become poor and empty; in melancholia it is the ego itself" (p. 246). Adam Phillips (1993) interestingly remarks: "And in boredom, we might add, it is both" (p. 72). To find the world full of interest, there must be an interested, a desiring and alive, self. What is worth wanting? This is not simply a medical question.

For Spinoza the primary affects, out of which all others are constituted, are pleasure, pain, and desire (all to be understood in his special senses). For the unfortunate Leopardi, pleasure, pain, and boredom are the basic passions. Black despair, *noia*, is pervasive: "All the intervals of human life between pleasures and displeasures are occupied by ennui" (Leopardi quoted in Kuhn, 1976, p. 280).

To retrace some steps: It might seem that in order to distinguish between reactive and endogenous boredom, one needs a notion of the objectively boring, and that to be objective a characteristic must be uniform if not universal in its effects. But if we understand by "reactive" something like "adequately explained by features of the object," then there is no need for a reaction to be universal in order for it to be recognized as a *reaction*. Indeed, either a very uncultivated or a very sophisticated person might be bored by something almost everyone else would find interesting, and we might all nonetheless recognize the emotion as a response to features of the object—while of course also recognizing that the response also depends on special features of the bored person. The uncultivated and the sophisticated are both bored, one because he notices and understands too little, the other because he notices and understands too much. Still the response would be adequately explained by features of the object, *given* the nature of the person (whose interests, we are supposing, are at least statistically not "normal"). Things would become different if they found *everything* boring, so features of particular objects were irrelevant. That would begin to seem like an extreme form of endogenous boredom, boredom from within. But can't one have a reaction to everything? Things seem, say, "always the same." Must the individual's nature at least allow for a spectrum of responses before we are prepared to say any particular response is adequately to be explained by features of the object, and so any boredom that appears is reactive? I don't see that there is any clear line to be drawn. An individual living in a lively and multi-colored society might nonetheless find their life and their world drab and it is not obvious at what point we must say they are wrong, their perception distorted, and their boredom pathological. They are not getting what they want. What should they want?

What is interesting depends on what one desires. But then are desires simply given or are they criticizable and changeable? Certainly desires are modifiable and manipulable—much advertising is based on this fact. It aims to create and to shape desires. Desire can also be made to go away. People fight even addictions—there are a variety of conditioning and other techniques. The question is whether we can modify our own desires, not by self-alienated manipulation, but by reasoning about what is desirable and by the intelligent appreciation of experience. Education depends on that hope, as do self-education and self-development. Asking what is desirable (objectively?) and how we might come to desire it may be the best way to think about

Berryman's claim that "Life, friends, is boring," the best way to confront Baudelaire's "monstre délicat."

Freud (1912b) concludes a discussion of "endogenous" versus "exogenous" factors in the causation of neurosis with the observation that

> psycho-analysis has warned us that we must give up the unfruitful contrast between external and internal factors, between experience and constitution, and has taught us that we shall invariably find the cause of the onset of neurotic illness in a particular psychical situation which can be brought about in a variety of ways. (p. 238)

He makes a similar point about innate disposition and accidental influences (infantile impressions) in shaping love and the erotic life (1912a, p. 99n). The contrast of endogenous and exogenous may be equally false in the etiology of emotions in general. An understanding of pathology in the emotions cannot simply rely on internal causation as a criterion if it turns out that inner and outer factors are always in play. A different kind of theory is needed if the failure of attention in boredom, the "pain caused by unused powers," is not simply an issue of incapacity (whether attributed to lacking inner resources or an uninviting world, bad attitude or enforced inactivity) but a question of what is worthy of and what repays attention, a question of the "right" fantasies. Nonetheless, in cases of reactive boredom one typically does not know what one would rather be doing. (Objects of desire are not pathologically repressed.) And perhaps that is enough to mark the crucial difference in ordinary life.

Notes

1. The extreme here is described in the literature of solitary confinement and of sensory deprivation experiments, where boredom may be the least of a person's problems. An early experiment in a rigidly monotonous environment, with resulting hallucinations, is reported in Heron (1957).

2. I owe this point to Bernard Williams.

3. I think it useful to regard boredom itself as an emotion, a psychological state with a characteristic structure. However, I do not think it useful to try here to work through the distinctions among emotions, moods, sensations, and other types of psychological states in order to set precise boundaries to the concept of emotion—this partly because I don't think those boundaries are precise: Emotions are not natural kinds. We use emotion terms to interpret complexes of sensation, desire, behavior, and belief. I attach most importance to the cognitive element because I, like Spinoza, regard thought as the essential defining element in characterizing particular emotions and differentiating them one from another (Neu, 1977).

"Interest" appears on many contemporary psychologists' lists of basic emotions (Oatley, 1992, pp. 59, 61), even if "boredom" does not. "Boring" has many possible opposites, including interesting, meaningful, and perhaps even wonderful. Descartes (1649), strangely to modern eyes, treated "wonder" as the first of his six primitive passions in *The Passions of the Soul*. He there writes wonder "has no opposite, for, if the object before us has no characteristics that surprise us, we are not moved by it at all and we consider it without passion" (§53), but it seems clear that the novel and the unusual that provoke wonder (i.e., attentive intellectual interest, §70–71) on Descartes's account are meant to be incompatible with boredom. Spinoza gives wonder no such importance, not regarding it as a distinct affect at all (*Ethics* III, Definitions of the Affects IV).

4. Much of that history is tellingly explored through its literary expressions by Reinhard Kuhn (1976). That emotions can have a history is a revealing fact about them, and that they have the particular histories they do is a revealing fact about us. Patricia Meyer Spacks (1995), in a volume that appeared after this chapter was completed, also sees the vocabulary of boredom as reflecting and expressing historical shifts in sensibility and social categories.

5. Do animals suffer from boredom? How would we know if they did? What would a bored dog do that would show it was bored, and how might that be distinguished from impatience? We don't usually think of animals as suffering from directionless longing. We think of them as more simply driven by instinctual needs. Animals may lack the self-consciousness that is a necessary condition of "boredom from within." But consider a caged monkey. Clearly it is agitated—is it bored? It knows it is missing something. It may not be disenchanted, but it is desperate. Reactive boredom may make sense for animals, even if "boredom from within" has trouble getting a foothold. (How different is the monkey from humans fidgeting at a boring lecture?)

References

Ayer, A. J. (1936). *Language, truth and logic.* London: Gollancz.
Bellow, S. (1975, August 7). On boredom (from *Humboldt's Gift*). *The New York Review of Books,* 22.
Berryman, J. (1969). *The dream songs.* New York: Farrar, Straus & Giroux.
Descartes, R. (1985). *The passions of the soul* (R. Stoothoff, Trans.). In J. Cottingham, R. Stoothoff, & D. Murdoch (Eds.), *The philosophical writings of Descartes* (Vol. 1, pp. 325–404). Cambridge: Cambridge University Press. (Original work published 1649)
Fenichel, O. (1953). On the psychology of boredom. In H. Fenichel and D. Rapaport (Eds.), *The Collected Papers of Otto Fenichel* (1st Ser., pp. 292–302). New York: Norton. (Original work published 1934)
Freud, S. (1912a). The dynamics of transference. *Standard Edition, 12,* 98–108. London: Hogarth Press.
Freud, S. (1912b). Types of onset of neurosis. *Standard Edition, 12,* 229–238. London: Hogarth Press.
Freud, S. (1915/1917). Mourning and melancholia. *Standard Edition, 14,* 239–258. London: Hogarth Press.
Freud, S. (1920). *Beyond the pleasure principle. Standard Edition, 18,* 3–64. London: Hogarth Press.
Greenson, R. (1953). On boredom. *American Psychoanalytic Association Journal, 1,* 7–21.
Hampshire, S. (1967/1972). Ethics: A defense of Aristotle. In his *Freedom of mind and other essays* (pp. 64–86). New York; Oxford University Press.
Heron, W. (1957). The pathology of boredom. *Scientific American, 196,* 52–56.
Jackson, S. W. (1986). *Melancholia and depression: From Hippocratic times to modern times.* New Haven, CT: Yale University Press.
Kierkegaard, S. (1959). The rotation method. In D. F. and L. M. Swenson (Trans.), *Either/Or* (Vol. 1, pp. 279–296). Princeton, NJ: Princeton University Press. (Original work published 1843)
Kierkegaard, S. (1983). *Repetition.* H. V. and E. H. Hong (Trans.). Princeton, NJ: Princeton University Press. (Original work published 1843)
Kuhn, R. (1976). *The demon of noontide: Ennui in Western literature.* Princeton, NJ: Princeton University Press.
Moore, G. E. (1903). *Principia ethica.* Cambridge: Cambridge University Press.

Neu, J. (1977). *Emotion, thought, and therapy.* Berkeley: University of California Press.

Nietzsche, F. (1974). *The gay science.* (W. Kaufmann, Trans.). New York: Vintage Books. (Original work published 1882)

Oatley, K. (1992). *Best laid schemes: The psychology of emotions.* Cambridge: Cambridge University Press.

Peyre, H. (1974, Spring). Creative boredom and French literature. *Centerpoint, 24–32.*

Phillips, A. (1993). On being bored. In his *On kissing, tickling, and being bored* (pp. 68–78). Cambridge, MA: Harvard University Press.

Spacks, P. M. (1995). *Boredom: The literary history of a state of mind.* Chicago: University of Chicago Press.

Spinoza, B. (1985). *Ethics.* In. E. Curley (Trans.), *The collected works of Spinoza* (Vol. 1, pp. 401–617). Princeton, NJ: Princeton University Press. (Original work published 1677)

Wenzel, S. (1960). *The sin of sloth: Acedia in medieval thought and literature.* Chapel Hill, NC: The University of North Carolina Press.

Williams, B. (1973). The Makropulos case: Reflections on the tedium of immortality. In his *Problems of the Self* (pp. 82–100). Cambridge: Cambridge University Press.

12

George W. Brown & Patricia Moran

Emotion and the Etiology
of Depressive Disorders

We outline in this chapter an approach to the study of psychosocial factors in the development of depressive disorders that has informed a research program started in the early 1970s. We must confess at the outset that our approach has been characterized for the most part by highly indirect attempts to study emotion. This strategy has been driven largely by methodological concerns rather than any desire to downplay the crucial role of emotion in depression. Therefore, rather than discussing the nature of emotion per se, what follows is an account of a particular set of concepts and measures we have found important in understanding the development of depression.

Methodological Considerations

First, in a book dealing with the emotions, we need to account for our adoption of a highly indirect method of investigating emotion. One reason is clear enough. There is often an uncomfortably small amount of time between the emotional experience following an etiological agent, such as a severely threatening life event, and the onset of an episode of depression. Of course, clinical depression goes beyond the "emotions" of distress and sadness to involve "symptoms" such as anhedonia, retardation, sleep disturbance, and lack of concentration. In addition, there are often feelings of self-derogation and hopelessness or defeat, the very emotional experiences some see as playing an etiological role. It was difficult at the start of the research program to believe that we could deal convincingly with these latter responses given that the gap between event and onset was often only a matter of a few days and that information had to be collected retrospectively.

We have attempted to overcome this by focusing on event and disorder. It is easier to date events such as an accident to a child, learning of a lover's infidelity, or being told of a child's delinquency than to date the array of feelings and thoughts that are provoked by such events. However, we could not avoid the need to deal with the *meaning* of a particular event for an individual.

To overcome various possible methodological pitfalls, including those of dating just discussed, we have employed investigator-based ratings, unlike most research in this area. In the research interviews respondents talk at some length about issues that concern them, and on the basis of relevant material occurring at any point in the interview, ratings are made by the investigator. The interviewers in making their ratings ignore anything they have been told by respondents about their emotional reaction to the event. Thus, *likely* emotional response is distinguished from *actual* emotional response, and the former is relied on to model onset. Emotion, in other words, was imported through the back door. Why, it may be asked, should such an estimate of emotion be taken seriously?

A recent review concludes that emotions are mental states usually elicited by external events relevant for goals or concerns (Oatley & Jenkins, 1992). The emotions relate to changes in action readiness, and in this way also set goal priorities. They also function to insert and maintain in consciousness information about the events that caused them and about their possible consequences (Oatley, 1992). Consider the experience of a woman interviewed in a population survey who developed a depressive disorder. Her husband had been killed in an accident when her daughter was three. She remained unmarried and devoted much of her time to her daughter and to her job, which had become increasingly demanding. There had been several unexpected crises over a matter of a few weeks concerning her 12-year-old daughter's behavior; the final one was a letter saying that she has been playing truant and seriously misbehaving at school. She told us,

> I was very disappointed. I felt absolutely wretched because I felt helpless. I felt ashamed—it was all my fault. What will people think? I had a daughter who was not a nice daughter any more. People had always said "Oh, you're wonderful, making a home and bringing her up so well." I must admit I liked that flattery, and here I was in a situation where she wasn't a well-brought-up daughter. It wasn't a wonderful situation. I had absolutely nothing to be proud of any more. It had all been shattered.

She developed fears that her daughter would become involved in the drug scene and become pregnant; she blamed herself and felt responsible "because I'm her mother." She also felt guilty because of working late—"I blame myself because maybe I didn't react. . . . I didn't notice what was coming. It hit me a little bit hard." She tried many ways of getting closer to her daughter. Nothing worked, and she described her developing feelings of helplessness, believing that everything she did was wrong and nothing was working: "It came gradually, but once there it stuck." She developed a depressive disorder within 7 weeks of the first event (discovering her daughter stealing) and within a day or so of receiving the letter from the school.

Her immediate emotional response was not unusual. Strong emotions such as despair, anger, shame, and anxiety are typically experienced after such events. There is often compulsive rumination of a kind following "trauma" (Horowitz, 1976). Her thoughts "just kept coming back" with a need to talk about the incident and its implications. The possible impact on self-esteem can be seen in comments made by other women about their response to similar events: "I somehow despised myself for becoming dependent on one person," "I found it difficult to tolerate the thought that I could not sustain a relationship," "I'm beginning to think it must be me—things are always happening to me and I wonder what the next thing will be." Clear goal priorities emerged from the jumble of feelings and thoughts about her life: to regain her perception of her daughter as well brought up and prevent any deterioration in her behavior.

Words such as *concern*, *plan*, and *goal* (we use them interchangeably) suggest that what they represent is easily accessible. This is certainly too narrow a view. We agree with Epstein's (1991) emphasis on the importance of implicit beliefs and values in terms of preconscious material. They may at times only be brought to awareness, if at all, by some act of attention provoked by a relevant event. Many goals are in any case caught up in the perpetuation of an ongoing setting rather than something yet to be achieved (Solomon, 1991). A trouble-free relationship may lull a person into accepting its routines with little thought of his or her dependence on the other person, something that may be rudely conveyed by a life event.[1] Goals are therefore not always readily articulated. In the example just given the mother had been increasingly involved in a full-time job, working long hours and sometimes away from home. Although she had, in fact, conveyed in an earlier interview that she might not be seeing enough of her daughter, her thoughts were certainly not dominated by any need to keep her daughter "nice." It was the event in the following year that brought home to her the centrality of this for her sense of well-being. The London Life Events and Difficulty Schedule (LEDS; Brown & Harris, 1978) was designed around the need to deal with such implicit meanings and "hidden" goals.

The Measurement of Life Events and Difficulties

The first step in the development of the LEDS measure was to establish what should count as an event. An event is accepted if on common sense grounds it is likely to produce significant emotion of any kind. (An extensive training manual details thousands of anchoring examples.) The interviewer collects full information about each using a semistructured interview and a standard list of events.

A second set of procedures then takes place. Events are rated on a 4-point scale of "long-term threat," which concerns the *likely* impact of the event on relevant plans and purpose. This is carried out in a deliberately indirect manner using a contextual method of measurement that takes into account relevant aspects of a person's biography and current circumstances in order to rate the person's likely response to the event. It has the advantage of being viable in cross-sectional enquiries when respondents will have already experienced both the event in question and any onset. It makes it possible to bypass reporting bias arising from the respondents' emotional response to the event (Brown, 1989).

By way of illustration, consider the example of the mother we described earlier. Rather than attempting to utilize the kind of complex material she reported, an estimate was made of the likely goals and concerns a mother in her position would have regarding such a daughter. Such "contextual" estimates are based on a detailed description of behavior and circumstances, but excluding any account of a person's actual emotional response to the event. The approach provides an estimate of likely emotional response with enough accuracy to get useful research underway. It is important to emphasize the word *likely* since ratings are at best probabilistic.

Investigators other than the interviewer are used to make contextual ratings. In doing so the interviewer withholds certain kinds of information from them, in particular the respondents' reports of what they felt and whether depression followed the event. It follows that there is no need to question about silent plans and concerns since they are estimated by the raters. The holding back of material and the probabilistic nature of the ratings also allow various types of possible bias to be controlled (Brown & Harris, 1986).

The scientific cost of withholding any information about the emotional impact of the event is not as serious as it may at first appear. Even if possible, a totally accurate assessment of the impact of an event would not necessarily be useful. How, for example, would it be possible to assess the protective effect of social support if its effect was taken into account in rating the event? It might be recorded as nonstressful when, in fact, it was only experienced as nonstressful because of the support received. A measure of *potential* stress would appear essential if the impact of such "extra" factors is to be explored. Therefore, information given to raters by the interviewer leaves out not only details about emotional response but anything concerning extraneous factors, such as level of self-esteem or support, which might have influenced the respondent's reaction to the event.

Research to be reviewed suggests that the approach allows a sufficiently accurate estimate of likely response to a particular event to make systematic research viable, a possibility discussed by Max Weber (1964) in terms of explanatory understanding, *erklarendes verstehen*. Such contextual ratings take into account not only the immediate situation (e.g., the event of losing a job), but the wider context (e.g., being unmarried, being in debt with a school-aged child). Serious long-term threat and unpleasantness persisting some 10 days after the occurrence of an event has been found to be important for onset of depression, and for other conditions such as anxiety disorder and multiple sclerosis (Brown & Harris, 1989). Such events have been termed *severe*. Typical examples are learning of a husband's infidelity and, as in the example given earlier, learning of a child's serious misbehavior.

In some 20 studies of depression from various parts of the world using the LEDS, between 67% and 90% of onsets have had a severe event occurring not long before (Brown & Harris, 1989, pp. 55–56). Table 12.1 gives results from a longitudinal study of women with a child at home living in Islington, an inner-city area of London. Women have been excluded who were already suffering from "major depression" at first interview. Around a fifth of women went on to develop an episode in the 6 months following a severe event occurring in the 1 year follow-up period and 91% (29 of 32) of the onsets were preceded by a severe event.

The Meaning of Events: Loss

So far we have dealt with the tasks of characterizing events reaching a minimum threshold of threat and a rating in terms of degree of long-term threat and unpleasantness. Another step in the measurement of events deals with a more *specific* assess-

Table 12.1 Onset rate among 303 women in terms of provoking agent status

Provoking Agent Status	Number of Onsets	Percentage Onset Rate
No provoking agent	2/153	1
Provoking agent		
Major difficulty only	1/20	5
Severe event	29/130	22
Total onset rate	32/303	11

$p < .001$.
Note. From Brown, Bifulco, & Harris, 1987.

ment of their meaning. Loss, for example, has been broadly defined to cover not only loss of a person, but loss of a role, loss of resources, and loss of a cherished idea (e.g., finding out about a daughter's delinquency), and danger in terms of the threat of future loss (Finlay-Jones, 1989). Again, ratings of loss and danger are made in probabilistic terms in the same manner as that of long-term threat. The community-based study carried out in Islington showed severe events involving loss more commonly led to onset of depression, and those involving danger often led to anxiety, with a tendency for mixed onsets to have either an event or events carrying both meanings, replicating an earlier study (see Brown, 1993; Finlay-Jones & Brown, 1981).

While research has confirmed the importance of loss, there is some reason to believe that the concept is not specific enough to get at the heart of the psychosocial processes leading to depression. This is suggested by a set of findings in which severe events characterized as "matching" on ongoing marked difficulty (lasting at least 6 months) had a much higher chance of being followed by depression. The event of a mother learning that her son had been arrested on a serious charge of drug dealing was said to match the difficulty she had been having with his long-standing delinquent and irresponsible behavior. The presence of such a matching difficulty event, which in practice had usually lasted much longer than 6 months, increased risk of onset of depression threefold compared with other severe events (Brown, Bifulco, & Harris, 1987).

The question arises as to why it is usually necessary to wait for such a matching event. Part of the answer appears to relate to the way our lives are most of the time run on the basis of routine. One way of conceiving of this is in terms of differing memory systems (Tulving, 1985). Procedural memory encodes information regarding recurrent patterns of sensory stimuli and behavioral responses. This contrasts with semantic memory, which encodes verbal representations of experience. Crittenden (1992) suggests that models derived from semantic memory are only used to derive meaning from experience and generate responses when models based on procedural memory fail to achieve expected ends. We act without conscious thought in much of our daily behavior. We propose that this can hold even when faced with significant hardship and deprivation. Fridja (1988) discusses a law of habituation; "Continued pleasures wear off; continued hardships lose their poignancy," (p. 353) because sequences of similar events lead to a decrease in the intensity of emotion. The question raised is how far adaptation holds for major hardships, those that if translated in "events" would be of an order of severity known to be able to provoke depression.

In a short story, *Albert Nobbs*, George Moore tells of a woman who had spent her life disguised as a male waiter in a Dublin hotel. A crisis occurs when someone discovers her secret: "I thought I would never cry again. . . . It is much sadder than I thought it was, and if I had known how sad it was I shouldn't have been able to live through it." This hints at a persistent sense of deprivation and dissatisfaction, but that such negative feelings were apparently kept within tolerable limits. In circumstances such as these, a "matching" event can tell us what in one sense we have known all along, and in doing so can dramatically increase the amount of dysphoric emotion. While by compartmentalization the full significance of a situation is in some way played down, certain difficulties are probably easier to accommodate than others — say, those characterized by what is *not* happening than by what is happening.

Matching events under such circumstances often fail to qualify as losses in LEDS terms. Returning to the woman with the delinquent son by way of example, what had been lost when the woman learned of her son's arrest? She had known of his feckless and troublesome behavior for some years and would be aware of the risk of his involvement in the local drug culture. She had certainly already lost any idea of him as an exemplary character. Matching severe events underlining what has *already* been lost (or perhaps were never really ever possessed) are not uncommon, at least for inner-city urban populations. In Islington some 12% of women not already depressed experienced such an event in the course of the follow-up year.

Hopelessness, Humiliation, and Defeat

Aside from the experience of loss, the literature on depression also emphasizes the likely etiological role of hopelessness, humiliation, and defeat. Such responses seem more likely following a difficulty-matching event irrespective of whether it is a loss. Bibring's (1953) key psychoanalytic chapter was perhaps the first to give an unequivocal role to the lowering of self-regarding feelings following an event as critical for the development of depression. Many studies have also emphasized the importance of a sense of a loss of control (Hammen, 1988).

Particularly interesting are views concerning ranking derived from ethological observations of evolutionarily based response tendencies, that is, responses of the same order as those involving anxiety and attachment. Those deriving from the experience of defeat are seen as particularly significant for the development of depression and, it is argued, have originated from either the activity of defending territory or submission following being "outranked" in a group living species (Price & Sloman, 1987). Gilbert (1989), with this perspective in mind, has also emphasized the importance of a sense of belonging and has outlined a number of depressogenic situations that follow closely those reached by life event research: (a) direct attacks on a person's self-esteem and forcing them into a subordinate position; (b) events undermining a person's sense of rank, attractiveness, and value, particularly via the consequences of the event for core roles; and (c) blocked escape. He notes that one consequence of "fresh-start events" that have been shown to relate to recovery (Brown, Lemyre, & Bifulco, 1992) is a reduced feeling of being trapped in a punishing situation.

Such ideas go beyond the concept of loss. In discussing human despair, Unger (1984) also underlines the key importance of the experience of imprisonment. This can occur in the "blocked escape" described by Gilbert, when we are unable to free ourselves from an unrewarding setting, but also in grief when despair arises from a disbelief in our ability to reaffirm an identity in the absence of the relationship. It is the idea of being blocked, being trapped with no way forward, that is most likely to be involved when depression follows matching difficulty events.

While the experience of loss is certainly common prior to an onset of depression, it is by no means necessarily associated with the experience of defeat and entrapment, and the latter may well arise from experiences other than loss. It may be asked, therefore, whether loss is of fundamental importance for depression or merely a likely correlate of a more basic set of experiences.

To answer this question another contextual measurement scale has recently been developed that deals with severe events in terms of the four broad themes of devaluation of self, entrapment, loss, and danger. We assume that severe events rated in terms of humiliation or entrapment are likely to be linked to the experience of defeat and hopelessness, and it is the latter that are critical in etiological terms. The woman's actual response to her daughter's delinquent acts described earlier involved shame and a sense of being devalued in other people's eyes. It is also of interest that she conveyed a sense of defeat: She felt helpless and nothing worked. This sense of helplessness "came gradually, but once there stuck." It needs to be borne in mind that by definition all severe events were unresolved after some 10–14 days and in most instances there was no sign of any immediate resolution. However, it is important to note again that such reported feelings were ignored when making the contextual estimate of feelings that were probably experienced. The "objective" characteristics of the event were quite enough for it to be rated on humiliation.

The hierarchial rating scheme shown in table 12.2 has been used in the analysis of all onsets occurring in a 2-year period among the 400 inner-city Islington women mentioned earlier. All severe events, or a closely related sequence of such events, occurring outside a period of depression have been utilized. For an assessment of etiological role, the event closest in time prior to the onset has been taken as the one related to onset. The fact that the rating scheme is hierarchial means that some of the types of experience may at times have overlapped (Brown, Harris, & Hepworth, 1995).

The first category (with three subcategories) concerning humiliation assumes that one consequence of the event was either a sense of being put down or a devaluation of self. Typical humiliation events were learning of a husband's infidelity, a boyfriend saying he wanted to end a year-long relationship, a woman criticized by a judge for failing to pay her son's fine and warned she could go to prison, and a woman who found out that her 12-year-old daughter had been stealing from her and playing truant from school.

The experience of being trapped, the second category, describes events likely to underline imprisonment in a punishing situation that had gone on for some time already. An example of such an event was a woman being told that nothing could be

Table 12.2 Onset by type of severe event over 2-year period in Islington community series

Hierarchical Event Classification	Number of Onsets	Percentage Onset Rate
All "humiliation events"	31/102	30
Humiliation: separation	12/34	35
Humiliation: other's delinquency	7/36	19
Humiliation: put down	12/32	38
All "trapped" alone events	10/29	34
All "loss" alone events	14/157	9
Death	7/24	29
Separation: subject initiated	2/18	11
Other key loss	4/58	7
Lesser loss	1/57	2
All "danger" alone events	3/89	3
All severe events	58/37	15

done about her arthritis that had crippled her. In terms of the hierarchy, none of the entrapping events were considered humiliating.

If those trapped were combined with the humiliated, risk of depression was three times more likely than those with a loss alone—31% versus 9%. The final group of danger events, without humiliation, entrapment, or loss, have a rate of depression onset of only 3%. What is more, a third of the humiliating and entrapping events leading to onset did not involve loss, suggesting that the latter is not essential or central.

These findings concerning the likely importance of the experience of defeat and hopelessness have been confirmed in a study of psychiatric patients treated for depression. It is important, however, not to overstate the case for such events. At least 10% of women in the general population who have an onset do not have an obvious provoking event and somewhat more than this proportion in a patient series. There are also some apparent exceptions to the kind of events we have argued to be critical. For example, it remains puzzling why one woman developed depression within a week or so of the death of an elderly parent whom she rarely saw and did not feel especially close to. However, a good case can be made for the central etiological importance of the kind of events outlined (Brown et al., 1995).

On the basis of both community and patient studies it can be concluded that events provoking depression will tend to have a number of characteristics: the experience of loss, ego-involvement, entrapment, a sense of being devalued in one's own or other's eyes, an interpersonal crisis, defeat, and a sense of harm. But there is equally clear evidence that this is not usually enough to bring about depression. More than an event, however unpleasant, is usually necessary. Recent work underlines the critical mediating role of other background psychosocial factors. These have been mainly conceived in terms of vulnerability.

Vulnerability to Depression

Vulnerability factors are defined as those that raise the risk of depression, but only in the presence of a provoking agent such as a severe event. In the longitudinal Islington inquiry, a full analysis of material collected at the time of first contact showed that two indices predicted onset of depression: *negative psychological*, consisting of either negative evaluation of self or chronic subclinical symptoms of anxiety or depression, or *negative environmental*, consisting of negative interaction in the home or, for single mothers, lack of a close confiding relationship where the person is seen regularly. Both indices were highly related to subsequent onset in the follow-up year and were additive in effect. The degree of prediction can be gauged from the fact that while only a fifth of the 303 nondepressed women had *both* such risk factors at first interview, three-quarters of those developing depression were in this small high-risk group (Brown, Bifulco, & Andrews, 1990). This finding has since been replicated in a specially selected group of high-risk women with vulnerability factors followed over a 12-month period. The strength of the prediction is remarkable and has obvious implications for prevention, bearing in mind that the population as a whole was chosen because of its likely high risk as an inner-city population of mothers.

It is also of note that severe events on their own rarely relate to onset without at least one of the background risk factors. This is shown in figure 12.1, which deals with type of event in terms of the humiliation–trapped–loss–danger ratings. (The figure shows only women developing depression in the first follow-up year since self-esteem was only measured at the time of first interview.) There is a marked interactive effect. The rate of onset was somewhat more than 40% following a severe event

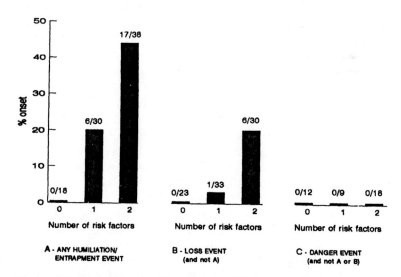

Figure 12.1 Rates of onset of depression in follow-up year by severe event type and background risk among 130 Islington women. (All onsets and severe events (or sequences) taken, only event nearest onset considered provoking)

involving humiliation or entrapment when two risk factors were present at first interview, compared with half this rate with one, and none in the absence of a risk factor. Onset associated with a loss event, without humiliation or entrapment, was 20% in the presence of both risk factors and practically absent otherwise, and danger without humiliation, entrapment, or loss was not associated with onset irrespective of number of risk factors.

Is it useful to see such background vulnerability in emotional terms? Some recent discussions would suggest that it is. Emotion is a constant accompaniment of daily life, providing a kind of running progress report of how a person is doing in terms of meeting plans and concerns involving the long-term and fundamental as well as the short-term and trivial.

> In contrast to those who argue that emotion occurs only when a motivational sequence is disrupted, this view suggests that emotion is a constantly occurring phenomenon, reflecting peacefulness and contentment when the organism is satisfied, as well as alarm when adaption is necessary. (Buck, 1985, p. 396)

Scheff (1990) takes a similar view in a discussion of pride and shame. He suggests that Cooley's (1922) well-known discussion of a looking-glass self can be summarized in terms of two propositions. First, that social monitoring of self is virtually continuous even in solitude, for we are, as Cooley put it, "living in the minds of others without knowing it" (p. 208). Second, that social monitoring always has an evaluation component and gives rise to either pride or shame.

Where self-esteem is concerned we have distinguished between negative (NES) and positive (PES) evaluation of self. These are rated quite separately, and it is possible to be both high on the negative and the positive measure. There is a strong link between NES and ongoing shortcomings in interpersonal relationships (the negative environmental index mentioned earlier—see Brown, Bifulco, Veiel, & Andrews, 1990). The association is, of course, hardly unexpected and has been confirmed in a 8-year follow-up of the women. Very few women in this time had moved from no-NES to NES, but nearly half with NES had moved to no-NES. The latter was highly related to favorable changes in the woman's life, particularly concerning marriage, children, employment, and further education (Andrews & Brown, 1995).

We assume that at any one point in time there is a store of more or less positive and more or less negative ideas about self, and that a person is rewarded and punished as these are drawn upon, in much the same way that comments from others can reward and punish. Scheff (1990) suggests that pride and shame provide an operational definition of self-esteem that represents the balance between the two states in a person's life. It seems reasonable to assume that aspects of this store of positive and negative self-evaluations can be activated by life events.

The key point in the present argument is the obvious conceptual closeness of the vulnerability factors and provoking life events involving humiliation and entrapment. For example, the "negative environmental" risk factor of lack of a close confiding relationship would tend to reduce self-esteem and also probably contribute to the perpetuation of chronic low-grade symptomatology. It would also appear safe to assume that the circumstances leading to an onset of depression will often be associated with a fall in self-esteem—with such a drop resulting either as a direct consequence of the event itself or from a failure to receive emotional support with the crisis from a particular core tie that might have been expected. Not infrequently there is therefore a double blow—a life event followed by a failure to gain support that might have been expected. Chronic subclinical symptoms (CSC), one of the two components of the negative psychological index, is fairly highly related to NES, the other component. This, together with the fact that there is some evidence that CSC only predicts onset when it is accompanied by a marked social difficulty (Brown, 1992; Brown, Bifulco, Harris, & Bridge, 1986; Harris,1992), suggests that the two measures may eventually best be seen in terms of a broader concept such as demoralization (Figueiredo & Frank, 1982).

In terms of the final cognitive and emotional experience of etiological significance, defeat (Gilbert , 1992; Price & Sloman, 1987) and generalized hopelessness (Brown & Harris, 1978) would appear to be strong contenders. However, there is the possibility that at times a situation involving entrapment and defeat may act via changes in the brain in a person with essentially high self-esteem. Gilbert (1992) discusses this possibility and we certainly have interviewed depressed women with surprisingly high self-esteem. In Islington 15% of the women suffering from caseness of depression had particularly high positive self-esteem (compared with 33% among women without a depressive or anxiety condition even at a subclinical level). Figures for those without NES were 27% and 81%, respectively (Brown, Andrews, Bifulco, & Veiel, 1990). It must be accepted that, if experiences such as hopelessness, entrapment, and defeat are etiologically important, it is possible for them to lead to onset without necessarily involving lowered self-esteem or self-denigration. However, low self-esteem will often be present, both because it is likely to increase the chances of such an emotional response to a severe event and because severe events capable of provoking such a response are likely at the same time to lower self-esteem.

Summary and Conclusions

An etiological model of depressive disorders has been outlined that considers how vulnerability factors and severe events lead to the onset of depression. Most of our work has concentrated on the measurement of environmental factors in terms of their *potential* for evoking strong emotions in most people, rather than focusing on the measurement of actual evoked emotion. This approach has involved a series of complex categorizations of life events according to their likely consequences for emotion, initially in terms of general threat, but then in more specific terms such as humiliation and entrapment as well as loss and danger.

In addition, the role of characteristics of the individual such as self-esteem and quality of close ties has been considered. The ability of these factors to increase the likelihood of emotion aroused by a severe life event and subsequent generalization into depressive symptomatology has been explored. Thus, the combination of a humiliating event for a woman with prior low self-esteem will increase risk in an additive, if not multiplicative, interactive sense (Brown & Harris, 1986). It is also assumed that the combination will link to core self-depreciative symptoms in any developing depressive disorder.

It is hoped that this discussion demonstrates the fruitfulness of our "backdoor" approach to the experience of emotion. It has enabled a convincing case for powerful psychosocial etiological effects to be made. However, now that this has been achieved, our research begins to encompass factors relating much more directly to the experience of emotion: We now additionally explore responses to events in terms of coping actions and cognitions. The latter includes self-blame, helplessness, pessimism, and denial. However, we would only recommend the use of such a "softer" approach in conjunction with the structure provided by "harder" contextual measures such as LEDS. With our knowledge of specific vulnerability factors, features of events, and now coping responses, we hope to pinpoint more closely the conditions under which strong emotions and ensuing depression may be elicited in a given individual. This is likely to have implications for clinical intervention; indeed, in the future *prevention* rather than postonset intervention may be possible given our increasing knowledge of factors that lead up to the onset of depression.

Note

1. Weiss (1994) in discussing adult relationships has emphasised the difficulty of gauging the presence of attachment outside this kind of crisis.

References

Andrews, B., & Brown, G. W. (1995). Stability and change in low self-esteem: The role of psychosocial factors. *Psychological Medicine, 25,* 23–31.

Bibring, E. (1953). Mechanisms of depression. In P. Greenacre (Ed.), *Affective disorders: Psychoanalytic contributions to their study.* (pp. 13–48). New York: International Universities Press.

Brown, G. W. (1989). Life events and measurement. In G. W. Brown & T. Harris (Eds.), *Life events and illness* (pp. 13–46). New York: Guilford Press.

Brown, G. W. (1992). Social support: An investigator-based approach. In H. O. F. Veiel & U. Baumann (Eds.), *The meaning and measurement of social support* (pp. 235–257). New York: Hemisphere Publishing.

Brown, G. W. (1993). Life events and affective disorder: Replications and limitations. *Psychosomatic Medicine, 55,* 248–259.

Brown, G. W. Andrews, B., Bifulco A., & Veiel. H. (1990). Self-esteem and depression: 1. Measurement issues and prediction of onset. *Social Psychiatry & Psychiatric Epidemiology, 25,* 200–209.

Brown, G. W., Bifulco, A., & Andrews, B. (1990). Self-esteem and depression: 3. Aetiological issues. *Social Psychiatry & Psychiatric Epidemiology, 25,* 235–243.

Brown, G. W., Bifulco, A., Harris, T. O. (1987). Life events, vulnerability and onset of depression: Some refinements. *British Journal of Psychiatry, 150,* 30–42.

Brown, G. W., Bifulco, A., Harris, T., & Bridge, L. (1986). Life stress, subclinical symptoms and vulnerability to clinical depression. *Journal of Affective Disorders, 11*, 1–19.

Brown, G. W., Bifulco, A., Veiel, H., & Andrews, B. (1990). Self-esteem and depression: 2. Social correlates of self-esteem. *Social Psychiatry & Psychiatric Epidemiology, 25*, 225–234.

Brown, G. W., & Harris, T. O. (1978). *Social origins of depression: A study of psychiatric disorder in women.* New York: Free Press.

Brown, G. W., & Harris, T. O. (1986). Establishing causal links: The Bedford College studies of depression. In H. Katschnig (Ed.), *Life events and psychiatric disorders* (pp. 105–187). Cambridge: Cambridge University Press.

Brown, G. W., & Harris, T. O. (1989). *Life events and illness.* New York: Guilford Press.

Brown, G. W., Harris, T. O., & Hepworth, C. (1995). Loss, humiliation and entrapment among women developing depression: A patient and non-patient composition. *Psychological Medicine, 25*, 7–21.

Brown, G. W., Lemyre, L., & Bifulco, A. (1992). Social factors and recovery from anxiety and depressive disorders: A test of the specificity. *British Journal of Psychiatry, 161*, 44–54.

Buck, R. (1985). Prime theory: An integrative view of motivation and emotion. *Psychological Review, 92*, 389–413.

Cooley, C. H. (1922). *Human nature and social order.* New York: Scribner's.

Crittenden, P. M. (1992). Quality of attachment in the pre-school years. *Development and Psychopathology, 4*, 209–242.

Epstein, S. (1991). The self-concept, the traumatic neurosis and the structure of personality. In R. Hogan (Ed.), *Perspectives in personality* (pp. 63–98). London: Jessica Kingsley.

Figueiredo, J. M. de, & Frank, J. D. (1982). Subjective incompetence, the clinical hallmark of demoralisation. *Comprehensive Psychiatry, 23*, 353–363.

Finlay-Jones, R. (1989). Anxiety. In G. W. Brown & T. Harris (Eds.), *Life events and illness* (pp. 95–112). New York: Guildford Press.

Finlay-Jones, R., & Brown, G. W. (1981). Types of stressful life event and the onset of anxiety and depressive disorders. *Psychological Medicine, 11*, 803–815.

Fridja, N. H. (1988). The laws of emotion. *American Psychologist, 43*, 349–358.

Gilbert, P. (1989). *Human nature and suffering.* New York: Erlbaum.

Gilbert, P. (1992). *Depression: The evolution of powerlessness.* Hove, UK: Erlbaum.

Hammen, C. (1988). Depression and cognitions about personal stressful life events. In L. B. Alloy (Ed.), *Cognitive processes in depression* (pp. 77–108). New York: Guilford Press.

Harris, T. O. (1992). Some reflections of the process of social support; and nature of unsupportive behaviours. In H. O. F. Veiel & U. Baumann (Eds.), *The meaning and measurement of social support* (pp. 171–189). New York: Hemisphere Publishing.

Horwitz, M. J. (1976). *Stress response syndromes.* New York: Jason Aronson.

Oatley, K. (1992). *Best laid schemes: The psychology of emotions.* New York: Cambridge University Press.

Oatley, K., & Jenkins, J. M. (1992). Human emotions: Function and dysfunction. *Annual Review Psychology, 43*, 55–85.

Price, J. S., & Sloman, L. (1987). Depression as yielding behavior: An animal model based on Schjelderup-Ebbe's pecking order. *Ethology and Sociology, 8*(Suppl.), 85–98.

Scheff, T. J. (1990). *Microsociology, discourse, emotion, and social structure.* Chicago: University of Chicago Press.

Solomon, R. C. (1991). E-type judgements, emotions and desire. In R. Hogan (Ed.), *Perspectics in personality* (pp. 169–190). London: Jessica Kingsley.

Tulving, E. (1985). How many memory systems are there? *American Psychologist, 40,* 385–398.

Unger, R. M. (1984). *Passion: An essay on personality.* New York: Free Press.

Weber, M. (1964). *The theory of social and economic organisation.* (T. Parsons, Ed. & Trans.). London: Collier-Macmillan.

Weiss, R. S. (1994). Is the attachment system of adults a development of Bowlby's attachment system of childhood? *Psychological Inquiry, 5,* 65–67.

13

Monique de Bonis

Thinking and Depression

Structure in Content

This chapter examines the nature of certain aspects of emotional disorders in depression from a structural perspective, thus complementing the content-oriented cognitive theories of depression. The main objective of a structural perspective is to describe precisely how different basic domains of knowledge or belief are organized. Although both content and structure are important concepts that sometimes interact, special emphasis is given in this chapter to the latter rather than to the former. The methods used to study structure were derived from Personal Construct Theory (PCT; Kelly, 1955).

In a first section, I reexamine the hypothesis that the cognitive world of depressed persons is governed by negativity and hence organized in a relatively unidimensional way of thinking. This section will be divided into two parts. In the first part, two conceptual difficulties, the overgeneralization and the exclusivity hypothesis, are discussed; I suggest that logical implication might be an alternative explanation to the overgeneralization principle advanced in the early Beckian formulations of thinking distortion. In the second part, without dismissing the importance of negative thinking in depression, I suggest that there are structural abnormalities of *both* positive and negative self-cognitions in depressed subjects. This latter point is illustrated by findings obtained from recent development of the PCT methodology in the field of stressful life events and of mood and memory.

Insofar as a cognitive approach necessarily takes into account representations not only of the self but also of other aspects of the world, in the second section I present empirical data on a second major knowledge domain: stressful life events (SLEs). The question addressed in this second section is whether similar structural abnormalities are also present in this knowledge domain.

Negativity Hypothesis about Self: Early and Recent Beckian Formulations Revisited

The main assumption of Beck's cognitive theory of depression is that the thoughts of depressive people are pervasively oriented in the direction of negativity, whatever the domain of knowledge or belief: the self, the world, and the future (i.e., cognitive triad; Beck, 1963, 1987). This theory has recently been confirmed on the basis of extensive dimensional measurement through the Self-Concept Test (Beck, Steer, Epstein, & Brown, 1990). Recent reviews have reaffirmed the "routinely confirmed" negativity bias, especially in the self-concept, one aspect of the cognitive triad (Haaga, Dyck, & Erst, 1991). Indeed, for some authors, the negativity bias remains a common-sense interpretation of the clinical symptoms of depression and a "thinly veiled tautology in research since subjects distinguished on the basis of BDI [Beck Depression Inventory] scores are then compared to other measurements taken of these specific negative tendencies" (Coyne & Gotlieb, 1983, p. 496).

The negativity bias has two features. The first is that it is unrealistic; the second is that it is illogical: "The typical depressive cognitions can be categorised according to the way in which they deviate from logical or realistic thinking" (Beck, 1963, p. 328). Only this deviation from realism has been questioned. For example, certain authors argue that normal subjects are also somewhat unrealistic because they tend to show a positive bias with an exaggerated optimism about their performances (Alloy & Abramson, 1988; Bonis, 1978; Bonis & Comiskey, 1991; Nelson & Craighead, 1977). The other deviation that Beck assumed to produce negative cognition — the departure from logical reasoning — has received comparatively little attention. In his typology of cognitive distortions related to an illogical way of reasoning, Beck makes a distinction between three kinds of logical errors: arbitrary inferences, selective abstractions, and overgeneralization.

I now examine conceptual limitations of the assumption that negativity involves being illogical, limiting our discussion to the principle of overgeneralization. Then, I explore the difficulties raised by some empirical findings.

Conceptual Difficulties

Negativity Hypothesis: A Consequence of Overgeneralization or of Logical Implication? The cognitive principle of overgeneralization is usually defined as a process that, on the basis of the observation of a certain number of elements, extends the properties of these elements in order to include them in a larger class. The generalization principle is characterized by the spreading of the semantic meaning across several aspects of the world.

As an example of overgeneralization, Beck presents the "depressed-father" scenario borrowed from clinical practice. This scenario starts with a father whose children are slow in getting dressed. The sequences of the scenario are as follows:

> He thought, "I am a poor father because the children are not better disciplined." He then noted a faucet was leaking and thought this showed he was also a poor husband. While driving to work he thought, "I must be a poor driver or other cars would not be passing me etc." (Beck, 1963, pp. 327–328)

An analysis of this scenario raises questions about the nature of the faulty cognitive operation leading to depressive thinking. Actually, the negative thoughts of "the depressed father" seem to be the result of a cognitive process belonging to logical implication rather than to overgeneralization. To clarify this argument, it is necessary to highlight some subtle differences between generalization and logical implication. Whereas generalization consists of constructing a class by using empirical observations of the elements of that class, logical implication refers to the abstract relationships among the elements of the class. Logical implication is a higher order cognitive process than generalization. In other words, whereas generalization is a cognitive operation that processes concrete thoughts, logical implication is concerned with more abstract aspects of thinking like themes or central ideas. In this view, the scenario of the depressed father is better seen as consisting of examples of logical implication, introduced by the connector *since*. The reasoning is as follows: *Since* I am a poor father, children are slow in getting dressed," *Since* I am a poor husband, a faucet is leaky," "*Since* I am a poor driver, other cars are passing me," and so on. The reasoning is driven by a centripetal movement, in which the different events that happen to the depressed father are interpreted according to a central idea of his self-concept. In the case of overgeneralization, the reasoning would have been: "I failed in bringing up my children (children slow in getting dressed), I failed in taking care of my house (faucet leaky), I failed in driving my car (car passing me), . . . *therefore*, I fail in *everything* I do." The process described by Beck as overgeneralization seems actually to be a form of inductive reasoning and this is the reason why one can suggest that it belongs to logical implication. It is worth mentioning that overly strong logical implication has been described in delusional disorders, especially in "Le délire d'interprétation" under the label of "systématisation" (see Ronis, 1992). Indeed, this kind of process consists of thinking that is very tightly structured around a central idea (a scheme), so that each new event is interpreted or misinterpreted in such a way that it provides support for the central idea. To quote Grize (1992): "Systematisation refers to a centripetal process that acts upon a theme, generalisation refers to a centrifugal process that acts upon thought contents" (p. 231).

Although these distinctions may appear to the reader somewhat subtle and difficult to isolate from the narrative of a depressed patient, it is important to acknowledge the fact that these two different cognitive mechanisms—overgeneralization and strong logical implication—would lead to opposite predictions about the structure of the mental world. In the case of overgeneralization, for instance, a structure would be expected to be loose and undifferentiated, whereas in the case of strong logical implication, it would be expected to be tighter. As we will see later, this question is not just speculative—it was examined empirically regarding self-concept of depressed people.

The Exclusivity Hypothesis: An Unfulfilled Corollary of the Negativity Bias   A corollary of the negativity bias initially suggested by Beck is that depressed people are led to ignore the positive elements present in the environment. The cognitive process thus activated corresponds to the principle of exclusivity, according to which depressed people will automatically exclude positive self-evaluations (Beck, 1987). Unfortunately for Beck's theory, an in-depth review carried out by Haaga et al. (1991)

has illustrated that "empirical results are inconsistent with this prediction" (p. 218). Other studies, they write, have shown that "depressed people rate at least as many positive adjectives as self descriptive as they do negative ones" and also that depressed people "average just at the mid point of the possible range on a self-concept test." However, according to such authors, say Haaga et al., the exclusivity hypothesis "could be deleted without loss in future revisions of cognitive theory" (p. 218). It is difficult to agree with such a conclusion because the corollary constitutes a basic element in the Beck model. To the extent that the empirical facts do not agree with a basic assumption of the theory, we may need to modify the theory. In any case, it is important that we scrutinize how positive aspects are actually structured in depressive thinking.

In the literature, some studies have examined the structural properties of self and other representations in depressives. The vast majority of these studies uses the methodological frame of reference of Kelly's (1955) PCT, whereas other studies are developed within the information processing and self-regulation frames of reference. One thing that makes these data interesting for the present discussion is the fact that these studies take into account wider structural aspects of the mental world of the depressive subject than just the negative content. Due to space limitations, we will focus the presentation to works conducted within PCT. We will neither look at studies of cognitive self-complexity (Linville, 1987), the discrepancy between different selves (Higgins, 1987; Strauman, 1989), nor the balance between positive and negative states of mind in relation to emotional disorders (Schwartz & Garamoni, 1989), which nevertheless offer interesting alternative specifications regarding the negative bias.

Empirical Limits on Testing, the Negativity Bias with Personal Construct Approaches

Personal Construct Theory and its application to depressive disorders have been well documented and they will not be described in detail here (see Button, 1982). The general principles will be summarized instead.

Personal Construct Theory: A Brief Summary   Personal Construct Theory offers a broad cognitive view of mental functioning, based on the core assumption that, as an incipient scientist, the layperson builds quasi-formal theories that enable interpretation and prediction about novel events. These interpretations are governed by a personal construct system composed of a set of self-constructs. According to Kelly (1955), a construct is a way in which "some things are construed as being alike and yet different from others" (p. 105). The nature of constructs is bipolar. The reality of constructs stands on their actual employment, in other words, the way constructs are actually *used* in context and not in the things themselves. Such an assumption refers to the notion of "constructive alternativism." For example, to paraphrase Kelly, supposing a person construes some of the elements of his or her environment in terms of a positive versus negative construct, the main concern will be to study the way in which this construct is used to classify the relevant elements of the environment. One major aspect of the use of a construct is its range of convenience. The "reality" of each contextual system is derived from a careful analysis of the way in which the constructs are assigned to the elements of the environment. This careful analysis is carried out through the use of a technique, the "Repertory Grid Technique," which can be briefly characterized as a two-way matrix with constructs as columns and rows as elements, and a multidimensional method of processing the data included in the matrix (for methodological details, see Slater, 1976, 1977; Rosenberg, 1977). As far as "Constructs are the channels in which one's mental processes run" (Kelly, 1955, p. 126), one of the possible ways to describe the disordered mental processes is to identify the context(s) in which the constructs are misapplied or inappropriately applied. One other major aspect of PCT is that the constructs are organized (or mapped) within a system in which it is possible to differentiate subordinate from superordinate constructs. The former are subsumed by the latter. A working personal construct system is a hierarchically organized structure. Another point of major interest of the general model proposed by Kelly is related to the general assumption that the self can be included in the system as an element. To quote Kelly, "when the person begins to use himself as a datum in forming constructs, exciting things begins to happen" and "thus much of his social life is controlled by the comparison he has come to see between himself and other" (p. 131).

Empirical Findings   Because the large body of evidence from the PCT in depression has been reviewed in detail by Neimeyer (1982), we will now only briefly summarize what kinds of "exciting things" foreseen by Kelly happened 30 years after the publication of his PCT. According to Neimeyer's review, the structure of self-concept in depression can be characterized by at least four properties: mixed self-valence, undifferentiation, monolithism, and polarized construing. Some of these properties, mixed self-valence and polarized construing, offer a number of alternative hypotheses to the negativity bias.

Mixed self-valence, an expression coined by Space and Cromwell (1980), consists of evaluating oneself with *both* the positive and negative constructs associated with a greater self-other distance. In another study, Space, Dingeman, and Cromwell (1983) concluded that "even severely depressed hospitalized patients rarely construe themselves in consistently negative terms, though they are more prone to higher level-devaluation than controls" (Neimeyer, 1985, p. 86). Polarized construing was observed in Rowe's (1971) single-case study of a patient whose construct system "divided people in her world into good and bad" (p. 293).

If the negativity bias was observed in some studies, such as that of Sheehan (1981), who concluded that depressive patients rated "themselves along the negative side of the construct dimensions approximately 62 percent of the time and, after treatment, 38.4 percent of the time" (p. 204), the results were not so clearcut in other studies. Comparing, in a cross-sectional approach, six groups of subjects, 20 depressed patients, 10 manics, 10 schizophrenics, 10 alcoholics, 10 physically ill patients, and 10 recovered depressed patients, Ashworth, Blackburn, and Mc Pherson (1982) found that "neither the depressed nor the manic group differed from all the other groups on any measure" (p. 247). Taken together, these results offer a mixed picture of the negative self of the depressed patient.

Another interesting aspect of PCT is about the deductive use of personal constructs. According to Kelly, there is an "if-then" relationship implied by the two-ended nature of the construct. Interestingly, the strength of the logical relationships has been studied by Slade and Sheehan (1979) and by Sheehan (1981). Combining both the PCT and the cognitive balance theory of Heider (1946), these authors devised a method and a computer program designed to analyze the implicative network of the personal constructs in depressed patients. The assessment of the degree of implicative relationship is derived from the analysis of triads of these concepts. The linkage between three concepts leads to two kinds of patterns called the balanced and the imbalanced triads. A triad is considered as balanced when all of the three relationships between the three concepts are positive (+++) or when one is positive, and the other two negative (+− −). A triad is considered to be imbalanced when all the three relationships are negative (− − −) or two are positive and one negative (++−). A construct system characterized by a high number of imbalanced triads is considered as a cognitive system that tolerates "conflict" and ambiguity (for examples of triads see Sheehan, 1981, p. 207). Using this paradigm Sheehan showed that the proportion of balanced triads was higher in depressed patients compared to normal controls, indicating a conceptual structure tightly organized in order to minimize incompatibilities between constructs. These results underline the importance of the logical structure in the content of self-concept.

Since the Neimeyer review, new statistical models have been applied in PCT to process different more or less sophisticated adapted versions of the original Repertory Grid Technique. The Rutgers group used a new clustering algorithm (HICLAS) to describe the structure of self and other descriptions in clinically depressed patients. The application of this new algorithm showed that depressed patients assign fewer positive attributes not only for the self but also for significant others (Gara et al., 1993). However, despite the important methodological improvements, the question of emotion differentiation (positive vs. negative) has led to mixed findings. In major depression, negative emotional constructs were found to be either undifferentiated (Goldston, Gara, & Woolfolk, 1992) or organized in a more complex way than positive constructs (Gara et al., 1993).

The picture of the depressed self may have been obscured by a number of methodological difficulties, especially those related to the assessment of complexity, a point already well documented (Chetwynd, 1977; Herhsberger, 1990). Another problem may be the spurious consequences of aggregating individual grids in the case of free-response formats. In such cases, the individual grids may differ in terms of the number of attributes generated for self and others. In such instances, proportional measures must be used to compare the self- and other differentiation (Bonis, De Boeck, Lida-Pudik, & Féline, 1995). In addition, most of the discrepancies among the findings may be due to the fact that multiple standards—self and ideal self, self versus more or less significant others—have been used as elements of the grid.

In sum, Beck's predictions on the semantic content of self-negative description always occur in studies using traditional questionnaires (Beck et al., 1990). With other methods, especially those derived from PCT, negative content of self-descriptions also occurs. However, the findings obtained from the personal construct approach suggest alternative assumptions on structural abnormalities in the balance of positive and negative cognitions. The question raised by this approach is whether depressed people see themselves more negatively or whether they differ in the way they organize the positive and the negative content of their self-descriptions.

In the next section of this chapter, I will examine the plausibility of such alternatives between structure and content in one aspect that is critical in depression — the stressful life event (SLE) domain.

Negativity Bias Revisited

A Personal Construct Approach to Stressful Life Events in Depression

Most clinical models of vulnerability to depression have emphasized that stressful events and current life experiences serve as a reinforcing agent, maintaining depressive affects (Cochran & Hammen, 1985). To quote Hammen, Ellicott, Gitlin, & Jamison (1989), studies of SLE

> have consistently indicated a relation between events or strains and depression in community samples and depressed patients. Nevertheless, the association is typically small, and the majority of individuals who experience even major stressors do not become depressed. (p. 154)

This is the reason why some theorists have argued that individual "meaning" of events needs to be considered (Brown & Harris, 1978). Several specific content dimensions in the meaning of stressful life events have been studied (Cochran & Hammen, 1985; Hammen et al., 1989; Shrout et al., 1989). To our knowledge few attempts have been made to clarify how SLEs are structured in the depressive mind.

Our investigation focused on how depressed patients structure a sample of SLEs. The experimental paradigm was based on the same principles as the one used in the field of personal construct approach to the perception of self and others (Dmitrieff, 1989). Instead of using persons as elements, they use SLEs, and the task consists of assigning attributes to these elements. The SLE list, chosen on the basis of previous studies in the field of stressful life event (Sarason, Johnson, & Siegal, 1978), is composed of 17 positive and negative environmental stress-related events. The affective valence was determined by 40 judges who rated each SLE on a 5-point graphic scale along a continuum between positive and negative. As an example, the two most positively rated SLEs are Health Recovery and Pregnancy, the most negatively rated are AIDS and Unemployment, and the neutral and widely varying are Minor Financial Problems and Divorce.

The technique employed to explore the patient's perceptions of SLEs was a modified version of Kelly's repertory grid technique (Bonis et al., 1995; Lida, Bonis, & Féline, 1992). Because it has been described in detail elsewhere, I will only briefly summarize the relevant features of the strategy of measurement used.

The procedure consists of four stages. First, the patient is presented a list of 17 SLEs. Second, each of the 17 SLEs have to be assigned one salient attribute. The subject is allowed to give either an adjective, a noun, or any other verbal expression, providing it is considered a salient feature of the target event to be described. Third, the list of self-generated attributes ($n = 17$) is presented to the patient, who is instructed to give the opposite noun or expression for each attribute. Finally, the 34 self attributes (17 salient and 17 opposites) are arranged in preestablished random order and the patient is asked to rate each of the 17 SLEs on the 34 self-generated attributes.

The SLEs (rows) and the attributes given by the patient (columns) are presented in a two-way matrix, to be filled out with binary codes 0 (does not apply) and 1 (does apply). Because of the format of the descriptions, the assignment of attributes on the raw matrix can be analyzed in several quantitative (number of attributes assigned) and qualitative aspects (semantic content of the attributes assigned).

Ten (five low and five high cultural level) patients, fulfilling the *Diagnostic and Statistical Manual of Mental Disorders* (3rd ed., rev.) criteria for major depression and having high scores (cutoff, 13) on the BDI, were compared to 10 paired controls exhibiting no sign of mental disorder; none of them scored above the cutoff point of 13 on the BDI.

The matrices corresponding to the 17 SLEs (columns) × attributes, collapsed over the five subjects (rows), were factor analyzed for each group of five subjects (depressed vs. controls and high vs. low cultural levels) separately. Since attributions are expressed on a nominal scale (yes/no format), a correspondence factorial analysis was carried out (Benzécri, 1973; Lebart, Morineau, & Warwick,. 1984). This statistical procedure enabled us to map the structure of the representation of SLEs for each group.

Results show that, for all groups, the first factor is an evaluative factor opposing positive and negative SLEs, with neutral elements in between. Although the overall configuration is very similar, several differences are noticeable, in particular when depressed subjects are compared to normal controls. Figures 13.1 and 13.2 give an illustration of the SLE representational space for low-cultural-level depressed and controls on the first and second axes. The results for high-cultural-level subjects are similar.

The SLE mapping on the first axis shows that positive SLEs are close together and negative SLEs are scattered in the control group, whereas a reverse pattern characterises the SLE mapping in the depressed group. Table 13.1 shows how positive, negative, and neutral SLE are differently structured within the overall space of representation. In the group of depressed patients, positive SLEs are significantly better differentiated from one another than in controls, whereas negative events are less differentiated in depressed than in controls. Depressed patients and controls do not differ regarding neutral SLEs on this first evaluative dimension.

In conformity with our predictions, the SLE mapping is semantically organized in the same way in both depressed and normal groups. Within the positive and the negative clusters, the pattern is the same. Nevertheless, structural differences are present. Among depressed subjects negative events are more tightly related to one another, a result that can be understood as the consequence of strong implicative meanings for negative events. Hence, a tighter construal of negative events and a greater complexity of positive life events seem to be critical features regarding the way in which the depressive mind is structurally organized.

What kind of clinical implications can be drawn from the structural differences within positive and negative SLE mapping and between depressed and nondepressed subjects observed in this study? Our interpretation is that, if a depressed patient encounters a negative event, it will be readily included in the structure reinforcing the implicative relationships within the negative pole. As a consequence, the imbalance between positive and negative aspects of the world will be increased. If the same depressive patient encounters a positive event, it is likely that the structure of positive

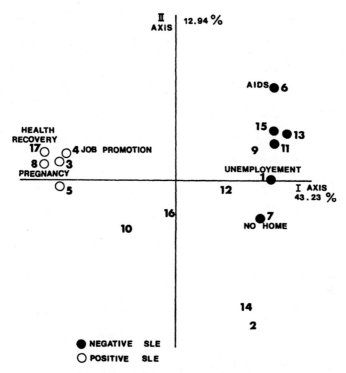

Figure 13.1 Factorial correspondence analysis. Mapping of stressful life events: low cultural level controls.

1=Unemployment, 2=Unneighborliness, 3=Job Promotion, 4=Marriage, 5=Win Gambling, 6=AIDS, 7=No Home, 8=Pregnancy, 9=Divorce, 10=Moving out, 11=Jail, 12=New Family Member, 13=Physically Handicapped, 14=Financial Problems, 15=Mourning, 16=Work Change, 17=Health Recovery. (Due to space limitation only the most relevant positive and negative events are specified in the graphs.)

events will not be modified as strongly. Because the positive events are better differentiated than the negative ones, a positive event will be processed with respect to many other dimensions than positivity alone. In other words, the occurrence of a negative event will maintain and amplify the negative content structure whereas the occurrence of a positive event will not have the same effect on the positive content structure.

The preceding remarks on the relation between the structure of positive and negative representations and their function in the adjustment to new events should be considered speculative at this time. To go beyond this point dynamic models of processing positive and negative affects are needed to understand how the observed differences in the structure of representations are related to differential cognitive functioning in depression. Such models have already been proposed by Carver and Scheier (1990), but the model has not yet been applied to affective disorders.

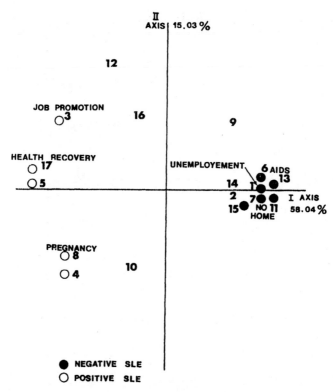

Figure 13.2 Factorial correspondence analysis. Mapping of stressful life events: low cultural level depressed.

1=Unemployment, 2=Unneighborliness, 3=Job Promotion, 4=Marriage, 5=Win Gambling, 6=AIDS, 7=No Home, 8=Pregnancy, 9=Divorce, 10=Moving out, 11=Jail, 12=New Family Member, 13=Physically Handicapped, 14=Financial Problems, 15=Mourning, 16=Work Change, 17=Health Recovery.
(Due to space limitation only the most relevant positive and negative events are specified in the graphs.)

Our interpretation of the structure of the depressive mind is far from being in contradiction with alternative hypotheses such as cognitive complexity (Linville, 1987) or negativity bias assumptions. However, our findings alter both assumptions slightly. Regarding the former, it is necessary to remember that the concept of cognitive complexity has more than one sense. In one sense, reduced cognitive complexity may mean a lack of differentiation. A second sense involves a lack of distinctiveness among the range of traits used to describe a sample of objects. In this sense, people use constructs crudely, as if everything were in black and white with no shades of gray in between. People who lack differentiation in this sense would recognize shades of gray, but would use every construct in the same way. The latter meaning is embodied in a quantitative definition of complexity, which has been adopted in most current research on the topic. However, high complexity also means low predictability. Our findings on the structure of negative life events show that depressed patients are, to a certain extent, less complex than normals within the sphere of negative life events, because depressed patient's representations of negative SLEs are more predictable. However, this is not true for positive SLEs, who show the opposite pattern. Indeed, overall the two groups are approximately equal in complexity.

Our interpretation of the role of implication in the mapping of SLEs is necessarily limited due to the fact that little work has been carried out so far to enable the structure of affect-loaded events to be described in depth. Further research is needed for this interpretation to be well founded. However, the negative thinking that we explain in terms of logical implication rather than overgeneralization resembles the cognitive processes that Tomkins (1963) described, accounting for negative affects with the monopolistic theory. Although the basic models of affect theory as related to depression are far more complex and more general than the assumptions discussed in this chapter, the idea that negative affects are based on a network of implicative relationships that amplify negativity fits in with the "snowball" metaphor suggested by Tomkins.

In addition, some supportive evidence can be found within a related field: memory of affect-loaded words, which seems congruent with the emphasis given here to the cognitive process of logical implication.

The Negativity Bias Problem in the Related Field of Mood and Memory

In their recent book *Affect, Cognition and Change*, Teasdale and Barnard (1993) propose a cognitive theory of depressive thinking based on a model of information processing: the Interacting Cognitive Subsystems (ICS). Although this model is mainly focused on mood and memory and is therefore somewhat different from the model that has been discussed here, research in this area is very relevant for understanding depressive thinking. The general model is very complex and only two points concerning theoretical and empirical foundations of the negativity bias will be out-

Table 13.1 Comparison between depressed and control stressful life events

	Positive	Negative	Neutral
Depressed	74.08	47.50	54.10
N = 10	(12.86)	(8.48)	(6.85)
Controls	64.33	56.58	62.60
N = 10	(10.41)	(7.86)	(14.59)
	$F = 4.16, p < .05$	$F = 7.39, p < .01$	$F = 2.72$, NS

Note: Within each cell mean distances and standard deviations of positive negative and neutral SLEs from the center of gravity are shown. The distance index corresponds to the inertia of each SLE in the factor space. The value of inertia is proportional to the squared distance of each SLE from the center of gravity of the set of points. Hence, larger values indicate greater differentiation.

lined. First, the model is based on a revision of the Bower Associative Network model (Bower & Cohen, 1982), and a critique of the concept of "spreading activation." This concept can be considered as a neuropsychological analog of the cognitive process of overgeneralization. The critiques proposed in this chapter concerning overgeneralization parallel those suggested by Teasdale and Barnard concerning the concept of spreading activation. From a detailed analysis of research carried out in the field of mood and memory, Teasdale and Barnard concluded that the assumption that negativity is the result of the overactivation of specific meanings and low-level constructs can no longer be accepted. There is a need to explain how multiple-meaning information is transformed in such a way as to maintain depressive affect. Second, Teasdale and Barnard's model takes into account positive and negative cognitions. The model relies on the core assumption that affect-biased information processing in depression is the result of higher level representation disorders. In these higher levels, as will be suggested below, implicative meaning is included in the processing of higher abstract levels.

The Teasdale and Barnard (1993) model proposes two basic processes: "The storage of patterns of information and the transformation of information into patterns of other qualitatively different kinds of information," and assumes that "two kinds of patterns, one propositional, the other implicational, organise the regularities at higher levels of abstraction" (p. 188). As an example, the implicational pattern is supposed to influence "the interrelationship between a constellation of constructs." Depressive thinking must be explained in terms of these higher level processes. These higher level processes are centered on central ideas or themes instead of concrete thoughts contents (as previously discussed in the first section of this chapter).

Within this frame of reference, Teasdale and Barnard have suggested some counter intuitive predictions regarding the negative bias hypothesis. According to their model, depressive patients were expected to make, in a completion task, at least in some instances, more positive than negative inferences than the nondepressed subjects, indicating that the whole structure of semantic meaning is differently organized in depressive thinking. Findings supporting these predictions are presented in their book (Teasdale & Barnard, 1993) and exemplified in Teasdale, Taylor, Cooper, Hayhurst, & Paykel (1995). These findings would bring further evidence against the Beck exclusivity corollary discussed in the first section of this chapter.

Conclusion

In this chapter, the importance of a structural representation of two affect-related aspects of the cognitive world in depressed patients was highlighted. The analysis of the structure of SLEs showed that, in depressed patients, the degree of belongingness, another word for logical implication, within the negative module is higher than within the positive one. Hence, at least for the domain of knowledge of SLEs, the architecture is not exactly the same for depressed and nondepressed subjects. Nevertheless, both groups attribute similar meanings to these events. It is likely that the different organization of events as they are construed will influence the way in which real events are experienced when they occur in real life, and in turn will modulate the emotional climate of the depressed patients. This chapter focused on the positive and negative aspects of SLEs. Reviewing previous studies on the structure of self-concept, some promising findings also suggested structural differences paralleling those evidenced in the SLE domain. However, some difficulties, due to an exclusive focus on the problem of self-complexity associated with methodological problems in processing positive and negative aspects of the depressive self-concept, still prevent definite conclusions to be drawn from being drawn with available findings (Bonis et al., 1996). In the field of SLEs, the patterning of structure in positive and negative content seems to be clear. However, these two major aspects of construing are far from being the only ways in which stressful events are interpreted. Further research is needed to know how other relevant dimensions of these events are integrated in the whole architecture of representations in the depressive world.

Acknowledgments Preparation of this manuscript was supported by the Institut National de la santé et de la Recherche Médicale (Grant 93 CN09) and by the Centre National de la Recherche Scientifique (CNRS, URA 316, Laboratoire de Psychopathologie, UFR Médecine-Sud, Université Paris XI, France). I gratefully acknowledge the advice of Ludovic Lebart for the statistical analysis and the assistance of Catherine Loridan in the data processing and of Janice Richardson and Todd Lubart for revising the translation.

References

Alloy, L. B., & Abramson, L. Y. (1988). Depressive realism: four theoretical perspectives. In L. B. Alloy (Ed.), *Cognitive processes in depression*. New York: Guilford Press.

Ashworth, C. M., Blackburn, I. M., & Mc Pherson, F. M. (1982). The performance of depressed and manic patients on some repertory grid measures: A cross-sectional study. *British Journal of Medical Psychology, 55*, 247–255.

Beck, A. T. (1963). Thinking and depression. *Archives of General Psychiatry, 9*, 324–333.

Beck, A. T. (1987). Cognitive models of depression. *Journal of Cognitive Psychotherapy, 1*, 5–37.

Beck, A. T., Steer, R. A., Epstein, N., & Brown, G. (1990). Beck self-concept test. *Journal of Consulting and Clinical Psychology, 2*, 191–197.

Benzécri, J. P. (Ed.). (1973). *L'analyse des données. L'analyse des correspondances* (1st ed., Vol. 2). Paris: Dunod.

Bonis, M. de. (1978). Une approche psychologique de la dépression. La théorie cognitive de A. T. Beck. In P. Pichot (Ed.), *Les voies nouvelles de la dépression* (pp. 101–108). Paris: Masson.

Bonis, M. de. (1992). Raisons et déraisons. Aalyse des figures de raisonnement illogique dans "Histoire du précédent écrit" de Jean-Jacques Rousseau. *Revue Internationale de Psychopathologie. 6*, 182–211.

Bonis, M. de, & Comiskey, F. (1991). Connaissances, cognitions et méta-cognitions: Trois questions pour une psychopathologie cognitive de la dépression. In A. Féline, P. Hardy, & Bonis, M. de (Eds.), *La dépression: Etudes* (pp. 74–87). Paris: Masson.

Bonis, M. de, De Boeck, P., Lida-Pulik, H., & Féline, A. (1995). Identity disturbances, self-other differentiation in schizophrenics, borderlines and normal controls. *Comprehensive Psychiatry, 36*, 362–366.

Bonis, M. de, De Boeck, P. Lida-Pulik, H., Hourtané, M., Féline, A. (1996). *Self-concept and mood: A comparative study between depressed patients with and without borderline personality disorder* (manuscript submitted for publication).

Bower, G. H., & Cohen, P. N. (1982). Emotional influences in memory and thinking: Data and theory. In M. S. Clark & S. T. Fiske (Eds.), *Affect and cognition*, (pp. 291–331). Hillsdale, NJ:. Erlbaum.

Brown, G. W., & Harris, T. (1978). *Social origins of depression*. New York: Free Press.

Button, E. (Ed.). (1982). *Personal construct theory and mental health. Theory, research and practice*. London: Croom Helm.

Carver, C. S., & Scheier, M. F. (1990). Origins and functions of positive and negative affect: A control-process view. *Psychological Review, 97*, 19–35.

Chetwynd, J. (1977). The psychological meaning of structural measures derived from grids. In P. Slater (Ed.), *Dimensions of intrapersonal space* (Vol. 2, pp. 175–194). London: Wiley.

Cochran, S. D., & Hammen, C. L. (1985). Perceptions of stressful life events and depression: A test of attributional models. *Journal of Personality and Social Psvchology, 48*, 1562–1571.

Coyne, J. C., & Gotlib, I. H. (1983). The role of cognition in depression: A critical appraisal. *Psychological Bulletin, 94*, 472–505.

Dmitrieff, L. (1989). *Structure des representations cognitives et dépression*. Unpublished DEA manuscript, Université Paris VI.

Gara, M. A., Woolfolk, R. L., Cohen, B. D., Goldston, R. B., Allen, L. A., & Novalany, J. (1993). Perception of self and other in major depression. *Journal of Abnormal Psychology, 102*, 93–100.

Goldston, R. B., Gara, M. A., & Woolfolk, R. L. (1992). Emotion differentiation: A correlate of symptom severity in major depression. *Journal of Nervous and Mental Disease, 180*, 712–718.

Grize, J. B. (1992). Logique et raisonnement: A propos de "Raisons et Déraisons", de Monique de Bonis. *Revue Internationale de Psychopathologie, 6*, 227–235.

Haaga, D. A. F., Dyck, M. J., & Ernst, D. (1991). Empirical status of cognitive theory of depression. *Psychological Bulletin, 110*, 215–236.

Hammen, C., Ellicott, A., Gitlin, M., & Jamison, K. R. (1989). Sociotropy/autonomy and vulnerability to specific life events in patients with unipolar depression and bipolar disorders. *Journal of Abnormal Psychology, 98*, 154–160.

Heider, F. (1946). Attitudes and cognitive organization. *Journal of Psychology, 21*, 107–102.

Herhsberger, P. J. (1990). Self-complexity and health promotion: Promising but premature. *Psychological Reports, 66*, 1207–1216.

Higgins, E. T. (1987). Self-discrepancy: A theory relating self and affect. *Psychological Review, 94*, 319–340.

Kelly, G. A. (1955). *The psychology of personal constructs* (Vols. 1 & 2). New York: Norton.

Lebart, L., Morineau, A., & Warwick, A. (1984). *Multivariate descriptive statistical analysis. Correspondence analysis and related techniques for large matrices*. New York: Wiley.

Lida, H., Bonis, M. de, & Féline, A. (1992). Structure du self-concept et schizophrenie. *European Review of Applied Psychology, 42*, 159–160.

Linville, P. W. (1987). Self-complexity as a cognitive buffer against stress-related illness and depression. *Journal of Personality and Social Psychology, 52*, 663–676.

Neimeyer, R. (1985). Personal constructs in depression: Research and clinical implications In E. Button (Ed.), *Personal construct theory and mental health. Theory, research and practice*, (pp. 82–102). London: Croom Helm.

Nelson, R. E., & Craighead, W. E. (1977). Selective recall of positive and negative feedback, self-control behavior and depression. *Journal of Abnormal Psychology, 86*, 379–388.

Rosenberg, S. (1977). New approaches to the analysis of personal constructs in person perception. In J. K. Cole and A. W. Landfield (Eds.), *Nebraska symposium on motivation* (Vol. 24, pp. 174–242). Lincoln: University of Nebraska Press.

Rowe, D. (1971). Poor prognosis in a case of depression as predicted by the repertory grid. *Psychiatry, 118*, 297–300.

Sarason, I. G., Johnson, J. H., & Siegal, J. M. (1978). Assessing the impact of life changes: Development of the life experience survey. *Journal of Consulting and Clinical Psychology, 46*, 932–946.

Schwartz, R. M., & Garamoni, G. L. (1989). Cognitive balance and psychopathology: Evaluation of an information processing model of positive and negative states of mind. *Clinical Psychology Review, 9*, 271–294.

Sheehan, M. J. (1981). Constructs and conflict in depression. *British Journal of Psychology, 72*, 197–209.

Shrout, P. E., Link, B. G., Dohrenwend, B. P., Skodol, A. E., Stueve, A., & Mirotznik, J. (1989). Characterizing life events as risk factors for depression: The role of fateful loss events. *Journal of Abnormal Psychology, 98*, 460–467.

Slade, P. D., & Sheehan, M. J. (1979). The measurement of 'conflict' in repertory grids. *British Journal of Psychology, 70*, 519–524.

Slater, P. (1976). *The measurment of intrapersonal space by grid technique: Vol. 1. Explorations of intrapersonal space.* London: Wiley.

Slater, P. (1977). *The measurement of intrapersonal space by grid technique: Vol. 2. Dimensions of intrapersonal space.* London: Wiley.

Space, L. G., & Cromwell, R. L. (1980). Personal constructs among depressed patients. *Journal of Nervous and Mental Disease, 168*, 150–158.

Space, L. G., Dingeman, P., & Cromwell, R. L. (1983). Self-construing and alienation in depressives, schizophrenics and normals. In J. Adams-Webber & J. Mancuso (Eds.), *Applications of Personal Construct Theory.* Toronto: Wiley.

Strauman, T. J. (1989). Self-discrepancies in clinical depression and social phobia: Cognitive structures that underlie emotional disorders? *Journal of Abnormal Psychology, 98*, 14–22.

Teasdale, J. D., & Barnard, P. J. (1993). *Affect, cognition and change. Re-modelling depressive thought.* Hillsdale, NJ: Erlbaum.

Teasdale, J. D., Taylor, M., Cooper, Z., Hayhurst, H., & Paykel, E. S. (1995). Depressive thinking: Shifts in construct accessibility or in schematic mental models. *Journal of Abnormal Psychology, 104*, 500–507.

Tomkins, S. S. (1963). *Affect, imagery, consciousness: Vol. 2. The negative affects.* New York: Springer.

14

Walter D. Scott & Rick E. Ingram

Affective Influences in Depression

Conceptual Issues, Cognitive Consequences,
and Multiple Mechanisms

There are two facts about depression that are inescapable. The first is that depression is an extremely widespread problem. In a large-scale project that interviewed approximately 19,000 people in five U.S. cities, the National Institute of Mental Health Epidemiologic Catchment Area Study found a lifetime prevalence rate of 6.3% and a 1-year prevalence rate of 3.7% for major depressive disorder (Weissman, Bruce, Leaf, Florio, & Holzer, 1991). In the same study, almost 30% of those assessed reported significant symptoms of depression. Projecting from these figures, then, literally millions of people in the United States suffer from substantial depressive symptoms.

Second, depression is an affective disorder. Although a number of symptoms can occur in depression, its essential feature according to the *Diagnostic and Statistical Manual of Mental Disorders* (4th ed.; American Psychiatric Association, 1994; hereinafter DSM-IV) is *sad or depressed affect*. In this chapter, our focus will be on the affective processes that are linked to unipolar depression.

Given the important linkage between depression and affect, the purpose of this chapter is to explore the affective foundations of depression. To do so, we begin by examining several conceptual issues, which include examining the meanings of depression and emotion as constructs. Another important conceptual issue concerns the use of affect induction studies to make statements about the role of affect in depression. After discussing these conceptual issues, we address the cognitive consequences of depression and negative affective states. We conclude the chapter by describing multiple mechanisms by which affect may produce the cognitive and motivational characteristics observed in unipolar depression.

Conceptual Issues

Nature of the Depression Construct

Depression is viewed by many investigators as a constellation of symptoms, affect being primary, that meet DSM-IV criteria. These criteria, however, represent but one operational definition of the construct. A variety of other potential operational definitions exist, which highlights the reality that depression is in large part a socially derived construct whose "nature" will vary depending on the particular operational definition in use (Ingram & Miranda, in press).

Consider in this regard that the DSM-IV syndrome that we call depression most likely has different treatment responses, diverse courses, and multiple etiologies. Additionally, depression can manifest clusters of symptoms that are considerably different from one case of the depressive disorder to another. DSM-IV criteria, for example, allow two people to share the same diagnosis of depression despite having only one symptom in common. Differences within the nature of the symptoms themselves are also frequently observed. For example, the symptom of "sleep disturbance" can be initial insomnia, middle insomnia, or terminal insomnia; likewise, the symptom of "appetite change" can refer to losses or gains in appetites.

Regrettably, rigid adherence to DSM-IV criteria has in many respects reified the depression construct. That is, by generating and employing formal diagnostic criteria, there has been a tendency by some researchers to remove the idea from the domain of a psychological construct and to give it a separate existence in its own right. Currently, however, there is too much ambiguity in our knowledge of depression to consider it anything but a psychological construct.

Acknowledging that depression represents a construct rather than an entity per se, a working definition is nevertheless needed for our discussion of affective processes in depression. In this regard, we use the conceptualization of depression offered by Ingram and Miranda (in press), who suggest that depression (a) represents a psychologically mediated disorder, (b) is reactive to life events, (c) is unipolar, and (d) reflects a state of both social and psychological dysfunction. The symptoms characterizing this disorder may or may not be sufficient at any given time to meet formal diagnostic criteria, though in numerous cases they will. Certainly this may describe only a subset of depressive disorders, although we believe that it is a considerably large subset.

Nature of the Emotion Construct

Understanding affective processes in depression requires a clear definition of emotion. Increasingly, researchers have come to view emotion as a coherent response pattern involving several prototypical features (e.g., Fehr & Russell, 1984). Emotion investigators commonly identify four prototypical features of an emotion: a cognitive appraisal, a change in the pattern of physiological arousal, an action tendency, and a characteristic behavioral expression (Ekman, 1992). Cognitive appraisals refer to the assessment of meaning that an individual constructs of a person-environment relationship that may have harmful or beneficial consequences for the individual's well-being. Appraisals can vary in the degree to which they involve automatic or controlled levels of information processing (Lazarus, 1991). Importantly, the appraisal process triggers several other prototypical features of the emotional state. Together, these features comprise the total emotional experience. Appraisals, for instance, evoke changes in the pattern of physiological arousal. Accompanying this alteration in arousal patterns is a state of action readiness or a behavioral tendency to respond in a particular manner (e.g., to flee, withdraw, or attack). Finally, the emotional response is typically communicated by means of overt expressive behavioral features, especially in facial movements, which may be inhibited or controlled.

In addition to some consensus on what constitutes the prototypical features of affective states, emotion researchers have also begun to identify several discrete emotions. Specifically, there is evidence supporting the existence for the following discrete emotions: sadness, anger, fear, disgust, and happiness (Ekman, 1992; Scherer, Wallbott, Matsumoto, & Kudoh, 1988). For each of these emotions, there appears to be specificity for each of the prototypical affective features, including cognitive appraisals (Smith & Lazarus, 1990), physiological arousal patterns (Levenson, Ekman, & Friesen, 1990), action tendencies (Frijda, Kuipers, & ter Shure, 1989), and overt behaviors such as facial expressions (Ekman, 1989).

Emotion researchers also recognize different types of affective states, typically differentiating affect, mood, and emotion. These states are distinguished primarily by the salience of the cognitive appraisal and by the intensity and duration of the subjective affective experience. *Emotions*, for instance, are defined as affective events in which the individual is relatively aware of the affect-eliciting event. Further, emotions are viewed as acute affective phenomena, with relatively quick onsets and brief durations. In contrast, the onset of a *mood* state is more difficult to discern because cognitive appraisals are generally less salient to the individual. In part due to the unfocused nature of these cognitive appraisals, the valence of mood states are less differentiated. That is, we recognize fewer mood states compared to emotional states. In addition, the physiological arousal patterns and behavioral tendencies of mood states are experienced as less intense but as persisting over a longer period of time (Lazarus, 1991). Finally, the term *affect* is used as a generic, superordinate category, encompassing both emotions and mood states (Forgas, 1992).

Generalizing from Affect-Induction Research to Depression

In seeking to understand affective processes in depression, researchers use a variety of experimental procedures to induce affective states, usually in normal, nondepressed college students (Martin, 1990). There are obvious advantages to such an approach. Although experimental control is one distinct advantage for inducing affect in the laboratory, there are several issues to consider when making generalizations to how affective processes may operate in depression. An important issue concerns the degree to which an experimentally induced negative affective state approximates negative affect in clinical depression. Although in both cases individuals may report feeling badly, the two affective states may differ on other important dimensions.

One dimension on which these affective states may differ is the intensity of the experienced affective state. There have been varying opinions in the literature as to how experimentally induced negative affect compares with depressive affect in intensity, with some researchers assuming that negative affect is more intense in depressive states (e.g., Bower, 1987), and others suggesting the possibility of the opposite, namely, that laboratory-induced negative affective states are more intense (e.g., Ellis & Ashbrook, 1988). In this regard, however, Martin (1990) compared the intensity levels, as indicated by self-report, of naturally occurring and experimentally induced "depressive" affective states. In general, she found no differences in intensity levels between depressed and induced affective states, but she based her conclusion on findings produced primarily in a single laboratory. Although empirical evidence has generally failed to support the notion that more intense affective states necessarily result in more robust cognitive consequences (Matt, Vazquez, & Campbell, 1992), there are other empirical findings (Singer & Salovey, 1988) and several theoretical arguments (Bower, 1981; Ingram, 1984b; Schwarz, 1990) suggesting that they do. Consequently, it is important to determine more conclusively whether intensity levels are matched between depression and affect-induction studies and, if so, whether varying levels of affective intensity can result in unique cognitive consequences.

Perhaps a more critical difference between negative affective states in affect-induction procedures and clinical depression is that they may differ in quality, that is, in *type* of affective state. Earlier we made a distinction between emotion and mood, in which mood states were described as having less salient cognitive appraisals and longer durations. In short, depression appears to be characterized more by negative *mood* states, whereas induction procedures appear to produce affect more similar to *emotional* states. In support of this assertion, stimuli used in the laboratory to induce affect have typically been highly salient to subjects. For instance, these procedures have subjects repeat negatively valenced sentences, imagine a depressive scenario, or listen to sad music. Furthermore, the duration of the affective experience has typically been transient, having dissipated by the debriefing stage of the experiment. In contrast, outside of the laboratory people may be less apt to identify the source of their negative affective states. Further, the affective experience in depression appears to be more chronic, lasting days and even weeks. Such qualitatively unique affective states may produce different cognitive effects. Indeed, there is some evidence to suggest that, as compared to emotions, mood states may have a stronger and a more pervasive impact on some cognitive processes (Schwarz, 1990).

Despite these caveats, affect-induction procedures can inform depression researchers about how basic affective processes operate in depression (Ingram & Reed, 1986). In fact, the use of affect-induction procedures has already elucidated important affective influences, such as whether affect influences memory in depression at the encoding or retrieval stage, or both (Martin, 1990). When affect-induction studies produce findings that parallel the cognitive features of depression, this type of evidence strengthens the case for the role of affective states in producing cognitive features in depression. In the next section, we briefly summarize the cognitive effects of depression and negative affective states. We then review several mechanisms by which negative affect may produce the cognitive effects observed in depression.

Cognitive Consequences

In a word, the cognitive features of depression are depressive. Depressed individuals selectively attend to negative information (Ingram, 1984a), and, when given a choice, seek out more information about sad people than about happy people (Wenzlaff & Prohaska, 1989). Depressed people are more likely to recognize negative as compared to neutral words when these words are presented at a subthreshold level (Powell & Hemsley, 1984). They also report more negative (Kendall, Howard, & Hays, 1989) and less positive automatic thoughts (Ingram, Slater, Atkinson, & Scott, 1990). Further, they display a pervasive negative evaluative bias for a variety of stimuli, including imagined activities (Grosscup & Lewinsohn, 1980) and other people (Hokanson, Hummer, & Butler, 1991). They are particularly critical in evaluating themselves (Bargh & Tota, 1988) and view the future with pessimism (Alloy & Ahrens, 1987). Finally, depressed individuals exhibit numerous memory biases for negatively valenced information, recalling more unpleasant than pleasant autobiographical memories (Blaney, 1986), more failures than successes on task performances (Craighead, Hickey, & DeMonbreun, 1979), and more negatively than positively valenced words and phrases (Ingram, Partridge, Scott, & Bernet, 1994).

The role of negative affect in producing these negative cognitive biases in depression is supported by increasing evidence (Segal & Ingram, 1994). For instance, Miranda, Persons, and Byers (1990) found that depressed psychiatric patients exhibited changes in negativistic thinking that matched natural diurnal fluctuations in negative affective states. Specifically, when these depressed individuals were experiencing high levels of negative affect, they reported more dysfunctional attitudes. When lower levels of negative affect were present, the same patients reported fewer dysfunctional attitudes. In short, negative cognition in depression appears to be "mood-state dependent" (Miranda & Persons, 1988).

Further support for the role of negative affect in producing the cognitive features of depression can be found in the affect-induction literature. Studies where negative affect is induced in nondepressed college students show results that generally parallel findings in clinical depression (Sedikedes, 1992). After the induction of a negative affective state, these otherwise "normal" individuals attend more to unfavorable self-information (Forgas & Bower, 1987). They exhibit a general negative evaluative judgmental bias (Mayer, Gaschke, Braverman, & Evans, 1992), rating imagined activities as less pleasant (Snyder & White, 1982) and indicating less satisfaction with political figures, controversial topics, and consumer products (Forgas & Moylan, 1987; Isen, Shalker, Clark, & Karp, 1978). They form more negative impressions of other people (Forgas & Bower, 1987) and perceive less support from others (Cohen, Towbes, & Flocco, 1988).

Importantly, these laboratory-induced affect-congruent effects are especially robust for self-related information (Sedikedes, 1992). Subjects induced to feel temporarily sad rate themselves lower on positively valued personality traits, such as intelligence, and higher on negatively valued personality traits, such as unfriendliness (Brown & Mankowski, 1993). When shown videotapes of their own social interaction skills, they also evaluate their behaviors as more antisocial, withdrawn, socially unskilled, and incompetent, despite the fact that objective judges rate them more favorably (Forgas, Bower, & Krantz, 1984). In addition, they report less satisfaction with imagined average academic and social interaction performances, such as earning a C in psychology or presenting an oral report in front of a small class (Cervone, Kopp, Schaumann, & Scott, 1994). They are more dissatisfied with their lives as a whole (Schwarz & Clore, 1983) and more pessimistic about future prospects (Forgas & Moylan, 1987). Finally, they exhibit a memory bias for negatively valenced information about the self, recalling more unpleasant personal memories (Teasdale & Fogarty, 1979), more unfavorable personal feedback (Ingram, 1984a), and more negatively valenced self-descriptive words and phrases (Bower, Gilligan, & Monteiro, 1981; Laird, Wagener, Halal, & Szegda, 1982).

To summarize, the evidence is quite strong in supporting the role of affective processes in producing negatively valenced cognition in depression. Negative cognitions appear to change with fluctuating levels of negative affect. Further, the negative cognitive biases found in depression have been created via experimental affect induction in normal, nondepressed college students. Consequently, it appears reasonable to conclude that a consequence of depressive affective states is negative cognition; however, the manner by which affect produces these cognitions is less clear.

Multiple Mechanisms

In accounting for the varied cognitive effects of negative affective states, emotion researchers have proposed several mechanisms. In the remainder of this chapter, we will focus on three mechanisms: priming, informational, and categorical. Although all three mechanisms have received a substantial amount of attention in basic research on affect and cognition, the mechanism of affective priming has generally constituted the theoretical bulwark in cognitive models of depression. By incorporating multiple affective mechanisms, however, we maintain that these models may account more comprehensively for dysphoric cognition in depression.

The Affect Priming Mechanism

Affect has a priming effect on similarly-valenced cognition. Just as the presentation of a category word (e.g., *tree*) cues or aids the recall of previously learned category members (e.g., *elm, spruce*), the experience of an affective state facilitates recall of memories that have the same affective valence (Singer & Salovey, 1988). In addition to increasing recall of previously learned material, affect also appears to prime or activate on-line thoughts, judgments, and associations with the same affective valence (Sedikedes, 1992).

In an attempt to account for all of these effects, Bower (1981) proposed a priming mechanism whereby emotions are viewed as special nodes embedded within a general semantic memory network. Each node is viewed as possessing connections to both the features of the emotion and to similarly valenced cognition in memory. For example, the node for sadness is linked to the prototypical features of sadness and to sad-valenced cognitions, including unpleasant memories and negative evaluations, judgments, and thoughts. Activation of the sadness node initiates a process of spreading activation. That is, when the sadness node is primed, activation spreads through interconnected links in the semantic network, with activation levels dissipating with distance from the originally primed node. When the level of activation exceeds a threshold for a particular emotion's node, two kinds of priming effects occur: (a) the individual experiences the prototypical features of the emotion (e.g., cognitive appraisal, change in physiological arousal, action tendency), and (b) there is increased accessibility for associated cognitions (Bower, 1981).

Bower's affect priming mechanism has subsequently been adapted and elaborated in several cognitive models of depression (Ingram, 1984b; Kuiper, Derry, & MacDonald, 1982; Teasdale, 1983). For example, in Ingram's (1984b) information-processing model, the onset of depression results from the priming of a sadness emotion node, which is activated by loss-related appraisals. The severity of the loss appraisal initially determines the duration and the intensity of the depressive mood state. However, activation in the sadness emotion node then spreads through associated connections to negatively valenced cognitive structures containing depressive self-statements, associations, attributions, and memories. The individual experiences priming of these structures as depressive rumination. This rumination of depressive cognition then reverberates within the sadness emotion node, resulting in a vicious cycle of spreading activation that maintains and potentially exacerbates depressive mood and cognition. The degree to which this cycling effect occurs depends on the degree of elaboration in the individual's depression-related cognitive structures. Individuals with well-elaborated, complex depressive memory structures are the ones who are the most vulnerable to prolonged, intense depressive mood states (Ingram, 1984b).

The affect priming model specifies several consequences for cognition in depression. Broadly, these cognitive consequences can be labeled *affect-congruent* learning (Bower, 1987). Affect-congruent learning is demonstrated when depressed individuals learn negatively valenced information more efficiently than they learn neutral or positive information. It occurs as a result of attentional, perceptual, and/or encoding biases that are driven by the depressed person's elaborate depressive cognitive structures. Specifically, when a depressive cognitive structure is primed, the salience of affectively congruent sad information is increased, causing it to "pop out" from the total informational array. Consequently, incoming negatively valenced information, which is more similar to the activated sadness node, receives greater attention (Ingram, 1984b). An encoding advantage exists for negatively valenced information because negative information is congruent with primed and well-elaborated depressive memory structures. As a result, the priming mechanism predicts that depressed individuals should more rapidly perceive and more easily cognitively elaborate on negatively valenced information, resulting in such information being processed at a deeper level of cognitive analysis.

In general, affect-priming mechanisms have received mixed empirical support (Blaney, 1986; Bower, 1991; Matt et al., 1992; Singer & Salovey, 1988). Basic research on affective processes has provided three kinds of evidence that are especially difficult to reconcile with models of affective influences that rely solely on affective priming mechanisms. First, there are instances of affect-*incongruent* cognition. Cervone et al. (1994) found that induced negative affect caused people to set higher performance standards. According to affect-priming models, negative affect ought to prime negative performance-related information (e.g., "I've done poorly on these types of things in the past" or "I'm just not very smart"), causing the person to set lower, not higher performance standards. The finding of affect-incongruent cognition for nondepressed people suggests the operation of a different affective mechanism.

Second, research on the influence of affect on evaluative judgments, where a robust affect-congruent effect exists, is not easily explained by an affect-priming account. In the priming model, affect-congruent judgment results from the increased accessibility, via spreading activation, of affectively congruent cognition. In fact, however, memory retrieval and evaluative judgments are often poorly correlated (Hastie & Park, 1986). For example, Fiedler, Pampe, and Scherf (1986) found that induced negative affective states caused people to form more unfavorable impressions of others. However, the negative affective state did not cause enhanced recall for negative information about those target persons. This finding would suggest that it was not increased accessibility of negative information that caused people to evaluate others more negatively. Rather, some other affective mechanism was at work.

Basic research on affective processes has implicated several nonpriming mechanisms. Specifically, we will review two affective mechanisms: affect-informational processes and categorical-affect processes. These two affective mechanisms have received some experimental support in studies with nondepressed college students, but have yet to be tested in subjects with clinical depression.

The Affect-as-Information Mechanism

In priming models, affect exerts an indirect influence on cognition: Affect primes cognitive structures, biasing subsequent cognitive activity. Although priming may account for many affective influences, accumulating evidence suggests the operation, at least in some instances, of a more direct process (Cervone et al., 1994; Schwarz & Clore, 1983; Scott & Cervone, 1996). Specifically, affect can function as information in the construction of evaluative judgments (Schwarz, 1990). Rather than engage in an effortful, systematic analysis of positive and negative features when evaluating a target, individuals may adopt a "how do I feel about it" heuristic, relying on the hedonic meaning of their affective states. In this case, preexisting affective states combine with any affective responses instigated by the target being judged, thereby exerting an unintended influence on the unrelated evaluative judgment. However, if the informative value of the preexisting affective state is attributed to some external stimulus, such as the actual inducing event, then the feeling state is discounted as a relevant source of information for the current judgment task.

There have been only a few empirical demonstrations of the affect-as-information mechanism. In the second of two studies from their landmark paper, Schwarz and Clore (1983) induced negative and positive affective states using an autobiographical-memory induction procedure. Prior to the affect manipulation, however, some of the subjects were told that the experimental setting itself (i.e., the room) might evoke "tense" or "elated" feelings. For these subjects an external source of attribution for the affective state was highly salient. Following the affect manipulation, subjects rated how satisfied they were with their lives as a whole. When no mention was made of affect-inducing features of the room, subjects in the negative affect condition rated their lives as less satisfying, a finding that duplicates the well-supported affect-congruent judgment effect. However, when the room was described as a possible cause of "tense" feelings, the affect-congruent judgment effect vanished: Subjects who were put in a negative mood did not rate their lives as any less satisfying than subjects who were put in a positive mood. When provided with a salient source of attribution for their feelings, these subjects appeared to discount the informational value of the negative affective state. As already described, this discounting effect has been found for naturally occurring mood as well (e.g., Schwarz & Clore, 1983, Study 1).

The identification of this alternative affective mechanism may have some implications for affective processes in depression. As one example, affect-informational processes may be involved in several motivational features of clinical depression. One of the hallmarks of depression is anhedonia, an impaired capacity to experience pleasure. In part, evaluative judgment processes may underlie this feature of depression. In fact, compared to the nondepressed, depressed individuals do evaluate common pleasant activities as less enjoyable (Lewinsohn & Hoberman, 1982). Some basic experimental research has supported the role of negative affect in low evaluations of activities. Specifically, nondepressed college students who are made to experience a negative affective state evaluate activities similarly to depressed people, namely, as less pleasant (Carson & Adams, 1980).

In a recent set of experiments, Martin, Ward, Achee, and Wyer (1993) provided some initial evidence suggesting that affect-as-information processes may underlie this affective influence on evaluative judgments. Specifically, Martin et al. had nondepressed college students view a film to induce negative and positive affective states. Subjects then participated in a person impression-formation task in which they had to read a series of cards that described various behaviors of the target person. Within each of the affect conditions, half of the subjects were told to continue reading the cards until they "no longer enjoyed" the task. The remaining half of the subjects were told to continue reading the cards until they "had enough information." Interestingly, the influence of negative affect on the amount of time spent reading the cards depended on the stop-rule given to the subjects. When told to work on the task until they no longer enjoyed it, subjects in the negative affect condition spent less time reading the cards. In effect, these subjects appeared to interpret their negative affective states as signifying that the task was not enjoyable. However, when told to read until they had enough information, subjects in the negative affect condition spent more time reading the cards than subjects in the positive affect condition. Subjects appeared to interpret their negative affective states as signifying that they had not yet acquired sufficient information to make a judgment.

After replicating these findings using a different task (listing category exemplars), Martin et al. (1993) argued that the motivational implications of affective states depend on how they are interpreted. When the situational context involves judging how enjoyable a particular activity is, people experiencing negative affect may interpret their feelings as signifying that an activity is unpleasant. For depressed individuals, who report chronic negative affectivity, a potential motivational consequence is that they will evaluate activities as affording minimal reinforcement or hedonic enjoyment value. As a result, they will be less motivated to engage in potentially rewarding activities (MacPhillamy & Lewinsohn, 1974).

Affect-informational mechanisms may also play a role in producing a maladaptive self-regulatory pattern observed in depression. Self-control models of depression propose that depressed individuals set relatively stringent personal standards that may exceed the performance levels that are judged to be achievable (Rehm, 1977). Although empirical findings have been somewhat equivocal, the evidence does suggest that depression is associated with the adoption of personal standards that are relatively perfectionistic (Hewitt & Flett, 1991), especially in relation to one's perceived capabilities (Ahrens, 1987). That is, depressed individuals tend to set minimal standards that are beyond the performance levels they view themselves as capable of achieving. This self-regulatory pattern has particularly pernicious consequences, resulting in increased negative affect, decreased effort and persistence on tasks, poorer use of behavioral strategies essential to successful task performance on complex tasks, and eventual goal abandonment (Bandura & Cervone, 1983).

Recent research has supported a causal role of negative affect in producing this maladaptive self-regulatory pattern (Cervone et al., 1994; Scott & Cervone, 1996). In a series of studies, Cervone et al. induced positive, negative, and neutral affective states and then assessed subject's performance standards and self-efficacy appraisals for different activities. The findings revealed that negative affect caused people to set higher standards for performance but had no effect on people's judgments of self-efficacy. The result was that people did not believe they had the capabilities to meet the high standards that they had adopted.

Several findings suggest that affect-informational processes produce this self-regulatory pattern. When people set performance standards, they may rely on their affective states to evaluate imagined outcomes (Cervone et al., 1994). In setting a standard for a minimally acceptable grade in psychology, for example, people in a negative mood may first evaluate a more moderate outcome, such as earning a C, consult their negative mood states, feel dissatisfied, and so evaluate that moderate outcome as dissatisfactory. This process would culminate in the establishment of higher minimal standards for performance: if a C is dissatisfactory, then an A or a B would be required in order to be minimally satisfied. According to this reasoning, induced negative affect would simultaneously cause lower evaluative judgments (e.g., dissatisfaction with a C) but higher performance standards (e.g., require earning a B or an A for minimal satisfaction). In fact, Cervone et al. found that people did set higher standards for performance while simultaneously lowering their evaluations of prospective performance outcomes.

More conclusive evidence for affect informational processes underlying perfectionistic standard setting was found by Scott and Cervone (1996), who provided a test of mood-as-information's discounting hypothesis. The discounting hypothesis predicts that feelings will be discounted as information when an external stimulus for the feeling state is made highly salient. In brief, this is exactly what Scott and Cervone found. Negative affect continued to lead to the adoption of high minimal performance standards but only when the salience of the induced negative mood state was minimized. However, when people's attention was drawn to the mood-inducing qualities of the induction procedure, induced negative mood no longer resulted in perfectionistic standard setting.

Although affect-informational processes may operate pervasively in depression, evaluative judgments may be particularly susceptible to the influence of affect used heuristically as informational input (Schwarz, 1990). For instance, a depressed person who chronically experiences negative affect may interpret these negative states as meaning that he or she is dissatisfied with important features of the self, the world, and the future (Beck, Rush, Shaw, & Emery, 1979). However, until there are direct tests of the affect-informational mechanism with clinically depressed populations, statements about affect-informational processes in depression must be regarded as hypothetical.

The Categorical Affect Mechanism

In the preceding discussions of affective mechanisms, we have treated negative affect as a unitary state. However, the evidence suggests that we must go beyond global distinctions of pleasant or unpleasant affect if we are to fully understand how affective processes operate in depression. Depressed individuals report experiencing a confluence of negative affective states, particularly sadness, anxiety, and hostility (Izard, 1977; Scott & Shadel, 1996). Although different negative affective states are often highly correlated, depressed individuals report varying levels of each, and they appear to experience stable predominant mood states. Basic research on emotion suggests that different negative mood profiles in depression may produce distinct cognitive consequences (Bodenhausen, Sheppard, & Kramer, 1994; Laird, Cuniff, Sheehan, Shulman, & Strum, 1989; Scott, 1993), a possibility that is currently being explored (Scott & Shadel, 1996). For instance, depressed individuals who report high levels of hostility would be expected to process information in ways similar to individuals prone to hostile moods, which is to selectively process hostile information and to perceive others as more hostile and less friendly (Allred & Smith, 1991).

In actuality, categorical affective processes do not constitute a separate mechanism, but specify the qualitatively different affective states that operate through the different mechanisms already discussed. Both priming and affect-informational explanations allow for the differential influence of discrete negative affective states. In Bower's (1981) priming model, rather than one global negative emotion node, he proposes separate memory nodes for each distinct negative affective state, such as sadness, fear, and anger. In turn, each of these nodes is linked to its own subset of negative cognitions. Thus, depending on the negative affective state activated, different kinds of negative cognition are primed. Similarly, Schwarz (1990) argues that an affect-informational mechanism can account for the specific cognitive effects of different negative affective states. Because different negative affective states are associated with distinct cognitive appraisals and action tendencies, a person who experiences a specific affect category receives information that is unique to that feeling state.

Summary and Conclusions

We wanted to document that the experience of a negative affective state exerts a strong influence on cognition, leaving a residue of dysphoric attributions, evaluations, memories, self-statements, and other types of cognition. In addition, negative affect appears to influence basic cognitive operations, such as attention, encoding, and retrieval processes. In a reciprocal fashion, biased cognitive processes and products intensify negative affective experiencing, resulting in the vicious cycle that is a predominant feature of many cognitive models of depression.

Models of these affective influences in depression need to be informed by basic research on affective and cognitive processes. Originally, cognitive models of depression drew on basic emotion research in incorporating affective priming mechanisms. Although affective priming mechanisms once promised a parsimonious explanation of the varied affective influences on cognition, they no longer appear able to account for the complete pattern of results. Indeed, in referring to the status of his affect priming model, Bower (1987) has commented that

> overall, the [affect-priming] theory has not fared well: it has had a few successes and several glaring failures, under conditions where it should reasonably have succeeded. Thus, we are left with a theory which is badly in need of repairs—or in need of a replacement theory. (p. 454)

Rather than repairing affect-priming theories or even replacing them altogether, we have argued that cognitive models of depression need to integrate multiple mechanisms of affective influence. In all likelihood, priming, informational, and categorical mechanisms are all involved in the mediation of affective influences on cognition (Forgas, 1995).

We began this chapter by reaffirming that depression represents a construct rather than a disease entity. Recognition of the diversity and variability of the features that characterize this construct has important implications for understanding the processes that contribute to depression. Costello (1993) has argued that because of the heterogeneity of symptoms that characterize depression, researchers who find significant relationships between variables and the syndrome cannot determine what causal mechanisms are at work. For example, are the causal processes underlying one set of symptoms different from those that underlie another set of symtoms, even though both symptom clusters are called depression? A multiple-mechanism-based approach to the study of depression allows for a useful analysis of depression in that it does not assume that all depression is equivalent; depressed individuals may possess different affective and cognitive characteristics that have considerably different consequences for the causal processes that are linked to their depression. Certainly such an approach underscores the complexity of the depression construct, but it is unlikely that any real progress will be made in understanding this disorder until we begin to fully appreciate such complexity.

Acknowledgments   We thank Robin Mermelstein, James Patrey, William Shadel, and members of the University of Illinois at Chicago Personality/Social Psychology Journal Club for their comments on earlier drafts of this chapter. We give special thanks to Daniel Cervone and Suzanna Penningroth for their many substantive comments and extensive editorial assistance.

References

Ahrens, A. H. (1987). Theories of depression: The role of goals and the self-evaluation process. *Cognitive Therapy and Research, 11*, 665–680.

Alloy, L. B., & Ahrens, A. H. (1987). Depression and pessimism for the future: Biased use of statistically relevant information in predictions for self versus others. *Journal of Personality and Social Psychology, 52*, 366–378.

Allred, K. D., & Smith, T. W. (1991). Social cognition in cynical hostility, *Cognitive Therapy and Research, 15*, 399–412.

American Psychiatric Association. (1994). *Diagnostic and statistical manual of mental disorders* (4th ed.). Washington, DC: Author.

Bandura, A., & Cervone, D. (1983). Self-evaluative and self-efficacy mechanisms governing the motivational effects of goal systems. *Journal of Personality and Social Psychology, 45*, 1017–1028.

Bargh, J. A., & Tota, M. E. (1988). Context-dependent automatic processing in depression: Accessibility of negative constructs with regard to self but not others. *Journal of Personality and Social Psychology, 54*, 925–939.

Beck, A. T., Rush, A. J., Shaw, B. F., & Emery, G. (1979). *Cognitive therapy of depression*. New York: Guilford.

Blaney, P. (1986). Affect and memory: A review. *Psychological Bulletin, 99*, 229–246.

Bodenhausen, G. V., Sheppard, L. A., & Kramer, G. P. (1994). Negative affect and social judgment: The differential impact of anger and sadness. *European Journal of Social Psychology, 24*, 45–62.

Bower, G. H. (1981). Mood and memory. *American Psychologist, 36*, 129–148.

Bower, G. H. (1987). Commentary on mood and memory. *Behavioral Research and Therapy, 25*, 443–455.

Bower, G. H. (1991). Mood congruity of social judgments. In J. P. Forgas (Ed.), *Emotion and social judgments* (pp. 31–53). Oxford: Pergamon.

Bower, G. H., Gilligan, S. G., & Monteiro, K. P. (1981). Selectivity of learning caused by affective states. *Journal of Experimental Psychology: General, 110*, 451–473.

Brown, J. D., & Mankowski, T. A. (1993). Self-esteem, mood, and self evaluation: Changes in mood and the way you see you. *Journal of Personality and Social Psychology, 64*, 421–430.

Carson, T . P., & Adams, H. E. (1980). Activity valence as a function of mood change. *Journal of Abnormal Psychology, 89*, 368–377.

Cervone, D., Kopp, D. A., Schaumann, L., & Scott, W. D. (1994). The influence of induced mood on personal standards, expectancies, and self-efficacy judgments. *Journal of Personality and Social Psychology Personality, 67*, 1–14.

Cohen, L. H., Towbes, L. C., & Flocco, R. (1988). Effects of induced mood on self-reported life events and perceived and received social support. *Journal of Personality and Social Psychology, 55*, 669–674.

Costello, C. G. (1993). The advantages of the symptom approach to depression. In C. G. Costello (Ed.), *Symptoms of depression* (pp. 1–22). New York: Wiley.

Craighead, W. E., Hickey, K. S., & DeMonbreun, B. G. (1979). Distortion of perception and recall of neutral feedback in depression. *Cognitive Therapy and Research, 3*, 291–298.

Ekman, P. (1989). The argument and evidence about universals in facial expressions of emotion. In H. Wagner & A. Manstead (Eds.), *Handbook of social psychophysiology* (pp. 143–164). Chichester: Wiley.

Ekman, P. (1992). An argument for basic emotions. *Cognition and Emotion, 6,* 169–200.

Ellis, H. C., & Ashbrook, T. W. (1988). Resource allocation model of the effects of depressed mood state on memory. In K. Fiedler & J. P. Forgas (Eds.), *Affect, cognition, and social behavior* (pp. 25–43). Toronto: Hogrefe.

Fehr, B., & Russell, J. A. (1984). Concept of emotion viewed from a prototype perspective. *Journal of Experimental Psychology: General, 113,* 464–486.

Fiedler, K., Pampe, H., & Scherf, U. (1986). Mood and memory for tightly organized social information. *European Journal of Social Psychology, 16,* 149–164.

Forgas, J. P. (1992). Affect in social judgments and decisions: A multiprocess model. In M. P. Zanna (Ed.), *Advances in experimental social psychology* (Vol. 24, pp. 227–275). New York: Wiley.

Forgas, J. P. (1995). Mood and judgment: The affect infusion model (AIM). *Psychological Bulletin, 117,* 39–66.

Forgas, J. P., & Bower, G. H. (1987). Mood effects on person-perception judgments. *Journal of Personality and Social Psychology, 53,* 53–60.

Forgas, J. P., Bower, G. H., & Krantz, S. E. (1984). The influence of mood on perceptions of social interactions. *Journal of Experimental Social Psychology, 20,* 497–513.

Forgas, J. P., & Moylan, S. (1987). After the movies: Transient mood and social judgment. *Personality and Social Psychology Bulletin, 13,* 467–477.

Frijda, N. H., Kuipers, P., & ter Schure, E. (1989). Relations among emotion, appraisal, and emotional action readiness. *Journal of Personality and Social Psychology, 57,* 212–228.

Grosscup, S. J., & Lewinsohn, P. M. (1980). Unpleasant and pleasant events and mood. *Journal of Clinical Psychology, 36,* 252–259.

Hastie, R., & Park, B. (1986). The relationship between memory and judgment depends on whether the judgment task is memory-based or on-line. *Psychological Review, 93,* 258–268.

Hewitt, P. L., & Flett, G. L. (1991). Dimensions of perfectionism in unipolar depression. *Journal of Abnormal Psychology, 100,* 98–101.

Hokanson, J. E., Hummer, J. T., & Butler, A. C. (1991). Interpersonal perceptions by depressed college students. *Cognitive Therapy and Research, 15,* 443–457.

Ingram, R. E. (1984b). Toward an information-processing analysis of depression. *Cognitive Therapy and Research, 8,* 443–478.

Ingram, R. E. (1984a). Information processing and feedback: Effects of mood and information favorability on the cognitive processing of personally relevant information. *Cognitive Therapy and Research, 8,* 371–386.

Ingram, R. E., & Miranda, J. (in press). *Cognitive vulnerability to depression.* New York: Guilford Press.

Ingram, R. E., Partridge, S., Scott, W. D., & Bernet, C. Z. (1994). Schema specificity in subclinical syndrome depression: Distinctions between automatically versus effortfully encoded state and trait depressive information. *Cognitive Therapy and Research, 18,* 195–209.

Ingram, R. E., & Reed, M. R. (1986). Information encoding and retrieval processes in depression: Findings, issues, and future directions. In R. E. Ingram (Ed.), *Information processing approaches to clinical psychology* (pp. 131–150). San Diego: Academic Press.

Ingram, R. E., Slater, M. A., Atkinson, J. H., & Scott, W. D. (1990). Positive automatic cognition in major affective disorder. *Psychological Assessment: A Journal of Consulting and Clinical Psychology, 2,* 209–211.

Isen, A. M., Shalker, T., Clark, M., & Karp, L. (1978). Affect, accessibility of material in memory and behavior; A cognitive loop? *Journal of Personality and Social Psychology*, *36*, 1–12.

Izard, C. E. (1977). *Human emotions*. New York: Plenum Press.

Kendall, P. C., Howard, B. L., & Hays, R. C. (1989). Self-referent speech and psychopathology: The balance of positive and negative thinking. *Cognitive Therapy and Research*, *13*, 583–598.

Kuiper, N. A., Derry, P. A., & MacDonald, M. R. (1982). Self-reference and person perception in depression. In G. Weary & H. Mirels (Eds.), *Integrations of clinical and social psychology*. New York: Oxford University Press.

Laird, J. D., Cuniff, M., Sheehan, K., Shulman, D., & Strum, G. (1989). Emotion specific effects of facial expressions on memory for life events. *Journal of Social Behavior and Personality*, *4*, 87–98.

Laird, J. D., Wagener, J. J., Halal, M., & Szegda, M. (1982). Remembering what you feel: Effects of emotion on memory. *Journal of Personality and Social Psychology*, *42*, 646–657.

Lazarus, R. S. (1991). *Emotion and adaptation*. New York: Oxford University Press.

Levenson, R. W., Ekman, P., & Friesen, W. V. (1990). Voluntary facial expression generates emotion-specific nervous system activity. *Psychophysiology*, *27*, 363–384.

Lewinsohn, P. M., & Hoberman, H. M. (1982). Depression. In A. S. Bellack, M. Hersen, & A. E. Kazdin (Eds.), *International handbook of behavior modification and therapy*. New York: Plenum Press.

MacPhillamy, D. J., & Lewinsohn, P. M. (1974). Depression as a function of desired and obtained pleasure. *Journal of Abnormal Psychology*, *83*, 651–657.

Martin, L. L., Ward, D. W., Achee, J. W., and Wyer, R. S., (1993). Mood as input: People have to interpret the motivational implications of their moods. *Journal of Personality and Social Psychology*, *64*, 317–326.

Martin, M. (1990). On the induction of mood. *Clinical Psychology Review*, *10*, 669–697.

Matt, G. E., Vazquez, C., & Campbell, W. K. (1992). Mood congruent recall of affectively toned stimuli: A meta-analytic review. *Clinical Psychology Review*, *12*, 227–255.

Mayer, J. D., Gaschke, Y. N., Braverman, D. L., & Evans, T. W. (1992). Mood-congruent judgment is a general effect. *Journal of Personality and Social Psychology*, *63*, 119–132.

Miranda, J., & Persons, J. B. (1988). Dysfunctional attitudes are mood-state dependent. *Journal of Abnormal Psychology*, *97*, 76–79.

Miranda, J., Persons, J. B., & Byers, C. N. (1990). Endorsement of dysfunctional beliefs depends on current mood state. *Journal of Abnormal Psychology*, *99*, 237–241.

Powell, M., & Hemsley, D. R. (1984). Depression: A breakdown of perceptual defense. *British Journal of Psychiatry*, *145*, 358–362.

Rehm, L. P. (1977). A self-control model of depression. *Behavior Therapy*, *8*, 787–804.

Scherer, K. R., Wallbott, H. G., Matsumoto, D., & Kudoh, T. (1988). Emotional experience in cultural context: A comparison between Europe, Japan, and the United States. In K. R. Scherer (Ed.), *Facets of emotion: Recent research* (pp. 6–30). Hillsdale, NJ: Erlbaum.

Schwarz, N. (1990). Feelings as information: Information and motivational functions of affective states. In E. T. Higgens & R. M. Sorrentino (Eds.), *Motivation and cognition: Foundations of social behavior* (Vol. 2, pp. 527–561). New York: Guilford Press.

Schwarz, N., & Clore, G. L. (1983). Mood, misattribution, and judgments of well-being: Informative and directive functions of affective states. *Journal of Personality and Social Psychology*, *45*, 513–523.

Scott, W. D. (1993). *A discrete approach to emotion: The effects of anger and sadness on self-referent cognition*. Unpublished master's thesis, University of Illinois at Chicago.

Scott, W. D., & Cervone, D. (1996). *The informative function of negative mood in the adoption of high performance standards: A test of the mood-as-information discounting hypothesis.* Unpublished manuscript.

Scott, W. D., & Shadel, W. G. (1996). Affective influences in depression. Poster presented at the annual meeting of the Association for the Advancement of Behavior Therapy, New York.

Sedikides, D. (1992). Changes in the valence of the self as a function of mood. In M. S. Clark (Ed.), *Emotion and social behavior: Review of personality and social psychology* (Vol. 14, pp. 271–311). Newbury Park, CA: Sage.

Segal, Z. V., & Ingram, R. E. (1994). Mood priming and construct activation in tests of cognitive vulnerability to unipolar depression. *Clinical Psychology Review, 14,* 663–695.

Singer, J. A., & Salovey, P. (1988). Mood and memory: Evaluating the network theory of affect. *Clinical Psychology Review, 8,* 211–251.

Smith, C. A., & Lazarus, R. S. (1990). Emotion and adaptation. In L. A. Pervin (Ed.), *Handbook of personality: Theory and research* (pp. 609–637). New York: Guilford Press.

Snyder, M., & White, P. (1982). Moods and memories: Elation, depression, and the remembering of events of one's life. *Journal of Personality, 50,* 149–167.

Teasdale, J. D. (1983). Negative thinking in depression: Cause, effect or reciprocal relationship? *Advances in Behavioral Research and Therapy, 5,* 3–25.

Teasdale, J. D., & Fogarty, S. J. (1979). Differential effects of induced mood on the recall of pleasant and unpleasant events from episodic memory. *Journal of Abnormal Psychology, 88,* 248–257.

Weissman, M. M., Bruce, M. L., Leaf, P. J., Florio, L. P., & Holzer, C. (1991). Affective disorders. In L. N. Robbins & D. A. Regier (Eds.), *Psychiatric disorders in America: The epidemiologic catchment area study* (pp. 53–80). New York: Free Press.

Wenzlaff, R. M., & Prohaska, M. L. (1989). When misery loves company: Depression and responses to other's moods. *Journal of Experimental Social Psychology, 25,* 220–233.

15

Susan Mineka & Eva Gilboa

Cognitive Biases in Anxiety and Depression

Emotions are thought to consist of several elementary components (e.g., expressive, subjective, physiological, cognitive) that are not in themselves emotional (e.g., Averill, 1992; Ortony & Turner, 1990; Scherer, 1993). In the present chapter, we adopt Scherer's definition of an emotion as an

> episode of temporary synchronization of all major subsystems of organismic functioning represented by five components (cognition, physiological regulation, motivation, motor expression, and monitoring/feeling) in response to the evaluation of an external or internal stimulus event as relevant to the central concerns of the organism. (Scherer, 1993, p. 4)

There is still some question regarding the extent to which each of the different components proposed by Scherer is a necessary part of an emotion. Whereas physiological, expressive, and subjective components are considered to be the "building blocks" of emotions by most theorists, there is less consensus regarding the cognitive component. In this chapter we argue that cognitive processes constitute an important part of the emotion process, and play an important role in the etiology and maintenance of emotional disorders.

Support for the proposition that cognition is an important part of the emotional experience derives from two different sources. First, subjective experiences of emotions often include intrusive thoughts and images involving the emotional event, its implications, and its meaning (e.g., Edwards & Dickerson, 1987, Seibert & Ellis, 1991). Such intrusions are the hallmark of the experience of anxiety and worry, but are also common in other emotional states. Second, a substantial body of literature supports the proposition that affective states influence cognitive processing (cf. Blaney, 1986). Two prominent theories, Bower's (e.g., Bower, 1981) and Beck's (e.g., Beck,

Rush, Shaw, & Emery, 1979), have been put forward to explain these effects. Although these models differ in a number of ways, they make similar predictions regarding the effects of various affective states on cognitive processing. For example, they predict that all affective states are associated with attentional, memory, and interpretative biases for valenced information. These cognitive biases are related to the selective or nonveridical processing of emotionally relevant information (e.g., Mineka, 1992; Mineka & Sutton, 1992; Mineka & Tomarken, 1989). Consequently, according to these models, although the *content* of their concerns might differ, anxious and depressed individuals should demonstrate a similar pattern of cognitive biases in the *processing* of valenced information.

The main goal of this chapter is to review the research literature on cognitive biases in emotional disorders. In the following, we first review the literature on cognitive biases associated with anxiety and depression. Next, we discuss the implications of these findings for theories of cognition and emotion. Finally, we discuss the causal status of these biases (i.e., their role in etiology and maintenance) for anxiety and depression.

Cognitive Biases in Anxiety and Depression

Two lines of research have examined cognitive biases in affective states. The first, conducted mostly with clinical populations, explored the role of cognitive biases in the etiology and maintenance of various emotional disorders. The majority of this research examined the effects of emotional disorders, particularly anxiety and depression, on memory and attention. The second line of research addressed the effects of induced positive and negative affective states on cognitive processing. In a typical study, college students were induced to experience a negative or positive affective state, following which their performance on various cognitive tasks was measured.

Attentional Biases

Dichotic listening, visual dot-probe detection, lexical decision tasks, and a modified Stroop task have been used to study attentional biases. The general conclusion from this body of research is that anxiety is associated with an automatic, preconscious, bias for threatening information. As we will review, the pattern of results concerning the effects of depressed, or sad mood, on attention is more mixed: Whereas some studies have shown that depression is associated with attentional biases, other studies have not. Recent research suggests that even if attentional biases can be demonstrated with depression, they are not likely to occur at the preconscious automatic level, but rather involve strategic or controlled processing.

Anxiety   Clinically, it has long been noted that anxious patients seem to have a tendency toward heightened perception of, and vigilance for, threat and danger cues (e.g., Beck, 1976; Beck & Emery, 1985). Experimental confirmation of such attentional biases comes from studies using information processing paradigms (cf. MacLeod & Mathews, 1991). Using a number of different experimental tasks, researchers have consistently demonstrated that anxious patients show evidence of their attention being diverted, without awareness, toward threatening cues in the environment when there is a mixture of threatening and nonthreatening cues (e.g., MacLeod, Mathews, & Tata, 1986; see MacLeod & Mathews, 1991, for a review). Nonanxious individuals, if anything, show an opposite bias, directing attention away from threatening stimuli.

Four important features of this attentional bias that should be noted. First, the bias appears to operate automatically and outside of conscious awareness, occurring at a very early stage of information processing (e.g., Mogg, Bradley, William, & Mathews, 1993). This conclusion is particularly compelling because it stems from studies that have used three very different kinds of paradigms (dot-probe reaction time task, dichotic listening with secondary reaction time task, and subliminal Stroop color naming task). Second, although most of the relevant studies have been conducted with high-trait anxious individuals or with generalized anxiety disorder patients (GADs), attentional biases seem to exist with nearly all of the anxiety disorders (e.g., Cassidy, McNally, Zeitlin, 1992; Ehlers, Margraf, Davies, & Roth, 1988; Foa & McNally, 1986; Watts, McKenna, Sharrock, & Trezise, 1986).

A third important issue concerns the relative role of state and trait anxiety in mediating these biases. It appears that high state anxiety had different effects on attentional functioning in low- and high-trait anxious individuals: Whereas high-trait anxious individuals demonstrated *increased* attention for threat words under high state anxiety—a mechanism likely to exacerbate their anxiety even further—low-trait anxious persons in this condition diverted their attention *away* from threat words—which is likely to protect them from becoming clinically anxious (e.g., Broadbent & Broadbent, 1988; MacLeod & Mathews, 1988).

A fourth important question addressed in this research concerns the specificity of the bias seen in anxious subjects. Do anxious subjects selectively attend to all *emotional* stimuli, all *negative* stimuli, all *threatening* stimuli, or only stimuli that are *relevant* to their concerns (e.g., social worries, physical worries)? Evidence on these issues is not entirely consistent across studies and paradigms. Yet it is possible that these inconsistencies are a function of temporal changes in selective attention: In early processing stages, only the valence of the word can be processed (Mogg et al., 1993), but later, when more controlled processing is involved, more differentiation is observed. Clearly, additional research is needed to clarify these results.

To summarize, it seems clear that anxiety leads one to focus increasingly on threat and danger cues when there is a mixture of threatening and nonthreatening cues available. Thus, it is easy to see how anxiety is likely to be maintained or exacerbated. Although empirical evidence is not yet available that such an attentional bias does in fact mediate the maintenance or exacerbation of anxiety, it certainly seems like a strong possibility.

Depression   As we already mentioned, two major contemporary theories of emotion and cognition predict that depression should also be associated with an attentional bias for mood-congruent information (cf. Williams, Watts, MacLeod, & Mathews, 1988). Yet, the empirical evidence of this for depression is less convincing than it is for anxiety. Some studies (e.g., Gotlib & Cane, 1987; Gotlib & McCann, 1984; McCabe & Gotlib, 1993) have shown that depression is associated with an attentional bias. However, few unequivocal conclusions can be drawn from those studies. First, these studies have generally not assessed the role of concomitant anxiety in depressed patients, which is of crucial importance given the high degree of comorbidity between anxiety and depression. Second, some of the studies suggesting that depression is associated with attentional biases have used tasks that may not assess "pure" attentional functioning. Further, when an association between attentional functioning and depression is observed, the relative bias is quite different from that seen in GADs. Whereas anxious individuals usually tend to show increased attention for negative, especially threatening material, mildly depressed subjects usually show no such tendency. Instead, findings indicate that depressives' attention is evenly deployed between positive and negative words. By contrast, nondepressed subjects demonstrated an attentional bias toward the positive words (e.g., Gotlib, McLachlan, & Katz, 1988).

Memory Biases

In general, when one examines the evidence for memory biases for mood-congruent information, the pattern of findings for anxiety versus depression appears to be opposite of that found for attentional biases. That is, whereas there is a good deal of evidence suggesting that depression is associated with a bias to recall mood-congruent information, there is little consistent evidence that anxiety is associated with a similar memory bias. Accordingly, we will discuss depression first, followed by anxiety.

Depression

EXPLICIT MEMORY   Most studies on mood-congruency effects in memory have employed traditional *explicit* memory tests, in which subjects are specifically directed to retrieve information that they had learned at an earlier time (e.g., recall and recognition). Self-referent encoding, incidental and intentional recall, depth-of-processing tasks, and autobiographical recall have been used to study the influence of affect on memory. The general approach to studying this type of memory bias in depression involves comparing individuals who experience high levels of depression with matched nondepressed controls (cf. Blaney, 1986). Stimulus items for the memory tasks are usually lists of words that vary in affective content, and the encoding task is usually self-referential (cf. Matt, Vazquez, & Campbell, 1992). Clinically depressed subjects typically show a strong bias to recall negative, especially self-referential, information. The bias occurs both when the negative material is autobiographical and when it is presented experimentally. Interestingly, the bias also appears to be the opposite of that shown by nondepressed subjects, who usually exhibit a bias favoring recall of positive material. Subclinically depressed subjects tend to show an intermediate "even-handed" memory, remembering approximately equal amounts of positive and negative material.

Two important features of the association between clinical depression and mood-congruent memory have to be noted. First, it appears that this bias is specific to depression-relevant words. For example, Watkins, Mathews, Williamson, and Fuller (1992) included not only depression-relevant words but also physical threat words, and found the bias only for the depression-relevant words. Relatedly, Bellew and Hill

(1990) found a recall bias in depressed subjects for self-esteem–threatening words, but not for negative words in general. Second, it seems that differences in retrieval of positive versus negative memories are due to the person's affective state, rather than to the real differences in past experiences. For example, Clark and Teasdale (1982) studied depressives with marked diurnal variations in their level of depression at different points in time. They found that the probability of retrieving negative autobiographical memories in response to neutral cue words increased as the subjects' depression level increased during the day. Similarly, the disappearance of mood-congruent biases when the depression remits is incongruous with the "different experiences" hypothesis (e.g., see Bradley & Mathews, 1988).

IMPLICIT MEMORY   In recent years researchers became increasingly interested in *implicit* memory tasks in which subjects are not explicitly directed to search their memory for previously learned material. Instead, memory is assessed indirectly, by, for example, asking participants to complete word stems with the first word that comes to mind. Evidence for the dissociations on these two kinds of memory tests comes from studies of amnesic patients, who show severe deficits on explicit memory tests, but relatively normal performance on tests of implicit memory (cf. Roediger, 1990; Schacter, 1987).

Given this dissociation, researchers have begun to address the question of whether depressed subjects also show mood-congruency effects in implicit memory, as they do in explicit memory. To date, no significant evidence of a mood-congruent implicit memory bias for negative information in depression has been found (see Roediger & McDermott, 1992, for a review and commentary). Yet, no final conclusions regarding the association between depression and implicit memory can yet be drawn, because the lack of evidence of mood-congruent implicit memory biases may well be due to the mismatch between the nature of the encoding task and the memory tests that have been used in *all* the studies done so far. Specifically, all of the studies to date have had subjects *encode* the mood-congruent target material in a conceptual manner, but have used *data-driven* or perceptual implicit memory tests; in contrast, explicit memory tasks used in this research have generally been conceptual in nature, providing a better match for the encoding process. Thus, one would not expect a mood congruent implicit memory with a conceptual encoding task and a data-driven implicit memory task because of the mismatch between the encoding and the retrieval process. Given that it is the semantic *meaning* of mood-congruent words that is so salient to emotionally disordered individuals, the lack of sensitivity of *data* driven tasks to mood-congruency effects may not be too surprising.

Anxiety

EXPLICIT MEMORY   As we noted earlier, in contrast to the strong evidence for mood-congruent memory biases in depression, the majority of studies of anxious patients have not found such effects even though highly similar studies have been conducted to those that do find a bias in depressed subjects (e.g., MacLeod & Mathews, 1991; Mineka & Nugent, 1995; Mogg, 1992; Nugent & Mineka, 1994). There are two possible exceptions to this conclusion. First, two studies of autobiographical memory in anxious subjects suggest that they may show superior autobiographical memory for anxiety-relevant material (e.g., Burke & Mathews, 1992; Richards & Whittaker, 1990). Second, in contrast to the generally negative pattern of results for mood-congruent memory biases with GADs, there appears to be a more consistent pattern of positive findings for explicit mood-congruent memory biases in individuals with panic disorder (e.g., Becker, Rinck, & Margraf, 1994).

IMPLICIT MEMORY   The pattern of findings regarding the association between anxiety and implicit memory has been equivocal: Whereas Mathews, Mogg, May, & Eysenck (1989) found that anxious patients may show a relative bias in implicit (but not in explicit) memory for threatening information, Nugent and Mineka (1994) have failed to find evidence for an implicit memory bias for threatening information in very high trait anxious subjects. However, as with depression, Roediger and McDermott's (1992) commentary suggests that performance on tests of conceptual nature need to be examined before the actual status of mood-congruent implicit biases in anxiety can be determined.

Summary   Different types of memory processes are differentially affected by emotional disorders. On explicit memory tasks, when individuals explicitly attempt to remember material (such as free recall or recognition) depressed individuals show mood-congruent biases. In contrast, on implicit memory tasks, which assess memory when individuals do not attempt to consciously recollect previously presented materials (e.g., by asking subject to complete word stems with the first word that comes to mind) the results concerning both depression and anxiety are inconclusive (see Mineka & Nugent, 1995, for a more complete discussion).

Judgmental Biases

The paucity of research on judgmental or interpretative biases in emotional disorders is surprising when compared to the vast literature on memory and attentional biases. The majority of studies in this domain have been conducted with subclinical populations, and have attempted to assess the influence of various affective states on the interpretation of ambiguous information. Judgments of event probabilities, interpretation of ambiguous homophones and sentences, text comprehension studies, categorization, impression formation, and causal attribution tasks have been used to study the effects of affect on judgment. Results of these studies generally suggest that negative emotional states increase judgments concerning the probabilities of negative and threatening events, as well as the likelihood of negative interpretation of ambiguous stimuli. Studies examining the influence of affect on social perception assessed the effects of positive, negative, and angry affective states on impression formation, stereotype judgment, and perception of responsibility in close relationships (e.g., Forgas, 1994; Forgas & Moylan, 1991). The results are consistent in demonstrating mood-congruent effects of emotional states on judgment processes. Because most experimental studies addressing the question of interpretation were conducted with anxious subjects, we discuss anxiety first.

Anxiety   There is considerable support for the proposition that anxiety is linked to distorted evaluation of risk (Butler & Mathews, 1983, 1987), biased interpretation of ambiguous stimuli (e.g., Eysenck, Mogg, May, Richards, & Mathews, 1991), and selective imposing of threatening interpretation on ambiguous sentences (MacLeod & Cohen, 1993). Butler and Mathews have shown that anxious individuals provide inflated estimates of the probabilities that they will experience negative events, and that the increase in subjective risk for negative events is mediated by both trait and state anxiety. Further, both state and trait anxiety are associated with an increased probability of imposition of a threatening meaning on homophones (i.e., words with one sound, but two different meaning, such as dye/die) (e.g., Eysenck et al., 1991; Mathews, Richards, & Eysenck, 1989). Similarly, interpretative biases seem to be linked to the comprehension of more complex information, such as sentences (e.g., "The man watched as the chest was opened," Eysenck et al., 1991). A similar tendency to impose a threatening interpretation on ambiguous stimuli, using a task that did not require subjects to consciously endorse a specific interpretation, was demonstrated by MacLeod and Cohen (1993). They found that high-trait anxious subjects tended to selectively impose threatening interpretations on unconstrained ambiguous sentences, whereas low-trait anxious subjects did not exhibit this tendency.

Depression   In contrast to anxiety, most research on interpretative biases in individuals with clinical depression has been conducted using self-report measures. Because most of these paradigms require that subjects explicitly report their interpretations of ambiguous information, the resulting data are subject to the problems and pitfall associated with the use of introspective techniques (e.g., Nisbett & Wilson, 1977). A consistent pattern of findings from mood-induction studies indicates that biased evaluation of social information is related to depression as a state (e.g., Forgas, 1994; Forgas & Bower, 1987), but not probably not as a trait (Miranda & Persons, 1988). Yet, given the dearth of experimental studies addressing the question of interpretative biases in clinical populations, conclusions regarding the association between these biases and clinical depression might be premature.

Theoretical Approaches to Understanding Cognitive Biases

Associated with Affective States

Recent research using cognitive-experimental paradigms suggests that anxiety and depression have different effects on cognitive processing. Whereas anxiety appears to be associated with an attentional bias for danger or threat cues that occurs at a preconscious level, depression appears to be associated with a memory bias for negative self-referential information that occurs at a later processing stage. In addition, current research suggests that anxiety is associated with the propensity to impose threatening interpretation on ambiguous stimuli. Although quite plausible, the association between depression and judgmental biases still lacks solid experimental support.

The two most prominent theories that have been used to account for the relation between affect and cognition (i.e., Beck's and Bower's) predict that memory, attentional, and judgmental biases should characterize *both* anxiety and depression, because both theories assume that there is one common cognitive mechanism that can be used to account for mood-congruency effects. Clearly, the empirical evidence indicates that these theories must be revised significantly. In the last few years investigators have begun to develop theoretical models that may help us understand the differential effects of anxiety and depression on attention, memory, and interpretative processes (Williams et al., 1988). These models are based on Oatley and Johnson-Laird's (1987) proposal that there may be unique modes of cognitive operation associated with the different primary emotions. This formulation makes intuitive sense given that different modes of information processing are likely to be particularly adaptive in facilitating the functions of different emotions. Depression and anxiety have probably evolved in response to different environmental needs and pressures: Anxiety, like fear, has probably evolved to aid in the anticipation and rapid identification of potentially threatening stimuli (e.g., Beck & Emery, 1985). Depression, in contrast, involves significant reflective consideration of events that have led to failure and loss (e.g., Beck, 1976; Bowlby, 1980). Thus, as Mathews (1993) has argued, whereas anxiety, as a forward-looking emotion, leads to attentional biases that will facilitate the rapid detection of threat and its subsequent avoidance, depression, as a more backward-looking emotion, leads to memory biases. The psychoevolutionary perspective is also consistent with the pattern of findings regarding interpretative biases: Reevaluation of risk and a conservative interpretation of ambiguous stimuli are likely to be beneficial in situations of threat, as well as loss.

The Casual Role of Cognitive Biases in Emotional Disorders: Etiology and Maintenance

The association between cognitive biases and emotional disorders is firmly established. Yet, the causal status of these biases is less clear. Their role may be threefold: (a) they may mediate the *course* of these disorders, (b) they may predict the vulnerability to *relapse*, and (c) they may contribute to the *onset* of anxiety and depression.

Although empirical evidence that attentional biases do, in fact, mediate the maintenance or exacerbation of anxiety is not yet available, it certainly seems plausible (e.g., MacLeod & Mathews, 1991; Mineka, 1992). Specifically, given the increased vigilance for, and interpretation of, threat-related stimuli, it is easy to see how an anxious state is likely to be maintained or exacerbated. Similarly, it is interesting to note that nonanxious subjects seem to have an opposite kind of bias, even under conditions of high-state anxiety (MacLeod & Mathews, 1988). This bias may serve to protect the nonanxious subjects from becoming clinically anxious. One might speculate that the attentional bias seen in high trait anxious subjects when their state anxiety is elevated, may mediate the increased risk that these individuals are thought to have for developing GAD. However, prospective longitudinal studies will have to be conducted before this intriguing hypothesis can be corroborated.

With respect to memory biases, Teasdale (1988) and others have argued that enhanced memory for negative self-referential material is important because, in combination with the interpretative and judgmental biases, it can be seen as creating a "vicious cycle of depression." Being in a depressed state, and having one's memory strongly biased to remember primarily negative events (e.g., losses and disappointments) is likely to contribute to the persistence of the depressive state. In fact, autobiographical memory biases were found to be highly correlated with a failure to recover from depression (Brittlebank, Scott, Williams, & Perrier, 1993).

Because in everyday life many events are inherently ambiguous and are, therefore, subject to both threatening and nonthreatening interpretations, the existence of interpretative biases is likely to contribute to the perpetuation of this state (e.g., MacLeod & Cohen, 1993). Thus, such a bias is likely to contribute to a vicious cycle of anxiety: Interpreting a situation in a threatening manner is likely to increase anxiety, which, in turn, increases the probability of imposing additional threatening interpretations.

Do the attentional, memory, and interpretative biases play an active causal role in the onset of emotional disorders? Because very few longitudinal studies examining cognitive biases in depressed and anxious patients have been conducted, the evidentiary basis for even preliminary conclusions regarding this issue is weak. Yet, existing evidence suggests that cognitive biases predict individuals' reactions to stressful life events. First, using a prospective design, Bellew and Hill (1991) assessed 156 pregnant women with a self-report measure of depression and with a measure of recall bias. They found that when women were assessed 3 months postnatally, those with a biased memory for self-esteem threatening nouns who also experienced negative life events showed a significant increase in depression levels, whereas other women showed a decrease. Thus, explicit memory bias was a significant and useful predictor of depression in subjects who experienced negative life events.

In the second study, MacLeod and Hagan (1992) examined the ability of automatic selective processing of threatening events to predict subsequent emotional reactions to a stressful life event. Women awaiting an appointment for a colposcopy test for cervical pathology participated in an experiment assessing attentional biases using subliminal and supraliminal Stroop tasks. MacLeod and Hagan found that the degree of subliminal threat interference was the *single best* predictor of the emotional response 8 weeks later for the 15 women who received a diagnosis of cervical pathology after the initial test session. This study provides a powerful demonstration that information processing measures can predict subsequent emotional reactions to stressful life events.

Summary and Suggestions for Future Research

Current research suggests that emotional disorders are associated with biases in attention, memory, and judgment. The general pattern of findings suggests that anxiety tends to be associated with biased attentional processes and interpretative judgments, whereas depression tends to be associated with biased recall of valenced information and, probably, with interpretative biases for social information. Beck's and Bower's models proposed to account for cognitive biases in emotional disorders may need to be refined to incorporate the differential pattern of associations between depression and anxiety on the one hand, and cognitive biases on the other. Recently, models accounting for this association pattern have appeared (e.g., Oatley & Johnson-Laird, 1987; Williams et al., 1988).

Despite much progress in understanding the nature of the cognitive biases associated with anxiety and depression, the role of cognitive biases in the onset and course of the emotional disorders is not fully understood. Do they have predictive validity with respect to the onset and course of depression or anxiety, as some studies suggest? Are they in evidence in individuals following recovery from anxiety or depression when the relevant mood is induced? Do they represent a vulnerability in currently nondisordered individuals? Given the high comorbidity between depression and anxiety, how can the differential association between these emotional disorders and attentional and memory processes be explained? And finally, from a broader perspective of emotion theory, how do these cognitive concomitants of the emotional states interact with other components of the emotional response (e.g., physiological, subjective)?

These questions dictate several design characteristics for studies aimed at elucidating the nature of the relation between emotional functioning and cognitive processes. A longitudinal design that allows examination of the same group of individuals in different affective conditions is more sensitive than a cross-sectional design. Only such designs can provide conclusive evidence regarding the causal status of cognitive biases. Finally, multiple measures of the emotional response in disordered individuals are needed to form a better understanding of the link between emotional states and cognitive processing.

References

Averill, J. R. (1992). The structural bases of emotional behavior. *Bulletin of Personality and Social Psychology, 13*, 1–23.

Beck, A. T. (1976). *Cognitive therapy and the emotional disorders.* New York: International Universities Press.

Beck, A. T., & Emery, G. (1985). *Anxiety disorders and phobias: A cognitive perspective.* New York: Basic Books.

Beck, A. T., Rush, A. J., Shaw, B. T., & Emery, G. (1979). *Cognitive therapy of depression.* New York: Guilford Press.

Becker, E., Rinck, M., & Margraf, J. (1994). Memory bias in panic disorder. *Journal of Abnormal Psychology, 103*, 369–399.

Bellew, M., & Hill, B. (1990). Negative recall bias as a predictor of susceptibility to induced depressive mood. *Personality and Individual Differences, 11*, 471–480.

Bellew, M., & Hill, B. (1991). Negative recall bias as predictor of susceptibility of depression following childbirth. *Personality and Individual Differences, 12*, 943–949.

Blaney, P. H. (1986). Affect and memory: A review. *Psychological Bulletin, 99*, 229–246.

Bower, G. H. (1981). Mood and memory. *American Psychologist, 36*, 129–148.

Bowlby, J. (1980). *Loss: Sadness and depression.* Harmondsworth, UK: Penguin.

Bradley, B., & Mathews, A. (1988). Memory bias in recovered clinical depressives. *Cognition and Emotion, 2*, 235–246.

Brittlebank, A. D., Scott, J., Williams, J. M., & Perrier, I. N. (1993). Autobiographical memory in depression: State or trait marker? *British Journal of Psychiatry, 162*, 118–121.

Broadbent, D., & Broadbent, M. (1988). Anxiety and attentional bias: State and trait. *Cognition and Emotion, 2*, 165–183.

Burke, M., & Mathews, A. (1992). Autobiographical memory and clinical anxiety. *Cognition and Emotion, 6*, 23–35.

Butler, G., & Mathews, A. (1983). Cognitive processes in anxiety. *Advances in Behavior Research and Therapy, 5*, 51–62.

Butler, G., & Mathews, A. (1987). Anticipatory anxiety and risk perception. *Cognitive Therapy and Research, 11*, 551–565.

Cassidy, K. L., McNally, R. J., & Zeitlin, S. B. (1992). Cognitive processing of trauma cues in rape victims with post-traumatic stress disorder. *Cognitive Therapy and Research, 16*, 283–295.

Clark, D. A., & Teasdale, J. D. (1982). Diurinal variation in clinical depression and accessibility of memories of positive and negative experiences. *Journal of Abnormal Psychology, 91*, 95–97.

Edwards, S., & Dickerson, M. (1987). On the similarity of positive and negative intrusions. *Behaviour Research and Therapy, 25*, 207–211.

Ehlers, A., Margraf, J., Davies, S., & Roth, W. (1988). Selective processing of threat cues in subjects with panic attacks. *Cognition and Emotion, 2*, 201–219.

Eysenck, M. W., Mogg, K., May, J., Richards, A., & Mathews, A. (1991). Bias in interpretation of ambiguous sentences related to threat in anxiety. *Journal of Abnormal Psychology, 100*, 144–150.

Foa, E. B., & McNally, R. J. (1986). Sensitivity to feared stimuli in obsessive-compulsives: A dichotic listening analysis. *Cognitive Therapy and Research, 10*, 477–485.

Forgas, J. P. (1994). Sad and guilty? Affective influences of the explanation of conflict in close relationships. *Journal of Personality and Social Psychology, 66*, 56–68.

Forgas, J. P., & Bower, G. H. (1987). Mood effects on person-perception judgments. *Journal of Personality and Social Psychology, 53*, 53–60.

Forgas, J. P., & Moylan, S. J. (1991). Affective influence on stereotype judgments. *Cognition and Emotion, 5*, 379–395.

Gotlib, I. H., & Cane, D. B. (1987). Construct accessibility and clinical depression: A longitudinal investigation. *Journal of Abnormal Psychology, 96*, 199–204.

Gotlib, I. H., & McCann, C. D. (1984). Construct accessibility and depression: An examination of cognitive and affective factors. *Journal of Personality and Social Psychology, 47*, 427–439.

Gotlib, I. H., McLachlan, A. L., & Katz, A. N. (1988). Biases in visual attention in depressed and non-depressed individuals. *Cognition and Emotion, 2*, 185–100.

MacLeod, C., & Cohen, I. (1993). Anxiety and the interpretation of ambiguity: A text comprehension study. *Journal of Abnormal Psychology, 102*, 238–247.

MacLeod, C., & Hagan, R. (1992). Individual differences in the selective processing of threatening information, and emotional responses to a stressful life event. *Behaviour Research and Therapy, 30*, 151–161.

MacLeod, C., & Mathews, A. (1988). Anxiety and the allocation of attention to threat. *Quarterly Journal of Experimental Psychology: Human Experimental Psychology, 38*, 659–670.

MacLeod, C., & Mathews, A. (1991). Cognitive-experimental approaches to the emotional disorders. In P. Martin (Ed.), *Handbook of behavior therapy and psychological science: An integrative approach*, (Pp. 116–150). New York: Pergamon.

MacLeod, C., Mathews, A., & Tata, P. (1986). Attentional bias in emotional disorders. *Journal of Abnormal Psychology, 95*, 15–20.

Mathews, A. (1993). Anxiety and the processing of emotional information. In L. Chapman & D. Fowles (Eds.), *Models and methods of psychopathology: Progress in expermental personality and psychopathology research*, (pp. 254–280). New York: Springer.

Mathews, A., Mogg, K., May, J., & Eysenck, M. (1989). Implicit and explicit memory bias in anxiety. *Journal of Abnormal Psychology, 98,* 236–240.

Mathews, A., Richards, A., & Eysenck, M. W. (1989). Interpretations of homophones related to threat in anxiety states. *Journal of Abnormal Psychology, 98,* 31–34.

Matt, G. E., Vazquez, C., & Campbell, W. (1992). Mood congruent recall of affectively tones stimuli: A meta-analytic review. *Clinical Psychology Review, 12,* 227–255.

McCabe, S. B., & Gotlib, I. H. (1993). Attentional processing in clinically depressed subjects: A longitudinal investigation. *Cognitive Therapy and Research, 17,* 1–19.

Mineka, S. (1992). Evolutionary memories, emotional processing, and the emotional disorders. In D. Medin (Ed.), *The Psychology of learning and motivation* (pp.161–206). New York: Academic Press.

Mineka, S., & Nugent, K. (Ed.). (1995). Mood congruent memory biases in anxiety and depression. In D. Schacter (Ed.), *Memory distortion: How minds, brains, and societies reconstruct the past* (pp. 173–193). Cambridge, MA: Harvard University Press.

Mineka, S., Sutton, S. (1992). Cognitive biases in the emotional disorders. *Psychological Science, 3,* 65–69.

Mineka, S., & Tomarken, A. J. (1989). The role of cognitive biases in the origins and maintenance of fear and anxiety disorders. In T. Archer & L. Nilsson (Eds.), *Aversion, avoidance, and anxiety: Perspective on aversively motivated behavior* (pp. 195–221). New York: Erlbaum.

Miranda, J., & Persons, J. B. (1988). Dysfunctional attitudes are mood-state dependent. *Journal of Abnormal Psychology, 97,* 76–79.

Mogg, K. (1992). Recollective experience and the recognition memory for threat in clinical anxiety states. *Bulletin of the Psychonomic Society, 30,* 109–112.

Mogg, K., Bradley, S. D., William, R., & Mathews, A. (1993). Subliminal processing of emotional information in anxiety and depression. *Journal of Abnormal Psychology, 102,* 304–312.

Nisbett, R. E., & Wilson, T. D. (1977). Telling more than we can know: Verbal reports on mental processes. *Psychological Review, 84,* 231–259.

Nugent, K., & Mineka, S. (1994). The effects of high and low anxiety on implicit and explicit mood congruent memory tasks. *Cognition and Emotion, 8,* 147–163.

Oatley, K., & Johnson-Laird, P. (1987). Towards a cognitive theory of emotions. *Cognition and Emotion, 1,* 29–50.

Ortony, A., & Turner, T. J. (1990). What's basic about basic emotions? *Psychological Review, 97,* 315–331.

Richards, A., & Whittaker, T. M. (1990). Effects of anxiety and mood manipulation in autobiographical memory. *British Journal of Clinical Psychology, 29,* 145–153.

Roediger, H. L. (1990). Implicit memory: Retention without remembering. *American Psychologist, 45,* 1043–1056.

Roediger, H. L., & McDermott, K. B. (1992). Depression and implicit memory: A commentary. *Journal of Abnormal Psychology, 101,* 587–591.

Schacter, D. L. (1987). Implicit memory: History and current status. *Journal of Experimental Psychology: Learning, Memory and Cognition, 13,* 501–518.

Scherer, K. (1993). Neuroscience projections to current debates in emotion psychology. *Cognition and Emotion, 7,* 1–41.

Seibert, P. S., & Ellis, H. C. (1991). Irrelevant thoughts, emotional mood states, and cognitive task performance. *Memory and Cognition, 19,* 507–513.

Teasdale, J. D. (1988). Cognitive vulnerability to persistent depression. *Cognition and Emotion, 2,* 247–274.

Watkins, P. C., Mathews, A., Williamson, D. A., & Fuller, R. D. (1992). Mood-congruent memory in depression: Emotional priming or elaboration? *Journal of Abnormal Psychology, 101,* 581–586.

Watts, F. N., McKenna, F. P., Sharrock, R., & Trezise, L. (1986). Colour naming of phobia related words. *British Journal of Psychology, 77,* 97–108.

Williams, M. J., Watts, F. N., MacLeod, C., & Mathews, A. (1988). *Cognitive psychology and the emotional disorders.* Chichester: Wiley.

16

Sandra C. Paivio & Leslie S. Greenberg

Experiential Theory of Emotion Applied to Anxiety and Depression

The Experiential View of Emotion

The experiential theory of emotion presented here summarizes views developed by Greenberg and associates (Greenberg, Elliott, & Foerster, 1990; Greenberg, Rice, & Elliott, 1993; Greenberg & Safran, 1987). It integrates traditional experiential concepts (Gendlin, 1981; Perls, Hefferline, & Goodman, 1957; Rogers, 1958) with recent developments in cognitive psychology and current emotion theory. Traditionally, the experiential/humanistic view of functioning is wholistic, positing an internal, tacit synthesizing process that guides the organism to adaptive action. In this view, emotion plays a central role and is intimately connected with cognitive, motivational, and physiological processes. Emotion is considered adaptive and a source of orienting information about self and the world. Perls and colleagues emphasized the role of emotion, particularly avoidance of painful emotion, in dysfunction. Other theorists (Gendlin, 1981; Rogers, 1958) have been concerned with the broader concept of experience, which consists of both emotion as sensorimotor response and the meaning of a feeling in context. The general assumption in this view is that being cut off from the adaptive information inherent in emotion impedes growth and healthy functioning.

Emotion Theory

Current experiential theory integrates bioevolutionary and cognitive appraisal models of emotion (e.g., Arnold, 1960; Lazarus, 1991; Leventhal, 1984). From the bioevolutionary perspective, emotion is seen as a wired-in, biologically adaptive orienting system (Izard, 1977; Plutchik, 1980; Tomkins, 1970). Cross-cultural studies (e.g.,

Izard, 1977) and infant research (e.g., Lang, 1984) suggest that there are a limited number of innate and discrete primary emotions—anger, sadness, fear, joy, and shame are commonly identified—each with a corresponding action tendency or response disposition. These action tendencies are hard-wired expressive motor responses that communicate to others and prepare the human organism to act. Anger, for example, is associated with aggressive self-protection and signals others to stay away, while fear is associated with escape or avoidance of harm and signals the need for protection from others.

A cognitive appraisal perspective on emotion, by comparison, puts more emphasis on generating processes and aspects of emotional responding that are socialized or learned. For example, Lazarus (1991) defines an emotional response as an automatic appraisal of a person-environment interaction with reference to one's goals or concerns. The type of appraisal determines the specific emotional response, and the innate action tendency inherent in emotion is modulated by a learned coping response that either coincides with or overrides the action tendency. For instance, the tendency to aggress in anger can be modulated by adaptive assertive behavior, maladaptive rage, or avoidance.

Integrating the two views, we define emotion as automatically generated information about our evaluations of situations that guides action and interaction. It tells us what is significant for our well-being. Emotion functions to motivate behavior for the attainment of survival-related goals and, furthermore, functions to direct attention through the salience of emotionally laden information (Fridja, 1986).

Cognitive Psychology

Recent developments in cognitive experimental psychology help specify and differentiate traditional experiential views of functioning. Centrally important in traditional experiential theories was the dichotomy between organismic experiential wisdom that is on the periphery of awareness and conscious cognition or intellect. This view is consistent with research in the areas of automatic and parallel processing (Neisser, 1976; Shiffrin & Schneider, 1977) indicating that large amounts of information are processed quickly and simultaneously, outside of awareness. Similarly, research on implicit learning (Kihlstrom, 1990) indicates that complex information is encoded in memory, is outside of conscious awareness, but influences behavior, experience, and functioning. Finally, schema theory (Kelly, 1955; Neisser, 1976) suggests that complex information is organized into molar information processing units. Accordingly, a schema is a system for representing various features of the physical or external environment and organizing them into clusters or sets. The information in such schematic structures is outside of awareness but, when automatically activated, it guides attention, perception, memory, and experience.

Schema theory, applied to emotional processes, states that similarities in emotional experiences are encoded in memory in a multilevel, multicomponent process. Leventhal (1984), for example, suggests that three levels of processing are synthesized in emotional experience: (a) sensorimotor responses that are nonvolitional, such as facial expression; (b) automatically activated schematic representations of previous emotional experience, which include episodic memories, environmental cues, and reactions of self and others; and (c) conceptual or conscious thinking about emotional experience. The entire complex is activated in an emotional response, making emotion a rich source of information.

We will employ the term emotion *scheme* (Piaget & Morf, 1958) because it emphasizes the action tendency component of emotion, that is, emotion as action structure rather than static representation. The action component of emotion is particularly important in complex emotion processes like anxiety and depression, because these disorders are characterized by particular types of autonomic arousal and corresponding action/inaction. These physiological and behavioral aspects are partly a function of the action tendency inherent in the core emotions associated with each disorder: sadness/withdrawal in depression and fear/arousal in anxiety. The action component of emotion also is important in therapeutic interventions that emphasize attention to bodily experience. These interventions can quickly evoke the entire emotion scheme, making it available for exploration and change. Overall, we view emotion as a complex action structure or system. The emotion system is composed of cognitive, affective, motivational, and behavioral components.

Attachment Theory

Finally, our understanding of the role of emotion in human functioning draws on attachment theory (Bowlby, 1988), which emphasizes the primary status of intimate emotional bonds. Bowlby states that, to a high degree, the underlying tone of a person's whole emotional life is determined by long-term committed relationships. When these bonds are threatened we become anxious and angry, and when broken we become sad. Therefore, attachment is central to an understanding of dysfunctions like anxiety and depression. Furthermore, Bowlby suggests that internal representations develop from the emotional quality of interactions between self and attachment figures, and these "object relations" influence one's core sense of self and interaction with others.

In our view, the internal representations that relate to one's sense of self, formed in early attachment relationships, are a particularly important class of emotion schemes. Such core self-related schemes develop from affect-laden responses to situations in which the state of self is enhanced or diminished by meeting or failure to meet needs (Greenberg & Johnson, 1988; Greenberg et al., 1993). These are basic survival, relatedness, and attachment needs, including autonomy and separation, exploration and mastery. Thus, one's sense of self as worthwhile, lovable, competent is more than simply a self-concept, but is a multidimensional complex, developed from early experience, including associated emotions, action tendency and physiology, reactions of self and others, implicit beliefs about self and others, coping responses or action. Distinctive experiences and schematic structures lead to different types of emotional dysfunction. In subsequent sections we present the specific self-organizations characteristic of anxiety and depression. Although adult trauma, loss, life stresses, and lack of support are precursors of anxiety and depression, core self-related emotion schemes that originate in development are major factors in generating these states.

Finally, we adopt a constructivist, rather than structural, view of self such that many schemes are continuously being constructed into a current self-organization. For example, people are at one time vulnerable and another time assertive depending on the emotion schemes that have been activated. Our view is also dialectical constructivist (Pascual-Leone, 1991; Stewart & Pascual-Leone, 1992). People's construals of self and reality are continually constructed from a synthesis of two sources of information and two types of processes. One source of information is conscious/cognitive, consisting of learned values and beliefs. The other source is information from immediate experience that is generated by automatically activated emotion schemes. There are two types of processes involved in construction. The first type is a set of hardware operations that are biologically wired in and serve functions such as activating, integrating, storing, or combining. The second type of process is the experientially constructed schemes that apply to a situation and carry information about events. The basic assumption is that personal reality is continually constructed; self experience and experience of self is created moment by moment through interaction of consciousness with external reality and activated emotion schemes (Greenberg et al., 1993; Greenberg & Pascual-Leone, 1995). A constructivist model emphasizes agency. It views people as active creators of meaning rather than simple information storage and retrieval systems. Core self-structures influence the construction of meaning attached to certain life events, and meaning, in turn, effects mood and coping responses.

Experiential View of Dysfunction

We present a general view of psychological dysfunction before specifically discussing anxiety and depression. Greenberg et al. (1993) posit two non-mutually exclusive categories of dysfunctional processes. The first is the failure to acknowledge immediate experience, such that adaptive information in emotion schemes is not integrated into current constructions of reality. This leaves the person disoriented. Adaptive information includes the action tendency, need or concern, and automatic appraisal associated with primary emotion—those innate and core emotions such as anger at violation, sadness at loss, fear of harm, which are a person's initial responses to external stimuli, that cannot be reduced into components. Painful primary emotions frequently are avoided or covered by secondary reactions for a variety of reasons, including fear of being overwhelmed, loss of control, familial or cultural injunctions against expression. Bowlby (1988) discusses the negative impact on children of "forgetting," or shutting off certain experiences, either because parents invalidate the child's experience or because the memories are unbearable. According to Bowlby, such selective exclusion from consciousness leads to disturbance because these experiences are encoded in memory and continue to influence thought, feeling, and behavior but the individual has no awareness of, and therefore no control over, their influence. In our view, such shutting off of primary experience also leaves the person disconnected from adaptive needs and action tendencies. This interferes with the ability to act in one's own best interests.

The second category of experiential dysfunction is the activation of maladaptive emotion schemes developed from negative learning experiences of loss and/or threat. These schemes are automatically triggered by current circumstance and guide the process of constructing reality and the current emotional response. Emotional responses, in this process, result from complex cognitive-affective sequences. Accordingly, primary emotion, that is, the initial response to an external situation, is associated with a set of learned beliefs and secondary emotional reactions. The latter can be defensive reactions to the more primary, initial emotion or reactions to cognitive processes. Thus, people are often afraid of their anger, ashamed of their fear, angry about sadness, and depressed when thinking about failure.

Maladaptive emotion schemes include rigid or distorted beliefs about self and reality, or about emotional experience itself resulting in maladaptive coping behavior. A clinical example is observed in men who experience insecurity at their wive's independence or unavailability. The initial emotion is fear of abandonment, but this fear is associated with internalized beliefs, such as "men shouldn't be weak" or "women should be supportive," and secondary blaming and anger. Angry and blaming behavior is maladaptive in this situation because it pushes the other away and deprives the person of needed reassurance and support. Secondary maladaptive reactions such as chronic anger or irritability frequently are the conscious "bad feelings" that clients want to change in therapy. One treatment objective in these circumstances is to access more core and adaptive emotional experience.

Anxiety and depression are complex secondary emotional reactions associated with a host of bad feelings. These disturbances can be generated by the blocking or interruption of primary emotion, such as anger, sadness, fear, and/or activation of a maladaptive emotion scheme. Furthermore, activation of maladaptive emotion schemes related to one's core sense of self renders a person susceptible to anxious and depressive states. The dysfunctional processes and content of emotion schemes for anxiety and depression are discussed next.

Anxiety and Depression

Common Features and Processes

The present discussion applies to diagnostic subtypes with mild to moderate symptomatology on Axis I (*Diagnostic and Statistical Manual of Mental Disorders*, 4th ed.; American Psychiatric Association, 1994) or "neurotic" disorders. This includes exogenous, unipolar depression and dysthymia among the depressive disorders, and anxiety subtypes such as generalized anxiety, social phobia, and post traumatic stress disorder. We will not consider those subtypes with strong biological or biochemical determinants (e.g., panic or bipolar depression) or those that respond well to simple behavioral intervention aimed at eliminating avoidant behavior (e.g., simple phobias).

Research indicates that anxiety and depression are strongly correlated with each other, that there is a high incidence of comorbidity, and therefore they probably should not be studied in isolation (Kendall & Watson, 1989). Common symptoms include a sense of powerlessness, restlessness, difficulty concentrating, insomnia, fatigue, loss of energy, irritability, and feeling incompetent or alienated. These symptoms have negative interpersonal and behavioral correlates such as deficits in social skills and support. Researchers also have identified maladaptive cognitive processes such as negative views of self and others, negative automatic thoughts, rigid and concrete cognitive structures, resistance to change, misinterpretation of events, and learned blocking of experience as common correlates of these disorders (Beck, 1976). As well, constitutional, developmental, and current interpersonal factors are frequently involved in the cause of, and vulnerability to, these states. Various theoretical orientations emphasize one of these aspects over others as the major causal factor in anxiety and depression. In our view, however, both disorders are complex, multicomponent processes in which cognitive, affective, and behavioral components interact.

First we examine the affective-cognitive-behavioral processes common to both anxiety and depression. This model is discussed in detail in a treatment manual for working with specific emotions in psychotherapy (Greenberg & Paivio, in press). Although we agree that constitution, current circumstances, stress and coping, and availability of support are factors in depression and anxiety, our model emphasizes early development as a predisposing factor. As well, autonomic arousal is emphasized because it gives each state its characteristic action/behavioral flavor, is related to primary emotion as action structure, and also reciprocally influences cognition. Unique features and contents of each disturbance will be presented later.

Model of Anxiety and Depression as Dynamic Processes

The following model (figure 16.1) is a useful heuristic for describing the dynamic relationship among the processes that constitute complex emotional states such as anxiety and depression. Accordingly, when a person with a particular negative learn-

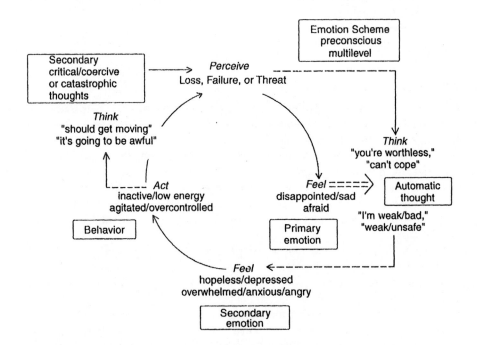

Figure 16.1 Model of anxiety and depression as dynamic processes.

ing history perceives loss or failure or potential threat, a multilevel, preconscious emotion scheme is activated. First, the perceptions of the situation generate a primary emotional response to the external situation, such as feeling disappointed/sad or afraid. Each primary emotion has an attendant response disposition, for example, to withdraw (low autonomic arousal) or escape (high arousal). The interaction between the situation and this sad or fearful state generates a "bodily felt sense" of meaning (Gendlin, 1981), or sense of self as weak/bad or insecure. Primary emotion generates this core sense of self by activating both automatic thoughts about self, such as "I'm worthless" or "I can't cope," and physiological and sensorimotor responses intrinsic to the emotional state. Furthermore, a weak/bad or insecure sense of self, when activated, leads to secondary emotional reactions or bad feelings, such as hopelessness, depression, or generalized anxiety. These depressogenic or anxious responses feed into the behavioral system and the person may be low in energy and inactive, or agitated and/or overcontrolled. Action, in turn, can generate secondary thoughts that are critical/coercive, or catastrophic, such as "I should get moving" or "it's going to be awful," and these feed back into perceptions of loss, failure, or threat. Secondary cognitions maintain the anxiety or depression but do not cause it. Importantly, when a weak/bad or insecure self-scheme is activated, the person is less able to combat negative cognitions. In our view, cognitions alone are not generators of anxiety and depression but are secondary to the anxious or depressive mood.

The close connection between anxious and depressogenic processes is evident when people collapse into a state of defeat after failed efforts to avoid harm. For example, a client who grew up terrorized by her father recalled desperate efforts to avert his rage by being a "perfect little girl," then giving up and withdrawing into herself when her repeated efforts proved futile. Simultaneously, she felt sad and unloved, hated her father for his cruelty and rejection, was unable to express her anger, and felt "bad" for hating her own father.

This same client responded similarly as an adult. The self-related emotion scheme was activated in situations when others were angry at her, or in response to her own experience of anger such that she attempted to "walk on eggshells" and then collapsed into resignation and depression. At the same time, she was chronically tense, and lacked self-confidence and self-esteem. As an adult, her sanctuary of withdrawal had become a prison.

This clinical example also illustrates the role of the two dysfunctional processes in generating anxiety and depression. The client is disoriented due to unacknowledged primary anger; she is cut off from the adaptive self-empowering action tendency of anger that is not integrated into her current view of self and reality. Thus, she feels weak, powerless, and worthless. The maladaptive emotion scheme that is activated in response to anger and sadness, as well as her view of self as helpless, bad, and unsafe, generates her anxiety and depression.

The point is that complex emotional responses like anxiety and depression are processes that unfold dynamically over time without a definite starting point. We apprehend the personal meaning of a situation, in terms of novelty, pleasantness, and personal significance, before we consciously appraise it. Different kinds of cognition enter into various stages of the emotional response but thinking does not have an executive role. Finally, the body contributes to subjective experience and is intimately connected with appraisal. This, again, is the view of emotion schemes as action structures, or emotion as "embodied" experience (Lakoff, 1987).

Anxiety

Distinctive Features and Processes

Consistent with current research (e.g., Barlow, 1988) we distinguish primary fear of imminent physical harm from anxiety about existential threat. Primary fear is the core emotion associated with situations of trauma and physical abuse, for example, and primary anxiety is an innate and adaptive response to the threat of abandonment or being left alone. According to Bowlby (1988), secure attachment is a fundamental human need; to know that an attachment figure is available and responsive gives one a strong and pervasive feeling of security. Separation anxiety is about losing or becoming separated from an attachment figure, and it signals an increased risk of harm. Anxiety is characterized by increased autonomic arousal, avoidant behavior, and anticipatory attempts to gain control. Adaptive anxiety is guided by an emotion scheme that generates adaptive behavior from attending to the response disposition to avoid anticipated danger, accurate symbolization as fear, and construction of complex situational meaning to explain the response. Anxiety generates an adaptive response to say one is afraid and elicit protection from others, or to take action in order to avoid harm. Thus, dysfunction results when primary adaptive anxiety is not attended to or inaccurately symbolized.

Dysfunction also results when anxiety is activated as part of a complex maladaptive emotion scheme. Aspects of this emotion scheme include stimulus generalization of anxiety-producing cues, learned inappropriate reactions, and faulty construals of self, others, and internal experience. There are individual differences, based on learning history, in susceptibility to maladaptive anxiety. Some anxiety responses are rooted in more extreme experiences of neglect, terror, or trauma, and the emotion schemes associated with these experiences are more readily activated than others.

Model of Anxiety as a Dynamic Process

The general model can now be applied to the nonlinear and dynamic processes that frequently underlie anxiety disorders. Maladaptive anxiety is a complex secondary reaction to perceived threat. The threat may derive either from an external situation, such as loss, abandonment, rejection, failure, or physical harm, or from core internal experience, such as feeling angry or sad. Perceptions of threat, regardless of the source, activate a multilevel emotion scheme (figure 16.1) that generates feelings of fear/arousal or anxiety, along with the attendant response dispositions. For an individual with a history of inconsistent or aversive attachment, this emotional state activates an insecure sense of self by eliciting both automatic thoughts, such as "I can't cope, I can't stand it," and physiological and sensorimotor experience. The latter is a bodily felt sense of self as unsafe, powerless, or trapped. A core insecure self-organization generates secondary anxiety and related bad feelings, such as anger and irritability, feeling overwhelmed and out of control, and shame at feeling weak and out of control. Together, these processes feed into the behavioral system to produce vigilance, agitation, and attempts to gain control through clinginess or avoidance. Action, in turn, can generate catastrophizing about imagined dangers ("It's going to be awful"), or self-castigation ("I'm such a wimp") that exacerbate maladaptive behavior and hypersensitivity to signs of threat. Thus, they perpetuate the anxiety-producing process.

This process is exemplified by a client who was abandoned by a critical, rejecting father, and who was angry and controlling in her current relationship. As an adult, signs of lack of support triggered her fear of abandonment, implicit beliefs that she was unwanted, and lack of confidence in her ability to cope on her own. Her reactive anger was generated by this insecure sense of self and need to secure proximity to an attachment figure. However, her angry responses pushed her partner further away, which leads to self-criticism about incompetence in relationships and catastrophizing about a life alone.

Self-Organizations Related to Anxiety

The two major categories of dysfunction that are relevant to anxiety are unacknowledged or avoided adaptive experience (anger, sadness, or fear) and activated maladaptive emotions schemes, particularly those schemes related to one's core sense of self. The latent self-organizations that predispose a person to anxiety are discussed below.

An insecure self-organization develops from repeated threats of harm, rejection or abandonment, or verbal and/or physical assaults in early attachment relationships. Bowlby (1988) states that the response of self in such situations is heightened arousal, vigilance, efforts to control the environment or self in order to avoid anticipated loss, and anger or clinginess to ensure the presence of the attachment figure. The person views attachment figures as untrustworthy or hurtful, and the future as insecure and unsure. This insecure self-organization consists of beliefs about self and other, sensorimotor arousal and vigilance, and memories of earlier experiences of existential threat or harm.

A common characteristic of an insecure self-organization is difficulty with self-soothing. This can result from a combination of temperamental factors and an invalidating and/or unprotective environment. Bowlby (1988) suggests that a child with a secure base develops the capacity to keep the mother in mind in order to self-soothe. However, the child who has not internalized a secure attachment figure is unable to explore and has a poor sense of mastery. The child has high dependency needs because of difficulty regulating anxiety on his or her own.

An avoidant self-organization is another emotion scheme that, when activated, generates anxiety. This sense of self develops from an extremely aversive learning history such that the person learns to avoid attachment, and learns to regulate anxiety by withdrawing into self-sufficiency. This self-organization may predominate in avoidant or schizoid interpersonal behaviors in which individuals are deeply suspicious and unable to form relationships, and distance themselves from others and from painful memories and internal experience. These people long for contact, although this longing may be on the periphery of awareness, and they remain alienated and untouched by life.

memories of earlier experiences of loss, physical or emotional injury and uncontrollable outcomes.

A self-critical self-organization is characteristic of one form of depression (Blatt, Quinlan, Chevron, McDonald, & Zuroff, 1982). Negative, critical, unsupportive interactions with significant others are internalized and can lead to self-persecution or self-denigration. Activation of this self-scheme also generates secondary anxiety in the form of fear of negative evaluation. Individuals can fear rejection because of implicit beliefs that they are flawed and they attribute self-critical cognitions to others.

Hostility toward self appears to be one core component of a depressive self-organization. People are able to tolerate knowledge of their shortcomings and failures so long as these are not accompanied by self-loathing. It is the contempt and disgust, disavowal or rejection of parts of self, that are damaging to self-worth and confidence.

Withdrawn or hidden essential self is the healthy self-organization that underlies depression; the life force that is unavailable and remains fearfully hidden when the depressive emotion scheme is activated. Initially the withdrawal may be self-protective and adaptive when efforts to protect the self become futile, as in the clinical example above. However, withdrawal becomes maladaptive when the vital part of the self remains unavailable. Again, clients in therapy frequently have had a taste of this authentic self, of feeling fully alive, and feel sad and despairing that this cherished part of themselves has disappeared. Such longing for contact can motivate assertiveness and risk-taking to recover the lost self.

Summary

Our theory of emotion integrates traditional experiential views with some recent developments in emotion theory and cognitive psychology (Izard, 1977; Leventhal, 1984). We view emotion as a complex system consisting of interacting cognitive, affective, motivational, and behavioral components. We also suggest that the internal representations that relate to one's core sense of self, formed in early attachment relationships, are an important class of preconscious emotion schemes and a major factor in generating maladaptive emotional states such as anxiety and depression. Furthermore, we believe that personal reality and self-experience is continuously constructed through the interaction of consciousness with both external reality and emotion schemes.

We distinguish between primary adaptive emotions, such as anger and sadness, and secondary emotional reactions, and view anxiety and depression as complex and secondary emotional responses with primary emotion as one component. These disorders are specific examples of maladaptive emotional reactions generated by two classes of dysfunctional processes: (a) lack of awareness of primary emotional experience (with sensorimotor and schematic components) such that adaptive information is not integrated into current constructions of self and reality, and (b) activation of preconscious emotion schemes, with learned maladaptive components that guide perceptions and behavior.

Anxiety and depression are highly correlated and researchers have identified numerous similarities in the two disorders (Kendall & Watson, 1989). In our view, anxiety and depression are both multilevel and interrelated processes that unfold dynamically over time. These processes involve the activation of core self-organizations as well as primary and secondary emotions, cognitions, and behavioral/action systems. Thinking contributes to these maladaptive states but does not play an executive role, and bodily experience is intimately connected to the appraisal system.

References

American Psychiatric Association. (1994). *Diagnostic and statistical manual of mental disorders* (4th ed.). Washington, DC: Author.

Arnold, M. B. (1960). *Emotion and personality.* New York: Columbia University Press.

Barlow, D. H. (1988). *Anxiety and its disorders: The nature and treatment of anxiety and panic.* New York: Guilford Press.

Beck, A. T. (1976). *Cognitive therapy and emotional disorders.* New York: International Universities Press.

Blatt, S. J., Quinlan, D. M., Chevron, E. S., McDonald, C., & Zuroff, D. (1982). Dependency and self-criticism: Psychological dimensions of depression. *Journal of Consulting and Clinical Psychology, 50,* 113–124.

Bowlby, J. (1988). *A secure base: Parent-child attachment and healthy human development.* New York: Basic Books.

Fridja, N. H. (1986). *The emotions.* New York: Cambridge University Press.

Gendlin, E. T. (1981). *Focusing.* New York: Bantam.

Gilbert, P. (1989). *Human nature and suffering.* Hillsdale, NJ: Erlbaum.

Greenberg, L. S., Elliott, R., & Foerster, F. S. (1990). Emotional processes in the psychotherapeutic treatment of depression. In C. D. McCann & N. S. Endler (Eds.), *Depression: New directions in treatment, research, and practice* (pp. 157–186). Toronto: Wall & Emerson.

Greenberg, L. S., & Johnson, S. (1988). *Emotionally focused therapy for couples.* New York: Guilford Press.

Greenberg, L. S., & Paivio, S. C. (in press). *Professional practice series* (M. Mahoney, Ed.), *Working with emotions.* New York: Guilford Press.

Greenberg, L. S., & Pascual-Leone, J. (1995). Experiential therapy from a dialectical constructivist perspective. In R. Neimeyer & M. Mahoney (Eds.), *Constructivism in Psychotherapy.* American Psychological Association.

Greenberg, L. S., Rice, L. N., & Elliott, R. (1993). *Facilitating emotional change: The moment by moment process.* New York: Guilford Press.

Greenberg, L. S., & Safran, J. D. (1987). *Emotion in psychotherapy.* New York: Guilford Press.

Izard, C. E. (1977). *Human emotions.* New York: Plenum Press.

Kelly, G. (1955). *The psychology of personal constructs.* New York: Norton.

Kendall, P. C., & Watson, D. (1989). *Anxiety and depression: Distinctive and overlapping features.* San Diego: Academic Press.

Kihlstrom, J. F. (1990). The psychological unconscious. In L. A. Pervin (Ed.), *Handbook of personality: Theory and research* (pp. 445–464). New York: Guilford Press.

Lakoff, G. (1987). *Women, fire and dangerous things: What categories reveal about the mind.* Chicago: University of Chicago Press.

Lang, P. J. (1984). The cognitive psychophysiology of emotion: Fear and anxiety. In S. H. Tuma & J. D. Maser (Eds.), *Anxiety and anxiety disorders* (pp. 131–170). Hillsdale, NJ: Erlbaum.

Lazarus, A. (1991). *Emotion and adaptation*. New York: Oxford University Press.

Leventhal, H. (1984). A perceptual-motor processing model of emotion. In L. Berkowitz (Ed.), *Advances in experimental social psychology* (pp. 117–182). New York: Academic Press.

Neisser, U. (1976). *Cognition and reality: Principles and implications of cognitive psychology*. San Francisco: Freeman.

Pascual-Leone, J. (1991). Emotions, development, and psychotherapy: A dialectical-constructivist perspective. In J. D. Safran & L. S. Greenberg (Eds.), *Emotion, psychotherapy, and change* (pp. 302–338). New York: Guilford Press.

Perls, F. S., Hefferline, R. F., & Goodman, P. (1957). *Gestalt therapy*. New York: Dell.

Piaget, J., & Morf, A. (1958). Les isomorpismes partiels entre les structures logiques et les structures perceptives. In J. S. Bruner, F. Bresson, A. Morf, & J. Piaget (Eds.), *Logique et perception* (pp. 83–108). Paris: Presses Universitaires de France.

Plutchik, R. (1980). *Emotion: A psychoevolutionary synthesis*. New York: Harper & Row.

Rogers, C. R. (1958). A process conception of psychotherapy. *American Psychologist, 13*, 142–148.

Shiffrin, R. M., & Schneider, W. (1977). Controlled and automatic information processing II: Perceptual learning, automatic attending and a general theory. *Psychological Review, 84*, 127–140.

Stewart, L., & Pascual-Leone, J. (1992). Mental capacity constraints and the development of moral reasoning. *Journal of Experimental Child Psychology, 54*, 251–287.

Teasdale, T. J., & Barnard, P. (1993). *Affect, cognition, and change*. Hillsdale, NJ: Erlbaum.

Tomkins, S. (1970). Affect as the primary motivational system. In M. B. Arnold (Ed.), *Feelings and emotions*. New York: Academic Press.

17

Paul McReynolds

The Role of Anxiety in Psychopathology

Of all the emotional states that the human species is susceptible to, the most ubiquitous, with respect to the range of psychopathologies, is anxiety. This is true in the sense that, first, severe anxiety, in any of several manifestations, is itself severely disabling, and second, that certain disorders are traced, in conventional theory, to attempts of the individual to avoid or to attenuate anxiety, or to the breakdown of such efforts. Anxiety, then, is implicated in a wide variety of behavior disorders, and plays a unique theoretical role in attempts to explain many disorders.

For these reasons it is important to examine the nature of anxiety and the manners in which it affects, and helps to determine, those behavioral patterns that are thought of as abnormal. In this chapter, first I present a brief historical review of the concept of anxiety. Next I consider the status of anxiety as an emotion. Following this I examine the concept of anxiety—what we mean by the term, its referents and its ambiguities. Then I summarize a theoretical interpretation of anxiety that I have developed, and finally, I apply this model to the understanding of certain psychopathologies.

The Nature of Anxiety

Historical Background

If anxiety is endemic to being human, as seems plausible, then it should follow that allusions to, and even descriptions of, anxiety should be found in early historical writings, and such is indeed the case (McReynolds, 1986). Thus, the earliest known human narrative, the Sumerian epic *Gilgamesh*, stresses the hero's inner anguish in the face of certain mortality. The early books of the Bible include numerous references to human fears and concerns. By the Hellenistic periods the basis of anxiety had been systematically explored, as evident in an essay by Epictetus (trans. 1944) translated as "On anxiety," which begins this way: "When I see anyone anxious, I say, what does this man want? Unless he wanted something or other not in his power how could he still be anxious?" (p. 117). Other early writers described some of the physiological and behavioral characteristics of states that we would classify as anxiety.

Passing over a number of medieval and Renaissance scholars, I turn next to the philosopher John Locke. Locke, in 1690, discussed the development in individuals of a state that he termed *uneasiness*, characterized by worry and mental distress (McReynolds, 1986). Then in 1758 a highly innovative work by William Battie included a systematic discussion of anxiety — by that name — and posited that it results from overstimulation. Battie (McReynolds, 1986) conceived of severe anxiety as a separate mental disorder. In the early to mid-nineteenth century several approaches to anxiety were published by other authors, and by the time Freud published his first article on anxiety in 1895, the theme of anxiety was already relatively common in works on psychopathology. Since Freud's book *The Problem of Anxiety* (1926/1936), the concept of anxiety has played a key role in virtually all broad models of psychopathology. The major inference to be drawn from this survey is that human experiences with anxiety, and attempts to conceptualize it in a meaningful way, have a long history.

Anxiety in the Overall Emotional Context

The ancient Stoic philosophers identified four basic *passions* (a concept roughly analogous to the current *emotions*): pleasure, grief, fear, and desire. Modern emotion theorists tend to be less restrictive. Thus, Ekman and his colleagues (Ekman, 1984) posit six fundamental, innate emotions (fear, surprise, anger, disgust, distress, and happiness), and Izard (1991) identifies 10 basic emotions (interest, enjoyment, surprise, sadness, anger, disgust, contempt, fear, shame, and shyness). Other emotion theorists have put forward slightly different but overlapping lists (see table 1 in Ortony and Turner, 1990). Ortony and Turner (1990) question the whole notion of basic emotions.

In any event my interest here is not in the overall lists of emotions as such, but rather in how the emotion of anxiety is to be construed. Notably, none of the emotion theorists just mentioned consider anxiety to be a basic emotion. The closest they come is to posit fear, as a basic affect, but fear, as I will elaborate below, is not identical to anxiety.

The question of whether anxiety is to be considered a basic emotion is not an easy one, and hinges in part on the question of how one defines "basic" (Ortony & Turner, 1990). Certainly anxiety is basic in the sense that it can plausibly be said to occur in all cultures and in all historical periods, and to be monumentally important in determining human behavior. Developmental psychologists identify a broad negative state in infants that can best be termed *distress*, and this can be seen as an early form of anxiety (Mandler, 1975). Spielberger (1985) views anxiety as a fundamental emotion, as does Akiskal (1985), who considers anxiety "to be a distinct emotion that has evolved over millions of years" (p. 796). In contrast, Izard (1991) argues that anxiety is a complex emotion, with the fundamental emotion of fear at its core, and also including certain additional associated elements, such as sadness, shame, or anger. The respects in which I consider anxiety a basic affect will become evident below.

Conceptual Analysis of Anxiety

The term *anxiety* is, first of all, a word. It has come into general usage because it has proved helpful in communicating an inner feeling of tension and anguish. Though such linguistic acceptance does not guarantee the commonality of the experience of anxiety among different individuals, it is at least presumptive evidence for that commonality, and thus for the meaningfulness of the concept of anxiety. Anxiety is, however, difficult to define in a way that is both clear and rigorous, and such a definition ultimately depends on a theoretical understanding of anxiety.

Like all personality characteristics, anxiety can be conceptualized in terms of a private feeling, as revealed in self-report data and/or in terms of particular overt behaviors accessible to observers. A third category is the physiological expression of anxiety, as represented, for example, in cardiovascular changes. Generally speaking, correlations between self-report assays of anxiety and corresponding behavioral or physiological measures are significant but low. Of the three approaches just noted — the phenomenal, the behavioral, and the physiological — by far the most important, as far as an understanding of psychopathology is concerned, is the subject's inner feeling of anxiety. This is because it is the feeling, when extreme, that the person finds intolerable, and which he or she seeks to relieve through behaviors that in some instances may be so maladaptive as to be considered pathological.

Anxiety is, of course, one of several negative emotions. In particular, it is closely related to fear and depression. Some writers treat fear and anxiety as essentially the same, but this seems to be an oversimplification. Fear is the affect accompanying the anticipation of an aversive future event, and while such anticipation frequently occasions the kind of tension and worry that we think of as anxiety, the fact is that anxiety may also be caused by nonanticipatory perceptions, for example, a woman overwhelmed and distressed by an excess of errands, chores, and obligations at Christmastime. It may also be noted that the word *fear* is customarily employed to cover events as widely divergent as the sudden terror that grips one when, for example, he suddenly sees a speeding car hurtling toward him, and the worry and rumination that characterizes a new graduate's fear that she may not find employment. Obviously, these are quite different phenomena — the former is probably a wired-in reaction to the immediacy of danger, whereas the latter is similar, if not identical, to what is ordinarily called anxiety. Other theorists who distinguish between fear and anxiety include Goldstein (1951) and Lazarus (1991).

Anxiety Theory

In order to usefully relate anxiety to psychopathology, it is necessary to work from a systematic theory that formally states the nature of anxiety, its causes, and the factors determining its occurrence. Thus, merely to say that since severe anxiety is unpleasant and therefore people engage in behaviors to reduce it is clearly inadequate. The problem is not that such a position is wrong, but that it lacks the theoretical rigor and specificity required for scientific analysis. Most theories of anxiety, it is fair to say, have not yet reached such a level of development. In the present chapter I will utilize the general conceptualization of anxiety that I have described elsewhere (McReynolds, 1976, 1987, 1989, 1990, 1991); in addition, several new extensions of the theory will be presented.

Anxiety, in the present model, is conceived to be a naturally occurring negative affect that arises, under certain specifiable conditions, as a function of the ongoing commerce of the person with his or her changing environment. This relationship, it is assumed, has been laid down through selective processes during the course of evolution, with the result that anxiety typically serves an adaptive function.

Cognitive Anxiety

The present model is based on the core conception of cognitive processing. It is assumed that the individual, as the result of early maturation and cognitive development, constructs an internalized, highly organized affecto-cognitive system that, as encoded in the brain, represents that person's conception of reality. New stimulus inputs are sorted, categorized, transformed into percepts, and typically assimilated into the overall cognitive structure, which for convenience I will refer to as the *category system*. This system at any given time represents, indeed constitutes, the individual's conception of reality. Throughout life the category system grows and changes as it is reorganized to conform with new inputs from both external and internal (thought) sources.

There is not sufficient space here to develop this general model in detail. The reader will recognize the above formulation as fairly conventional and, indeed, in its essence as going back to Herbart's notion of the apperceptive mass. Modern theorists to whom I am indebted include Bruner, Goodnow, and Austin (1960), Kelly (1955), Piaget (1952), and Sarbin, Taft, and Bailey (1960). The concept of anxiety enters the picture, in my theory, when we conceive of inputs—that is to say, perceptual experiences—that do not fit into the structure of the category system because of discrepancies between the characteristics of the input and the relevant portions of the category system. In such instances one of two things tends to occur: (a) Either the category system is modified to accommodate the new input—indeed, such restructuring is the primary manner by which the category system grows and develops, or (b) the input data remain unassimilated. The occurrence of cognitive discrepancies of the type just noted (whether referred to as cognitive dissonance, disparity, incongruence, or by some other term) tends to provoke a transient degree of discomfort and arousal. In my view, however, such discrepancies are not sufficient, in themselves, to account for the agonizing affect that we know as anxiety. For that to occur something additional is needed, and that something else, in my model, is the assumption that unassimilated perceptual data tend to accumulate, in a kind of suspended, un-worked-through status. If this accrual is protracted enough, it can be thought of as constituting a *cognitive backlog*.

This backlog, I posit, is the fundamental basis of anxiety. It is not itself anxiety, since anxiety is an affect. Rather, it is conceived that the cognitive backlog leads directly to anxiety. I refer to this kind of anxiety as *primary*, or *cognitive*, anxiety. It is assumed that the amount of cognitive anxiety is a direct function of the magnitude of the cognitive backlog (a distinction must be made, however, between *amount* and *intensity* of anxiety, as I will elaborate below). There are two sorts of dynamic processes that can contribute to an increment in the cognitive backlog of an individual.

The first of these processes consists of the phenomenal occurrence of percepts, based on life experiences, thoughts, and recollections, that are discrepant with the relevant specifications of the category system and thus cannot be assimilated. The general affect associated with a buildup of the backlog is, I suggest, a feeling of distress and unsettledness. More specifically, the feeling is a mixture of anxiety per se and the contents of the unassimilated material, the latter of which would give its name to the affect, for example, test anxiety, social anxiety, and the like. As an example of an experience yielding inassimilable input, suppose a man, taking a qualifying exam for a position, yields to the temptation to cheat, and then learns that he barely outscored his best friend, depriving him of the job. The man's perception of his own behavior would be difficult to assimilate because it would be discrepant with the dimensions of his ongoing self-structure, as embedded in his category system. More devastating instances of input-system discrepancies could easily be stated; they would concern disturbances in the self-concept, interpersonal problems, and worries about the future.

It should be noted at this point that the anxiety aroused by an unassimilable experience may be out of all proportion to the magnitude of the newly unassimilable data. This is because the level of anxiety would be a function of the total amount of unassimilated material, not just of the new input. This explains why persons may flare up with great distress and anger over seemingly minor frustrations.

When the magnitude of the cognitive backlog is sufficient to cause an unpleasant feeling of anxiety, efforts are initiated to reduce the anxiety; this requires that the category system be restructured, in some instances drastically, to accommodate the new material. This process clearly involves seeing oneself and one's world in somewhat different ways, and amounts, in essence, to cognitive problem solving. Such efforts, as manifested in everyday life, may be called rumination, worrying, seeing oneself anew, and the like.

So far I have focused on the occurrence of new experiences that are unassimilable. Another, and on occasion much more potent, process contributing to the magnitude of the cognitive backlog is the disassimilation of previously assimilated material. A striking example would be a woman who, having largely built her life around interactions with her husband, is suddenly asked for a divorce. Such an experience would result in a flood of unassimilated material, and an intense surge of anxiety. In some instances radically new conceptions of one's self, of one's whole identity, or of some major newly perceived personal problem, could occur suddenly and lead to a state of panic, perhaps similar to what Goldstein (1951) referred to as "an inner experience of catastrophe" (p. 46).

The second kind of process, in the context of the present theory, that can cause an increase in the cognitive backlog is the input of new percepts at a more rapid rate than they can be assimilated, even though in terms of raw discrepancies they do not present major problems. Examples of this sequence would be a business man suddenly beset with more critical problems than he can cope with immediately, or the woman, noted above, overwhelmed with Christmas chores. This whole phenomenon, in a different theoretical context, is sometimes referred to as input overload (Miller, 1960), and is related to those theories (e.g., Battie, noted above; Freud 1926/1936) that attribute anxiety to overstimulation.

Conditioned Anxiety

A second type of anxiety—in addition to cognitive anxiety—is conditioned anxiety. I refer to this as *secondary anxiety* because it is based on the association of situational cues with the existence of strong states of cognitive, or primary anxiety. Although details of the process remain somewhat obscure (McReynolds, 1989; Rachman, 1978), there is little doubt that anxiety is conditionable. For my present purposes the implication is that certain perceptions and settings may, as the result of having previously been experienced in the presence of severe anxiety, come to elicit anxiety directly, that is, independently of the process of assimilation, and irrespective of whether the cognitive backlog that led originally to the severe anxiety has since been assimilated.

Phenomenally, conditioned anxiety, I believe, has the same "feel" as cognitive anxiety. It differs in one major respect, however: Whereas one can avoid the settings that trigger conditioned anxiety, and thus to a considerable extent control its occurrence, susceptibility to cognitive anxiety is constant, since one cannot escape the underlying cognitive backlog.

Discussion

Earlier I suggested a distinction between amount and intensity of anxiety. What I have in mind is something analogous to the difference between calories and degrees in the physics of heat. In the present model the *amount* of anxiety is reflected in the magnitude of unassimilated material (cognitive backlog); the *intensity* of anxiety is indicated by the degree of the affect at any given moment. Recall that earlier I posited that anxiety is a function of the magnitude of the cognitive backlog; this affect, however, may be attenuated, or even temporarily eliminated, by various factors. Some of these are commonplace; thus, an individual may become temporarily so involved in some distracting activity, such as music, tennis, or a film, as to be oblivious to otherwise distressful anxiety. Antianxiety drugs, by a different process, evidently also have the capacity to reduce the intensity of anxiety, without, however, ameliorating the cognitive problems underlying the anxiety.

We can now examine further the question of whether anxiety is a basic emotion. To the extent that the present theory is valid, anxiety is certainly fundamental, in the sense that it is conceived that the human organism is genetically wired such that anxiety necessarily arises under certain prescribed conditions.

Psychopathology

Before considering how the present theory of anxiety may illuminate certain instances of psychopathology, it will be useful to examine the concept of psychopathology.

Literally, the term means "sickness of the psyche"; since a precise definition of the psyche is elusive at best, however, this interpretation is of little value. It is doubtful that a brief, rigorous definition of psychopathology can be framed. For one thing, there is the matter of cultural relativism; for example, in some societies a person who sees visions is considered special and important, whereas in contemporary America such a person, except in occasional religious contexts, is likely to be labeled schizophrenic. Further, there is the problem of sifting out moral and pejorative judgments (Sarbin & Mancuso, 1980) in identifying behaviors that are to be called pathological. These problems aside, the existence of behaviors that are grossly deviant and/or personally agonizing, and that cannot be attributed to transient circumstances, such as drunkenness or a great personal disappointment, can hardly be denied, and need to be understood.

As just implied, the two cardinal criteria of psychopathology are behavioral deviance and psychological discomfort. From the public perspective it is the former that is the more conspicuous and bothersome, but from the subject's perspective it is the latter that constitutes the main problem. The two perspectives are not unrelated, however; thus, certain cognitive maneuvers carried out by individuals to reduce anxiety, for example, the formation of delusions, as discussed below, may lead to behaviors perceived by others as unacceptably deviant.

Pathological Anxiety

Anxiety as such is, of course, not pathological; on the contrary, it is only through the existence of unassimilable inputs, with the subsequent revisions of the category system, that a person's conception of reality grows and develops. The transition from normal to pathological anxiety is not a lien set in the nature of things, but rather is a matter of judgment and cultural consensus. Nevertheless, severe, protracted anxiety is extremely excruciating and debilitating.

Generalized anxiety is due, in my theory, to the existence in an individual of a large mass of unassimilated experiential material. This backlog, in turn, is due to the existence in the individual's category system of mental discrepancies that make assimilation difficult. My treatment here is not particularly different from that of conventional psychodynamic and cognitive theory, to which I am much indebted. However, I have attempted (McReynolds, 1987, 1991) to be as explicit as possible about the taxonomy of the mental discrepancies—which can also be thought of as intrapsychic conflicts—that prevent assimilation. Thus, the mental elements among which such conflicts may exist include desires, values, attitudes, intentions, and affects, among others.

The individual's natural reaction to the high degree of anxiety engendered by massive unassimilated cognitive material is to attempt to restructure the category system to make assimilation possible. This is the area covered by the Freudian concept of defense (against anxiety) mechanisms. Elsewhere (McReynolds, 1987) I have identified certain "assimilation strategies" that I believe to be involved in such cognitive efforts.

If it is true, as seems likely, that anxiety can be conditioned to certain particular situations only when the degree of existent anxiety is high, then it follows that those individuals afflicted with high levels of cognitive conflicts are especially susceptible to conditioned, or situational, anxieties. Instances of such anxiety appear to cover a wide scope, ranging from, say, discomfort in social situations to full-blown phobias. Modern research (Bower & Hilgard, 1981) does not support a simple contiguity model of conditioning; instead, the most plausible paradigm is that a particular stimulus situation comes to be *predictive* of anxiety. Thus, the individual learns to avoid that situation. In this context a phobia, though in the long run maladaptive, can be seen as a mental device signaling the likelihood of intense anxiety, and thereby permitting avoidance behavior to eliminate that possibility.

It is unnecessary to assume a logical connection between the phobic stimulus and anxiety. For example, consider an individual with a phobia against driving a car: It is *not* required that the person have previously had a serious automobile accident when driving. Instead, the present assumption is that the individual must have suffered a severe anxiety attack, of panic proportions, when driving a car. Such an attack—which is similar to what Barlow (1988) has termed a "false alarm"—could arise from sudden massive disassimilation that might have occurred, through thought processes, while the person was driving, but which was totally unrelated to the driving.

Therapeutically, the reduction of cognitive anxiety requires some sort of category system restructuring, whether under the guidance of psychodynamic, cognitive-behavioral, gestalt, or some similar type of therapy. The reduction of conditioned anxiety, in contrast, appears to require the application of techniques in which the patient is systematically exposed to the feared cues (Foa & Kozak, 1986).

Schizophrenic Solutions

In this section I will focus on certain highly deviant behaviors that characterize the schizophrenic disorders, and will show how, in terms of the present theory of anxiety, these behaviors can be understood as serving to reduce an individual's mass of unassimilated material, and hence anxiety. Though this approach assumes a high level of anxiety in such individuals, at least in the disorder's initial stages, it does not get into the questions of the role of genetic, physiological, or cultural factors in the etiology of the disorder. The three deviant behaviors that I will summarize, while effective in reducing or preventing intolerable anxiety, are, however, highly maladaptive, in the sense that they limit the individual's capacity to cope successfully with the everyday problems of living.

The first drastic defensive maneuver that I wish to consider is the formation of delusions. A delusion is a way of conceiving reality that is outside the normal consensus, but that makes sense to the individual involved. It is, in other words, a major restructuring of the individual's category system that permits the assimilation of previously unassimilable material (McReynolds, 1960; McReynolds, Collins, & Acker, 1964). Though the delusion can itself be very frightening, it is less so than the cognitive material it rationalizes. This conception of delusions is not new and is roughly similar to that proposed by Cameron (1947) under the concept of "sudden clarification."

The second major feature of schizophrenia that is at least partially explicable in terms of the present anxiety theory is disorganized thinking, or thought disorder. My interpretation here (McReynolds, 1960; McReynolds and Collins, 1961) is based on the notion of degree of fit between input data and the relevant characteristics of the category system into which they would be assimilated. When the individual's cognitive processing system requires close fits, then obviously it is more difficult for inputs to be assimilated, and contrariwise, when the assimilation standards are loose then assimilation can more readily occur. A reduction in assimilation standards, as manifested in thought disturbances, functions to permit assimilation of otherwise unassimilable materials, and thus reduce anxiety.

The third solution to the problem of intolerable anxiety to be noted here is withdrawal behavior. The extreme, generalized withdrawal that is characteristic of schizophrenia would have the effect of shielding the individual from new perceptual inputs, particularly novel inputs, that might be difficult to assimilate (McReynolds, 1960, 1963), and would thus tend to prevent increments in anxiety.

Concluding Comments

In this chapter, rather than simply reviewing the numerous behavior disorders in which anxiety is a major symptom, I have opted for a broader perspective. I have emphasized that it is essential, in order to adequately understand the role of anxiety in psychopathology, to have a reasonably comprehensive theory of the affect. Such a theory should explain both the causes and the effects of anxiety, should rationalize the reactions of persons to anxiety, and should cover normal as well as pathological anxiety.

As a contribution to such a theoretical understanding I have proposed a two-component conceptualization, which conceives that experiential data that a person is unable to assimilate build up (cognitive backlog) and lead to the emotion of anxiety (cognitive component), and further, that under certain circumstances adventitious stimuli occurring in tandem with such anxiety gain the power (conditioned component) to elicit anxiety.

There are three ways, in the present model, in which anxiety symptoms in an individual can be accounted for. The first is due to the buildup of a large backlog of unassimilated mental data, which is felt as extreme personal discomfort. Second, the anxiety may be conditioned to certain stimulus arrays, limiting the individual's freedom of action. And third, the person may develop certain cognitive-behavioral methods for containing or reducing the backlog, and these may hinder the individual's overall effectiveness, and/or make him or her appear socially deviant.

Acknowledgments I appreciate the helpful suggestions of John Altrocchi, Richard Baldo, and Duane Varble in the preparation of this chapter.

References

Akiskal, H. S. (1985). Anxiety: Definition, relationship to depression, and proposal for an integrative model. In A. H. Tuma & J. D. Maser (Eds.), *Anxiety and the anxiety disorders* (pp. 787–797). Hillsdale, NJ: Erlbaum.

Barlow, D. H. (1988). *Anxiety and its disorders*. New York: Guilford Press.

Battie, W. A. (1969). *A treatise on madness*. New York: Brunner/Mazel (Originally published 1758).

Bower, G. H., & Hilgard, E. R. (1981). *Theories of learning* (5th ed.). Englewood Cliffs, NJ: Prentice-Hall.

Bruner, J. S., Goodnow, J. J., & Austin, G. A. (1960). *A study of thinking*. New York: Wiley.

Cameron, N. (1947). *The psychology of behavior disorders*. New York: Houghton Mifflin.

Ekman, P. (1984). Expression and the nature of emotion. In K. R. Scherer & P. Ekman (Eds.), *Approaches to emotion* (pp. 319–343). Hillsdale, NJ: Erlbaum.

Epictetus (trans. 1944). *Discourses*. (T. W. Higginson, Trans.). Roslyn, NY: Walter J. Black.

Foa, E. B., & Kozak, M. J. (1986). Emotional processing of fear: Exposure to corrective information. *Psychological Bulletin, 99,* 20–35.

Freud, S. (1895/1959). The justification for detaching from neurasthenia a particular syndrome: The anxiety-neurosis. In Joan Riviere (trans.) *Sigmund Freud: Collected papers*. vol. 1 (pp. 76–106). New York: Basic Books.

Freud, S. (1926/1936). *The problem of anxiety*. New York: Psychoanalytic Press.

Goldstein, K. (1951). On emotions: Considerations from the organismic point of view. *Journal of Psychology, 31,* 37–46.

Izard, C. E. (1991). *The psychology of emotions*. New York: Plenum Press.

Kelly, G. A. (1955). *The psychology of personal constructs*. New York: Norton.

Lazarus, R. S. (1991). *Emotion and adaptation*. New York: Oxford University Press.

Mandler, G. (1975). *Mind and emotion*. New York: Wiley.

McReynolds, P. (1960). Anxiety, perception and schizophrenia. In D. D. Jackson (Ed.), *The etiology of schizophrenia* (pp. 248–292). New York: Basic Books.

McReynolds, P. (1963). Reactions to novel and familiar stimuli as a function of schizophrenic withdrawal. *Perceptual and Motor Skills, 16,* 847–850.

McReynolds, P. (1976). Assimilation and anxiety. In M. Zuckerman & C. D. Spielberger (Eds.), *Emotions and anxiety* (pp. 35–86). Hillsdale, NJ: Erlbaum.

McReynolds, P. (1986). Changing conceptions of anxiety: A historical review and a proposed integration. In C. D. Spielberger & I. G. Sarason (Eds.), *Stress and anxiety* (Vol. 10, pp. 131–158). New York: Hemisphere.

McReynolds, P. (1987). Self-theory, anxiety and intrapsychic conflicts. In N. Cheshire & H. Thomae (Eds.), *Self, symptoms and psychotherapy* (pp. 197–223). New York: Wiley.

McReynolds, P. (1989). Toward a general theory of anxiety. In C. D. Spielberger, I. G. Sarason, & J. Strelau (Eds.), *Stress and anxiety* (Vol. 12, pp. 3–14). New York: Hemisphere.

McReynolds, P. (1990). The concept of anxiety: Background and current issues. In D. G. Byrne & R. H. Rosenman (Eds.), *Anxiety and the heart* (pp. 3–28). New York: Hemisphere.

McReynolds, P. (1991). The nature and logic of intrapsychic conflicts. In C. D. Spielberger, I. G. Sarason, J. Strelau, & J. M. T. Brebner (Eds.), *Stress and anxiety* (Vol. 13, pp. 73–83). New York: Hemisphere.

McReynolds, P., & Collins, B. (1961). Concept-forming behavior in schizophrenia and non-schizophrenic subjects. *Journal of Psychology, 52,* 269–378.

McReynolds, P. Collins, B., & Acker, M. (1964). Delusional thinking and cognitive organization in schizophrenia. *Journal of Abnormal and Social Psychology, 69,* 210–212.

Miller, J. G. (1960). Information input overload and psychopathology. *American Journal of Psychiatry, 116,* 695–704.

Ortony, A., & Turner, T. J. (1990). What's basic about basic emotions? *Psychological Review, 97,* 315–331.

Piaget, J. (1952). *The origins of intelligence in children.* New York: International Universities Press.

Rachman, S. (1978). *Fear and courage.* San Francisco: Freeman.

Sarbin, T. R., & Mancuso, J. C. (1980). *Schizophrenia: Medical diagnosis or moral verdict?* New York: Pergamon.

Sarbin, T. R., Taft, R., & Bailey, D. E. (1960). *Clinical inference and cognitive theory.* New York: Holt, Rinehart & Winston.

Spielberger, C. D. (1985). Anxiety, cognition and affect: A state-trait perspective. In A. H. Tuma & J. D. Maser (Eds.), *Anxiety and the anxiety disorders* (pp. 171–182). Hillsdale, NJ: Erlbaum.

18

Jill H. Rathus & William C. Sanderson

The Role of Emotion in the Psychopathology and Treatment of the Anxiety Disorders

Adaptive Value of Anxiety

The focus of this chapter is on the role of the emotion of anxiety in the development and treatment of anxiety disorders. First, we highlight the significance of anxiety from an evolutionary perspective, portraying anxiety symptoms in terms of their adaptive roles. Specifically, we discuss the impact of anxiety on moment to moment functioning, outline the response systems involved in the emotion of anxiety, and differentiate various manifestations of anxiety. In the second part of this chapter we discuss the psychopathological manifestations of anxiety—the anxiety disorders. We postulate a specific function for each of the essential features of the *Diagnostic and Statistical Manual of Mental Disorders* (4th ed.; hereinafter DSM-IV; American Psychiatric Association, 1994) anxiety disorders, taking the perspective that each anxiety disorder represents an exaggerated form of an adaptive mechanism. Finally, we conclude with a discussion of the theory and process of anxiety reduction.

Evolutionary Significance: Survival of Species Through Protection

The basic premise of evolutionary theory is that features that best equip organisms to pass on their genes are naturally selected and continue to be expressed in future generations. Organisms must continuously evaluate and respond to stimuli that either enhance or endanger their ability to survive and mate, and those that develop successful features to accomplish these goals are more likely to pass on their genes. Emotions have evolved as one mechanism to direct the organism toward this purpose. As noted by Lazarus (1991), emotions reflect the evaluation of the relationship between the organism and the environment. Specifically, negative emotions (e.g., anxiety, anger, sadness) indicate a "goal incongruent" (harmful) organism-environment transaction, whereas positive emotions indicate a "goal congruent" (beneficial) transaction. As a result of these signals, the organism is compelled to take action to eliminate negative emotions and maximize positive emotions.

Our premise is that anxiety is a hard-wired phenomenon that enhances the odds of survival by providing regulation of actions that may ultimately lead to harm or injury. This approach to anxiety, and emotions in general, originates with the work of Charles Darwin (1872), and has been supported by the work of several emotion theorists (e.g., Beck, 1985; Izard, 1977; Plutchik, 1980), yet largely neglected by clinicians in the field of psychopathology.

While the primary function of anxiety is to prepare an organism for protective action, a secondary function involves communicating danger to other members of a species through facial expression, posture, vocal responses, and so on (cf. Barlow, 1988). In addition to individual mobilization, emotional expression of fear also allows observers to respond protectively to potential harm, enhancing their chances for survival as well, and potentially eliciting aid in a vulnerable situation. Since members of a kin group may be interdependent (e.g., mating partners) and may share genes with one another (e.g., offspring, siblings), then passing on one's genes may be related to the survival of members of the group as well. Lines of evidence supporting the hard-wired and functional nature of emotions include research demonstrating the presence of emotional expressiveness at birth (before learning could occur), and strong consistency of emotional expression within and across species.

When an organism is under threat, there are essentially two functional strategies to cope with the threat: eliminating it or escaping it. This is best known as the "fight or flight" response, which activates the organism to cope with the situation. This response, first formulated by Cannon (1929), reflects the alternate strategies of hostile/attacking (anger) responses versus fearful/escape (anxiety) strategies. These reactions occur across species and occur automatically. Beck and Emery (1985) suggest a further elaboration of this response termed the "fight-flight-freeze-faint reaction," which incorporates the immobilizing reactions that under certain threat circumstances may best serve the organism (e.g., freezing may result in being overlooked by a predator; fainting in response to an injury may reduce blood, due to decreased blood pressure). In fact, as will be detailed below, each symptom that occurs during the anxiety response serves a protective function for the organism.

Since survival is the most important goal for the organism, one would expect that anxiety should be a highly aversive emotional experience that supersedes other cognitive or affective states and compels the organism to attend to the source of anxiety. Attention becomes narrowed as a function of the intensity of the emotion. Specifically, as the emotion intensifies, one becomes more focused on cues congruent with the particular emotion, and less attentive to mood-incongruent cues. From our functional perspective, this cue restriction magnifies those stimuli important to process for adaptive coping, and "weeds out" irrelevant stimuli that may distract from the goal of taking protective action. For example, if an organism encounters a predator, it is adaptive for resources to be directed toward escaping from an imminent threat, rather than on other functional behaviors, such as feeding or mating.

In addition, the discomfort of anxiety motivates one to take some action to reduce the state of arousal. The action may involve retreating from dangerous situations (e.g., fleeing from an attacker), inhibiting careless actions (e.g., proceeding cautiously when on a ledge), or behaving in a defensive manner (e.g., avoid provoking a potential enemy). If these strategies successfully avert the dangerous cue, anxiety will subside; it not, the unpleasant emotional state persists, motivating the organism to take further action.

The Activation of Emotion

Anxiety is expressed in multiple, integrated systems that operate to respond most adaptively to threats of danger: the behavioral, physiological, cognitive, and affective systems. Once threat in the environment is processed, an emotional response is triggered. This process appears to be automatic and extremely rapid, and can occur out of one's awareness. Lang (1985) has proposed an information processing theory that links each system involved in the emotional response. According to Lang, fear and anxiety are triggered by fear-relevant stimuli that are encoded in propositional form in memory. Memory structures (networks) integrate environmental inputs, semantic information, and action patterns. An emotion information structure is conceived to be a conceptual network containing representations of *stimuli* (information about prompting external stimuli and the context in which they occur), *responses* (information about responding in the context, including overt acts, and visceral and somatic events that support attention and action), and *meaning* (information that elaborates or defines the meaning of the stimulus and response data).

Emotions are produced when input cues match concepts in the network, and therefore activate the affective network. The probability of a network activation (emotional production) is determined by the number of matching propositions *irrespective* of their taxonomic category (i.e., stimulus, response, meaning) that are present in short-term memory. The likelihood of accessing an emotion is increased by presenting information that maximizes the number of propositions matched. For example, an actual phobic object (e.g., a snake) is a greater provocation than a picture of the object because it is a closer match. Once the stimulus is processed, the entire network is activated, and symptoms are produced within each sphere: physiological (increased heart rate, blood pressure, muscle tension, and respiration), behavioral (flight, avoidance), cognitive (focus of attention on the stimulus), and affective (subjective discomfort). Thus, the organism becomes motivated and equipped to appropriately respond to the danger.

Emotion in the Anxiety Disorders

So far, we have focused on the functional, adaptational value of anxiety. In this section, we will focus on the psychopathological manifestations of anxiety. While the experience of anxiety is commonplace, for some anxiety is pervasive, interfering with one's lifestyle, resulting in impaired social and/or occupational functioning, and decreasing the quality of life. Individuals suffering from severe anxiety often meet the diagnostic criteria for one or more DSM-IV (American Psychiatric Association, 1994) defined "anxiety disorders." The anxiety disorder category represents the pathological expression of anxiety and is composed of several specific disorders, including panic disorder (with and without agoraphobia), social phobia, specific (formerly simple) phobia, generalized anxiety disorder, obsessive-compulsive disorder, and posttraumatic stress disorder (PTSD). (Several new disorders have been included in the DSM-IV for the first time, but very little information is available about these disorders at the present time.)

Throughout the history of abnormal psychology, anxiety has been considered to be a key emotion in psychopathology (Lazarus, 1991). In fact, recent data concerning the prevalence of psychiatric disorders support this notion, demonstrating that within a 12-month period, anxiety disorders are the most commonly occurring psychiatric disorder, affecting 17.2% of the population (Kessler et al., 1994). Moreover, one out of every four individuals suffers from an anxiety disorder at some point in their life (Kessler et al., 1994). Clearly, individuals suffering from excessive anxiety represent a significant proportion of patients with psychological disorders.

Dimensions of Anxiety Disorders

As stated earlier, emotion is generated by the individual's appraisal of what is happening in their adaptational relationships with the environment (Lazarus, 1991). It is our contention that the mechanisms underlying functional and psychopathological anxiety are the same. Indeed, symptoms experienced by patients with anxiety disorders are present in the "normal" population, although to a lesser degree (Barlow, 1988). The difference between normal and psychopathological anxiety is a direct result of differences in the degree of cognitive threat appraisal within a situation. Specifically, patients with anxiety disorders either (a) overestimate the danger of a situation or (b) underestimate their ability to cope with the demands of a situation, resulting in an increased perception of threat (danger) and the subsequent generation of anxiety. Several lines of research have confirmed that patients with anxiety disorders possess cognitive structures that facilitate the processing and increase the salience of threat-related information (cf., Litz & Keane, 1989; McNally, 1990).

Within the spectrum of anxiety disorders, there are two broad-based phenomena, shared to some extent by all anxiety disorders: generalized anxiety and panic (Barlow, 1988). Interestingly, this parallels Lazarus's theory, which distinguishes the concepts of anxiety and fright. Both panic (fright) and anxiety are related to threat. Panic is a reaction to a direct and imminent threat, often when there is an immediate prospect of death or injury. In contrast, anxiety is a future-oriented mood state related to uncertainty about threat that may occur in the future.

Patients with anxiety disorders can experience both anxiety and panic depending on the context and the immediacy of the fear provoking stimulus. For example, a patient with a specific phobia of flying may experience weeks of anxiety prior to the flight itself (future threat), and experience panic when getting onto the plane (imminent threat). When the threat is immediate, the panic experienced by individuals is similar regardless of the specific anxiety disorder (Rapee, Sanderson, McCauley, & DiNardo, 1992). Likewise, there is similarity across the anxiety disorders in the anticipatory anxiety state generated by a future threat (Barlow, Blanchard, Vermilyea, Vermilyea, & DiNardo, 1986; Sanderson & Barlow, 1990).

While anxiety and panic cut across each of the anxiety disorders, they represent the essential features of generalized anxiety disorder and panic disorder, respectively. As will be detailed below, the essential feature of each anxiety disorder may in fact represent an aspect of adaptive anxiety. Specifically, under certain circumstances, intrusive thoughts, compulsive behaviors, evaluation anxiety, and phobias serve a useful function and are present to some degree in everyone.

However, patients with anxiety disorders may share basic biological and psychological predispositions or vulnerabilities that result in the overdevelopment of these features. Indeed, data on psychiatric symptom and syndrome comorbidity demonstrate that symptoms of various anxiety disorders, as well as anxious personality features, typically occur in each patient suffering from any one anxiety disorder (Rapee, Sanderson, & Barlow, 1988; Sanderson, DiNardo, Rapee, & Barlow, 1990; Sanderson & Wetzler, 1991; Sanderson, Wetzler, Beck, & Betz, 1994). These data suggest that a common underlying mechanism leads to exaggerations in various anxiety features.

In view of the high rates of comorbidity, we have proposed elsewhere that a more useful classification system might identify the presence of an "anxious personality" (Sanderson & Wetzler, 1991) and then rate the presence of a variety of specific features (e.g., panic attacks, intrusive thoughts, evaluation anxiety) that warrant treatment (Sanderson et al., 1990). This anxious personality may be a result of temperament (e.g., Eysenck, 1981) or of negative, uncontrollable life events that lead to the development of a style of information processing based on perceptions of vulnerability (Barlow, 1988; Beck & Emery, 1985). Whatever the etiology, the nature of this anxious personality predisposes one to excessive anxiety within each of the dimensions mentioned above.

Fear and Anxiety in Patients with Anxiety Disorders

Essentially, in humans, two types of events define the spectrum of threat: events that threaten our *physical well-being* (i.e., physical dangers) and events that threaten our *psychological well-being* (i.e., self-esteem, self-concept; Beck & Emery, 1985; Lazarus, 1991). Consequently, in each of the various anxiety disorders, the focus of danger concerns physical or psychological threats. Although by definition, patients suffering from anxiety disorders are experiencing maladaptive anxiety, from our functional perspective, the nature of each anxiety disorder should have survival benefits. In this section we describe the essential feature for each anxiety disorder and propose its adaptive function.

Generalized Anxiety Disorder   The essential feature of generalized anxiety disorder is persistent and excessive/unrealistic worry (i.e., apprehensive expectation) focused on a variety of life situations (e.g., family, finances, work) accompanied by somatic arousal (American Psychiatric Association, 1994). Worry accompanied by negative affect and somatic arousal compels one to focus on future events that may have a negative outcome (threat). By focusing attention on the event, and experiencing a negative mood state, the person is motivated to solve or prepare for the event, thereby reducing or terminating the unpleasant arousal. For example, a person who worries about his or her health may engage in positive behaviors (e.g., exercise, diet), reducing the threat to his or her physical well-being and thereby reducing anxiety. Likewise, a person who worries about an upcoming exam may be motivated to study to reduce the anxiety and in turn reduce the likelihood of performing poorly (threat to self-esteem). However, for excessive worriers such as those with generalized anxiety disorder, worrying becomes disproportionate to the situation. Instead of generating solutions, excessive worriers tend to generate all of the negative *possibilities* in a situation, regardless of their *probability*. In these cases, worry is no longer serving a functional purpose.

Obsessive Compulsive Disorder The essential feature of obsessive compulsive disorder (OCD) is the experience of obsessive thoughts and compulsive behaviors (American Psychiatric Association, 1994). Obsessions are defined as recurrent and persistent thoughts, impulses, or images that are intrusive and inappropriate and are accompanied by significant anxiety. Compulsions are defined as repetitive behaviors (e.g., hand washing, checking) or mental acts (e.g., counting, repeating words silently) aimed at preventing some dreaded event or situation (e.g., checking the stove to make sure it is off to prevent a fire). However, the compulsive behavior either (a) is not connected in a realistic way to prevent the event or (b) is excessive. For the most part, the focus of obsessions and compulsions is on concerns maintained by normal individuals: health, death, sex, religion, welfare of others. From a functional perspective, if a behavior can eliminate a negative outcome in a situation, it makes sense to repeat the response more than once to ensure that the response has been emitted. For example, if a person is going to parachute from a plane, it is not unreasonable for him or her to check several times that the belts attaching the parachute to the body are fastened—even though he or she may remember checking this 10 minutes earlier. Along the same line, it is considered normal to "double-check" (perhaps more than twice) that one has his or her airline tickets before leaving for home. The concern (anxiety) about not having one's tickets provides a hypervigilance about a situation that could result in a problem (i.e., not having the tickets and missing the flight), and checking reduces the anxiety by confirming that he or she has the tickets.

However, in the case of OCD, the person exaggerates the potential for negative consequences, or repeats a behavior beyond what is reasonable to eliminate the threat. For example, checking to see that one has turned off a gas stove once or twice may be appropriate; however, the OCD patient may stare at the stove for 15 minutes, checking over and over. Or a patient obsessed with religious guilt who fears that when he passes a church he may be punished for not being a perfect Christian (obsession) will attempt to think only positive thoughts about Christianity as he passes the church to avoid the punishment (compulsion).

Panic Disorders (with and without Agoraphobia) The essential feature of panic disorder is the presence of recurrent, unexpected panic attacks. Panic attacks are defined as bouts of fear or a feeling of impending doom, accompanied by accelerated autonomic nervous system activity (American Psychiatric Association, 1994). In addition, patients typically develop agoraphobia (anxiety about being in places or situations from which escape might be difficult or in which help may not be available).

As mentioned above, panic is a component that is present among all anxiety disorders, although in the other disorders, the panic is a response to an imminent danger (e.g., social humiliation, contamination, etc.). In panic disorder, the patient experiences a so-called spontaneous panic attack, and then develops a fear of the attack itself. While the first attack may be the result of a misfiring of the fear system (cf. Barlow, 1988), perhaps provoked by stress, the patient then develops a fear of bodily sensations associated with the attacks (i.e., fear of fear). Patients typically "catastrophize" about the consequences of the symptoms, believing that they may die, lose control, or go crazy during the attack (Clark, 1986). This further accelerates the autonomic activity, thus resulting in an increase in fear. The fear of panic attacks often results in the development of agoraphobia, where the patient begins to fear and avoid situations that may either cause a panic attack, or where the person would have difficulty escaping from if a panic attack occurred.

Thus, panic attacks appear to be a hard-wired response to dangerous situations (Barlow, 1988). From our perspective, the experience of repeated panic attacks that are *not focused on a specific danger* offers no adaptive function. However, the subsequent maneuvers (i.e., agoraphobia, persistent worry about the attacks) aimed at reducing the chance of further occurrences of the attacks reflect functional strategies. For example, if a person believes he or she is having a heart attack (a common belief that occurs during panic attacks), he or she should not travel alone, or go into places where escape is difficult or where help is not available (typical concerns of the agoraphobic).

Posttraumatic Stress Disorder   Posttraumatic stress disorder (PTSD) involves development of anxiety and other characteristic somatic symptoms (e.g., intrusive recollections of the event, autonomic arousal, persistent avoidance of stimuli associated with the traumatic event) following exposure to a traumatic event in which actual or threatened death, or serious injury occurred (American Psychiatric Association, 1994). The person may have either been involved in the event itself, or merely witnessed it. From a functional perspective, the organism should be able to develop new associations to dangerous situations (stimuli) that arise in the environment. Posttraumatic stress disorder appears to reflect this mechanism, whereby individuals experiencing or witnessing life threatening events experience a host of symptoms that cause them to avoid that situation in the future (e.g., intrusive recollections of the event), consequently reducing the likelihood that they will be endangered in the same situation.

Posttraumatic stress disorder allows for the development of a fear response to novel situations that may not be biologically prepared. As we will discuss below, certain fears (e.g., heights, predators) represent stimuli that have been threatening throughout the history of evolution. Other fears (e.g., airline flights, guns) represent responses to contemporary danger cues. Although fear responses to specific stimuli are typically characterized by specific phobia, their development appears to be the result of a plastic, adaptive mechanism that allows the organism to respond to "novel" threats not typically encountered throughout evolutionary history, an important process necessary to adapt to an ever-changing environment. This mechanism is central to PTSD.

Specific Phobia   The essential feature of specific phobia is a marked and persistent fear of a specific object or situation (American Psychiatric Association, 1994). For the most part, specific phobic stimuli have a realistic potential for danger, although in the case of the phobic patient, the probability of danger is often overestimated. For example, a fear of heights (falling out of a window), flying on an airplane (crashing), and snakes (being bitten) all reflect potential danger, although the possibility may be remote (e.g., the odds of dying in a plane crash are substantially less than those while driving in a car, yet many people who will not fly calmly drive to work each day). As mentioned above, there appear to be two types of specific phobias: those that develop as a result of vicarious or experiential learning, and those that have been acquired through evolutionary selection. Seligman's (1971) preparedness theory addresses those stimuli that have been biologically selected; many phobic situations or objects were dangerous to pretechnological humans in their natural environment and thus developed if the "prepared" stimulus was linked with an aversive outcome. For example, although most of us rarely encounter poisonous snakes, many respond with fear to an innocuous snake, even when we know it is not dangerous.

Social Phobia   The essential feature of social phobia is marked and persistent fear of social or performance situations (American Psychiatric Association, 1994). From our functional perspective, concern about another's evaluation may have important adaptive value. How one is perceived by others may affect one's ability to gain important resources (e.g., sexual partner, promotion at work) that allow for survival and procreation. Therefore, one would expect concern (anxiety) to develop that would compel individuals to avoid being viewed negatively. In fact, typically, social anxiety is increased in situations where approval from others could result in the acquisition of important resources that are desired by the individual. For example, for an unmarried person, having a casual conversation with a person of the opposite sex who is attractive, unmarried, and about the same age, will generate more anxiety than speaking with someone who is 30 years older, married, and unattractive. Likewise, giving an academic presentation to prospective employers during a job interview will generate more anxiety than giving that same presentation to a group of students.

However, in the case of social phobia, the patient often exaggerates the potential and significance of negative evaluation by others and, as a result, feels as though a positive evaluation is essential in almost every situation. In addition, the patient often magnifies his or her own shortcomings, consequently feeling ineffective and undesirable in most social situations. These processes result in significant anxiety in a host of social evaluative situations.

Taking Emotion into Consideration When Treating Patients with Anxiety Disorders

As noted above, anxiety is a compelling emotion composed of cognitive, affective, somatic, and behavioral expressions. Patients suffering from anxiety disorders enter treatment to gain relief in each of these spheres. Perhaps more than for any other emotional disorder, when engaging in psychotherapy with anxiety disorder patients, effective treatment must address the entire spectrum of emotional expression.

The most widely studied psychotherapy for anxiety disorders is cognitive behavior therapy (CBT). Cognitive behavior theory has shown to be an effective treatment for each of the anxiety disorders (cf., Barlow, 1988; Brown, Hertz, & Barlow, 1992). While the specific details of treatment vary among the disorders, in general, each of these therapies directly addresses the specific emotional psychopathology of the patient. As stated earlier, anxiety as an emotional disorder arises when individuals consistently appraise situations in the following manner: (a) overestimate the danger of a situation, or (b) underestimate their ability to cope with the demands of a threatening situation. In both scenarios, the result is an exaggerated perception of threat (danger) and the subsequent generation of anxiety or panic. Depending on the disorder present, various stimuli provoke anxiety, whether it be a social situation for the social phobic patient, heart palpitations for the panic disorder patient, or germs for the obsessive compulsive disorder patient.

The primary aim of CBT is to extinguish the association between the stimulus and the anxiety/panic (emotion) response. While several comprehensive theories have been proposed to account for the anxiety reduction observed during CBT with anxiety disorder patients (Barlow, 1988; Foa & Kozak, 1986; Rachman, 1980; Sanderson & Wetzler, 1993), we detect a common mechanism: CBT attempts to remediate the exaggerated threat appraisal of the patient by (a) increasing the accuracy of the patient's appraisal and (b) increasing the patient's ability to cope with the demands of the situation.

To accomplish this, the most common strategies employed are cognitive restructuring and systematic exposure. (Due to space limitations, a very brief discussion of treatment will be provided here. For those interested in a further elaboration see Barlow [1988] or Beck and Emery [1985].) During cognitive restructuring, the therapist attempts to modify the patient's fearful thoughts by guiding the patient to access contradictory information incompatible with the anxiety response. Processing of information is automatic and extremely rapid; thus, the emotional response comes on suddenly. During cognitive restructuring, the therapist works with the patient, first, to uncover fear-related cognitions, and second, to learn to "challenge" the accuracy of his or her threat appraisal of the stimulus. Since patients with anxiety disorders typically exaggerate the threat in their respective anxiety-provoking situations, consciously reappraising the situation, by using various structured exercises, will ultimately decrease the anxiety and panic response.

During systematic exposure, patients confront specific "phobic" stimuli that trigger their anxiety and panic attacks. Since this exposure is done in a systematic, hierarchical fashion, patients learn to tolerate manageable levels of anxiety as they confront low-grade phobic situations. Methods such as relaxation and breathing exercises are often used to decrease the patients' arousal in anxiety-provoking situations. This will result in a perception of increased efficacy in coping with higher level phobic situations. Hence, exposure provides a "corrective" experience, allowing the patient to disconfirm the threatening appraisal by facing progressively more threatening experiences in the absence of the feared consequences.

While cognitive behavioral theories may differ regarding their emphasis on the importance of cognition (e.g., Beck, 1985; Beck & Emery, 1985) versus exposure (e.g., Barlow, 1988) in this fear reduction process, all cognitive behavioral theories are to some degree based on the principle that repeated exposure to anxiety-provoking stimuli in a systematic fashion, while accessing information incompatible with the fear appraisal, results in anxiety reduction (Barlow, 1988; Foa & Kozak, 1986; Rachman, 1980; Sanderson & Wetzler, 1993). Provoking the entire emotional response (cognitive, affective, somatic, and behavioral aspects) in the context of therapy signals that processing of the threat stimulus is occurring, thereby allowing the fear-reduction process to occur. For patients suffering from anxiety disorders, the anxiety- and panic-provoking stimuli do not represent true threats. Therefore, the emotional response is not functional. As a result of the corrective experiences gained in therapy, the anxious response will extinguish.

References

American Psychiatric Association. (1994). *Diagnostic and statistical manual of mental disorders* (4th ed.). Washington, DC: Author.

Barlow, D. H. (1988). *Anxiety and its disorders.* New York: Guilford Press.

Barlow, D. H., Blanchard, E. B., Vermilyea, J., Vermilyea, B., & DiNardo, P. A. (1986). Generalized anxiety and generalized anxiety disorder: Description and reconceptualization. *American Journal of Psychiatry, 143,* 40–44.

Beck, A. T. (1985). Theoretical perspectives on anxiety. In A. H. Tuma & J. D. Maser (Eds.), *Anxiety and the anxiety disorders* (pp. 183–196). Hillsdale, NJ: Erlbaum.

Beck, A. T., & Emery, G. (1985). *Anxiety disorders and phobias.* New York: Basic Books.

Brown, T. A., Hertz, R. M., & Barlow, D. H. (1992). New developments in cognitive behavioral treatments of anxiety disorders. In A. Tasman & M. B. Riba (Eds.), *Review of psychiatry* (Vol. 11, pp. 285–306). Washington, DC: American Psychiatric Press.

Cannon, W. B. (1929). *Bodily changes in pain, hunger, fear, and rage: An account of recent researches into the functions of emotional excitement* (2nd ed.). New York: Appleton-Century-Crofts.

Clark, D. M. (1986). A cognitive approach to panic. *Behaviour Research and Therapy, 24,* 461–471.

Darwin, C. (1872). *The expression of emotions in man and animals.* London: John Murray.

Eysenck, H. J. (1981). *A model for personality.* New York: Springer-Verlag.

Foa, E. B., & Kozak, M. S. (1986). Emotional processing of fear: Exposure to corrective information. *Psychological Bulletin, 99,* 20–35.

Izard, C. (Ed.). (1977). *Human emotions.* New York: Plenum Press.

Kessler, R. C., McGonagle, K. A., Zhao, S., Nelson, C. B., Hughes, M., Eshlemna, S., Wittchen, H., & Kendler, K. S. (1994). Lifetime and 12-month prevalence of DSM-III-R psychiatric disorders in the United States. *Archives of General Psychiatry, 51,* 8–19.

Lang, P. J. (1985). The cognitive psychophysiology of fear. In A. H. Tuma & J. D. Maser (Eds.), *Anxiety and the anxiety disorders* (pp. 131–170). Hillsdale, NJ: Erlbaum.

Lazarus, R. S. (1991). *Emotion and adaptation.* New York: Oxford University Press.

Litz, B. T., & Keane, T. M. (1989). Information processing in anxiety disorders: Application to the understanding of post-traumatic stress disorder. *Clinical Psychology Review, 9,* 243–257.

McNally, R. J. (1990). Psychological approaches to panic disorder: A review. *Psychological Bulletin, 108,* 403–419.

Plutchik, R. (1980). *Emotion: A psychoevolutionary synthesis.* New York: Harper & Row.

Rachman, S. (1980). Emotional processing. *Behaviour Research and Therapy, 18,* 51–60.

Rapee, R. M., Sanderson, W. C., & Barlow, D. H.(1988). Social phobia symptoms across the DSM-III-Revised anxiety disorder categories. *Journal of Psychopathology and Behavioral Assessment, 10,* 287–299.

Rapee, R. M., Sanderson, W. C., McCauley, P. A., DiNardo, P. A. (1992). Differences in reported symptom profile between panic disorder and other DSM-III-R anxiety disorders. *Behaviour Research and Therapy, 30,* 45–52.

Sanderson, W. C., & Barlow, D. H. (1990). A description of patients diagnosed with DSM-III-R generalized anxiety disorder. *Journal of Nervous and Mental Disease, 178,* 588–591.

Sanderson, W. C., DiNardo, P. A., Rapee, R. M., & Barlow, D. H. (1990). Syndrome comorbidity in patients diagnosed with a DSM-III-Revised anxiety disorder. *Journal of Abnormal Psychology, 99,* 308–312.

Sanderson, W. C., & Wetzler, S. (1991). Chronic anxiety and generalized anxiety disorder: Issues in comorbidity. In R. M. Rapee & D. H. Barlow (Eds.), *Chronic anxiety, generalized anxiety disorder and mixed anxiety-depression* (pp. 119–135). New York: Guilford Press.

Sanderson, W. C., & Wetzler, S. (1993). Observations on the cognitive behavioral treatment of panic disorder: Impact of benzodiazepines. *Psychotherapy, 30,* 125–132.

Sanderson, W. C., Wetzler, S., Beck, A. T., & Betz, F. (1994). Prevalence of personality disorders in patients with anxiety disorders. *Psychiatry Research, 51,* 167–174.

Seligman, M. E. P. (1971). Phobias and preparedness. *Behavior Therapy, 2,* 307–320.

19

Martha S. Stretton & Peter Salovey

Cognitive and Affective Components of Hypochondriacal Concerns

Hypochondriasis is a disorder that interests professionals in both physical and mental health care settings. For the medical professional, the anxious, symptomatic patient who presents repeatedly without objective signs of illness can test the limits of tolerance and clinical compassion. Similarly, the psychotherapist may find the rigidity and persistence of the hypochondriacal patient's apparently irrational and exaggerated health concerns a daunting challenge to any sense of therapeutic efficacy.

Although the word *hypochondriac* has a pejorative connotation today, there is a resurgence of interest in this form of health preoccupation (Barsky, 1988; Baur, 1988; Meister, 1980). It appears that exaggerated health concerns are one result of our society's increasingly intense focus on illness and wellness, and that for some individuals, these concerns lead to hypochondriacal preoccupations. The popular press is saturated with sensational news stories and features about new ways to catch new diseases, so it seems only logical that some individuals would respond to this zeitgeist with exaggerated, anxious concerns about their health.

The question of how this response occurs is the focus of this chapter. We review and discuss research bearing on a model of "amplifying somatic style" offered by Barsky and Klerman (1983) as a way of thinking about individual variability in health concerns. This review then takes a more fine-grained look at some particular components of their model and offers some suggestions about the central role that affect may play in this somatic style. We begin, however, with a brief overview of some of the formulations that have guided thinking about hypochondriasis over the years — as context for a discussion of whether hypochondriasis is best thought of as a categorical or a dimensional attribute.

Formulation of Hypochondriasis: A Disorder and a Characteristic

Early psychodynamic conceptualizations of hypochondriasis had their beginnings in Freud's (1914/1957) libido-based theory that physiological disturbances could be unconsciously perceived as erotogenic and thus command sexually charged attention that would otherwise be directed toward others. Subsequent formulations have not relied specifically on a libido-based interpretation but have retained an emphasis on the role of unconscious forces in the initiation and maintenance of symptoms. One such approach suggests that hypochondriasis "represents an internalized persecutor" (Hunter, Lohrenz, & Schwartzman, 1964, p. 150). Similarly, Lesse (1974) has suggested that hypochondriasis may function as an equivalent to depression in some patients. In addition, certain symptoms have been interpreted psychodynamically, with the location of symptoms in the body thought to provide an indication of the importance of those body areas in the individual's image of the self (Kreitman, Sainsbury, Pearce, & Costain, 1965; Zborowski, 1975). For example, individuals highly invested in their intellect would complain of headaches. This formulation calls to mind traditional models of psychosomatic medicine, such as Alexander's (1950) proposals about the direct relationship between psychological disorders and organ pathology.

Clearly, hypochondriasis has a long history as a particular form of psychopathology, and it remains a discrete diagnostic category in the current nomenclature. Current diagnostic criteria include "preoccupation with fears of having, or the idea that one has, a serious disease based on a misinterpretation of one or more bodily signs or symptoms" when "a thorough medical evaluation does not identify a general medical condition that fully accounts for the person's concerns about disease or for the physical signs or symptoms" (American Psychiatric Association, 1994, pp. 462–463). Befitting the purpose of the current *Diagnostic Statistical Manual* approach, these criteria serve to classify individuals as hypochondriacs or not. However, some investigators (Barsky & Klerman, 1983; Barsky, Wyshak, & Klerman, 1986; Kenyon, 1976; Ladee, 1966; Pilowsky, 1975) have suggested that individuals' health concerns vary along a continuum and that hypochondriacal concerns form a dimensional attribute rather than a categorical one. Kenyon (1976) and Ladee (1966) in particular have argued for abandonment of the term *hypochondriasis* in favor of the adjective *hypochondriacal* to capture this distinction.

In the dimensional viewpoint, individual variability could underlie differences in many levels of health concerns that could be labeled hypochondriacal. Granting that it is necessary and desirable to have a cutoff for determining individual status for diagnostic and research purposes, subclinical individual variability remains a worthy subject of investigation in its own right. The dimensional approach is consistent with current, cognitive formulations of hypochondriacal concerns, which emphasize the roles of factors such as attention, information processing biases, and misattribution. For example, Mechanic (1972) invoked Schachter and Singer's (1962) two-factor model of emotional arousal to explain "medical students' disease" (Hunter et al., 1964), a sort of transient hypochondriasis observed in about 70% of medical students, but apparently not restricted to this population (Kellner, Wiggins, & Pathak, 1986). This syndrome is characterized by the fear or conviction that one has the disease about which one is studying. The physical symptoms likely to accompany the stress of medical school provide the material for a misattribution process, which makes use of the new data provided by the environment (regarding disease) to reach hypochondriacal conclusions. Mechanic also suggested other social psychological factors that may produce hypochondriacal outcomes, such as cultural influences (Zborowski, 1975). These formulations involve extremely common psychological phenomena and allow for the occurrence of hypochondriacal concerns at varying levels of intensity in people not considered to have mental disorders.

Consistent with this approach, Barsky and Klerman (1983) have described an "amplifying somatic style," in which individuals have a "perceptual and/or cognitive abnormality" (p. 276) involving three non-mutually exclusive forms: (a) amplification and augmentation of bodily sensations, (b) misinterpretation of sensations, and (c) a tendency toward "thinking and perceiving in physical and concrete terms rather than in emotional and subjective terms" (p. 276). They suggest that individual variability in this domain is similar to variability in political beliefs or affiliation with other causes, and that individuals may range from apathetic to zealous in their degree of involvement. Using the word *style* to describe the clinical phenomena of varying levels of health concerns clearly indicates an adoption of the dimensional view. Our frequent preference for the adjective *hypochondriacal* over the noun *hypochondriasis* reflects our similar orientation on this point.

Amplification of Sensations

Perceptual Inaccuracy

The cornerstone of models such as Barsky and Klerman's is the tendency in individuals with an amplifying somatic style to augment and amplify normal bodily sensations and to experience them as more intense than other people. This style implies a basic inaccuracy in perception of body state, a concept for which there is considerable empirical support. Pennebaker and his colleagues (Pennebaker, 1982) conducted a program of research addressing the issue of accuracy in perception of physiological states and events. In general, individuals possess rather poor accuracy in perception of heart rate, hand temperature, and skin conductance.

Perceptual accuracy is influenced by a variety of factors, however. Intensity is one; obviously, it is easier to perceive a sharp, intense sensation than a vague, weak one. Further, accuracy is not a unidimensional construct. It may be possible for an individual to perceive hand temperature accurately, for example, without being able to sense heart rate accurately (Pennebaker, 1982). Perhaps it is more adaptive to be aware of certain physiological indicators than others, and so we have developed the ability to discern states like hunger or fatigue but have not developed comparable skill at detecting changes in hand temperature.

Even though we may identify some domains where accuracy seems to be better than in others, inaccuracy remains. Individuals vary widely in their perceptions of what is going on inside their bodies, and individual differences and situational characteristics may play a role in determining the exact nature of this inaccuracy (Pennebaker, 1982; Petrie, 1978). Indeed, it is variability of this sort that makes possible the responses subsumed under Barsky and Klerman's (1983) "amplifying somatic style."

Variables Influencing Amplification and Augmentation

Clinically, it would be useful to understand the basis for the tendency to amplify bodily sensations. Is it a "wired-in" characteristic that is not amenable to change, or is it a learned behavior that could be modified? Do hypochondriacal individuals perceive more body sensations because they *have* more, or do they simply attend to sensations others ignore? The answer may lie in a combination of these influences.

There may be an "arousal-based" form of hypochondriasis (Hanback & Revelle, 1978), wherein hypochondriacal individuals report more symptoms because their bodies produce more symptoms via a chronic arousal state. Individuals with relatively high baseline levels of arousal may be predisposed to perceive symptoms; students scoring higher than their peers on a hypochondriasis scale showed greater sensitivity on a two-flash fusion (TFF) task, a task with empirical support as an index of arousal (Hanback & Revelle, 1978; Maley, 1967; Rose, 1966). These results do not allow us to determine whether the arousal is antecedent or consequent to hypochondriacal concerns, however. Perhaps the individuals reporting more symptoms were also worried about them and thus remained in an aroused, anxious state. It is also possible that the relationship between hypochondriacal concerns and arousal is a reciprocal one.

Further research could clarify these issues. First, multiple dependent variables could be measured to provide more precise physiological data. Arousal is no longer viewed as a unidimensional construct (Hassett, 1978; Lacey, 1967; McHugo & Lanzetta, 1983), and more sophisticated equipment for gathering physiological data is available than was the case 10 years ago. A more refined understanding of physiological states is thus possible. Second, repeated-measures designs using time series or path analyses should be helpful in determining the direction of influence between the variables. Finally, manipulation of the physiological parameters initially used as dependent variables could help to determine the malleability of the tendency to report symptoms and sensations.

Augmentation/Reduction

Several other variables have been proposed to influence the processes of amplification and augmentation of bodily sensation (Barsky & Klerman, 1983). Two of these are augmentation/reduction tendencies (Petrie, 1978) and direction of attention (e.g., Pennebaker, 1982). Petrie and his colleagues (Petrie, 1978) classified subjects as augmenters, reducers, or moderates based on performance on a psychophysical task requiring estimation (while blindfolded) of the size of a block before and after exposure to a block that is larger or smaller than the original. Individuals who tended to increase their estimate of the size of the original block after exposure to another block, regardless of whether the other block was larger or smaller than the original, were classified as "augmenters." Individuals who did the reverse were classified as "reducers," and individuals who provided judgments between the cutoff points designated for classification were "moderates." Overall, augmenters had lower pain tolerance, dreaded pain more, feared "sensory bombardment in general" (Petrie, 1978, p. 24), and experienced greater pain relief from aspirin and alcohol than did reducers. Conversely, there was a negative correlation between tendency to reduce and the number of items on the Minnesota Multiphasic Personality Inventory (MMPI) Hypochondriasis scale endorsed. Many of these studies used experimentally induced pain so that the physical qualities of the stimulus were held constant across subjects, and "varied reactions to physical pain . . . may, in part, be due to ways of *experiencing* the environment that vary according to the perceptual modulation of the individual" (Petrie, 1978, p. 98).

One shortcoming of the augmentation/reduction research, at least for a general theory of hypochondriasis, is its emphasis on pain. Not all symptoms are painful per se. Many hypochondriacal symptoms are, on the contrary, vague and diffuse. Many symptoms under scrutiny are limited to different, nonpainful symptoms (e.g., dizziness, nasal congestion, stiffness of joints, shortness of breath, etc.). The MMPI scale used in one of the studies allows for some generalization of findings from pain, but further research is needed to determine if the same results obtain when nonpainful stimuli are used. Second, it would be useful to know whether a common underlying process gives rise to augmentation (as operationalized in Petrie's task) and to augmentation of physical sensations. It is also important to determine whether manipulations inducing a change in augmenting/reducing tendencies (if such changes are possible) result in changes in symptom reporting. If augmenting/reducing tendencies drive other perceptual processes, they could be a powerful locus for clinical intervention.

Attentional Influences

Focusing attention on the body increases perception of symptoms and sensations (Pennebaker, 1982). Attentional focus plays a role in the amplifying somatic style (Barsky & Klerman, 1983). An individual's awareness of internal states is a function of the ratio of internal to external information. Therefore, an individual in an environment that provides little stimulation is more likely to focus on body sensations than someone in a highly stimulating environment.

There are descriptive data consistent with the focus of attention hypothesis. For example, the National Center for Health Statistics reported during the 1970s that individuals who presumably have fewer attention-grabbing stimuli in their environment because they live alone, are not married, or are not working report more symptoms than individuals who do not fall into these three categories (Pennebaker, 1982). In a more recent study of general clinic outpatients, however, those who were separated, widowed, or divorced were no more likely to report symptoms than other patients (Barsky et al., 1986). Clearly, these sociodemographic variables are imperfect indices of the amount of stimulation provided by the individual's environment, and little can be concluded about this apparent discrepancy without further data. It is generally acknowledged that even if these correlational findings were completely reliable, they would not allow us to determine whether individuals who report a lot of symptoms do so because of the relative imbalance of internal and external stimuli in their lives, or whether they are in those presumably less stimulating environments because their symptoms keep them from moving into more enriched ones. Another possibility is that a confounding variable such as depression is responsible for these patterns of findings. We devote fuller attention to the possible role of depression in hypochondriacal concerns in a later section addressing affective distress.

It is also important to note that a certain degree of internal focus is adaptive. For example, individuals who scored high on a private self-consciousness scale, a measure assessing the tendency to focus attention on private aspects of the self (Fenigstein, Scheier, & Buss, 1975), were *less* likely to report health problems following life stresses than individuals low in private self-consciousness (Suls & Fletcher, 1985). The underlying mechanism suggested by the investigators was that attending to the self facilitated regulatory actions that prevented physical problems. For example, focusing attention on the self may have allowed individuals to perceive stress reactions (e.g., tension headaches) and thus take some corrective action (e.g., relax). Even though it is not clear at what point internal focus of attention becomes problematic, several studies have revealed differential patterns of symptom reporting in different attentional conditions.

Experiments testing the internal versus external focus of attention hypothesis have used a variety of manipulations designed to alter subjects' focus of attention. For example, Pennebaker and Lightner (1980) asked participants to wear headphones while running on a treadmill. Participants who heard a tape of their own breathing over the headphones reported significantly more symptoms than subjects who heard a tape of street sounds or nothing at all over their headphones. In addition, there was a trend for participants who heard nothing to report more symptoms than those who heard street sounds. There were no differences across conditions on any of the physiological measures included in the study. Other manipulations have included the setting in which jogging took place (cross-country vs. track; Pennebaker & Lightner, 1980, Study 2), use of an auditory monitoring task during jogging (Fillingim & Fine, 1986), and the degree of interest or boredom generated by segments of a film (Pennebaker, 1980). In all cases, participants in more boring and/or less cognitively demanding conditions were more likely to report symptoms. These experimental findings lend support to the hypothesis that individuals who have relatively less external stimulation on which to focus will repoɩ more symptoms.

Beyond Direction of Attention

Use of the self-environment dimension to examine allocation of attention or consciousness (Buss, 1980; Carver & Scheier, 1981) is basic to the paradigms discussed above. This distinction is probably an oversimplification; Carver and Scheier (1981) note "the difficulty of maintaining a dichotomy based solely on the point of origin of the perceptual information being processed" (p. 37) and go on to suggest that the content and not just the source of the information be considered when classifying perceptions. The characteristics of the objects of perception and the individual's physical and psychological responses to them could be expected to contribute to the observed effects of attentional manipulations. For example, a test-taking situation is one that could be considered to provide adequate external stimulation, yet Wine (1971) reported that test-anxious people have difficulty with tests because they attend more to internal sensations than to the test. This result suggests that it is not just the amount but also the perceived quality of the stimuli present in the environment that determine the individual's cognitive and physiological responses.

Attention and Habituation

One of the stimulus qualities that could be expected to affect the perceiver's evaluation is its predictability. Unpredictable environments preclude habituation and so may keep the individual in an aroused, vigilant state. This can lead not only to affective distress but also to physical symptoms via continually elevated levels of autonomic nervous system activity.

Research exploring the role of stimulus predictability in symptom reporting has yielded mixed findings (Matthews, Scheier, Brunson, & Carducci, 1980). Sometimes predictable events produced positive effects (i.e., lower levels of symptoms), but at other times they did not. These investigators provided evidence in support of the argument that these discrepant findings were actually due to differences in the allocation of attention. Specifically, they hypothesized that the more predictable a stressor, the more quickly habituation could occur. Habituation would lower attention and arousal and thus reduce the reported symptoms, even though attention would presumably be available for internal allocation. In their study, participants who heard predictable noise bursts reported fewer symptoms, even though attention would presumably be available for internal allocation. However, they were able to "eliminate the benefits of predictability" by instructing participants to attend to the noise bursts. They argued that this instruction prevented habituation and thus blocked the reduction in symptom reporting. In a related vein, experiments manipulating degree of perceived control over unpleasant noise bursts indicated that lower perceived control was associated with higher levels of symptom reporting (Pennebaker, Burnam, Schaefer, & Harper, 1977). The mechanisms underlying these results are unclear, but the differences did not appear to be due to physiological changes.

Regardless of the underlying mechanisms, however, these studies demonstrate that it is not just the amount of stimulation present in the environment but the individual's response to it that determines effects on symptom reporting. Returning to Carver and Scheier's (1981) claim that using the self-environment dichotomy is an oversimplification, it is clear that direction of attention matters in symptom perception, but the quality of what is being attended to is a powerful influence as well.

Amplification of physical sensations is determined by a combination of physiological activity levels and perceptual tendencies. These perceptual tendencies are influenced by such individual differences as an augmenting perceptual style and the tendency to allocate attention inward, toward the self, both of which have been demonstrated to affect individual's experiences of physical sensations. The role of attention is complicated by the fact that the quality of the content being attended to may have its own effects on the perceiver.

Emotional Distress

So far, our discussion of hypochondriasis has centered around cognitive processes such as allocation of attention and eventual perception and encoding of physical sensations. It has not addressed affective distress in hypochondriasis. In fact, the relationship between hypochondriasis and other forms of psychopathology has been of interest to clinicians for some time. It is popularly believed that hypochondriasis often appears in the psychiatric clinic in constellation with and secondary to other pathologies, especially depression (Diamond, 1985; Kellner, Abbott, Pathak, Winslow, & Umland, 1983–1984; Kenyon, 1964). For example, the clinical literature on masked depression (e.g., Lesse, 1974) suggests that hypochondriasis may function as a depressive equivalent in some patients. Kenyon (1976) warned of the dangers of misdiagnosis when depression is "entirely masked by somatic symptoms" (p. 9), noting that the clinician misses not only the chance for positive outcome through use of antidepressant medication or psychotherapy but also the possibility of suicide.

It is also possible, as Zborowski (1975) has suggested regarding responses to pain in different cultures, that hypochondriacal individuals use the language of symptoms when they cannot use verbal means of expressing their emotional concerns. It may be more socially acceptable to have a physical complaint than an emotional one, for example, a fact communicated via cultural expectations. It may also be the case that hypochondriacal individuals are predisposed to experience phenomena in physical rather than emotional ways (Apfel & Sifneos, 1979; Barsky & Klerman, 1983). Similarly, Brink (1982) suggested that depression in the elderly gives rise to hypochondriacal behavior, which is then used to defend against the depression itself. In fact, Brink (1982) and Kenyon (1976) argued that because hypochondriasis is so often secondary to other pathologies, especially depression, treatment should be directed toward the underlying disorder rather than toward undermining the hypochondriacal "defense" against it.

In this light, it is interesting to note that the literature contains several reports of successful treatment of hypochondriasis in depressed patients with antidepressants (Kellner, Fava, Lisansky , Perini, & Zielezny, 1986; Ladee, 1966; see Brink, 1982, for a summary of their use in geriatric populations). The mechanism underlying this effectiveness is not clear. Clearly, a biological substrate for hypochondriacal concerns cannot be ruled out; exploration of such an approach, although not incompatible with our views, is beyond the scope of this chapter. Ladee (1966) suggested that the medications alter the quality of the patient's bodily experience; Kellner et al. (1986) argued that the amelioration of the underlying depression caused the reduction in hypochondriacal symptoms. There is no indication that antidepressants are effective in cases of primary, nonpsychotic hypochondriasis or where it accompanies other forms of psychopathology. In sum, although these findings are consistent with the hypothesis that in some patients depression causes hypochondriacal concerns, we are currently unable to verify any such mechanism based on the studies to date.

Further complicating the picture is the fact that most prevalence studies have been conducted within psychiatric populations. Therefore, the perceived co-occurrence of hypochondriasis with other forms of psychopathology could be an artifact of the settings in which epidemiological data traditionally have been collected (Barsky &

Klerman, 1983), and thus the strength of the relationship between the two disorders may be overestimated. Because hypochondriacs tend to seek treatment for somatic rather than psychological complaints, they are likely to be found in nonpsychiatric settings as well. Kellner et al. (1983–1984) compared levels of distress, hypochondriacal concerns, and somatic complaints among nonpsychotic psychiatric outpatients, family practice patients, and a group of randomly selected employees. They found that family practice and psychiatric patients did not differ significantly on scores indicating level of hypochondriacal concern, but both groups scored significantly higher than the randomly selected employees.

It is not clear, then, to what degree the clinical observations linking hypochondriasis and depression would be supported in a broader empirical analysis. Even in cases of reoccurrence, the causal relationship between these two disorders or their mutual relationship to a third unknown variable, such as a biological substrate, is impossible to determine from the evidence accumulated. However, current research on mood, focus of attention, and symptom reporting suggests several mechanisms that lead to predictions of the co-occurrence of hypochondriasis and depression. These findings suggest that affect may play a central role in hypochondriacal concerns, via the reciprocal influence between self-focused attention and negative mood, and will be discussed next.

Mood and Focus of Attention

Salovey and Rodin (1985; Salovey, 1992) noted that studies examining mood and focus of attention on the self indicate that "during emotional experiences—and particularly when they are negative—there is a tendency for individuals to focus their attention on themselves" (Salovey & Rodin, p. 157). Increased focus of attention on the self has been demonstrated to be associated with depression (Ingram & Smith, 1984; Smith & Greenberg, 1981; Wood, Saltzberg, & Goldsamt, 1990). Indeed, Pyszczynski and Greenberg (1987) have proposed that persistent self-focus plays a role in the onset, maintenance, and exacerbation of unipolar reactive depression. Their theory builds on earlier work (Carver & Scheier, 1981; Duval & Wicklund, 1972) suggesting that allocation of attention to the self serves a regulatory purpose and helps the individual maintain goal-directed behavior. A complete discussion of this theory is beyond the scope of this chapter (see Pyszczynski & Greenberg, 1987; Pyszczynski, Holt, & Greenberg, 1987), but the main point relevant here is that self-focus seems to be associated with depression (see also Ingram, 1990). The evidence suggests that perseverative focus on the self could be responsible for many of the observed phenomena of depression (e.g., low self-esteem, the tendency to make internal attributions for failures, and performance difficulties).

Given the role of attention in perception of physical symptoms, it seems reasonable to hypothesize that exaggerated self-focus could be a common mechanism giving rise to both hypochondriacal concerns and depression. The same attention processes that maintain and exacerbate depressive phenomena could lead to continued augmentation and amplification of body sensations and symptoms. In fact, Pyszczynski and Greenberg (1987) suggest that self-focus could also be partially responsible for the patient's perception of neurovegetative signs of depression via an increased awareness of bodily sensations (Gibbons, Carver, Scheier, & Hormuth, 1979; Scheier, Carver, & Gibbons, 1979).

Similarly, the tendency of self-focus to produce internal attributions for negative events would lead to the prediction that such individuals would be more likely to interpret a physical sensation as indicating a disease process rather than as a result of a stressful environment. For example, a self-focused individual would be more likely to attribute an upset stomach to a virus (internal) than to a stressful, demanding day (external). As we have seen, such an interpretive set is a key component in the "amplifying somatic style."

Evidence supporting the instrumental role of self-focused attention in depression, along with evidence supporting its role in symptom reporting and risk perception, leads naturally to predictions of the co-occurrence of hypochondriasis and depression. It does not address the question of why some individuals seem to develop these concerns while others do not, however. Studies of the differences between depressed individuals with and without hypochondriacal concerns and vice versa should lead to suggestions about how the mechanisms vary. Perhaps the degree to which the individual is generally aware of somatic sensations is a mediating variable. Participants who scored highest on the Private Body Consciousness Scale, a scale measuring tendencies to focus on bodily sensations, were more likely than low scorers to report physical arousal after unknowingly consuming caffeine. Further, this tendency was stronger among those individuals who scored high on the Private Self-Consciousness Scale (Miller, Murphy, & Buss, 1981). These results suggest that a combination of inward focus and body awareness may be necessary to induce symptom reporting.

Mood, Symptom Appraisal, and Perceptions of Vulnerability

One of the most striking features of hypochondriacal concerns is that they demonstrate an absence of the optimistic bias observed in many domains, including health (e.g., Weinstein, 1980, 1982, 1984). Normatively, we view ourselves as "uniquely invulnerable" (Perloff & Fetzer, 1986, p. 502; see also Kulik & Mahler, 1987; Weinstein & Lachendro, 1982). Hypochondriacal concerns go against the grain in this regard, reflecting a tendency to view the self as imminently vulnerable to health threats.

Studies have, however, revealed a group of people who show less of the expected optimistic bias. Experiments comparing healthy and ill individuals have shown the bias to be attenuated in ill subjects (Salovey & Birnbaum, 1989), but the mechanism underlying this effect remains unclear. Recent research suggests that mood plays a role in perceptions of vulnerability (Johnson & Tversky, 1983). Further, mood has also been found to influence symptom reporting. Salovey and Birnbaum (1989) found that inducing negative mood caused acutely ill subjects to increase their report of symptoms (Croyle & Uretsky, 1987). Among healthy subjects, negative mood increased perceptions of vulnerability to future negative health events, such as contracting various diseases. Thus, depressed mood may influence hypochondriacal concerns in two ways: by increasing the perception of symptoms and by biasing their interpretation as indicators of negative health status.

Further research is needed to clarify the role of mood in both these domains of hypochondriacal distress. First, understanding the degree of generalization of increased vulnerability would be useful. Johnson and Tversky (1983) found quite general effects of mood, where negative mood resulted in an increase in perceived likelihood of negative events across many domains. Different patterns of findings emerged in studies comparing healthy and ill individuals, where the results tended to be more domain specific (Salovey & Birnbaum, 1989). Second, exploration of the sequelae of heightened perceptions of personal vulnerability is needed. It seems reasonable to hypothesize that feeling more at risk leads to negative mood, thus perpetuating the cycle of pessimistic evaluations. Perhaps education about risk assessment could, via its effect on mood state, be as useful as direct efforts to alter affective status.

Negative Affectivity and Symptom Reporting

Symptom reporting does not necessarily index objective health status. It is significantly correlated with measures of neuroticism and negative affectivity (Costa & McCrae, 1985, 1987; Watson, 1988; Watson & Pennebaker, 1989). Evidence reviewed by these authors supports the hypothesis that symptom reporting is, in part, an expression of distress just as are psychological complaints. The distinction between psychological and physical complaining may be arbitrary and inadequate. Internal focus of attention is an important component of this argument, as negative affectivity is associated with tendencies toward introspection (Watson & Clark, 1984).

Conclusion

Mood is an important component of hypochondriasis. First, affective distress is clearly a feature of the disorder. Second, mood is one of a group of variables implicated in processes underlying hypochondriacal concerns, such as inward focus of attention, and symptom and risk perception. It appears that focus of attention may be associated with both perception of symptoms and negative mood, and that negative mood in turn affects symptom reporting and risk perception. We have hypothesized further that pessimistic risk perception could lead to negative mood. Research clarifying the extent and direction of influence of these variables is needed.

In this chapter, we have selected for discussion some areas of research that bear on a new formulation of hypochondriacal concerns, the amplifying somatic style. We have focused our discussion on cognitive and affective components, especially attention and mood. Intriguing relationships between focus of attention and somatic symptoms on the one hand and concern about the meaning of those symptoms on the other raise several questions for further research. A similar dual role for mood was suggested. Other sources of variability in somatic concerns were also discussed, both internal (arousal) and external (presence or absence of stimulation in the environment, and sources of secondary gain). A dimensional rather than categorical view of hypochondriacal concerns is tenable (Stretton, Salovey, & Mayer, 1992). We suggest that a reasonable next step in understanding variability along this continuum is exploration of the interrelationships among attention, mood, and hypochondriacal concerns within a context that can be evaluated along the internal and external dimensions of arousal, stimulation, and reinforcement.

Acknowledgments We thank J. L. Singer, D. T. Kraemer, and J. D. Mayer for their comments on an earlier version of this manuscript. We also acknowledge the support of NIH Biomedical Research Support Grant S07 RR07015, the John C. and Catherine T. MacArthur Foundation–supported Program on Conscious and Unconscious Mental Processes, a National Science Foundation Presidential Young Investigator Aware (BNS-9058020), and a grant from the American Cancer Society (PBR-84).

References

Alexander, F. (1950). *Psychosomatic medicine: Its principles and applications.* New York: Norton.

American Psychiatric Association. (1994). *Diagnostic and statistical manual of mental disorders* (4th ed.). Washington, DC: Author

Apfel, R. J., & Sifneos, P. E. (1979). Alexithymia: Concept and measurement. *Psychotherapy and Psychosomatics, 32,* 180–190.

Barsky, A. J. 91988). *Worried sick: Our troubled quest for wellness.* Boston: Little, Brown.

Barsky, A. J., & Klerman, G. L. (1983). Overview: Hypochondriasis, bodily complaints, and somatic styles. *American Journal of Psychiatry, 140,* 273–283.

Barsky, A. J., Wyshak, G., & Klerman, G. L. (1986). Hypochondriasis: An evaluation of the DSM-III criteria in medical outpatients. *Archives of General Psychiatry, 43,* 493–500.

Baur, S. (1988). *Hypochondria: Woeful imaginings.* Berkeley: University of California Press.

Brink, T. L. (1982). Geriatric depression and hypochondriasis: Incidence, interaction, assessment, and treatment. *Psychotherapy: Theory, Research, and Practice, 19,* 506–511.

Buss, A. H. (1980). *Self-consciousness and social anxiety.* San Francisco: Freeman.

Carver, C. S., & Scheier, M. F. (1981). *Attention and self-regulation: A control-theory approach to human behavior.* New York: Springer.

Costa, P. T., Jr., & McCrae, R. R. (1985). Hypochondriasis, neuroticism, and aging: When are somatic complaints unfounded? *American Psychologist, 40,* 19–28.

Costa, P. T., Jr., & McCrae, R. R. (1987). Neuroticism, somatic complaints and disease: Is the bark worse than the bite? *Journal of Personality, 55,* 299–316.

Croyle, R. T., & Uretsky, M. B. (1987). Effects of mood on self-appraisal of health status. *Health Psychology, 6,* 239–253.

Diamond, D. B. (1985). Panic attacks, hypochondriasis, and agoraphobia: A self-psychology formulation. *American Journal of Psychotherapy, 34,* 114–125.

Duval, S., & Wicklund, R. A. (1972). *A theory of objective self-awareness.* New York: Academic Press.

Fenigstein, A., Scheier, M., & Buss, A. H. (1975). Public and private self-consciousness: Assessment and theory. *Journal of Consulting and Clinical Psychology, 43,* 522–527.

Fillingim, R. B., & Fine, M. A. (1986). The effects of internal vs. external information processing on symptom perception in an exercise setting. *Health Psychology, 5,* 115–123.

Freud, S. (1957). On narcissism: An introduction. In J. Strachey (Ed. & Trans.), *The standard edition of the complete psychological works of Sigmund Freud* (Vol. 14, pp. 67–102). London: Hogarth Press. (Original work published 1914)

Gibbons, F. X., Carver, C. S., Scheier, M. F., & Hormuth, S. E. (1979). Self-focused attention and the placebo effect: Fooling some of the people some of the time. *Journal of Experimental Social Psychology, 15,* 263–274.

Hanback, J. W., & Revelle, W. (1978). Arousal and perceptual sensitivity in hypochondriacs. *Journal of Abnormal Psychology*, 87, 523–530.

Hassett, J. (1978). *A primer of psychophysiology*. San Francisco: Freeman.

Hunter, R. C. A., Lohrenz, J. G., & Schwartzman, A. E. (1964). Nosophobia and hypochondriasis in medical students. *Journal of Nervous and Mental Disease*, 139, 147–152.

Ingram, R. E. (1990). Self-focused attention in clinical disorders: Review and a conceptual model. *Psychological Bulletin*, 107, 156–176.

Ingram, R. E., & Smith, T. W. (1984). Depression and internal versus external focus of attention. *Cognitive Therapy and Research*, 8, 139–152.

Johnson, E. J., & Tversky, A. (1983). Affect, generalization, and the perception of risk. *Journal of Personality and Social Psychology*, 45, 20–33.

Kellner, R., Abbott, P., Pathak, D., Winslow, W. W., & Umland, B. E. (1983–1984). Hypochondriacal beliefs and attitudes in family practice and psychiatric patients. *International Journal of Psychiatry in Medicine*, 13, 127–139.

Kellner, R., Fava, G. A., Lisansky, J., Perini, G. I., & Zielezny, M. (1986). Hypochondriacal fears and beliefs in DSM-III melancholia: Changes with amitriptyline. *Journal of Affective Disorders*, 10, 21–26.

Kellner, R., Wiggins, R. G., & Pathak, D. (1986). Hypochondriacal fears and beliefs in medical and law students. *Archives of General Psychiatry*, 43, 487–489.

Kenyon, F. E. (1964). Hypochondriasis: A clinical study. *British Journal of Psychiatry*, 110, 478–488.

Kenyon, F. E. (1976). Hypochondriacal states. *British Journal of Psychiatry*, 129, 1–14.

Kreitman, N., Sainsbury, P., Pearce, K., & Costain, W. R. (1965). Hypochondriasis and depression in out-patients at a general hospital. *British Journal of Psychiatry*, 111, 607–615.

Kulik, J. A., & Mahler, H. I. M. (1987). Health status, perceptions of risk, and prevention interest for health and non-health problems. *Health Psychology*, 6, 15–27.

Lacey, J. I. (1967). Somatic response patterning and stress: Some revisions of activation theory. In M. H. Appley & R. Trumbull (Eds.), *Psychological stress: Issues in research* (pp. 14–37). New York: Appleton-Century-Crofts.

Ladee, G. A. (1966). *Hypochondriacal syndromes*. Amsterdam: Elsevier.

Lesse, S. (1974). Hypochondriasis and psychosomatic disorders masking depression. In S. Lesse (Ed.), *Masked depression* (pp. 53–74). New York: Jason Aronson.

Maley, M. J. (1967). Two-flash threshold, skin conductance and skin potential. *Psychonomic Science*, 9, 361–362.

Matthews, K. A., Scheier, M. F., Brunson, B. I., & Carducci, B. (1980). Attention, unpredictability, and reports of physical symptoms: Eliminating the benefits of predictability. *Journal of Personality and Social Psychology*, 38, 525–537.

McHugo, G. J., & Lanzetta, J. T. (1983). Methodological decisions in social psychophysiology. In J. T. Cacioppo & R. E. Petty (Eds.), *Social psychophysiology: A sourcebook* (pp. 630–665). New York: Guilford Press.

Mechanic, D. (1972). Social psychologic factors affecting the presentation of bodily complaints. *New England Journal of Medicine*, 286, 1132–1139.

Meister, R. (1980). *Hypochondria: Toward a better understanding*. New York: Taplinger.

Miller, L. C., Murphy, R., & Buss, A. H. (1981). Consciousness of body: Public and private. *Journal of Personality and Social Psychology*, 41, 397–406.

Pennebaker, J. W. (1980). Perceptual and environmental determinants of coughing. *Basic and Applied Social Psychology*, 1, 83–91.

Pennebaker, J. W. (1982). *The psychology of physical symptoms*. New York: Springer.

Pennebaker, J. W., Burnam, M. A., Schaeffer, M. A., & Harper, D. C. (1977). Lack of control as a determinant of perceived physical symptoms. *Journal of Personality and Social Psychology, 35,* 167–174.

Pennebaker, J. W., & Lightner, J. M. (1980). Competition of internal and external information in an exercise setting. *Journal of Personality and Social Psychology, 39,* 165–174.

Perloff, L. S., & Fetzer, B. K. (1986). Self-other judgments and perceived vulnerability to victimization. *Journal of Personality and Social Psychology, 50,* 502–510.

Petrie, A. (1978). *Individuality in pain and suffering* (2nd ed.). Chicago: University of Chicago Press.

Pilowsky, I. (1975). Dimensions of abnormal illness behaviour. *Australian and New Zealand Journal of Psychiatry, 9,* 141–147.

Pyszczynski, T., & Greenberg, J. (1987). Self-regulatory perseveration and the depressive self-focusing style: A self-awareness theory of reactive depression. *Psychological Bulletin, 102,* 122–138.

Pyszczynski, T., Holt, K., & Greenberg, J. (1987). Depression, self-focused attention, and expectancies for positive and negative future life events for self and others. *Journal of Personality and Social Psychology, 52,* 994–1001.

Rose, R. J. (1966). Anxiety and arousal. A study of two-flash fusion and skin conductance. *Psychonomic Science, 6,* 81–82.

Salovey, P. (1992). Mood-induced self-focused attention. *Journal of Personality and Social Psychology, 62,* 699–707.

Salovey, P., & Birnbaum, D. (1989). Influence of mood on health-relevant cognition. *Journal of Personality and Social Psychology, 57,* 539–551.

Salovey, P., & Rodin, J. (1985). Cognition about the self: Connecting feeling states and social behavior. In P. Shaver (Ed.), *Self, situations, and social behavior: Review of personality and social psychology* (Vol. 6, pp. 143–166). Beverly Hills, CA: Sage.

Schachter, S., & Singer, J. E. (1962). Cognitive, social, and physiological determinants of emotional state. *Psychological Review, 69,* 379–399.

Scheier, M. F., Carver, C. S., & Gibbons, F. I. (1979). Self-directed attention, awareness of bodily states, and suggestibility. *Journal of Personality and Social Psychology, 37,* 1576–1588.

Smith, T. W., & Greenberg, J. (1981). Depression and self-focused attention. *Motivation and Emotion, 5,* 323–331.

Stretton, M. S., Salovey, P., & Mayer, J. D. (1992). Assessing health concerns. *Imagination, Cognition, and Personality, 12,* 115–137.

Suls, J., & Fletcher, B. (1985). Self-attention, life stress, and illness: A prospective study. *Psychosomatic Medicine, 47,* 469–481.

Watson, D. (1988). Intraindividual and interindividual analyses of positive and negative affect: Their relation to health complaints, perceive stress, and daily activities. *Journal of Personality and Social Psychology, 54,* 1020–1030.

Watson, D., & Clark, L. A. (1984). Negative affectivity: The disposition to experience aversive emotional states. *Psychological Bulletin, 96,* 465–490.

Watson, D., & Pennebaker, J. W. (1989). Health complaints, stress, and distress: Exploring the central role of negative affectivity. *Psychological Review, 96,* 234–254.

Weinstein, N. D. (1980). Unrealistic optimism about future life events. *Journal of Personality and Social Psychology, 39,* 806–820.

Weinstein, N. D. (1982). Unrealistic optimism about illness susceptibility. *Health Psychology, 2,* 11–20.

Weinstein, N. D. (1984). Why it won't happen to me: Perceptions of risk factors and susceptibility. *Health Psychology, 3,* 431–457.

Weinstein, N. D., & Lachendro, E. (1982). Egocentrism as a source of unrealistic optimism. *Personality and Social Psychology Bulletin, 8,* 195–200.

Wine, J. (1971). Test anxiety and direction of attention. *Psychological Bulletin, 76,* 92–104.

Wood, J. V., Saltzberg, J. A., & Goldsamt, L. A. (1990). Does affect induce self-focused attention? *Journal of Personality and Social Psychology, 58,* 899–908.

Zborowski, M. (1975). Cultural components in response to pain. In T. Millon (Ed.), *Medical behavioral science* (pp. 561–571). Philadelphia: Saunders.

Part III

SCHIZOPHRENIA
AND PSYCHOSIS

20

Luc Ciompi

Is Schizophrenia an Affective Disease?

The Hypothesis of Affect-Logic and Its Implications
for Psychopathology

Since the fundamental classificatory work of Emil Kraepelin at the end of the nineteenth century, major "functional" or "endogenous" psychoses are subdivided into mania and melancholia on the one hand, and dementia praecox—which after E. Bleuler (1911) became schizophrenia—on the other hand. Classically, the former two are considered as affective diseases according to the prevailing psychopathologic picture, whereas the latter is supposed to be a predominantly cognitive disease, as thinking disorders are in fact in the foreground. There are, however, intermediate forms—the so-called schizo-affective psychoses—and important cognitive disturbances exist also in melancholia and mania, as there are affective disturbances in schizophrenia. Despite various attempts to replace this basic dichotomy by the perhaps more adequate notion of a unitary psychosis with variable phenomenological aspects (Kühne, Morgner, & Koselowski, 1988), the Kraepelinian subdivision continues to form a cornerstone of current psychopathologic and diagnostic systems, such as the International Classification of Diseases (ICD-10), or the *Diagnostic and Statistical Manual* (DSM-III and -IV) of the American Psychiatric Association.

Dissatisfaction with this purely descriptive approach has, however, repeatedly been expressed, because it has not led to a deeper understanding of the observed phenomenological differences, or of the underlying etiologic or pathogenetic mechanisms. This failure may, at least partly, be related to a lack of clarity concerning the nature of cognitive and affective phenomena and their fundamental interactions, as mirrored by a confusing multiplicity of definitions and theories. During the last 10 years, the debate on these issues was dominated—and perhaps somewhat obscured—by the question of primacy of cognition over emotion or, vice versa (Izard, 1993a; Lazarus, 1982, 1991; Leventhal & Scherer, 1987; Zajonc, 1980, 1984). In the following pages, an alternative approach—the concept of affect-logic—will be presented which is mainly focused on operational aspects of affective-cognitive interactions and obligatory functional links, with circular relations between emotion and cognition. This concept has first been proposed by this author in a German book in 1982 that was eventually translated into English and further developed since (Ciompi, 1982/ 1988b; 1986, 1989, 1991, 1993). The term *affect-logic* is not an entirely satisfactory translation of an appropriated German neologism meaning, simultaneously, "the logic of affectivity" and "the affectivity of logic." It points to the central conceptual basis of the model, which postulates that in all normal and most pathological mental functions, emotions and cognitions—or affective and cognitive functions, feeling and thinking, affectivity and logic—are inseparably connected and interact in regular but not yet sufficiently well understood ways.

Psychotic disturbances are viewed, under this hypothesis, as specific modifications of affective-cognitive patterns of interaction, with characteristic differences between mania and melancholia on one side, and schizophrenia on the other. All three psychoses are, however, understood as essentially *affective diseases*, given that specific modifications of postulated fundamental organizing and integrating functions of affects on cognitions seem to play a major role in all three conditions.

The concept of affect-logic is based on long-standing clinical observation and research in the long-term evolution, psychopathology, and rehabilitation of schizophrenia (Ciompi, 1980, 1988; Ciompi, Dauwalder, & Augé, 1979), and on a theoretical approach that integrates basic elements both of Piaget's genetic epistemology and of psychoanalysis, with current psychological and neurophysiological theories on affective-cognitive interactions (Derryberry and Tucker, 1992; Izard 1993a, 1993b; Kernberg, 1980; Lazarus, 1982, 1991; Leventhal & Scherer 1987; Piaget, 1977a, 1977b, 1981; Zajonc, 1980, 1984). The overall theoretical framework is system-theoretic (Bertalanffy, 1950; Miller, 1975), including current notions on self-organization and nonlinear (chaos-theoretical) dynamics of complex systems far from equilibrium (Haken, 1982, 1990; Prigogine & Stengers, 1983; Tschacher, Scheier, & Aebi, 1994; Tschacher, Schiepek & Brunner, 1992).

The main theses that are developed below are:

1. In almost all mental functioning, affective, cognitive and behavioral components are functionally connected in integrated affective-cognitive systems of reference, or "feeling-thinking-behaving programs." These are self-generated through action and store in their configuration the relevant past experience. Affective-cognitive programs on different hierarchical levels form the essential "building blocks" of the psyche.
2. Energizing, organizing, and integrating functions of affects on cognition play an essential role in generating, storing, and reactivating these affective-cognitive programs.
3. Their neurophysiological basis consists of functionally integrated neuronal pathways with cognitive, affective, sensorimotor, and vegetative-hormonal components that are differentiated through action by neuronal plasticity. Specific structural-anatomical configurations may correspond to cognitive aspects, and activating neurotransmittory flows may correspond to emotional aspects.
4. Normal as well as pathological ways of functioning correspond to specific overall patterns of interactions between affective and cognitive elements that operate— formulated in chaos-theoretical terms, which will be explained below—as

supraordinated self-organized attractor-basins, or dissipative structures. Nonlinear phase transitions (bifurcations) toward psychotic patterns of functioning can occur under energetically overtaxing conditions far from equilibrium, with basic affects functioning as crucial control-parameters, and emerging aberrant cognitions as predominant order-parameters.

5. Stability (or rigidity), flexibility, and lability of affective-cognitive connections play an essential role in organizing normal as well as psychotic mental functioning. In mania and melancholia, these connections are too rigid and unilateral, in opposite directions, and in schizophrenia they are too loose. Schizophrenia, too, thus appears as an affective disease, albeit of a distinct kind.

Basic Concepts of Affect-Logic

The notion of *affects* was introduced into psychopathology by Eugen Bleuler (1911, 1926). Emphasizing the "switching power of affects," Bleuler considered that understanding the dynamic effects of affects is the most important key to understanding psychopathology. According to the central basic assumption of affect logic, the whole multiformity of normal and pathological mental phenomena can most economically be understood by the *obligatory* operational complementarity of two fundamentally different systems: an affective one and a cognitive one. Overlapping terms such as *affects, emotions, feelings,* and *moods* are, however, used across the literature, with widely variable significations (Izard, 1993a; Kleinginna & Kleinginna, 1981; Murphy & Zajonc, 1993; Panksepp, 1982). On the basis of their major common denominator, affects such as joy, fear, sadness, and rage are defined, in affect-logic terms, as *global psychophysiological states that obligatorily "affect" not only the mind, but also the brain and the whole body.* Psychomotor-expressive, autonomous, and behavioral aspects of affects in this sense are deeply rooted in phylogenesis and ontogenesis, as illustrated by sympathicotonic, or ergotropic, states related to aggressivity or fear (fight or flight), and parasympathicotonic, or trophotropic, states characterized by pleasant feelings related, for example, to food intake, sexuality, care of the brood, or sleep. Affects are not necessarily conscious, and their duration may vary between a few seconds (emotions in the neurophysiological sense, which actually correspond to transitions from one affective state to another) up to hours, days, and even weeks (moods in the sense of psychology and psychopathology). They are overall qualitative conditions that involve the whole organism. A far reaching implication of this definition is the fact that it is impossible not to be in a certain affective state. Body and mind are always "tuned" in some way, even when we feel neutral, apathetic, or indifferent.

Cognition (or cognitive-intellectual functioning, "thinking"), on the other hand, is defined in affect-logic as the *perception and further elaboration of sensory differences* on widely different levels of complexity, from elementary sensory stimuli up to highly differentiated concepts and theories.

Thus defined, cognitive functions, too, have deep roots in phylogenesis and ontogenesis. Wimmer (1995) actually follows the origin of cognition, as well as of inseparably linked emotions, right back to the elementary regulations of unicellular organisms reacting to perceptions of environmental differences. (Wimmer is an Austrian ethologist in the tradition of Konrad Lorenz and Jean Piaget whose ideas are very close to our own conceptualization.) This broad definition covers narrower ones such as, for example, the definition recently advanced by Izard (1993a): While recognizing elementary cellular, organismic and biopsychosocial forms of information processing, Izard proposes to restrict the term *cognition* to information processing on higher levels that involve memorization, mental representations, and appraisal. Phylogenetically and ontogenetically, it is, however, practically impossible to delimit the beginning of mental representations. A broad definition of cognition also has the advantage of leading to a remarkable conceptual consistency not only with the given definition of affects, but also with other theoretical approaches of cognitive evolution. The British mathematician Spencer-Brown (1979), for example, has convincingly shown that our whole cognitive world is based on the perception and further processing of a system of differences. This remains true for most elementary differences perceived by primitive organisms. Distinguishing between differences (variances) and nondifferences (invariances) corresponds to one of the most basic performances of neuronal networks. The proposed definition is also in agreement with the cybernetic concept of information based on the notion of "a difference which makes a difference" (Bateson, 1979). Moreover, it leads to an unbroken ontological continuity from primitive to highly abstract cognitive phenomena, because the perception of any difference presupposes a comparison, hence a relation, and a relation implies even in its most elementary forms an abstract logicomathematical component. Simultaneously, a sharp contrast appears between the global qualitative and body-near nature of affects, on the one hand, as defined above, and the essentially quantitative and logicoabstract nature of cognition, on the other hand.

Logic, finally, is defined, on these bases, as *the way in which cognitions are linked together*. Purposefully, this definition too is broad: As cognitive elements can be selected and linked in various ways, it leads to the notion of different types of logic — a very useful notion, as we will see, especially regarding the influence that different affects have on selection and linkage of cognitive elements. Moreover, this notion is in good agreement with modern scientific, mathematical, and even philosophical concepts that all imply multiple definitions of logic, truth, or reality[1] (Glasersfeld, 1987; Piaget, 1977b; Vattimo, 1985; Watzlawick, 1981).

Focusing, as mentioned, on the operational aspects of affective-cognitive interactions, the theory of affect-logic proposes that affects are continually and systematically linked, through experience, to specific cognitions and corresponding behavioral sequences. They are stored in functionally integrated affective-cognitive systems of reference, or "feeling-thinking-behaving programs." An ever more differentiated hierarchical network of context-related programs for feeling, thinking, and behavior is generated through repetitious actions. By neuronal plasticity, these "programs" are encoded in privileged neuronal pathways that eventually provide the functional matrix for all further cognition and communication. The range of learned affective-cognitive-behavioral patterns goes from simplest conditioned reflexes (e.g., of the type "burnt children fear the fire" — a German proverb), up to highly complex transference phenomena in the psychoanalytic sense (e.g., stereotyped aggressive or submissive behavior with typical father figures). Similar affective-cognitive programs exist for interactions with inanimate objects, with places and spaces, and other sensory-motor activities. According to psychoanalytic concepts, too, interpersonal relations are essentially determined by experience-based internalized programs of increasing complexity, under the form of so-called self-representations and object-representations (Jacobson, 1964; Kernberg, 1976, 1980; Mahler, 1968). It therefore seems justified to understand those programs, systems of reference, or affective-cognitive structures as the essential building blocks of the psyche. What we call the psyche appears, thus, as a complex hierarchy of internalized affective-cognitive-behavioral programs.

These basic assumptions of affect-logic are supported by an extended body of scientific evidence ranging from experimental psychology to current ethology and neurophysiology, reviewed below. They are, in particular, grounded on Piaget's central notion of the genesis of all cognitive concepts through action, on the base of innate sensorimotor schemata that are continually differentiated, equilibrated, automatized, internalized, and finally "mentalized" by complementary assimilatory-accommodatory processes since the first days of life (Piaget, 1977a, 1977b). Despite the fact that Piaget repeatedly emphasized inseparable functional links between cognition and emotion, and also postulated mobilizing and energizing effects of emotions on cognition as well as unconscious aspects of both (Piaget 1973, 1977a, 1981), he did not include, or systematically conceptualize, the participation of affects in the evolution of cognitions. But actions without emotions do not exist, and the effects of emotions on cognition go far beyond a bare energizing, or motivating and activating function.

Organizing and Integrating Functions of Affects on Cognitions

There are at least the following five aspects of organizing and integrating effects of emotions on cognitions. First, the focus of attention is continuously conditioned by basic emotional states. Therefore, these states have a decisive influence on selection and linkage of relevant cognitive stimuli. Specific types of logic in the above-mentioned sense are thus generated by different emotional states. In addition to conventional forms of logic and of culturally determined cognitive *self-evidences* that are characterized by an average state of relaxation, a specific "fear-logic," "anger-logic," "sadness-logic," "happiness-logic," and so on, must therefore be postulated and does in fact exist: In a melancholic state, for instance, only negative facts are recalled, perceived, and combined into an entirely negative perspective; in mania, in contrast, a euphoric "logic" is created on an analog base. Similarly, affect-specific cognitive contents and logical chains are activated when being in love, or in hate, and so on.

Second, storage and remobilization of cognitive material, also, are state dependent for the same reasons, and can be illustrated by the same examples. This is already obvious in everyday experience: Cognitive information without a specific emotional connotation is hardly noticed or stored, and emotion-specific memories are remobilized in corresponding states. By experimental work, too, affect-specific memorization has been widely demonstrated: Under hypnosis or specific drug-induced emotional states, cognitively very different life-events scattered over many years, which however were linked by common affective connotations such as shame, or rage, or pleasure, were remembered "en bloc" (Bower, 1981, 1990; Grof, 1975).

Third, both above-mentioned phenomena contribute to create affect-specific diachronic and synchronic coherence and continuity of experience according to context: Context-relevant cognitive stimuli are activated, while irrelevant stimuli are suppressed by specific affects. In a fearful situation caused by a fire, for instance, all other cognitive elements but those directed on salvation—which are highlighted—are eliminated from the field of consciousness. It is obvious that this has a high survival value. More subtle mechanisms of the same type are, however, also at work in less dramatic situations. In scientific work, for instance, the focus of attention, as well as the storage and mobilization of mnesic material, is continuously directed and conditioned, consciously or not, by specific underlying states with clearly emotional connotations, for example, interest, ambition, competition.

Fourth, this last example may show that emotional factors also play an important role in the reorganization of cognitive material at higher levels of abstraction. In these "majorizing equilibrations," as Piaget (1977a) calls them, unpleasant feelings caused by contradictions or inconsistencies furnish the needed energy for looking for new solutions that, when found, are immediately linked to pleasant feelings. In addition, several pleasant (because tension-reducing) cognitive elements are eventually linked together and combined into positively connotated higher order cognitive structures, for instance, a new theory or hypothesis. More efficient (tension-reducing) thinking is therefore pleasurable. Common pleasant and unpleasant feelings, thus, literally guide and connect relevant cognitive elements, and, respectively disconnect irrelevant ones. These initially intense and quite conscious emotions are stored—this is the hypothesis of affect-logic—together with the corresponding cognitive elements and continue, eventually, to manifest themselves, for example, in what has been called pleasure of function, which accompanies all easy-going mental and psychomotor activities. On the other hand, strongly unpleasant feelings (anger, aggressivity, sadness, or fear) are immediately activated when long-lasting automatized cognitive paradigms are suddenly questioned and disturbed by new scientific evidence (Kuhn, 1962).

Last but not least, dominant and subordinate affective states reduce complexity by creating a hierarchical order of cognitive functions, with important implications for motivation and so-called free will—a phenomenon that represents an "affective regulation of regulations," that is, something like a compact supraordinate affect, according to Piaget (1981).

All these affective-cognitive interactions may be mutually reinforcing, or circular. They are not only observed on the individual level, but also on the collective level (see also Collins, 1981). Affects are, in fact, highly contagious; they create common patterns of feeling-thinking-behaving in couples, groups, and even in whole nations (Hatfield, Caciopo & Rapson, 1994). Extreme examples are collective hysteria, panic, enthusiasm, and aggressivity. On the social level, too, affects create continuity and coherence of experience and activity, both diachronically and synchronically. Common actions without common feelings are practically impossible. Collective storage and mobilization of cognitive memories, too, are highly influenced by basic emotions, as demonstrated by sudden reactivations of remote collective memories under the influence of specific emotions as, for example, occurs in nationalistic groups. Hence, affects have analog mobilizing, organizing, and integrating effects on cognitive material both on the individual and on the social level.

Biological Bases

Virtually all postulates of affect-logic are supported by basic biological findings. The biological substratum of the assumed affective-cognitive "building blocks of the psyche" are integrated neuronal circuits self-organized by means of neuronal plasticity[2]—that is, through action. Different affect-specific neuronal systems with integrated cognitive, affective, sensorimotor and vegetative components have been identified, or are on the way to being identified, during the last 10–15 years, among them a so-called reward-system characterized by pleasant feelings, an anger-aggression system, a fear-anxiety system, and a panic system (Panksepp, 1982; Ploog, 1986, 1989; Routtenberg, 1978). Furthermore, five global cerebral states corresponding to so-called basic emotions (interest, fear, anger, sadness, and joy) have been detected by spectral electroencephalographic (EEG) methods (Machleidt, 1992). Other EEG research confirms the phenomenon of state-dependent information processing, learning, and memory in different functional states of the brain, including wake, sleep, dream, trance, and psychosis (Koukkou & Lehmann, 1983; Koukkou & Manske, 1986). The fact that limbic and paralimbic structures that regulate emotions are closely connected with those involved in memorization underscores the crucial role of emotions in learning processes not only on the clinical, but also on the neurophysiological level. Recently detected rich ascending and descending connections between limbic system, neocortex, thalamus, and hypothalamus provide the neuronal basis for close mutual interactions between emotions, cognitions, sensorimotor activity, and hormonal tuning of the whole body (Derryberry & Tucker, 1992; LeDoux, 1993; McNeal, 1993; Panksepp, 1982). Of particular interest is the discovery of direct connections between thalamus and amygdala, allowing for emotional emergency reactions to sensory inputs without previous high-level cognitive processing (LeDoux, 1989). These same structures are richly innervated by all major neurotransmitter systems related to specific affective states, for example, noradrenaline to aggression, dopamine to anxiety and fear, serotonin to depression, and endorphins to pleasant feelings. Their projections toward distant brain areas provide the functional basis for the postulated far-reaching effects of emotions.

The following tentative hypothesis may explain a multitude of closely connected phenomena such as affects obligatorily linked to cognitions and to mnesic functions, state-dependent learning and memory, mobilizing, organizing and integrating functions of affects: On the basis of the assumption that specific combinations of neuro-transmittory flows correspond to specific affects, and specific functional-neuroanatomical bifurcations to specific cognitive configurations, a specific *emotional inprint* may be necessary for generating, as well as for reactivating, specific neuronal pathways (Ciompi, 1991). All above-mentioned phenomena would in fact be functionally linked, if such an "inprint" was provided by a mechanism through which the same neurotransmitters that reactivate emotion-specific pathways already contributed to create these same pathways by stimulating dendritic growth and the genesis of new neuronal connections (neuroplasticity). Thus, the postulated *obligatory* connection between affective and cognitive functions as well as the described organizing and integrating functions of emotions could be elegantly explained by a single biological mechanism.

Psychopathologic Implications

Affect-logic has implications for several domains of psychopathology. Here, however, only those concerning schizophrenia will be discussed in some detail. They include, mainly, the following four domains.

1. Affect-logic leads to a psychosociobiologically integrative model of the long-term evolution of schizophrenia in three phases, centered on a modified version of the vulnerability hypothesis.
2. It deepens the understanding of psychopathologic core phenomena such as ambivalence, incoherence, and emotional flattening.
3. It generates new hypotheses concerning the role of nonlinear dynamics in the short-term and long-term evolution of schizophrenia.
4. It leads to innovative therapeutic approaches.

The above-mentioned model of *long-term evolution of schizophrenia* (Ciompi 1982/1988, 1988) is based on the notion of feeling-thinking-behaving programs generated through action, and encoded in correspondingly configured neuronal networks. During the *first phase*, premorbid evolution from conception until the outbreak of psychosis, affective-cognitive-behavioral programs of less than average stability are generated by interacting unfavorable biological and/or psychosocial factors known to increase the risk of psychosis. These include genetic factors, perinatal traumatisms, severe early developmental discontinuities, and confusing familial communication patterns (Gottesman & Shields, 1978; Kringlen, 1986; Mednick, Schulsinger, & Schulsinger, 1975; Singer, Wynne, & Toohey, 1978; Tienari et al., 1985). This creates a specific vulnerability (Ciompi, 1982/1988; Nuechterlein & Dawson, 1984; Zubin & Spring, 1977) that may consist primarily of a critical lability of affective-cognitive connections, with far-reaching behavioral effects especially when high-ranking affective-cognitive programs such as the mentioned self-representations and object-representations in the psychoanalytic sense (Kernberg, 1976, 1980) are touched.

During a *second phase*, characterized by acute psychotic decompensation, additional biological and/or psychosocial stressors including, alternately or in combination, hormonal changes, drug abuse, severe emotional trauma and conflicts, mating, and childbirth gradually overtax this vulnerable coping system. At a critical point (the "point of no return" in Manfred Bleuler's formulation; see Bleuler, 1984) that represents a typical bifurcation in chaos-theoretical terms (Ambühl, Dünki, & Ciompi, 1992; Ciompi, 1989, in press), the global pattern of affective-cognitive functioning is more or less suddenly forced into a radically different "regime" corresponding to psychosis.

The *third phase*, long-term evolution, which has been shown to be much more variable and often also more favorable than traditionally assumed (Bleuler, 1978; Ciompi, 1980, 1988; Harding, Brooks, Ashikaga, Strauss, & Breier, 1987a, 1987b; Huber, Gross, Schinttler & Linz, 1980; McGlashan, 1988; Tsuang, Woolson & Fleming, 1979), is again determined by complex interactions between numerous biological and psychosocial variables, including premorbid vulnerability, personality structure and social adaptation, familial communication patterns and "expressed emotions," socioeconomic and cultural conditions, therapeutic and preventive interventions, institutional milieu, and care system (Ciompi, 1988; Leff, Kuipers, Berkowitz, Eberlein-Vries, & Sturgeon,1982; Singer et al., 1978; Tienari et al., 1985; Wing & Brown, 1970; World Health Organization, 1979). The concept of affect-logic provides the theoretical framework, or metatheory, for integrating all these seemingly heterogeneous findings under one common denominator: All these biological and social factors can have a critical impact on the described feeling-thinking-behaving programs, respectively, on their neuronal substratum.

Concerning specific *psychopathological phenomena*, the concept of integrated programs for feeling, thinking, and behaving contributes to explain the striking parallels among these three aspects in schizophrenic core symptoms like ambivalence and incoherence, or (mainly in chronical residual states) affective-cognitive flattening—actually, not only feelings and thoughts, but also behaviors become highly unstable and finally discontinuous or, on the contrary, highly restricted and leveled. On the bases of the preceding conceptualizations, this could be explained by a primarily *affective, respectively affective-cognitive disorder* with only secondary effects on organization and integration of corresponding cognitive functions. Not only melancholia and mania, but also schizophrenia may thus primarily be an "affective disease," as also suggested by increasing evidence for structural or functional defects in limbic and paralimbic areas and their relations with the prefrontal cortex (Berman et al., 1994; Buchsbaum, 1990; Shapiro, 1993). All three major psychoses (mania, melancholia, schizophrenia) would thus not only have a common denominator, but also characteristic differences: They may all be primarily based on affective disorders, with secondary effects on cognitive functions. In mania and melancholia, however, affective-cognitive connections appear as too rigid and unilateral (in opposite directions), whereas in schizophrenia, these same connections are too loose, with possible overcompensatory counterregulations in chronic states both on a psychodynamical and on a biological level (Ciompi, 1991; Lecrubier & Douillet, 1983).

Finally, the postulated notion of integrated affective-cognitive-behavioral systems of reference organized and integrated by specific affects leads to a *chaos-theoretical interpretation* of short-term and long-term dynamics of schizophrenia. Focusing on the energetic (activating, motivating, mobilizing) aspects of emotions, normal as well as psychotic patterns of functioning can be understood as characteristic distributions of affect-mediated energy among available cognitions, or state-specific patterns of dynamic affective-cognitive organization. In chaos theory, specific patterns of energy distribution, which have already been described in a great number of self-organizing physical, chemical, biological and also socioeconomical systems, are known as "dissipative structures," or attractor-basins (Babloyantz, 1986; Prigogine & Stengers, 1983). New patterns of organization, or energy distribution, can suddenly appear far from the state of equilibrium, at a critical bifurcation point, under increasing energy input. Something very similar seems to happen when a normally functioning but vulnerable feeling-thinking-behaving system is progressively decompensated by overtaxing emotional charges, and finally switches to a psychotic "regime." Haken's (1982, 1990) physicomathematical theory of synergetics shows that such nonlinear phase transitions may occur when certain crucial control parameters, or basic energetic conditions, undergo a critical change. At this point, formerly peripheral elements of the dynamic system can suddenly become predominant and function as new so-called order parameters that will eventually "enslave," as Haken calls it, the dynamics of the whole system. In psychotic decompensations, increasing emotional tensions (as, e.g., provoked by "high expressed emotions," or by critical life events, drug abuse, hormonal changes, and other known psychosocial or biological triggers of psychosis) can be understood as typical control parameters whereas certain formerly marginal cognitive elements such as paranoid ideas, or hallucinations, function as emerging order parameters. Under the metaphor of "butterfly effect" (metaphorically, the minimal atmospheric movement caused by the wing of a butterfly in Japan under critical conditions may eventually provoke a thunderstorm in Hawaii; Lorenz, 1963), chaos theory describes also a typical high sensitivity of the whole systems-dynamics to initial conditions and minimal environmental influences close to bifurcation points—a dynamic pattern that seems to correspond to the clinical phenomena of oversensitive reactions to very small perceptual inputs such as a colored spot, a suspicious word, or a glimpse that may provoke psychosis during critical periods of instability. Other striking parallels between phenomena described in chaos theory and clinical observations in psychotic states concern typical ("ambivalent") fluctuations close to bifurcation points, and unpredictable behavior of the system over time remaining, however, within the range of certain "attractive" global patterns. Preliminary empirical evidence for chaos-like time series in schizophrenic short-term psychopathology over 1–2 years, and in long-term relapses over decades, with different types of attractors and dissipative structures, has in fact recently been detected by our own research group, and by other authors (Ambühl et al., 1992; Ciompi, in press; Ciompi, Ambühl & Dünki, 1992; Schiepek & Schoppek, 1992; Tschacher, Scheier & Aebi, 1994).

Therapeutic Consequences

As the focus of this chapter is on theoretical conceptualization, only a few practical implications shall be mentioned briefly. One of them is the importance of the basic "emotional atmosphere" of therapeutic settings and style of care that is understood as a critical "control parameter" in the mentioned sense. The hypothesis that psychotic cognitive functioning can be critically improved by an emotionally relaxed, supportive, and stimulus-protected small-scale milieu has been clinically confirmed over now more than 13 years by the pilot project "Soteria Berne," derived from a similar program realized in San Francisco by Mosher and colleagues (Mosher & Menn, 1978; Mosher, Menn, & Matthews, 1975). Equivalent therapeutic results concerning psychopathologic state, relapse rate, working, and housing situation over 2 years were in fact obtained with three to five times lower doses of neuroleptics than in a control population (Ciompi, Dauwalder, Aebi, Trütsch & Kupper, 1992; Ciompi, Knepper, Aebi, Dauwalder, Hubschmid, Trütsch, & Rutighauser, 1993). The similarity of therapeutic effects of neuroleptics on emotional relaxation provided by a specific therapeutic milieu and type of care speaks for a primary effect of neuroleptics on limbic and paralimbic emotional regulations, and thus provides additional support for the hypothesis of schizophrenia as a primarily affective disease.

Other practical applications of affect-logic are based on the notion of state-dependent learning and memory. They include the crucial importance of a positive emotional atmosphere for successful cognitive information processing, learning, and communication in psychotherapy, pedagogy, advertising, and rhetoric. Interesting implications exist also in social psychology, where basic emotions are determinant for the overall cognitive structure of collective ideologies, or prejudices. Affect-logic theory may furthermore explain why basic emotions are often more important than cognitive content for deciding whether messages become true "in-formations" in a literal sense, which are built into the preexisting affective-cognitive systems of references, or not.

Perspectives for the Future: Toward a New Psychopathology?

In summary, the proposed theory seems capable of integrating a wide range of normal and psychopathological phenomena under one general view. It leads to a comprehensive psychosociobiological model of the psyche in which the "mental apparatus" is understood as a complex hierarchy of functionally integrated affective-cognitive-behavioral programs that are generated by action and store in their structure the relevant past experience. Affects in circular interactions with cognitions are supposed to play a key role in all normal and pathological mental functioning. They operate not only as energy vectors, but also as organizing and integrating forces: Normal as well as pathological patterns of functioning correspond to diagnosis-specific distributions, or dissipative structures, of affect-energy among available cognitions. Nonlinear shifts from one global affective-cognitive "regime," or "attractor basin," to another are understood as the emergence of new dissipative structures. They are provoked by modifications of crucial control parameters, among them basic emotions that facilitate the emergence of new order parameters, such as critical perceptions, paranoid ideas, or hallucinations that eventually "enslave" the whole affective-cognitive field. In contrast to manic or depressive states where affective-cognitive linkages are too rigid (in opposite directions), the emergence of schizophrenia or schizophreniform states seems to be facilitated by initially too unstable affective-cognitive connections. In this sense, not only mania and depression, but also schizophrenia could actually correspond to a basically *affective* disorder, albeit of a particular kind. A fundamentally new understanding of psychopathology and psychotherapy could emerge from such a view.

It seems also promising to further explore the hypothesis that a specific *affective inprint*, mediated by interacting neurotransmitters as vectors of specific emotions, may be necessary for generating, as well as for activating, privileged affective-cognitive-behavioral pathways on the neurophysiological level. This single hypothesis seems capable of explaining not only the postulated obligatory connections between emotion and cognition, but also the described integrating and organizing functions of affects.

Notes

1. For instance, euclidean vs. noneuclidean geometry, relativistic vs. nonrelativistic physics, and postmodern constructivism.

2. Repeated stimulation of the same synaptic connections facilitates stimulus transmission and dendritic growth; see Haracz (1984) and Changeux and Konishi (1987).

References

Ambühl, B., Dünki, R. M., & Ciompi, L. (1992). Dynamical systems and the development of schizophrenic symptoms. *Series in Synergetics*, 58, 195–203.

Babloyantz, A. (1986). *Molecules, dynamics, and life. Introduction to self-organisation of matter.* New York: Wiley.

Bateson, G. (1979). *Mind and nature. A necessary unit.* New York: Bantam Books.

Berman, K. F., Ostrm, J. L., Mattay, V. S., Esposito, G., Van Horn, J. D., Abi-Dargham, A., Fuller Torrey, E., & Weingberger, D. R. (1994). The role of the dorsolateral prefrontal cortex and hyppocampus in working memory and schizophrenia [Abstract]. *Biological Psychiatry*, 35, 615–747.

Bertalanffy, L. von. (1950). An outline of general systems theory. *British Journal of Philosophical Science*, 1, 134–165.

Bleuler, E. (1911). Dementia praecox oder die Gruppe der Schizophrenien. In G. Aschaffenbrurg (Ed.), *Handbuch er Psychiatrie, specieller Teil*, 4. Leibzig: Deuticke.

Bleuler, E. (1926). *Affektivität, suggestibilität, paranoia.* Halle: Carl Marhold Verlag.

Bleuler, M. (1978). *The schizophrenic disorders. Long-term patient and family studies.* New Haven, CT: Yale University Press.

Bleuler, M. (1984). Das alte und das neue Bild des Schizophrenen. *Schweizer Archiv für Neurologie Neurochirurgie und Psychiatrie*, 135, 143–149.

Bower, G. H. (1981). Mood and memory. *American Psychologist*, 36, 129–148.

Bower, G. H. (1990). Awareness, the unconscious, and repression: An experimental psychologist's perspective. In J. L. Singer (Ed.), *Repression and dissociation: Implications for personality theory, psychopathology, and health* (pp. 209–231). Chicago: University of Chicago Press.

Buchsbaum, M. S. (1990). Frontal lobes, basal ganglia, temporal lobes—Three sites for schizophrenia? *Schizophrenia Bulletin*, 16, 377–378.

Changeux, J. P., & Konishi, M. (1987). *The neuronal and molecular bases of learning.* Chichester: Wiley.

Ciompi, L. (1980). Catamnestic long-term studies on the course of life of schizophrenics. *Schizophrenia Bulletin*, 6, 606–618.

Ciompi, L. (1986). Zur Integration von Fühlen und Denken im Licht der "Affektlogik". Die Psyche als Teil eines autopoietischen Systems. In Kisker, K. P., Lauter, H., Meyer, J.-E., Müller, C., & Strömgren, E. (eds.) *Psychiatric der Gegenwart* (pp. 373–410). Berlin: Springer.

Ciompi, L. (1988). Learning from outcome studies. Toward a comprehensive biological-psychological understanding of schizophrenia. *Schizophrenia Research*, 1, 373–384.

Ciompi, L. (1988). *The psyche and schizophrenia. The bond between affect and logic.* Cambridge, MA: Harvard University Press. (Original work published 1982)

Ciompi, L. (1989). The dynamics of complex biological-psychosocial systems. Four fundamental psycho-biological mediators in the long-term evolution of schizophrenia. *British Journal of Psychiatry*, 155, 15–21.

Ciompi, L. (1991). Affects as central organising and integrating factors. A new psychosocial/biological model of the psyche. *British Journal of Psychiatry*, 159, 97–105.

Ciompi, L. (1993). Die Hypothese der Affektlogik. *Spektrum der Wissenschaft*, 2, 76–82.

Ciompi, L. (in press). The chaos-theoretical approach to schizophrenia. On non-linear dynamics of complex systems. *British Journal of Psychiatry*.

Ciompi, L., Ambühl, B., & Dünki, R. (1992). Schizophrenie und Chaostheorie. Methoden zur Untersuchung der nicht-linearen Dynamik komplexer psycho-sozio-biologischer Systeme. *System Familie*, 5, 133–147.

Ciompi, L. Dauwalder, H. P., Aebi, E., Trütsch, K., & Kupper, Z. (1992). A new approach of acute schizophrenia. Further results of the pilot-project "Soteria Berne". In A. Werbart & J. Cullberg (Eds.), *Psychotherapy of schizophrenia: Facilitating and obstructive factors* (pp. 95–109). Oslo: Scandinavian University Press.

Ciompi, L. Dauwalder, H. P., & Augé, C. (1979). Ein Forschungsprogramm zur Rehabilitation psychisch Kranker. III. Längsschnittuntersuchung zum Rehabilitationserfolg und zur Prognostik. *Nervenarzi, 50*, 366–378.

Ciompi, L. Kupper, Z. Aebi, E., Dauwalder, H. P., Hubschmid, T., Trütsch, K., & Rutishauser, C. (1993). The pilotproject "Soteria Berne" for the treatment of acute schizophrenics. II. Results of a comparative prospective study over 2 years. *Nervenarzt, 64*, 440–450.

Collins, R. (1981). On the microfoundations of macrosociology. *American Journal of Sociology, 86*, 984–1014.

Derryberry, D., & Tucker, D. M. (1992). Neural mechanisms of emotion. *Journal of Consulting and Clinical Psychology, 60*, 329–338.

Glasersfeld, E. (1987). *Wissen, Sprache und Wirklichkeit.* Braunschweig: Vieweg.

Gottesman, J., & Shields, J. (1978). A critical review of recent adoption, twin, and family studies on schizophrenia: Behavioural genetics perspectives. *Schizophrenia Bulletin, 2*, 360–398.

Grof, S. (1975). *Realms of the human inconscious.* New York: Viking.

Haken, H. (1982). *Evolution of order and chaos.* Berlin: Springer.

Haken, H. (1990). *Synergetics. An introduction.* Berlin: Springer.

Hatfield, E., Cacioppo, J. T., & Rapson, R. L. (1994). *Emotional contagion.* Paris: Cambridge University Press.

Haracz, J. L. (1984). A neuronal plasticity hypothesis of schizophrenia. *Neuroscience and Biobehavior Review, 8*, 55–71.

Harding, C. M., Brooks, G. W., Ashikaga, T., Strauss, J. S., & Breier, A. (1987a). The Vermont longitudinal study of persons with severe mental illness. I. Methodology, study sample, and overall status 32 years later. *American Journal of Psychiatry, 144*, 716–726.

Harding, C. M., Brooks, G. W., Ashikaga, T., Strauss, J. S., & Breier, A. (1987b). The Vermont longitudinal study of persons with severe mental illness. II. Long-term outcome of subjects who retrospectively met DSM-III criteria for schizophrenia. *American Journal of Psychiatry, 144*, 727–737.

Huber, G., Gross, G., Schüttler, R., & Linz, M. (1980). Longitudinal studies of schizophrenic patients. *Schizophrenia Bulletin, 6*, 592–605.

Izard, C. E. (1993a). Four systems for emotion activation: Cognitive and noncognitive processes. *Psychology Review, 100*, 68–90.

Izard, C. E. (1993b). Organizational and motivational functions of discrete emotions. In M. Lewis & J. Haviland (Eds.), *Handbook of emotion* (pp. 631–641). New York: Guilford Press.

Jacobson, E. (1964). Das Selbst und die Welt der Objekte. Frankfurt a.M.: Suhrkamp.

Kernberg, O. (1976). *Object relations theory and clinical psychoanalysis.* New York: Jason Aronson.

Kernberg, O. (1980). *Internal world and external reality.* New York: Jason Aronson.

Kleinginna, P. R., & Kleinginna, A. M. (1981). A categorized list of emotion definitions, with suggestions for a consensual definition. *Motivation and Emotion, 5*, 345–355.

Koukkou, M., & Lehmann, D. (1983). Dreaming: The functional state-shift hypothesis. A neuropsychophysiological mode. *British Journal of Psychiatry, 142*, 221–231.

Koukkou, M., & Manske, W. (1986). Functional states of the brain and schizophrenic states of behaviour. In C. Shagass, R. C. Josiassen, & R. A. Roemer (Eds.), *Brain electrical potentials and psychopathology* (pp. 91–114). Amsterdam: Elsevier.

Kringlen, E. (1986). Genetic studies of schizophrenia. In G. D. Burrows, T. Norman, & G. Rubinstein (Eds.), *Handbook of studies on schizophrenia: Part I. Epidemiology, aetiology and clinical features* (pp. 45–49). Amsterdam: Elsevier.

Kuhn, T. S. (1962). *The structure of scientific revolutions* (2nd ed.). Chicago: University of Chicago Press.

Kühne, G. E., Morgner, J., & Koselowski, G. (1988). The model of unitary psychosis as a basis for understanding affective processes in psychoses. *Psychopathology, 21*, 89–94.

Lazarus, R. S. (1982). Thoughts on the relations between emotion and cognition. *American Psychologist, 37*, 1019–1024.

Lazarus, R. S. (1991). Cognition and motivation in emotion. *American Psychologist, 46*, 352–367.

Lecrubier, Y., & Douillet, P. (1983). Neuroleptics and the bipolar dopaminergic hypothesis of schizophrenia. In M. Ackenheil & N. Matussek (Eds.), *Special aspects of psychopharmacology*. Paris: Expansion Scientifique Française.

LeDoux, J. E. (1989). Cognitive-emotional interactions in the brain. *Cognition and Emotion, 3*, 267–289.

LeDoux, J. E. (1993). Emotional networks in the brain. In M. Lewis & J. M. Haviland (Eds.), *Handbook of emotions* (pp. 109–118). New York: Guilford Press.

Leff, J. P., Kuipers, L., Berkowitz, R., Eberlein-Vries, R., & Sturgeon, D. (1982). A controlled trial of social intervention in the families of schizophrenic patients. *British Journal of Psychiatry, 141*, 121–134.

Leventhal, H., & Scherer, K. (1987). The relationship of emotion to cognition: A functional approach to a semantic controversy. *Cognition and Emotion, 1*, 3–28.

Lorenz, E. N. (1963). Deterministic nonperiodic flow. *Journal of Atmospheric Sciences, 20*, 130–141.

Machleidt, W. (1992). Typology of functional psychosis—A new model on basic emotions. In F. P. Ferrero, A. E. Haynal, & N. Sartorius (Eds.), *Schizophrenia and affective psychoses. Nosology in contemporary psychiatry* (pp. 97–104). New York: Libbey.

Mahler, M. S. (1968). *Symbiose und Individuation: Band I. Psychosen im frühen Kindesalter*. Stuttgart: Klett-Cotta.

McGlashan, T. H. (1988). A selective review of recent North American long-term followup studies of schizophrenia. *Schizophrenia Bulletin, 14*, 515–542.

McNeal, P. (1993). Cerebral evolution of emotion. In M. Levine & J. M. Haviland (Eds.), *Handbook of emotions* (pp. 67–83). New York: Guilford Press.

Mednick, S. A., Schulsinger, F., & Schulsinger, H. (1975). Schizophrenia in children of schizophrenic mothers. In W. Davis (Ed.), *Childhood personality and psychopathology. Current topics*. New York: Wiley.

Miller, J. G. (1975). General systems theory. In A. M. Freedman, H. J. Kaplan, & B. J. Sadock (Eds.), *Comprehensive textbook of psychiatry*. Baltimore: Williams & Wilkins.

Mosher, L. R., & Menn, A. J. (1978). Community residential treatment for schizophrenia: Two-year follow-up data. *Hospital and Community Psychiatry, 29*, 715–723.

Mosher, L. R., Menn, A. J., & Matthews, S. (1975). Evaluation of a homebased treatment for schizophrenics. *American Journal of Orthopsychiatry, 45*, 455–467.

Murphy, S. T., & Zajonc, R. B. (1993). Affect, cognition, and awareness: Affective priming with optimal and suboptimal stimulus exposures. *Journal of Personality and Social Psychology, 64*, 723–739.

Nuechterlien, K. H., & Dawson, M. E. (1984). A heuristic vulnerability/stress model of schizophrenic episodes. *Schizophrenia Bulletin, 10*, 300–312.

Panksepp, J. (1982). Toward a general psychobiological theory of emotions. *Behavioral and Brain Sciences, 5*, 407–467.

Piaget, J. (1973). The affective unconscious and cognitive unconscious. *Journal of the American Psychoanalytic Association, 21*, 249–261.

Piaget J. (1977a). *The development of thought: Equilibration of cognitive structure*. New York: Viking Press.

Piaget, J. (1977b). *The essential Piaget*. In H. von Gruber & J. Voneche (Eds.). New York: Basic Books.

Piaget, J. (1981). Intelligence and affectivity. Their relationship during child development. In T. A. Brown & C. E. Kaegi (Eds.), *Annual review monograph*. Palo Alto: University of California Press.

Ploog, D. (1986). Biological foundations of the vocal expressions of emotions. In R. Plutchik & H. Kellerman (Eds.), *Emotion: Theory, research and experience: Vol. 3. Biological foundations of emotion* (pp. 173–197). New York: Academic Press.

Ploog, D. (1989). Human neuroethology of emotion. *Progress in Neuro-Psycho-Pharmacology and Biological Psychiatry, 13*, 15–22.

Prigogine, I., & Stengers, I. (1983). *Order out of chaos*. London: Heinemann.

Routtenberg, A. (1978). The reward system of the brain. *Scientific American, 239*, 122–131.

Schiepek, G., & Schoppek, W. (1992). Synergetik in der Pychiatrie: Simulation schizophrener Verläufe auf der Grundlage nicht-linearer Differenzengleichungen. *Systeme, 6*, 22–57.

Shapiro, R. M. (1993). Regional neuropathology in schizophrenia. Where are we? Where are we going? *Schizophrenia Research, 10*, 187–239.

Singer, M. T., Wynne, L. C., & Toohey, B. A. (1978). Communication disorders in the families of schizophrenics. In L. C. Wynne, R. L. Cromwell, & S. Matthysse (Eds.), *The nature of schizophrenia* (pp. 499–511). New York: Wiley.

Spencer-Brown, G. (1979). *Laws of form*. New York: Durron.

Tienari, P., Sorri, A., Lathi, I., Naurala, M., Wahlberg, K. E., Pohojola, J., & Moring, J. (1985). Interaction of genetic and psychosocial factors in schizophrenia. *Acta Psychiatrica Scandinavia, 71*, 19–30.

Tschacher, W., Schiepek, G., & Brunner, E. J. (Eds.). (1992). *Self-organization in clinical psychology*. Berlin: Springer.

Tschacher, W., Scheier, C., & Aebi, E. (1994). Nichtlinearität und Chaos in Psychoseverläufen—eine Klassifikation der Dynamik auf empirischer Basis. In W. Böker & H. D. Brenner (Eds.), *Auf dem Weg zu einer integrativen Therapie der Schizophrenie* (pp. 48–65). Bern: Huber.

Tsuang, M. T., Woolson, R. F., & Fleming, J. A. (1979). Long-term outcome of major psychoses: I. Schizophrenia and affective disorders compared with psychiatrically symptom-free surgical conditions. *Archives of General Psychiatry, 39*, 1295–1301.

Vattimo, G. (1985). *La fine della modernità*. Milan: Garzanti.

Watzlawick, P. (1981). *Die erfundene Wirklichkeit*. München: Piper.

Wimmer, M. (1995). Evolutionary roots of emotion. *Evolution and Cognition, 1*, 38–50.

Wing, J. K., & Brown, G. W. (1970). *Institutionalism and schizophrenia*. London: Cambridge University Press.

World Health Organization. (1979). *Schizophrenia: An international follow-up study*. New York: Wiley.

Zajonc, R. B. (1980). Feeling and thinking: Preferences need no inferences. *American Psychologist, 35*, 151–175.

Zajonc, R. B. (1984). On the primacy of affect. *American Psychologist, 39*, 117–124.

Zubin, J., & Spring, B. (1977). Vulnerability—a new view on schizophrenia. *Journal of Abnormal Psychology, 86*, 103–126.

21

Ross Buck, Cheryl K. Goldman, Caroline J. Easton,
& Nanciann Norelli Smith

Social Learning and Emotional Education

Emotional Expression and Communication in Behaviorally
Disordered Children and Schizophrenic Patients

This chapter presents a model of the role of emotional expression and communication that seeks to explain how normal emotional development can go awry, contributing to emotional disregulation and to psychopathology; and a measurement procedure—the slide-viewing technique—that arguably provides reliable, valid, and efficient measures of emotional expression and communication that can be applied to psychiatric patients. We begin by presenting the general viewpoint and formally defining basic terms.

Developmental-Interactionist Theory

Emotional Education and Competence

We approach emotional expression and communication from the viewpoint of a broad developmental-interactionist (DI) model of motivation, emotion, and cognition. Both subjectively experienced emotion and spontaneous emotional expression are conceived as "readouts" of biologically based motivational-emotional systems (Buck, 1985, 1988, 1994). DI theory argues that motivational-emotional systems contribute structured information to the organism in the form of subjective experience that is itself a kind of knowledge, an immediate knowledge-by-acquaintance of feelings and desires, or of *affects* (Buck, 1990, 1993b).

The Social Biofeedback Process   Affects—feelings and desires—are based on biological systems structured by phylogeny. Through an emotional communication process, the child must *learn about* the "internal environment" of affects in the context of specific personal relationships that themselves reflect social, cultural, and historical conditions. This is *emotional education*, defined as the child's learning about feelings and desires: how to attend to them, to recognize and label them, and to express them in specific contexts (Buck, 1983). Emotional education proceeds via a *social biofeedback* process in which others give feedback about feelings and desires based on the child's expressive behavior.[1] Emotional education may or may not produce *emotional competence* in dealing with one's feelings and desires; this is defined as the ability of the child to attend to, label, and express emotions appropriately in specific social/relational contexts.

Emotional Expression and Communication   From this point of view, critical to developing emotional competence is *emotional communication*, which involves both sending accuracy and receiving ability. Sending accuracy is the accuracy by which information about a sender's emotional state is relayed to a receiver via expressive behavior, whereas receiving ability is an individual's ability to attend and respond appropriately to such information. *Emotional expression* is hypothesized to be related to communication accuracy in a curvilinear manner: Levels of expression that are either too high or too low will tend to disrupt emotional communication because of a deficit or surfeit of signal, respectively. In a developmental context, both high or low levels of expressiveness will disrupt the social biofeedback process, thus resulting in deficits in emotional education and competence. This account can explain the poorly defined clinical phenomenon of *alexithymia*, meaning no words for mood.

Alexithymia has been invoked in the etiology of a number of pathological conditions. The concept is not well defined, but its central aspect is a "striking incapacity for the verbal description and expression of feelings" (Nemiah & Sifneos, 1970, p. 155). We suggest that the verbal deficit has roots in emotional communication deficits: that alexithymia reflects deficits in emotional education that can occur when a child is either too expressive or not expressive enough. If expression is too high we predict disinhibitory psychopathology; if too low we predict inhibitory psychopathology. This implies that expressive and nonexpressive alexithymia must be distinguished.

Suggested relationships between emotional expression, communication, alexithymia, and psychopathology are presented in figure 21.1, which also relates them to an hypothesized excitatory-inhibitory dimension of behavior (Gray's [1982] Behavioral Activation and Behavioral Inhibition Systems), and to autonomic nervous system responses (skin conductance deflections [SCDs]). Briefly, a highly internalizing or introverted pattern is associated with high inhibition and SCD responding; low emotional expression, with consequent deficits in emotional communication and education, and nonexpressive alexithymia. Conversely, a highly externalizing or extroverted pattern is associated with low inhibition and SCD responding, a surfeit of emotional expression with consequent deficits in emotional communication and education, and expressive alexithymia. The suppression hypothesis holds that events that increase inhibition should simultaneously (albeit independently) increase SCDs and decrease spontaneous expressiveness, resulting in a negative between-subject correlation of SCDs and expressiveness (Buck, 1984, 1983a).

Operationalization and Measurement   Communication accuracy is measured by the slide-viewing technique (SVT), in which senders watch emotionally loaded color

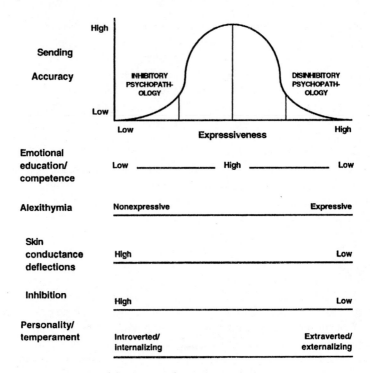

Figure 21.1 Model: Emotional expressiveness, communication, emotional education/competence, and alexithymia.

slides while, unknown to them, their facial/gestural expressions are televised and viewed by receivers, who make judgments about the slides and the sender's reactions. *Sending accuracy* is operationally defined as the accuracy of response generated by a specific sender across receivers, and *receiving ability* as the accuracy of response of a specific receiver across senders. *Emotional expression* is defined operationally as the total number of facial/gestural behaviors in response to an emotional stimulus, and as we shall see it is measured by a segmentation technique that can both identify events in the stream of expressive behavior responsible for accuracy, and assess general emotional expressiveness that may not be communicative.

The Social Learning of Emotion

Developmental-interactionist theory is fundamentally a social learning theory in the mold of Miller and Dollard (1941) and Bandura and Walters (1963), but unlike them DI theory stresses the features that distinguish the social learning of emotion from social learning as traditionally conceived.

Special- and General-Purpose Systems   In DI theory, emotion involves an interaction between biologically based special-purpose processing systems (SPPSs) structured by phylogeny, and general-purpose processing systems (GPPSs) involving classical conditioning, instrumental learning, and/or higher-order cognitive processing structured during ontogeny. Developmental-interactionist theory emphasizes the developmental dimension of the interaction: In the emotional education process children learn *about* their feelings and desires just as they learn about the external environment. Primary motivational-emotional systems, or *primes*, are SPPSs organized hierarchically within the brain (Buck, 1985, 1988). They include reflexes, instincts, drives, and primary affects. *Motivation* is defined as the potential for response built into the prime; *emotion* as the *readout* of such potential when activated by a challenging stimulus. There are three sorts of readout: autonomic, endocrine, and immune system responses that serve functions of bodily adaptation and homeostasis (*Emotion I*), expressive responses that serve functions of communication and social organization (*Emotion II*), and subjective experiences that inform about bodily states (feelings and desires involving hunger, sexual arousal, happiness, anger, and so on) and function to provide knowledge of bodily responses important to self-regulation (*Emotion III*). *Affect* refers to Emotion III responses — subjectively experienced feelings and desires (Buck, 1991a, 1993b).

Accessibility and Emotional Education   A major point of DI theory is that these different sorts of emotional response are differentially *accessible* to the individual and the socialization agent, and that this has important consequences for social learning. Affects, or Emotion III responses, are accessible to the individual but not others, expressive Emotion II responses are more accessible to others than the individual, and Emotion I responses are generally not accessible without special equipment. The individual thus *knows* affects or Emotion III responses immediately and directly, but *learns about* them indirectly, through the responses of others to his/her Emotion II expressive behaviors.

Spontaneous Versus Symbolic Communication   The social learning process on which emotional education is based has another distinguishing feature from social learning as usually conceived: The process is based on *spontaneous communication*. Spontaneous communication, discussed in detail by Buck (1984), is a species-specific communication system that includes expressive displays that constitute social affordances that, given attention, activate emotional preattunements and are directly perceived.[2] The "meaning" of these displays is known directly by the receiver, as, given attention, the feel of one's shoe on one's foot is known directly: It is not propositional knowledge, but rather knowledge by acquaintance (Buck, 1990).

This spontaneous communication system constitutes a *conversation between limbic systems* that occurs simultaneously and interactively with intentional symbolic communication. The emotional displays and preattunements on which spontaneous communication is based have evolved as phylogenetic adaptations. This biologically based communication system involves human beings *directly* with one another: The individuals in spontaneous communication constitute literally a biological unit (Buck & Ginsburg, 1991).

Emotional Competence   The child learns about biologically based affects — feelings and desires — in a process of emotional communication with others, hence the developmental aspect of DI theory. The result of such learning embodies an interaction between biologically based affects on one hand and personal, sociocultural, linguistic and historical factors on the other, hence its interactionist aspect. Emotional education results in a greater or lesser competence in dealing with one's own feelings and desires, or emotional competence. Emotional competence is the ability to deal effectively with the "internal environment" of feelings and desires, just as social competence is the ability to deal effectively with other people, and competence in general is the ability to deal effectively with the external environment.

The child learns about feelings and desires in culturally and individually variable ways. Individual differences can arise from both responses socialization agents give to one's expressions (social biofeedback) and models available for imitation. If it is easy to communicate a given motivational/emotional state, both emotional and social competence should be enhanced. Thus, spontaneously communicative people should tend to be both emotionally and socially competent. However, the most *expressive* person is not always the most *communicative*: As noted previously, communication is as much disrupted by a surfeit of expression as a deficit.

Studies of Emotional Expression and Communication: The Slide-Viewing Technique

Communication Accuracy

Developmental-interactionist theory grew out of the results of studies employing the slide-viewing technique (SVT), which itself was developed out of the cooperative conditioning procedure used by Robert E. Miller to study communication of affect in monkeys (Miller, Banks, & Ogawa, 1963). Senders are shown a series of emotionally loaded color slides and rate their affective response to each while their facial/ gestural reactions are televised with a hidden camera. The slides show familiar persons, pleasant scenery, unpleasant and unusual scenes, and in some cases sexual content. They are not designed to evoke specific emotions, but rather emotion blends. Receivers viewing the film judge what kind of slide is shown on each trial, and how the sender felt about it. These judgments are related to the actual slide shown and the sender's rated reactions, resulting in percent correct and specific-emotion correlation scores: accuracy scores that can be evaluated against chance. The SVT has been used with male and female adults and preschoolers, dating and married couples, and persons from differing cultures (see Buck, 1991a). Particularly relevant from a clinical point of view are studies of elderly brain-damaged patients.

Brain-Damaged Patients

The SVT was used successfully with hospitalized brain-damaged patients, its simplicity and lack of complex verbal instructions proving highly useful. Buck and Duffy (1980) found left-hemisphere-damaged (LHD) aphasic patients to be as communicative as non-brain-damaged (NBD) comparison patients in the SVT, while right-hemisphere-damaged (RHD) patients were significantly less communicative and in fact did not differ from patients with Parkinson's disease. Segmentation revealed a similar pattern, with LHD and NBD patients receiving more segmentation points than Parkinson's disease patients, and with RHD patients in between (Easton, Norelli, & Buck, 1992). Also using the SVT, Borod, Koff, Perlman Lorch, and Nicolas (1985) found anterior RHD patients to be rated as less expressive than LHD patients, with evidence of less prosodic expression as well.

Social Factors and Expression

One factor that must be taken into account in the measurement of emotional expressiveness is that the display rules inherent in the social situation should be expected to affect markedly the individual's pattern of expressiveness (Ekman & Friesen, 1975). The "social" versus "emotional" determinants of expressive behavior have lately been a source of controversy (Buck, 1991b, 1994; Chovil, 1991; Chovil & Fridlund, 1991; Fridlund, 1991). There is evidence that the presence of other persons may have both inhibitory and facilitatory effects on expression; thus, an individual who is normally unexpressive may be expressive in the presence of a significant other, while a normally expressive person may "clam up" in the presence of a certain person. These effects depend on the emotion involved and the personal relationship with the other. Buck, Losow, Murphy, and Costanzo (1991) found that people become less accurate senders in the presence of a stranger, but in the presence of a friend were more communicative on sexual slides but less communicative on unpleasant and unusual slides. Wagner and Smith (1991) similarly found friendship to influence expressiveness. In general, any measure of expressiveness that is made in the presence of another person is both a measure of individual expressiveness and a measure of the nature of the personal relationship involved. An effective measure of emotional expressiveness must either minimize social cues or provide an independent means for assessing the effects of the personal relationship.

Segmentation

Communication accuracy scores do not assess the behaviors on which communication is based. The segmentation procedure is employed as a first step in analyzing these behaviors (Buck, Baron, & Barrette, 1982). In segmentation observers viewing a videotape are told to press a button when something meaningful occurs (Newtson, Engquist, & Bois, 1977). Observers tend to agree about the location of meaningful events, so a number of potentially useful measures of spontaneous expressive behavior can be analyzed. Specifically, the total number of events identified as meaningful may be taken as a measure of *expressiveness*, as opposed to *sending accuracy*, while points where observers agree that something meaningful occurred are defined as consensual points (CPs), which can guide the application of notation systems to determine specific behaviors underlying observers' judgments. Segmentation is a general tool that provides a way of approaching the behavior stream without preconceptions (Buck, 1984).

Therapeutic Implications

Developmental-interactionist theory presents a conceptual orientation, with specific definitions of important terms, and the SVT provides operational definitions for many of these terms and procedures of measurement relevant to studying emotional expression and communication. This view of emotion is consistent with what we know about the linguistic and cultural nature of human beings emphasized in cognitive theories, but goes beyond them by regarding the body itself as a source of knowledge that a child must deal with in a special sort of social learning process termed *emotional education*. Moreover, the principles of DI theory are relevant to therapy, for insofar as it deals with feelings and desires therapy can be considered a process of *emotional reeducation*, in which one learns to deal with bodily realities. Such realities may include a new bodily condition such as a serious illness (Reardon & Buck, 1989), or they may be feelings and desires that are poorly understood and inappropriately expressed. This appears to be the case with behaviorally disordered children and with schizophrenic patients, as we shall see.

Emotional Communication in Psychopathology

Behaviorally Disordered Children

Behaviorally disordered (BD) children are aggressive, disruptive, and often socially maladjusted. They often act out rather than explore and deal with their emotions in a controlled manner, and seem unable verbally to describe, label, and interpret their feelings. They may deny that they have feelings. They are regarded as difficult to treat clinically, and are at risk for antisocial and criminal behavior (Walker, Shinn, O'Neill, & Ramsey, 1987).

There is evidence that BD children are deficient in the kinds of labeling and understanding that should be gained during emotional education (Dodge & Crick, 1990). They may be unable to experience their own affect fully because they fail to differentiate among feelings and desires, or because they do not attend to them. Or, they may fully experience affect but be unable to label it. We suggest that BD children may be unable to verbalize emotions that are in fact subjectively experienced, occurring physiologically and/or being expressed, and that this is a result of deficits in emotional education that in turn is at least in part a result of extreme (high or low) expressiveness and consequently poor social biofeedback.

The Goldman Study   Goldman (1993) studied BD children's affective communication and its relationships with self-reported and other-reported emotion, as well as self- and other-reported social competence, externalizing-internalizing, and alexithymia. Thirty BD children and 30 age-matched comparison-group (CG) children served as senders in the SVT. Groups of undergraduates, blind to the clinical nature of the sample, served as receivers. Four types of slides were used: familiar people (pictures of the child him/herself and the child's teacher), unfamiliar people, unpleasant, and unusual. Measures of social competence were taken from the child, teacher, and parent using the Gresham and Elliott (1990) Social Skills Rating System.

Communication Accuracy   Results indicated that BD children were markedly poorer senders than CG children. Undergraduate receivers were better at guessing the type of slide viewed by CG (60% correct) than BD children (44% correct; $F(1,56) = 25.30$, $p < .001, E_{ta} = .56$). CG children were superior senders on all of the slide categories.

BD children were also consistently poorer senders on the emotion correlation measures ($F(1,56) = 13.16$, $p = .0006$, $E_{ta} = .44$). The emotion correlations are communication measures based on correlations between the children's ratings of their own feelings on each slide and others' judgments of their feelings (see Wagner, Buck, & Winterbotham, 1993). Children rated the feelings evoked by each slide on emotion rating scales (five 5-point differential emotion scale affects, from *not at all* to *very* happy, sad, afraid, angry, surprised; and one 5-point bipolar pleasant-unpleasant scale). Judges viewing the child's expressions rated how happy, sad, afraid, angry, surprised, and pleasant the child looked on each slide using the same scales. Correlations between the child's and judges' ratings across the slides for each emotion constituted the accuracy measure. These emotion correlations are given in figure 21.2. It is noteworthy that BD children did not significantly communicate anger. Also, abilities to communicate fear and anger were more highly correlated with other-rated social competence than other emotion communication measures.

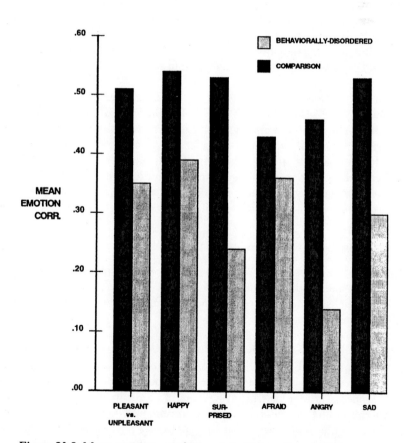

Figure 21.2 Mean emotion correlations (specific emotion sending accuracy) for behaviorally disordered and comparison group children.

Thus, as expected BD children were poorer senders, though they were not necessarily less *expressive* than CG children. This will be revealed by future segmentation analysis.

Ratings of Subjective Experience   BD children's ratings of *their own* feelings toward the slides did not differ significantly from that of the CG children, although the BD children were *judged by others* to be significantly more sad, afraid, and angry and less happy and pleasant (Group × Emotion interaction, $F(5,280) = 6.37$, $p <$ .001, $E_{ta} = .32$).

Response to Familiar Photographs   Of particular interest was the response of children to familiar pictures. Both BD and CG children rated their own and their teacher's picture as highly positive, but when others rate how happy they *look* when they see their picture BD children are seen as significantly less happy (CG = 5.72, BD = 4.34, $p < .001$). Inspection reveals negative looks suggesting disgust and contempt when BD children view pictures of themselves. A similar but less marked pattern exists for the BD childrens' response to the picture of the teacher (CG = 5.03, BD = 4.23, $p <$ .01). This illustrates the potential of the SVT for revealing emotionally laden responses not tapped by self-reports, and indeed such dissociations between self-report and expressive behaviors are of particular interest in the investigation of emotional expression and communication in psychiatric groups.

Implications   This research has important implications for the treatment of BD children in terms of the emphasis that is placed on emotional education during social skills training. These children may need to learn to recognize when they are experiencing certain feelings, how to label them accurately, and how to express them appropriately. Increasing their understanding of their own affect may enhance their sensitivity to others. The potential here is for an empirically based theory of therapy that accounts in a coherent way for the "dark side," unknown, not evil side, of human nature in ways impossible with cold cognitive approaches.

Emotional Expression and Communication in Schizophrenia

"Inappropriate affect" has long been cited as characteristic of schizophrenia, but there are no reliable and valid measures of this concept. We suggest that schizophrenia has roots in deficits in emotional communication, and that the SVT provides a paradigm for measuring such deficits.

Expressed Emotion and Schizophrenia   Many studies have suggested that high levels of expressed emotion (EE), including hostility, criticism, and "emotional overinvolvement" within the family is associated with a high probability of relapse in schizophrenia. A meta-anslysis of 24 studies, involving a total of 1,321 patients, showed that schizophrenic persons with family members and/or close relatives high in EE are more likely to experience clinical relapse (57%) than persons from low-EE families (21%; Bebbington, 1992). There is cross-cultural evidence for the importance of EE in schizophrenia (Jenkins & Karno, 1992). These data are puzzling on the surface, as one might expect that, everything else being equal, high levels of emotional expression would be associated with an ability to cope with emotional disorders.

Affective Sensitivity and Schizophrenia   Another part of this question concerns the sensitivity of schizophrenia patients to EE. Perhaps persons with predispositions to schizophrenia are abnormally sensitive to negative emotion, thus responding in ways that tend to exacerbate the effects of EE in a vicious circle. Many schizophrenic persons, particularly those who manifest negative symptoms, are thought to have "flat affect," suggesting that their expression and perhaps experience of emotion is less than that of normal individuals. This has been repeatedly demonstrated in studies of affect *expression*, but Krause, Steiner, Sanger-Alt, and Wagner (1989) suggest that the affective *experience* of the schizophrenic person may be actually heightened, and negative.

Krause et al. (1989) found that the emotional expression of healthy persons *interacting with* schizophrenic persons is greatly reduced: Only half the facial expressions normally shown are manifested by healthy persons when conversing with schizophrenic persons. Also, Hufnaegel, Steimer-Krause, and Krause (1991) found that 57% of the variance of the emotion self-ratings of schizophrenic persons can be accounted for by the expressive behavior of the interaction partner, while this is the case for only 20% of the variance in the emotion self-ratings in healthy dyads. Thus, the self-ratings of emotion are actually more predictable for schizophrenic than for healthy persons, the prediction depending on the expressive behavior of the partner. The implication is that schizophrenic persons are actually quite sensitive—perhaps abnormally sensitive—to the displays of others during face-to-face interaction. Moreover, there was evidence that the experiential response of schizophrenic persons even to smiles appears to be negative (Hufnaegel et al., 1991).

Krause et al. (1989) suggest that the schizophrenic's usual lack of expression may actually be a protective device to "turn off" the expressions of others, because the schizophrenic person is in reality affectively labile and prone to respond uncontrollably, and negatively, to the affective expressions of others. Thus, the normal preattunements to respond to emotional expressions in others may be abnormally sensitive in schizophrenic persons. This could explain why schizophrenic persons from high-EE families have higher rates of relapse.

Emotional Sensitivity   If schizophrenic persons are extraordinarily sensitive to emotional displays as Krause et al. (1989) suggest, they may show this in increased receiving ability when viewing spontaneous expressions. Studies have found deficits in schizophrenic patients' ability to label emotional expressions (Mandal, 1987, 1989a, 1989b, 1990; Walker, McGuire & Bettes, 1984), but such expressions are usually posed, so that their true status as "emotional" is in some doubt. The only study using spontaneous expression known to the present authors is that of LaRusso (1978), who found that paranoid subjects were *superior* to healthy subjects in recognizing true displays anticipating pain, but poorer in recognizing posed expressions of anticipated pain.

Implications   The question is, then, whether EE constitutes a social stress that interacts with genetic potential relevant to schizophrenia, whether the affective sensitivity of the schizophrenic person exacerbates the effects of EE, or both. Perhaps EE works by increasing negative affective sensitivity, in a vicious circle. In any case, emotional expression and communication appear to play an important role in schizophrenia, and indeed it has been suggested that schizophrenia is a disorder of nonverbal communication that impairs social functioning (Flack, Miller, & Cavallaro, 1992). It was with this background that a study of schizophrenic patients using the SVT was undertaken.

The Easton Study

Sample   Clinical subjects included 17 psychiatric patients and one family member. The patients included 13 diagnosed with schizophrenia (11 male, 2 female), 2 with depression (both female) and 2 with schizoaffective disorder (both female). Five schizophrenic patients (four male, one female) and one schizoaffective patient were retested within approximately 1 week of the first testing. The mother of one of the schizophrenic patients was tested, viewing her son's picture as one of the slides. Later, he was retested and viewed a slide of his mother. Comparison-group (CG) subjects were from a study of 44 adults (Buck, Maxon, & Norelli, 1991).

Communication and Expressive Behavior   Mean percentage correct scores showed that, as expected, schizophrenic patients were poorer senders (39.68%) compared with CG adults (45.10%: $F(1,50) = 7.73$, $p = .0076$, $E_{ta} = .366$). However, as figure 21.3 shows, these particular patients were *more expressive* than CG persons on the segmentation measure ($F(1,50) = 6.43$, $p = .0144$, $E_{ta} = .338$).[3] It should be noted that in the analysis of data from a larger sample, schizophrenic patients did not differ significantly from comparison patients on the segmentation measure (Easton, 1994). However, the latter study included a larger proportion of chronic schizophrenic patients than the initial data. It is possible that acute schizophrenic patients may show a pattern of high but disorganized expression, while chronic patients may become less expressive.

Ratings of Subjective Experience   Rating scales were similar to those used in the Goldman (1993) study, except that 7-point scales were used. Ratings were found to be remarkably reliable both between and within SVT sessions. The mean emotion ratings across the slides for the five schizophrenic patients who were retested showed a correlation from Time 1 to Time 2 of .90, $p < .01$. The correlations for mean level of rated emotion across the five slide categories for Times 1 and 2 are as follows: Happy = .98, $p = .0039$; Sad = .93, $p = .0242$; Fear = .91, $p = .0312$; Anger = .92, $p = .0268$; Surprise = .89, $p = .0455$; and Pleasant-Unpleasant = .58, NS. Thus, even though different slides were presented at Times 1 and 2, the slide categories elicited highly reliable patterns of rated emotion in these schizophrenic patients.

Ratings of Self Versus Experimenter   The pattern of ratings within the SVT session showed that schizophrenic patients *rated the picture of themselves similarly to their ratings of the unpleasant pictures* and unlike pictures of pleasant scenery and the picture of the experimenter. Figure 21.4 shows that patients rated their responses to

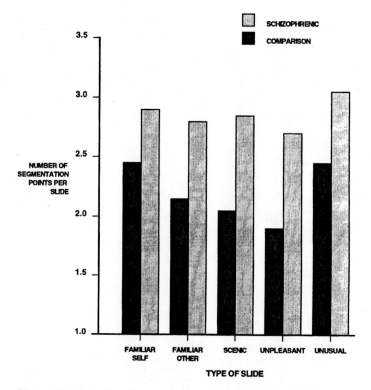

Figure 21.3 Emotional expressiveness: Number of segmentation points per slide for schizophrenic and comparison subjects.

their own picture as low in happiness and pleasantness, and high in sadness, fear, and anger, compared with CG adults (Group × Emotion interaction, $F[5,155] = 60.02$, $p < .001$, $E_{ta} = .812$). However, they rated the picture of the experimenter similarly to CG adults (Group × Emotion interaction, NS).

Other Observations   One of the most remarkable observations from the initial study comes from the one family member who was tested. Her first facial expression on seeing her son's picture included a broad, open-mouth smile and an unmistakably angry upper face. This changed quickly into a smile with "distress brow" upper face suggestive of fear and sadness. It is known that the upper face is more difficult to control than the lower face, and therefore may be "leakier" of one's "true feelings." Certainly, the only slide that evoked such a response in this woman's upper face was the picture of her son. The son's response to the picture of his mother was more muted, but included an initial flash of an expression suggesting fear.

Significance

In these studies of emotional expression and communication in clinical groups, several findings stand out. First, both groups showed deficits in spontaneous emotional

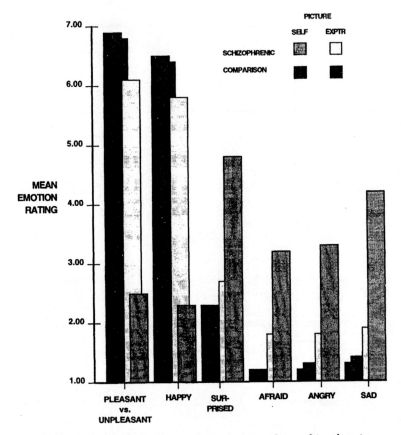

Figure 21.4 Self-rated emotions to familiar picture from schizophrenic and comparison subjects.

communication. Second, it was demonstrated that emotional *communication* can be dissociated from emotional *expressiveness*. Third, both groups were able to *report* their feelings to the slides appropriately and reliably. Fourth, both groups showed negative reactions to the picture of the self.

The deficits in communication accuracy were expected, and should theoretically contribute to deficits in emotional education and competence, and to alexithymia, as outlined earlier. The fact that BD children were unable to communicate anger at all, and that the accurate communication of fear and anger were most strongly related to social competence in the children, is of particular interest. If such negative feelings are not accurately conveyed, others cannot know and respond appropriately to them at relatively low levels. Instead, anger may "build up" until it is expressed intensely, a common occurrence in BD children.

The fact that communication and expressiveness can be dissociated has important implications for research. Typically researchers have concentrated on expressive behaviors—the nature of facial expressions, postures, vocalizations, and the like that are associated with emotion (Ekman & Friesen, 1978). The present results emphasize that the occurrence of these behaviors does not guarantee that communication occurs, and that it is *communication*, not necessarily expressive behaviors, that is deficient in these clinical groups.

The reliability and appropriateness of self-reported emotional experience in these clinical groups were not anticipated. Indeed, a major reason for the initial study with schizophrenic patients was to determine whether such patients could use the emotion rating scales at all. These results imply that some cognitive concomitants of emotion are near normal in these groups: They apparently know when they *should* feel happy, sad, surprised, and so on. Their actual subjective feelings are, of course, conjectural, but the present results are not inconsistent with the suggestion of Krause et al. (1989) that the subjective experience of schizophrenic patients is heightened and negative.

The fact of the negative responses of these groups to a picture of themselves, and in one case a relative, is significant. It reveals the possibility of using expressive behaviors as unobtrusive measures of self-esteem and social relationship that are not influenced as much by self-presentational rules as are self-reports.

This analysis of emotional expression and communication in clinical groups has therapeutic implications that could be beneficially applied both to the patient and the family dynamic system as a whole. First, the SVT can potentially provide a useful diagnostic and prognostic tool. It is well known that BD children and schizophrenic patients have disorganized emotional patterns and symptoms, but little research has been done to specify the precise nature of these symptoms. Studying specific patterns of emotional expression and communication has potential to being able to distinguish types of schizophrenia. The SVT may also serve as a useful prognostic tool. As noted above, much research has been done illustrating that schizophrenic patients who are in a high-EE family environment are more likely to experience clinical relapse, have a longer duration of illness, show less effective coping response, and respond poorly to drug treatment (Kuipers, 1988; Mintz, 1989; Priebe, 1989). The processes responsible for this relationship are not well understood, but we believe that emotional expression and communication, and how they contribute to emotional education and competence, are central. Indeed, it may be that distorted emotional communication is involved in the etiology and maintenance of schizophrenia, as well as playing a role in relapse.

Second, this research has important therapeutic implications. It can reveal the emotional communication style of the individual patient and his or her emotional interactions with specific family members. It is important—perhaps vital—to teach patients about their own feelings and desires (emotional reeducation) and also to teach them how to judge appropriately emotional stimuli. Also, family members and relatives could be taught how to be sensitive to the patient's emotional communication style. This could help in reducing the stress associated with emotional miscommunication. This would be in effect an "emotional reeducation" of the dynamic family system.

In conclusion, the SVT is a fast, efficient, inexpensive, and proven way to "tap into" the emotional expressiveness and communication in patients and their families. In the future, it should be possible to learn about the emotional styles of *each* of the family members involved and how they interpret *each others'* emotions. In this way, emotional communication within specific family relationships can be analyzed.

Notes

1. The process by which a child learns about affects or Emotion III responses is termed *social biofeedback* because it constitutes a naturally occurring social process that has all of the essential ingredients of the biofeedback paradigm. The biofeedback signal gives one information about an otherwise inaccessible bodily response, affording some control over it. Just so, others give information about the feelings and desires we are experiencing by responding to our expressive behaviors.

2. Spontaneous communication does not function at the level of reflexes and instincts, as some (e.g., Fridlund, 1991) have averred. Although it is in itself an SPPS based on phylogenetic adaptation, it functions at levels in the hierarchy of control systems in the brain where there is considerable interaction with GPPSs involving conditioning, learning, and higher order cognitive processing, and consequently great flexibility of functioning (Buck, 1985, 1988, 1994). The primes on which spontaneous communication is based are SPPSs that are biologically based, phylogenetically structured, and therefore pancultural. They are not inflexible, but rather are *inherently flexible*, insofar as they interact with GPPSs.

3. Figures are given for the comparison of scenic, unpleasant, and unusual slides. Familiar slides were analyzed separately.

Acknowledgments   Preparation of this chapter was supported by NIMH Grant RO1 40753 to Ross Buck, and by the University of Connecticut Research Foundation.

References

Bandura, A., & Walters, R. H. (1963). *Social learning and personality development*. New York: Holt, Rinehart & Winston.

Bebbington, P. E. (1992, July). A meta-analysis of predictive studies of expressed emotion in schizophrenia. Paper presented at the twenty-fifth International Congress of Psychology, Brussels.

Borod, J. C., Koff, E., Perlman Lorch, M., & Nicholas, M. (1985). Channels of emotional expression in patients with unilateral brain damage. *Archives of Neurology, 42*, 345–348.

Buck, R. (1983). Emotional development and emotional education. In R. Plutchik & H. Kellerman (Eds.), *Emotion in early development* (pp. 259–292). New York: Academic Press.

Buck, R. (1984). *The communication of emotion*. New York: Guilford Press.

Buck, R. (1985). Prime theory: An integrated view of motivation and emotion. *Psychological Review, 92*, 389–413.

Buck, R. (1988). *Human motivation and emotion* (2nd ed.). New York: Wiley.

Buck, R. (1990). William James and current issues in emotion, cognition, and communication. *Personality and Social Psychology Bulletin, 16*, 612–625.

Buck, R. (1991a). Motivation, emotion, and cognition: A developmental-interactionist view. In K. T. Strongman (Ed.), *International review of studies of emotion* (vol. 1, pp. 101–142). Chichester: Wiley.

Buck, R. (1991b). Social factors in facial display and communication: A reply to Chovil and others. *Journal of Nonverbal Behavior, 15*(3), 155–162.

Buck, R. (1993a). Emotional communication, emotional competence, and physical illness: A developmental-interactionist view. In J. Pennebaker & H. Traue (Eds.), *Emotional expressiveness, inhibition, and health* (pp. 32–36). New York: Hogrefe & Huber.

Buck, R. (1993b). What is this thing called subjective experience? Reflections on the neuropsychology of qualia. *Neuropsychology, 7*, 490–499.

Buck, R. (1994). Social and emotional functions in facial expression and communication: The readout hypothesis. *Biological Psychology, 38*, 95–115.

Buck, R., & Duffy, R. J. (1980). Nonverbal communication of affect in brain-damaged patients. *Cortex, 16*, 351–362.

Buck, R., Baron, R., & Barrette, D. (1982). The temporal organization of spontaneous emotional expression: A segmentation analysis. *Journal of Personality and Social Psychology, 42*, 506–517.

Buck, R., & Ginsburg, B. (1991). Emotional communication and altruism: The communicative gene hypothesis. In M. Clark (Ed.), *Altruism. Review of personality and social psychology* (Vol. 11, pp. 149–175). Newbury Park, CA: Sage.

Buck, R., Losow, J., Murphy, M., & Costanzo, P. (1991). Social facilitation and inhibition of emotional expression and communication. *Journal of Personality and Social Psychology, 63*, 962–968.

Buck, R., Maxon, A., & Norelli, N. (1991). *Emotional communication and coping in hearing-impaired persons* (UCONN Research Foundation Grant B91 923501). University of Connecticut, Storrs, CT.

Chovil, N. (1991). Social determinants of facial display. *Journal of Nonverbal Behavior, 15*(3), 141–154.

Chovil, N., & Fridlund, A. J. (1991). Why emotionality cannot equal sociality: Reply to Buck. *Journal of Nonverbal Behavior, 15*(3), 163–168.

Dodge, K., & Crick, N. R. (1990). Social information-processing bases of aggressive behavior in children. *Personality and Social Psychology Bulletin, 16*, 8–22.

Easton, C. J. (1994). *Expression and communication of emotion in schizophrenic patients.* Unpublished doctoral dissertation, University of Connecticut.

Easton, C. J., Norelli, N., & Buck, R. (1992, August). Spontaneous facial/gestural expression in brain-damaged patients: A segmentation analysis. Paper presented at the meeting of the International Society for Research on Emotions, Carnegie-Mellon University, Pittsburgh, PA.

Ekman, P., & Friesen, W. V. (1975). *Unmasking the face.* Englewood Cliffs, NJ: Prentice-Hall.

Ekman, P., & Friesen, W. V. (1978). *The facial action coding system (FACS): A technique for the measurement of facial action.* Palo Alto, CA: Consulting Psychologists Press.

Flack, W. F., Jr., Miller, D. R., & Cavallaro, L. A. (1992, July). Nonverbal communication and social cognition in psychosis. Paper presented at the twenty-fifth International Congress of Psychology, Brussels.

Fridlund, A. J. (1991). Sociality of solitary smiling: Potentiation by an implicit audience. *Journal of Personality and Social Psychology, 60*, 229–240.

Goldman, C. K. (1993). *The relationship of emotional communication to social competence: The role of communication accuracy in behaviorally disordered children's social functioning.* Doctoral dissertation, University of Connecticut, Storrs.

Goldman, C. K., & Buck, R. (1992, August). *Communication of specific emotions in emotionally disturbed and comparison children.* Paper presented at the meeting of the International Society for Research on Emotions, Carnegie-Mellon University, Pittsburgh, PA.

Gray, J. A. (1982). Precis of *The neuropsychology of anxiety* (with commentaries). *The Behavioral and Brain Sciences, 5*, 469–534.

Gresham, F. M., & Elliott, S. N. (1990). *Social Skills Rating System.* Circle Pines, MN: American Guidance Service.

Hufnaegel, H., Steimer-Krause, E., & Krause, R. (1991). Facial behavior and emotional experiencing within schizophrenic patients and healthy subjects. *The German Journal of Psychology, 20,* 356–370.

Jenkins, H., & Karno, M. (1992). The meaning of expressed emotion: Theoretical issues raised by cross-cultural research. *American Journal of Psychiatry, 149,* 9–20.

Krause, R., Steimer, E., Sanger-Alt, C., & Wagner, G. (1989). Facial expression of schizophrenic patients and their interaction partners. *Psychiatry, 52,* 1–12.

Kuipers, L. (1988). Expressed emotion research in schizophrenia. *Psychological Medicine, 18,* 893–909.

LaRusso, L. (1978). Sensitivity of paranoid patients to nonverbal cues. *Journal of Abnormal Psychology, 8,* 463–471.

Mandal, M. K. (1987). Decoding of facial emotions, in terms of expressiveness, by schizophrenics and depressives. *Psychiatry, 50,* 271–376.

Mandal, M. K. (1989a). Identification of brief presentations of facial expressions of affects in schizophrenics. *International Journal of Psychology, 24,* 605–616.

Mandal, M. K. (1989b). Identifying the components of facial emotion and schizophrenia. *British Journal of Psychiatry, 22,* 295–300.

Mandal, M. K. (1990). Identification of brief presentations of facial expressions of affects in schizophrenics. *International Journal of Psychology, 25,* 351.

Mintz, M. K. (1989). The initial onset of schizophrenia and family expressed emotion. *British Journal of Psychiatry, 154,* 212–217.

Miller, N. E., & Dollard, J. (1941). *Social learning and imitation.* New Haven, CT: Yale University Press.

Miller, R. E., Banks, J., & Ogawa, N. (1963). Role of facial expression in "cooperative avoidance conditioning" in monkeys. *Journal of Abnormal and Social Psychology, 67,* 24–30.

Nemiah, J. C., & Sifneos, P. E. (1970). Psychosomatic illness: Problem in communication. *Psychotherapy and Psychosomatics, 18,* 154–160.

Newtson, D., Engquist, G., & Bois, J. (1977). The objective basis of behavior units. *Journal of Personality and Social Psychology, 35,* 847–862.

Priebe, S. (1989). Lithium prophylaxis and expressed emotion. *British Journal of Psychiatry, 154,* 396–399.

Reardon, K., & Buck, R. (1989). Emotion, reason, and communication in coping with cancer. *Health Communication, 1,* 41–54.

Wagner, H., Buck, R., & Winterbotham, M. (1993). Communication of specific emotions: Sending accuracy and communication measures. *Journal of Nonverbal Behavior, 17*(1), 29–53.

Wagner, H., & Smith, J. (1991). Facial expression in the presence of friends and strangers. *Journal of Nonverbal Behavior, 15*(4), 201–214.

Walker, E., McGuire, M., & Bettes, B. (1984). Recognition and identification of facial stimuli by schizophrenics and patients with affective disorders. *British Journal of Clinical Psychology, 23,* pp. 37–44.

Walker, H. M., Shinn, M. R., O'Neill, R. E., & Ramsey, E. (1987). A longitudinal assessment of the development of antisocial behavior in boys: Rationale, methodology, and first-year results. *Remedial and Special Education, 8,* 7–16, 27.

22

William F. Flack, Jr., James D. Laird,
Lorraine A. Cavallaro, & Daniel R. Miller

Emotional Expression and Experience

A Psychosocial Perspective on Schizophrenia

Basic research on emotion and clinical investigations of emotion in the various psychopathologies have proceeded largely independently of one another. In this chapter, we describe a program of research in which ideas and methods developed by academic social psychologists to study emotions are employed to investigate the problem posed by discrepancies between emotional behavioral expression and subjective experience of emotion in schizophrenia. We begin by summarizing our concepts of emotion and of schizophrenia, then review briefly the work that has been conducted on expressive behaviors and subjective emotional experiences of normals and of people diagnosed as schizophrenic. Finally, we describe how our perspectives on schizophrenia and on emotion might be linked up in a single theory.

Basic Concepts

Emotion

Numerous definitions of emotion are proposed in various chapters of this book. We find it most useful to think of emotion as a pattern of response that includes an eliciting stimulus, such as a bear or a baby; some appraisal of that stimulus event as threatening or inviting; an instinctive behavioral response, such as fleeing or cuddling; expressive behavior, such as the facial expression of fear or happiness; a set of psychophysiological reactions; and a subjective experience or feeling, such as fear or happiness. Investigators are agreed that these are all important aspects of emotional response (Kleinginna & Kleinginna, 1981), but they are decidedly at odds when they postulate the ones that occur in every emotional episode, their sequential ordering, their relative importance, and their respective roles in an emotional episode. Workers reared in different scientific traditions differ in their emphasis on one or more of the component processes over others. Although we have focused on the expressive and experiential aspects of emotional response in our own work, we believe that any adequate theory of emotion must account for the functioning of each component process relative to the others.

Among the disagreements about the organization of emotional processes, we are most interested in those regarding the relationship between feelings and overt emotional behavior. The controversy over the relationship between emotional feelings and behavior arose with William James's theory of emotion.

James, Tomkins, and the Role of Expression in Emotional Experience

Our work on emotion is based on the theory of emotion that is most often associated with William James (1884). James proposed that common sense leads to the incorrect assumption that emotional feelings are the causes of emotional behavior. Instead, he argued, emotional behaviors occur automatically in response to appropriate instigating circumstances, and the subjective experience of these "bodily changes" as they are occurring is the emotional feeling. He concludes, then, that the feeling is a consequence of experiencing the behavioral reaction.

While James came to emphasize autonomic changes occurring during emotions, other investigators, such as Tomkins (1962, 1963, 1982), feel that expressive behavior, especially of the face, is the most important determinant of emotional feelings. Because Tomkins's publications have had a significant influence on subsequent workers in this field, the largest proportion of the research has focused on facial expressions.

One means of exploring the relationship between emotional expression and experience is to manipulate expressive behavior directly, and then assess the emotional feelings that follow the expression. The results of numerous studies are consistent with James's basic prediction: When people are induced to adopt the facial expressions commonly associated with particular emotions, they report corresponding feelings (for reviews see Adelman & Zajonc, 1988; Izard, 1990; Laird, 1984; Laird & Bresler, 1992).

The same kinds of effects have been observed with emotional behaviors other than facial expressions as well, including bodily postures (Duclos et al., 1989; Flack, Laird, & Cavallaro, 1995), gaze (Kellerman, Lewis, & Laird, 1989), tone of voice (Siegman & Boyle, 1993), and breathing patterns (Couture et al., 1995; Phillippot, Chapelle, & Blairy, 1994). The evidence indicates that any kind of behavior that we recognize as distinctively associated with a particular emotional feeling is capable of generating that feeling.

If expressive behaviors are specific to individual categories of emotion, then their impact on subjective experiences should be equally specific. For example, expressions of anger and fear should produce feelings of anger and fear, and not experiences of, for instance, sadness and happiness. Exactly this specific effect has been observed with facial expressions and bodily postures (Duclos et al., 1989). Furthermore, the impact of expressions and postures of the same emotion are additive when they are combined (Flack et al., 1995).

In sum, a great deal of evidence demonstrates that, contrary to the common-sense assumption, feelings are generated by emotional behaviors. Feelings seem to be information about ongoing emotional behavior (Laird & Bresler, 1992).

Schizophrenia

Our view of schizophrenia overlaps partially with that contained in the current psychiatric nosology (*Diagnostic and Statistical Manual of Mental Disorders*, 4th ed.; hereinafter DSM-IV; American Psychiatric Association, 1994), but is derived more directly from theory and observation than historical clinical tradition (Flack & Miller, 1991). Schizophrenia, we think, is most usefully defined as one of a number of disorders of interpersonal functioning (Miller & Jaques, 1988). More specifically, schizophrenic behavior consists principally of unusual frequencies, sequences, and qualities of nonverbal behavior (Flack & Miller, 1991). These unusual nonverbal behaviors are severely disruptive to the sort of communication that usually takes place when two people are conversing face to face. Schizophrenic conduct has extreme consequences for the welfare of the social group, and is thereby identified by the group because it interferes with the social interactions required to accomplish the work of the society.

Note that this is an alternative *definition* of, or way of recognizing, schizophrenia, and not another etiological proposal. This concept does not imply any particular assumptions about cause, such as the proposition that schizophrenia is a disease (as is the case in the medical model), but rather is open to a wide range of etiological hypotheses—genetic, neurodevelopmental, biochemical, neuroanatomical, psychological, interpersonal, and/or sociological ones. What we are emphasizing is that, whatever the etiology, the critical, defining feature of schizophrenia is the disruption of nonverbal behaviors that are essential to full and effective social communication.

Where our conception overlaps with that in the DSM-IV is in the notion of negative symptoms, which denotes the absence of certain behaviors such as emotional expressions. We agree that people who come to be identified as schizophrenic often fail to behave in ways that others expect. This is both the central defining feature of negative symptoms, and the reason that communication with others most often breaks down in schizophrenia. Positive symptoms, such as delusions and hallucinations, are perhaps more flagrant and "noticeable," but as criteria for identifying schizophrenia, they are inadequate because they usually occur sporadically even in acute stages of the disorder.

Emotional Expression and Experience in Schizophrenia

One negative symptom that has recently received increased attention from investigators is the diminution of emotional expression, usually called *blunted* or *flattened affect*. Inexpressiveness is destructive to social interaction. Any of the meanings of verbal utterances are conveyed, modified, or "commented on," by their nonverbal concomitants, such as facial expression, bodily posture, prosody, and volume of speech. Talk without expression is talk in which meaning has been distorted. When partners to an interaction are not able to understand each other because of a fundamental rent in conversation, communication can be markedly disrupted.

If people who are schizophrenic diminish their expression of emotions, can they experience them? Despite the emphasis placed on disturbances of emotion in psychopathology and, more specifically, in schizophrenia, both historically (Bleuler, 1911/1950; Kraepelin, 1909/1917) and currently (American Psychiatric Association, 1994), very few attempts have been made to understand the connections between the components of emotional episodes in this disorder by empirical means (Berrios, 1985). Results of the four investigations (Berenbaum & Oltmanns, 1992; Brown, Sweeney, & Schwartz, 1979; Krause, Steimer-Krause, & Hufnagel, 1992; Kring, Kerr, Smith, & Neale, 1993) in which the relationship between overt expression and subjective emotional feeling in schizophrenia has been studied can be summarized in two broad conclusions. First, discrepancies of emotional expression and feeling do not appear to be specific to schizophrenia, as has been proposed by some authors (Lehmann & Cancro, 1985). Second, inexpressiveness, or blunted affect, does not necessarily correspond to an absence of reported emotional feeling in this disorder.

These studies leave some interesting questions unanswered. If schizophrenics report emotional experiences in the event of diminished, or even absent, emotional expression, what is the relationship between expression and feeling in this disorder? Does this mean that James's account of the development of emotion lacks relevance to schizophrenia? Our first study of emotional processes in psychological disorder was designed to assess the impact of expressive behavior on emotional experience.

The Role of Expressive Behavior in Emotional Experience in Schizophrenia

In our first clinical study (Flack, 1993), we manipulated five facial expressions and four bodily postures in outpatient groups: male schizophrenics, unipolar depressives, and nonpsychiatric controls. The clinical study was also replicated with college students. The findings reveal that the normals react to their own expressive behavior pretty much as previous, nonclinical samples of normals had. Depressives fail to show any statistically significant association between their facial expressions or bodily postures and their emotional feelings. Schizophrenics tended to fall somewhere in between the other two groups. On the one hand, regarding their responses to facial expressions, the schizophrenic group was largely comparable to the normals. That is, when instructed unknowingly to adopt a facial expression of sadness, for example, subjects in the schizophrenic group tended to report more sadness than in the other, non-sad expression conditions. On the other hand, schizophrenics did not perform as well in responding to their bodily postures. In fact, in three out of four conditions, the schizophrenic group tended to report greater feelings of emotions that did not match a particular posture. These results represent an anomaly, and may be attributable to difficulties in producing manipulations of some postures, especially one for happiness (Flack et al., 1995). In this chapter, we concentrate on the results for facial expressions, which indicate that schizophrenics often show effects similar to those routinely found among normals.

In the context of a Jamesian perspective on emotion, one theoretically interesting difference between the findings from normal, nonclinical samples and the clinical data we have gathered from psychiatric patients is the signal-to-noise ratio with respect to subjects' ratings of their feelings across conditions of expression or posture. This ratio consists of the difference between the rating of a feeling matching a given expression and ratings of the same feeling during nonmatching expressions. At least in the case of the impact of facial expressions on feelings, this difference is consistently greater in the normal samples than in the clinical ones. If the smaller ratio in schizophrenia is reliable, this may provide one explanation as to why such patients have difficulty in identifying their own emotions. That is, facial expressions in normals tend to cause both a relatively high level of emotional feeling that matches the expression, and a low level of generalized emotional arousal that is reflected in ratings (which tend to be greater than zero) of the same emotional feelings in noncorresponding expression conditions (Duclos et al., 1989; Flack et al., 1995). In schizophrenics, this level of generalized arousal is greater, resulting in less differentiation between the feeling being expressed and other, "competing" feelings. Confusion about how one is feeling is the most likely result, and such confusion is commonly reported by schizophrenic patients.

So what do we know about emotional expressions and feelings in schizophrenia? On the one hand, we know that many schizophrenics show little or no expressive behavior. On the other, they report normal levels of emotional feelings (Kring et al., 1993). And if unknowingly instructed to adopt emotional expressions, they often tend to respond with increases in the appropriate feelings. Perhaps, then, if schizophrenics produced more expressive behavior naturally, they would be better able to experience their own emotional feelings; workers in the tradition of psychiatric rehabilitation claim that this is one effect of social skills training (Liberman, DeRisi, & Meuser, 1989). Schizophrenics' flattened affect might, then, be an attempt to control and dampen the intensity of their own emotional experiences (Strauss, Rakfeldt, Harding, & Lieberman, 1989).

The deliberate dampening of expressive behavior does reduce the intensity of emotional feelings in normals. If normal subjects are prevented from expressing themselves spontaneously, in effect demonstrating "flattened affect," they report diminished emotional responses while watching films (Laird et al., 1994) and to relived unpleasant memories (Duclos, 1992). Interference with expressiveness even reduces the unpleasantness of electric shocks (Lanzetta, Cartwright-Smith, & Kleck, 1976). Among normals, inhibiting one's expressive behavior is clearly a good technique for controlling one's feelings (Laird & Apostoleris, 1996).

The evidence, although sketchy, suggests that flattened expressive behavior in schizophrenics may be a self-control strategy adopted to reduce the intensity of their emotional feelings. Such a "strategy" is not, of course, adopted consciously, since self-perception processes usually take place outside of awareness (Laird & Bressler, 1992). The problem with such dramatic inhibition of expressive behavior is that the person can no longer give an outward indication of their emotional state in face-to-face interaction. The price of emotional self-control for the schizophrenic is further disruption of social interaction, which in turn will produce more distress, and perhaps greater flattening, in another of those negative spirals so common in psychological disorder.

Expressive Abnormality and Disruptions of Social Interaction

Social interaction may be disrupted because schizophrenics are unable to understand, or empathize with, others with whom they are interacting. Capella (1993) and Hatfield, Caccioppo, and Rapson (1993) note that the effects of peripheral feedback from facial expressions may play a crucial role in the successful face-to-face interaction. Their position can be traced to Mead (1934, 1982), who attributed the development of a sense of self to the adoption of expressive conduct similar to that of social partners; the feelings that are a direct result of such behavior contribute to a sense of mutual emotional understanding, or empathy.

The process assumed by Capella, Hatfield et al., and Mead entails this reasoning. Assume an ongoing interaction between participants A and B. In order for A to understand B during a conversation, A must not only listen to and comprehend what B says, but A must also understand B's nonverbal behavior in order to know what B means and feels. Since A cannot experience B's feelings, A must (a) be sensitive to B's expressive behavior, (b) express that behavior herself, perhaps in an attenuated form, and then (c) identify in herself the emotional feeling that corresponds to that behavior. If A's ability to perceive the impact of peripheral feedback from her own conduct is working properly, then she is able to understand, both cognitively and emotionally, B's communication.

Problems will arise, however, when either or both partners cannot employ this sequence with sufficient skill. If A attempts to adopt the smile that she perceives (correctly) on B's face, and then feels happy, all is well. If, however, A also adopts a slouched-over posture at the same time, she is likely to feel a combination of both happiness and sadness, which may or may not correspond to B's emotional experience. To make matters worse, if the adoption of A's bodily posture does not result in a feeling matching the posture, A may experience another feeling entirely, or even feel confused about how she is feeling, thus making it impossible for A to be clear about what is going on in B.

Consider another instance of communication, in which A mimics B's bodily posture of sadness and, consequently, feels sad. Suppose that B's sad posture causes B to feel angry rather than sad. In that event, even though A's expressions are having the normal impact on her feelings, since B's are not, A cannot know how B is feeling, and they cannot make meaningful, successful contact with each other. Interpersonal communication can also be disrupted when other aspects of partners' emotional responses are disordered as well, including the perception, or decoding, or expressive behavior. And disordered responses can occur in any of the nonverbal channels, including facial expression, bodily posture, vocal expression, and gesture.

In this section, we have suggested ways in which abnormalities of the expression-experience relationship may interfere with interpersonal communication. Obviously, these speculations await empirical verification. But the findings to date regarding both normal and abnormal relationships between emotional expression and subjective feeling in schizophrenia suggest that this research may prove fruitful in providing an explanation of why emotions and social interactions break down in this disorder.

References

Adelman, P. K., & Zajonc, R. B. (1988). Facial efference and the experience of emotion. *Annual Review of Psychology, 40,* 249–280.

American Psychiatric Association. (1994). *Diagnostic and statistical manual of mental disorders* (4th ed.). Washington, DC: Author.

Berenbaum, H., & Oltmanns, T. F. (1992). Emotional experience and expression in schizophrenia and depression. *Journal of Abnormal Psychology, 101,* 37–44.

Berrios, G. E. (1985). The psychopathology of affectivity: Conceptual and historical aspects. *Psychological Medicine, 15,* 745–758.

Bleuler, E. (1950). *Dementia praecox or the group of schizophrenias.* New York: International Universities Press. (Original work published 1911)

Brown, S. L., Sweeney, D. R., & Schwartz, G. E. (1979). Differences between self-reported and observed pleasure in depression and schizophrenia. *Journal of Nervous and Mental Disease, 167,* 410–415.

Capella, J. N. (1993). The facial feedback hypothesis in human interaction: Review and speculation. *Journal of Language and Social Psychology, 12,* 13–29.

Couture, J., Bourgeois, P., Herrera, P., Blairy, S., Hess, U., & Phillipot, P. (1995). *Induction d'emotions par feedback facial et respiratoire.* Paper presented at the eighteenth annual meeting of the Societe Quebecoise de la Recherche en Psychologie, Ottawa, Ontario, Canada.

Duclos, S. E. (1992). *The self-determination of emotional experience.* Unpublished Ph.D. dissertation, Clark University, Worcester, MA.

Duclos, S. E., Laird, J. D., Schneider, E., Sexter, M., Stern, L., & Van Lighten, O. (1989). Emotion-specific effects of facial expressions and postures on emotional experience. *Journal of Personality and Social Psychology, 57,* 100–108.

Flack, W. F., Jr. (1993). Emotions in schizophrenia. (From *Dissertation Abstracts International, 54-04B,* 2197 [University Microfilms No. 9323639])

Flack, W. F., Jr., Laird, J. D., & Cavallaro, L. A. (1995). *Separate and additive effects of facial expressions and bodily postures on emotional feelings.* Unpublished manuscript.

Flack, W. F., Jr., & Miller, D. R. (1991). Social interaction and schizophrenia: Problem, theory, and research. *Schizophrenia Research, 4,* 303.

Hatfield, E., Caccioppo, J. T., & Rapson, R. L. (1993). Emotional contagion. *Current Directions in Psychological Science, 2,* 96–99.

Izard, C. E. (1990). Facial expressions and the regulation of emotions. *Journal of Personality and Social Psychology, 58,* 487–498.

James, W. (1884). What is an emotion? *Mind, 9,* 188–205.

Kellerman, J., Lewis, J., & Laird, J. D. (1989). Looking and loving: The effects of mutual gaze on feelings of romantic love. *Journal of Research in Personality, 23,* 145–161.

Kleinginna, P. R., Jr., & Kleinginna, A. M. (1981). A categorized list of emotion definitions, with suggestions for a consensual definition. *Motivation and Emotion, 5,* 345–379.

Kraepelin, E. (1917). *Clinical psychiatry: A textbook for students and physicians.* New York: Macmillan. (Original work published 1907)

Krause, R., Steimer-Krause, E., & Hufnagel, H. (1992). Expression and experience of affects in paranoid schizophrenia. *European Review of Applied Psychology, 42,* 131–138.

Kring, A. M., Kerr, S. L., Smith, D. A., & Neale, J. M. (1993). Flat affect in schizophrenia does not reflect diminished subjective experience of emotion. *Journal of Abnormal Psychology, 102,* 507–517.

Laird, J. D. (1984). The real role of facial response in the experience of emotion: A reply to

Tourangeau and Ellsworth, and others. *Journal of Personality and Social Psychology,* 47, 909–917.

Laird, J. D., Alibozak, T., Davainis, D., Deignan, K., Fontanella, K., Hong, J., Levy, B., & Pacheco, C. (1994). Individual differences in the effects of spontaneous mimicry on emotional contagion. *Motivation and Emotion, 18,* 231–246.

Laird, J. D., & Apostoleris, N. H. (1996). Emotional self-control and self-perception: Feelings are the solution, not the problem. In R. Harre & G. W. Parrott (Eds.), *The emotions: Social, cultural and physical dimensions.* London: Sage.

Laird, J. D., & Bressler, C. (1992). The process of emotional feeling: A self-perception theory. In M. Clark (Ed.), *Emotion: Review of Personality and Social Psychology* (Vol. 13, pp. 223–234). Newbury Park, CA: Sage.

Lanzetta, J. T., Cartwright-Smith, J., & Kleck, R. E. (1976). Effects of nonverbal dissimilation on emotional experience and autonomic arousal. *Journal of Personality and Social Psychology, 33,* 354–370.

Lehmann, H. E., & Cancro, R. (1985). Schizophrenia: Clinical features. In H. I. Kaplan & B. J. Sadock (Eds.), *Comprehensive textbook of psychiatry* (4th ed., Vol. 4) (pp. 680–712). Baltimore: Williams & Wilkins.

Liberman, R. P., DeRisi, W. J., & Mueser, K. T. (1989). *Social skills training for psychiatric patients.* New York: Pergamon Press.

Mead, G. H. (1934). *Mind, self, and society: From the standpoint of a social behaviorist.* Chicago: University of Chicago Press.

Mead, G. H. (1982). *The individual and the social self: Unpublished work of George Herbert Mead.* Chicago: University of Chicago Press.

Miller, D. R., & Jaques, E. (1988). Identifying madness. In H. J. O'Gorman (Ed.), *Surveying social life: Essays in honor of Hubert H. Hyman.* Middletown, CT: Wesleyan University Press.

Phillippot, P., Chapelle, G., & Blairy, S. (1994). Respiratory feedback in the generation of emotion. In N. Frijda (Ed.), *Proceedings of the VIIIth Conference of the International Society for Research on Emotion* (pp. 265–286). Cambridge.

Siegman, A. W., & Boyle, S. (1993). Voices of fear and anxiety and sadness and depression: The effects of speech rate and loudness on fear and anxiety and sadness and depression. *Journal of Abnormal Psychology, 102,* 430–437.

Strauss, J. S. Rakfeldt, J., Harding, C. M., & Lieberman, P. (1989). Psychological and social aspects of negative symptoms. *British Journal of Psychiatry, 155*(Suppl. 7), 128–132.

Tomkins, S. S. (1962). *Affect, imagery, consciousness: Vol. 1. The positive affects.* New York: Springer.

Tomkins, S. S. (1963). *Affect, imagery, consciousness: Vol. 2. The negative affects.* New York: Springer.

Tomkins, S. S. (1982). Affect theory. In P. Ekman (Ed.), *Emotion in the human face* (2nd ed.) (pp. 355–395). Cambridge: Cambridge University Press.

23

Heiner Ellgring & Marcia Smith

Affect Regulation During Psychosis

Affective disturbance is a hallmark of psychopathological disorders. In this chapter, we describe dysregulation of the affect system as it applies to psychosis, specifically to individuals with schizophrenia. We then present data related to facial expression, an efferent component of the affect system, and its role in affect regulation in schizophrenia.

Use of Terms

In accordance with most theorists, emotional reactions are regarded here as comprising affective arousal, subjective feeling, and expressive behavior, such as facial expression, although the nature of emotional experience and the relationships among the components are still in debate. The terms *affect, emotion*, and *feeling* are frequently used interchangeably. Such use may obscure important structural and functional differences, but reflects the current state of knowledge. According to Batson, Shaw, and Oleson (1992), *affect* refers to the physiological activity of the organism in response to current conditions. Its function is to inform the organism about changes in conditions to more or less valued states; thus, affect has both valence and intensity. Humans show an innate preference for positive affect over negative. Affects function as signals that homeostasis no longer exists, and mobilize or terminate actions and cognitions that serve to regain homeostasis. Batson et al. (1992) state that *emotion* refers to a specific type of affective state in relation to a specific goal. *Feeling* or *feeling state* is used by other theorists (e.g., Izard, 1990) synonymously with *emotion experience*, referring to the subjective representation of the autonomic components.

Thus, we will use the term *affect* to mean physiological responses to changes in internal or external stimulus conditions, *feeling* to refer to the subjective interpretation of these experiences, and *emotion* to refer more generally to both affect and feeling: the bodily reaction together with its subjective representation. We acknowledge, however, that there is no clear consensus regarding use of these terms.

Understanding the relationships among these components is important for understanding emotional disturbances, and, conversely, the study of disorders may be useful for understanding normal interrelationships.

Models of Emotion Regulation in Healthy Individuals

Synchronization of Subsystems

Most emotion theorists assume that the components of an emotional response are closely interrelated, but these relationships are given a particularly important role in Scherer's (1993) component process theory. Scherer maintains that a key concept regarding emotion is that it represents a "temporary synchronization" through the central nervous system, of all principal subsystems. In component process theory these include physiological response, subjective feeling, motor system, cognition, and motivation. This synchronization occurs when the organism is faced with a stimulus that is judged to be relevant to its concerns. During nonemotional states, these systems are thought to function independently. The subsystems are all interrelated through a complex network of feedback and feedforward processes. Cognition, for example, which affects each of the other subsystems directly, may be particularly important for triggering the onset of the emotional process, and is involved in subjective feeling. Subjective feeling is seen as part of a monitoring system that reflects the current state of all other systems.

Synchrony Within a Social System

Synchrony is important not only for interactions within an individual, but also for interactions between individuals. Social factors can exert an important influence on emotional regulatory processes. This influence is described by Krause, Steimer, Sänger-Alt, and Wagner (1989), who believe that facial and vocal expressions are themselves part of an interactive social and emotional regulatory system. This notion is based on the idea that emotion has both externally motivated and self-motivated functions. Externally motivated functions include informing others of the person's current disposition and intentions, and inducing others to react. Self-motivated functions include the regulation of needs and preferences, preparation for action, and interruption of ongoing action.

Multiple Functions of Emotion

From the foregoing it seems appropriate to recognize the multiple functions of emotion. We suggest that these functions be grouped under the categories of social regulation and internal regulation, focusing on the target of regulation.

Social Regulation

The expression of emotions can stimulate and influence the social environment, providing social regulation, which may affect the relationships within a dyad, group, or society. Social distance, level of personal intimacy, and dominance hierarchies are examples of social homeostatic processes that can be created, maintained, or disrupted through the communication of emotional expressions. This social regulation is normally performed without conscious awareness.

Internal Regulation: Direct Influence

The expression of emotions can influence internal homeostasis through direct routes or indirect routes. Direct influence may be achieved through facial feedback, according to some theorists, although the idea has remained controversial for decades. Izard (1990) maintains that the degree to which expressive behavior may influence experience depends on the person's own stage of development and ability to regulate emotion. Controversy likewise surrounds the mechanisms by which facial feedback is believed to exert its effects; postulated mechanisms include the early notion of direct peripheral effects of sensory feedback from facial receptors (Tomkins, 1962), a central effect through efferent commands from the motor cortex to subcortical centers (Izard, 1977), self-perception (Laird, 1974), a spread in activation networks (Scherer, 1993), and even regulation of venal blood flow in the brain (Zajonc, 1985). An important aspect of facial feedback may be an increase in synchrony, consistent with Scherer's component process theory of emotion activation.

A distinction between voluntary control (via the motor cortex and pyramidal tract) and spontaneous control (via the limbic and extrapyramidal circuits) of facial expression is widely recognized (Rinn, 1984). Izard (1990) asserts that the most direct means of regulating emotions is by learning to manage spontaneous, involuntary expressions. He suggests that voluntary expressions *can* also activate emotional experiences, but that connections between these expressions and emotional feeling states must first be learned.

We further suggest the possibility that if these connections are well learned, or overlearned, they can become "automatic," in that they are performed without conscious intention or awareness, just as limb movements can come under automatic control with practice. Some facial expressions that are frequently used in social interactions within specific cultures, such as lifting of eyebrows or smiling in certain situations, may fall into this category, and may be particularly vulnerable to disruption in psychopathology. This disruption could have implications not only for social regulation, but also for internal regulation, if the learned connections with feeling states are likewise affected. To our knowledge, however, this type of overlearning of voluntary expression has not been investigated.

Internal Regulation: Indirect Influence Through Social Interactions

A more important route to internal regulation is indirect, through relationships with the environment. This regulation can be achieved in several ways.

1. The individual may try to adapt the social environment to his or her own capacity. This aspect of internal regulation has been the focus of our research on emotion regulation in psychosis. As will be described in more detail, schizophrenics tend to behave as if to prevent social communication, through a reduction of gaze and lack of social signals.
2. The individual may approach or avoid certain types of social or nonsocial stimulation, thereby affecting the degree of exposure to potential emotion-eliciting situations. For example, a depressed individual may tend to avoid social activities.
3. Emotion and its expression may become an interrupt between stimulus and action. The individual may be able to withhold or delay direct action toward others through the use of expression as a symbolic action, that is, information about possible action that may occur if demands continue or increase.

Changes in Emotion Regulatory Systems in Psychosis

From a neuroethological viewpoint, Ploog (1972) has claimed that the breakdown of the social communication system is a key process in the development of schizophrenia. We propose that in psychosis, the need for internal regulation becomes dominant, with a decreased capacity for mutual social regulation. There is considerable evidence supporting a reduction in facial expression in schizophrenia. Rather than assume a general emotional deficit, however, it can be argued that it is the association between components that is changed. A brief overview of studies on the expression of emotion in schizophrenia will next be presented, followed by our proposal for integrating these findings in a model of affective regulation during psychosis.

Prior Studies of Expression of Emotion in Schizophrenia

Jones and Pansa (1979) reported that schizophrenics tended to smile less and show less overall facial movement than controls, giving the impression of "emotional blankness," and that these characteristics did not change with clinical improvement. Similarly, Pansa-Henderson, de L'Horne, and Jones (1982) found that schizophrenics displayed detached facial expressions and averted their gaze when being interviewed.

This decrease in expression has been shown to be particularly pronounced for positive expressions. Martin, Borod, Alpert, Brozgold, and Welkowitz (1990) videotaped blunted schizophrenics while they were discussing a pleasant and an unpleasant emotional experience, and found that schizophrenics were rated as showing less positive emotion and more negative emotion, regardless of which experience they were discussing, with less overall intensity of expression.

The dissociation between expression and feeling has also been assessed. Kring, Kerr, Smith, and Neale (1993) tested whether flattened affect reflected a true diminution of emotional experience. They found that medication-free schizophrenics showed less positive expressiveness while watching a happy film, despite reporting *more* positive affect than controls. In addition, they showed less negative expressiveness during sad- and fear-inducing films. The researchers concluded that schizophrenics exhibit greater discrepancies between experience and expression than do controls, although it was not clear whether they actively inhibit expressions, are unable to show their feelings, or are not aware that they do not show normal levels of expression.

Social dynamics of facial display were addressed by Krause et al. (1989), who studied schizophrenic patients as they discussed politics in a dyad. The results indicated that although schizophrenics did not show less total facial activity, they displayed a smaller repertoire of facial movements, fewer upper face movements, fewer symmetric smiles, and less talking than control subjects. In addition, schizophrenics produced a higher percentage of negative expressions than controls, with fewer expressions of happiness. Krause et al. concluded that schizophrenics tend to react less to their partner, giving the impression of greater distance. In a later study of paranoid schizophrenics, Krause, Steimer-Krause, and Hufnagel (1992) emphasized how interactions with the patients affected normal partners. The healthy partners showed more negative affect, and reported that the talk was stressful for them.

Although the studies described above concern spontaneous expression of emotion, there is some evidence that schizophrenics also show reduced *posed* emotional facial expression in comparison to controls (Borod et al., 1989). Braun, Bernier, Proulx, and Cohen (1991) showed that when expressions were posed to auditory command, the deficit was greater for emotional than nonemotional displays.

Mechanisms Responsible for Disruption of Emotional Regulation

Role of Cognitive Deficit

What would cause this decrease in expressiveness or, as we propose, the increased need to control internal emotional processes that can lead to a decrease in expressiveness? Several lines of research have suggested that schizophrenics are in a state of sensory overload, and that some sort of *cognitive* deficit is responsible for this overload. For example, Hemsley (1992) has submitted that stimuli that should be treated as "familiar" are instead treated as "novel" because schizophrenics cannot automatically make use of redundant information. Thus, while normal individuals cease attending to redundant information, schizophrenics do not. The cognitive deficit is a disruption of the integration of past regularities of experience with current stimulus information. Although this specific model, and the integration of these concepts into a larger model of schizophrenia (Gray, Feldon, Rawlins, Hemsley, & Smith, 1991), are still in preliminary stages of validation, there is considerable evidence that a cognitive deficit of some type, most likely related to or including the disruption of attentional processes (Levin, Yurgelun-Todd, & Craft, 1989), is characteristic of schizophrenia.

Regulation of Stimulation in Response to Overload

Strauss (1987) has suggested that the functioning of schizophrenics must be adjusted to regulate the amount of external stimulation or demand, to fit the reduced capacity of the individual. This change in functioning may be manifested as negative symptoms, such as reduced speech and social withdrawal. These characteristics could thus be viewed from this perspective as adaptive strategies that are learned over time, ways of coping with the effects of positive symptoms (Carpenter, Heinrichs, & Wagman, 1988). Consistent with this notion, Ellenbroek and Cools (1990) reported in a review of animal models that negative symptoms appear to function as a "compensatory mechanism" to protect the animals from sensory overload.

Development of negative symptoms, including decreased facial expression, certainly does not appear to represent a consciously adopted coping mechanism on the part of individuals with schizophrenia, and it may be doubtful whether it could be viewed as adaptive in any true sense. However, decreased abilities to process environmental stimuli effectively may be associated with a decrease in the level of communication and synchrony with the environment, even if this adaptation is not particularly beneficial for the individual.

Evidence Against a Cognitive Basis for Emotion Dysregulation

There is also evidence that related information-processing deficits may *not* be the basis for the disruption of emotional processes found in schizophrenia. Berenbaum and Oltmanns (1992) investigated whether differences in spontaneous facial reactions depended on the cognitive demand of the stimuli. They compared facial responding to film clips, assumed to be high in cognitive demands, with tasting drinks, a task assumed to be low in cognitive demands. Blunted and nonblunted schizophrenics (all on neuroleptic medication), depressed, and normal subjects were compared. Results showed that the blunted schizophrenics and depressed subjects showed fewer facial responses in response to positive stimuli than normals or nonblunted schizophrenics, although there were no differences in levels of reported emotions. No interactions between group and cognitive demand were found, however. Thus, these results do not support the idea that deficits in emotional expression are due simply to cognitive deficits. It could be argued, however, that these negative results were obtained because the specific type of cognitive deficit proposed by Hemsley (1992) and Gray et al. (1991)—difficulty integrating past regularities with current information—was not tested in this experiment.

The Same Mechanism for Both Positive and Negative Symptomatology?

Although the sensory loading hypothesis has intuitive appeal as well as substantial supporting research, it does not explain why some schizophrenics show positive symptoms as opposed to negative symptoms, or why individuals may fluctuate between the two conditions. In an early article, Hemsley (1977) had suggested that this cognitive deficit may be responsible for *negative* symptoms, consistent with the line of reasoning presented above. In Gray et al.'s (1991) more recent elaboration of the model, however, the cognitive deficit is seen as producing *positive* symptoms. As Gray et al. speculate, a deficit of this type could in fact be responsible for both: positive symptoms occurring as schizophrenics attempt to rationalize their increased sensory experiences, to cognitively reinterpret alien perceptions; negative symptoms functioning to compensate for this overload through avoidance. Gray et al. further suggest that individual differences, severity of disease, and environmental factors may influence whether negative or positive symptoms are displayed, although there are as yet few data addressing this issue.

If this idea is true, the same patterns should be found regarding facial expression. That is, schizophrenics should show normal or increased levels of facial expression during periods of positive symptomatology, expressions that may in fact be appropriate facial expressions to abnormal (internal) emotional stimuli; and reduced facial expression during periods of negative symptomatology, reflecting avoidance of such stimuli. The type of symptoms exhibited should reflect, in some way, the person's current adaptive capacity and strategies, and may be predictable from other factors, such as severity of the psychotic state. We will argue, however, that in both conditions facial expressions would be dissociated from their social function.

Longitudinal Studies of Facial Expression in Schizophrenia

In the following, we will present longitudinal research from our group, to illustrate the changes in schizophrenic behavior on which many of our ideas were based. Ellgring and Gaebel (1995) compared three groups of subjects: patients with schizophrenia ($n = 37$), depression ($n = 28$, including neurotic depressed and endogenous depressed), and healthy controls ($n = 30$). Patients were tested at three different time points: at the beginning of their clinical stay (T0), 4 weeks later (T1), and at discharge (T2).

Spontaneous facial expressions were videotaped while subjects watched positive and negative emotion-eliciting films and were administered standardized interviews. Videotapes were coded using Ekman and Friesen's (1978) Facial Action Coding System (FACS), which describes visible facial movement based on an anatomical analysis of facial action, requiring examination of 44 separate action units (AUs). These AUs can occur alone or in combination with other AUs.

Results showed that facial expression was reduced in the schizophrenics and depressed patients in comparison with controls, consistent with prior research. The facial repertoire (number of different action units) remained low for schizophrenics from T0 to T2; in contrast, however, depressed subjects showed an increase at discharge.

The pattern of less general facial activity for schizophrenics in comparison with controls was shown both when subjects were being interviewed and while they watched positive films. Although there were no differences between groups during the sad films, this lack of differences appeared to be because control subjects also showed little expression.

Besides looking at overall activity, differences between upper and lower face movements were investigated. It was found that the differences between patients and controls were due to reduced activity in the *upper* face. Specifically, controls showed a conversational pattern that included brow raises (AUs 1 & 2) and smiles (AU 12), whereas schizophrenics more often showed movements associated with anger and disgust (AUs 14 & 17). These patterns are consistent with the findings of Krause et al. (1989), providing support for the notion that partner-oriented, socially active facial expressions are particularly lacking in this disorder.

Expressions During Speech

As an additional measure of the degree of social coordination shown by subjects, Ellgring (1986), in an earlier study, calculated the percentage of time that facial expressions occurred while speaking. For controls and relatives of schizophrenics, 80–90% of the expressions occurred while speaking. For schizophrenics, in contrast, the differences between the rates while speaking and not speaking was only at chance level. The figures for the other groups fell in between (neurotic depressed group, 75%; endogenous depressed, 60%; relatives interacting with schizophrenics, 60%).

This independence of facial expression from the speaker role indicates a dissociation of facial expression from its communicative function. In an earlier study of one schizophrenic, Condon and Ogston (1966) had reported that videotaped analyses revealed a similar pattern of lack of head movements when speaking. This result was not found by Krause et al. (1989), however. There are several possible reasons for this discrepancy. For one, Krause et al. studied schizophrenics who were in remission, whereas Ellgring (1986) tested patients during their clinical stay. Further, in the Krause et al. study, patients interacted with strangers and discussed politics; in the Ellgring study, patients interacted with relatives and discussed topics of disagreement. There was no doubt a higher level of emotional involvement in the latter study. Prior findings by Tarrier, Vaughn, Lader, and Leff (1979) that the arousal level of schizophrenics increases when relatives enter the room support this notion.

Medication Effects

Medication effects were investigated in a parallel study (Schneider et al., 1992). A group of drug-naive patients with schizophrenia or schizophreniform disorder ($n = 8$) was compared with a similar group of patients who were already medicated ($n = 8$). Subjects were tested at admission (T0), beginning at which time all subjects received medication, and 3 weeks later (T1). The previously drug-naive subjects showed a reduction in facial activity and facial expression at T1, whereas the facial behavior in the already medicated group remained unchanged. This difference thus appears to be due to effects of neuroleptics on facial expression, and suggests that without medication a substantially higher level of behavior, and presumably a higher level of emotion, is present.

Relationship to Negative Symptoms

To help clarify the role of facial expression in relation to negative symptomatology, in the study by Ellgring and Gaebel (1995) the level of general facial activity was correlated with ratings on the Scale for the Assessment of Negative Symptoms (SANS; Andreasen, 1979). At admission, this correlation was not significant, apparently due to floor effects. At discharge, however, there was a significant negative correlation for the schizophrenic group, meaning that the higher subjects scored on the negative symptom scale, the lower was their level of facial activity. This correlation was not found for the depressed group.

Implications of Findings

In sum, these results suggest the following:

1. A lack of facial activity in the upper face of schizophrenics gives the impression of less social orientation.
2. The predominance of negative affect displays shown by the schizophrenics tends to prevent the social interaction from achieving another social function, namely, continuous reassurance between participants.
3. Schizophrenics' dissociation of facial expression from the speaker role suggests that the presence of others is not an important factor for them in producing facial expression, although this presence could have increased emotion that would then have to be regulated.
4. Psychosis appears to change the relative weight of the subsystems that control emotions, at least with regard to facial expression. Normally, social regulation is very important. During psychosis, however, the main function of the affective system becomes internal regulation of physiological events whose origin cannot be traced or attributed by the patient to any outside experience or stimulus. The lack of expressive behavior can thus be seen either as an attempt to control internal affective bursts, or as an inability to produce the appropriate social expressions because of distraction by sensory overload. Under normal conditions, many of the behaviors that contribute to social regulation are "automatic" in that they are not consciously attended to (Rinn, 1984). In psychosis, however, these behaviors are no longer performed because the individual might not attend to social stimuli that would evoke such behaviors.

Conclusions and Directions for Future Research

Normally, emotional expression and experience are controlled or activated to a large degree by external stimuli, mainly social in nature (Scherer, Wallbott, & Summerfield, 1986). Facial expressions under normal conditions are thus relational actions, actions that modify the individual's relationship with the environment and express different levels of action readiness (Frijda & Tscherkassof, 1995). During psychosis, the dominance of internally generated stimuli appears to reduce the individual's ability to engage in normal interactions in the social environment. The psychotic is in a state of sensory overload (Hemsley, 1977; Strauss, 1987), presumably due to a disruption of normal information processing. This disruption, in turn, affects emotional systems—individuals may be *unable* to regulate social interactions because they are overburdened or distracted by internal physiological events, and are no longer attending to social stimuli that normally evoke interactive facial expressions. Thus, psychotic patients attend to internal regulation at the expense of social interactions, and expressive behavior loses its normal social signaling and communication function. Whether a *decrease* in facial expression is shown or not may be related to whether the individual exhibits other negative or positive symptomatology, which may, in turn, be dependent on the current coping mechanisms of the individual and may vary over time with clinical course. Even if the amount of facial behavior remains normal, however, the timing and character of the expressions show a reduced influence of social stimuli.

Future Research

Although these ideas remain speculative, they suggest several avenues for future research. For one, it is not yet clear what factors are most likely to disrupt social communication. According to the ideas presented here, however, disruption should depend in part on the degree to which stimuli arouse emotions in the individuals. Thus, increasing the emotional content of interviews, for instance, by discussing disease-related topics compared with neutral topics, should decrease the level of socially responsive facial communication. Similarly, the expressive level should decrease, while physiological arousal rises, when subjects talk with relatives (who presumably arouse more emotions) as compared with neutral strangers.

In addition, these findings have implications for the large body of research on expressed emotions (Vaughn & Leff, 1976). The impact of the patients' emotional dysfunction on the behavior of their relatives needs further clarification. Acknowledging the importance of a social theory of emotions (Rimé, Mesquita, Phillippot, & Boca, 1991), deficits in schizophrenia that reflect a lack of social sharing deserve special attention.

Another open question is the degree to which schizophrenics *could* increase their attention to social stimuli and, correspondingly, their socially relevant facial expressions, if they were aware of the problem and motivated to change. In other words, are the differences in expression due primarily to an inability to regulate affect appropriately, a lack of awareness, or a lack of motivation? To test this question, schizophrenics could be specifically instructed to interact in such a way that their emotions would be known, or concealed, from an interactant. They could also be asked to judge the intensity of their own facial expressions, and watch videotapes of themselves to see if they can identify their own emotional states. An alternative method of assessing the degree of social communication is to focus on the reactions of others, similar to Krause et al.'s (1992) study of paranoid schizophrenics, measuring subjective and behavioral reactions, including facial activity, in the partners.

To better assess the relationship between the appearance of positive versus negative symptoms, and facial expression, further longitudinal studies specifically targeting different subtypes of patients would be important. We would predict that schizophrenics who show predominantly positive symptoms would be more likely to show more, perhaps different, facial expressions compared with schizophrenics who show predominantly negative symptoms, although in neither group would expressions be normally synchronized with social cues. Similarly, intensity and type of facial expression should change as other symptoms change, for example, if an individual switched from positive to negative symptomatology.

Finally, if the reduction in facial expression in schizophrenia is indeed due to sensory overload, it may be possible to achieve the same pattern of results in normal individuals that occurs in schizophrenia by providing extraneous stimuli that must be attended to during ongoing social interactions. For example, the subjects could be instructed to attend to such stimuli through headphones while carrying on a conversation.

Clinical Implications

This line of research has relevance for the clinical assessment and treatment of psychotic disorders. Objective coding of facial expressions may provide a more sensitive measure of the level of social functioning than current global ratings, and can be used to assess patients' emotional states and capacities for social interaction through recovery. Assessment of emotions in specific contexts could become an integral part of functional diagnostics, to complement nosological concepts. This research also suggests that treatment aimed at improving the emotional condition of patients should take into account the internal as well as social consequences of the affective dysregulation, for example, by considering the emotional costs for patients when they increase social interactions. Further, relatives of individuals with psychotic disorders could be trained to recognize and respond to nonverbal emotional behaviors of the patients, and to understand their dysfunctional aspects.

In conclusion, we suggest that psychosis is associated with a breakdown of the normal balance between social and internal regulation of stimuli. Psychotic patients must devote a disproportionate amount of attention to regulate internal processes. This imbalance results in a conscious or subconscious disregard for expressions that function to facilitate social interactions.

Acknowledgments   This chapter was prepared with the assistance of the members of the CERE group, and the support of the Maison des Sciences de l'Homme, Paris. The research described was supported by DFG Grant EL67-6. The help of Katja Beck-Dossler and Norbert B. A. Wirth in developing the ideas and research discussed is very much appreciated.

References

Andreasen, N. (1979). Affective flattening and the criteria for schizophrenia. *American Journal of Psychiatry, 135,* 226–229.

Batson, C. D., Shaw, L. L., & Oleson, C. C. (1992). Differentiating affect, mood, and emotion: Toward functionally based conceptual distinctions. In M. S. Clark (Ed.), *Emotion.* London: Sage.

Berenbaum, H., & Oltmanns, T. F. (1992). Emotional experience and expression in schizophrenia and depression. *Journal of Abnormal Psychology, 101,* 37–44.

Borod, J. C., Alpert, M., Brozgold, A., Martin, C., Welkowitz, J., Diller, L., Peselow, E., Angrist, B., & Lieberman, A. (1989). A preliminary comparison of flat affect schizophrenics and brain-damaged patients on measures of affective processing. *Journal of Communicative Disorders, 22,* 93–104.

Braun, C., Bernier, S., Proulx, R., & Cohen, H. (1991). A deficit of primary affective facial expression independent of bucco-facial dyspraxia in chronic schizophrenics. *Cognition and Emotion, 5,* 147–159.

Carpenter, W. T., Heinrichs, D. W., & Wagman, A. M. I. (1988). Deficit and nondeficit forms of schizophrenia: The concept. *American Journal of Psychiatry, 145,* 578–583.

Condon, W. S., & Ogston, W. D. (1966). Sound film analysis of normal and pathological behavior patterns. *The Journal of Nervous and Mental Disease, 143,* 338–347.

Ekman, P., & Friesen, W. V. (1978). *The Facial Action Coding System (FACS)*. Palo Alto, CA: Consulting Psychologists Press.

Ellenbroek, B. A., & Cools, A. R. (1990). Animal models with construct validity for schizophrenia. *Behavioral Pharmacology, 1*, 469–490.

Ellgring, H. (1986). Nonverbal expression of psychological states in psychiatric patients. *European Archives of Psychiatry and Neurological Sciences, 236*, 31–34.

Ellgring, H., & Gaebel, W. (1995). Facial expression in schizophrenic patients. In A. Beigel, J. J. Lopez Ibor, Jr., & J. A. Costa e Silva (Eds.), *Past, present, and future of psychiatry*, vol. 1 (pp. 435–439). London: World Scientific Publisher.

Frijda, N., & Tscherkassof (1995). *Facial expression and modes of action readiness*. Manuscript in preparation.

Gray, J. A., Feldon, J., Rawlins, J. N. P., Hemsley, D. R., & Smith, A. D. (1991). The neuropsychology of schizophrenia. *Behavioral and Brain Sciences, 14*, 1–84.

Hemsley, D. R. (1977). What have cognitive deficits to do with schizophrenic symptoms? *British Journal of Psychiatry, 130*, 167–173.

Hemsley, D. R. (1992). Disorders of perception and cognition in schizophrenia. *Revue Europeenne de Psychologie Appliquee, 42*, 105–114.

Izard, C. E. (1977). *Human emotions*. New York: Plenum Press.

Izard, C. I. (1990). Facial expressions and the regulation of emotions. *Journal of Personality and Social Psychology, 58*, 487–498.

Jones, I. H., & Pansa, M. (1979). Some nonverbal aspects of depression and schizophrenia occurring during the interview. *The Journal of Nervous and Mental Disease, 167*, 402–409.

Krause, R., Steimer, E., Sänger-Alt, C., & Wagner, G. (1989). Facial expression of schizophrenic patients and their interaction partners. *Psychiatry, 52*, 1–12.

Krause, R., Steimer-Krause, E., & Hufnagel, H. (1992). Expression and experience of affects in paranoid schizophrenia. *Revue Europeenne de Psychologie Appliquee, 42*, 131–138.

Kring, A. M., Kerr, S. L., Smith, D. A., & Neale, J. M. (1993). Flat affect in schizophrenia does not reflect diminished subjective experience of emotion. *Journal of Abnormal Psychology, 102*, 507–517.

Laird, J. D. (1974). Self-attribution of emotion: The effects of expressive behavior on the quality of emotional experience. *Journal of Personality and Social Psychology, 29*, 475–486.

Levin, S., Yurgelun-Todd, D., & Craft, S. (1989). Contributions of clinical neuropsychology to the study of schizophrenia. *Journal of Abnormal Psychology, 98*, 341–356.

Martin, C. C., Borod, J. C., Alpert, M., Brozgold, A., & Welkowitz, J. (1990). Spontaneous expression of facial emotion in schizophrenic and right-brain-damaged patients. *Journal of Communicative Disorders, 23*, 287–301.

Pansa-Henderson, M., de L'Horne, D., & Jones, I. H. (1982). Nonverbal behaviour as a supplement to psychiatric diagnosis in schizophrenia, depression, and anxiety neurosis. *Journal of Psychiatric Treatment and Evaluation, 4*, 489–496.

Ploog, D. (1972). Breakdown of the social communication system: A key process in the development of schizophrenia? *Neurosciences Research Progress Bulletin, 10*, 394–395.

Rimé, B., Mesquita, B., Phillippot, B., & Boca, S. (1991). Beyond the emotional event: Six studies on the social sharing of emotion. *Cognition and Emotion, 5*, 435–465.

Rinn, W. E. (1984). The neuropsychology of facial expression: A review of the neurological and psychological mechanisms for producing facial expressions. *Psychological Bulletin, 95*, 52–77.

Scherer, K. R. (1993). Neuroscience projections to current debates in emotion psychology. *Cognition and Emotion, 7*, 1–41.

Scherer, K. R., Wallbott, H., & Summerfield, A. B. (1986). *Experiencing emotions: A cross-cultural study*. Cambridge: Cambridge University Press.

Schneider, F., Ellgring, H., Friedrich, J., Fus, I., Beyer, T., Heimann, H., & Himer, W. (1992). The effects of neuroleptics on facial action in schizophrenic patients. *Pharmacopsychiatry, 25*, 233–239.

Strauss, J. (1987). Processes of healing and chronicity in schizophrenia. In H. Hafner, W. F. Gattaz, & W. Janzarik (Eds.), *Search for the causes of schizophrenia* (pp. 75–87). Heidelberg: Springer-Verlag.

Tarrier, N., Vaughn, C. E., Lader, M. H., & Leff, J. P. (1979). Bodily reactions to people and events in schizophrenia. *Archives of General Psychiatry, 36*, 311–315.

Tomkins, S. S. (1962). *Affect, imagery, consciousness: Vol. 1. The positive affects*. New York: Springer.

Vaughn, C., & Leff, J. (1976). The measurement of expressed emotion in the families of psychiatric patients. *British Journal of Social and Clinical Psychology, 15*, 157–165.

Zajonc, R. B. (1985). Emotion and facial efference: A theory reclaimed. *Science, 228*, 15–21.

24

Jack J. Blanchard

Hedonic Capacity

Implications for Understanding Emotional
and Social Functioning in Schizophrenia

Disturbances of emotion have been considered an essential aspect of the clinical presentation of schizophrenia. Eugen Bleuler (1911/1950) described a range of emotional characteristics observed in schizophrenia, including a paucity of emotional expression and emotional indifference, as well as affective lability and inappropriate affect. Bleuler, however, considered these disturbances in affect as secondary symptoms (in his model the disturbance of association was primary). Kraepelin (1919/ 1971) described changes in the emotion of patients with schizophrenia, which he termed "emotional dullness" (p. 32), involving indifference and the lack of joy and affection. Kraepelin did not consider all affect to be lacking as he observed instances of inappropriate affect and intense emotional outbursts. An alternative conceptualization of affective symptoms in schizophrenia is represented by Rado (1962) and Meehl (1962), both of whom placed greater theoretical emphasis on emotion with a focus on the decreased capacity to experience pleasure, or anhedonia. Rado (1962) viewed anhedonia not merely as a symptom of schizophrenia but rather as a central, genetically based, deficit. For Rado every phase of life and area of behavior was altered by this pleasure deficit. Anhedonia had the following effects:

> (1) it weakens the motivating power of the welfare emotions, such as pleasurable desire, joy, affection, love and pride; (2) it weakens the counterbalancing effect ordinarily exerted by the welfare emotions on the emergency emotions, thus allowing fears and rages to rise to excessive strength; (3) it reduces the coherence of the action-self, which is viewed as the highest integrative system of the organism, and the very basis of self-awareness; (4) it undermines the schizotype's self-confidence and sense of security in relation to both himself and his social environment; (5) it makes the development of a well-integrated sexual function impossible; (6) it limits the schizotype's capacity for the appropriate enjoyment of his life activities, as well as for love and affectionate give and take in human relationships. (Rado, 1962, p. 2)

Meehl (1962), expanding on the views of Rado, thought that the diminished capacity to experience pleasure, anhedonia, was a "quasi-pathognomonic sign" of schizophrenia. Meehl proposed that anhedonia might be fundamental, the primary cause of social isolation, aberrant interpersonal behavior, and cognitive deviance. In this model, Meehl suggested that anhedonia was the expression of a genetic defect in the limbic brain regions involved with reward.

Meehl (1990) has revised his theory involving anhedonia. Meehl clarified that he conceptualizes anhedonia as an individual difference in the experience of pleasure that should best be referred to as *hypohedonia*. Hypohedonia reflects the dimensional view of this trait and acknowledges that even in severe instances individuals may nonetheless retain the capacity to experience pleasure in some domains. Meehl no longer posits a central role for anhedonia in the genesis of schizophrenia, but rather proposes that hypohedonia is "one of a dozen *normal-range (nontaxonic) individual difference factors (dimensions)* that raise or lower the probability of decompensation" (Meehl, 1990, p. 24, emphasis in original). He has also proposed that anhedonia may arise either (a) as a result of genetic causes, or (b) secondary to the pervasive experience of negative affect, which Meehl considers an important element of the affective lives of schizophrenics. In the first case Meehl (1990) terms the pleasure deficit *primary hypohedonia*, and for the nongenetic case the deficit is referred to as *secondary hypohedonia*. In the present discussion, the term *anhedonia* will be used for purposes of historical consistency; however, the dimensional view of this construct is adopted.

Despite the diminution of anhedonia as a causal agent in Meehl's recent theorizing, anhedonia continues to be considered prominently in contemporary investigations of schizophrenia as reflected in studies of its relation to schizophrenia-related characteristics and the liability for the development of schizophrenia or psychosis proneness (e.g., Chapman, Chapman, Kwapil, Eckblad, & Zinser, 1994; Erlenmeyer-Kimiling et al., 1993; Katsanis, Iacono, & Beiser, 1990), and its inclusion in the negative symptom complex (Andreasen, 1982; Carpenter, Heinrichs, & Wagman, 1988; Kirkpatrick & Buchanan, 1990). The focus of this review is on examining the occurrence of anhedonia in schizophrenia and in other disorders, and on the hypothesized association between anhedonia and the liability for the development of this disorder. Subsequently, the relationship between anhedonia and other dimensions of affect and social functioning in schizophrenia is evaluated. First, current methods to measure anhedonia are reviewed briefly.

The Measurement of Anhedonia

The study of anhedonia was greatly facilitated by the development of methods to measure this construct. These methods include clinical interviews as well as self-report questionnaires. Because of anhedonia's inclusion as one of the negative or deficit symptoms, several structured clinical interviews to measure these symptoms include items relating to anhedonia (e.g., Andreasen, 1982; Kirkpatrick, Buchanan, McKenney, Alphs, & Carpenter, 1989). However, perhaps the most widely used instruments for the measurement of anhedonia are the self-report scales developed by Chapman, Chapman, and Raulin (1976).

Chapman et al. (1976), influenced by the writings of Meehl and Rado, developed self-report measures that were designed to measure "a life-long characterological defect in the ability to experience pleasure" (p. 376). These scales were intended to measure trait-like dimensions of anhedonia rather than the transitory anhedonia associated with depression. True–false scales were constructed to tap two sources of pleasure, physical and social. The revised 61-item Physical Anhedonia scale (PAS; Chapman & Chapman, 1978) consists of pleasures relating to such experiences as eating, seeing, touching, and smell. Examples of items on the PAS are: "*The beauty of sunsets is greatly overrated*" (keyed true); "*When I have walked by a bakery, the smell of fresh bread has often made me hungry*" (keyed false).

The 40-item revised Social Anhedonia scale (SAS; Eckblad, Chapman, Chapman, & Mishlove, 1982) samples interpersonal pleasures such as talking and being with people. The SAS was developed to measure schizoid withdrawal rather than social anxiety. Example items from the SAS are: "*I attach very little importance to having close friends*" (keyed true); "*If given the choice, I would much rather be with others than be alone*" (keyed false). The PAS and SAS have been shown to have good internal consistency and test-retest reliability (Blanchard, Mueser, & Bellack, in press; Chapman, Chapman, & Miller, 1982). Because of the widespread use of the Chapman scales in research on anhedonia in both clinical and nonclinical populations, the present review is limited to investigations utilizing these self-report measures. The Chapman scales have been used extensively in studies examining various aspects of Meehl's original conjectures, including (a) the liability for the development of schizophrenia, (b) other aspects of emotion, and (c) social impairment.

Anhedonia and the Liability for the Development of Schizophrenia

Several strategies have been employed in testing the conjectures of Rado and Meehl regarding the genetic basis of anhedonia and the role of this pleasure deficit in the development of schizophrenia. These include (a) the comparison of various diagnostic groups to determine the specificity of anhedonia to schizophrenia, (b) the study of relatives of schizophrenics to examine if individuals who have an increased genetic risk for schizophrenia manifest schizophrenia-related traits such as anhedonia, and (c) the prospective study of individuals identified as high in anhedonia in order to determine if anhedonia is related to an increased risk of developing schizophrenia.

In the first study examining the occurrence of anhedonia in schizophrenia, Chapman et al. (1976) found that schizophrenics reported greater anhedonia than did normal controls. Several other studies have consistently found that schizophrenics report greater physical or social anhedonia than do controls (Berenbaum & Oltmanns, 1992; Clementz, Grove, Katsanis, & Iacono, 1991; Grove et al., 1991; Schuck, Leventhal, Rothstein, & Irizarry, 1984). Anhedonia, however, does not always discriminate between schizophrenics and patients with other psychiatric disorders such as major depression or bipolar disorder. In a study by Schuck et al. (1984) the PAS failed to discriminate schizophrenics from a group of psychiatric controls composed of patients with depression, bipolar disorder, and personality disorders; however, all patient groups scored higher than normal controls. Similarly, Berenbaum and Oltmanns (1992) found that schizophrenics, with or without blunted affect, and depressed patients reported significantly greater scores on the SAS than did controls. Schizophrenics with blunted affect and depressed patients also reported greater physical anhedonia than did controls (Berenbaum & Oltmanns, 1992). Finally, Katsanis et al. (1990) found that there were no differences between first episode patients with schizophrenia, schizophreniform, or affective disorders (depression and bipolar) with psychotic features on either the SAS or PAS. These results suggest that anhedonia may not be specific to schizophrenia but rather may be secondary to psychopathology.

Although anhedonia may occur in disorders other than schizophrenia, the underlying causes of anhedonia may differ as a function of diagnosis. In this view, anhedonia in schizophrenia is the expression of an enduring trait-like deficit while in the affective disorders anhedonia is secondary to depressed mood and covaries with symptom state (Bernstein & Riedel, 1987). In an evaluation of this hypothesis, Katsanis, Iacono, Beiser, and Lacey (1992) demonstrated that for individuals with schizophrenia, the PAS and SAS were unrelated to various measures of symptomatology and functioning at intake or at 18-month follow-up. This finding is consistent with other studies that have also shown a lack of a significant association between anhedonia and depression in schizophrenia (Chapman et al., 1976). However, Katsanis et al. (1992) found that for individuals with psychotic affective disorders the measures of anhedonia were significantly correlated with symptomatology and functioning at both assessments. Furthermore, poor premorbid adjustment (discussed more fully below) was significantly related to higher scores on the PAS and SAS in schizophrenia, but there was no such relation between anhedonia and premorbid adjustment in the affective disorders (Katsanis et al., 1992). These authors concluded that anhedonia represents a long-term trait deficit in schizophrenia, while in psychotic affective disorders it reflects current clinical state.

Blanchard, Bellack, and Mueser (1994) sought to examine further the role of depression in the failure to discriminate schizophrenics from other patient groups with respect to anhedonia. Specifically, Blanchard et al. reasoned that a patient sample *not* characterized by depression, namely, bipolar patients most recently in a manic phase, should be discriminable from schizophrenics (i.e., report less anhedonia). Consistent with this hypothesis, these authors found that patients with schizophrenia and schizoaffective disorder reported greater social and physical anhedonia than did patients with bipolar affective disorder. Furthermore, the PAS and SAS were uncorrelated with symptom ratings in this sample of stabilized inpatients. These findings are consistent with those of Katsanis et al. (1992) in supporting the hypothesis that anhedonia is a trait-like characteristic in schizophrenia unrelated to current symptomatology, including depression. In other patient groups anhedonia may be a transient deficit secondary to current symptomatology. It is important to note, however, that no study has directly tested this hypothesis. Ideally, such a study would involve a longitudinal assessment of anhedonia and symptomatology in affective disorder patients to determine if anhedonia decreases with remitting symptomatology.

Anhedonia has also been investigated in the relatives of schizophrenics in an attempt to determine if the diminished capacity to experience pleasure is associated with a genetic risk for the development of schizophrenia. In studying schizophrenics and their first degree relatives Grove et al. (1991) found that schizophrenics had higher PAS scores than did controls, and that probands' relatives also reported greater physical anhedonia than did controls. In a related report combining data from different geo-graphical regions in the United States and Canada, Clementz et al. (1991) also found that schizophrenics and their relatives had higher PAS scores than did normal sub-jects. Furthermore, Clementz et al. (1991) found a pattern of correlations suggest-ing that physical anhedonia may be familial in schizophrenics and their relatives. These data are consistent with the hypothesis that physical anhedonia may be an indicator of liability to schizophrenia.

Despite the above findings suggesting the specificity of anhedonia to schizophre-nia, other results complicate the matter. In the same sample reported on in their 1992 study, Katsanis et al. (1990) found that anhedonia was elevated in the relatives of schizophrenics but was also elevated in the first-degree relatives of patients with psy-chotic affective disorders. Additionally, in a 10-year follow-up study of college stu-dents, Chapman et al. (1994) found that social anhedonia and magical ideation were not related to an increased risk for the development of schizophrenia but rather these scales were associated with risk for psychosis and dimensional scores of schizotypal personality at follow-up. Physical anhedonia was not related to psychosis in this study. In summary, a number of studies indicate that anhedonia is a replicable feature of schizophrenia. However, other data suggest that anhedonia may not be specific to the risk for the development of this disorder but may instead be related to a risk of psychosis. Further study of anhedonia in schizophrenia and in other psychotic dis-orders will be necessary to clarify anhedonia's role in the liability for psychosis.

Anhedonia and Other Dimensions of Emotion

Although anhedonia is defined as a diminished capacity to experience pleasure, the actual emotional correlates of anhedonia remain an empirical question. Specifically, is anhedonia characterized by a diminished experience of positive affective states or are negative affective states affected as well? In order to better understand the potential dimensions of affect that may be affected by a pleasure deficit, it will be useful to re-view briefly current models of personality and affect (Tellegen, 1985; Watson & Clark, 1992a, 1992b; Watson & Tellegen, 1985). Two broad dimensions that have emerged in self-report data of affect have been identified as positive affect (PA) and negative affect (NA). These dimensions have been identified in both short-term state ratings as well as in long-term trait ratings of affect (e.g., Watson, 1988b; Watson & Clark, 1992a, 1992b; Watson & Tellegen, 1985; Tellegen, 1985; Zevon & Tellegen, 1982). Importantly, these dimensions of affect are viewed as orthogonal dimensions that may have differ-ential (not just opposite) correlations with other variables. Thus, PA but not NA has been found to be associated with social activity (e.g., Watson, 1988a; Watson, Clark, McIntyre, & Hamaker, 1992), exercise (Watson, 1988a), and personality indices of extraversion (Costa & McCrae, 1980; Tellegen, 1985; Watson et al., 1992). Alterna-tively, NA but not PA is related to physical problems (Clark & Watson, 1988) and personality markers of neuroticism (Costa & McCrae, 1980; Tellegen, 1985; Watson et al., 1992). Several studies have examined the relationship between anhedonia and self-reported PA and NA. Space limitations require that the present discussion focus on investigations of anhedonia and affect in schizophrenia, though there have been several such studies conducted with nonpsychiatric populations (e.g., Berenbaum, Snowhite, & Oltmanns, 1987; Fitzgibbons & Simons, 1982).

Several recent studies have examined the relationship between anhedonia and other dimensions of emotion in schizophrenia. In a study of outpatient schizophrenics, depressives, and normal controls, Berenbaum and Oltmanns (1992) evaluated self-reported mood and facial expressions in response to films and flavored drinks intended to elicit positive and negative emotions. Additionally, all subjects completed the Chapman scales of physical and social anhedonia. Although all three psychiatric groups reported greater social anhedonia than did controls, and blunted schizophrenics and depressives reported greater physical anhedonia than did controls, there were *no* group differences in self-reported mood regardless of manipulation (films or drinks). Furthermore, schizophrenics with blunted affect did not differ from the nonblunted schizophrenics in anhedonia or self-reported mood, although the blunted schizophrenics did display less facial expression.

Blanchard et al. (1994) studied the association between physical and social anhedonia and self-reported mood in response to affect eliciting films in inpatient schizophrenics, schizoaffectives, and bipolars most recently in a manic phase. As discussed above, both schizophrenia groups reported greater physical and social anhedonia than did bipolars. Analyses of self-reported positive affect in response to the films indicated that the positive and negative film clips differed in the expected direction and the combined group of schizophrenia-schizoaffective patients reported less positive affect than did bipolars across films. Similar analyses conducted on ratings of negative affect again indicated that the films differentially elicited negative affect. However, there were no differences between the patient groups in negative affect. Correlational analyses indicated that physical anhedonia, but not social anhedonia, was negatively correlated with self-reported positive affect in schizophrenics-schizoaffectives across films. Neither physical or social anhedonia was related to negative affect in the schizophrenics-schizoaffectives. The findings of this study suggest that anhedonia, at least as measured by the PAS, is associated with decreased positive affect in response to affect eliciting stimuli.

The reasons for the above variability in results in both nonclinical samples and schizophrenics is not clear. One possibility is the methods used to rate mood. In Berenbaum and Oltmanns' (1992) study, self-reported mood was rated with the adjectives *happy* or *disgusted*, rated on 7-point scales. In the Blanchard et al. (1994) study, mood was rated with a 22-item adjective list, 11 items each for PA and NA. The broader assessment of positive affect and negative affect in Blanchard et al. (1994) may have provided an index of affect more sensitive to the effects of anhedonia. Additionally, the 11-item scales could be expected to be somewhat more reliable than the single item assessment utilized by Berenbaum and Oltmanns.

The focus on *state* measures of affect used in these laboratory mood induction studies may also be relevant to understanding the variability in findings. Correlations between state ratings and anhedonia may be attenuated due to the lack of reliability or poor generalizability of point assessments of mood (Epstein, 1979, 1980). This is not to suggest that personality markers do not correspond to state indices of affect (e.g., Larsen & Ketelaar, 1989, 1991). However, such state-trait correlations are typically attenuated in comparison to trait-trait correlations.

Another concern with laboratory mood induction studies relates to the methods used to elicit affect. The available data clearly indicate that anhedonia is not related to affective responsivity to all forms of stimuli. This is consistent with Meehl's original conjectures in which anhedonia was *not* construed as a pan deficit in the capacity to experience pleasure. Meehl (1962) originally observed that anhedonia is mainly interpersonal and that "schizotypes seem to derive adequate pleasure from esthetic and cognitive rewards" (p. 833). Similarly, Meehl (1990), in explaining his preference for the term *hypohedonia*, indicated that even the most deteriorated schizophrenic can achieve pleasure from a few sources such as smoking or watching television. Thus, the variable findings of laboratory mood induction studies may be a consequence of the failure to examine social-interpersonal factors that are presumed to be central to the construct of anhedonia. The neglect of social stimuli in mood manipulation procedures is also problematic because social-interpersonal activity has repeatedly been found to be a robust predictor of positive affect (Clark & Watson, 1988; Watson, 1988a; Watson et al., 1992).

In a recent study Blanchard, Mueser, and Bellack (in press) addressed these concerns in an examination of the *trait* affect correlates of anhedonia. Several advantages were expected to be derived from measuring affect using trait ratings. First, trait indices should provide more reliable and generalizable markers of affect than do single point assessments of mood. Second, in assessing trait affectivity, issues arising from the nature of the evocative stimuli that might be used in a mood induction paradigm are not of concern. Importantly, trait markers of PA have been shown to be sensitive to social-interpersonal activity (e.g., Watson, 1988a; Watson et al., 1992). Finally, the utilization of trait indices should allow for a better understanding of anhedonia in the context of prevailing models of personality and affect (e.g., Costa & McCrae, 1980; Tellegen, 1985; Watson & Clark, 1992a, 1992b; Watson & Tellegen, 1985).

Blanchard et al. (in press) hypothesized that anhedonia, as a construct reflecting the decreased capacity to experience pleasure, should be associated with decreased trait PA. The hypothesized relationship between anhedonia and trait NA was less clear. One might expect anhedonia to be unrelated to NA given that the Chapman scales of anhedonia were developed to be independent of negative affective states such as social anxiety (Mishlove & Chapman, 1985). Furthermore, personality models that posit independent dimensions of PA and NA would suggest the independence of anhedonia and trait NA. Alternatively, Meehl (in both his original, 1962, and revised, 1990, theories) has proposed that anhedonia is an important contributor to, or in some cases a consequence of, what he describes as "aversive drift" in schizophrenia, or the tendency for activities, people, and places "to take on a burdensome, threatening, gloomy, negative emotional charge" (Meehl, 1990, p. 21). Meehl's proposal would indicate that anhedonia might be characterized by decreased PA and increased NA. Emotion and personality research in normals also suggests that anhedonia, especially social anhedonia, would be related to both trait PA and trait NA, given findings that self-descriptions based on words reflecting sociability (e.g., *friendly*) and happiness (e.g., *happy, joyful*) are markers of both high PA and low NA (Watson, 1988; Watson, Clark, & Tellegen, 1988; Watson & Tellegen, 1985). Socially anhedonic schizophrenics, presumably low in sociability and happiness, may demonstrate low PA and high NA.

Therefore, Blanchard et al. (in press) sought to test the hypothesis that anhedonia would be related to elevated trait NA in addition to low trait PA. Outpatient schizophrenics and normal controls were assessed at a baseline evaluation and again at approximately a 90-day follow-up for physical and social anhedonia (the Chapman scales), trait PA and NA (as measured by the Well-Being and Stress Reaction scales of the Multidimensional Personality Questionnaire; Tellegen, 1982), and social anxiety (assessed with the Interaction Anxiousness scale [IAS; Leary, 1983b] and the brief Fear of Negative Evaluation scale [FNE; Leary, 1983a; Watson & Friend, 1969]). Consistent with the dispositional view of these affective dimensions, test-retest correlations indicated that anhedonia and trait affectivity were reliable across the two assessment periods in both patients and controls. In support of the hypothesized pleasure deficit in schizophrenia, schizophrenics reported significantly greater physical and social anhedonia, and less trait PA, than controls. Schizophrenics also reported greater trait NA and social anxiety than controls. These findings converge with other reports indicating low PA and high NA in schizophrenics and their affected co-twins (DiLalla & Gottesman, unpublished study cited in Torrey, Bowler, Taylor, & Gottesman, 1994), and with findings of decreased extraversion (a personality dimension thought to reflect PA) and increased neuroticism (reflecting NA) in schizophrenia (Berenbaum & Fujita, 1994).

In examining the affective correlates of anhedonia within schizophrenics, Blanchard et al. (in press) found that in schizophrenics the SAS was significantly negatively correlated with trait PA and was significantly positively correlated with trait NA and social anxiety. Although the PAS did share a significant amount of variance with the SAS (25%), the PAS was not significantly correlated with trait PA, trait NA, or social anxiety. These results suggest that schizophrenia may be characterized by both low PA and high NA and are consistent with Meehl's proposal that anhedonia and aversive drift co-occur in schizophrenia. Additionally, anhedonia, in particular social anhedonia, appears to be a marker of both low PA and high NA. Despite the attempt to develop the SAS to reflect schizoid rather than anxious withdrawal (Mishlove & Chapman, 1985), Blanchard et al. (in press) found that the SAS was significantly correlated with social anxiety. The SAS has also been found to correlate with indices of anxiety in college students (Laurenceau, Feldman, & Blanchard, 1994; Leak, 1991; Peterson & Knudson, 1983) and in patients with personality disorders (Bailey, West, Widiger, & Freiman, 1993). Bailey et al. (1993) also found the SAS to be significantly correlated with the *Diagnostic and Statistical Manual of Mental Disorders* (3rd ed., rev.) criteria set for avoidant personality disorder and the schizotypal criterion item of social anxiety. Individuals low in hedonic capacity who also have social-interpersonal deficits may experience an accumulation of negative social experiences that lead to social anxiety. Alternatively, social anxiety may result in the decreased experience of pleasure form social encounters. Longitudinal studies will be required to examine the developmental trajectory of anhedonia and negative affects such as anxiety.

The preceding review indicates that schizophrenia cannot be adequately characterized by simply a diminished capacity to experience pleasure. Rather, it is clear that this disorder involves both diminished positive affectivity and increased negative affectivity. Future studies will be required to examine the potential differential clinical correlates of these affective changes in schizophrenia. Additionally, future research will need to go beyond self-reports of emotion and to examine the cognitive, physiological, and behavioral dimensions of emotion in schizophrenia.

Anhedonia and Social Functioning

The significance of interpersonal impairment in schizophrenia is reflected in its inclusion in current diagnostic criteria (American Psychiatric Association, 1994) and the research that has documented impairments in the social skills of schizophrenics (e.g., Bellack, Morrison, Wixted, & Mueser, 1990; Mueser, Bellack, Morrison, & Wade, 1990). Presently, little is known about the origins of these interpersonal deficits, although symptomatology, attentional impairment, and cognitive deficits have been identified as possible contributors (Bellack et al., 1990; Mueser, Bellack, Douglas, & Wade, 1991). Anhedonia may also provide a clue to better understanding impairments in the social-interpersonal functioning of schizophrenics. Rado (1962) and Meehl (1962) theorized that anhedonia underlies schizophrenics' reduced social interest, social isolation, and interpersonal deficits. Studies have focused on the association between anhedonia and (a) premorbid functioning and (b) current social functioning.

Premorbid Competence

Chapman et al. (1976) demonstrated that for schizophrenics with higher scores on the PAS and SAS, anhedonia was associated with poorer premorbid social-sexual activity or achievement—consistent with Meehl's theory that anhedonia underlies schizophrenics' social withdrawal and isolation. Similarly, Katsanis et al. (1992) found physical and social anhedonia to be related to poor premorbid adjustment in first-episode schizophrenics, but not in patients with psychotic affective disorders.

Two studies have failed to find anhedonia to be uniquely related to premorbid adjustment in schizophrenics. Schuck et al. (1984) examined the association between the PAS and premorbid adjustment in outpatients with schizophrenia, depression, and a psychiatric control group composed mostly of patients with personality disorders as well as patients with bipolar affective disorders. Schizophrenics did not differ from other patients on the PAS. The PAS was found to be significantly correlated with premorbid adjustment in the schizophrenics as well as the combined psychiatric control group which included depressives and other diagnoses.

In a recent study, Garnet, Glick, and Edell (1993) examined the association between the PAS and premorbid competence in young (mean age = 16.9 years) nonpsychotic inpatients. The most frequent diagnoses were major depression (57%), conduct disorder (19%), and other mood disorders (9%). Subjects scoring higher on the PAS had lower premorbid adjustment ratings. In examining only those patients with nonpsychotic affective disorder, physical anhedonia was again found to be associated with poorer premorbid adjustment.

The results of Schuck et al. (1984) and Garnet et al. (1993) are at odds with those reported by Katsanis et al. (1992), who found that the relation between anhedonia and premorbid adjustment was specific to schizophrenia. Although it might be concluded that anhedonia's link with premorbid adjustment is not unique to schizophrenia, several methodological issues should be noted. First, Schuck et al. (1984) used a self-report scale of the process-reactive continuum (Ullmann & Giovannoni, 1964) to assess premorbid adjustment. The validity of this self-report scale for assessing premorbid adjustment is unknown. However, many items in this questionnaire refer to recent or current functioning and no item explicitly refers to functioning prior to onset of the illness. Thus, the premorbid ratings in the Schuck et al. (1984) are likely confounded by chronicity. Furthermore, since these ratings did not utilize treatment records or other informants to assess early, premorbid functioning, the validity of this measure is questionable.

Concerns also arise regarding the interpretability of the interview ratings utilized by Garnet et al. (1993). Although these authors studied young patients they apparently were not in their first-episode. Unfortunately, Garnet et al. do not provide data on the duration of the illness or the number of prior episodes. To the degree that this sample had early onset with multiple episodes of the illness, ratings of premorbid adjustment may be confounded by functioning postonset. Even though ratings were limited to childhood and early adolescence, Garnet et al. do not specifically indicate that competence ratings were only derived from the period preceding the illness. As noted by Lenzenweger and Dworkin (1987), if competence ratings are not limited to behavioral data from the premorbid period such ratings may be contaminated by the effects of chronicity and institutionalization. Thus, although the findings of Schuck et al. (1984) and Garnet et al. (1993) suggest that anhedonia's association with long-term social functioning is not unique to schizophrenia, these studies are characterized by potential methodological issues that should be considered in their interpretation.

Current Social Skill and Functioning

In addition to examining poor premorbid adjustment, it may be informative to study how anhedonia is related to current social skill and functioning. The PAS has been related to various indices of social competence assessed with role play measures in college students (Beckfield, 1985; Haberman, Chapman, Numbers, & McFall, 1979; Numbers & Chapman, 1982). Although poor premorbid adjustment has been shown to be related to poor social skill in role play tests (Mueser, Bellack, Morrison, & Wixted, 1990), no study has evaluated the relation between the Chapman anhedonia scales and *behavioral* indices of social competence in schizophrenia. If anhedonia underlies a lack of interest in social activities and relationships, it may also be related to the failure to acquire and develop interpersonal competencies that are expressed as social skill deficits observed in schizophrenia. In two recent studies Blanchard and colleagues (Blanchard et al., 1994, in press) have sought to examine the association between anhedonia, and social skill and current social functioning in the community.

Blanchard et al. (1994) studied inpatients with schizophrenia, schizoaffective disorder, and bipolar disorder. Utilizing a behavioral role play test, patients' skills in responding to negative social interactions were studied. Although the patient groups demonstrated skills deficits in comparison to normal controls (Mueser, Blanchard, & Bellack, 1995), neither the PAS or the SAS was correlated with social skill in any patient group. Blanchard et al. (1994) proposed that although anhedonia was unrelated to skill in the negative valenced social interaction, anhedonia may play a role in skills required for positive valenced, affiliative, interactions.

In a subsequent study, Blanchard et al. (in press) sought to determine if anhedonia was related to the social functioning of outpatients in the community. As reviewed above, outpatient schizophrenics completed the PAS and SAS as well as trait scales for positive affect and negative affect, and measures of social anxiety. They were also interviewed regarding their current social functioning. Correlational analyses indicated that both the SAS and PAS were significantly correlated with social functioning in schizophrenics such that greater anhedonia scores were related to poorer current functioning. Poor social functioning was also positively correlated with trait NA and social anxiety. Alternatively, trait positive affect was negatively correlated with poorer functioning (i.e., greater positive affect was associated with better social functioning). The results of partial correlations, controlling for all other affective measures, indicated that only trait positive affect remained a significant predictor of social functioning in schizophrenics. This finding is consistent with a number of studies with normals indicating that positive affect is positively correlated with social activities (e.g., Watson, 1988a; Watson et al., 1992) and with the quantity and quality of relationships (Hotard, McFatter, McWhirter, & Stegall, 1989).

In summary, anhedonia has been found to be related to poor premorbid adjustment in schizophrenia. However, the specificity of this relationship to schizophrenia is unclear, with some studies finding such a link in other patient groups. Methodological concerns with these later studies underscore the need to further examine the question of anhedonia's relationship with premorbid adjustment in schizophrenics as well as other patient groups. Anhedonia's association with current social skill deficits in schizophrenia is less clear. Although one study found anhedonia to be unrelated to social skill, this finding was limited to conflictual interactions. The link between anhedonia and affiliative skills has not been studied. Finally, anhedonia has been found to be associated with poor current social functioning in schizophrenics. These results indicate that anhedonia and PA are clearly relevant to understanding the debilitating social impairment seen in schizophrenia. The precise nature of anhedonia's contribution to various spheres of social functioning and the uniqueness of anhedonia's role in social impairment to schizophrenia requires further study.

Neurobiological Origins of Anhedonia

One question regarding anhedonia that has not been addressed empirically is the neurobiological basis of this presumed genetically based deficit. Meehl (1962) speculated that impairment in limbic systems involved in reward was responsible. Contemporary neuropsychological models of affect are likely to be informative in the search for the neurological system(s) involved in anhedonia. One promising model has been proposed by Depue and Iacono (1989) who propose a behavioral facilitation system (BFS), which is involved in the initiation of behavior, incentive-reward motivation, and positive affect. The BFS is thought to be composed of the ascending dopamine (DA) projections of the ventral tegmental area (VTA). (For recent reviews of the role of DA in emotion see Phillips, Blaha, Pfaus, & Blackburn, 1992; White & Milner, 1992.) These VTA DA projections innervate limbic system structures including the nucleus accumbens, amygdala, substantia innominata, septum, and hippocampus. Additionally, DA fibers project to cortical regions, especially the frontal lobes. Depue and Iacono propose that the mesolimbic DA system is involved in the self-initiation of locomotor activity and that mesocortical DA pathways mediate reward. In this model, the functional activation of the BFS results in signals of reward initiating behavior, incentive-reward motivation, and pleasurable arousal. Alternatively, the failure of stimuli (signals of reward) to activate the BFS leads to a decreased likelihood of behavioral engagement, incentive motivation, and positive affect.

The frontal lobes have also been implicated in the neuropsychological models of emotion put forth by Davidson (1984, 1992) and Heller (1990, 1993). Both Davidson and Heller proposed a lateralized division of emotion based on the valence distinction of positive-approach and negative-withdrawal emotions. Relative activation of the left frontal lobe is involved in the production of approach or positive valenced affects. Alternatively, relative activation of the right frontal region is seen as related to withdrawal or negative valenced affects. Heller (1990, 1993) has further proposed that the right parietotemporal region is involved in autonomic arousal.

In summary, neuropsychological models of emotion have placed great emphasis on DA neurotransmitter systems and the frontal lobes. Importantly, dysfunction of both DA systems and the frontal lobes have been identified as central aspects in theorizing regarding the neurobiology of schizophrenia (e.g., Davis, Kahn, Ko, & Davidson, 1991; Weinberger, 1987). Both Davis et al. (1991) and Weinberger (1987) have proposed that mesocortical DA function is *underactive* in schizophrenia and subserves frontal lobe dysfunction. Weinberger (1987) hypothesizes that corticolimbic feedback is disrupted secondary to this mesocortical DA dysfunction. The consequence of this failed feedback is *overactivation* of mesolimbic DA systems. As summarized by Weinberger (1987), "a lesion that affects prefrontal dopamine projections and/or their connections could account for both mesocortical dopaminergic underactivity and mesolimbic overactivity and, thereby, the defect and 'positive' symptoms of schizophrenia" (p. 664).

Evidence from brain imaging studies utilizing regional cerebral blood flow, single-photon emission computed tomography (SPECT), and positron emission tomography (PET) provide support for this model, indicating that at least some schizophrenia patients are characterized by a reduced physiological activation of the frontal region (e.g., Andreasen et al., 1992; Buchsbaum et al. 1992; Siegel et al., 1993; Weinberger, Berman, & Zec, 1986; Wolkin et al., 1992). Given the proposed role of mesocortical DA projections and frontal regions in incentive-reward and positive affect (Depue & Iacono, 1989), it may be that anhedonia in schizophrenia derives, in part, from underactive mesocortical DA function and associated hypofrontality. Although no study has examined this directly it is interesting to note that investigations have found an association between overall negative symptom scores (of which anhedonia is a part) and hypofrontality using SPECT (Andreasen et al., 1992) and PET (Wolkin et al., 1992). However, at least one PET study has failed to find negative symptoms to be related to hypofrontality (Siegel et al., 1993). The lateralized models of Davidson and Heller would further suggest that decreased positive affect in schizophrenia may relate more specifically to relative inactivation of the left frontal lobe. Finally, the finding that positive affect is linked with social activity, and that the BFS is proposed to be associated with behavioral engagement, further suggests that mesocortical and frontal dysfunction may be associated with the social impairment in schizophrenia. Investigations combining brain imaging technology with detailed assessments of trait dimensions of affectivity and social functioning will be required to better understand the neurobiological correlates of anhedonia and social impairment in schizophrenia.

Directions for Future Research

The above review suggests that the decreased capacity to experience pleasure is a replicable feature of schizophrenia. However, despite the historical and theoretical importance of anhedonia, much remains unknown about this construct. Importantly, available research suggests that the affectivity in schizophrenia is likely more complex than a simple focal impairment in the experience of pleasure. The theorizing of both Rado and Meehl explicitly indicates alterations in negative affectivity that either precede or follow the development of anhedonia. Furthermore, recent empirical evidence supports at least the co-occurrence of decreased trait positive affect and elevated trait negative affect in schizophrenia (Blanchard et al., in press). Future investigations should attempt to ensure a broad assessment of affective experience that assesses both positive valenced and negative valenced affects. Longitudinal assessments of anhedonia and emotion in schizophrenia may help to clarify the developmental sequence of various aspects of emotion in schizophrenia.

Regarding social functioning in schizophrenia, the evidence indicates that anhedonia is meaningfully associated with social impairment in schizophrenia either measured premorbidly or currently. These results converge with findings in normals indicating a robust link between social activity and positive affect. The available evidence, therefore, would indicate that the proper study of emotion in schizophrenia must also involve the study of social-interpersonal aspects of this disorder. To neglect social functioning is to neglect an apparently important determinant of emotional experience.

Acknowledgments Preparation of this chapter was supported in part by National Institute of Mental Health Grant MH51240 to Jack J. Blanchard.

References

American Psychiatric Association. (1994). *Diagnostic and statistical manual of mental disorders* (4th ed.). Washington, DC: Author.

Andreasen, N. C. (1982). Negative symptoms in schizophrenia: Definition and reliability. *Archives of General Psychiatry, 39*, 784–788.

Andreasen, N. C., Rezai, K., Alliger, R., Swayze, V. W., Flaum, M., Kirchner, P., Cohen, G., & O'Leary, D. S. (1992). Hypofrontality in neuroleptic-naive patients and in patients with chronic schizophrenia: Assessment with xenon 133 single-photon emission computed tomography and the Tower of London. *Archives of General Psychiatry, 49*, 943–958.

Bailey, B., West, K. Y., Widiger, T. A., & Freiman, K. (1993). The convergent and discriminant validity of the Chapman scales. *Journal of Personality Assessment, 61*, 121–135.

Beckfield, D. F. (1985). Interpersonal competence among college men hypothesized to be at risk for schizophrenia. *Journal of Abnormal Psychology, 94*, 397–404.

Bellack, A. S., Morrison, R. L., Wixted, J. T., & Mueser, K. T. (1990). An analysis of social competence in schizophrenia. *British Journal of Psychiatry, 156,* 809–818.

Berenbaum, H., & Fujita, F. (1994). Schizophrenia and personality: Exploring the boundaries and connections between vulnerability and outcome. *Journal of Abnormal Psychology, 103,* 148–158.

Berenbaum, H., & Oltmanns, T. F. (1992). Emotional experience and expression in schizophrenia and depression. *Journal of Abnormal Psychology, 101,* 37–44.

Berenbaum, H., Snowhite, R., & Oltmanns, T. F. (1987). Anhedonia and emotional responses to affect evoking stimuli. *Psychological Medicine, 17,* 677–684.

Bernstein, A. S., & Riedel, J. A. (1987). Psychophysiological response patterns in college students with high physical anhedonia: Scores appear to reflect schizotypy rather than depression. *Biological Psychiatry, 22,* 829–847.

Blanchard, J. J., Bellack, A. S., & Mueser, K. T. (1994). Affective and social-behavioral correlates of physical and social anhedonia in schizophrenia. *Journal of Abnormal Psychology, 103,* 719–728.

Blanchard, J. J., Mueser, K. T., & Bellack, A. S. (in press). Anhedonia, positive and negative affect, and social functioning in schizophrenia. *Schizophrenia Bulletin.*

Bleuler, E. (1950). *Dementia praecox or the group of schizophrenias* (J. Zinkin, Trans.). New York: International University Press. (Original work published in 1911)

Buchsbaum, M. S., Haier, R. J., Potkin, S. G., Nuechterlein, K., Bracha, H. S., Katz, M., Lohr, J., Wu, J., Lottenberg, S., Jerabek, P. A., Trenary, M., Tafalla, R., Reynolds, C., & Bunney, W. E. (1992). Frontostriatal disorder of cerebral metabolism in never-medicated schizophrenics. *Archives of General Psychiatry, 49,* 935–942.

Carpenter, W. T., Heinrichs, D. W., & Wagman, A. M. I. (1988). Deficit and nondeficit forms of schizophrenia: The concept. *American Journal of Psychiatry, 145,* 578–583.

Chapman, L. J., & Chapman, J. P. (1978). *Revised Physical Anhedonia scale.* Unpublished test, University of Wisconsin, Madison, WI.

Chapman, L. J., Chapman, J. P., Kwapil, T. R., Eckblad, M., & Zinser, M. C. (1994). Putatively psychosis-prone subjects ten years later. *Journal of Abnormal Psychology, 103,* 171–183.

Chapman, L. J., Chapman, J. P., & Miller, E. N. (1982). Reliabilities and intercorrelations of eight measures of proneness to psychosis. *Journal of Consulting and Clinical Psychology, 50,* 187–195.

Chapman, L. J., Chapman, J. P., & Raulin, M. L. (1976). Scales for physical and social anhedonia. *Journal of Abnormal Psychology, 85,* 374–382.

Clark, L. A., & Watson, D. (1988). Mood and the mundane: Relations between daily life events and self-reported mood. *Journal of Personality and Social Psychology, 54,* 296–308.

Clementz, B. A., Grove, W. M., Katsanis, J., & Iacono, W. G. (1991). Psychometric detection of schizotypy: Perceptual aberration and physical anhedonia in relatives of schizophrenics. *Journal of Abnormal Psychology, 100,* 607–612.

Costa, P. T., & McCrae, R. R. (1980). Influence of extraversion and neuroticism on subjective well-being: Happy and unhappy people. *Journal of Personality and Social Psychology, 38,* 668–678.

Davidson, R. J. (1984). Affect, cognition and hemispheric specialization. In C. E. Izard, J. Kagan, & R. Zajonc (Eds.), *Emotion, cognition and behavior* (pp. 320–365). New York: Cambridge University Press.

Davidson, R. J. (1992). Prolegomenon to the structure of emotion: Gleanings from neuropsychology. *Cognition and Emotion, 6,* 245–268.

Davis, K. L., Kahn, R., Ko, G., & Davidson, M. (1991). Dopamine in schizophrenia: A review and reconceptualization. *American Journal of Psychiatry, 148,* 1474–1486.

Depue, R. A., & Iacono, W. G. (1989). Neurobehavioral aspects of affective disorders. *Annual Review of Psychology, 40,* 457–492.

Eckblad, M. L., Chapman, L. J., Chapman, J. P., & Mishlove, M. (1982). *The Revised Social Anhedonia scale.* Unpublished test, University of Wisconsin, Madison, WI.

Epstein, S. (1979). The stability of behavior: I. On predicting most of the people much of the time. *Journal of Personality and Social Psychology, 37,* 1097–1126.

Epstein, S. (1980). The stability of behavior: II. Implications for psychological research. *American Psychologist, 35,* 790–806.

Erlenmeyer-Kimling, L., Cornblatt, B. A., Rock, D., Roberts, S., Bell, M., & West, A. (1993). The New York High-Risk Project: Anhedonia, attentional deviance, and psychopathology. *Schizophrenia Bulletin, 19,* 141–153.

Fitzgibbons, L., & Simons, R. F. (1992). Affective response to color-slide stimuli in subjects with physical anhedonia: A three-systems analysis. *Psychophysiology, 29,* 613–620.

Garnet, K. E., Glick, M., & Edell, W. S. (1993). Anhedonia and premorbid competence in young, nonpsychotic psychiatric inpatients. *Journal of Abnormal Psychology, 102,* 580–583.

Grove, W. M., Lebow, B. S., Clementz, B. A., Cerri, A., Medus, C., & Iacono, W. G. (1991). Familial prevalence and coaggregation of schizotypy indicators: A multitrait family study. *Journal of Abnormal Psychology, 100,* 115–121.

Haberman, M. C., Chapman, L. J., Numbers, J. S., & McFall, R. M. (1979). Relation of social competence to scores on two scales of psychosis proneness. *Journal of Abnormal Psychology, 88,* 675–677.

Heller, W. (1990). The neuropsychology of emotion: Developmental patterns and implications for psychopathology. In N. Stein, B. L. Leventhal, & T. Trabasso (Eds.), *Psychological and biological approaches to emotion* (pp. 167–211). Hillsdale, NJ: Erlbaum.

Heller, W. (1993). Neuropsychological mechanisms of individual differences in emotion, personality, and arousal. *Neuropsychology, 7,* 476–489.

Hotard, S. R., McFatter, R. M., McWhirter, R. M., & Stegall, M. E. (1989). Interactive effects of extraversion, neuroticism, and social relationships on subjective well-being. *Journal of Personality and Social Psychology, 57,* 321–331.

Katsanis, J., Iacono, W. G., & Beiser, M. (1990). Anhedonia and perceptual aberration in first-episode psychotic patients and their relatives. *Journal of Abnormal Psychology, 99,* 202–206.

Katsanis, J., Iacono, W. G., Beiser, M., & Lacey, L. (1992). Clinical correlates of anhedonia and perceptual aberration in first-episode patients with schizophrenia and affective disorder. *Journal of Abnormal Psychology, 101,* 184–191.

Kirkpatrick, B., & Buchanan, R. W. (1990). Anhedonia and the deficit syndrome of schizophrenia. *Psychiatry Research, 31,* 25–30.

Kirkpatrick, B., Buchanan, R. W., McKenney, P., Alphs, L. D., & Carpenter, W. R. (1989). The schedule for the deficit syndrome: An instrument for research in schizophrenia. *Psychiatry Research, 30,* 119–123.

Kraepelin, E. (1971). *Dementia praecox and paraphrenia* (R. M. Barclay, Trans.). Huntington, NY: Krieger. (Original work published in 1919)

Larsen, R. J., & Ketelaar, T. (1989). Extraversion, neuroticism and susceptibility to positive and negative mood induction procedures. *Personality and Individual Differences, 10,* 1221–1228.

Larsen, R. J., & Ketelaar, T. (1991). Personality and susceptibility to positive and negative affect. *Journal of Personality and Social Psychology, 61,* 132–140.

Laurenceau, J. P., Feldman, L. A., & Blanchard, J. J. (1994, August). *Construct validity of the Social Anhedonia scale.* Paper presented at the 102nd annual meeting of the American Psychological Association, Los Angeles, CA.

Leak, G. K. (1991). An examination of the construct validity of the Social Anhedonia scale. *Journal of Personality Assessment, 56,* 84–95.

Leary, M. R. (1983a). A brief version of the Fear of Negative Evaluation scale. *Personality and Social Psychology Bulletin, 9,* 371–375.

Leary, M. R. (1983b). Social anxiousness: The construct and its measurement. *Journal of Personality Assessment, 47,* 66–75.

Lenzenweger, M. F., & Dworkin, R. H. (1987). Assessment of premorbid social competence in schizophrenia: A methodological note. *Journal of Abnormal Psychology, 96,* 367–369.

Meehl, P. E. (1962). Schizotaxia, schizotypy, schizophrenia. *American Psychologist, 17,* 827–838.

Meehl, P. E. (1990). Toward an integrated theory of schizotaxia, schizotypy, and schizophrenia. *Journal of Personality Disorders, 4,* 1–99.

Mishlove, M., & Chapman, L. J. (1985). Social anhedonia in the prediction of psychosis proneness. *Journal of Abnormal Psychology, 94,* 384–396.

Mueser, K. T., Bellack, A. S., Douglas, M. S., & Wade, J. H. (1991). Prediction of social skill acquisition in schizophrenic and major affective disorder patients from memory and symptomatology. *Psychiatry Research, 37,* 281–296.

Mueser, K. T., Bellack, A. S., Morrison, R. L., & Wade, J. H. (1990). Gender, social competence, and symptomatology in schizophrenia: A longitudinal analysis. *Journal of Abnormal Psychology, 99,* 138–147.

Mueser, K. T., Bellack, A. S., Morrison, R. L., & Wixted, J. T. (1990). Social competence in schizophrenia: Premorbid adjustment, social skill, and domains of functioning. *Journal of Psychiatric Research, 24,* 51–63.

Mueser, K. T., Blanchard, J. J., & Bellack, A. S. (1995). Memory and social skill in schizophrenia: The role of gender. *Psychiatry Research, 57,* 141–153.

Numbers, J. S., & Chapman, L. J. (1982). Social deficits in hypothetically psychosis-prone college women. *Journal of Abnormal Psychology, 91,* 255–260.

Peterson, C. A., & Knudson, R. M. (1983). Anhedonia: A construct validation approach. *Journal of Personality Assessment, 47,* 539–551.

Phillips, A. G., Blaha, C. D., Pfaus, J. G., & Blackburn, J. R. (1992). Neurobiological correlates of positive emotional states: Dopamine, anticipation and reward. In K. T. Strongman (Ed.), *International review of studies on emotion* (Vol. 2, pp. 31–50). New York: Wiley.

Rado, S. (1962). *Psychoanalysis of behavior. In Collected papers: Vol. 2. 1956–1961.* New York: Grune & Stratton.

Schuck, J., Leventhal, D., Rothstein, H., & Irizarry, V. (1984). Physical anhedonia and schizophrenia. *Journal of Abnormal Psychology, 93,* 342–344.

Siegel, B. V., Buchsbaum, M. S., Bunney, W. E., Gottschalk, L. A., Haier, R. J., Lohr, J. B., Lottenberg, S., Najafi, A., Nuechterlein, K. H., Potkin, S. G., & Wu, J. C. (1993). Cortical-striatal-thalamic circuits and brain glucose metabolic activity in 70 unmedicated male schizophrenic patients. *American Journal of Psychiatry, 150,* 1325–1336.

Tellegen, A. (1982). *Brief manual of the Multidimensional Personality Questionnaire.* Unpublished manuscript, University of Minnesota.

Tellegen, A. (1985). Structures of mood and personality and their relevance to assessing anxiety, with an emphasis on self-report. In A. H. Tuma & J. D. Maser (Eds.), *Anxiety and the anxiety disorders* (pp. 681–706). Hillsdale, NJ: Erlbaum.

Torrey, E. F., Bowler, A. E., Taylor, E. H., & Gottesman, I. I. (1994). *Schizophrenia and manic-depressive disorder: The biological roots of mental illness as revealed by the landmark study of identical twins.* New York: Basic Books.

Ullmann, L. P., & Giovannoni, J. M. (1964). The development of a self-report measure of the process-reactive continuum. *Journal of Nervous and Mental Disease, 138*, 38–42.

Watson, D. (1988a). Intraindividual and interindividual analyses of positive and negative affect: Their relation to health complaints, perceived stress, and daily activities. *Journal of Personality and Social Psychology, 54*, 1020–1030.

Watson, D. (1988b). The vicissitudes of mood measurement: Effects of varying descriptors, time frames, and response formats on measures of positive and negative affect. *Journal of Personality and Social Psychology, 55*, 128–141.

Watson, D., & Clark, L. A. (1992a). Affects separable and inseparable: On the hierarchical arrangement of the negative affects. *Journal of Personality and Social Psychology, 62*, 489–505.

Watson, D., & Clark, L. A. (1992b). On traits and temperament: General and specific factors of emotional experience and their relation to the five-factor model. *Journal of Personality, 60*, 441–476.

Watson, D., Clark, L. A., McIntyre, C. W., & Hamaker, S. (1992). Affect, personality, and social activity. *Journal of Personality and Social Psychology, 63*, 1011–1025.

Watson, D., Clark, L. A., & Tellegen, A. (1988). Development and validation of brief measures of positive and negative affect: The PANAS scales. *Journal of Personality and Social Psychology, 54*, 1063–1070.

Watson, D., & Friend, R. (1969). Measurement of social evaluative anxiety. *Journal of Consulting and Clinical Psychology, 33*, 458–468.

Watson, D., & Tellegen, A. (1985). Toward a consensual structure of mood. *Psychological Bulletin, 98*, 219–235.

Weinberger, D. R. (1987). Implications of normal brain development for the pathogenesis of schizophrenia. *Archives of General Psychiatry, 44*, 660–669.

Weinberger, D. R., Berman, K. F., & Zec, R. F. (1986). Physiologic dysfunction of dorsolateral prefrontal cortex in schizophrenia: I. Regional cerebral blood flow evidence. *Archives of General Psychiatry, 43*, 114–124.

White, N. M., & Milner, P. M. (1992). The psychobiology of reinforcers. *Annual Review of Psychology, 43*, 443–471.

Wolkin, A., Sanfilipo, M., Wolf, A. P., Angrist, B., Brodie, J. D., & Rotrosen, J. (1992). Negative symptoms and hypofrontality in chronic schizophrenia. *Archives of General Psychiatry, 49*, 959–965.

Zevon, M. A., & Tellegen, A. (1982). The structure of mood change: An idiographic/homothetic analysis. *Journal of Personality and Social Psychology, 43*, 111–122.

25

John M. Neale, Jack J. Blanchard, Sandra Kerr,
Ann M. Kring, & David A. Smith

Flat Affect in Schizophrenia

Although regarded by Bleuler (1950) as a fundamental symptom of schizophrenia, until recently flat affect, a lack of overt emotional expressivity, was not a prominent part of the diagnosis of schizophrenia because it was believed that it could not be rated reliably. In the last decade, however, reliable rating scales have appeared and an accumulation of evidence has supported Bleuler's position on the relative importance of flat affect in schizophrenia.

Diagnostically, flat affect has been shown to be important in making differential diagnoses as evidenced by its occurrence with 11 other symptoms in an equation that best discriminated schizophrenics from non schizophrenics (Carpenter, Strauss, & Bartko, 1974). Flat affect has also been shown to be of prognostic importance since treatment response is correlated with the degree of emotional blunting (Abrams & Taylor, 1978). Furthermore, of a variety of symptom variables, blunted affect was one of only two that predicted short-term outcome (Endicott, Nee, Cohen, Fleiss, & Simon, 1986).

Scales for rating flat affect are based on observations made during a clinical interview, and they differ somewhat in the domains that they assess. Andreasen's (1983) 10-item scale of affective flattening is based principally on observed behavioral components (e.g., decreased spontaneous movements, paucity of expressive gestures). Abrams and Taylor's (1978) measure of emotional blunting is a 16-item, trichotomous scale that assesses the domains of affect (i.e., mood), thought (e.g., indifference/lack of affection for family), and behavior (e.g., expressionless face). The various clinical ratings of flat affect all include judgments of overt emotional expressivity (e.g., facial reactivity, vocal intonation) as well as ratings of other variables (e.g., poor eye contact) that may more properly be conceptualized as correlates of emotional expressivity, and still others that may not be part of the concept at all (e.g., inappropriate affect).

But there is a good deal more to affect than expressivity. Many researchers in the field of emotion believe that no single indicator provides a complete assessment of the concept. Instead, they propose that emotion is best assessed via multiple measures from different domains—self-report, behavioral, and physiological. Data from these indicators are sometimes positively correlated (Levenson, Ekman, & Friesen, 1990). As applied to flat affect in schizophrenics, the implication is that their meager expressiveness would be congruent with behavioral or psychophysiological indicators of low levels of emotion. But there are also data indicating negative relationships among emotion indicators from different domains. For example, self-reports of affective experience and psychophysiological indices of emotionality have been found to correlate *negatively* with emotional expressivity (Notarius & Levenson, 1979). This is not just one of the usual modest to low correlations found among the different facets of affectivity, but rather is a situation where nonexpressive people actually report and demonstrate psychophysiologically intense emotion. Thus, the different subsystems of affect can, in some circumstances, be decoupled. Consequently, although affective flattening may imply diminished emotionality, as indicated by phenomenological and physiological data, results from the existing literature on schizophrenics do not bear on this issue, and there are indications in the literature on normals that the direction of the relationship can at times be reversed. Schizophrenics' affectively flat exterior may mask an emotionally volatile interior.

It is therefore apparent that the clinical term *flat affect* implies too much. Although we may conclude that some schizophrenics are low in emotional expressivity, this does not necessarily imply experiential or physiological deficits. A broader assessment of affect in schizophrenia is clearly needed, including indices of expression, self-report, and psychophysiology. It is also unclear whether the typical clinical ratings of flat affect have any relationship at all to emotion. Facial, gestural, and vocal actions can serve a number of purposes and it is possible that during an interview the ratings are more related to a person's interpersonal style or social behavior (Dworkin, 1992) than to emotion per se.

In recent years, empirical studies of emotion in schizophrenia that do not focus on clinical rating scales have begun to appear in the literature. For example, Krause, Steiner, Sanger-Alt, and Wagner (1989) and Berenbaum and Oltmanns (1992) have studied facial responses in laboratory contexts. Both studies found schizophrenics to be facially nonexpressive. With respect to phenomenology, Brown, Sweeney, and Schwartz (1979) studied self-reported and observer-reported pleasure and found low to moderate levels of pleasure in their schizophrenics as well as a low correlation between self and observer reports. In another study using experience sampling methods, Hurlbert (1989) found that schizophrenics' diary entries in response to random "beeps" during the day were quite emotional in content.

There is also a large literature on psychophysiology in schizophrenia, but it has in recent years been focused more on cognition (the orienting response or evoked potentials) than emotion (for reviews, see Freedman & Mirsky, 1991; Zahn, Frith, Steinhauer, 1991). Notably, no study except the one we report here has simultaneously examined the three domains of affective response—expression, self-report, and psychophysiology. The closest is Berenbaum and Oltmanns (1992), who examined both expressivity and self-report. They found that schizophrenics' self-reported as much emotion as normals, despite being quite facially nonexpressive.

To develop a model of flat affect in schizophrenia, it is necessary to examine referents of emotion from all three domains. If schizophrenics show a congruent relationship between their low levels of expressiveness and data from other emotion indicators, the theoretical implication would be very different than if a disjunctive relationship exists among the indicators. In the former case, for example, a deficit in processing affective information may lead to the entire emotion system being unresponsive. In the latter case, we might consider the possibility that while emotions are being elicited their overt display is being inhibited.

Major theorists in schizophrenia have held differing opinions about these interrelationships. Kraepelin (1904), for example, seemed to believe that flat affect reflected a lack of emotional experience: "All his movements are languid and expressionless—and the patient remains quite dull throughout, experiencing neither fear, nor hope, nor desires" (p. 23). Bleuler (1950), for whom affective disturbance was one of the four primary characteristics of schizophrenia, described a disjunction between emotional expression and experience as evidenced by discrepancies between observer and patient reports of emotion. Another influential position is Rado's (1953) notion concerning the fundamental importance of anhedonia, the inability to experience pleasure. Rado's position suggests that experience and expression would be congruent, at least for positive emotions. Regarding negative emotional states, Rado believed that schizophrenics experience them more strongly than normals.

Although our primary goal was gathering descriptive data on the components of emotion in schizophrenia, our findings will be relevant to the different viewpoints just described. Our intuition on beginning the study was that Bleuler's position seemed to be the most promising. Several indirect lines of evidence suggest that the components of emotion may be dissociated in schizophrenics. We know that a large percentage of schizophrenics are outwardly flat. What some studies also hint at is that the outward picture may not reflect well their internal state.

For example, in studies following up child guidance clinic samples, preschizophrenics have been described as high in anxiety, vulnerable, and having little self-control (Fleming, 1969; Fleming & Ricks, 1970). Perhaps the outward expression of emotion is punished during the preschizophrenic years but other emotion domains are unaffected. Similarly, psychophysiologically, a subgroup of schizophrenics (principally chronic patients) demonstrate a high frequency of nonspecific skin conductance responses (SCRs; see Zahn et al., 1991, for a review). This is a clear reflection of a high level of sympathetic activation that is often thought of as an indicator of emotional arousal. Recent work on precipitants of relapse also suggests that schizophrenics may experience intense emotions. For example, Ventura, Nuechterlein, Lukoff, & Hardesty (1989) found that about 50% of clinical relapses were preceded by a stressful life event in the month before the relapse. Similarly, a number of studies have found that a high level of expressed emotion (EE), typically defined by critical comments, hostility, and emotional overinvolvement of key relatives, is related to relapse (see Kavanagh, 1992, for a review). In both cases, the mediating mechanism could be the elicitation of high levels of negative affect. In the case of EE this hypothesis is strengthened by data indicating either higher levels of SCR by schizophrenics in the presence of a relative or a failure for SCR to habituate after the relative had left the room (Sturgeon, Turpin, & Berkowitz, 1984; Tarrier, Vaughn, & Lader, 1979). A classic series of studies by Rodnick and Garmezy (1959) also indicated that schizophrenics' performance on various tasks was more disrupted by censure than was normals' performance. Finally, regarding psychosocial interventions in schizophrenia, it is often recommended that intrusive, intense and, presumably emotion-eliciting treatments be avoided (McGlashan, 1994). To sum up, there is abundant reason to suspect that schizophrenics experience emotions, especially negative ones. What is unclear is whether patients who experience intense emotions are the same as those who are outwardly nonexpressive.

Empirical Investigations

The male schizophrenic patients in our studies were selected from the research units at Mt. Sinai Medical Center, the Bronx Veterans Administration Hospital, and Pilgrim Psychiatric Center. For most patients, diagnoses based on the *Diagnostic and Statistical Manual of Mental Disorders* (3rd ed., rev.) criteria were derived from a standard research protocol (Keefe, Mohs, Losonczy, et al., 1987), which included the Schedule for Affective Disorders and Schizophrenia (SADS; Endicott & Spitzer, 1978) conducted by trained interviewers. Hospital diagnoses were obtained for those patients who had not yet completed the standard diagnostic work-up. Any participant with a history of head trauma, severe alcohol or drug abuse, or known neurological disease was excluded from the study. Additionally, patients with evidence of tardive dyskinesia were excluded so as not to confuse uncontrollable facial movements with facial expressions of emotion. Mean age was in the upper thirties. Mean number of years of education was slightly over 12. On average the patients had been hospitalized about eight times.

Because many neuroleptic medications can reduce SCR via their anticholinergic effects and can produce a lack of movement in facial muscles, it was crucial that we test unmedicated patients. Therefore all patients were medication-free for at least 2 weeks prior to testing. Serum neuroleptic levels were analyzed to confirm drug-free status. Because depot neuroleptics often lead to the maintenance of plasma drug levels for several months following their discontinuation, patients who had received depot neuroleptics in the past 3 months were not included.

Normal males were recruited from the nonprofessional staff of SUNY, Stony Book and Pilgrim Psychiatric Center. They were screened for psychopathology and family history of psychopathology. They did not differ from the patients in age or education but were more likely than the patients to have been married.

The major goal of the present research was to gather further data on nonverbal aspects of emotion in schizophrenics. With data from multiple sources we should be able to draw firmer conclusions concerning whether the lower level of facial activity among schizophrenics is occurring despite equivalent experience of emotion or whether their lack of facial activity actually reflects a lack of emotional response.

There are many methods for eliciting emotion in the laboratory. We chose film clips because they have been used successfully with schizophrenics by Berenbaum and Oltmanns (1992). Additionally, film clips allowed us to assess changes in emotion over time. Subjects were randomly assigned to view one of two sets of stimulus tapes. Each set included neutral (nature films), happy, sad, and fear/disgust segments ranging in length from 285 to 360 seconds. Multiple sets were used to ensure that responses were not due to the unique characteristics of a single film. Film set had no effect on the main results and will not be discussed further. In previous research with these clips we had validated that they each elicit the intended emotion to a significantly greater extent than the others. At the end of each film, participants completed the Positive and Negative Affect Schedule (PANAS; Watson, Clark, & Tellegen, 1988), a 20-item, mood adjective checklist designed to measure two orthogonal factors: positive affect (PA) and negative affect (NA). Finally, the number of nonspecific SCRs (minimum amplitude, .05 microsiemens) and heart rate were continuously recorded with a Colbourn Instruments constant-voltage coupler and cardiotachometer using standard recording methods. (For further details, see Kring, 1991; Kring, Kerr, Smith & Neale, 1993.)

Because our interests were in positive and negative facial expressivity and its correspondence to self-reports of PA and NA, a dimensional facial coding system was deemed most appropriate to our needs. We thus developed a new system for coding facial expression (the Facial Expression Coding System, FACES), both to assess dimensional expressivity and to allow for an analysis of over 20 continuous minutes of expression. Although highly sophisticated methods (such as Ekman and colleagues' Facial Action Coding System) exist, they are time consuming to implement, are typically used with relatively short video segments, and they assess discrete emotions rather than dimensions.

In FACES, an expression is defined as a change from a neutral expression to a non-neutral expression and back to neutral. The rating dimensions were drawn from the literature suggesting that two dimensions, valence and arousal, provide an effective description of emotion (Russell, 1980). Coders rate the expression on valence (positive or negative) and intensity, and record its duration (see Kring & Sloan, 1991, for more details). Average intraclass correlations between raters was high (.87–.93). For the present analysis, the individual variables (frequency, intensity, and duration) were converted to z scores and aggregated to yield a single positive and negative expression score for each film.[1]

The facial expression data were analyzed separately for positive and negative expressions in 2 (Group) × 4 (Film Type) MANOVAS, followed by simple effects analyses of significant interactions. The interaction was significant in both analyses. For positive expressions, the schizophrenics were markedly lower than the normals for the happy film, and for negative expressions schizophrenics were lower than normals during both the sad and fear/disgust films (see figure 25.1). Parallel analyses were conducted for the PANAS ratings of PA and NA. Importantly, the self-reports of schizophrenics and normals were equally reliable as measured by coefficient alpha. In one sample (Kring et al., 1993), schizophrenics reported more PA than the normals during the happy and neutral films. However, in another sample (Kring, 1991) there were no between group differences in PA. Regarding NA, for both samples the reports of schizophrenics were higher than those of the normals during the happy and neutral films. Finally, nonspecific SCRs and heart rate were analyzed with a Group × Film type analysis of covariance (using baseline as a covariate). For SCRs there

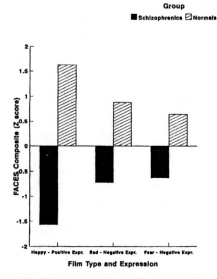

Figure 25.1 Facial expressions of schizophrenics and normals for each film type. Scores are z-ed and aggregated over the components of FACES.

were no significant between-group differences during baseline, but schizophrenics were higher than normals during each film (see figure 25.2). For heart rate, schizophrenics were higher than the normals during *both* baseline and while viewing the films. Therefore, the heart rate data are not readily interpretable.[2] To sum up, there was a striking dissociation among the three emotion indicators in schizophrenics: Their marked lack of expression was coupled with a higher than normal rate of nonspecific SCRs and phenomenological reports of considerable emotion.

Causes of Flat Affect

To examine some possible correlates of flat affect, we had included measures of emotion perception and neuropsychological performance as part of our overall research protocol. A failure to perceive correctly the emotional displays of others could be related to flat affect. To assess this possibility we devised new measures of the perception of both facial and vocal affect and linked them to control tasks assessing visual and auditory perceptual abilities. New measures were needed because existing ones were far from optimal in their psychometric properties (see Kerr & Neale, 1993, for full details). We found that unmedicated schizophrenics were considerably impaired in perceiving both facial and vocal displays but did not find a differential deficit. That is, the patients were equally impaired on both emotion and nonemotion perception tasks. Although schizophrenics were very poor in emotion perception, this finding does not fit well with the dissociative relationship we found among the emotion indicators. If schizophrenics were failing to perceive the emotional content of the films, it is unlikely that we would have found the SCR and self-report data that we did.

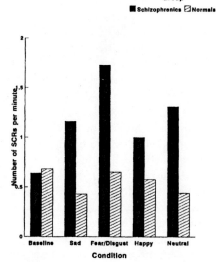

Figure 25.2 Number of skin conductance responses per minute of schizophrenics and normals for baseline and each film type.

Blunted affect may arise from neurological impairment of brain regions involved in emotion. Specifically, both the right hemisphere and the frontal lobes have been implicated in either the experience or expression of emotion. Regarding the right hemisphere, impairment in this region can result in blunted affect or emotional indifference, which is strikingly similar to the clinical picture of flat affect seen in schizophrenia (Denny-Brown, Meyer, & Horenstein, 1952; Gainotti, 1972). Right-hemisphere pathophysiology has been found to be associated with deficits in the ability to express emotions, both facially (Borod, Koff, Lorch, & Nicholas, 1986; Buck & Duffy, 1980) and through vocal intonation (Ross, 1981; Ross, Harney, deLacoste-Utamsing, & Purdy, 1981; Tucker, Watson, & Heilman, 1977; Weintraub, Mesulam, & Kramer, 1981). Frontal lobe dysfunction has also been related to restricted affective behavior or lack of emotional reactivity (Blumer & Benson, 1975; Damasio & Van Hoesen, 1983; Stuss, Grow, & Hetherington, 1992). Additionally, decreased facial expressions have been noted in patients with frontal lobe lesions (Kolb & Milner, 1981; Weddell, Miller, & Trevarthen, 1990).

In the first study to examine the role of neuropsychological impairment in blunted affect, Mayer, Alpert, Stastny, Perlick, and Empfield (1985) found that right hemisphere functioning was related to flat affect. Unfortunately, this study was conducted on medicated schizophrenics and did not examine frontal lobe functioning. In a recent study, we (Blanchard, Kring, & Neale, 1994) sought to replicate and extend Mayer et al.'s findings in a study of unmedicated schizophrenics, utilizing neuropsychological tasks sensitive to functioning of both the right and left hemisphere and the frontal lobes.

Unmedicated schizophrenics performed more poorly than normals on every test with the exception of the Tactile Performance Test, left hand, and the Purdue Pegboard, right hand. These results indicate a pattern of generalized impairment among schizophrenics that is further supported by the high correlation, .88, between composite variables created for right and left hemisphere tests. There was some differentiation, however, between the frontal tasks and the right and left hemisphere composites.

The high correlation between the right and left hemisphere tests clearly compromised our ability to test for a specific association between the right hemisphere and flat affect. Nonetheless, we report the correlations that were obtained. Neuropsychological performance was uncorrelated with clinical ratings of flat affect. Several reliable correlations did emerge between neuropsychological performance and facial expressions assessed while the patients viewed films. One of the frontal tests was associated with fewer expressions during the fear/disgust film and better performance on both right and left hemisphere tasks was associated with more expression during the happy film. These correlations do not readily fit into extant theories of the neuropsychology of emotion. In summary, the neuropsychological hypotheses could not really be well evaluated because of the generalized impairment of the patients and the high correlation between left and right hemisphere tests.

Interpreting Our Findings

Our main finding is a possible dissociation between expressive and other (self-report, psychophysiological) indicators of emotion in schizophrenics. The dissociation we have found could be interpreted as indicating that emotion is being elicited in schizophrenics, but the overt expression of emotion is being inhibited or suppressed. Two recent experiments in which normals were asked to suppress their expressions (Gross & Levenson, 1993a, 1993b) revealed a pattern of findings that is similar to what we have observed in schizophrenics. Subjects in Gross and Levenson's studies were indeed able to successfully inhibit facial displays and inhibiting did not alter their self-reports. In both studies, suppression increased sympathetic arousal as indexed by increased skin conductance, decreased finger pulse amplitude, and shortening of pulse transmission time to the finger. Thus, when normals actively inhibit emotional expression, their behavior in other emotion domains (self-report and psychophysiological) resembles the pattern we have found among schizophrenics. (But also see Lanzetta, Cartwright-Smith, & Kleck, 1976, and Vaughn & Lanzetta, 1981, for other data from normals with different results.)

Lang's (1984) bioinformational analysis of emotion is also of some relevance to a dissociative relationship among emotion indicators in schizophrenics. In brief, he hypothesizes that the activation of an emotion prototype (a specific information structure in memory) leads to self-reports of emotion and also to the activation of the somatomotor and visceral aspects of emotion. He also proposes, and has collected supporting data, that the information in an emotional stimulus can be processed as "knowledge about" an emotional situation. In this case, verbal reports will be appropriate to the context, but the deep structure of the emotion prototype and its motor and visceral components are not activated. Given the well-known cognitive deficits of schizophrenics, it is possible that they do not process the filmed stimuli in depth and hence the emotion prototype is not activated. The prediction would be "normal" self-reports but low levels of facial expression. The high level of SCR could be due to "nonemotional" aspects of the testing situation, such as changes in the intensity of background music. In fact, some of our own data may indicate that the high rate of SCRs among schizophrenics is not due to emotional arousal. For example, the frequency of SCRs was as high during the "neutral" film as during those designed to elicit fear/disgust, happiness, and sadness. Thus, it remains possible that schizophrenics' emotion system as a whole is not being activated. A possible explanation of this pattern could involve cognitive deficit.

To evaluate these contrasting positions, more data are needed on nonverbal indicators of emotional state. Two such measures have emerged from the recent literature. One is Lang's startle response paradigm (Lang, Bradley, & Cuthbert, 1990). In a series of studies, Lang and colleagues have shown that the response (eye blink magnitude) to acoustic startle probes is reduced when viewing a "positive" slide, and augmented when viewing a "negative" one. That the slides elicit their intended positive and negative emotional states is demonstrated by self-ratings, behavioral measures, and heart rate. Thus, it appears that the magnitude of the startle response can provide a nonverbal indicator of whether the person is in a positive or negative affective state. Applied to the question being asked here, we would expect that if schizophrenics are indeed experiencing emotional states, the magnitude of their startle response would vary as a function of stimulus valence.

A second measure is covert facial activity that is detected by electromyography (EMG) even when no facial expressions are apparent to observers. Positive emotional states are related to high levels of zygomatic activity (cheek muscles) and negative emotional states to high levels of activity in the corrugator (eyebrow) and orbicularis oculi (surrounds lower eye; e.g., Dimberg, 1990). Not only does this pattern appear without observable facial movement, it occurs among subjects who are specifically asked to inhibit facial response (Cacioppo, Bush, & Tassinary, 1992). Based on these findings we would expect that if schizophrenics are experiencing different emotional states we would find that EMG activity would change according to stimulus valence. Data from these paradigms should allow a more definitive answer to the question of whether schizophrenics, despite being nonexpressive, are experiencing emotional states.

Acknowledgments This research was supported by Grant MH4411602 from the National Institute of Mental Health. We thank the staff and patients at the Bronx Veterans Administration Hospital, Mount Sinai Medical Center, and Pilgrim Psychiatric Center for their support and cooperation.

Notes

1. It is interesting to note that Kring and Tomarken (1993) have found a good deal of agreement between one of Ekman and colleagues' systems (EMFACS) and FACES. For example, EMFACS codes of felt and unfelt happiness were related to FACES ratings of positive expressivity, and EMFACS codes of disgust were related to negative expressivity.

2. Although the baseline differences in heart rate make the data difficult to interpret, our findings are consistent with those of other studies examining heart rate response to films in both medicated (Corrigan, Stolley, & Davies-Farmer, 1989) and unmedicated (Goldstein & Acker, 1967) schizophrenics.

References

Abrams, R., & Taylor, M. A. (1978). A rating scale for emotional blunting. *American Journal of Psychiatry, 135,* 226–229.

Andreasen, N. C. (1983). *The scale for the assessment of negative symptoms (SANS).* Iowa City, IA: University of Iowa.

Berenbaum, H., & Oltmanns, T. F. (1992). Emotional experience and expression in schizophrenia and depression. *Journal of Abnormal Psychology, 101,* 37–44.

Blanchard, J. J., Kring, A., & Neale, J. M. (1994). Flat affect and deficits in affective expression in schizophrenia: A test of neuropsychological models. *Schizophrenia Bulletin, 20,* 311–325.

Bleuler, E. (1950). *Dementia praecox, or the group of schizophrenias* (J. Zinkin, Trans.). New York: International University Press.

Blumer, D., & Benson, D. F. (1975). Personality changes with frontal and temporal lobe lesions. In D. F. Benson & D. Blumer (Eds.), *Psychiatric aspects of neurologic disease,* (pp. 151–170). New York: Grune & Stratton.

Borod, J. C., Koff, E., Lorch, M., & Nicholas, M. (1986). The expression and perception of facial emotion in brain-damaged patients. *Neuropsychologia, 24,* 169–180.

Brown, S., Sweeney, D. R., & Schwartz, G. E. (1979). Differences between self-reported and observed pleasure in depression and schizophrenia. *The Journal of Nervous and Mental Disease, 167,* 410–415.

Buck, R., & Duffy, R. J. (1980). Nonverbal communication of affect in brain-damaged patients. *Cortex, 16,* 351–362.

Cacioppo, J. T., Bush, L. K., & Tassinary, L. G. (1992). Micro expressive facial actions as a function of affective stimuli. *Personality and Social Psychology Bulletin, 18,* 515–526.

Carpenter, W. T., Strauss, J. S., & Bartko, J. J. (1974). An approach to the diagnosis and understanding of schizophrenia: Part 1. Use of signs and symptoms for the identification of schizophrenic patients. *Schizophrenia Bulletin, 1,* 37–49.

Corrigan, P. W., Stolley, M. R., & Davies-Farmer, E. M. (1989). Cardiovascular reactivity in schizophrenics to videotaped social vignettes. *Psychological Reports, 65,* 847–850.

Damasio, A. R., & Van Hoesen, G. W. (1983). Emotional disturbances associated with focal lesions of the frontal lobe. In K. Heilman & P. Satz (Eds.), *The neurophysiology of human emotion: Recent advances* (pp. 85–110). New York: Guilford Press.

Denny-Brown, D., Meyer, J. S., & Horenstein, S. (1952). The significance of perceptual rivalry resulting from parietal lesions. *Brain, 75,* 434–471.

Dimberg, U. (1990). Facial electromyography and emotional reactions. *Psychophysiology, 27,* 481–493.

Dworkin, R. H. (1992). Affective deficits and social deficits in schizophrenia: What's what? *Schizophrenia Bulletin, 18,* 59–64.

Endicott, J., Nee, F., Cohen, J., Fleiss, J. L., & Simon, R. (1986). Diagnosis of schizophrenia: Prediction of short-term outcome. *Archives of General Psychiatry, 43,* 13–19.

Endicott, J., & Spitzer, R. L. (1978). A diagnostic interview: The Schedule for Affective Disorders and Schizophrenia. *Archives of General Psychiatry, 35,* 837–844.

Fleming, P. (1969). *Prediction of adult psychopathology through early emotional experiences.* Paper presented at the conference on Life History Research in Psychopathology, Minneapolis, MN.

Fleming, P., & Ricks, D. F. (1970). Emotions of children before schizophrenia and before character disorder. In M. Roff & D. F. Ricks (Eds.), *Life history research in psychopathology* (pp. 240–264). Minneapolis: University of Minnesota Press.

Freedman, R., & Mirsky, A. (1991). Event-related potentials: Exogenous components. In S. H. Steinhauer, J. Gruzelier, & J. Zubin (Eds.), *Handbook of schizophrenia* (Vol. 5, pp. 71–90). New York: Elsevier.

Gainotti, G. (1972). Emotional behavior and hemispheric side of lesion. *Cortex, 8*, 41–45.

Goldstein, M. J., & Acker, C. W. (1967). Psychophysiological reaction to films by chronic schizophrenics. *Journal of Abnormal Psychology, 72*, 23–39.

Gross, J. J., & Levenson, R. W. (1993a). *Emotional suppression.* Paper presented at the annual meeting of the Society for Psychophysiological Research, Rottach-Egern, Germany.

Gross, J. J., & Levenson, R. W. (1993b). Emotional suppression: Physiology, self-report, and expressive behavior. *Journal of Personality and Social Psychology, 64*, 970–986.

Hurlbert, R. (1989). *Sampling normal and schizophrenic inner experience.* New York: Plenum Press.

Kavanagh, D. J. (1992). Recent developments in expressed emotion and schizophrenia. *British Journal of Psychiatry, 160*, 601–620.

Keefe, R. S. E., Mohs, R. C., Losonczy, M. F., Davidson, M., Silverman, J. M., Kendler, K. S., Horvath, T. B., Nora, R., & Davis, K. (1987). Characteristics of very poor outcome schizophrenia. *American Journal of Psychiatry, 144*, 889–895.

Kerr, S., & Neale, J. M. (1993). Emotion perception in schizophrenia: Specific deficit or further evidence of generalized impairment? *Journal of Abnormal Psychology, 102*, 312–318.

Kolb, B., & Milner, B. (1981). Observations on spontaneous facial expression after focal cerebral excisions and after intracarotid injection of sodium amytal. *Neuropsychologia, 19*, 505–514.

Kraepelin, E. (1904). *Lectures on clinical psychiatry* (T. Johnstone, Trans.). New York: Wood.

Krause, R., Steiner, E., Sanger-Alt, C., & Wagner, G. (1989). Facial expression of schizophrenic patients and their interaction partners. *Psychiatry, 52*, 1–12.

Kring, A. M. (1991). *The relationship between emotional expression, subjective experience, and autonomic arousal in schizophrenia.* Unpublished Ph.D. thesis, SUNY, Stony Brook.

Kring, A. M., & Sloan, D. (1991). *The Facial Expression Coding System (FACES): A users guide.* Unpublished manuscript.

Kring, A., Kerr, S., Smith, D. A., & Neale, J. M. (1993). Flat affect in schizophrenia does not reflect diminished subjective experience of emotion. *Journal of Abnormal Psychology, 102*, 507–517.

Kring, A. M., & Tomarken, A. J. (1993, June). *Measuring facial expression of emotion: A comparison of methods.* Paper presented at the annual meeting of the American Psychological Society, Chicago, IL.

Lang, P. J. (1984). Cognition in emotion: Concept and action. In C. Izard, J. Kagan, & R. Zajone (Eds.), *Emotions, cognitions, and behavior* (pp. 192–226). New York: Cambridge University Press.

Lang, P. J., Bradley, M. M., & Cuthbert, B. N. (1990). Emotion, attention, and the startle reflex. *Psychological Review, 97*, 377–395.

Lanzetta, J. T., Cartwright-Smith, J., & Kleck, R. E. (1976). Effects of nonverbal dissimulation on emotional experience and autonomic arousal. *Journal of Personality and Social Psychology, 33*, 354–370.

Levenson, R. W., Ekman, P., & Friesen, W. V. (1990). Voluntary facial action generates emotion-specific autonomic nervous system activity. *Psychophysiology, 27,* 363–384.

Mayer, M., Alpert, M., Stastny, P., Perlick, D., & Empfield, M. (1985). Multiple contributions to clinical presentation of flat affect in schizophrenia. *Schizophrenia Bulletin, 11,* 420–426.

McGlashan, T. H. (1994). Psychosocial treatments of schizophrenia: The potential of relationships. In N. C. Andreasen (Ed.), *Schizophrenia: From mind to molecule* (pp. 189–215). Washington, DC: American Psychiatric Press.

Notarius, C. I., & Levenson, R. W. (1979). Expressive tendencies and physiological response to stress. *Journal of Personality and Social Psychology, 37,* 1204–1210.

Rado, S. (1953). Dynamics and classification of disordered behavior. *American Journal of Psychiatry, 110,* 406–416.

Rodnick, E., & Garmezy, N. (1957). An experimental approach to the study of motivation in schizophrenia. In M. R. Jones (Ed.), *Nebraska symposium on motivation* (Vol. 5, pp. 109–183). Lincoln: University of Nebraska Press.

Ross, E. D. (1981). The aprosodias: Functional-anatomic organization of the affective components of language in the right hemisphere. *Archives of Neurology, 38,* 561–569.

Ross, E. D., Harney, J. H., deLacoste-Utamsing, C., & Purdy, P. D. (1981). How the brain integrates affective and propositional language into a unified behavioral function: Hypotheses based on clinicoanatomic evidence. *Archives of Neurology, 38,* 745–748.

Russell, J. A. (1980). A circumplex model of affect. *Journal of Personality and Social Psychology, 39,* 1161–1178.

Sturgeon, D., Turpin, G., & Berkowitz, R. (1984). Psychophysiological responses of schizophrenic patients to high and low expressed emotion relatives: A follow-up study. *British Journal of Psychiatry, 145,* 62–69.

Stuss, D. T., Grow, C. A., & Hetherington, C. R. (1992). "No longer Gage": Frontal lobe dysfunction and emotional changes. *Journal of Consulting and Clinical Psychology, 60,* 349–359.

Tarrier, N., Vaughn, C., & Lader, M. H. (1979). Bodily reactions to people and events in schizophrenia. *Archives of General Psychiatry, 36,* 618–624.

Tucker, D. M., Watson, R. T., & Heilman, K. M. (1977). Discrimination and evocation of affectively intoned speech in patients with right parietal disease. *Neurology, 27,* 947–950.

Vaughan, K. B., & Lanzetta, J. T. (1981). The effect of modification of expressive displays on vicarious emotional arousal. *Journal of Experimental Social Psychology, 17,* 16–20.

Ventura, J., Neuchterlein, K. H., Lukoff, D., & Hardesty, J. D. (1989). A prospective study of stressful life events and schizophrenia relapse. *Journal of Abnormal Psychology, 98,* 407–411.

Watson, D., Clark, L. A., Tellegen, A. (1988). Development and validation of brief measures of positive and negative affect. *Journal of Personality and Social Psychology, 54,* 1063–1070.

Weddell, R. A., Miller, J. D., & Trevarthen, C. (1990). Voluntary emotional facial expression in patients with focal cerebral lesions. *Neuropsychologia, 28,* 49–60.

Weintraub, S., Mesulam, M., & Kramer, L. (1981). Disturbances in prosody: A right-hemisphere contribution to language. *Archives of Neurology, 38,* 742–744.

Zahn, T., Frith, H., & Steinhauer, S. (1991). Psychophysiological studies. In S. Steinhauer, J. Gruzelier, & J. Zubin (Eds.), *Handbook of schizophrenia* (Vol. 5, pp. 185–226). New York: Oxford University Press.

Part IV

DISORDERED PERSONALITY

26

Robert Plutchik

Emotions, Diagnoses, and Ego Defense

A Psychoevolutionary Perspective

The psychoevolutionary theory of emotions has been described in a number of previous publications (Plutchik, 1980a, 1980b, 1983, 1989, 1990, 1993, 1994a). The focus of the present chapter is on some implications of the theory for an understanding of psychopathology—more specifically, the contributions the theory makes to an understanding of clinical test development, personality disorders, and the nature of ego defenses are discussed.

The Psychoevolutionary Theory of Emotion: An Overview

There are six basic postulates that define the characteristics of emotions: (a) Emotions are communication and survival mechanisms based on evolutionary adaptations, (b) emotions have a genetic basis, (c) emotions are hypothetical constructs based on various classes of evidence, (d) emotions are complex chains of events with stabilizing feedback loops that produce some kind of behavioral homeostasis, (e) the relations among emotions can be represented by a three-dimensional structural model, and (f) emotions are related to a number of conceptual domains that are derived from emotions.

Evolutionary theory assumes that the natural environment creates survival problems for all organisms that must be successfully dealt with if they are to survive. These problems include, for example, differentially communicating with and responding to prey and predators, potential mates, and caregivers and care solicitors. Emotions can be conceptualized as basic adaptive patterns that deal with these survival issues and that can be identified at all phylogenetic levels. These patterns involve approach and avoidance reactions, fight and fight reactions, attachment and loss reactions, and riddance or ejection reactions. The evolutionary perspective suggests that these patterns are the prototypes of what we call emotions in higher animals and in humans. The subjective feelings that are often identified as emotions are a relatively late evolutionary development and should not be used as the only criterion of the presence of an emotional state. Although the details of the adaptive processes vary among different animals, species, and phyla, depending on the nature of the environment and genetics, the *function* of each pattern of adaptation has remained unchanged throughout all phylogenetic levels. From the evolutionary point of view, emotions are patterns of adaptation that increase the chances of individual and genetic survival.

Another way to describe the psychoevolutionary theory is in terms of its component models. There are three: the *sequential model*, the *structural model*, and the *derivatives model*.

The Sequential Model

In the sequential model, an emotion is a complex chain of events that begins with a stimulus event and is followed by a cognitive evaluation of the stimulus as relevant to the well-being or integrity of the individual. If such a determination is made, various feelings as well as a pattern of physiological changes will result. These physiological changes have the character of anticipatory reactions associated with various types of exertions or impulses, such as the urge to attack, to retreat, or to mate. Depending on the relative strengths of these various impulses, a final result will occur in the form of overt action that is designed to have an effect on the stimulus that triggered this chain of events in the first place. For example, distress signals by a puppy or the crying of an infant will increase the probability that the mother or a mother-substitute will arrive on the scene. The overall effect of this complex negative feedback system is to reduce the threat or to change the emergency situation in such a way as to achieve a temporary behavioral homeostasis (Plutchik, 1994a).

The Structural Model

In the structural model the relations among emotions are represented by a three-dimensional structural model shaped like a cone. The vertical dimension represents the intensity of emotions, the circle defines the degree of similarity of emotions, and polarity is represented by the opposite emotions on the circle. This model also includes the idea that some emotions are primary and others are blends or mixtures, in the same sense that some colors are primary and others are mixed. A number of studies have been published showing that the relations among emotion concepts can be described by means of a circle or circumplex (Conte & Plutchik, 1981; Fisher, Heise, Bohrnstedt, & Lucke, 1985; Plutchik, 1980a; Russell, 1989; Wiggins & Broughton, 1985).

In examining the concept of mixtures of emotion (Plutchik, 1980a), it gradually became evident that the terminology used by raters to label the mixtures included many terms that are usually considered to describe personality traits. For example, the mixture of anger and disgust was often labeled by such terms as hostile, scornful, and sarcastic. The mixture of sadness and fear was given such labels as forlorn or passive. These connotations suggested that the combining of primary emotions into blends or compounds created long-lasting, dispositional traits that are part of the language of interpersonal interactions. These observations led to the idea that interpersonal personality traits are *derivatives* of emotions. It led also to the idea that there are other derivative concepts as well.

The Derivatives Model

The concept of emotion derivatives gradually evolved to include a large number of conceptual domains. For example, based on the circumplex structure of emotions, it was hypothesized that personality traits would also show a circumplex structure. This was demonstrated by Conte and Plutchik (1981), who used two independent methods to examine the similarity structure of a large sample of personality terms. One method was direct similarity scaling, and the other was based on the semantic differential. The two methods produced angular locations of the personality traits that correlated over +.95. The study also revealed that the language of emotions and personality overlapped to a considerable degree and thus further supported the notion of their intimate connection.

Based on these observations two new tests of emotion/personality were developed. The first, called the Emotions Profile Index (EPI; Plutchik & Kellerman, 1974), provides measures of the intensity of the eight basic emotions present in an individual. It is based on the idea that when individuals choose personality traits as descriptive of themselves, they are automatically revealing something about the underlying emotions that are the theoretical components of the traits. This means that those who describe themselves as shy or gloomy are implicitly telling us something about the primary emotions that make up these traits. Shyness, for example, implies frequent feelings of fear, whereas gloominess implies frequent feelings of sadness.

The EPI is a forced-choice test. The person taking it is simply asked to indicate which of two paired words is more personally descriptive; for example, is he or she more quarrelsome or shy? The choices are scored in terms of the primary emotions implied by the trait word. Each time the respondent makes a choice between two trait words he or she adds to the score on one or more of the eight basic emotion dimensions. The test measures not only anxiety, but also anger, sadness, joy, and so on. Because the implications of the choices are not always clear to the respondent, the test has something of a projective quality since the subject does not usually recognize the implicit scoring system. Finally, because of the forced-choice format of the EPI, it tends to reduce response bias associated with a set to choose socially desirable traits. This is true because many of the choices must be made between two equally undesirable or two equally desirable traits. In addition, a bias score is built into the test as a measure of the respondent's tendency to choose socially desirable or undesirable traits in those cases where the items are not matched. Figure 26.1 shows what a depression profile looks like. It is based on a group of hospitalized manic-depressive patients while they were in the depressed phase of their illness. With the norm at the 50th percentile based on a large group of nonpatients, it is evident that these depressed patients are very high on the depression scale (90th percentile), relatively low on the gregarious scale (38th percentile), very low on the dyscontrol ("interested in new experiences") scale (26th percentile), and moderately high on timidity

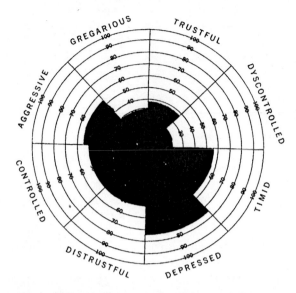

Figure 26.1 Depression profile based on the *Emotions Profile Index* obtained from a group of manic-depressive patients

(anxiety) (66th percentile) and aggressiveness (60th percentile). Some inferences can be made about the presence of conflicts based on the magnitudes of opposite scales.

The second personality test based on the theory is called the Personality Profile Index (PPI; Plutchik & Conte, 1989). This 89-item test provides an assessment of eight personality dimensions labeled accepting, submissive, passive, assertive, sociable, rejecting, aggressive, and depressed. The PPI yields measures of both social desirability and conflict. Patients rate (on a 5-point scale) how often they show various behaviors. Items are stated in the following ways: "I am easy to get along with," "I enjoy doing things that are risky," "I let people know what is wrong with their opinions," "I get embarrassed easily." Internal reliabilities of the subscales are high. The scales correlate in clinically meaningful ways with measures of self-esteem, diagnoses and ego functions.

To illustrate this point, figure 26.2 shows PPI scores for a normal group of subjects and for a group of 20 patients diagnosed as having a borderline personality disorder (Plutchik & Conte, 1989).

Since the normal subjects serve as the norm group, their mean scores are all at approximately the 50th percentile. In contrast, the borderline patients are very low on assertiveness, sociability, and acceptance. They are very high on depression, passivity, rejection and aggressiveness. Other profiles have been obtained for different diagnostic groups. The concept of derivatives of emotion has other implications as well.

Personality Disorders as Derivatives of Emotion

Table 26.1 provides a theoretical statement of the relations among subjective emotion terms and words that are used in other conceptual domains. Seven different

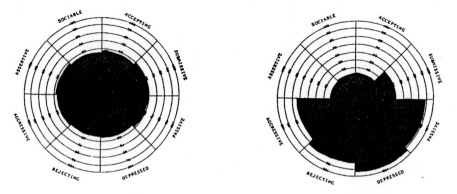

Figure 26.2 Personality profiles obtained from a normal group (N=170) and a group of borderline outpatients (N=20)

domains are represented, although these are not exhaustive. To illustrate the ideas consider one emotion, anger. In the *subjective language* this state has various aspects, depending on intensity, which can be represented by such terms as annoyed, irritated, and furious. The *behavioral language* that is associated with anger in a probabilistic way, would be represented by such terms as attacking, fighting, biting, or hitting. The *functional language* would be described by a term such as *destruction*, implying that the function of attack is the destruction of a barrier to the satisfaction of one's needs. As emotions mix, fuse, or interact, new families of states are derived that we call *personality traits*. Thus, "quarrelsome" or "rebellious" would be traits derived from anger as an emotion. These traits may be thought of as within "normal" limits. However, when these traits exist in an individual at an extreme level the language of personality diagnoses is then used. Thus, the extremely quarrelsome or rebellious individual might be given the diagnosis of antisocial personality, just as the extremely gloomy person would be called dysthymic, or the extremely timid person, avoidant.

The *language of ego defenses* has usually been considered an independent domain of mental functioning, yet the clinical literature implies a strong connection to emotions. For example, a child who is punished by his mother may feel angry or vengeful, yet be afraid to express these emotions directly to his mother because of fear of further punishment, or fear of loss of love. Instead the child may kick his dog, beat up his younger brother, or smash his mother's favorite vase "by accident." These are classical examples of displacement reactions. The interaction of anger and anxiety leads to the use of the ego defense of displacement. A similar case can be made for the other ego defenses and this issue will be discussed in more detail shortly.

The last derivative domain to be illustrated here is the *language of coping styles*. In contrast to defenses, which are presumably unconscious, rigid attempts at self-protection, coping styles are conscious, flexible modes of problem-solving. If, for example, an adult is faced with threat or punishment from a boss that he or she believes would not be wise to handle by direct confrontation, he or she might use an indirect method of coping such as jogging, meditation, or having an extra cocktail at

Table 26.1 Emotions and Their Derivatives

Subjective language	Behavioral language	Functional language	Trait language	Diagnostic language	Ego-defense language	Coping-style language
Fear	Escape	Protection	Timid	Avoidant, Dependent	Repression	Suppression
Anger	Attack	Destruction	Quarrelsome	Antisocial	Displacement	Substitution
Joy	Mate	Reproduction	Sociable	Manic	Reaction-Formation	Reversal
Sadness	Cry	Reintegration	Gloomy	Depressed	Compensation	Replacement
Acceptance	Groom	Incorporation	Trusting	Histrionic	Denial	Minimization
Disgust	Vomit	Rejection	Hostile	Paranoid-Narcissistic	Projection	Fault finding
Expectation	Map	Exploration	Demanding	Obsessive-Compulsive	Intellectualization	Mapping
Surprise	Stop	Orientation	Indecisive	Borderline	Regression	Help seeking

dinner. Such coping styles are substitutes for anger because of the fear of further punishment or loss. In the same general way, denial may be an unconscious ego defense, while its derivative, minimization, may be a conscious way of handling a frustrating situation by minimizing its relative importance.

The Circumplex Structure of Personality Disorders

One of the important implications of the concept that various clinical domains are derivatives of emotion is that these domains should have some of the properties of emotions. Since the structural model of the psychoevolutionary theory assumes that emotions are related to one another in terms of a circular or circumplex similarity structure, it is likely that the circumplex model applies to these other domains, such as personality, personality disorders, and ego defenses. The study by Conte and Plutchik (1981), as well as others (e.g., Wiggins and Broughton, 1985), has already demonstrated that the language of interpersonal personality traits may be represented by a circumplex. Other work, to be described here, has shown that the circumplex idea applies to personality disorders and to ego defenses as well. A recent book reveals a number of other domains to which the circumplex idea applies (Plutchik & Conte, 1997).

Comorbidity of Personality Disorders

Low agreement on personality disorder diagnoses has continued to be reported both for the *Diagnostic and Statistical Manual of Mental Disorders* (3rd ed.) (DSM-III) and DSM-III-R (3rd ed., rev.; Frances, 1985; Melsop, Varghese, Joshua, & Hicks, 1982; Serban, Conte, & Plutchik, 1987; Skodal, Resnick, Kellman, Oldham, & Hyler, 1988). The low reliability of Axis II categories and corresponding overlap of diagnoses have led to the observation that certain diagnoses overlap with each other much more than they do with other diagnoses. Thus, in three studies, reporting correlations between the symptoms of the 11 DSM-III personality disorders, it was found that the highest degrees of overlap were obtained in the following pairs of disorders — avoidant/dependent, histrionic/narcissistic, and schizotypal/paranoid (Hyler et al., 1988; Kass, Skodol, Charles, Spitzer, & Williams, 1985). This overlap of diagnoses has led in recent years to an increased interest in comorbidity issues, as well as to attempts to create clusters of Axis II disorders. For example, Francis (1985) has suggested that the personality disorders may be grouped into three broad clusters on the basis of relative similarity. The first cluster consisting of the paranoid, schizoid, and schizotypal diagnoses has been called the "eccentric" cluster. The second, consisting of the antisocial, borderline, histrionic, and narcissistic diagnoses, has been labeled as the "dramatic" or "erratic" cluster. The third or "anxious" cluster consists of the avoidant, dependent, obsessive-compulsive, and passive-aggressive diagnoses.

An issue that has been largely ignored, however, concerns the *degree* of overlap, or degree of similarity between the various diagnoses, as well as the degree of relationship between the clusters themselves. The research to be described is based on the assumption that a circumplex similarity model will provide a more adequate description of the overlap of diagnostic concepts than will the assumption of "independent" clusters or simple comorbidities.

In the past few decades, the idea of a circular set of personality descriptions has been applied specifically to the personality disorders. For example, Plutchik and Schaefer (1966) asked experienced clinicians to judge the extent to which a person who was described by a diagnostic label such as dependent or compulsive would exhibit each of a number of traits or emotions. The data were factor-analyzed and the factor loadings for each diagnosis plotted. The results showed a circumplex with schizoid and compulsive diagnoses at very similar locations, while dependent and psychopathic were opposite each other and independent of the first group. In a later study, Plutchik and Platman (1977) asked psychiatrists to select personality traits that they believed to be associated with each diagnostic label. Factor analysis of these ratings demonstrated a circumplex with hysterical and cyclothymic diagnoses being relatively similar, but quite opposite to the paranoid and schizoid diagnoses. Kiesler (1983) described his Interpersonal Circle, which included both personality traits and personality disorders. In this circumplex, histrionic was opposite inhibited, submissive was opposite dominant, and paranoid was near both hostile and competitive. Plutchik and Conte (1985) presented a circumplex of DSM-III-R personality disorders based on psychiatrists' judgments of similarity using a paired comparison technique. The results indicated great similarity of four diagnoses: schizoid, schizotypal, passive-aggressive, and avoidant. This cluster was almost opposite the histrionic diagnosis and independent of another closely related group of diagnoses: antisocial, narcissistic, and borderline. These findings are consistent with those of Kass et al. (1985), as well as the groupings proposed by Francis (1985). However, they add the important concept of polarities.

If the circumplex structure of Axis II diagnoses can be established, there are a number of potential benefits. First, the model will clearly indicate which diagnoses are most difficult to differentiate from one another. Second, by recognizing that co-occurrence of symptoms of different disorders is a frequent phenomenon rather than a rare event, it may provide a more refined basis for diagnosis of patients. Third, it may provide a systematic framework for examining the effects of psychotherapy interventions.

In the new study to be described here, the method used was a modified paired-comparison procedure (Conte & Plutchik, 1981; Plutchik & Conte, 1985). This procedure was used to estimate the similarity and dissimilarity of the 11 DSM-III-R Axis II personality disorders plus the proposed diagnostic categories of sadistic personality disorder and self-defeating personality disorder. A category for dysthymia as another possible personality disorder was also added. Sixteen clinicians (eight psychiatrists and eight psychologists) independently rated the 14 disorders against three reference disorders, using a 7-point bipolar scale. These terms were selected on the basis of previous work by Plutchik and Conte (1985) that demonstrated a circular ordering of the 11 personality disorders listed in DSM-III and that also represented each of the diagnostic clusters, A, B, and C, of the personality disorders listed in DSM-III-R. The diagnoses that were selected as reference points were schizotypal, narcissistic, and dependent. Clinicians were asked to rate for similarity the other diagnostic categories against each of them.

However, in the present study, it was decided not to use single diagnostic terms such as *antisocial, narcissistic,* or *schizoid,* simply because such terms in isolation may have somewhat different meanings to different clinicians. Instead, we prepared a brief descriptive paragraph for each personality diagnosis based explicitly on the criteria given in DSM-III-R. The adequacy of each description was rated and revised by an independent group of clinicians. The average similarity ratings for the diagnostic descriptions relative to each reference description were then transformed into angular placements on a circle. This transformation is related to the geometrical convention stating that no relation (i.e., independence) between two variables can be represented by a 90-degree angle on a circle, that polar opposites can be represented by 180-degree separation on a circle, and that all other degrees of similarity will fall between identity and polarity. Once all the diagnostic descriptions received angular placements relative to each of the three reference descriptions, an average angular placement on a circle was determined for each disorder. The results of these similarity ratings are plotted on a circle shown in figure 26.3. The paranoid schizotypal and schizoid diagnoses are sequential on the circle and clearly form the "eccentric" cluster defined by Francis (1985). The "erratic" or "dramatic" cluster as defined in DSM-III-R is not confirmed. For example, borderline and histrionic are not found in this segment of the circle. It is interesting to note, however, that sadistic fits nicely with narcissistic and antisocial. This cluster seems to be centered around aspects of aggression. We therefore believe that this "cluster" or segment of the circle should more properly be labeled the "aggressive" cluster.

The traditional "anxious" cluster purportedly consisting of avoidant, dependent, obsessive-compulsive, and passive aggressive is also not confirmed. Our findings

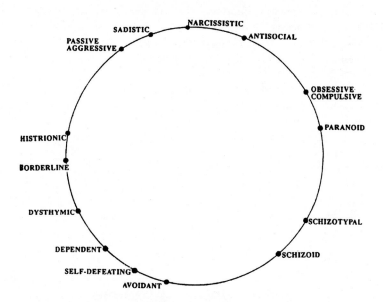

Figure 26.3 Circumplex structure of personality disorders

indicate that avoidant and dependent are highly similar to one another, and are similar to self-defeating and dysthymic disorders. We suggest calling this empirical grouping the anxious/depressed cluster. From our empirical data, the passive-aggressive and obsessive-compulsive disorders appear to be quite dissimilar to the anxious/depressed grouping.

Of some interest is the fact that the histrionic and borderline diagnoses are near each other on the circumplex and also near the dysthymic diagnosis. If one were trying to identify a cluster into which they fit, it would seem to be the anxious/depressive cluster. The presence of strong features of both anxiety and depression in these two diagnoses supports this placement.

In terms of opposition of personality disorders, we find that the aggressive cluster is opposite the anxious/depressed cluster. We also see that the eccentric cluster is opposite the histrionic and borderline diagnoses.

These findings help us to understand that some degree of comorbidity exists for all personality disorders, and that there is a gradual transition from one personality disorder to another in terms of degree of similarity. Strictly speaking, this implies that clusters are somewhat arbitrary and are based on an arbitrary selection of boundaries. The circumplex concept implies that all personality disorders, those we now recognize and those that may be clinically labeled in the future, can be represented by placements on a circle as a function of degree of closeness.

Another implication of these findings is that the concept of comorbidity is a narrow way of describing the more fundamental similarity structure of personality disorders. Comorbidity applies only to pairs of overlapping disorders. The concept of the circumplex implies that all personality disorders overlap in different ways and to different degrees. For example, an opposite placement of two disorders on the circumplex implies that they will almost never be mistaken for one another, which might be called a kind of negative comorbidity.

Finally, we believe that these findings have relevance to the issue of whether personality disorders should be thought of in terms of discrete categories or in terms of dimensions. The present data suggest that personality disorders are not discrete categories and that various kinds of overlap and comorbidity exist for all disorders. All disorders vary in degrees of similarity to one another, and in this sense there is a dimension of similarity that relates all personality disorders. In addition, for any single diagnostic label there are different numbers of symptoms that can be used to define it. This implies a dimension of intensity for each diagnosis, even though many clinicians prefer to use an arbitrary criterion to decide when a diagnosis is said to exist. The selection of patients for psychotherapy research should be based on a recognition of the arbitrary nature of single diagnoses and on the need to provide a meaningful profile for each individual on all personality disorders.

A Theory of Ego Defenses as Derivatives of Emotion

The classical psychoanalytic view of ego defenses assumed that anxiety was the trigger that initiates defensive functioning in a weak or immature ego. Freud assumed that defensive processes emerge during a very early stage of mental development and that they have one or more of three functions: (a) blocking or inhibition of mental contents, (b) distortion of mental content, or (c) screening and covering of mental contents by the use of opposite contents. This concept of defense is at the core of Freud's theory of neurosis. Defenses invariably lead to self-deception. Since defenses by definition are theoretical constructs, they can only be inferred from overt behavior and from the contents of communications.

The literature on ego defenses implies that many defenses are similar and overlap to varying degrees. It also implies that some defenses are polar opposites of others. For example, introjection is the opposite of projection, just as acting-out is the opposite of repression (Plutchik, 1994b). These ideas suggest that the circumplex idea applies to defenses as well as to emotions. In a study designed to test this hypothesis, experienced psychiatrists were asked to make paired comparisons of 16 ego-defense concepts in terms of degree of similarity. The details of the method are described in Plutchik, Kellerman, and Conte (1979). The results of this study are shown in figure 26.4.

The results of the analysis revealed an approximate circumplex showing the degree of nearness of all defenses, and polarities as well. Thus, for example, denial, repression, and undoing are considered to be relatively similar in meaning, just as intellectualization, rationalization, and isolation are relatively similar in meaning. The cluster of projection, displacement, and acting-out are also found near one another and thus represent similar methods by which the ego defends itself.

Polarities may also be seen in figure 26.4. Displacement is clearly opposite the defenses of fantasy and introjection; sublimation is opposite regression and reaction

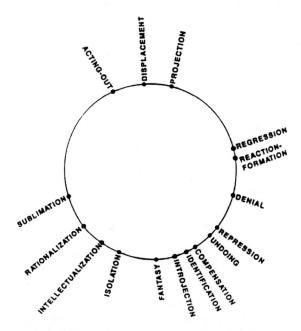

Figure 26.4 Similarity scaling of 16 ego defenses by the method of paired comparisons

formation; acting-out is opposite repression. These are all relations that make clinical sense.

Implications

In humans, particularly during early stages of growth and development, the infant and young child are relatively helpless and have few methods for dealing with dangers. These reactions include calling for help (distress signals), ignoring the danger, and making believe that the danger is not serious, as well as a few others. They are the prototypes of the ego defenses that we recognize in adults. Defenses are relatively limited, rigid, unconscious, and primitive methods that both children and adults use to deal with anxiety-provoking situations. They are related not only to the eight basic emotions postulated by the psychoevolutionary theory of emotions but also to clusters of personality traits, and to diagnoses of personality disorders. As the ego strengthens and matures, dangers and difficulties are seen as problems to be dealt with in relatively more conscious ways. These conscious and therefore flexible problem-solving methods are coping styles, and although they bear some resemblances to defenses, they have emergent properties that make them different. The development of appropriate coping styles is the basis for successful psychotherapy.

References

Conte, H. R., & Plutchik, R. (1981). A circumplex model for interpersonal traits. *Journal of Personality and Social Psychology*, 2, 823–830.

Fisher, G. A., Heise, D. R., Bohrnstedt, G. W., & Lucke, J. Z. (1985). Evidence for extending the circumplex model of personality trait language to self-reported moods. *Journal of Personality and Social Psychology*, 49, 233–242.

Francis, A. (1985). The DSM-III personality disorders: Perspectives from psychology. *Archives of General Psychiatry*, 42, 615–623.

Hyler, S. E., Lyons, M., Rieder, R. O., Young, I. L., Williams, J. B., & Spitzer, R. L. (1990). The factor structure of self-report DSM-III Axis 2 symptoms and their relationship to clinicians ratings. *American Journal of Psychiatry*, 147, 751–755.

Kass, F., Skodol, A. E., Charles, E., Spitzer, R. L., & Williams, J. B. (1985). Scaled ratings of DSM-III personality disorders. *American Journal of Psychiatry*, 142, 627–630.

Kiesler, D. (1983). The 1982 interpersonal circle: A taxonomy of complementarity in human transactions. *Psychological Review*, 90, 185–214.

Mellsop, G., Varghese, F., Joshua, S., & Hicks, A. (1982). The reliability of Axis II of DSM-III. *American Journal of Psychiatry*, 139, 1360–1361.

Plutchik, R. (1980a). *Emotions: A psychoevolutionary synthesis*. New York: Harper & Row.

Plutchik, R. (1980b). A general psychoevolutionary theory of emotion. In R. Plutchik & H. Kellerman (Eds.), *Emotions: Theory, research and experience: Vol. 1. Theories of emotion* (pp. 3–34). New York: Academic Press.

Plutchik, R. (1983). Emotions in early development: A psychoevolutionary approach. In R. Plutchik & H. Kellerman (Eds.), *Emotions: Theory, research and experience: Vol. 2. Emotions in early development* (pp. 221–258). New York: Academic Press.

Plutchik, R. (1989). Measuring emotions and their derivatives. In R. Plutchik & H. Kellerman

(Eds.), *Emotions: Theory, research and experience: Vol. 4. The measurement of emotions* (pp. 1–36). New York: Academic Press.

Plutchik, R. (1990). Emotions and psychotherapy: A psychoevolutionary perspective. In R. Plutchik & H. Kellerman (Eds.), *Emotions: Theory, research and experience: Vol. 5. Emotions, psychopathology and psychotherapy* (pp. 3–42). New York: Academic Press.

Plutchik, R. (1993). Emotions and their vicissitudes: Emotions and psychopathology. In M. Lewis & J. M. Haviland (Eds.), *Handbook of emotions* (pp. 53–66). New York: Guilford Press.

Plutchik, R. (1994a). *The psychology and biology of emotion.* New York: Harper Collins.

Plutchik, R. (1994b). A theory of ego defenses. In H. R. Conte & R. Plutchik (Eds.), *Theory and measurement of ego defenses* (pp. 13–37). New York: Wiley.

Plutchik, R., & Conte, H. R. (1985). Quantitative approaches to the measurement of personality disorders. In R. A. Michels et al. (Eds.), *Psychiatry* (vol. 1, pp. 1–13). Philadelphia: J. B. Lippincott.

Plutchik, R., & Conte, H. R. (1989). Measuring emotions and their derivatives: Personality traits, ego defenses, and coping styles. In S. Wetzler & M. Katz (Eds.), *Contemporary approaches to psychological assessment* (pp. 239–269). New York: Bruner/Maxel.

Plutchik, R., & Conte, H. R. (Eds.). (1997). *Circumplex models of personality and emotions.* Washington, D.C.: American Psychological Association Press.

Plutchik, R., & Kellerman, H. (1974). *Manual of the Emotions Profile Index.* Los Angeles: Western Psychological Services.

Plutchik, R., Kellerman, H., & Conte, H. R. (1979). A structural theory of ego defenses and emotions. In C. E. Izard (Ed.), *Emotions in personality and psychopathology* (pp. 229–257). New York: Plenum Press.

Plutchik, R., & Platman, S. R. (1977). Personality connotations of psychiatric diagnoses. *Journal of Nervous and Mental Disease, 165,* 418–422.

Plutchik, R., & Schaefer, E. S. (1966). Interrelationships of emotions, traits, and diagnostic constructs. *Psychological Reports, 18,* 399–410.

Russell, J. A. (1989). Measures of emotions. In R. Plutchik & H. Kellerman (Eds.), *Emotions: Theory, research and experience: Vol. 4. The measurement of emotions* (pp. 83–112). New York: Academic Press.

Serban, G., Conte, H. R., & Plutchik, R. (1987). Borderline and schizotypal personality disorders: Mutually exclusive or overlapping? *Journal of Personality Assessment, 51,* 15–22.

Skodol, A. E., Rosnick, L., Kellman, O., Oldham, J. M., & Hyler, S. E. (1988). Validating structured DSM-IIIR, personality disorder assessments with longitudinal data. *American Journal of Psychiatry, 145,* 1297–1299.

Wiggins, J. S., & Broughton, R. (1985). The interpersonal circle: A structural model for the integration of personality research. *Perspectives in Personality, 1,* 1–47.

27

Carol Magai & Jill Hunziker

"To Bedlam and Part Way Back"

Discrete Emotions Theory and Borderline Symptoms

Anne Sexton, the popular poet of the mid-twentieth century, one of America's most talented, accessible, and short-lived poets, suffered from symptoms consistent with what today would be called borderline personality disorder. Emblematic of this disorder, as described in the *Diagnostic and Statistical Manual of Mental Disorders* (4th ed.; American Psychiatric Association, 1994), is a "pervasive pattern of instability of interpersonal relationships, self-image, and affects, and marked impulsivity that begins by early adulthood and is present in a variety of contexts" (p. 650). Further features of this disorder, which were observable within Sexton's personality structure, include (a) a profound fear of real or imagined abandonment; (b) a disturbed and unstable self-concept; (c) recurrent suicidal behavior and ideation; (d) chronic feelings of emptiness; (e) intense, inappropriate, and often uncontrollable anger; and (f) transient dissociative states. This clinical description, however, does not provide any clues to the developmental origins of the disorder, or any formulations about the role of particular kinds of emotional experience in forging borderline predispositions.

In the present chapter we consider how Sexton's clinical symptoms and personality can be understood within the context of contemporary theories of emotion and emotional development, especially ethological and functionalist models of emotion. Although we focus on the life of Anne Sexton and borderline symptoms in this chapter, it is important to point out that this is but one application of emotions theory to clinical work. We use it here as an illustration of the potential that emotions theory has to illuminate the developmental origins of psychopathology.

Discrete emotions theory (Izard, 1971, 1977, 1991; Plutchik, 1962, 1980; Tomkins, 1962, 1963, 1991, 1993) is grounded in the premise that there are a limited number of basic or fundamental emotions, each with unique experiential and motivational features. Fear motivates escape and avoidance behavior, shyness motivates protection of privacy, anger motivates behavior designed to overcome obstacles to barriers, and so forth. Our own developmental application of discrete emotions theory focuses on how certain affects become structuralized in the personality of individuals (Magai & Hunziker, 1993; Magai & McFadden, 1995; Malatesta, 1990; Malatesta & Wilson, 1988). A central thesis is that salient and repetitive emotional experiences in early childhood, as well as in later development, produce emotion traits or affective biases that then function to regulate emotion and govern interpersonal relations in adulthood. In the case of Sexton, we will show that her adult personality, organized around shame with intrusion affects of rage and despair, and her alternately agoraphobic and exhibitionistic behavior, constituted a personal strategy—albeit a maladaptive one—for survival, that had deep roots in a disturbance in attachment relationships and affect balance, and which were multiply magnified by significant life experience beyond infancy.

We draw on biographical material to inform our analysis—specifically, Diane Middlebrook's (1992) thickly detailed biography of Sexton—rather than actual clinical records because of the richer historical and developmental context that is offered. Many years ago, Wilhelm Stern (1911, 1919), the father of personalistic psychology, made a distinction between psychography and biography. Psychography deals with the multiplicity of traits that constitute a given personality, which have no historical organization. In contrast, and as an essential supplement to psychography, biography is concerned with the unity of a goal-oriented personality as described over time; the emphasis on goal-related behavior is entirely consistent with the functionalist framework of much of contemporary emotions theory. Apropos, we begin our analysis with a biographical sketch.

Sketch of the Main Events and People in the Life of Anne Sexton

Sexton was born November 9, 1928, in Newton, Massachusetts. Her father, Ralph Harvey, was a prosperous wool merchant and businessman; her mother, Mary Gray Staples, was a status-conscious and socially ambitious woman who also believed she had a talent for writing that she inherited from her father. As Middlebrook describes, the Harveys led a life reminiscent of the faded abandon and self-absorption of F. Scott and Zelda Fitzgerald. Children in this narrowly and superficially defined world were relegated to a somewhat peripheral existence, valued as emblems of social standing and image rather than as people.

Anne was the third of three daughters. The eldest, Jane, was her father's favorite; Blanche, the middle child, was "the brain," and Anne, being the youngest, was "the baby" of the family. She recalled being very shy as a child and feeling lonely and acutely disconnected from the rest of the family. "I was a nothing, crouching in the closet" (Middlebrook, 1992, p. 8). She experienced her mother as "elusive," self-absorbed, emotionally inconsistent, and unpredictable. While Anne was still a child her father began abusing alcohol, alternating between secretive drinking and uncontrolled, "ugly" binges.

At age 11, an unmarried great-aunt, Nana, came to live with the family and in short order developed an intense bond with Anne. Both would sometimes refer to themselves as "twins." The approach of Anne's adolescence and attempts at more autonomous functioning threatened the idealized and symbiotic bond the two had established. The aunt could not tolerate her great-niece's need to be separate and withdrew from her when Anne began dating; at the same time she suffered a sudden loss of hearing, and subsequently developed symptoms consistent with a psychotic depression. Nana was hospitalized and later transferred to a nursing home. In some deep and basic way, Anne felt responsible for Nana's decline and these feelings were to plague her the rest of her life.

As an adolescent, Anne began to express her need for intense attention, recognition, and belonging in the form of seductive and flirtatious behavior toward the opposite sex. By high school she had developed a steady relationship, but the relationship, which was tumultuous and punctuated with both real and feigned suicide attempts, was not to survive, and it was in the aftermath of its rupture that she first began to write poems. Her parents were hardly supportive of this activity. Her father disparaged her creativity, comparing her literary talents unfavorably with those of his wife. Her mother was provoked to jealous competition and even sent Anne's poems to a New York academic to determine whether they were plagiarized, a revelation that Anne found devastating. She did not write poetry for another 10 years.

Anne met her future husband, Kayo Sexton, in May of 1948 and three months later they eloped. Two daughters were born to this marriage. Kayo abandoned his medical career aspirations early on and, like Anne's father, found work as a wool merchant to support his family. He was frequently away from home on long business assignments, absences that Anne was later to relate experientially to abandonments. In 1950 she was hospitalized for three weeks at Westwood Lodge for symptoms of depression, rage, and fears that she would harm her children. This was to be the first of several hospitalizations. Sexton was discharged but several months later her condition worsened and she attempted suicide. Shortly after this she entered a therapeutic relationship with psychiatrist Martin Orne, who encouraged her to begin writing again as a means of shoring up her self-esteem, and as a means of consolidating her fragmented and diffuse self identity. In 1960 she published her first volume of poetry, *To Bedlam and Part Way Back*, describing her experiences on a mental ward in vivid and emotionally evocative terms. Her star rose rapidly but she continued to be plagued with serious mental illness. In addition to firmly entrenched characterological difficulties, Sexton suffered from agoraphobic-like symptoms that necessitated the construction of elaborate rituals to get from place to place. Later on, as she became increasingly sought after for poetry readings, she had to sedate herself with alcohol and pills to overcome her dread of leaving the house. At the same time, and despite her distress at the exposure and inspection she would have to face at these readings, she was aroused and stimulated by the recognition, acceptance, and adulation of her fans. She dressed in a provocative and seductive fashion and threw herself passionately into her readings. Over the course of the years she was to publish a number of other acclaimed volumes of poetry including *All My Pretty Ones* (about emotional losses), *Live or Die* (about her struggles with bouts of depression), *Love Poems* (about her elusive quest for symbiotic love), and several later volumes in which she dealt with more religious themes, including *The Awful Rowing Towards God*.

Anne Sexton was a woman of many moods and emotions. Indeed, raw, primitive emotion was a signature feature of her poetry, and it was perhaps this more than anything else that explains her great popular appeal during the 1950s and 1960s. Her cohort consisted of a generation of Americans reared under the influence of Watson's *Psychological Care of the Infant and Child* (1928), in which parents were directed to refrain from kissing or hugging their children and to restrict their emotional displays. To the buttoned-down generation of the Eisenhower years who cut their eye-teeth on the cerebral, academic, and esoteric poetry of T. S. Eliot and his peers, Sexton's primitive effusion of emotion must have come as rather startling but welcomed breath of fresh air. Beneath the surface of Sexton's emerging identity as a poet, however, was the powerful undercurrent of her profound psychological distress.

Anne continued in therapy with Martin Orne for seven years. Ultimately, he relocated to accept a research and teaching position out of state and proceeded to transfer Sexton to another therapist. However, this therapist severely compromised Sexton's treatment by becoming sexually involved with her. Sexton was again transferred to another therapist, who, perhaps unadvisedly, encouraged her tentative plans to separate from her husband, Kayo, a man who had been one of the few anchors in an otherwise chaotic life. This therapist abruptly terminated treatment with Sexton, although it is not clear why. With many of her emotional supports suddenly gone, Sexton rapidly deteriorated and in 1974 she committed suicide at the age of 46.

The above chronology provides the bare outline of events and people in Sexton's life that had a bearing on her development as an individual and as an artist. It does not begin to reflect the full emotional undercurrents and their ramifications. At this juncture we turn to the more clinically and developmentally relevant aspects of her emotional development. We do so within the context of attachment theory and discrete emotions theory.

Significance of Affect in Early Development: Attachment and Fundamental Affective Goals

Two of the most significant events in the history of ideas concerning emotion and its centrality in social and personality development were the publication of John Bowlby's three-volume work, *Attachment, Separation, and Loss* (1969, 1973, 1980), and Silvan Tomkins's four-volume work, *Affect, Imagery, Consciousness* (1962, 1963, 1991, 1993). Both of these original theoretical works have stimulated empirical work on the emotions that has been instrumental in bringing emotions back into mainstream psychology after a long hiatus (Magai & McFadden, 1995). Each has its own special emphasis: Bowlby's ethologically grounded attachment theory is more concerned with interpersonal process and social development whereas Tomkins's affect theory is more a theory of individual personality. In our own work, we have attempted to integrate these two different theories into a working model that situates individual differences in personality within a sociohistorical and lifespan developmental framework (e.g., Magai & Hunziker, 1993; Magai & McFadden, 1995; Malatesta, 1990; Malatesta & Wilson, 1988); this description of what we might call "embedded individualism" is consistent with an emerging trend in developmental and clinical psychology in which individuality is conceptualized in other-oriented terms (Emde, 1994). In this chapter we consider the formulations of attachment theory, affect theory, and other contemporary models of emotional development as they relate to clinical issues, and specifically to the symptomatology of borderline personality disorder. Some of the symptoms that we address in this context with reference to Sexton are fears of abandonment, problems with affect regulation, certain dissociative phenomena, boundary/merger problems, issues of identity, and problems with anger.

Attachment and Its Relation to Abandonment Issues

It has long been recognized that one of the most important emotional experiences of early life revolves around relationships with caregivers, although this idea gained renewed emphasis and respect with the emergence of attachment theory and subsequent laboratory-based research on attachment patterns (Ainsworth, Bleher, Waters, & Wall, 1978; Bowlby, 1969, 1973, 1980). Infants who receive care that is sensitive and responsive come to experience "felt security" and over time develop internal working models of the world in which others can be trusted and are seen as sources of support and comfort. On the other hand, infants who receive insensitive care develop insecure attachments to their caregivers. When the care is *inconsistent*, the attachment pattern tends to be characterized by ambivalence, signaled by anger and/ or withdrawal, and approach-avoidance behavior; when it is *intrusive and overstimulating*, avoidance, including emotional overcontrol and exaggerated self-reliance, is more characteristic.

Sexton had three important attachment figures — mother, father, and Nana — but none served as an adequate model for the internalization of a secure sense of self and a trust in interpersonal relationships. Anne's attachment objects were singularly inconsistent, unpredictable, and even frightening: "Daddy was either drunk or he was sober. . . . But you never knew with Mother, when she was going to be horrible or nice. The minute you thought you knew where you were, she'd turn on you" (Middlebrook, 1992, p. 13). Sexton's mother was often absent from the home due to her many social engagements; more important, perhaps, when she was available, she seemed preoccupied with her own needs, and was alternately critical and neglectful. Nana, the much loved great-aunt, seemed to offer her that which was missing from her mother — unstinting attention and affection; unfortunately, the aunt also used Anne for the gratification of her own needs and, from Anne's point of view, ultimately abandoned her as she went into mental decline and withdrew emotionally. Another significant feature of Sexton's childhood, as pieced together in therapy, was that she was sexually abused by this aunt as well as by her father.

As an adult, Anne's style of relating to intimate others reflected continuing problems with attachment. The relationship with her husband was dependent, tension filled, and contentious with occasional physical abuse. Her love affairs with both men and women were similarly conflicted. Finally, she replicated a pattern of inconsistency, insensitivity, and neglect with her own children. During Anne's protracted episodes of illness and hospitalization, her mother-in-law took over the rearing of Anne's eldest, who in turn came to care for both her younger sibling and her mother. Sexton's masturbatory/seductive behavior with at least one daughter replicated her own abuse and confusion over separateness and merger. Thus, both in her relations with her parents and in intimate adult relationships, she was often conflicted, dissatisfied, angry, and distressed. Attachment theory refers to the adult analog of the ambivalent attachment style of childhood as the "preoccupied" individual, one who is virtually consumed with attachment issues. These issues clearly surfaced in Sexton's therapy sessions and were pivotal to much of her poetry.

Relation Between Attachment Style and Affect Regulation

As a poet, Anne consciously allowed herself to be very transparent with her emotions and to give reign to, if not amplify, them. But this was more than adroit exploitation of a successful literary style. Lability and intensity of emotion were key elements in her persona as well, and over this she had less control. Part of this relates to her borderline symptoms, but part also may reflect a constitutionally based vulnerability to mood swings. In any case, Sexton was given to flights of ebullience and sociability, fits of rage that led to dissociative trances, deep despairs, and episodes of exhibitionism alternating with paralyzing agoraphobia-like symptoms.

In addition to or beyond any constitutional bias, there were two socially mediated sources of her affective lability, both traceable to early childhood, but not limited to infancy. Attachment theory notes that attachment styles in infancy and childhood are linked to internalized representations of self and other and to particular patterns of affect regulation in childhood as well as in adulthood. The consistent caregiver promotes the internalization of a secure and stable sense of self. The inconsistent caregiver sets up conditions of confusion. In Anne's case, there was more than one source of confusion—there were three inconsistent, disturbing, and dysfunctional attachment objects with whom she had to contend. In adulthood, ambivalently attached individuals also tend to have overly emotional and enmeshed relationships with intimates characterized by dependency and anger. This pattern clearly obtained in Sexton's relationship with her husband, with other men and women in her life, and with her therapists.

Anne's experience with inconsistent parenting and ambivalent attachment also created conditions for the acquisition of attention-getting patterns that had life-long ramifications but were ultimately unfulfilling. Throughout her life, Sexton desperately sought connection with others—through her demanding and dependent behavior in therapy, through the poetry that reached out and seized her reading public, and through her seductive attempt to capture and merge with the men and women she lured into her field of sexuality.

In terms of affect regulation, ambivalently attached individuals appear to be especially sensitive to the detection of distressing events; they tend to become distressed themselves more readily than others and to express their distress in a less modulated fashion. Anne's whole life was absorbed in contending with affect: Poetry allowed her to amplify her emotions in a way that filled the void inside; trances, alcohol, and sleeping pills allowed her to tranquilize the affect when it got too intense; therapy assisted her in releasing emotions but she was not able to integrate them with any meaningful insight.

Given these circumstances, it becomes clear why, as an adult, Sexton was intensely drawn to people but also repelled by them. This pattern underlay the instability of her interpersonal relationships—a characteristic emblematic of the borderline personality. Anne found herself in the same circumstances, emotionally, time and time again: longing for connection, being deeply disappointed, and turning away in despair. In adult life, the conflict between desiring and resisting connection with others can be seen as well in some of her other symptoms. The agoraphobia expressed her fear of others; her exhibitionism can be seen as a counterphobic measure.

The attachment literature's descriptions of internal working models of self and interpersonal relationships, and of affect regulation, are astute and penetrating observations. However, attachment theory as yet does not explain how problematic attachment patterns of the ambivalent type might speak to issues of identity confusion of the kind that is so common in borderline personalities, nor does it offer a very satisfying explanation of why the ambivalently attached individual should have the particular pattern of affect regulation problem that is characteristic of this attachment pattern. For this we need to turn to affect theory.

Affect Theory and Affect Regulation

First let us expand on the emotional profile we have drawn of Sexton. Anne was not only often very intense and overt in her emotional expressivity, but she also experienced periods of deadly torpor and inertia. Thus, her difficulties entailed a more fundamental disturbance in affect regulation, meaning she had difficulty controlling the quality, range, frequency, and occasion of her affects. Tomkins's (1962, 1963, 1991) affect theory addresses the motives behind the intensity of the affective drive.

One of the theory's fundamental premises is that humans are motivated not only by the specific qualities of specific affects, but that there are certain more overarching goals of human behavior. According to Tomkins, humans are ruled by four "general images" or desires, namely, to (a) maximize positive affect, (b) minimize negative affect, (c) keep affect inhibition to a minimum, and (d) maximize the power to achieve a balance among the other goals. In this formulation, Tomkins goes beyond the psychoanalytic tenet that human behavior is governed by only two motives—the avoidance of pain and the pursuit of pleasure. What Tomkins means by the third principle is that humans *need to feel*, that is, to experience and express their feelings, and that the suppression of emotion is punishing or unpleasant. Lack of feeling gives rise to boredom and even depersonalization. Moreover, emotion that is blocked (what Tomkins called "backed-up affect") continues to press for release and may become transmuted by lack of release. The fourth goal is about having a sense of efficacy with respect to emotion regulation. We want to feel that we have the power to avoid negative affect, to achieve positive affect, and to live fully and intensely as emotional beings.

Sexton often seemed to be maximizing her ability to feel. Indeed, she often deliberately placed herself in the direct path of circumstances that were guaranteed to intensify her already intense affective state. To be more specific, she was frankly and chronically flirtatious and provocative—with many men, with several women, and with her therapists. In the end, in one form or another, all of her therapists unwittingly enacted a repetition of childhood themes of seduction, betrayal, and abandonment during the course of their relationships with Anne.

Sexton's promiscuous and impulsive behavior was obviously dangerous and risky, more so because she lacked the ability to stay on top of her experiments in affectivity. She constantly seemed to be ricocheting between too much emotion and not enough—between being and nothingness. During her periods of decompensation, she oscillated between extremes of "stupefied vacancy and panicky agitations" (Middlebrook, 1992, p. 4). In the effort to overcome the internal emptiness and feel more fully—Tomkins's third goal—she veered between too little restriction (her "trances" and alcoholic stupors), and thus was always in essential conflict with the fourth goal of achieving balance.

The dread of nothingness must have been a powerful motivating force, for she did more than react to her world in an emotionally intense and unregulated manner. What was the origin of this lack of modulation? Part of it, we submit, is due to the sexual abuse she experienced as a child. But her borderline symptoms accrued not from the existence of abuse alone, but because it was part of a more pervasive pattern of boundary violation that was linked to the development of shame as an organizing structure in her personality. At this point we want to turn to another of Sexton's borderline symptoms—the sense of emptiness that drove her to extreme of behavior, her identity confusion, and related dissociative phenomena.

Self, Identity, and Dissociative Phenomena

As indicated above, Anne had inordinate difficulty regulating her affect. She had a similar problem with her thought processes. Her ability to keep in mind events from previous sessions was almost nonexistent. One therapist, Orne, suggested taping her sessions and having her replay them so that she "could really remember and learn about her feelings" (Middlebrook, 1992, p. xvi). She also had periods during which she would go into a catatonic-like trances for minutes, hours, and on occasion, days.

We turn presently to examine this aspect of Sexton's symptoms from that of skills theory—a cognitive-affective theory of development (Fischer, Shaver, & Carnochan, 1990); we then return to Tomkins's affect theory. Skills theory suggests that negative self-concepts and dissociative patterns of mental activity—both features of the borderline personality and clearly true of Sexton—are linked to patterns of sexual abuse, though there may be other developmental origins as well.

Skills Theory and Self-Concept

According to skills theory, in normal development, affects and thoughts help organize each other; they get bound up with one another and segregated according to content (Calverley, Fischer, & Ayoub, in press; Fischer & Ayoub, in press; Haviland, 1995). Fischer and Ayoub (in press) have proposed that in normal development, children naturally split the world along an evaluative dimension such as nice versus mean, good versus bad, friendly versus unfriendly, and so on, and that these are linked to positive and negative affect. In further development, splitting is replaced by coordination and integration as children develop more mature mental processes and as they develop a more skilled grasp of the way the world works. The growth in cognitive skills is accompanied by corresponding changes in the representation of the self.

Early in development children switch from a preference for "mean" stories to a positivity bias, especially for stories about the self. The positivity bias appears to be a relatively mature form of affective splitting, and in normal development there is a natural tendency toward a positive representation of the self. However, if the child experiences traumatic emotional experiences, such as sexual or physical abuse, this bias is reversed and a negative representation of self is internalized; as a consequence, the individual experiences "malignant feelings of inner badness and basic fragmentation in self" (Fischer & Ayoub, in press). This seems to capture what happened to Sexton, and it appears to have affected her adult personality. As an adult she acted out the bad self—the bad, neglecting mother; the bad, withdrawing, nonremembering client; the bad unfaithful wife; the bad quixotic lover. Split off from these central identities and roles, however, was another identity, added later in her development, of the good poet. Tragically, she conformed so well to the twentieth-century American genre of good poet—skilled, engaging, mad, and suicidal—that she took her own life in the end.

The above analysis indicates that Sexton's dissociative trances may well have been linked to her repetitive experiences with sexual abuse. The abuse is also relevant to understanding problems that Sexton had with separation and merger—issues that relate to the borderline's unstable self-concept and lack of boundaries.

The Borderline's Problems with Separation and Merger

Middlebrook (1992) described Sexton as "not a private person" (p. xxii), meaning that she was open, impulsive, and exhibitionistic. Boundaries between self and others were not clearly demarcated in Sexton's private world; moreover, her impairment in affect regulation meant that the typical modulatory brakes could not be applied. Sexton was boldly exhibitionistic in her confessional poetry and in her dramatically staged readings, driven to display herself at the service of seeking approval. Finding that the public was responsive to her self-revelatory style, she used this natural dramaturgical talent to further seduce her audiences. But the impulsivity that underlay the exhibitionism she cultivated spilled over into her everyday interpersonal affairs. Thus, instead of learning to modulate her affect and impulsivity, she was, in a sense, being rewarded for doing just the reverse. In her "confessional" noninhibited mode she made connections not only with her readers but with a whole cohort of poets. Perversely, even though her identity as a poet gave Sexton a badly needed source of self-esteem, her very success made it difficult to learn more restraint in the expression of emotion. Well into her forties, she continued to veer between eruptions of rage and despair, on the one hand, and stupor and coma-like trances on the other.

Sexton's lack of boundaries and poor affect modulation may have been predicated on the antecedent of an ambivalent attachment, as already discussed, but it is our thesis that it is not ambivalent attachment per se that makes a borderline personality. Other circumstances—in Anne's case, sexual abuse and the repetitive recruitment of shame—can be considered pivotal. Indeed, much of Sexton's behavior, interpersonal process, and experiential world was structured around the affect of shame. Her exposures to events and circumstances that would shame, humiliate, and mortify her were massive and ongoing. To be specific, what can be more humiliating than to be seduced, abandoned, and betrayed, over and over again — mother, father, aunt, lovers, and therapists. Of course, by the time Anne was an adult she contributed to this pattern since her own behavior began to mimic that of the seductive/rejecting attachment objects of her childhood. Nevertheless, her early experiences with shame involving seduction and abandonment were multiply amplified by developmentally continuous experiences of exposure and belittlement, as described below. We discuss her shame organization within the context of Tomkins's theory of personality development.

Ideoaffective Organizations and Personality Development

One of the more important concepts to emerge from Tomkins's writings on affect is the idea that people organize their life experiences into strategies that Tomkins called "ideoaffective" organizations — ideoaffective because they had both affective and cognitive components. These organizations are described as having two cardinal features: (a) They serve as filters to scan incoming information for relevance to a particular emotion or emotions, and (b) they contain organized strategies for coping with a variety of contingencies specific to particular affects in order to avoid or attenuate them. In our own developmental analysis of affect theory (Magai and Hunziker, 1993; Malatesta & Wilson, 1988), we have emphasized that individuals are characterized by prevailing mood states that color their everyday interactions; these are roughly equivalent to Tomkins's ideoaffective organizations. However, we have also attempted to specify the conditions under which such biased information processing strategies accrue developmental importance.

As described elsewhere (Malatesta, 1990; Malatesta & Wilson, 1988), children learn how to identify emotional states in others and how to assign meaning to their own emotional experiences as a part of normal development. More idiosyncratically, individual children learn how to screen for certain affective stimuli and how to avoid others. As the child develops, certain emotional states become ever more highly centered in experience and, through repetition and thematic variation, become associated with self-feeling and self-identity. When these patterns become consolidated over time, they function in a way that qualifies them as personality traits, which then influence wide domains of behavior. Some of the experiences in development that lead to the structuralization of emotions include chronic or repetitive elicitation of particular emotional states as well as chronic or repetitive exposure to certain classes of emotion. Sexton's history was such that shame affect was continually recruited and developmentally magnified. Apropos, we turn now to a more detailed consideration of shame and clinical symptoms and, in particular, the role that shame plays in boundary problems.

The Role of Shame in Boundary and Merger Problems

As mentioned earlier, a photograph from Sexton's girlhood presents the portrait of a shy youngster who can hardly bear to look at the camera (see Middlebrook, 1992, p. 8). Also recall her statement that as a young girl she was "a nothing, crouching in the closet" (p. 8.). This sense of loneliness and insignificance appears to have roots in a fundamentally insecure attachment pattern, though it was amplified by later social experiences and by her poor school performance. Most important, from an affective and developmental theoretical point of view, there was a recurring theme in Anne's early development of physical and mental violation. Sexual violation was historically preceded by other kinds of invasive disregard for her emotional boundaries, and she was constantly exposed to the contempt and derogation of her parents.

Sexton's biography indicates that she was repeatedly subjected to intrusive questioning and physical probing by her mother for a case of constipation that was so severe that it required hospitalization. On another occasion her mother became aggressively involved in inspecting a genital condition in Anne, and examined her daughter almost daily. As such, Sexton was exposed to constant violations of her physical boundaries. She endured her mother's constant criticism as a child, and jealous competition as an adolescent and adult. The mother, instead of providing praise and encouragement to Anne for her first tentative forays into poetry, offered discouragement and belittlement, and this was echoed and amplified by her husband. Moreover, Anne's father was particularly cruel in his comments on her adolescent acne. She was consequently also exposed to constant violations of her self-worth and self-confidence. These experiences constitute some of the most powerful innate elicitors of shame—a painful affect most closely associated with self-identity. On an early, continuing, and repetitive basis, Anne was derogated, intruded upon, invaded, and invalidated. From the perspective of discrete emotions theory, it was through such humiliating exposures and immersion in shame that feelings of vulnerability and inadequacy were consolidated. Indeed, it is our thesis that shame formed a central core of Anne's personality. But how does shame figure into the problem that borderlines experience with separation and merger? According to Helen Block Lewis (1971), shame sets up conditions in which the boundaries of self become permeable. While shame/shyness is normally an adaptive affect that motivates protection of the self through withdrawal from negative social contact, when it is chronically activated it creates painful feelings of inferiority and insecurity, both of which are antithetical to the establishment of a stable and clear identity with a firm sense of boundaries. In the absence of trust in the self's intrinsic self-worth, identity is diffuse and susceptible to influence. The shame that Sexton experienced on an almost daily basis was also the condition that created intense, if sequestered, anger.

Anger and Borderline Personality

As indicated earlier, intense, inappropriate, and often uncontrollable anger are features of the borderline personality. In Sexton as well, the emotion of anger was close to the core structure of her personality, but was less stable. Here we suggest that anger accrued as a natural consequence of shame through the mechanism of the shame/rage spiral (Lewis, 1971; Retzinger, 1991; Sheff, 1987) and as a reaction to multiple experiences with seduction and betrayal. However, because of her tenuous and ambivalent attachment feelings, in childhood she could hardly dare to express her anger overtly and directly. In her adult life as well, rage was typically submerged, but evidence of its presence as "backed up" affect (Tomkins, in Demos, 1994) could be found in her clinical symptoms.

Anne suffered from fits of blinding rage and episodes during which she would become virtually comatose. One of her therapists, Orne, hypothesized that her dissociative trances were self-induced and that Sexton used her anger instrumentally as a means of punishing others. However, it is our view that the trances represented attempts to escape from the sense of utter helplessness that was associated with the rage. Sexton herself notes, "It seems to me that my whole childhood was powerless, and feeling angry about it" (Middlebrook, 1992, p. 409). Multiply and frequently shamed, and physically violated by her mother, her father, and her great-aunt, she must have felt enormous anger. However, the expression of direct anger was too risky because of her tenuous attachment and was fruitless as well in the Harvey household. Sexton's mother was an impotent witness to her husband's drunken binges; Anne was powerless to get her mother to attend to her. These encounters with ineffectuality are prototypical circumstances for the establishment of learned helplessness and depression. It is our impression that Sexton's unexpressed anger—which was her particular form of backed-up affect—strangled her symbolically and physically. The pent-up anger was so intense it threatened to overwhelm, even annihilate her; withdrawal became an avenue of escape. Her therapist suggested that Anne used the trance episodes to play the role of dying (Middlebrook, 1992, p. xvii), which then also suggests that her suicide may have been an act of desperation *and* rage. In the end, her strangulated rage and fatalistic despair overcame the competing urge to find connection and meaning in her life.

Summary and Conclusions

In this chapter we considered the interpersonal and developmental origins of the borderline personality, as exemplified by the case of Anne Sexton, and as interpreted through the lens of a discrete emotions, functionalist, and lifespan developmental framework. Details of the life of this talented and complex individual, as described by Diane Middlebrook (1992), permitted us to examine the interpersonal and affective roots of borderline symptoms. Although space limitations preclude a more in-depth specification of the multiple organizing and consolidating forces that were at work developmentally in the forging of Sexton's flawed but charismatic personality, her clinical illness, and her talent as a poet, we have tried to highlight some of the more central affective dynamics from an emotions-theoretical account. In particular, we highlighted the fact that there were multiple antecedents for the formation of borderline symptoms, including, in this particular case, ambivalent attachment, sexual abuse, neglect, and massive recruitment of shame. These sources of personality influence were not limited to oedipal or pre-oedipal periods of development but involve adolescent experiences as well, and even experiences in adulthood. It is our thesis that it was not ambivalent attachment alone that destined her for borderline symptoms. This attachment pattern is associated with a variety of clinical syndromes, as the accumulating clinical literature now illustrates. The movement toward borderline personality disorder in Sexton's case entailed sexual abuse as well, but was not limited to this experience either. Indeed, we surmise that an important component was the experience of multiple daily humiliations from a variety of sources—poor scholastic performance, parental belittlement and derogation, and intrusions on her personal physical boundaries. These conditions laid the groundwork for the massive recruitment of shame that engulfed her fragile identity. Sexton's sense of personal self-worth was restored to a limited extent by the nurturing of her poetic identity in adulthood, but the gratification she found in the adulation of her fans worked against, rather than for, the acquisition of effective affect regulation during her adult years.

Anne Sexton's life was a fascinating and developmentally complex one, as the reader may gather from even the very short synopsis provided in this chapter. While it was a very unique life, we have examined it from the perspective of locating important developmental principles that relate to clinical issues. In introducing a developmentally informed, emotions-analytic framework for the exposition of Sexton's life, we hope to have identified some of the critical experiences that underlay the development of the borderline personality. Whether the conditions we discussed—ambivalent attachment, sexual exploitation, and the massive recruitment of shame—obtain in other borderline patients is a question for systematic clinical research.

References

Ainsworth, M. D. S., Blehar, M. C., Waters, E., & Wall, S. (1978). *Patterns of attachment: A psychological study of the strange situation.* Hillsdale, NJ: Erlbaum.

American Psychiatric Association. (1994). *Diagnostic and statistical manual of mental disorders* (4th ed.). Washington, DC: Author.

Bowlby, J. (1969). *Attachment and loss: Vol. 1. Attachment.* New York: Basic Books.

Bowlby, J. (1969). *Attachment and loss: Vol. 2. Separation.* New York: Basic Books.

Bowlby, J. (1969). *Attachment and loss: Vol. 3. Loss, sadness and depression.* New York: Basic Books.

Calverley, R. M., Fischer, K. W., & Ayoub, C. (in press). Complex splitting of self-representations in sexually abused adolescent girls. *Development and Psychopathology.*

Emde, R. N. (1994). Individuality, context, and the search for meaning. *Child Development, 65,* 719–737.

Fischer, K. W., & Ayoub, C. (in press). Affective splitting and dissociation in normal and maltreated children: Developmental pathways for self in relationships. In D. Cicchetti & S. Toth (Eds.), *Rochester Symposium on Developmental Psychopathology: Vol. 5. The self and its disorders.* Rochester, NY: University of Rochester Press.

Fischer, K. W., Shaver, P., & Carnochan, P. G. (1990). How emotions develop and how they organize development. *Cognition and Emotion, 4,* 81–127.

Haviland, J. (1995). Passionate thought. In C. Magai & J. Haviland (Eds.), *The emotional archaeology of personality.* In preparation.

Izard, C. E. (1971). *The face of emotion.* New York: Appleton-Century-Crofts.

Izard, C. E. (1977). *Human emotions.* New York: Plenum Press.

Izard, C. E. (1991). *The psychology of emotions.* New York: Plenum Press.

Lewis, H. B. (1971). *Shame and guilt in neurosis.* New York: International University Press.

Magai, C., & Hunziker, J. (1993). Tolstoy and the riddle of developmental transformation: A lifespan analysis of the role of emotions in personality development. In M. Lewis & J. Haviland (Eds.), *Handbook of Emotions* (pp. 247–260). New York: Guilford Press.

Magai, C. Z., & McFadden, S. (1995). *The role of emotions in social and personality development: History, theory, and research*. New York: Plenum Press.

Malatesta, C. Z. (1990). The role of emotion in the development and organization of personality. In R. Dienstbier & R. Thompson (Eds.), *Nebraska Symposium on Motivation* (Vol. 36, pp. 1–56). Lincoln: University of Nebraska Press.

Malatesta, C. Z., & Wilson, A. (1988). Emotion/cognition interaction in personality development: A discrete emotions, functionalist analysis. *British Journal of Social Psychology, 27,* 91–112.

Middlebrook, D. (1992). *Anne Sexton: A biography*. New York: Vintage Books.

Plutchik, R. (1962). *The emotions: Facts, theories, and a new model*. New York: Random House.

Plutchik, R. (1980). *Emotions: A psycho-evolutionary synthesis*. New York: Harper & Row.

Retzinger, S. M. (1991). *Violent emotions: Shame and rage in marital quarrels*. Newbury Park, CA: Sage.

Scheff, T. J. (1987). The shame-rage spiral: A case study of an interminable quarrel. In H. B. Lewis (Ed.), *The role of shame in symptom formation* (pp. 109–150). Hillsdale, NJ: Erlbaum.

Stern, W. (1911). *Die differentiele Psychologie*. Leipzig: Barth.

Stern, W. (1919). *Die menschliche Perseonlichkeit*. Leipzig: Barth.

Tomkins, S. S. (1962). *Affect, imagery, consciousness: Vol. 1. The positive affects*. New York: Springer.

Tomkins, S. S. (1963). *Affect, imagery, consciousness: Vol. 2. The negative affects*. New York: Springer.

Tomkins, S. S. (1991). *Affect, imagery, consciousness: Vol. 3. The negative affects: Anger and fear*. New York: Springer.

Tomkins, S. S. (1993). *Affect, imagery, consciousness: Vol. 4. Cognition–Duplication and transformation of information*. New York: Springer.

Watson, J. B. (1928). *Psychological care of infant and child*. New York: Norton.

28

Drew Westen

Affect Regulation and Psychopathology

Applications to Depression and Borderline
Personality Disorder

In a number of areas of psychology, particular developmental, personality, and clinical, researchers have begun focusing on affect regulation (Aronoff, Stollak, & Woike, 1994; Eisenberg & Fabes, 1992; Fox, 1994; Garber & Dodge, 1991; Kobak, Cole, Ferenz-Gillies, & Fleming, 1993; Kopp, 1989; Mayer, Salovey, Gomberg-Kaufman, & Blainey, 1991; Thayer, 1989; Tile & Baumeister, 1993; Tronick, 1989). Much of this research has centered on the way infants and young children learn to regulate their emotions in the first 2 years of life. Researchers have focused comparatively less attention on affect regulation in adults and psychopathology. Psychoanalytic theorists have written extensively about defensive processes, and many researchers have studied coping responses, but neither have typically conceptualized these primarily as mechanisms of affect regulation (but see more recent work by Lazarus, 1991, 1992).

After defining the domain of affect regulation and psychopathology, in this chapter I outline a model of affect regulation informed by evolutionary, behaviorist, cognitive, and psychodynamic theory and research. I then describe methodological issues confronting the attempt to assess affect regulation strategies in adults and report on preliminary research using an observer-rated affect regulation Q-sort. Finally, I apply the model and measure to depression and borderline personality disorder. Because of space constraints, each of these sections is necessarily brief and occasionally telegraphic, but hopefully the verbiage, if not the affect, is well regulated.

Affect Regulation and Psychopathology: Delimiting the Domain

Clinicians and researchers have long recognized affect to be a central aspect of many forms of psychopathology. By the early part of the twentieth century, physicians had begun to write clear descriptive accounts of melancholia, pathological anxiety (notably phobias), and flattened or inappropriate affect in schizophrenia. The recognition of affect *regulation* as a central aspect of many forms of psychopathology, however, has in some respects waited another century. In one sense, this appears paradoxical: If dysfunctional affect is a problem, then surely the flipside is a problem with affect regulation.

We must therefore be careful in defining the term *affect regulation* lest it become a meaningless restatement of the fact that people with psychological troubles have psychological troubles. I will use the term *affect regulation*, or *affect regulation strategies*, to refer to conscious and unconscious procedures used to maximize pleasant and minimize unpleasant emotions. By this definition, affect regulation is purposive. It is aimed at a goal: managing affect.

Affect *dysregulation*, on the other hand, simply means that one or more affects are not optimally regulated—they may be too strong, weak, labile, and so on—for any number of reasons, some psychologically meaningful and some not. The affective dysregulation of the melancholic major depressive who comes in with her first episode of major depression at age 45 and reports a family history of severe depression may not, by this definition, reflect a problem with her affect regulation strategies. Rather, her disorder may be one of neurotransmitter dysregulation. Her pathology is not purposive; that is, it is not an attempt to manage an affect but in fact *presents* an affect that must now be managed.

Matters are not, however, usually so simple. As we shall see, the etiology of her depression may indeed have an affect regulation component to the extent that her ways of dealing with her emotions readily contributed to her vulnerability to depression, which they frequently do. Her depression may also *come to serve* an affect regulation function. She may receive secondary gains from the sick role, such as an excuse to quit an ungratifying job; she may feel a comforting identification with her deceased, depressive mother; she may feel like her painful depression helps her atone for some perceived sins; and so forth. Thus, even a symptom reflecting a primarily biological diathesis may come to take on affect-regulatory properties (which is one reason psychotherapy can be essential even in the most clearly biogenic depressions).

Similarly, the flattened affect of the schizophrenic is not primarily a problem of affect regulation as defined here. Rather, it presumably reflects the failure of midbrain dopaminergic tracts and other limbic inputs to the frontal lobes to perform their normal activating functions, creating flattened affect along with other negative symptoms (Breier, Wilkowitz, Roy, Potter, & Pickar, 1990; Davis, Kahn, Ko, & Davidson, 1991; Tamminga et al., 1992). Again, this does not constitute an affect regulation problem because flattened affect is not purposive or strategic. To the extent that a schizophrenic patient numbs himself to the intense pain of the shattered dreams, social ostracism, and inability to trust his own mind that so frequently accompany the disorder, then that aspect of his flattened affect can be considered an affect regulation strategy because its aim is to protect against intolerable affect. In this sense, the response of the schizophrenic patient is similar to the patient with posttraumatic stress disorder who numbs herself, except that the stress to which the schizophrenic individual is numbing himself is the trauma of losing his mind. (Again, this suggests that even if psychological factors had absolutely no role in the etiology of schizophrenia, psychotherapy would be essential. We would not consider treating any other posttraumatic patient without attending to the psychological trauma, and there is no worse trauma that can befall a human being than losing trust in one's own mental processes.)

At the risk of belaboring the point, the distinction, then, is not between psychological and neurophysiological processes per se. The defensive and coping strategies people use to regulate affect are biophysiological events with neural correlates, just as all psychological events are. To be classified as an affect regulation problem, a pathological process or symptom must be initiated in an effort to maximize pleasurable or minimize unpleasant affect. The effort may ultimately prove misguided or maladaptive to later circumstances, so that the procedure itself causes more pain than it alleviates, as when a physically or emotionally abused child learns to hate himself instead of his parent as a way of minimizing his rage or maintaining some sense that he is loved and safe and hence deserves the abuse. Nevertheless, the process of affect regulation is defined by its function.

Perhaps the grayest areas are cases in which what begins as a purposive attempt to regulate affect becomes hardwired. This probably occurs in some childhood sexual abuse victims, who shut down some of their verbal intelligence to prevent associative thinking that can lead to unpleasant memories (Westen, Ludolph, Block, Wixom, & Wiss, 1990), or whose dissociative efforts may conceivably trigger later seizure activity (A. Celenza, personal communication, 1994). In these cases, we simply do not know the extent to which addressing the trauma and the affect regulation strategy psychologically would change pathological brain processes.

A Model of Affect Regulation

Elsewhere I have proposed an integrative model of affect regulation that can be applied to individual differences in personality in the normal spectrum as well as to psychopathology (Westen, 1985, 1994). The model holds that feelings (including both emotions and other sensory feeling states that have a positive or negative valence) are mechanisms for the selective retention of behavioral and mental responses. In other words, of the behavioral and mental processes a person produces, those that regulate aversive affective states or maximize pleasurable feelings will be more likely to be used again in similar situations.

With evolutionary theorists, this model holds that feeling-states channel behavior in adaptive directions in organisms whose behavior is not rigidly controlled by instinct (see Plutchik, 1980; Tomkins, 1980). Innate affective proclivities interact with learning to motivate people to act in ways that serve their own interests and those of others with whom they are genetically related or cooperatively engaged. Just as humans and other organisms are prepared to associate tastes with nausea (Garcia & Koelling, 1966), they are *emotionally prepared* to care about the welfare of those with whom they are most familiar (an evolutionary proxy for degree of relatedness), to avoid sexual contact with people with whom they familiar early in life, to fear infidelity in partners in whom they invest resources or on whose resources they rely, and so forth (see Buss, 1991; Buss, Larsen, Westen, & Semmelroth, 1992; Westen, 1985, 1994).

With behaviorist theories, the model holds that action follows its consequences. Contrary to the antimentalism of radical behaviorism, however, it proposes that the feelings elicited by a behavior determine its reinforcing or punishing quality and hence its future occurrence. Thus, rats injected with adrenalin, which increases anxious arousal, are superior to control rats in avoidance learning tasks (Latane & Schachter, cited in Schachter & Singer, 1962), whereas rats administered anxiolitic medications are inferior to controls at learning to avoid behaviors associated with negative consequences (Gray, 1979). When anxiety or fear is minimized, so is motivation to avoid. Indeed, Gray (1990) has proposed neurologically distinct motivational systems for appetitive and avoidant behavior associated with positive and negative affect, respectively.

From a cognitive perspective, conditioning processes of this sort involve the associative connection of affects with representations. These representations may be quite primitive, as when a pattern of activation of neurons in the lateral geniculate nucleus of the thalamus activate a limbic response without cortical involvement (see LeDoux, 1995). Alternatively, these representations may be quite complex, as when a person who is vulnerable to feelings of inadequacy and self-criticism becomes depressed upon anticipating not receiving a promotion, as processing of current information matches an affect-laden prototype. Cognitive processes (though not necessarily conscious ones) are also involved in discrepancies between cognitions about reality and desired or feared goal-states, such as goals involving proximity to an attachment figure (Bowlby, 1969) or standards for one's own behavior (Freud, 1933; Higgins, 1990; Rogers, 1959). These discrepancies produce emotional feedback, which in turn motivates conscious coping strategies (such as self-distraction, seeking advice, or seeking information that could be useful in solving the problem) or defensive processes (such as ingesting substances that eliminate the affect directly, or using distorted logic to conclude that one has not really done something wrong, when in fact one's behavior has violated an internal standard). (For other control-theory models, see Horowitz, 1987; Menninger, Mayman, & Pruyser, 1963; Miller, Gallanter, & Pribram, 1960; Powers, 1973; Scheier & Carver, 1982.) If these strategies regulate affect in a hedonically desired direction, they are likely to be maintained and used again in similar circumstances, as when an infant whose mother is uncomfortable with physical or emotional intimacy learns to shut off wishes for close contact after repeatedly experiencing them as distressing, leading to an attachment style similar to that of the mother (Dozier & Kobak, 1992; Main, Kaplan, & Cassidy, 1985; van IJzendoorn, 1994). Thus, affect regulation strategies are a form of procedural knowledge; that is, they are largely implicit, often automatic processes activated when an emotionally relevant situation matches a representation or prototype of the kinds of situations or affects for which they have been encoded as successful solutions.

From a psychodynamic perspective, mental processes, like behaviors, can also be conditioned or selectively retained by their perceived utility in regulating affect. If keeping memories or wishes from consciousness minimizes anxiety or guilt, the "operant" of repression will be reinforced—that is, made likely to recur. Psychoanalytic theory emphasizes, however, that people rarely associate representations of any important person or state with a single affect, so their actions often reflect compromise solutions to several simultaneous affect regulation tasks (see Brenner,

1982, on compromise formations). This is frequently the case with people with highly critical parents, who want to achieve but for whom success is also associated with fears of being a fraud or of being disappointed at the response of significant others. As a consequence, they may achieve (and thus satisfy one of the active goals) but be unable to feel any self-satisfaction or accept compliments (thus regulating the unpleasant emotions on the other side of the conflict).

Measuring Affect Regulation in Adults

Literature on adult affect regulation has historically been split between psychodynamic research on unconscious defenses and stress research on conscious coping strategies. Each body of literature, however, suffers from considerable limitations. Measures of stress and coping uniformly tend to violate many of the theoretical postulates proposed by stress theorists such as Lazarus (1991). For example, research on coping strategies has relied almost exclusively on self-report questionnaires, even though models of stress and coping explicitly recognize that many ways of coping are not conscious, such as denial, rationalization, or forms of cognitive reframing that place adversity in a more tolerable light. This methodological shortcut is highly problematic for two reasons (Westen, 1995). First, cognitive research documents that much of procedural knowledge (i.e., skills, of which coping strategies can be considered one) is unconscious and inaccessible to conscious self-report (see Holyoak & Spellman, 1993; Nisbett & Wilson, 1977). Second, self-report methods assume away the defensive biases that not only psychodynamic theory but also stress and coping theory postulates. These defensive biases have now been documented empirically by several independent research programs linking defensive response styles to physiological reactivity, physical illness, and immune functioning (Dozier & Kobak, 1992; Pennebaker, 1990; Shedler, Mayman, & Manis, 1993; Weinberger, 1990).

With the exception of research by Haan (1977) and Vaillant (1977; Roston, Lee, & Vaillant, 1992), which made use of a Q-sort procedure, the literature on defense mechanisms has been plagued with problems of reliability (Perry & Cooper, 1989). Self-report measures (e.g., Bond et al., 1983) show little resemblance to defense as conceptualized clinically and have serious problems with face validity since defenses are by definition inaccessible to consciousness. Although Bond's self-report measure has shown positive correlations with some measures, it failed to correlate with Vaillant's defense Q-sort, which is probably not surprising (Roston et al., 1992).

Jonathon Shedler and I have recently developed an Affect Regulation and Experience Q-sort (AREQ), an observer-rated instrument to assess both the pattern of affects the person chronically experiences (specific affects and their intensity) and the mechanisms she or he uses to regulate them. The initial item pool was drawn from a number of sources, including clinical experience, theoretical and empirical literature on defense, research instruments on coping (Carver, Scheier, & Weintraub, 1989; Folkman & Lazarus, 1985), self-report questionnaires assessing emotional experience (e.g., Watson & Clark, 1992), and the author's own prior self-report research on situational and dispositional affect regulation strategies (Westen, 1994). After initial item selection, 23 clinicians rated each item on a scale from 1 to 9 for three of their patients (where 1 is highly nondescriptive and 9 is highly descriptive of the patient) and were asked to comment on items that were unclear or missing. This initial set of ratings was also used to eliminate redundant items and to set a distribution for the Q-sort. This procedure led to the creation of a 96-item instrument.

To assess the validity of the measure (Westen, Muderrisoglu, Fowler, Koren, & Shedler, in press), we asked clinicians at Harvard Medical School to Q-sort three patients they were currently treating and knew well and to provide additional information, such as whether or not the patient had made suicide attempts or been hospitalized, the patient's current and lowest Global Assessment of Functioning (GAF; American Psychiatric Association, 1994) score, the patient's diagnosis, whether the patient had a personality disorder, and other variables. Thirty-one clinicians reported on a total of 90 subjects. Based on theoretical considerations and previous empirical findings (Westen, 1994), the items were split into two categories: affective experience (such as whether the subject tends to experience depression, whether affective expression seems peculiar or incongruent with verbal communications, etc.) and affect regulation (coping and defensive strategies). Each set of items was subjected to a factor analysis, with Promax oblique rotation. All factors showed substantial internal consistency, with alphas ranging from .71 to .91.

For affect regulation, factors included *adaptive regulation* (items with high positive loadings on this factor included "is able to remain goal-directed even in distressing circumstances" and "is able to anticipate problems and develop realistic plans for dealing with them," and items with high negative loadings included "tends to give up easily when faced with difficult or frustrating circumstances" and "behaves in manifestly self-destructive ways when distressed"), *externalizing defenses* ("tends to blame others for own mistakes and misdeeds" and "tends to deny any responsibility for his/her own problems" versus "tends to remain passive in the face of conflict or distress" and "tends to avoid confrontations even when has legitimate grievances"), and *avoidant defenses* ("consciously and deliberately avoids thinking about distressing wishes, feelings, or experiences" and "tends to describe relationships in abstract or general terms without providing supporting details, or providing incongruent details" versus "tends to become clingy, dependent, and needy when distressed" and "tends to ruminate or dwell on concerns when distressed").

For affective experience, factors included *socialized negative affect* (items with high positive loadings on this factor included regret, guilt, and shame, and items with high negative loadings included peculiar affect, labile affect, and inability to take other perspectives when affects are strong), *positive affect* ("tends to feel positive emotions intensely" and "tends to be happy" versus "tends to be angry" and "tends to be bored"), and *intense negative affect* ("tends to feel unpleasant emotions intensely," "tends to feel anxious," and "tends to have panic attacks," versus "tends to have a limited ability to recognize emotions" and "tends to show very little emotion"). The first factor was labeled socialized negative affect, in contradistinction to the third factor, because items with high positive loadings suggest internalization of moral standards and concerns for others' feelings or points of view, whereas those with high negative loadings reflect gross pathology of affective experience (either peculiarities or the results of deficits in affect regulation capacities). The distinction between two negative affect factors accords with clinical experience (see Kernberg, 1975) and suggests the importance of going beyond normal or undergraduate samples, because the first factor, which includes unpleasant emotions such as guilt and regret, correlated *positively* with mental health measures, such as GAF score, quality of relationships, and work history. It also correlated positively ($r = .43$) with the pleasurable affect factor as well as with active coping ($r = .57$), and it correlated negatively with externalizing defenses ($r = -.61$). In contrast, the other negative affect factor correlated negatively with mental health measures as well as with adaptive regulation and avoidant defenses, which tend to be found in healthier patients.

Among the affect regulation factors, the one that was the most clearly predictive of all mental health measures was adaptive regulation, although externalizing defenses were also correlated (negatively) with mental health. Patients high in adaptive regulation were less likely to have been hospitalized or to have made suicide attempts and were less likely to have personality disorder diagnoses. Adaptive regulation also correlated strongly with clinicians' ratings of quality of relationships ($r = .62$), employment stability ($r = .58$), GAF ($r = .53$), and a Likert rating of personality organization (using Kernberg's scheme, from borderline to high-functioning neurotic; ($r = .73$). Externalizing defenses generally correlated negatively with these variables, whereas correlations were moderately positive for avoidant defenses, as one would expect, since people who use defenses such as suppression, repression, and intellectualization tend to have relatively stable and functional lives.

Affect Regulation in Borderline Personality Disorder and Depression

Another way we assessed the validity of the Q-sort was to see if we could predict the profiles of different diagnostic groups. To establish convergent and discriminant validity, we examined three diagnoses prevalent in the sample — borderline personality disorder (BPD), narcissistic personality disorder (NPD), and dysthymic disorder (DD) — and correlated hypothesized prototype Q-sorts for each disorder (made by the author) with the average actual obtained profile. If the measure is valid, the BPD prototype, for example, should correlate strongly with the mean BPD profile of actual patients but less highly with the mean NPD profile. This would be a very conservative test of the validity of the measure because these two disorders are in the same Axis II cluster and have proven difficult to discriminate by current personality disorder instruments. In fact, the BPD prototype correlated at $r = .63$ with the obtained mean BPD profile ($p < .0001$) but at only $r = .08$ with the NPD profile.

For our purposes here, perhaps more significant is the lack of convergence of the BPD prototype and the dysthymic profile ($r = -.14$), despite the fact that most borderline patients in the sample were depressed. Thus, although BPD and DD subjects tend to share an Axis I diagnosis, their patterns of affective experience and affect regulation are quite different, as can be seen in Table 28.1, which lists the items that were, on the average, placed highest in the Q-sorts of patients given these diagnoses. As can be seen from the table, BPDs tend to regulate their affects behaviorally, with manifestly self-destructive behaviors, alcohol or drug use, or avoidance through restricting activities or sleeping, and they rely on defenses such as repression, dissociation, and global, impressionistic thinking when distressed. The dysthy-

Table 28.1 Items most descriptive of borderline and dysthymic patients

Borderline Personality Disorder		Dysthymic Disorder	
Item	Mean	Item	Mean
Behaves in manifestly self-destructive ways when upset (e.g., fast driving, wrist cutting)	8.13	Tends to feel sad or unhappy	7.12
Tends to become overwhelmed or disorganized by emotion	6.63	Tends to feel bad or unworthy instead of feeling appropriately angry at others	7.06
Tends to feel unpleasant emotions (sadness, anxiety, guilt, etc.) intensely	6.63	Is able to use and benefit from support and advice when distressed	6.82
Tends to use drugs or alcohol to avoid facing distressing feelings or situations	6.63	Tends to feel ashamed, embarrassed, or humiliated	6.76
Tends to feel sad or unhappy	6.50	Tends to feel guilty	6.76
Tends to feel anxious	6.50	Is able to express impulses in ways that are social acceptable or desirable	6.64
Can plunge into deep despair that lasts for several weeks	6.38	Tends to experience regret	6.23
Has trouble recognizing or remembering anything positive when feeling bad; when things are bad, everything is bad	6.38	Is able to anticipate problems and develop realistic plans for dealing with them	6.18
Tends to remain at home or restrict travel or activities to escape distress	6.00	Tends to feel anxious	6.12
Tends to make suicide attempts or threaten suicide when distressed	5.88	Tends to feel unpleasant emotions (sadness anxiety, guilt, etc.) intensely	5.94
Tends to think in impressionistic, global ways in the face of distressing circumstances	5.88	Tends to ruminate or dwell on concerns when distressed	5.94
Unpleasant memories or powerful emotions seem to "come out of the blue" and intrude on consciousness	5.88	Is able to remain goal-directed even in distressing circumstances	5.82
Often seems unaware of own wishes, needs, and feelings	6.23	Often seems unaware of own wishes, needs, and feelings	5.70
Tends to feel bad or unworthy instead of feeling appropriately angry at others	6.23	Tends to avoid confrontations even when has legitimate grievances	5.53
Appears to sleep excessively to escape distress	6.23	Is able to draw comfort from being with others when distressed	5.53

mics in the sample, in contrast, tend to turn their anger inward, to dwell on negative events, or to respond passively when they should be more assertive, but they also show a number of active and effective coping strategies, which fits with their considerable higher GAF scores and Kernberg personality organization ratings.

The BPD and DD subjects also differed substantially in their affective experience. BPD subjects were more likely to have intense unpleasant emotions and affects that "seem to come from nowhere," reflecting a failure in affect regulation. DD subjects, like BPDs, were also unhappy, but they showed a constellation of emotions not prevalent in the BPD subjects: guilt, regret, remorse, shame, and embarrassment. These findings are in accord with previous findings with both adolescent and adult inpatient samples comparing BPD subjects with patients with either DD or major depressive disorder: The depression may be similar in intensity, but it differs in quality. BPD patients have a qualitatively distinct depression characterized by emptiness, loneliness, rejection sensitivity, global self-loathing, and labile, diffuse negative affectivity (Westen et al., 1992; Wixom, Ludolph, & Westen, 1993). Nonborderline depressed patients may also feel lonely or show signs of dependency (Blatt & Zuroff, 1992), but their depression frequently centers on feelings of failure, inadequacy, and guilt. The pattern of intense, desperate negative affect *combined with* maladaptive strategies for regulating it seems to be what defines borderline affective pathology in contradistinction to affective pathology in non-BPD depressed patients, including depression defined in recent research as dependent or anaclitic.

Conclusion: Affect Regulation and Depression

Perhaps two points deserve special note here. First, we cannot assume that depression is a homogeneous category—and that it is somehow more important diagnostically than personality pathology—simply because it happened to find its way onto Axis I. Borderline patients typically present for treatment because they are depressed, and their scores on measures of depression are often just as high as nonborderline depressed patients (Westen et al., 1992). Yet something clearly distinguishes borderline from nonborderline "depressives": the intensity and quality of their depression and the affect regulation strategies they use to try to manage their distress.

Second, with respect to affective experience and affect regulation, causality undoubtedly runs in both directions. People whose emotions are intense, or who tend to experience particular emotions (such as guilt or anger), tend to respond with different patterns of affect regulation (Westen, 1994). People who feel chronically anxious require different strategies for dealing with their moods and emotions than people who do not, and people whose emotions are extremely intense typically have difficulty making use of adaptive coping strategies that require anticipation or planning. Conversely, people who use particular affect regulation strategies are likely to experience different feelings and intensities of emotion because their actions create more or less havoc in their lives and their defenses and coping strategies have differing impacts on their consciousness of emotion. Wrist cutting, suicide threats, and precipitously breaking off relationships are affect regulation strategies used by borderline patients that in turn create new situations and affect states that must now be managed.

Feeling chronically depressed itself can also reflect a pattern of affect regulation; that is, depression can be a compromise formation and not simply an instigator of affect-regulatory procedures. The data reported here suggest that relatively high-functioning dysthymic patients tend to feel depressed instead of feeling angry. Depressogenic patterns of thought or behavior can in fact be a solution to a number of problems, selected as a way of regulating affect during childhood and not readily changed without intervention because these procedures are automatized and unconsciously maintained through their association with reduction of anxiety and other emotions. Depression may stem, for example, from identification with a belittling or critical parent, and attempts to break the identification may elicit feelings of loss, anxiety, or rage (which in turn evokes guilt). Self-hate may also feel preferable to feeling alone in a hateful world, so that a child with emotionally or physically abusive parents may blame herself instead of them in a paradoxical effort to protect her feelings of security. Alternatively, maintaining chronically negative feelings and beliefs about the self may prevent disappointment at the reactions of significant others, may keep hopes low, or may avoid conflict engendered by the possibility of outdoing a parent or sibling. For other patients, depression can be a means of self-punishment or a paradoxical way of attaining moral standards. As one patient put it, "The only way to be good is to know how bad you are" (a sentiment that may have a familiar ring to readers who learned as children about theological concepts of original sin). Or as Neitzsche put it, "He who despises himself nevertheless esteems himself as a despiser."

References

American Psychiatric Association. (1994). *Diagnostic and statistical manual of mental disorders* (4th ed.). Washington, DC: Author.

Aronoff, J., Stollak, G., & Woike, B. (1994). Affect regulation and the breadth of interpersonal engagement. *Journal of Personality and Social Psychology, 67,* 105–114.

Bandura, A. *Social foundations of thought and action.* Englewood Cliffs, NJ: Prentice-Hall.

Blatt, S., & Zuroff, D. Interpersonal relatedness and self-definition: Two prototypes for depression. *Clinical Psychology Review, 12,* 527–562.

Bowlby, J. (1969). *Attachment and loss: Vol. 1. Attachment.* New York: Basic Books.

Breier, A., Wolkowitz, O., Roy, A., Potter, W. Z., & Pickar, D. (1990). Plasma norepinephrine in chronic schizophrenia. *American Journal of Psychiatry, 147,* 1467–1470.

Brenner, C. (1982). *The mind in conflict.* New York: International Universities Press.

Buss, D. M. (1991). Evolutionary personality psychology. *Annual Review of Psychology, 42,* 459–591.

Buss, D. M., Larsen, R. J., Westen, D., & Semmelroth, J. (1992). Sex differences in jealousy: Evolution, physiology, and psychology. *Psychological Science, 3,* 251–255.

Carver, C. S., Scheier, M. F., & Weintraub, J. K. (1989). Assessing coping strategies: A theoretically based approach. *Journal of Personality and Social Psychology, 56,* 267–283.

Davis, K. L., Kahn, R. S., Ko, G., & Davidson, M. (1991). Dopamine in schizophrenia: A review and reconceptualization. *American Journal of Psychiatry, 148,* 1474–1486.

Dollard, J., & Miller, N. (1950). *Personality and psychotherapy: An analysis in terms of learning, thinking, and culture.* New York: McGraw-Hill.

Dozier, M., & Kobak, R. (1992). Psychophysiology in attachment interviews: Converging evidence for deactivating strategies. *Child Development, 63,* 1473–1480.

Eisenberg, N., & Fabes, R. A. (Eds.). (1992). *New directions for child development: Vol. 55. Emotion and its regulation in early development*. San Francisco: Jossey-Bass.

Folkman, S., & Lazarus, R. S. (1985). If it changes it must be process: A study of emotion and coping during three stages of a college examination. *Journal of Personality and Social Psychology, 48*, 150–170.

Fox, N. (Ed.). (1994). Development of emotion regulation: Biological and behavioral considerations. *Monographs of the Society for Research on Child Development, 59*(2/3, Serial No. 240).

Freud, S. (1933). The dissection of the psychical personality. *New introductory lectures on psychoanalysis*. New York: Norton.

Garber, J., & Dodge, K. (Eds.). (1991). *The development of emotion regulation and dysregulation*. Cambridge: Cambridge University Press.

Garcia, J., & Koelling, R. (1966). Relation of cue to consequences in avoidance learning. *Psychonomic Science, 4*, 123–124.

Gray, J. A. (1979). A neuropsychological theory of anxiety. In C. E. Izard (Ed.), *Emotions in personality and psychopathology*. New York: Plenum Press.

Gray, J. A. (1990). Brain systems that mediate both emotion and cognition. *Cognition and Emotion, 4*, 269–288.

Haan, N. (1977). *Coping and defending: Processes of self-environment organization*. New York: Academic Press.

Higgins, E. T. (1990). Personality, social psychology, and person-situation relations: Standards and knowledge activation as a common language. In L. Pervin (Ed.), *Handbook of personality: Theory and research* (pp. 301–338). New York: Guilford Press.

Holyoak, K., & Spellman, B. (1993). Thinking. *Annual Review of Psychology, 44*, 265–315.

Horowitz, M. J. (1987). *States of mind: Configurational analysis of individual psychology* (2nd ed.). New York: Plenum Press.

Kernberg, O. (1975). *Borderline conditions and pathological narcissism*. New York: Jason Aronson.

Kobak, R., Cole, H. E., Ferenz-Gillies, R., & Fleming, W. S. (1993). Attachment and emotion regulation during mother-teen problem solving: A control theory analysis. *Child Development, 64*, 231–245.

Kopp, C. (1989). Regulation of distress and negative emotions: A developmental view. *Developmental Psychology, 25*, 343–354.

Lazarus, R. S. (1991). Progress on a cognitive-motivational-relational theory of emotion. *American Psychologist, 46*, 819–834.

Lazarus, R. S. (1992). Cognition and motivation in emotion. *American Psychologist, 46*, 352–367.

LeDoux, J. (1995). Emotion: Clues from the brain. *Annual Review of Psychology, 46*, 209–235.

Main, M., Kaplan, N., & Cassidy, J. (1985). Security in infancy, childhood, and adulthood: A move to the level of representation. In I. Bretherton & E. Waters (Eds.), *Growing points of attachment theory and research. Monographs of the Society for Research in Child Development, 50*(1–2), 67–104.

Mayer, J., Salovey, P., Gomberg-Kaufman, S., & Blainey, K. (1991). A broader conception of mood experience. *Journal of Personality and Social Psychology, 60*, 100–111.

Menninger, K., Mayman, M., & Pruyser, P. (1963). *The vital balance*. New York: Viking.

Miller, G. A., Gallanter, E., & Pribram, K. H. (1960). *Plans and the structure of behavior*. New York: Holt, Rinehart, & Winston.

Nisbett, R., & Wilson, T. (1977). Telling more than we can know: Verbal reports on mental processes. *Psychological Review, 84*, 231–259.

Pennebaker, J. (1990). Stream of consciousness and stress: Levels of thinking. In J. S. Uleman & J. A. Bargh (Eds.), *Unintended thought* (pp. 327–350). New York: Guilford Press.

Perry, J. C., & Cooper, S. (1989). An empirical study of defense mechanisms. I. Clinical interview and life vignette ratings. *Archives of General Psychiatry, 46*, 444–460.

Plutchik, R. (1980). A general psychoevolutionary theory of emotion. In R. Plutchik & H. Kellerman (Eds.), *Emotion: Vol. 1. Theories of emotion*. New York: Academic Press.

Powers, W. T. (1973). *Behavior: The control of perception*. Chicago: Aldine.

Rogers, C. (1959). A theory of therapy, personality, and interpersonal relationships, as developed in the client-centered framework. In S. Koch (Ed.), *Psychology: The study of a science* (Vol. 3). New York: McGraw-Hill.

Roston, D., Lee, K., & Vaillant, G. (1992). A Q-sort approach to identifying defenses. In G. Vaillant (Ed.), *Ego mechanisms of defense: A guide for clinicians and researchers* (pp. 217–233). Washington, DC: American Psychiatric Association.

Schachter, S., & Singer, J. (1962). Cognitive, social, and physiological determinants of emotional state. *Psychological Review, 69*, 379–399.

Scheier, M. F., & Carver, C. S. (1982). Cognition, affect, and self-regulation. In M. S. Clark & S. T. Fiske (Eds.), *Affect and cognition: The 17th annual Carnegie symposium on cognition*. Hillsdale, NJ: Erlbaum.

Shedler, J. Mayman, M., & Manis, M. (1993). The illusion of mental health. *American Psychologist, 48*, 1117–1131.

Tamminga, C., Thaker, G., Buchanon, R., Kirkpatrick, B., Alphs, L., Chase, T., & Carpenter, W. T. (1992). Limbic system abnormalities identified in schizophrenia using positron emission tomography with fluorodeoxyglucose and neocortical alterations with deficit syndrome. *Archives of General Psychiatry, 49*, 522–530.

Thayer, R. (1989). *The biopsychology of mood and arousal*. New York: Oxford University Press.

Tice, D., & Baumeister, R. (1993). Controlling anger: Self-induced emotion change. In D. Wegner & J. Pennebaker (Eds.), *Handbook of mental control* (pp. 393–409). Englewood Cliffs, NJ: Prentice-Hall.

Tomkins, S. (1980). Affect as amplification: Some modifications in theory. In R. Plutchik & H. Kellerman (Eds.), *Emotions: Vol. 1. Theories of emotion*. New York: Academic Press.

Tronick, E. (1989). Emotions and emotional communication in infants. *American Psychologist, 44*, 112–119.

Vaillant, G. E. (Ed.). (1987). *Empirical studies of ego mechanisms of defense*. Washington, DC: American Psychiatric Press.

Van IJzendoorn, M. (1994). Attachment representations in mothers, fathers, adolescents, and clinical groups: A meta-analytic search for normative data. *Journal of Consulting and Clinical Psychology, 64*, 8–21.

Watson, D., & Clark, L. A. (1992). Affects separable and inseparable: On the hierarchical arrangement of the negative affects. *Journal of Personality and Social Psychology, 62*, 489–505.

Weinberger, D. (1990). The construct validity of the repressive coping style. In J. Singer (Ed.), *Repression and dissociation*. Chicago: University of Chicago Press.

Westen, D. (1985). *Self and society: Narcissism, collectivism, and the development of morals*. New York: Cambridge University Press.

Westen, D. (1994). Toward an integrative model of affect regulation: Applications to social-psychological research. *Journal of Personality, 62*, 641–667.

Westen, D. (1995). A clinical-empirical model of personality: Life after the Mischelian ice age and the NEO-lithic era. *Journal of Personality, 63*, 495–524.

Westen, D. (in press). A model and a method for uncovering the nomothetic from the idiographic: A comparison with the Five Factor Model. *Journal of Research in Personality*.

Westen, D., Muderrisoglu, S., Fowler, C., Shedler, J., & Koren, D. (in press). Affect regulation and affective experience: Individual differences, group difference, and measurement using a Q-sort procedure. *Journal of Consulting and Clinical Psychology*.

Westen, D., Ludolph, P., Block, J., Wixom, J., & Wiss, F. C. (1990). Developmental history and object relations in psychiatrically disturbed adolescent girls. *American Journal of Psychiatry, 147*, 1061–1068.

Westen, D., Moses, M. J., Silk, K. R., Lohr, N. E., Cohen, R., & Segal, H. (1992). Quality of depressive experience in borderline personality disorder and major depression: When depression is not just depression. *Journal of Personality Disorders, 6*, 382–393.

Wixom, J., Ludolph, P., & Westen, D. (1993). Quality of depression in borderline adolescents. *Journal of the American Academy of Child and Adolescent Psychiatry, 32*, 1172–1177.

29

John Altrocchi

Evidence for Theories of Emotion from Dissociative Identity Disorders

> Looking at emotion through the window of illness can pro-
> vide empirical evidence with respect to issues of major con-
> cern to emotion theorists and can reveal theoretically im-
> portant aspects of emotion processes that might otherwise
> remain hidden.
>
> Leventhal & Patrick-Miller, 1993, p. 365

This chapter derives empirical evidence about emotion processes from the observations of many thoughtful professionals and patients who have worked with a specific
kind of serious psychopathological disorder–dissociative identity disorder (DID),
formerly known as multiple personality disorder or multiple personality response. In
this disorder *extreme negative emotional states* play a central role. Emotional states,
which are inferred constructs, are defined as particular constellations of changes in
somatic and/or neurophysiological activity, and in facial, bodily, and vocal behavior
(Lewis, 1993). Emotional states may include, but are not the same as, conscious
emotional experiences. Because of the probable origins of DID at times of unbearable repetitive traumas in early childhood, the resulting emotional states are also
intense and unbearable. Understanding the importance of intense and unbearable
emotional states in a severe disorder of human functioning may help us understand
the roles of emotion in memory, cognition, psychopathology, healing, and human
functioning in general.

Definition and Phenomena of DID

DID is diagnosed when the individual displays two or more different "alters," each
of which takes control at different times, has somewhat different memories, and claims
a distinctly different identity from the others (American Psychiatric Association, 1994).
The term *alter* is replacing *personality* in this area because the latter term implies an
"internal time-line of memories encompassing a person's chronology" (Yates & Nasby,
1993, p. 310). Each alter usually "leaves" when another alter is "out" (in control)

so that there are continuing amnesic barriers among them. Each alter usually has a very limited range of emotions and a particular set of personally central emotions. The following is a composite example of uncomplicated DID (i.e., without other accompanying abnormalities such as borderline personality disorder).[1] The summary of the case omits some of the complexities of diagnosis and treatment of DID that are not central to this chapter and focuses on the roles and effects of extreme negative emotional states.

> Judith, a 24-year-old, single woman, presented herself as meek, cooperative, pleasing, and dependent in seeking admission to a mental hospital, as she had several times before, for depression, "mental overload," and extremely suicidal thoughts. When the examiner discovered that Judith remembered only small fragments of her life before age 9, but did remember that she had had nightmares and was told that she sleep-walked as a child, the examiner asked Judith focused (but not leading) questions about whether she ever heard voices inside her head, found clothes in her possession that were not hers, or was called different names by people she did not know. Judith showed surprise at each question, but answered yes to each, ending by asking, "How did you guess all of that?" The examiner referred Judith to a DID specialist.
>
> This specialist, in the third session, while exploring what the voices said, was suddenly confronted with a different facial expression and very different and aggressive behavior by an alter who said she was Jude, and, "Who the f___ are you?" Over a series of psychotherapy sessions Jude revealed, slowly and grudgingly, that she remembered "what those bastards" (stepfather and brother) had done (repeated and severe sexual, physical, and mental abuse, often in the context of loud drunken brawls in a family who saw themselves as moral pillars of their community). Jude was usually angry and often furious, said she did not trust any man (yet the therapist was a man and Jude continued to see him), and said she had no idea what love or tenderness was. She said she was very strong, however, and protected "that wussy" (Judith) from men and other dangers.
>
> During one therapy session, from the hallway next to the therapist's office, there was sudden loud yelling and Judith instantly looked very frightened, and switched to "Judy," a terrified "little girl" who eventually said she was 5. Judy occasionally had flashbacks of a few of the traumas and said that the most recent traumas happened "yesterday." So Judy "hid" almost all the time in her (fantasized) isolated home in the woods. (Actually Judith and her alters have been living with kindly relatives and then roommates 700 miles from her home town since age 14 and there is no evidence that Judith or her alters have been molested or assaulted in the last 10 years.)

These phenomena indeed partly represent rule-governed, socially constructed behavior that is guided by current cultural expectations on the part of some people in North America and by sections of the mental health community (Spanos, 1994). It would be extremely unwise to assume, without corroborating evidence, that Jude's memories are veridical, because all memories must be considered to be reconstructions (Frankel, 1993) based not only on past events, but on intervening events, cultural expectations, prejudices, cognitive assumptions, and present emotions. Nevertheless, for purposes of this chapter we can ignore those contentious issues and note that (a) Judith's behavior was dramatically changeable, far beyond what all but a very few accomplished actors or actresses can portray; (b) the alters gave every evidence of not knowing much of what other alters remembered or felt; (c) each alter's memories and emotions were dramatically real to the alter experiencing them; and (d) the intense emotional states shown separately by the different alters—suicidal despair, fury, and terror—were extreme. Furthermore, seven periods of pharmacological and psychiatric treatment in inpatient and outpatient settings, each guided by other diagnoses (various kinds of depressions or schizoaffective disorder) had had no lasting positive effects on Judith's life. There had also been no "spontaneous remissions" because DID is *a self-perpetuating rather than a self-limiting disorder*. And her recent treatment for DID, characterized by bringing the alters to know each other and work together, teaching reduction in habits of dissociating when there was no major stress, fostering expression and constructive handling of the previously sequestered emotions, and reprocessing the "memories," all guided by a DID diagnosis, has resulted in a considerably improved life so far for Judith-Jude-Judy. At the time of this writing, her life was relatively calm, she had a part-time job and was back in college part-time, and the alters usually cooperated with each other. She can teach us a great deal about emotions.

Causes of DID

[I]nformation is at least partially organized through affect (Shapiro, 1995, p. 316).

Thus, while a person's beliefs, stated via language, are clinically useful distillations of experience, it is the affect feeding them that is the pivotal element in the pathology (Shapiro, 1995, p. 43).

DID in adults (ignoring child cases here for the sake of simplicity) can be conceived as a kind of posttraumatic stress disorder (American Psychiatric Association, 1994; Lowenstein, 1994) that began in early childhood (there are no reliable reports of DID developing *only* as a result of late adolescent or adult traumas, no matter how severe). The traumas were usually repetitive, but also unpredictable (Kluft, 1984; Putnam, 1989; Ross, 1989), and were usually carried out in a context of extreme dominance and enforced secrecy (e.g., "If you ever tell anyone, your mother will die"). The child lacked close attachment bonds in the family (Barach, 1991) and evidently had been unable to develop a distinct and cohesive self (Albini & Pease, 1989) and/ or had multiple self-schemas (Horowitz, 1991; Horowitz & Reidboard, 1992). And there was heavy use of dissociation—*disconnection or separation of elements of mental functioning, such as emotions, memories, and thoughts, from each other* (American Psychiatric Association, 1994; Putnam, 1989; Ross, 1989). Automatic dissociation can be triggered by an overwhelming trauma, but it is believed that what produce and maintain separated alters are repeated, overwhelming traumas (Yates & Nasby, 1993). Dissociation of events and emotions then become overgeneralized, habitual, and deeply ingrained. It should be noted that emotions that are dissociated, although temporarily unavailable to consciousness, sometimes indirectly indicate their presence, for example, when the person shows unusual sensitivity to cues that remind her (or an alter) of the trauma(s) (Li & Spiegel, 1992); and the event or emotion can be retrieved when certain conditions occur (Yates & Nasby, 1993).

The Role of Emotions in the Development and Phenomenology of DID

> Emotions are related to psychopathology in four ways: 1) when some emotions are extreme; 2) when some emotions are absent or too limited; 3) when strong emotions are in conflict; and 4) when there are disconnections between such components of the emotional chain as cognition, feeling, physiology, and behavior.
>
> Plutchik, 1993 (p. 54)

Clearly DID entails all four of the above relationships. Judith was, periodically, suicidally depressed; Jude was, at first, at least angry, and often furious, threatening to "go back and castrate" her brother; and Judy was usually terrified. Such extreme negative affects have been shown to lead often to (a) disorganization of emotional and other functioning (Horowitz & Reidboard, 1992)—clearly Judy showed severe disorganization; (b) reduction of and/or focusing of attention and memory (Braun & Frischolz, 1992; Horowitz & Reidboard, 1992; McGaugh, 1992)—Judith's disorganization developed into separate parts, each of which showed reduced and focused attention and memory; (c) helplessness (Horowitz & Reidboard, 1992)—Judith's repeated appeals for outpatient and inpatient treatment demonstrated her helplessness; (d) avoidant and defensive tendencies (Lang, Bradley, & Cuthbert, 1990)—dramatic in Judith; and (e) severing of ties between aspects of mental functioning (Harber & Pennebaker, 1992). (The disconnections comprise Plutchik's fourth way in which emotions and psychopathology can be related above.) That is where dissociation comes in.

Many DID investigators (e.g., Braun & Sacks, 1985) believe that humans differ in the degree to which they have an inborn capacity to dissociate, to artificially separate elements of mental functioning from each other, a capacity that enables a person to keep contrary emotional states side by side without having any impact on each other. There is abundant clinical evidence that severe and prolonged or repeated physical, sexual, and psychological traumas in early childhood are associated etiologically, for some people, with the tendency to dissociate to such a degree that the dissociation, although enhancing psychosocial survival at the time (Cohen, Gilles, & Lynn, 1991), becomes maladaptive in the long run, since it continues to be used when protection is not essential (Branscomb & Fagan, 1992; Sanders & Giolas, 1991; Sanders, McRoberts, & Tollefson, 1989). As Putnam (1989) puts it,

> Dissociative states have long been recognized as adaptive responses to trauma, because they provide: 1) escape from the constraints of reality; 2) containment of traumatic memories and affects outside of normal conscious awareness; 3) alteration or detachment of sense of self (so that the trauma happens to someone else or to a depersonalized self); and 4) analgesia. (p. 53)

If the child has developed a habit of dissociation in response to trauma, and since most young children have not developed a distinct and cohesive sense of self (Albini & Pease, 1989) and/or tend to have multiple self-schemas (Horowitz, 1991; Horowitz & Reidboard, 1992), the child may develop several dissociated states that are the beginnings of different alters. Then the person can, in different dissociated states, focus on, enhance, and endlessly repeat, as child, adolescent, and adult, different sets of emotions and memories, consciously or unconciously. At the same time, the child can reduce, essentially to "nothing," all the memories and emotions connected with the traumas, and can prevent their appearance in awareness in the "host" personality.

Regarding Plutchik's (1993) second criterion relating emotions to psychopathology (when some emotions are absent or too limited), and turning again to the case described earlier: Judith at first seemed almost incapable of experiencing any of the angry emotions. Jude fiercely claimed that she felt no affection or love and did not even know what the terms meant, and Judy experienced some affection and a lot of fear and terror, but denied other emotions. The dissociative system kept all these emotions separate and prevented direct conflict (items 3 and 4 in the Plutchik quote above).

It has long been thought that highly emotional stimulation may "almost leave a scar" in the cerebral tissue (James, 1890) and there is now experimental evidence supporting such thinking (McGaugh, 1992). Similarly, van der Kolk and van der Hart (1989, 1991) have modernized Pierre Janet's views of the effect of "vehement" emotions on the brain and "the engraving of trauma." The best current theories of the features of brain functioning that underlie the processing of emotional trauma focus on the limbic system and especially the amygdyla (van der Kolk, 1994).

Current "network" models of memory have been adapted to include consideration of the dissociation of strong affects (Li & Spiegel, 1992; Yates & Nasby, 1993). It is proposed that strong negative affect may increase inhibition of links between items of memory. Thus, a highly charged, negatively toned affect may make specific memories inaccessible (Yates & Nasby, 1993). Emotions and memories that are thus inaccessible but are present may guide the person to behave as if still exposed to traumatic input (Li & Spiegel, 1992).

The Role of Emotions in Psychotherapy with DID

> Theories of emotions need to have implications for change and remediation.
> Plutchik & Kellerman, 1992 (p. xviii)

While dissociation, splitting, and multiple alters may have been appropriate and lifesaving as initial ways of coping with unbearable, repeated, and unpredictable abuse (Cohen et al., 1991), the habitual use of these ways of coping when abuse is no longer occurring comprises disordered or abnormal behavior because (a) dissociation is not usually adaptive if used well beyond the time of traumas; (b) usually at least one of the alters engages in one or more kinds of abnormal and/or dangerous behaviors, such as being paralyzed when she needs to say no, or behaving promiscuously or antisocially, behaviors that often occur outside of the awareness and control of the host personality; and (c) the person is dealing with life by means of a very limited set of emotional responses at any one time, being unable, for instance, to experience normal anger or love.

There are no specific medications for DID, although medications are sometimes used to reduce specific symptoms such as anxiety or depression. DID is, as far as we know, a psychological disorder and must be dealt with psychotherapeutically. This is a lengthy task and is often difficult for all concerned (Kluft, 1984; Putnam, 1989; Ross, 1989). It is evidently necessary for recovery, as is generally true for other post-traumatic stress disorders, for the person to recover and experience enough of the previously unbearable emotions to allow her or him to "work through" the emotions, just as one works through the grief of losing a loved one. Interestingly, for a theory of emotions, the working through of the negative emotions tends to be followed by increased experiencing of positive emotions.

> Let us revisit Judith. She had been desperately tired of feeling "crazy" and of repeated failures in treatment and evidently was ready to try to get her life in order. A therapeutic alliance was established (Jude was slow to trust a man, of course) and the psychotherapist reassured himself that Judith's present life situation was safe. He then slowly tried to persuade Judith to listen to the voices, to "hang around" when Jude or Judy was in control, and then to interact with them. Slowly each of them learned to hear, accept, and then feel each other's strong emotions—fury, terror, and despair. The experiencing of each other's emotions led slowly to sharing of and much fully remembering of the traumas—and those memories led to more strong emotions. Judith, with consultation from Jude and Judy, decided to detach even further from her family of origin and to not even telephone them. The "team" of Judith-Jude-Judy then slowly learned to reconceptualize the memories as events that were past but not present or "forever," and to reintegrate them into a new vision of "herself" as a survivor rather than a victim, and as a person with a future—perhaps even with a male partner some day. Judith's and Judy's liking of men slowly overcame Jude's serious reservations, but the therapist assured all three that it would be important to maintain some reservations too. Very limited telephone contacts were reinstituted with the geographically distant family of origin.

It is now recognized that it is not just the experiencing or abreaction of the dissociated emotions that is therapeutic, but also cognitive acknowledgment of disavowed affect, owning disclaimed action tendencies (Greenberg, 1993), and allowing previously unacceptable aspects of experience into awareness and accepting them as one's own (Greenberg & Safran, 1990). One can partially facilitate such processes by gradually persuading the personalities not to leave totally, to hear each other, to feel each other's feelings, to talk to each other, and to come to know each other (Putnam, 1989), all of which helps in developing a coherent sense of self. Some clinicians believe that total integration or "fusion" of all the alters is not always necessary as long as the parts are cooperating with each other. Many people with differentiated or pluralistic selves evidently function normally. But for satisfactory healing, the person needs to be relatively unhindered by the background presence of powerful negative emotions that emerge in undercontrolled ways and at unpredictable times, and needs to have good communication among all major parts—as is true of all of us. Being able to call into play all aspects of yourself, when necessary, is a hallmark of effective and healthy personality functioning.

Implications for Theories of Emotions

The data presented here are highly selected, uncontrolled but consistent, primarily from women patients, and focus on very strong and extreme trauma-based negative emotions engendered in childhood. How can these clinical data contribute usefully to our dealing with theoretical controversies about emotions?

One controversy is, "Do we simply 'have' them (emotions) or do we perhaps, to some extent, construct, cultivate and 'do' them to ourselves?" (Solomon, 1993, p. 13); or, put another way, to what extent are emotions best seen as cognitive constructions to attempt to deal with an object, usually an interpersonal object (Averill, 1988; Frijda, 1993; Goldsmith, 1993)? The data from DID suggest that extremely strong negative emotional states were experienced during the original traumas when the small (sometimes preverbal) child had little cognitive understanding of what was happening. Such traumas can evidently produce emotional states that are *relatively* uninfluenced by cognition. According to Lewis's (1993) definition of emotions adopted here, emotional states can occur without the person's conscious knowledge (p. 223). Also, DID switches are evidently triggered by emotions, and patients often respond involuntarily to such stimuli as "yelling" or "anger" before cognizing or processing what is being said and (sometimes) by whom, seeming to automatically respond as if huge danger were still present. One patient even said, "We did not know what emotions were until we were diagnosed DID." (Notice the plural pronouns.) These powerful emotions, when not dealt with by the child, evidently remain forceful in dissociated form and can be recovered from sequestering, in seemingly unchanged form, in psychotherapy. Therefore, it is probably much more useful and valid to theorize that powerful emotions guide social constructions, that they strongly affect current interpersonal relationships, than to postulate the opposite causal sequence.

Furthermore, evidence is accumulating that the neuroanatomy or brain circuitry of emotional processing is different from the circuitry of cognitive processing, but that the two processes may strongly interact in the brain under normal circumstances (Davidson & Ekman, 1994; Ledoux, 1994; Panksepp, 1994). The data outlined here suggest that under abnormal circumstances—that is, when trauma-based, overwhelming emotions are engendered in childhood—these emotions may be more likely to influence cognition than vice versa. Extreme emotional arousal early in life can produce lasting changes in synaptic conductivity (McGaugh, 1992), and such processes can be accommodated by modern network theory (Li & Spiegel, 1992; Yates & Nashby, 1993). The data suggest that extreme negative emotions produce disorganization, dissociation, and splitting and not vice versa. The different alters predominantly organize themselves around different sets of emotions and "the problems of post-traumatic thought intrusions lie not so much with the memories themselves, as with the unassimilated emotions that drive these memories to the surface of consciousness" (Harber & Pennebaker, 1992, p. 362). It seems that overwhelming emotions originally produced in childhood can continue to be a major force in a person's adult functioning.

Another and related controversy has concerned the degree to which emotion or cognition has primacy over the other in time and degree of influence (Lazarus, 1984; Zajonc, 1984). Under current broad research definitions of emotion (i.e., to include nonconscious emotional states; Lewis, 1993) and of cognition (to include a wide spectrum ranging from simple informational to conscious reflective processing; Davidson & Ekman, 1994), it is clear that emotion and cognition can influence each other at many brain circuitry levels. The data reviewed here suggest that investigating the brain circuitry of clinical subjects who have dissociated strong emotions and accompanying memories, and investigating the changes in their brain circuitry as they recover and cognitively integrate the emotions and the memories, might help us move toward further clarity in the extremely complex interactions of emotion and memory in the brain.

These conclusions and suggestions do not undermine but actually help to explain the major roles of social constructions and cognitions in DID. Many of the behavioral features of DID, as is true for much of psychopathology, are influenced by cultural and role demands, and diagnosticians and therapsits need to be acutely aware of such cultural phenomena (Spanos, 1994). Also, the emotions that drive DID are almost always, as is congruent with constructionists' views, responses to the actions of people (perpetrators) in a family situation that is lacking in attachment (Barach, 1991): Only a tiny proportion of the original traumas were impersonal, such as natural disasters (Putnam, 1989; Ross, 1989). The emotions themselves are intimately intertwined with memories. And, the cognitive variable of extent of multiple self schemas versus cohesion of the self concept is probably a key etiological variable for DID; cognitive acknowledgment of disavowed emotions and cognitive reorganization are key healing principles in psychotherapy with DID. But strong emotions must be dealt with in order to heal, whether or not they have been sequestered. Thus, this review of data regarding overwhelming emotions engendered early in life suggests that we must pay attention to powerful as well as weak emotions produced in a laboratory in order to see the full role of emotions in psychological functioning.

Finally, however, construction and cognition are central in healing, too. It is not simply the relief after expression of emotion that comprises healing, but also cognitive reorganization, which then leads to emotional restructuring (Greenberg & Safran, 1990). Evidently healing occurs in DID when those strong, previously sequestered emotions are recalled, cognitively acknowledged, and reorganized into new cognitive appraisals of past traumas, present life, and future functioning.

Acknowledgments I am especially grateful to my inspiring emeritus colleague, Paul McReynolds, with whom I have worked on research and theory in self pluralism and DID for several years and who carefully reviewed a draft of this chapter. I also appreciate the conferences and exchanges of letters I have had with Ondra Williams, a trailblazer in Auckland, New Zealand (one of whose deft phrases I used here); the constructive criticisms of drafts of this chapter by Laurel Altrocchi, Dean Hinitz, Denise Trease, and one person who prefers to remain anonymous; and the many contributions to my knowledge from people who are working on resolving this disorder and moving ahead with their lives.

Note

1. This case example is composed of pieces of the histories and therapies of several different patients so that none of them can be identified. Identification is an especially sensitive issue for people who have been severely abused by people who are still alive. The case example—and the whole chapter—were given a careful critique by a patient in the late stages of long-term therapy for this disorder. She suggested several small changes designed to assure that the case and the chapter properly represent clinical reality for patients as well as for therapists.

References

Albini, T. K., & Pease, T. E. (1989). Normal and pathological dissociations of early childhood. *Dissociation*, II, 144–150.

American Psychiatric Association. (1994). *Diagnostic and statistical manual of mental disorders* (4th ed.). Washington, DC: Author.

Averill, J. F. (1988). Disorders of emotion. *Journal of Social and Clinical Psychology, 6*, 247–268.

Barach, P. M. M. (1991). Multiple personality disorder as an attachment disorder. *Dissociation*, IV, 117–123.

Branscomb, L. P., & Fagan, J. (1992). Development of a scale measuring childhood dissociation in adults: The Childhood Dissociative Predictor scale. *Dissociation*, V, 80–86.

Braun, B. G., & Frischolz, E. J. (1992). Remembering and forgetting in patients suffering from multiple personality disorder. In S. A. Christianson (Ed.), *The handbook of emotion and memory* (pp. 411–427). Hillsdale, NJ: Erlbaum.

Braun, B. G., & Sacks, B. G. (1985). The development of multiple personality disorder: Predisposing, precipitating and perpetuating factors. In R. P. Kluft (Ed.), *Childhood antecedents of multiple personality* (pp. 37–64). Washington, DC: American Psychiatric Press.

Cohen, B. M., Gilles, E., & Lynn, W. (1991). *Multiple personality from the inside out*. Baltimore: Sidran Press.

Davidson, R. J., & Ekman, P. (1994). Afterward: What are the minimal cognitive prerequisites for emotion? In P. Ekman & R. J. Davidson (Eds.), *The nature of emotion: Fundamental questions* (pp. 232–234). New York: Oxford University Press.

Frankel, F. H. (1993). Adult reconstruction of childhood events in the multiple personality literature. *American Journal of Psychiatry, 150*, 954–959.

Frijda, N. H. (1993). Moods, emotion episodes, and emotions. In M. Lewis & J. M. Haviland (Eds.), *Handbook of emotions* (pp. 381–403). New York: Guilford Press.

Goldsmith, H. H. (1993). Temperament: Variability in developing emotions systems. In M. Lewis & J. M. Haviland (Eds.), *Handbook of emotions* (pp. 353–364). New York: Guilford Press.

Greenberg, L. S. (1993). Emotion and change processes in psychotherapy. In M. Lewis & J. M. Haviland (Eds.), *Handbook of emotions* (pp. 499–508). New York: Guilford Press.

Greenberg, L. S., & Safran, J. D. (1990). Emotional-change processes in psychotherapy. In R. Plutchik & H. Kellerman (Eds.), *Emotion: Theory, research, and experience: Vol. 5. Emotion, psychopathology, and psychotherapy* (pp. 59–85). San Diego: Academic Press.

Harber, K. D., & Pennebaker, J. W. (1992). Overcoming traumatic memories. In S. A. Christianson (Ed.), *The handbook of emotion and memory* (pp. 359–387). Hillsdale, NJ: Erlbaum.

Horowitz, M. J. (1991). Introduction. In M. J. Horowitz (Ed.), *Person schemas and maladaptive interpersonal patterns* (pp. 1–10). Chicago: University of Chicago Press.

Horowitz, M. J., & Reidboard, S. P. (1992). Memory, emotion, and response to trauma. In S. A. Christianson (Ed.), *The handbook of emotion and memory* (pp. 343–357). Hillsdale, NJ: Erlbaum.

James, W. (1890). *The principles of psychology*. New York: Henry Holt.

Kluft, R. P. (1984). Treatment of multiple personality disorder: A study of 33 cases. *Psychiatric Clinics of North America, 7*, 9–29.

Lang, P. J., Bradley, M. M., & Cuthbert, B. N. (1990). Emotion, attention, and the startle reflex. *Psychological Review, 97*, 377–395.

Lazarus, R. S. (1984). The primacy of cognition. *American Psychologist, 39*, 124–129.

Ledoux, J. E. (1994). Cognitive-emotional interactions in the brain. In P. Ekman & R. J. Davidson (Eds.), *The nature of emotion: Fundamental questions* (pp. 216–223). New York: Oxford University Press.

Leventhal, H., & Patrick-Miller, L. (1993). Emotion and illness: The mind is in the body. In M. Lewis & J. M. Haviland (Eds.), *Handbook of emotions* (pp. 365–379). New York: Guilford Press.

Lewis, M. (1993). The emergence of human emotions. In M. Lewis & J. M. Haviland (Eds.), *Handbook of emotions* (pp. 223–235). New York: Guilford Press.

Li, D., & Spiegel, D. (1992). A neural network model of dissociative disorders. *Psychiatric Annals, 22*, 144–147.

Lowenstein, R. J. (1994). Diagnosis, epidemiology, clinical course, treatment, and cost effectiveness of treatment for dissociative disorders and MPD: Report submitted to the Clinton administration task force on health care financing reform. *Dissociation, VII*, 3–11.

McGaugh, J. L. (1992). Affect, neuromodulatory systems, and memory storage. In S. A. Christianson (Ed.), *The handbook of emotion and memory* (pp. 245–268). Hillsdale, NJ: Erlbaum.

Panksepp, J. (1994). A proper distinction between affective and cognitive process is essential for neuroscientific progress. In P. Ekman & R. J. Davidson (Eds.), *The nature of emotion: Fundamental questions* (pp. 224–226). New York: Oxford University Press.

Plutchik, R. (1993). Emotions and their vicissitudes: Emotions and psychopathology. In M. Lewis & J. M. Haviland (Eds.), *Handbook of emotions* (pp. 53–66). New York: Guilford Press.

Plutchik, R., & Kellerman, H. (Eds.). (1992). *Emotion: Theory, research, and experience: Vol. 5. Emotion, psychopathology, and psychotherapy.* San Diego: Academic Press.

Putnam, F. W. (1989). *Diagnosis and treatment of multiple personality disorder.* New York: Guilford Press.

Ross, C. A. (1989). *Multiple personality disorder: Diagnosis, clinical features, and treatment.* New York: Wiley.

Sanders, S., & Giolas, M. H. (1991). Dissociation and childhood trauma in psychologically disturbed adolescents. *American Journal of Psychiatry, 148*, 50–54.

Sanders, S., McRoberts, G., & Tollefson, C. (1989). Childhood stress and dissociation in a college population. *Dissociation, II*, 17–23.

Shapiro, F. (1995). *Eye movement desensitization and reprocessing.* New York: Guilford Press.

Solomon, R. C. (1993). The philosophy of emotions. In M. Lewis & J. M. Haviland (Eds.), *Handbook of emotions* (pp. 3–15). New York: Guilford Press.

Spanos, N. P. (1994). Multiple identify enactments and multiple personality disorder: A sociocognitive perspective. *Psychological Bulletin, 116*, 143–165.

van der Kolk, B. A. (1994). The body keeps the score. *Harvard Review of Psychiatry, 1*, 253–265.

van der Kolk, B. A., & van der Hart, O. (1989). Pierre Janet and the breakdown of adaptation in psychological trauma. *American Journal of Psychiatry, 146*, 1530–1540.

van der Kolk, B. A., & van der Hart, O. (1991). The intrusive past: The flexibility of memory and the engraving of trauma. *American Imago, 48*, 425–454.

Yates, J. L., & Nasby, W. (1993). Dissociation, affect and network models of memory: An integrative proposal. *Journal of Traumatic Stress, 6*, 305–326.

Zajonc, R. B. (1984). The primacy of affect. *American Psychologist, 39*, 117–123.

30

Joseph de Rivera

Some Emotional Dynamics Underlying the Genesis of False Memory Syndrome

You thought you had got away with it. The "good" daughter had repressed forever. Not a chance, Dad. No, I do remember. I remember almost everything, and the things I do remember are with great horrible detail. *I hate that I remembered, for I deserve no more pain.* As far back as age 5, I do remember the fondling of me and [sister], the demanding to watch me naked, and then the repeated rapes all of which were called punishments, Ma, I believe in my heart that you at least had an idea of what was going on. But you chose to look the other way. Why didn't you save me? I am your child. Was your fear of Dad so great it came before my safety? Was that the price of Dad's love and comfort and peace for you? Me?

Two months after mailing the letter from which the above segment is excerpted, a turn of events led the woman who wrote it to stop seeing her therapist, to completely retract her accusation, and to reconcile with her family. Letters, such as the one excerpted above, have been received by thousands of bewildered families in the United States. They are a reflection of what has come to be called *false memory syndrome,* a disorder in which a person's identity and relationship are centered about a belief in memories of traumatic experiences that are objectively false (Kihlstrom, in press).

Since real child abuse is all too frequent, it is important to distinguish between memories of real abuse and false memory syndrome. False memory syndrome may be suspected whenever a person claims to have completely repressed or dissociated from traumatic events. Ordinarily, people remember traumatic events, often all too well. Of course, there are numerous cases in which a person in therapy discloses memories of abuse for the first time, or gradually comes to realize that what they experienced was abusive, or appears not to have dealt with important affective aspects of the abuse. However, there is no convincing evidence that persons can completely repress or dissociate entire episodes of traumatic abuse (Pope & Hudson, 1995). Hence, if a person begins to suspect that they may have been abused and then begin to remember details of the abuse, it is quite possible that pseudomemories are developing. When other members of the family are open to dialogue, are unable to confirm instances of abuse and offer evidence contrary to abuse, when medical and school records are not supportive of abuse, and when the abused person and her or his therapist are not open to dialogue, it seems highly likely that the person is suffering from false memory syndrome. If the person retracts the charges of abuse and her or his psychological health improves, we may conclude that they did, in fact, suffer the disorder.

In the case at hand, the person had no memories of abuse until she went into psychotherapy. Her family was open to discussing the allegations, her sisters had never experienced her father as sexually intrusive, and the sister who slept with her in the same bedroom could not understand why she would not have woken up during the purported rapes. By contrast, the patient and her therapist would not discuss the possibility that the memories were mistaken and cut off communication with the family, which they considered to be in denial. After retracting, the person was much less depressed and disorganized, required much less medication, and was able to again love and work.

While there can be little doubt as to the empirical existence of cases of false memory syndrome, and eight autobiographical accounts have been presented in Goldstein and Farber (1993), the processes that are involved in its creation are not fully understood. It is possible to induce isolated pseudomemories (Loftus & Pickrell, in press), and Yapko (1994) has convincingly argued that cultural context and therapeutic power of suggestion can account for the development of counterfactual beliefs. However, it is difficult to understand how a normal person could replace memories of a normal childhood with a completely fictitious account of childhood sexual abuse. How could a reasonably healthy parent-child relationship be turned into accusations of sexual abuse? How could loving parents be turned into fearful monsters?

This chapter attempts to use the structural theory of the emotions and an understanding of situational dynamics to understand some of the emotional processes that appear to be involved in some false memory syndrome cases. Theoretical background is presented first, followed by two brief case histories that illustrate the emotional dynamics.

The Structural Theory of Emotions

From the perspective of the structural theory of emotions, emotions are transformations of personal relationships that function (ideally) to reveal and enhance what is good and avoid what is bad (de Rivera, 1985). That is, just as actions occur in relation to motives, emotions occur in relation to values. The "it" emotions (e.g., love, anger, admiration, fear) have objects that deal with the value of another's actions as perceived by the self. There is an "it" toward which the emotion is directed. The "me" emotions (e.g., joy, depression, pride, anxiety) are perceptions of the self as valued in the eyes of the other and the emotion is directed toward that "me." For example, when we love someone else we perceive their essence as valuable; when we perceive the self as valuable, we experience joy.

It should be noted that, from this viewpoint, emotions are *not* inherently subjective phenomena. That is, they need not only exist in the mind (or body) of the subject rather than in the perceived object. Rather, they exist in the personal relationship *between* person and others and they may either be a response to the objective value of the other *or* a subjective evaluation that has nothing to do with the real value of the other or self (see Macmurray, 1961). The transformation of love may either allow a person to see the objective value of the revealed other (Murdoch, 1970; Ortega y Gassett, 1957), or simply be a wishful fantasy (Stendahl, 1822/1957) or a mistake (Merleau-Ponte, 1962, p. 378).

In either case there is a profound transformation of the body, perceptions, and "life space" of the person who is having the emotion, and a change in the field of psychological forces between that person and others. Thus, the body of the angry person becomes filled with tension as she or he perceives the others as challenging what ought to exist. Forces to remove this challenge arise in the life space, and if changes in the other do not occur, psychological distance may increase (de Rivera, 1977). In the case of the me-emotions, the person's self-image may become profoundly altered as he or she "floats" in elation (Lindsay-Hartz, 1981), is weighted down in depression, or feels the tension of anxiety or the calmness of serenity.

In the terms of the structural theory these different transformations are understood to be alternative structures that reflect "choices" about how to deal with one's personal situation. The term *choice* is not meant to imply a conscious decision but, rather, to signify that alternative perceptions are possible. Thus, in the transactional theory of perception, an increase in the apparent size of an object may either mean that an object is expanding or that it is approaching (Ames 1951). In a similar manner, emotions always involve an implicit judgement (Solomon, 1984). If a person is given a surprise party, the person has a "choice" between becoming joyful, embarrassed, or even hurt and angry (as Cezanne once felt when he mistook a party that was given in his honor to be a mocking gesture). As mentioned above, the emotion that is chosen in any particular situation may either be an objective response to the actual situation or a subjective reaction. If it is objective, that is, if it is a reasonable response to the value of what is other than self, then the person's development will be supported. If it is an irrational, subjective reaction that is dominated by self-concern, then development will be retarded (de Rivera, 1989).

We ordinarily think of the ego or self as distinct from the situation in which it finds itself. And we experience action as intended by the self and as creating change in the environment, in what is other than self. However, emotion occurs when the boundary between ego and other has become porous such that the self is no longer as distinct and separated. That is why emotion is experienced as transformative. In contrast to action, the self is being moved and the other as environment is perceived physiognomically, as majestic, lovely, puny, evil. While there are many different factors that can weaken the self boundary so that emotion occurs — fatigue, satiation certain rhythms, and drugs — we shall focus on the factor of tension.

The Dynamics of Tension in "Impossible" Situations

In 1930, Tamara Dembo, a student of Kurt Lewin's, performed an experimental study that became the basis for much of field theory (Dembo, 1976). She had her subjects stand within a rectangle that was marked out on the floor by wooden lathes and gave them the problem of grasping a flower that was out of reach. The subjects, who were told that they had to keep both feet within the rectangle, discovered possible solutions to this problem by kneeling on the ground, or by placing the chair outside the rectangle and leaning upon it so they could reach the flower. However, they were unable to discover the third solution that they were instructed to find. In fact, no third solution existed, and Dembo, who was interested in the dynamics of anger, simply observed how persons behaved in this frustrating situation.

She observed that when a barrier prevents people from reaching their goal, when they cannot find how to reach the flower, they do *not* become angry. After becoming convinced that there is no solution they simply try to leave. At this point, however, they discover that an "outer barrier" holds then in the situation, for the experimenter tells them that there *is* a solution and if they try, they can discover it. In life outside the laboratory this "outer barrier" is often a commitment that the person may feel they cannot abandon.

All subjects try again to discover a solution to the problem. This time, however, the barrier to the goal of finding a solution begins to acquire negative valence. In part, this occurs because it is beginning to become clear that finding a solution is the only way out of this difficult situation. Hence the frustration of not discovering the solution cannot be avoided. Of course, subjects again try to give up, but the outer barrier is held in place by the will of the experimenter, who was granted authority when subjects entered experiment. The experimenter simply insists that they *can* find a solution.

By now there is some tension in the field and subjects often take a respite from this tension by going into fantasy. In her diagrams of the situation, Dembo shows this level of fantasy above the "level of reality." The subjects may escape into a daydream or they may imagine solutions to the problem such as hypnotizing the flower and bidding it to come. At this point there is a clear boundary between fantasy and reality and subjects know that they cannot really solve the problem in such a fanciful way, and realize that they must eventually return to reality. However, crossing the boundary into fantasy has made the boundary between fantasy and reality a bit more permeable.

Subjects may also create a subregion within reality by using their own will to stake out a space that they can dominate. For example, a subject may tell the experimenter that he is just going to give up and read the newspaper. But after a while it becomes clear that the larger field of reality remains with all its oppressive features.

As the subject begins to move back and forth, trying another solution, trying again to leave, moving again into fantasy, finding the self still trapped in the situation, the *tension* steadily increases. The tension is not only experienced in the self but also in the situation and between the subject and the experimenter. In Dembo's conceptualization, as the tension increases it begins to obliterate the boundaries that exist between subject and environment, subject and experimenter, and the level of fantasy and the level of reality. It also begins to weaken the boundary between the experimental situation and the rest of the subject's life. And it stresses boundaries that separate deeper layers of the personality from superficial layers, and that separate different regions of the environment. At first, this weakening of boundaries is only manifested in irrational thinking. The person may find that they have a hard time relinquishing an incorrect solution, or have the brief thought that perhaps he or she could really hypnotize the flower, or that the experimenter's smile appears scornful. However, as the tension mounts irrational behavior also begins to occur. Subject may find themselves grasping a nearby flower that clearly is *not* the flower that is the out-of-reach goal. Subjects may begin speaking about private matters that they will later regret having said. Subjects may swear at the experimenter, or storm angrily out of the experiment. What is remarkable is that no one simply leaves. The subject has been trapped by a situation that admits of no solution, a situation that generates so much tension that normal boundaries are weakened such that irrational thoughts and behavior occur. Dembo was able to obtain these effects in 1–3 hours of time.

Let us see how similar dynamics appear to be useful in accounting for the genesis of some cases of false memory syndrome. The following cases are based on lengthy (2- to 4-hour) interviews using the method of conceptual encounter (de Rivera, 1981). While some identifying information has been omitted, no details have been altered and the respondents have reviewed the material for accuracy.

Application to the Genesis of False Memory Syndrome

Case 1

A highly intelligent and self-sufficient 30-year-old woman in a managerial position experienced job harassment from a competitive male. She allowed herself to be intimidated by him and developed panic attacks when she tried to go to work. She entered therapy to learn how to manage this situation, was impressed with the intelligence of her therapist, felt consoled by her empathy, and "handed her myself right away." Instead of teaching her skills to cope with the situation in which she found herself, the therapist elected to search for the cause of the panic attacks. Why had she let herself be intimidated by a man? The therapist raised the issue of whether the client had been emotionally abused as a child. She showed her client how the parents could have been more sensitive to her needs and the client began to feel that her parents really could have done better by her. The therapist then told her that she had the symptoms of someone who had been sexually abused. The client forcefully resisted this suggestion and the therapist backed off but continued talking about the past wounds that had caused her to be susceptible to her nemesis at work. Rather than encouraging her to accept responsibility, the therapist made it clear that she should trust her therapist. The therapist had her pay for the session and make an appointment for the next session before the current session began. When she, occasionally, spoke of leaving therapy, her therapist warned her that if she did she might have a breakdown and have to be institutionalized. She felt she had to find out what was wrong. Why had she let herself be intimidated by a man. What had happened to her as a child?

After about a year of therapy the client experienced an illness that she interpreted as a case of the flu and delayed seeing her physician. In fact, she had underestimated her illness and barely got to the doctor in time. This shook her confidence.

Her therapist pointed out that she never took care of herself and again brought up the possibility that she had been sexually abused. This time she did not resist as strenuously. The therapist gave her a book that accurately described her perfectionism. Whereas previously she had been proud of her self-sufficiency, she now began to agree with her therapist's view of herself as quite sick. Then the therapist bought her a copy of *Courage to Heal* (Bass & Davis 1988) and gave it to her client to read.

While she was not really able to remember concrete instances of abuse, when her therapist had her relax, close her eyes, and spoke "soft-type affirmations," she could imagine her father entering her room at night. She began becoming terrified and finally became convinced that she had been abused. In retrospect, she felt that her ability to resist the therapist's reality had been eroded. She said her "will was broken." The therapist encouraged her to write her parents and tell them that she now realized how they had abused her. This led her to write the letter excerpted at the beginning of the chapter.

She said that she had felt desperate, and that her time was running out. The therapist mentioned that it might be best if she were institutionalized but she was afraid she might be given shock treatments and tried to display herself as in a better mental state than she actually was. She stated, "I definitely did not know the difference between what I felt and what she was telling me was right to do."

Retraction occurred because the patient discovered that she got worse rather than better after writing the accusatory letter, and when her husband took charge of the situation on discovering that the therapist was encouraging her to leave him.

Note that the patient was trapped in a situation analogous to Dembo's experimental situation. To get better she had to recover a memory of abuse that did not actually exist. She was afraid to leave the situation because the authoritative therapist told her she would become insane and be subjected to shock treatment if she did. Her only way out of the situation was to remember what did not actually exist. The tension was extremely high (in fact, the patient had difficulty sleeping, could not relate to her children, and "accidentally" hit her car against a parked car), and boundaries were broken as indicated by the failure to distinguish between her own feelings of reality and what the therapist was telling her was real.

Case 2

A 35-year-old woman with three children came into therapy to learn how to deal with one of her children who was acting out at home. Her therapist seemed very bright, had an excellent understanding of what it was like to have an alcoholic parent, and had worked with children. He was kind and she "gave him all my power" quite soon in the course of therapy. He soon had her searching for memories of abuse and soon had her feeling that her background was "quite horrendous." She had felt she had been an active, together sort of person, but learned that these characteristics were actually dysfunctional and that she was an "overachiever" who kept busy to avoid feeling the pain of her childhood.

She began feeling depressed and suicidal and became quite dependent on her therapist, who encouraged her to call him at home every night. She wanted to please him and continued her search for memories. After her therapist began doing "relaxation techniques" with her, she began going into trance states and recalled some apparently real memories that her therapist interpreted as memories of sexual abuse. For example, her mother had given her an enema and the therapist had seen this as a sexual act. She was hospitalized and placed in a unit for sexually abused women. She tried desperately to retrieve memories but was unable to recall any specific ones. However, she began to have "flashbacks." She described these as altered states of very high anxiety. Her body felt extremely tense and she would feel as though she was in another world. During these states she was given a lot of attention. People would come and sit with her and hold her hand. She was told that this was a way to get better and going into the states became habitual. At one point she was told that she had had a "spontaneous age regression" and had a little girl in her.

After leaving the hospital her therapy became centered around these "flashbacks." Memories of real events would be incorporated into these trance-like states and her therapist would help her elaborate imagery that would fit into a narrative of abuse. He asked, for example, "What was the look on your mother's face as she was giving you the enema?" The images were painfully sharp and she experienced a great deal of physical tension. Her therapist would come and sit by her, hold her, and nurture her through it until she felt relief. He referred to her as his sweet little girl.

When she emerged from these states she would sometimes angrily state that in fact nothing abusive had really happened. However, her therapist would tell her that that was her "angry little girl" speaking and they should ask her to leave the room. In retrospect, she stated, "The sick thing about this was that I was getting a lot of attention from this and so I continued the process. I was very special to this guy. . . . he kept telling me I was teaching him so much." After these sessions she would sometimes slash her wrist. At the time this was taken to be a sign of the traumatic abuse she had suffered, but she now believes this was a cutting of herself out of guilt and a cutting of *him*, the therapist, out of anger.

The disintegration of her marriage finally led her to a family therapist who helped validate her underlying belief that she had not really been abused. The death of her mother led her to leave the first therapist and to fully repudiate her "memories."

As in Case 1, the patient was told that she would not get better until she did the work of recapturing the abuse memories. She, too, felt that the degree of tension was important. She stated, "The tension would be incredible because you went into the therapy office and you never knew what you were going to come out like." However, in contrast to Case 1, where the patient was held in the field by her fear that she would go crazy if she left, this patient described herself as more trapped by her feelings for the therapist.

Summary

In both cases the client gave authority to a therapist who insisted that the client could only solve her problem if she remembered the abuse that occurred in childhood. The client's confidence in her own reality was undermined and she was encouraged to be dependent on the therapist. While the cases differ in how the outer barrier was constituted, in both cases the client felt herself trapped in a field of forces that generated so much tension that boundaries between fantasy and between self and therapist were seriously eroded.

In both cases there appears to have been three features in addition to those described by Dembo. First, the focus on what was wrong with the patient and her family contributed to a depression that enhanced the patient's dependence on the therapist. Second, multiple sessions were involved so that more extreme irrational beliefs could be gradually developed over time. Finally, the nature of the accusation and the encouragement of the therapist led the client to stop communicating with people who did not support her belief system.

It is all too easy to understand how the therapist, too, becomes trapped in a *folle a deux*. From the therapist's perspective, she or he is helping a person who is unable to function in the way the client desires. The lack of function is due to repressed or dissociated memories of abuse and the client must be helped to face this awful reality so that recovery can occur. The client grants authority to the therapist and follows his or her suggestions. When the therapist suggests that the client will improve when she or he talks about the abuse suffered at the hands of the parents, the client begins talking about all the unpleasant things that happened. When people think about unpleasant events they become depressed (Carr, Teasdale, & Broadbent, 1991), and when the client's concern is focused on how they have been mistreated, fear increases and the client's emotions become more subjective. At the same time, confidence is weakened and clients become more dependent on the therapist. The therapist responds by giving more nurturance and concern.

When the client is not able to retrieve memories of abuse that are sufficiently traumatic to explain her or his problems, the client may attempt to leave the therapy. The therapist discourages this because of the client's fragile state. Clients then discover, as in the Dembo experiment, that the only way out is to go further in. They *must* recover the postulated memories of abuse. As tension builds, the boundaries between client and therapist and between fantasy and reality weaken until the person finds themselves believing that they were abused although they have no real memory of abuse. When the boundaries are further relaxed by means of hypnosis or equivalent methods, the person begins to have images that support the beliefs. The fear and rage that are present are subjectively real and help motivate actions such as talking about the abuse, writing letters, and so on, that reinforce the belief.

We cannot assume that these particular dynamics are at work in all cases of false memory syndrome. However, we believe that the basic tenets of the structural theory will be applicable in all cases. The structural theory posits that the way we perceive reality is based on emotional choices that either relate us to objective reality or ensnare us in subjective delusions. The latter occurs when our fear for ourself dominates our concern for others. When a therapist encourages a person to replace the me-emotion of confidence with the me-emotion of depression, there is a risk that the person may be led away from her or his true value as a person. This will lead a person to become preoccupied with the self, and this concern will become dominate over the concern for what is other than self (objective truth). Hence, defenses will be reinforced and the person will be unavailable for dialogue and an exploration of what is actually true.

In a similar manner, the tactic of encouraging a patient to search for memories of how she or he was abused encourages the patient to replace the emotions of trust, gratitude, and love with the emotions of fear and anger. This is apt to lead a person to become concerned for the self at the expense of a concern for others, and to lose the ability to take the perspective of others. The person becomes completely dependent on the therapist and psychological growth cannot occur until their joint delusional system is breached and new behavior leads to better emotional choices.

We are not, of course, arguing that only "positive" feelings should be emotional choices and that feelings of confidence and love reflect defensive operations. However, the emotion that is chosen must relate a person to the objective other if psychological growth is to occur. If the emotion maintains a concern for the self at the expense of a concern for the objective nature of the other, psychological growth cannot be maintained.

References

Ames, A., Jr. (1951). Visual perception and the rotation trapezoidal window. *Psychological Monographs*, 65(7). Whole number 325 (pp. 1–27)

Bass, E., & Davis, L. (1988). *The courage to heal*. New York: Harper & Row.

Carr, S. J., Teasdale, J. D., & Broadbent, D. (1991). The effects of induced elated and depressed mood on self-focused attention. *British Journal of Clinical Psychology, 30*, 273–275.

Dembo, T. (1976). The dynamics of anger. In J. de Rivera, (Ed.), *Field theory as human science*, (pp. 324–422). New York: Gardner Press.

de Rivera, J. (1977). *A structural theory of the emotions*. New York: International Universities Press.

de Rivera, J. (1985). Biological necessity, emotional transformation, and personal value. In S. Koch & D. E. Leary (Eds.), *A century of psychology as science* (pp. 364–389). New York: McGraw-Hill.

de Rivera, J. (1989). Choice of emotion and ideal development. In L. Cirillo, B. Kaplan, & S. Wapner (Eds.), *Emotions in ideal human development* (pp. 7–31). Hillsdale, NJ: Erlbaum.

de Rivera, J. (1981). *Conceptual encounter: A method for the explanation of human experience*. Washington, DC: University Press of America.

Goldstein, E. & Farmer, K. (1993). *True stories of false memories*. Boca Raton, Fla: SIRS Books.

Kihlstom, J. F. (in press) Exhumed memory. In S. J. Lynn & N. P. Spanos (Eds.), *Truth in memory*. New York: Guilford Press.

Lindsay-Hartz, J. (1981). Elation, gladness, and joy. In J. H. de Rivera (Ed.), *Conceptual Encounter* (pp. 163–224). Washington, DC: University Press of America.

Loftus, E. F., & Pickrell, J. E. (1995). The formation of false memories. *Psychiatric Annals, 25*, 720–725.

Macmurray, J. (1961). *Persons in relation*. Atlantic Highlands, NJ: Humanities Press.

Merleau-Ponty, M. (1962). *Phenomenology of perception*. New York: Humanities Press.

Murdoch, I. (1970). *The sovereignty of good*. London: Routeledge & Kegan Paul.

Ortega y Gassett, J. (1957). *On love*. Cleveland, OH: World.

Pope, H. G. Jr., & Hudson, J. I. (1995). Can memories of childhood sexual abuse be repressed? *Psychological Medicine, 25*, 121–126.

Solomon, R. C (1984). Emotions and choice. In C. Calhoun & R. C. Solomon (Eds.), *What
is emotion?* (pp. 305–326). New York: Oxford University Press.

Stendahl, M. H. B. (1957). *On love.* Garden City, NY: Doubleday. (Original work published
1822)

Yapko, M. D. (1994). *Suggestions of abuse.* New York: Simon & Schuster.

Index